A Travel Guide to Basque America

The Basque Series

A Travel Guide to Basque America

Families, Feasts, and Festivals ■ Nancy Zubiri

SECOND EDITION

University of Nevada Press / Reno, Las Vegas

Basque Series Editor: William A. Douglass

University of Nevada Press, Reno, Nevada 89557 USA

Manufactured in the United States of America
Design by Carrie Nelson House
Library of Congress Cataloging-in-Publication Data
Zubiri, Nancy, 1959–
A travel guide to Basque America : families, feasts, and festivals / Nancy Zubiri.—2nd ed.
p. cm. — (The Basque series)
Includes bibliographical references and index.
ISBN 0-87417-632-8 (pbk. : alk. paper)
1. Basque Americans. 2. United States—Guidebooks. I. Title. II. Series.
E184.B15Z83 2006
305.89′992073—dc22
2005036574

The paper used in this book meets the requirements of American National Standard for Information Sciences—Permanence of Paper for Printed Library Materials, ansi z39.48-1984. Binding materials were selected for strength and durability.

First Printing
14 13 12 11 10 09 08 07 06 5 4 3 2 1

TO MY FATHER, JEAN BAPTISTE ZUBIRI

CONTENTS

PREFACE TO THE SECOND EDITION

Six years after my book was first published, I began the revision of *Travel Guide to Basque America.* I wanted new and old readers to have the latest information when they set off to follow the Basque trails across America. Unfortunately, for many months the mantra at my house became, "when Mama's book is done." Many activities with my children were postponed or done only with Papa, while I stayed home to write on my computer. Despite the sacrifices, there were many moments when it was all worth the effort—such as the thrill I felt during the summer of 2004 as I sat at the computer in my living room, listening to the voice of the late Basque-American author Robert Laxalt. He spoke about the foresight of his mother, sending her children to college because she knew the time was ending when people (the Basques in particular) would be able to earn a living with their hands. I laughed when he talked about the fact that his father never spanked him—he didn't need to. He just gave his children "that murderous Basque look" and that was enough to correct their behavior.

This is the wonder of the Internet. You can hear voices from the past in the privacy of your own home. Laxalt's interview is part of the oral history site, Oroitzapenak (*www.basquemuseum.com /oralhistory/*) sponsored by the University of Nevada, Reno, and the Basque Museum. I heard his interview after I had spent three months checking out hundreds of Basque-related Web sites—probably thousands of web pages. None of this was available when I wrote the first edition of my book. Through e-mail and my journalistic skills, I was easily able to track down the sources I needed for this update. The first time I wrote the book, I interviewed perhaps five hundred people. This time I spoke with at least half that many. I reconnected with old friends, and made new ones in the process.

And just as I made discoveries about my personal history the first time I wrote the book, such as finding the cousin whose family had welcomed my father when he first arrived in 1928, I encountered a similar exhilarating surprise this time, too. On the Internet, I found the list of passengers of the ship that brought my grandfather to this country in 1902. I never met my grandfather, Barthelemy Zubiri. He died in the Basque Country the year I was born. He had come to the United States to herd sheep for only a few short years. Yet there was his name, handwritten and easily readable on the Internet. This is due to the fabulous work that has been done by the Statue of Liberty–Ellis Island Foundation (*www.ellisisland.org*) in cataloging the millions of immigrants who arrived in the U.S. via this important port.

No one who is interested in Basque culture should miss the opportunity to look into the many facets of Basque life that are available today on the Internet. See a music video of acclaimed accordionist Kepa Junkera (*www.kepajunkera.com*) or watch a little television in Basque (*www.eitb.com*). I had always wanted to learn the words to the famous song "Gernikako Arbola," and now I can, at home, via Lisa Corcostegui's fabulous Web site for the Ontario Basque Club. Visit *www.ontariobasqueclub.dantzariak.net* and click on the Txildren's Txoko. You can listen to Euskara-language lessons on her site, too. And Buber's Basque Page, *www.Buber.net/Basque/*, the first important English-language Web site on Basques, continues to be a fantastic page to go to for information on many interesting topics.

The Internet also led me to the newest Basque restaurants and festivals. All that and more is included in this revised version of my book for you to enjoy.

PREFACE

My father was a sheepherder for many years. I never hesitated to tell people what he did because it had an aura of romance about it. But the particulars of that lonely rural lifestyle were a mystery to me. My father eventually married and settled in San Francisco—where my sister and I grew up.

I remember some of his stories, but only in bits and pieces. I knew he had spent time in Fresno and Bakersfield and traveled with the sheep around Mono Lake. But many of the details were lost on me simply because I was young and didn't realize the significance of his experiences, until it was too late to ask him to repeat those stories.

There is one aspect of that life, however, that is imbedded in my memory. In the kitchen, we were influenced by habits my father developed from years spent hunkered over a campfire. For as long as I can remember, he ate the exact same breakfast: hot coffee and milk (*kafesnea*) sweetened with sugar and poured over a bowl full of day-old pieces of "French" (sourdough) bread. He cooked dinner for the family on weekends, and the menu inevitably included lamb—most frequently lamb stew or vegetable soup flavored with fat chunks of sautéed lamb.

The rest of the family refused to join him in one of his favorite dishes: lamb's head. He would bring the head home from the butcher's, and we'd watch him, repelled yet fascinated, as he sawed it in half in the kitchen. An entire head was too much for him to eat by himself. After baking it in the oven, he would take special delight over the eyeball and cheek meat. My sister and I would sometimes taste a piece of the latter just to please him, and I have to admit it wasn't bad. For dessert he often ate canned peaches topped with red wine.

I always considered my ethnic background unique. I would proudly tell my friends, "I'm half-Basque and half-Peruvian," a comment that was often followed by the question, "What's Basque?" The mystique surrounding the Basques made me feel even more special.

To me, being Basque meant eating those dishes my dad cooked and drinking wine with dinner. It meant hearing my aunts and uncles speak Euskara with my dad. It meant occasional Sunday-night dinners at the Sorhondos' Pyrenees boardinghouse on Broadway, where my father had lived before he married my mother. It meant summer visits to my uncle's farm near Fresno and to my cousins' Basque restaurants. And then there was the annual Basque picnic.

I was always fascinated by the dance performances at the picnic. When I was a young teenager, I begged my parents to find out how I could join the dance group. That was the beginning of my family's serious involvement with the local Basque community. The Zazpiak Bat dance group was at its peak membership in those years—sixty youngsters or more were involved. It was quite a social circle. I insisted that we go to all the nearby Basque festivals. I also begged my parents to take me to the frequent dinner dances, which led them to become members of the San Francisco Basque Club.

My mother loved to travel, and she and I convinced my father, the homebody, to go back to the Old Country to see his family after forty-one years. That trip, when I was sixteen, opened my eyes. I realized that many aspects of my family life that I had thought were unique were part of longtime cultural traditions.

It became clear, however, that I had roots not only in Euskal Herria, but in this country as well. I embarked on this book seven years after my father's death. When I began following the trails of the Basques across America, I learned the answers to many of the questions I wished I could have asked him. Because my father's experiences in this country, as well as many of my own, were quite common among Basque-Americans. Almost every Basque man of his generation had started his life here in the same way as my father. Like my uncle in Fresno, many of them left sheepherding and went into farming. Many Basque families had gone into the restaurant business, like my cousins. Even the locations where my relatives had settled were common Basque focal points: San Francisco, Fresno, Bakersfield, and La Puente. The image of a land of opportunity had fed the dreams of these immigrants, who took a great leap of faith in crossing the Atlantic. But once here, they took the safest paths, the ones that had already been proven successful by fellow villagers or other family members.

While writing this book, I made some amazing discoveries. When I searched for the owners of San Francisco's former *kantxa,* (the court where handball is played; also known as a fronton) I found a long-lost relative, Juanita (Meabe) Fieldsoe. It was to her family's house that my father first came when he arrived in America. Her family and mine had lost touch over the years. She told me my father had initially gone to work for cousins with a sheep business near Winnemucca. Armed with that information, I traced some photos in my father's album to the Winnemucca Hotel, including a photo of its *kantxa,* which was torn down long ago.

When I investigated the Basque aspen tree carvings, researcher Joxe Mallea-Olaetxe told me it was impossible to know how many sheepherders had been here, because so many had returned to the Basque Country, especially at the beginning of the century. My aunt told me that my grandfather had been one of these. That astonished me, because my grandfather, who died before I was born, seemed ancient. He must have traveled by ship here and back, just as my father did when he first arrived in 1928.

I realized that my family's personal history was part of this bigger picture—part of the history of the West. My uncle told me how during the depression my father lost five years' worth of wages, which he had been banking with his cousins, as many sheepherders did. When he decided to make a visit home in 1934, during the height of the Great Depression, there was no money to pay him. What a blow! Suddenly, the depression was a part of my life, too.

So what began as an attempt to record one slice of the history of the American West also turned into a voyage of self-discovery. My ethnic background was not unique after all. In the course of my research I even met a couple of half-Basque, half-Peruvians, as well as some Basque Peruvians along the way.

I cannot begin to thank all the fine and wonderful personalities who, in one way or another, helped me with this book. The many people I interviewed provided me with the greatest pleasures in writing this book. Your inclusion here is my tribute to you. A special thanks goes to talented photographer Averie Cohen, who gave me a new perspective on my subjects and to painter and computer whiz Pierre Igoa, who provided his expertise for the map making. And to William A. Douglass and to editors Sara Vélez Mallea and H. Maggie Carr for their dedication to a polished and accurate manuscript. My family and my husband, Robert Lopez, deserve the greatest thanks.

INTRODUCTION

In the past, Basque immigrants in the United States lived in tight-knit neighborhoods in the West's sheep towns. To find their history, we studied the churches and cemeteries of these towns as well as the boardinghouses and old handball courts. Some predicted the demise of Basque culture in the United States, because the immigrant generation is passing away and there are very few functioning boardinghouses. Along with many other ethnic populations, more and more Basques live in big metropolises, mostly in the suburbs. Historically, the Basques settled in the cities of San Francisco, New York, and Boise. But today there are significant numbers in Las Vegas, Nevada; Seattle, Washington; Portland, Oregon; and Denver, Colorado. Yet a new phenomenon is occurring within the Basque-American community, and it bodes well for the future of Basque culture in this country. Basque-Americans are seeking out fellow Basques through cultural clubs and festivals in order to preserve their culture. Even though they may not know their compatriots, just being Basque is enough reason to get together.

Many new clubs have sprouted in the past ten to fifteen years, their missions to serve as focal points for local Basques to congregate and to share their culture. "We're a new breed," said Mike Matassa, the 2005 president of the Colorado Euskal Etxea, referring to the creation of his club in an area where there was no significant Basque community in the past. These new gatherings are not occurring without some struggle. Some big city clubs have been created only to disband within just a few years, such as the one in Portland.

"People have been living a long time in Colorado without a Basque club in their lives and it's hard to fit it in," explained Matassa acknowledging that they have had a hard time bringing Basques together. Each club needs to figure out the type of events that will appeal to the largest number of people. The Denver group is experimenting with different activities to attract members, such as afternoon movies, cooking sessions, and a cultural exchange with a school in Iruñea/Pamplona. The clubs that are surviving are those with organizers like Matassa, who are willing to work hard to keep the culture alive. Pride in being Basque keeps them going, too. And the Internet is serving as an important tool to help them grow. The clubs are promoting themselves via their own Web sites, hoping to attract new people and keep members enlightened. Thus the Internet is not only helping to bring Basques together, but it is also providing them with a wealth of new information about their culture. The history and the future of Basques in America, the restaurants, festivals, clubs, and dance groups are now all documented on the Internet.

This book is a travel guide to places of importance for the U.S. Basque colony. My intent has been to take a nonacademic, reader-friendly approach. As a result, many of the stories that go with these places are told through the eyes of Basques, both young and old, who live in this country. I interviewed over four hundred people. Nevertheless, much background information did come from books, as they are essential to putting together a picture of Basque culture in this country.

Much of the historical information on Basque settlement in the United States was derived from the 1975 publication *Amerikanuak*, by William Douglass and Jon Bilbao, which is probably the most comprehensive book on the subject to date. Professor Jeronima Echeverria's book, *Home Away from Home: A History of Basque Boardinghouses*, also provided a significant amount of background on early Basque communities. Many other students' dissertations and theses on individual Basque communities proved important in relating early history and identifying places of Basque importance. These are cited specifically within the text and in the reference list at the end of each chapter. I focused on only the most significant historical events in each community, placing particular emphasis on those that relate to existing Basque establishments and organizations.

For decades Basques who immigrated to the United States maintained their unique language and centuries-old traditions by gathering together for food and dance at Basque boardinghouses. With time these get-togethers were transformed into organized social clubs and annual festivals. But since the 1970s, immigration from the Basque homeland has trickled down to almost nothing. Meanwhile, the assimilation of the generations of U.S.–educated Basques into American culture threatens to overshadow the unique culture of their parents. Second- and third-generation Basque-Americans are losing the language. And except for a few urban areas where the Basque community is fairly significant, fewer and fewer U.S.–born Basques have the opportunity to participate in traditional Basque customs. This book is an attempt to help keep the rich Basque culture alive in the United States by recording the many Basque establishments and activities that are still in existence today.

A small group of Basques have worked to promote Basque culture at the Basque Educational Organization in San Francisco, incorporated as a nonprofit group in 1984. As a board member of the BEO, I saw many letters over the years from people who know that they are of Basque heritage but know little about the Basques in America. I hope this book will help them travel to some places of significance to Basques and get a flavor for the culture their ancestors left behind. But this book is also for non-Basques, to introduce them to the unique culture and to let them experience it firsthand.

I did not automatically include in this book any business with Basque ownership. Only businesses and institutions that impart Basque culture in an obvious manner or have historical value were included. Consequently, many different kinds of businesses owned by Basques were left out, and at the same time a few Basque restaurants or other Basque establishments that are not owned by Basques can be found in these pages.

As you begin your travels following the trails of the Basque immigrants across the United States, take note:

Many former boardinghouses that are still standing are now private homes. They are mentioned here so readers can drive by and get a feel for an earlier era in Basque communal life. Please don't disturb the occupants. Also keep in mind that many events sponsored by local Basque clubs are primarily for the enjoyment of the club members and their guests. I mentioned such groups to give readers an idea of what each organization is up to and to interest Basque-Americans who might be tempted to join a club. If you want to find out whether an event is open to the public, because that information is not indicated in the book, call the information numbers provided for the individual clubs involved. As for the festivals, you are typically heartily welcome to attend one and all of them . . . and bring your friends!

Entry Examples

The **Basque Cultural Center,** with its handball court, bleachers, restaurant, and banquet hall, opened in South San Francisco in 1982. The San Francisco Basque Community now has the largest Basque Center in the country, as well as the largest handball court in the West. [A full entry giving business name, owner, address, and telephone number is provided at the end of the relevant section.]

Basque Cultural Center, 599 Railroad Avenue, South San Francisco, CA 94080. Restaurant: (650) 583-8091; event information: (650) 583-7018 (Anita Arduain); *www.BasqueCulturalCenter.com*

A small contingent of the Hegoaldetarrak have always been members of the **Union Española,** the city's Spanish organization, which started as far back as 1923. For years the Union Española had its own hall in North Beach, first on Pacific and then on Broadway.

[This organization is not Basque, so even though the address might be given in the text, no further information is provided.]

General directions are provided for most locations in this book, but if you go on a road trip in search of some of the more remote places, be sure to take along a map of the region.

Places to visit are listed at the end of each topical section. The full name, address, and phone number are listed for each place to visit. If the place information is highlighted in bold, with an address immediately following, that is the extent of the information I will provide on these places because these locations had some association with Basques but not enough to warrant additional information.

Place names in the Basque Country are in Basque. Some of these terms and their spellings may seem awkward, since they haven't been in use for very long. In fact, they may even be unfamiliar to Basque immigrants, who left their homeland many years before cultural awareness reached its current level in the Basque Country. These immigrants know these places by their Spanish or French names. All words represented in italics are usually in Basque, but they may be in Spanish or French as well—they reflect the term most commonly used by Basques to refer to a place or thing. A glossary of Basque words is included at the end of the book.

The recipes included here are simply a few chefs' specialties chosen to reflect the typical boardinghouse meal that later evolved into Basque-American cuisine. In an effort to represent food from several regions, the recipes were selected from chefs across the West.

Use this book as a resource guide, carry it with you when you travel, or simply peruse it at home and take an armchair voyage along the Basque trails across America.

Ondo Ibili! Happy travels!

Basque-American History, Culture, & Traditions

With the discovery of gold in 1848, fortune seekers from around the globe poured into California. The Basques were no exception. Young Basque men who had migrated to South America were lured by the stories of quick fortunes and caught ships for the three-month trip north on the Pacific to San Francisco. A brave few, eager to escape their poor rural villages in the Pyrenees Mountains, scraped together money for the passage across the Atlantic Ocean. The trip entailed a long treacherous journey around the southernmost tip of South America or an overland trek across the malaria-infested Isthmus of Panama. Once in California they found that a few of their countrymen had preceded them, as part of the Spanish and Mexican settlement in what is now the southwestern United States.

The notion of California was inextricably linked with the gold rush—the name conjured up images of a limitless frontier where economic opportunity was plentiful. After the discovery of gold, people flowed in, hoping, like everyone, to haul in a bonanza of gold nuggets. Most were disappointed. Very few miners were actually able to extract enough gold to make a living. But the Basques were a determined bunch, and most of them found more reliable livelihoods, primarily in the livestock industry.

Life in the rugged undeveloped American West was not easy. But the Basques' strong work ethic and characteristic tenacity saw them through hard times. The Basques who came to America at this time had little education and were mainly from rural villages. Their values of hard work and thriftiness helped them to make their way in a foreign country where they did not speak the language. They got their foot in the door through their experience with sheepherding. It was solitary work that did not require the ability to speak English. The Basque herders saved their money and watched for their opportunity to acquire assets—for many, it was sheep. Later it was property.

Since those early days, not only have Basque immigrants managed to survive economically, but they have also embraced this country's entrepreneurial spirit. They have been lucky enough to know America as the land where initiative is rewarded. By working hard, many of them have established successful businesses in a single generation. In the rural areas, the businesses were ranching and dairies. In the cities, boardinghouses, restaurants, bakeries, and construction and gardening businesses were among the most common.

Today most of the Basque immigrants and their descendants are scattered throughout the American West and can be found at all economic and educational levels. Compared to the numbers of other immigrant groups, the number of Basques in this country is small. According to the most recent U.S. Census, in 2000, 58,000 Americans identified themselves as Basque, up 8,000 from 1990. (In the 2000 U.S. Census, 20,868 Californians identified themselves as Basques; in Idaho the number was 6,637.) But these figures do not represent an accurate picture of the total number of Americans of Basque descent. Probably a large number of Americans with some Basque heritage chose not to report this aspect of their ethnicity. Those most likely to identify themselves as Basque were immigrants and first-generation Basque-Americans. A large but unknown percentage of this group probably speaks Basque. The numbers obviously do not reflect the many immigrants who have died, or those who came, worked for several years and went home to the Basque Country. (If we could expand the total population to include second-, third-, and fourth-generation descendants of immigrants, the Basque-American population would be considerably larger. But just like people of any other extraction, many of these descendants simply do not care about their Basque heritage.) The number of Basques immigrating to the United States has been extremely low since 1970. Some Basques have returned to the Basque Country since then. The improved European economy has essentially stopped the flow of Basque immigrants to this country.

Nevertheless the Basque traditions are carried on by many of those who have claimed the United States as their home. They celebrate their heritage through singing and dancing and their competitive spirit through games held at large festivals and banquets. They have taught their youngsters about their unique ethnicity and taken them, when they could, to visit the Old Country. Many of the children, in turn, participate in folk dancing groups or bugle corps, attend Basque cultural camp, or learn to play pelota (handball). Some college students and others have even spent summers or a year studying in the Basque Country. If you ask any of those young people about their heritage, you're likely to see a fierce pride in their eyes as they explain to you who the Basques are.

San Francisco *klika* player Michael Curutchet, *tronpeta* in hand, cheers alongside Marc Sorhouet at the Saturday afternoon competitions in Elko. (Photo by Averie Cohen.)

The Origins of the Basques

The Basques are considered Europe's oldest surviving culture. Their homeland—despite being called "the Basque Country"—is not a sovereign state. Euskal Herria (as it is called in Basque) straddles the border between France and Spain, at the western end of the Pyrenees Mountains, where the mountains meet the Cantabrian coast. Therefore the Basque people are subject to the rule of two nations. Although anthropologists have determined that the Basque people did not originate in that area, they have not pinned down a time when the Basques' ancestors first arrived there. One Roman historian dates their presence in the region back to at least 77–79 B.C., and another scholar estimates that the Basques were already subject to Roman rule approximately two hundred years before the birth of Christ. In fact, some experts claim that the Basques are distinguished by physical differences, such as unique cranial features, that suggest they are descendants of the Stone Age inhabitants of the Pyrenees. Remarkably, as a people they have one of the world's highest incidences of Rh negative blood for one particular ethnic group (30 percent of the native population). Type B blood is extremely rare among Basques, yet they have one of Europe's highest levels of type O blood.

The most distinguishing ethnic marker of the Basque people is their language. The language, called Euskara or Eskuara by its speakers, is the culturally identifying feature that binds Basques together. The word for someone who is Basque, "Euskalduna" or "Eskualduna," means "speaker of the Basque language." The variations in the term reflect the dialects that developed in isolated villages across the Pyrenees Mountain range.

Euskara is vastly different from the Romance languages spoken by the Basques' European neighbors, and its origins remain a mystery to this day. Scholars have studied it for centuries, seeking some link to other languages, and thus to other peoples. Although minor similarities with other languages, such as Finnish, Georgian, and even the Inca language Quechua, have been found, none of the evidence is conclusive. It is this linguistic isolation that primarily supports the belief that Euskara is the oldest language of Europe, and one of the oldest in the world. The uniqueness of the Basque language is also one of the primary tenets of the argument that the Basques are directly descended from Stone Age inhabitants of the Pyrenees. Some experts believe the Basques are the authors of ancient cave paintings in the region, such as the famous Lascaux site.

Euskal Herria—The Basque Country

Euskal Herria's population is about 3 million, although only about one million Basques speak the language. Despite their small numbers, the Basques have managed to maintain their unique culture and language through the centuries, despite invasions and battles that have raged through the 12,000-square-mile region of broad, flat expanses, rolling foothills, and mountains they call home. The region is about the area of the state of Maryland. Basques have never had a country to call their own, although they had one of the earliest working democratic systems in the world. (In the early years of their immigration to the United States, Basques left their homeland because of the Carlist Wars of 1833 and 1876, during which Basques in Spain lost political rights they had held for centuries.)

The Basques were supposedly among the last European people to be introduced to Catholicism in the sixth century. But by the twelfth century they had embraced it wholeheartedly, and later attempts to convert Basques to Protestantism were unsuccessful.

The Basque Country consists of seven regions (formerly provinces): Araba, Gipuzkoa, Bizkaia, and Nafarroa in Spain; and Lapurdi, Nafarroa Beherea, and Zuberoa in France. The seven are sometimes referred to as Zazpiak Bat—the seven are one. Many U.S. groups pay tribute to the Basque Country by naming themselves Zazpiak Bat. Although the political division created by the border between countries is undeniable, today the popular terms emphasize the geographic rather than the political divisions. Thus the French side is referred to as Iparralde (the North) and the Spanish side as Hegoalde (the South). The desire for cultural unity in modern times has brought an overall strengthening of the Basque traditions. Nevertheless, many people, including Basques themselves, often insist there are great distinctions between Iparraldetarrak and Hegoaldetarrak.

The history of Spain and France affected the two territorial divisions differently. In the last two decades of the nineteenth century, a movement for greater political autonomy and cultural expression founded by Sabino Arana took hold, primarily in Hegoalde. The most significant modern influence in Spain was the repressive nearly forty-year reign of dictator Francisco Franco. He banned the use of the Basque language and sent the Spanish Guardia Civil to the region to crack down on any expressions of nationalism or Basque culture. The development of the violent separatist group Euzkadi 'ta Askatasuna (Basque Homeland and Freedom), better known as ETA, was born in Spain in 1968 of the frustration Franco's policies generated. Under Franco, ETA had popular support—a lasting reminder of the region's history with Basque nationalism—but that support has vanished under the current situation of regional autonomy.

The two economies developed differently because of the geographic differences on either side of the border. The southwest corner of France (all of France's Basque territory), except for its biggest coastal cities, is poorer than other parts of the country, and its economy is based on agriculture and tourism. Its rural inhabitants tend to be aloof and distrustful when they first meet people. They wear this cautiousness like defensive armor. This tendency can also be seen

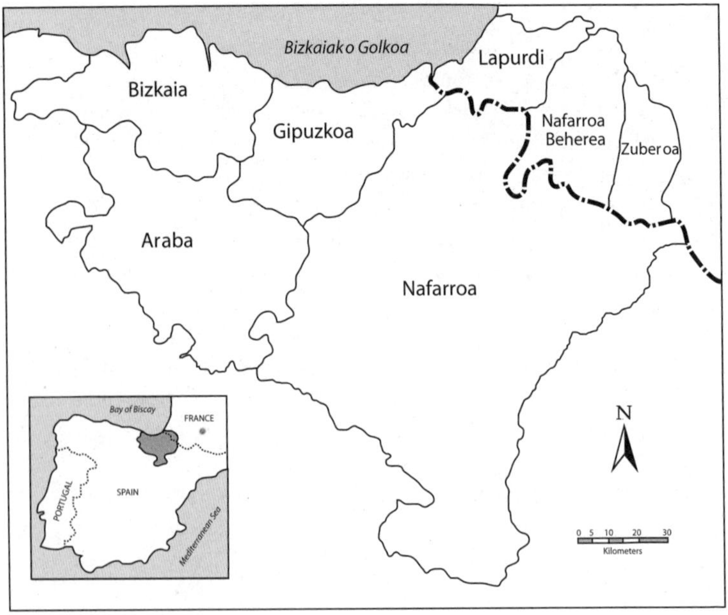

Euskal Herria.

among the Nafarrak, just on the other side of the border, who also come from farming backgrounds. The mineral richness along the Spanish Basque coast, on the other hand, was discovered and exploited early on, and it was probably a factor in the area's eventual industrial development. The Spanish Basque region is Spain's most industrialized area. It has a large population (2.4 million compared to about 500,000 in France's Basque region) and many more city dwellers. For those in Hegoalde, living mainly in heavily populated urban areas has created among them a broader social tolerance. They are much more extroverted. After years of living under Franco's repression, they tend to be more nationalistic as well. Despite an overriding disapproval of ETA's violent tactics, Hegoaldetarrak support an expansion of cultural expression.

Four years after the death of Franco in 1975, the Spanish government signed agreements with the Basque Country and other regions of Spain to allow for the creation of semiautonomous regional governments. Three of the four Hegoalde regions voted in 1979 to be governed by their own president and parliament. This arrangement allows Basques to resume collecting taxes and to provide their own Basque police protection; it also gives them great autonomy over their own budget. The geopolitical area governed by the parliament is referred to as Euskadi. Nafarroa opted for its own regional government. A small section of this province speaks Euskara, but a larger portion has lost the language and much of the Basque culture.

The political recognition of the Basques in Spain has inevitably brought with it a stronger cultural identification among the Hegoaldetarrak, who are pushing, through education and government programs, to revive the unique culture. These developments are generating a mirror effect in Iparralde, where similar changes are beginning to take place, although much more slowly.

Past Emigration Patterns to Other Parts of the World

Although significant Basque immigration to the United States began in the mid-1800s, emigration from the Basque Country was nothing new. Indeed, there is evidence dating back to the 1500s that Basques visited the northeastern coast of North America. Some historians say that it is conceivable that Basque fishermen were exploring the area as early as the 1300s, before Christopher Columbus, but there's no proof.

The Basques apparently were using iron weapons in the battlefield as early as the fifth century, indicating they had an abundant supply of iron. The remains of at least one iron foundry in the Basque Country date back to the year 871. By 1200 they had already begun building ships in which iron anchors, chains, and nails were crucial elements. By that time the Basques had already industrialized the production of iron, which was in high demand by the reigning powers of Europe.

In all likelihood, Basques pursued shipbuilding in order to support whaling. Fishermen probably first discovered the value of the huge mammal's oil, meat, and bones when dead whales occasionally washed up on the Atlantic shoreline along the Bay of Biscay. The Basques may have been the first Europeans to turn whaling into a commercial venture. As the whalers depleted the number of whales closer to home, they were probably forced to venture farther out to sea to capture them. Bigger ships were needed. And as the seafaring hunters followed whales along their migration paths, they were propelled to lands where Europeans had never been before.

Directly across the Atlantic Ocean from the Basque coast is the eastern coast of what is now Canada. Whale hunting and cod fishing took Basques, along with other European seafarers, mostly French, into the bays and straits in and around the entry of the St. Lawrence River. Today their early presence is reflected in several Basque place names in that region, such as Channel-Port aux Basques and Placentia in Newfoundland. During the late 1500s and early 1600s Europeans converged on this icy area inhabited by the native Inuit people and turned it into a busy whale-oil producing region. Shipwrecks and other recent archeological finds indicate that Basques were present in the area in significant numbers from about 1540 to 1610. Basques themselves like to promote the unproved theory that it was a Basque who told Christopher Columbus about the existence of the New World.

The New World

In *Colonizadores de la Epopeya Americana,* published in 1966 in Argentina, the author Xamurre presents the findings of several historians who reported that Columbus learned of the New World from a Bizkaian navigator who was shipwrecked at the Portuguese island of Madeira, where Columbus was living at the time. The historians wrote that Columbus confirmed the information by consulting the Basque navigator's marine charts. The late Joe Eiguren of Boise was extremely interested in the legend and studied Xamurre's work. "Everybody talks about the Basques coming to Idaho, and that is relatively unimportant," said Eiguren. "I would like them to know that they did something besides herd sheep—I'd like them to know that they were very prominent explorers and colonizers."

Although the primary motivation pushing people to leave the Basque Country was likely economic, some historians have speculated that the early overseas forays of the Basques show that they have an inherent propensity for exploration. "It seemed that the Basques' natural instinct was to go and discover the world," wrote scholar Marie Pierre Arrizabalaga. Yet even the Basques' earliest voyages to the Canadian coast for whale and codfish were financially motivated, so we should suppose that they expected to gain some material wealth by joining the many voyages of discovery from Europe to different parts of the world.

Juan de Lakotsa, navigator on Columbus's historic 1492 voyage, was Basque, and there is no question that many of his seamen were Basque. The expedition of Magellan, who was attempting to circumnavigate the globe when he was killed in the Philippines in 1521, was taken over by second-in-command Juan Sebastian Elcano—a Basque. In the history books, the expedition is always associated with Magellan, and Elcano, who completed the trip, is given short shrift. In his hometown of Getaria, Gipuzkoa, Elcano's accomplishments are celebrated annually.

In the 1500s and 1600s, Basques were heavily involved in the French and Spanish exploration and colonization of the New World and Asia. Basque mariners traveled primarily to Latin America and the Philippines. They left behind descendants bearing Basque names. Basques can be most easily identified by their last names. Typically the surname refers to the location of the family's house. For example, Carricaburu is a common Basque last name and means "the head (or upper part) of the street."

The bay on Baja California's west coast, Bahía Sebastián Vizcaíno is named for the sixteenth-century Basque explorer who eventually traveled all the way up the Pacific Coast. Cape de Alava, at the northernmost tip of the coast of Washington State, was likely named for Basque explorations. On the East Coast, in Florida, numerous Bizkaia-related place names—among them Key Biscayne, Biscayne Bay, the Vizcaya Castle—reflect the contributions made by other Basque seamen. (At one time, *Vizcaíno* was a generic Spanish term used to refer to all Basques.)

In the 1700s and 1800s many Basques followed their pioneering countrymen to Argentina, Uruguay, Chile, Peru, and Venezuela. There they became heavily involved in the sheep industry, and many of them became wealthy landowners and civic leaders. Juan de Garay, for instance, founded the Argentine city of Buenos Aires. When movements for independence from Spain spread through South America in the early nineteenth century, Basques were in the thick of the battles. South American liberator Simón Bolívar was part Basque.

In the chapter "Sheepmen of South America," in their book *Amerikanuak*, authors William Douglass and Jon Bilbao noted that colonial South America attracted Basque immigrants from a more educated strata of society, people who often became landowners and participated in civic and religious affairs. Abroad they saw opportunities for advancement in commerce and trade, in ranching and in civil, military, and religious institutions. Of course, it helped that the Basques had the Spanish language in common with the other settlers of the area. A statistic in a 1961 bulletin from Donostia/San Sebastián bears out Douglass and Bilbao's observation: 108 presidents in sixteen Latin American countries had Basque heritage. After the Latin American countries had achieved independence (by 1825), a much larger portion of those Basques who arrived there took up jobs as laborers, some as meat-salting plant workers, milk vendors, loggers, and brick or charcoal makers.

Mexico

Basque navigators and sailors took part in the Spanish exploration of Mexico, and as the land was settled, many were given powerful military and political positions. In the early 1800s many Basques joined the Mexicans in their fight for independence from Spain, so Basque names run throughout the history of Mexico's many important battles. Basques also served as civic and religious leaders in Mexico's northern settlements, which at the time included parts of what is now the American Southwest. Francisco Ibarra explored northern Mexico, where he founded the province of Nueva Vizcaya. He named its capital Durango after his birthplace. Some historians credit Juan de Oñate, an early colonizer of the area that is now New Mexico, with founding the city of Santa Fe in 1598, although most U.S. history books give Governor Don Peralta credit for doing so in 1610.

Today the influence of Basques in Mexico has spread extensively, as evidenced by the many Mexicans who carry Basque names. The continuous large immigration of Mexicans to the United States has added an abundant number of Basque names to the U.S. population. Ethnically, however, the vast majority of this group is Mexican. For those Mexicans who actually have Basque heritage, their Basque forebears date back so far that they know little about their Basque family tree.

As an occupational group, Catholic clergymen from the Basque Country can probably claim the longest presence in America, starting with the missionaries who came as early as the late 1500s. In Mexico the first Catholic archbishop, Juan Zumarraga, was Basque. Basque priests and friars helped in the development of the missions that were California's first settlements. Basque Fermín Francisco de Lasuen was president of the missions for eighteen years starting in 1785, right after founding father Junipero Serra. Another Basque, Vicente de Sarria, followed Lasuen. Many came on missions to Christianize the indigenous people, some of whom were given Basque family names.

In addition to expanding the missions, a number of Basques also joined Spain's efforts to establish military bases in the California territory. Several became officers and administrators. Three Basques served as consecutive governors to Alta California from 1793 until at least 1815—Joaquín de Arrillaga, Diego de Borica y Retegui, and Pablo Vicente de Sola—seeing through the governorship of the territory from Spanish to Mexican rule. Later, when the region was part of Mexico, José Maria de Echeandia had the top post from 1825 to 1830, and the controversial Mexican Basque Manuel Micheltorena took over from 1842 until he was forced to resign in 1845.

Forty years before the Gold Rush, local indigenous tribes still dominated the outpost that later became California. As late as 1810 there were only 2,000 Europeans in the state. When Mexico took over in 1812, colonization efforts continued. Mexican dons were given large land grants for ranching. A few Basques settled in the territory during this period. Most of them were Basque merchants in Mexico and South America who began a shipping trade with clients in California. Some of them, such as Jose Antonio Aguirre, Cesareo Lataillade, and Miguel de Pedrorena, became wealthy landowners and socialized with California's elite Spanish families.

■ Immigration to the United States

Alta California belonged to Mexico until February 1848, exactly two months before the first gold strikes. But after California was annexed by the United States, Europeans from all over began arriving at its ports. During the initial Gold Rush years, Basques were present in the mining camps in sufficient numbers to be mentioned specifically by newspaper reporters of the time.

During the 1850s and 1860s, Basques did not venture beyond California. The destruction of cotton fields in the South during the Civil War, as well as the need to supply meat to the growing mining towns, increased the demand for sheep and wool. Once the transcontinental railway was completed in 1869, the number of European Basque arrivals increased, since they could sail directly to New York City and catch a train for the long trip across the country. Unlike other immigrant groups who sought jobs in industrialized East Coast cities, the early Basques made the West their sole destination.

In the beginning, almost all Basque immigrants were single young men who saw the opportunities in this country as being mostly rural, manual labor jobs. This work appealed to poor disinherited farm folk, who usually had little formal education. As a result, the general perception of Basques in this country in those early days may have been somewhat skewed.

One of the most significant factors propelling so many Basques to leave their homeland was the unwritten single-heir law of the Basques that prevailed in the rural areas. Despite a national French law that called for equal division of a family's property among the children, Basque peasant families were unwilling to break up their land. Traditionally they passed the land on to one child, usually the oldest, and the remaining family members had to find other ways to earn their livelihood. Those who did not inherit land had an incentive to emigrate. Some estimates suggest that approximately 5,000 Basques left Europe every year during the 1800s.

The strongest influence on Basque immigration patterns to the United States was the typical practice of sending for other family members and neighbors. It is not surprising then that Basques in the United States were typically concentrated in areas according to their villages or regions. Among the Basques who settled in California in the mid-1800s most were Nafarrak from the inland farming communities on both sides of the Pyrenees. (At one time the region of Nafarroa extended into what is now France, but the political border split it into two provinces, Nafarroa and Nafarroa Beherea [Lower Nafarroa]. The dialects of the two provinces are very similar.) A majority came from a cluster of villages around Donibane-Garazi. Meanwhile, Spain's Bizkaitarrak, who started arriving in the United States a little later in the 1880s, were concentrated in Idaho. Giputxes, as Giputzak were often called, and those from Zuberoa and Lapurdi in France never came to the United States in large numbers.

Reno, Winnemucca, and Elko, Nevada, which were at railroad crossroads and a midway point on the sheep trails, have quite a mixture of Hegoaldetarrak and Iparraldetarrak. Yet Nevada towns were dominated by people from two or three villages alone. Indeed, Father Adrien Gachitéguy, who wrote a book about the three months he spent traveling around the West during the 1950s, found that the largest numbers of Basque immigrants to this country came from the towns of Aldudes, Esterenzubi, and Arnegi, all in Nafarroa Beherea.

In South America the Basques had established themselves as experts in the sheep industry that dominated the southern pampas.

In California the early arrivals from South America were quickly disappointed in their mining efforts and turned to their acquired expertise in cattle and sheep raising. "For these men, California offered the opportunity to replay the South American scenario, with the added advantage of a ready and inflated market for meat products in the nearby gold camps," wrote Richard Lane and William Douglass in *The Basque Sheepherders of the American West.*

Basques began arriving in great numbers as word spread to those back home of the money to be made working as *artzainak* (sheepherders). For the poor farmers' sons, the money to be earned constituted a small fortune, despite the low wages. Sheep businessmen in the United States sought out the Basques in greater numbers as they realized their dependability and ability to withstand the lonely herder life.

Despite their apparent willingness and ability to spend months on end with no one to talk to except the camp tender during his visit every few days, a few herders did go mad. Others were eager to leave the business as soon as they could. In many cases it was only pride that kept them from fleeing back home. Judging by the carvings they left on the aspen trees along their trails, they obsessed about women and sex. Some sheepherders, though, saw the occupation's solitude as an advantage because there were no distractions on which to waste their money. Many would work for three to five years, saving every penny they earned for their return to the Basque Country. Others chose to pursue their fortunes here and asked to be paid in ewes, which they herded along with their other charges until they had enough to break off on their own.

Settlement Patterns

As the number of Basque sheep outfits expanded, so did the amount of grazing land they needed. In time the sheep owners moved from Los Angeles to California's interior valleys, where land was still open and there was enough grazing land on which to feed their herds during the wet winter months. Quickly, the herders discovered the benefits of trailing sheep to the high green pastures of the Sierra Nevada and the San Bernardino Mountains during the dry summers.

Thus did the traveling sheepherding pattern known as *transhumance* develop. The owners were known as tramp or gypsy sheep operators because they were constantly on the move and did not own their own land.

Increased homesteading and the shrinking of open range in California pushed sheepmen east, first into Nevada during the 1870s, and from there into Oregon and Idaho. They were following on the heels of miners who had ventured beyond California. As miners and settlers realized the economic potential in agriculture in the inland states, small ranching communities began to develop, and the demand for meat in these areas increased. There were early reports that in order to meet this need, Basques were running sheep from Arizona, New Mexico, and Texas up north to the new mining communities in Nevada, Idaho, and Oregon to sell them.

By the turn of the century, Basques had settled throughout the Great Basin states, between California's Sierra Nevada and Utah's Wasatch Mountains—Nevada, Idaho, Oregon, Wyoming, and Montana—where the public lands were not so crowded, because the use of public land was crucial to the survival of small-time sheep operators.

Although the seasonal back-and-forth pattern appeared ideal for raising sheep, it had its adverse side too. Cattle ranchers felt the sheepherders were trespassing on land that rightfully belonged to them. This led to fights and harassment of Basque sheepherders by cattle ranchers. Sheepherders were shot at or dragged behind horses, their sheep were killed, and their camps were burned. They gained a bad reputation, exacerbated by biased newspaper reports of the day, for ignoring rules and feigning ignorance. The Basques were criticized for being foreigners who saved their money and then left the country. It didn't help that the earliest arrivals spoke no English, and they spent months to years in the mountains where they could not practice or learn the language. But a few newspaper editors and forest rangers in the early 1900s provided alternative views, praising the Basques as conscientious workers who were simply trying to please their employers.

But it was true that many immigrants stayed only as long as they had to, to accumulate enough money to buy property back home—a desire that had brought them to America in the first place. "By all indications, there was a very, very large number of people going back," said Professor William Douglass, adding that there's no way to estimate how many. "It waxed and waned depending on economic conditions here and the political situation there." Both French and Spanish Basques avoided military conscription during different periods because they felt no allegiance to the countries they were being asked to serve. "Under no circumstances did I want to go into the army for Mr. Franco," said Elko restaurateur Tony Leniz, from the small town of Gizaburuaga, Bizkaia, voicing a common sentiment. "It would have been a waste of two years."

Basque settlement patterns across the American West followed logical paths along major transportation routes, particularly the railroad. As the sheepmen headed farther and farther inland, Basque boardinghouses cropped up along the way, most notably at the major train stops where Basques would debark for their first view of the West or at towns where the sheepherders would come to load their sheep. Soon significant concentrations of Basque families and ranchers settled around the hotels and boardinghouses, creating Basque neighborhoods. From the 1920s on, transcontinental highway routes began crisscrossing many of these towns, bringing even more people.

Migration across America to the West continued steadily without interruption from the turn of the century until 1924, when a national quota system was adopted, seriously restricting entry to immigrants according to country. The influx from Spain, whose large Basque population had filled a majority of the sheepherder ranks until then, was limited to 131 immigrants for the entire United States per year. While the French were also limited by a quota, it had much less of an impact on them because they immigrated in fewer numbers. For years afterward, many Spanish Basques entered the country illegally by jumping ship.

The Taylor Grazing Act

In the early 1930s a combination of overgrazing and serious drought conditions chased a few sheepherders east to state-owned grazing lands in Colorado, with cooler weather and greener pastures. But a few territorial cattle ranchers got mad and sought protection of their interests. At their request, U.S. Senator Edward Taylor introduced the Taylor Grazing Act in 1934, which essentially put all the country's

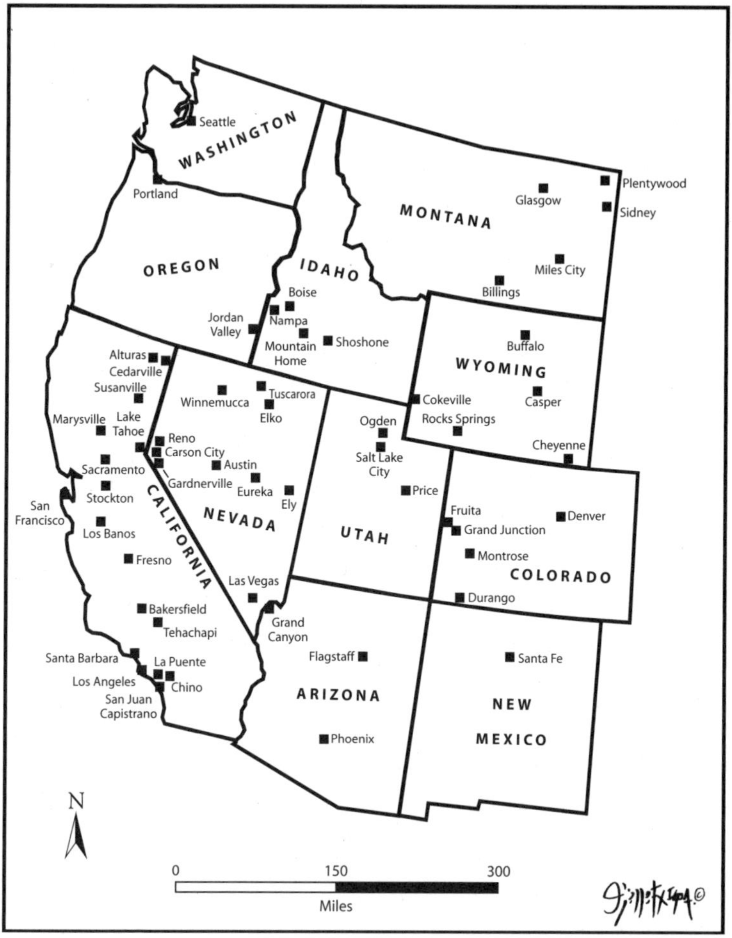

The Western states.

remaining public lands under federal control and under the same restrictions as the national forests, effectively blocking the foreign herders' access to the free grazing areas because it gave grazing privileges only to landowning ranchers. The typical tramp sheepherder, who packed all his possessions on his donkey as he traveled from place to place with his band of sheep, had avoided buying property, because it would tie him to this country when all he really wanted was to make some money and return home. The Taylor legislation marked the end of a viable way of life for the gypsy sheepherder. It also coincided with the years of the Great Depression, when many a sheep owner lost his entire band to the bank and herders lost years' worth of wages that they had been banking with their bosses.

Discouragement over the obstacles to continued sheepherding in the Western United States led many Basques to return home, complaining that herding was no longer a viable occupation. But for those who had built up their outfits and already acquired land, the new law posed no problems. In fact, the late Basque sheepman Jean Urruty saw it quite differently. He acquired a wealth of property in Colorado, and he was tired of the poor reputation shouldered by Basques in the sheep business. He had buried more than one herder because he would not be accepted by a funeral home. "The Taylor Grazing Act in 1934 was a blessing for sheepmen. The allotment system settled the battles which were pretty much a moonshine business anyway," he said. Herders who stayed went to work for large property-owning sheep operations or moved into other ranching jobs. Those who could bought land and continued raising sheep. Most, however, preferred to leave life on the range, if possible, and integrate into the ever-growing urban areas. This was especially true in California, where city jobs were more abundant.

Postwar Immigration Upswing

After the passage of the Taylor Grazing Act, U.S. citizenship took on more importance for those who stayed, since it facilitated many other goals Basque immigrants strived for, such as owning land and gaining permission to graze animals on federal land. But even those who were not ranch owners sought citizenship. Some of the earliest Basque organizations were mutual aid societies, which included among their objectives helping Basques learn English and achieve citizenship. A few Basques signed up for the U.S. Army as a way of obtaining citizenship. Those who served in the military learned English much more quickly, which propelled them up the economic ladder faster than their compatriots.

The wave of Basque arrivals here slowed considerably in the 1940s, in large part because of World War II. Soon the demand for herders became greater than the supply. Sheep ranchers would offer Basques a contract guaranteeing payment of their voyage in exchange for a commitment of several years' work. But they always needed more men because the herders they employed would eventually leave and go into other lines of business once they paid off their debt. Western senators pushed through special bills that gave permanent residency to Basques who had entered the country illegally, even identifying the illegal immigrants by name. But it was not enough, and the high demand led the powerful Senator Pat McCarren and Congressman Walter Baring, both of Nevada, to push for approval of legislation that became commonly known as the "Sheepherder Bills." Under these measures, passed during the 1950s, hundreds of Basque herders were brought in to replenish the dwindling supply. The California Range Association (which later became the Western Range Association), comprised of ranchers, became a powerful lobby for Basque sheepherders. More changes in immigration laws authored by McCarren allowed skilled laborers to enter if employers specified that the job they had come to fill could not be filled by U.S. citizens. Ranchers noted that no group could withstand the isolated job like the Basques could.

Frank Maitia Sr. of Bakersfield remembers the years after the war, between 1947 and 1955, when immigration was on the upswing. He helped his in-laws manage the Amestoy Hotel, and then later he bought the Basque Café, where all the young Basque immigrants in the area liked to spend their Saturday nights. "They were coming every month. Sometimes twenty-five to thirty of them would come in one month."

Southern California's warm weather allowed many workers to take advantage of two lambing seasons. In the summer they would head for Nevada, where cold winters caused the lambing season to arrive earlier. In September or October the lambing season would start for the Bakersfield operations. The sheepherders would come into town in between, for a week, maybe a month. "By the end of October," Maitia remembered, "everybody was gone."

Despite the increased influx of Basques to this country to satisfy demand for ranchers, the problem of herders leaving once their contracts were up was not resolved. Because of their low wages, they couldn't afford to buy their own land, which they needed to start an operation. It was natural that they would get into other lines of business when they could no longer afford to get into the sheep business as owners. As they sought jobs other than sheepherding, they moved away from the rural areas to the cities. Basque communities in the small towns died a small death. The only areas that were able to keep Basques in the second half of the century were those that provided lots of employment opportunities for manual laborers. In San Francisco, it was gardening. In Chino, it was milking cows at the dairies. A few small towns, like Burns, Oregon, had lumber mills that employed Basques. In northern Utah, southwestern Wyoming, and northeastern Nevada, Basques were drawn by mining operations that continue to this day.

The End of the Basque Sheepherder

Even though the majority of the Basques arriving in the United States eventually went into other lines of work, the sheepherder roaming the Western range with his burro, his dog, and a herd of thousands of sheep has become the stereotypical image of the Basque immigrant.

Today that chapter of the history of the Basques in this country is closed. The sheep industry in the United States is on the decline, and Basques no longer immigrate to fill the herder ranks. Today the Basques that are still involved in the sheep business are all owners and managers. At that level, they still carry significant weight in the industry, as they do in the cattle business, to which more and more Basque ranchers are shifting their resources. "In the West, Basques are still a potent force," said Bob Erreca, head of Erreca Cattle Company, based in Los Banos.

Ironically, some of the Basque restaurants that serve lamb dishes, which were the sheepherders' main fare, now import the meat from Australia and New Zealand. Sheep business owners point to many changes in legislation over the years as the main contributors to the slow death of the sheep business in this country over the past fifty years: Pro-environmental laws, prohibiting the shooting or poisonous baiting of coyotes—sheep's biggest enemy—are causing some of the worst damage, according to many. The protection of endangered species has also decreased the amount of available grazing lands. Grazing fees are more expensive. There's not much demand for wool these days. And foreign competition is undercutting the price U.S. ranches can get for sheep at market. "They can raise them so much cheaper," said Paco Iturriria, president of the Kern County Woolgrowers Association, about the sheep business in Australia and New Zealand. "But the quality of our meat is much, much better." The one bright spot is that consumption of lamb in the United States is higher today than it was ten years ago, and the total remains steady.

Grace and John Mainvil operated sheep outfits in California and in Idaho. For many years they pastured their sheep in California, around the Riverside and Chino areas, but in the 1960s they decided to move to Idaho, where urban intrusion was not such a problem. But Grace said that eventually ranching became just as difficult in Idaho. In 1973 the poison bait they had used for years to eliminate sheep predators such as coyotes was outlawed. That was the beginning of the population explosion among coyotes, cougars, and bears. She remembered the time when a bear stampeded a herd of four hundred head of their sheep in Hells Canyon, forcing them over a cliff, where they piled up on top of each other and suffocated to death. The Mainvils sold their sheep in 1974. "We were just fighting a losing battle," she said. "Running sheep is a very, very difficult operation."

The Basque-owned Mendiburu Land and Livestock Company of Bakersfield was at one time the largest single open-range sheep enterprise in the West, controlling huge properties across California, Arizona, and Texas. At one time or another, most Basques across the West have herded sheep for the Mendiburu company. But the industry is not what it once was, according to industry spokesman Paco Iturriria. At its peak, during the 1970s the Mendiburu business ran twenty-five thousand to forty thousand sheep. Today Mendiburu raises more cattle than sheep, and several other sheep growers have grown larger. But these days, even the biggest sheep companies do not run more than ten thousand to twelve thousand head of sheep.

The economic position of sheepherders in this country is deteriorating. The wages no longer buy what they once did. The California Range Association, hoping to stop losing herders to other jobs, had fought for legislation to allow herders to enter the country under contract with a specific rancher for only three years. Although some Basques may not have cared to stay any longer—and in fact some did go home and then returned for additional three-year stints—others were discouraged because the program didn't allow them to stay long enough to obtain legal residency, which requires a five-year stay.

Today's herders are likely to be Mexican, Peruvian, or Chilean. Few Basques remain in the occupation. "I asked everywhere—but I only know of one," said Father Jean Eliçagaray, who traveled around the eleven western states from 1991 to 1994 serving as chaplain to the American Basques. "There are none anymore."

Even though the sheepherder era is over, the ethos still lives on. Older Basques who lived the life still tell stories from the days when they participated in the development of the Old West. "They left the mountains as soon as they could," said Eliçagaray. "There they had the most difficult moments of their life . . . and the greatest joys." The spirit of that time and a certain nostalgia for it is likely to linger in the collective heart of the U.S. Basque colony forever.

Basque Immigration Slows to a Trickle

Basque immigration has slowed down significantly in the second half of this century. Most of the decrease can be attributed to the industrial development of the Basque Country since World War II. Basques who once lived a poor, rural existence now have the option of leaving the countryside for jobs in the cities. The economy in the Basque Country has been growing at a healthy pace for many years, providing more local job opportunities and improving salaries. Workers' disability and social security are now available in Europe. France even provides monthly subsidies to families with three children or more. None of these programs were available in the early part of the century. In Spain, too, the economy has vastly improved over the last two decades, so even Hegoaldetarrak, who once came to America in great numbers, are unwilling to come to the United States today to fill the demand for herders.

For additional factors to explain the lack of Basque immigration to the United States in recent years, we can look at some of the very forces that drove Basques out of their homeland in the first place. In the past, given that the economy was land based, farming families were large, and the laws of inheritance placed the family land in the hands of only one child. There were a significant number of Basques who would not own their own land and thus could not be sure of an income in the Basque Country. Today's families are much smaller, and, ironically, on some of these small farms, parents even fear none of their children will want to take over the farm when they die. The exodus from rural villages to the Basque Country's larger cities is growing, as youngsters from farming families opt to learn trades or other less backbreaking livelihoods.

Over time the lonely herder life became less and less appealing. The number of Basque women immigrating to the United States slowed significantly, because with many boardinghouses closing down, fewer jobs were available. The most recent wave of immigrants, during the 1960s, was made up predominantly of men from Hegoalde. "They're making the same money as we make over here," said Joe Garde of Bakersfield. "That was the reason we immigrated here before—to make more money. They don't have to leave." Garde, now a bartender, arrived in the United States in 1964 to work for the Bidart brothers' sheep operation in Bakersfield, one of the biggest in the area. "I think we're the last Basques to immigrate here," said Garde.

In the past twenty years, immigration from the Basque Country has dropped so low that it has been offset by the many families who have returned to their homeland.

Education Levels Rise and Occupations Change

Basque-Americans in ever greater numbers are going into white-collar jobs as their assimilation into U.S. life increases. Maite Curutchague, past owner of Bakersfield's Chalet Basque, said that she never pushed her two children to join the family business. "Go to college," she told them. "You don't want to have to work hard like we did."

Many of the immigrant generation, like Curutchague, realize the value of higher education in this country. Yet within the traditional culture there is an overriding work ethic that reveres hard, manual labor. "Basques admire the self-made man. The industrious man is superior to the well-educated man," summed up Carol Pagliarulo in her master's thesis, "Basques in Stockton." Some of the immigrant generation that grew up laboring on the family farm complain that today's young people don't want to work. The criticism may reflect the immigrants' unwillingness to let go of their traditional respect for manual labor. They may resent the fact that many of the members of the younger, U.S.–born generations are not interested in taking on the labor-intensive jobs (sheepherding, milking, gardening) or time-consuming occupations (hoteliers or restaurant owners) that their elders engaged in. Some of the older Basques may think that the young people who work for big white-collar companies are relinquishing their personal autonomy. And sometimes, children's resistance to following in the parents' footsteps means the end of businesses family members have spent lifetimes building.

Yet the old ideas seem to be changing as the world becomes more technological. "Now you need college for any job," said Jess Guerrica of the Lagun Onak Las Vegas Basque Club and father of three. "Now there will be more [Basques] going to college." In fact, as early as 1948 John Edlefsen remarked on the "commendable" pattern of greater schooling among second- and third-generation Basque-Americans in southwest Idaho. Many of the Basque clubs today are offering scholarships to the children of their members to encourage them to go to college.

Today Basques are just as likely to express pride in the members of their communities who have excelled in professions such as law or academics, or made their way into public life, such as former Nevada governor Paul Laxalt, good friend of former president Ronald Reagan; the longtime secretary of state in Idaho Pete Cenarrusa; and former California senator and insurance commissioner John Garamendi, who ran for governor in 1994.

Youngsters Immigrate to the Basque Country

In a turnaround of the prior practice, in which Basque men returned to the Basque Country to find a wife and bring her to the United States, some of today's youth are finding love and marriage in the Old Country. As more and more of the high school and college-age students travel to study or vacation in the Basque Country, the number of reported marriages between Basque-Americans and Basques seems to be on the rise.

"I'd go over to Spain and find myself a Basque husband any day," exclaimed Melissa Guerrica when she was a high school senior in Las Vegas. Her mother, Mary Guerrica, smiled at the comment, adding that her daughter has traveled to her grandparents' hometowns and found the young Basque men over there very attractive.

Almost every Basque community can count a handful of young people, mostly women, who have married in the Basque Country and stayed there to live—a reverse migration, in effect. During a trip back to see his family in Aldudes, Franxoa Bidaurreta ran into a young woman who had grown up in San Francisco, but who had fallen in love during a trip to her parents' small hometown, stayed, and got married. "She seemed real satisfied with her life right there."

Basque Traits

The Basques' tenacity for survival is arguably their greatest attribute. An interesting question to consider is whether the common characteristics of these hardy people have helped the culture survive through the centuries, or whether they developed those characteristics in order to survive. In addition to being hard workers, Basques are known for being honest, loyal, and very independent. They can also be stubborn to the point of frustration. They are used to following their own minds. Manuel Villanueva puts it simply: "Knowing us . . . you'd have five guys and six different opinions."

The very same attributes that distinguish this small cultural group and have helped it survive in its native region may also have been instrumental in the Basques' successful adaptation to life in the United States. Like other immigrant groups, the Basques who arrived here tended to be clannish. They married Basques and associated mostly with other Basque immigrants. The Basques shared some similarities with some other prominent immigrant groups, such as the Italians and Irish; namely, many of them also came from poor farming backgrounds, and they held tight to Catholicism.

Most of the Basques who arrived here came from farms that were completely self-sufficient. They raised all their own fruits and vegetables, and they kept cows for milk and pigs for meat. They typically sold a pig or a cow once or twice a year to have money for the few items they could not make themselves, like salt and sugar. All the members of the family had to learn many trades just to maintain the farm. They had to have business sense, in addition to knowing about farming, carpentry work, and a host of other work. This versatility proved very useful to them in the United States, where they were willing and qualified to do many jobs. Although almost all started as herders, very few stayed with that job. They changed occupations, sometimes two or three times in one lifetime, typically seeking jobs that gave them more independence and money. Because of their farming background, they had some familiarity with most of the jobs they took—agricultural jobs, ranching, dairy work, and gardening. Many of those who went into hotel and restaurants or bakeries came from families who operated such businesses back in the Basque Country. In other cases, they learned such trades after joining relatives who were running such businesses here.

The Basques' reputation as hard workers helped pave their way in this country, because employers knew they could rely on their Basque employees. But once a Basque had some money tucked away, his employer was likely to lose him, because inevitably Basques would seek the opportunity to start their own business.

One Basque put it quite simply: "If you're going to work hard, you might as well work for yourself." Thus spoke Manuel Villanueva of Downey, California, who runs his own wholesale meat-selling business. Owning one's own business does bring headaches and worries twenty-four hours a day, seven days a week, but, says Villanueva, "I'd rather work for myself."

Basques helped one another financially by doing business with other Basques. They started businesses with the help of the entire family, and children were likely to take over when their parents got old. As they became more successful, Basques took greater risks. Basque sheepmen would take out more loans to buy more property or sheep. A few, the wealthiest, were known for giving out loans to other Basques without a second thought, based solely on a verbal agreement. And then there were a couple who even started small local banks.

Perhaps because of their small numbers and extensive networking, many Basques have stuck together and maintained their customs in this country better than many other ethnic groups, despite the disintegration of Basque communities. "You don't have the ethnic identity on a daily basis that a Chinese in Chinatown does," said Basque expert William A. Douglass. "Those people live an ethnic reality that is not even available to the Basques." Consequently, acting out their ethnic traditions is a much more conscious decision for Basques than for larger, stronger ethnic groups in the United States. "Basque social life really does center on the Basque centers and social clubs," Douglass said.

In a country that admires independence and initiative, the Basques' possession of both traits eventually brought them social acceptance and economic well-being. At the same time, Basques have maintained a certain aloofness, keeping their culture to themselves. While many of their ethnic customs, such as their cuisine, folk dancing, and festivals, have gained a growing audience of non-Basque admirers, they organize their festivals and banquets primarily for their own pleasure. Pierre Lhande, who wrote about Basque emigration in 1910, said it well:

> The Basque knows well how to become part, externally, of his new environment: he has realized that it is very important for him to understand men and their customs well because this flexibility of character and judgment would be important for his achievements.
>
> But if it is true that the Basque is capable of adapting to the customs and ways of life of his new environment, it is also true that this adoption is totally superficial, and that, basically, he is

> one of those types of foreigners who maintains more vividly and intact his national individualism.

It will be interesting to follow the development of the Basque community in the United States now that emigration from the Basque Country has ceased almost completely. Will it be possible to preserve the Basque culture in this country without a constant influx of immigrants from the native land? Will the Basque people's strong survival traits help the culture to survive in the United States? Basques appear to have maintained certain practices and customs in other countries where they migrated in large numbers, such as Argentina, Chile, and Mexico, where most immigration took place in the nineteenth century. In those countries, the culture has survived, but it has taken on intrinsic Argentinean, Chilean, or Mexican ways to create slightly different cultural practices, just as it has become American, roundly defined by the sheepherding experience.

Basque Culture and Traditions

Basque culture and traditions have developed in the United States based on practices brought from the Old Country but also based on the patterns of life Basques established in their new homes through the work they chose, the places where they chose to live, and the rhythms of their lives.

The Herder Life

The herder lived a rough and lonely life for many months of the year. During the winter and early spring, there was sufficient feed for sheep to graze at lower elevations, and getting supplies was not a problem. During the winter months, herders lived in sheep wagons, which contained a stove and an oven in which they could bake bread as needed. But in the dry summers, the sheep were taken to the greener pastures in the high mountain ranges, where the wagons couldn't go. "Sheepherders always took their tents into the high country," relates Basque historian Joxe Mallea of the University of Nevada, Reno.

The rhythm of the sheepherder's year was built upon the winter grazing places, the lambing periods, the summer months spent in high mountain ranges with plenty of grass and fresh water, and the trip to town to send the sheep off to market. There would be a few weeks spent in town, living in the boardinghouses, buying new clothes, and enjoying a bit of civilization. Based on these yearly activities, the sheepherder led a life of loneliness, solitude, and self-sufficiency out with the elements in the grazing months, with little contact except to pick up supplies from the camp tender or talk with herders should their trails meet. Some left messages to friends or sketches of women or poems engraved on the aspen trees.

Basque Boardinghouses

The Basque boardinghouse, with its dining room and bar, served as a home away from home for newly arrived Basques, but it was also home to the itinerant sheepherder for those months when he did not need to be with the sheep, and to mine workers. The boardinghouses tended to be located near the town's rail depot so as to be easy to find and also to attract travelers stopping over for a few days on their way west or north. Oftentimes Basque families would simply rent out rooms in their homes, and their boardinghouse would be known by the family name. The woman of the house would serve up good home cooking, family-style, to her boarders.

The earliest Basque boardinghouses or rooming houses, referred to by Basques as *ostatuak* or *hotelak,* were two stories with a balcony on the second story and a large kitchen occupying an important place. They had all the features of a European boardinghouse, with individual rooms and common bathrooms down the hall. This setup remained unchanged throughout the life of the boardinghouses. Meals were served in one main dining room. For the holidays, the boarders became part of the extended family. "They would eat what we put out there, and it was a darn good meal," said Lyda Esain, of Fresno. In the early days of the *ostatuak,* the dining rooms were only for the boarders during the week, but on the weekends the hotel keepers welcomed Basques from the community who were friends of boarders or of the owners.

The social life of the early Basque communities revolved around the boardinghouse. The families that operated the boardinghouses mixed with the guests, and those Basques who had once stayed in the boardinghouses later brought their families there to socialize. They would come for dinner at the long tables, to play *mus* or pelota, to listen to music and to dance. Many Basque women coming to America to marry their Basque sweetheart would rendezvous with him at a Basque boardinghouse, where they would celebrate the marriage and the honeymoon. Some establishments took in sick people and women were ready to deliver babies in towns that didn't have a hospital.

In the earliest days, the boardinghouses were dependent on Basques and their sheepherder wages, yet that was sufficient. That situation eventually turned around. Many of the old-time boardinghouse owners turned their dining rooms into restaurants. A majority of the clientele who patronize today's Basque restaurants is American. Nevertheless, Basque restaurants, where Basques are likely to see a familiar face or two, have played an integral part in maintaining the culture. Even those who have grown out of touch with the Basque community enjoy taking their families out for a Basque dinner where a flicker of nostalgia over past family outings is likely to grab hold of them and remind them of their roots.

The boardinghouses, and even the restaurants that evolved from the boardinghouses, were all run by immigrants. "There was not one who took on a hotel who was born here," said former San Francisco hotel owner Aña Iriartborde. That is still true for the most part, but there are a number of exceptions as U.S.-born family members realize there's money to be made in the Basque restaurant business. The primary reason is because the clientele has changed. "We have a lot of Basque customers, but the American is constant," said Elvira Cenoz of Gardnerville, Nevada. "We make our living from the American," she said, repeating a comment made by many other Basque restaurant owners.

Food

Typically the first contact most non-Basques have with the culture is through the many Basque restaurants to be found in the Western states. The unique family-style dinners—with their huge tureens of vegetable soup, plates full of lamb or beef, and never-ending bottles of red wine linger in the memory of even the most finicky eater.

Because the first Basque restaurants were simply extensions of the boardinghouse dining room, the American public established an association between Basque cuisine, long tables, and the large family-style servings. "That is Basque-American," emphasized Roger Minhondo, of San Rafael's Chalet Basque. "That family-style doesn't exist in France." (Although food is served that way in some small village restaurants.) Americans didn't know what Basque cuisine was before it was introduced in the boardinghouse setting.

The Basques take food seriously in the tradition of their French and Spanish neighbors. Cooking and eating take a central place in the Basque family life. Meals are meant to be lingered over, in the company of friends and family, and are always accompanied by the essential red wine.

The sheepherder out on the range relied heavily on beans, potatoes, and the abundant supply of lamb meat. Although his only companions besides the sheep were his dog and his burro, he nevertheless took time every day to make a fire and cook himself a hearty meal. Sheepherders adapted the familiar Basque dishes they knew, developing their own style of cooking. Lamb stew was a staple. Most of those sheepherder dishes, with their emphasis on red meat, have been incorporated into the menus of most Basque restaurants in this country. The late Jean Baptiste Larrateguy, of Millbrae, who was trained as a chef in France, once described Basque cooking in this country as essentially home cooking produced in mass quantities.

Wine or other alcoholic drinks have always been in plentiful supply at every hotel, restaurant, and Basque festival, and the rowdy crowds at the end of a good Basque party are often inspired by alcohol. Basques' determination in sidestepping Prohibition laws to have their alcohol is proof of its integral role in Basque daily life. Red wine was part of the food supply delivered to many sheepherders out on the range every few days. In fact, "it was part of the contract that they had to have a gallon of wine every five days," said DeLoyd Satterthwaite, of the Basque herders he hired at the Spanish Ranch in Nevada. In comparison, he notes that today's herders, who are mostly Peruvian and Mexican, drink soda, not wine.

Barbecues

Big barbecues were common in early ranch life. The actual killing of the lamb, sometimes hauled up on a rope by its hind legs, was somewhat ceremonial, witnessed by the men and others who could stand to watch. Killing a hog was also a group activity. These were farm rituals they had practiced in their homeland.

Today these practices continue, although in a different form. Local Basques usually butcher the meat for the festival barbecues. At Basque restaurants, many Basques make their own chorizos and cure their own ham. Just like in the Old Country, the blood is typically saved to make blood sausage. "People think that is gross, but that is part of the culture," said Linda Alzaa of Gooding, Idaho, who grew up on a ranch among Basques.

Early ranching barbecues were in one sense the precursors to today's festival. Families would get together, sometimes to help each other with big jobs on the farm or with the lambing or cattle roundups. The hosting family would kill a pig or a lamb to share with those who came to help. Sometimes they didn't even need an excuse to get together, but the barbecue was typically the central part of the reunion. The same could be said for today's festivals. The midday meal

Seafood

In Europe Basque cuisine is best known for its seafood specialties. But this specialization did not make the transition across the Atlantic to a significant degree for several reasons. Most of the herders who came to California came from mountain villages, where seafood was not commonly served. "They were not used to eating fish," said former California hotel owner Ganix Iriartborde. And the boardinghouses catered to the herders' tastes. If they didn't ask for it, the cook didn't make it. Idaho, on the other hand, was full of Bizkaitarrak, who ate lots of fish in their coastal region. But fresh seafood was not readily available so far inland in the early part of the century. So Basque-American cuisine developed without the emphasis on fish. Yet within the last twenty years more restaurants, particularly the higher-priced ones, have added more of the traditional seafood specialties from the Basque coastal region to their menus. Serving fish is also part of an effort to cater to Americans' healthier eating habits.

with barbecued lamb is sacrosanct, the highlight of the day for many. The meat is typically accompanied by a ladleful of beans, lettuce salad, a fat sourdough roll, and wine. For those who attend several festivals each summer, the food is the point of comparison.

The study of food's role in culture is gaining popularity among academics. "In preparing and serving and eating food, people say who they are. They say to themselves who they are," said David Wilson, director of American Studies at the University of California, Davis, in a November 18, 1993, article in the *Los Angeles Times.* Anthropologist Sidney Mintz, of Johns Hopkins University, remarked in the same article, "We never just feed. We always surround our eating behavior with all kinds of ceremony." For the Basques, sitting down to eat together has always been an essential part of any celebration.

Catholicism

A TRAVELING PRIEST

Since about 1960 a Basque priest from France has been assigned to the West Coast. Based out of San Francisco, he usually remains for several years and travels around the Western states, visiting families and celebrating Basque Masses on different occasions, including every festival. The U.S. Catholic Conference sponsors the priest, who is selected by the Bishop of Bayonne. Father Martxel Tillous arrived in 1994, replacing Father Jean Eliçagaray, who was here for three years. Father Jean Pierre Cachenaut enjoyed one of the longest stays in this country, from 1977 to 1986, and became a much loved member of the Basque community. Odette Etcheverry served as Father Cachenaut's answering service for the nine years he was in this country and saw the great number of invitations he received. "They want the priest there. It's an honor for them," she said.

CATHOLIC TRADITIONS

Catholic traditions are an integral part of the Basque culture. Young lives are celebrated with baptisms and First Communions. Marriages can be huge affairs, to which the majority of the local Basque

The Mass is an important part of the festival ritual for Basques, even for the youngest ones, like these young Elko Arinak dancers. (Photo by Averie Cohen.)

community is invited. For funerals, Basques feel compelled to show their support, even if they were only slightly acquainted with the person who died.

"When Basques died here," said Mary Gaztambide of Salt Lake City, "we'd go to the funeral whether we knew them or not. It was out of respect. We worried that nobody would go. A lot of these guys didn't know anybody," she said, referring to the sheepherders who had been here just a few years, and had spent most of their time in the mountains.

During his stay in the United States, Father Eliçagaray visited Basque families in the eleven western states. "The farther away they live, the more they anticipate my visit," said Eliçagaray about his travels. One tiny community in Miles City, Montana, organizes its picnic around the priest's annual visit—no matter when he arrives. In states where the few Basque families are spread out, such as New Mexico, Colorado, Utah, Montana, Oregon, and Washington, the priest makes house calls. "In California, there are lots of events where people can come to see the priests," said Eliçagaray. "I don't need to go house to house."

In large Basque communities like San Francisco's, special Basque Masses are organized to celebrate important Catholic holidays and festivals, and they are usually well attended. These occasions are the glue that holds the Basque community together. Old friends have a chance to find each other and renew old ties, while their children make new ones. In an effort to reach those who do not speak Euskara, Father Martxel Tillous has begun projecting onto the wall English translations, so parishioners can follow the Mass. The words to the hymns are printed and distributed so they can sing along.

Second-generation Basques, as they too marry and have children, are carrying on some of the religious traditions. Every year Bernard and Ann Marie Goyhenetche, of Marysville, California, take their two children to the Basque Mass on Palm Sunday at Notre Dame de Victoires in San Francisco. "We never miss that," said Ann Marie. The Goyhenetches, like other families, attend their own local parish most of the year, but they turn out for the special Basque Masses because it's an opportunity for their own extended family to get together as well as to see old friends. "We see people that we don't see all year until then," she said.

Festivals and Celebrations

Today's summer festivals are typically referred to as "Basque picnics," but they are so much more than picnics. Festival dates were often chosen to reflect a saint's day celebrated back home, such as San Inazio de Loyola in Boise. For that reason a one-day festival is likely to start with an early-morning Mass. It's followed by a massive barbecued lamb lunch, an afternoon of folk dance and singing exhibitions, as well as some fun competitions of wood chopping, weightlifting, and tug-of-war, and then, after dinner, there is a lively dance that will last late into the night.

The biggest annual festivals, like Winnemucca's and Elko's, last two days and are twice as much fun, with even more competitions thrown in. Almost all are held on a regular date every year, planned so that they don't overlap. A few Basques, young men in particular, will spend the entire summer traveling from one festival to another every weekend. This is a modern-day fad that resembles the summers spent in similar fashion by carefree youths roaming from festival to festival in the Basque Country.

For the most part Basques aren't interested in accommodating curiosity seekers, although they aren't unfriendly to them—especially later in the evening, when everyone has gotten warmed up after a few drinks and a few fandangos. Just don't expect to find friendly people doling out advice at the entrance to welcome you to these festivals. The events are organized primarily for Basques' own entertainment. They provide a welcome annual gathering where old friends can find each other, and new friendships are always being established.

If you're invited by a Basque, you'll be heartily welcomed. The Basques are proud of their heritage, and they are glad to see outsiders interested in their culture. J. B. Aguerre, president of the Chino Basque Club, sees that in the future the celebration of Basque culture will be expanded for the enjoyment of all Americans.

Athletics

Several Basque traditions practiced in the United States provide clues to the origins of Basque communities' members. The athletic contests organized most often at U.S. Basque festivals were practiced primarily on the Spanish side, and it is mostly in communities with large numbers of Hegoaldetarrak that you'll see them. The festivals in California, dominated by Iparraldetarrak, don't typically feature these competitions. Wood chopping developed in the high forested areas of Nafarroa. Weight carrying and stone lifting are closely related to mining and Old World stone quarry work. These also developed in Hegoalde.

"Play for Basques is not removed from everyday life," wrote scholar Sonia Eagle in her dissertation, "Work and Play Among the Basques of Southern California." "Rather, social and sports events are a way of transforming work into play. And just as work is best understood in terms of hard physical labor, play in the Basque world is always a test of strength and endurance more than it is a test of skill. The brute strength demonstrated in wood chopping, weight lifting and handball illustrate the value of strenuous physical exertion in the typical Basque work experience."

In early picnic days there were plenty of strapping young men trained in wood chopping and weight-lifting. But today no one has replaced the older athletes, so the traditional sports have lost much of their steam. "It's harder and harder to get people who can compete," said Janet Inda, and it's too expensive to bring them from the Basque Country. Mark Etcheberry, originally of Reno, became an extremely proficient *aizkolari* (wood chopper), after competing for years in

The biggest Basque festivals, like this one in Elko, always feature wood-chopping competitions. (Photo by Averie Cohen.)

Australia. He put on quite a show when he occasionally popped in at Reno for the festival. Weight-carrying is still popular, since anyone can easily participate. Crowds get a big kick out of watching young or older men huffing and puffing around the track.

Pelota

The game of pelota, or handball, developed from a medieval game known as *jeu de paume,* which was played face to face, like today's court tennis. The Basques are credited with the development of the modern game along with about a dozen variations. The most famous variation is jai alai, which Basques created by inventing the *txistera,* or basketlike extension worn on the hand. (For more information on jai alai, see the section on Connecticut and Rhode Island.) The simplest version of pelota is bare-handed handball, and this game is an integral part of the Basque culture. Other variations, such as *pala,* played with a wooden racket, can be played on the typical handball court. Different courts create different versions of the game, such as *trinket,* which is played against all four walls. Only one such court exists in the United States, in Chino, California.

Basque immigrants to this country began building courts so they could practice their favorite sport, and the game became a strong unifying factor for the U.S. Basque communities. Weekend competitions of pelota or *pala* brought together many Basques spread out in rural areas. Although the public commonly associates the sport of jai alai with the Basques, in the Western United States pelota was the much more commonly played sport. It was fairly easy to set up—a court can consist of a single exterior wall. It is also much easier to learn. With enthusiasm and a willingness to withstand pain, most nonplayers can quickly learn it well enough to compete. (Hitting the small, hard ball with the open palm of the hand for the length of a game can cause serious swelling and pain.)

In tracing the path of Basque migration in this country, one has merely to seek out the places where handball courts were built. The existence of a court implied there was or once had been a significant knot of Basques in the surrounding area. In the Basque Country, the pelota court was typically built along the back wall of the town church. In the United States a few courts were built on large Basque ranches, but mostly they were set up in the center of town, alongside the boardinghouses. Through the first half of the 1900s every significant Basque community had at least one, if not several, pelota courts. Competitions between teams from different communities became popular. The game went a long way toward promoting intrastate relations among Basques.

Pelota among the Basques suffered somewhat of a decline after the 1940s, as Basques began scattering, and interest in the sport declined. Second- and third-generation Basques were not taught the game, so they opted for American sports. Pelota courts were torn down during urban renewal and not replaced. A few—a very few—old pelota courts survive as historical markers of former Basque communities. In Fresno, Bakersfield, and Chino, California; and Boise, Idaho, old boardinghouse frontons are still used regularly. Historic courts in Jordan Valley, Oregon, and Mountain Home, Idaho, have been restored in recent years. The Basque immigrants who arrived during the 1950s and 1960s included a fair number of pelota enthusiasts who kept up interest in the sport.

Mus

Although the origins of the card game *mus* are unknown, the Basques have definitely made it their own. Two teams of two people play against each other, and the goal is for a team to win bets on individual hands in order to be the first to reach a total number of points (usually 40). Team members cannot show their cards, so they devise facial expressions to reveal their hand to their partner without being noticed by the other team, in order to gain an advantage in the betting. There are standard comic expressions, such as sticking out the tip of the tongue to indicate two aces. Bluffing is accepted.

There is also a basic vocabulary of more than thirty words that are used to bet your hand, and as tournaments have popularized the game, a standard vocabulary in Euskara has become the norm.

In Boise, Basques developed an early pattern of men playing *mus* and women playing *briska,* a Spanish card game similar to hearts. In all communities, *mus* was relegated to "the old folks" who had come

The card game *mus*, played here by a group of men at the annual San Francisco picnic, is growing in popularity among all age groups. (Photo by Averie Cohen.)

from the Old Country. Today, however, the game is played among young and old alike and is increasing in popularity.

Clubs sponsor annual tournaments, and the winners meet up at the annual *mus* tournament sponsored by the North American Basque Organizations (NABO) ever since 1977. This event has probably become the primary event strengthening ties among Basque clubs around the United States. It has also greatly increased interest in the game of *mus*. And since 1979, organizations in the United States, Europe, and South America have sponsored an international *mus* tournament, which rotates to different countries every year. (For more information, see the section on NABO.)

"If you're a card player, this is your Olympics. The chance to go across the world and play is very exciting," said Dominic Etcheberria, when he was president of the Southern California Basque Club. He said his club probably would not have joined NABO if it weren't for the *mus* tournament.

Mus appears to be growing in popularity in the Basque Country as well. "I heard that in those little towns, they're going crazy with *mus*—even the women," said Tony Espinal of San Francisco, and men are even competing against women, which they never would have considered doing in the past. More and more Basque-American teens are becoming interested in the game as well, since NABO organized a junior *mus* tournament. Some clubs have had more success than others in piquing the youngsters' interest. For example, about twenty youngsters have participated in the tournament of California's Marin-Sonoma club. Mayie Galzagorry of San Rafael is amazed at the interest her two young daughters have taken in the game, which requires knowledge of some Basque words. "It was real cute when we went to France and they were playing *mus* with their cousins," she said.

Music

Music, in many different forms, has always been a significant feature of Basque culture, and the enjoyment of music has been evident among the Basque communities in this country since the arrival of the earliest immigrants.

For many people, music is the heart of the Basque culture. No Basque gathering is complete without it. In earlier days Basques got together without all the fanfare that accompanies today's festivals. There were no wood-chopping or weight-lifting or tug-of-war competitions, no bread-baking contests or *irrintzi* (war-whoop) contests. But there was always an accordion player or two, and there was always dancing. Impromptu choruses of men singing around the bar were probably also likely. In fact, Basque men, or women for that matter, are not shy about singing in public.

BERTSOLARIAK

Bertsolariak, or the Basque version of troubadours, represent the singing art of the Basques. The singers are given a topic, and they then compose impromptu verses on the spot, usually as part of a competition that passes between two or three singers. This highly respected art has been kept alive for centuries in the Basque Country and has also served to keep up the love for the unique Basque language. Although *bertsolariak* in the United States are few and far between, they typically love a good party, and at least two of them can frequently be

If you're lucky, you'll be around when a Basque crowd breaks out in song, like they did here at the Overland Hotel, during the breakfast that follows the annual Gardnerville picnic.

rounded up at most Basque celebrations. If you do get the chance to see them perform, take a look around at the old-timers in the audience. They'll probably be laughing or crying, or maybe both.

Bertsolari competitions were a common feature at Basque picnics, but the lack of new immigration bodes ill for its continuation in the U.S. Mastering the art of verse-making requires complete fluency in Euskara, and it is one Basque tradition that did not make the transition to the U.S.-born generation. All of today's *bertsolariak* come from the Basque Country. "To be a *bertsolari*, you have to be pretty much raised among them," said Johnny Curutchet, one of four *bertsolariak* recipients of the 2003 National Heritage Fellowship. Although he was born in San Francisco, Curutchet was taken back to the Basque Country as a young child and stayed there until he was nineteen years old. "A few times a year when they killed a pig, the old-timers would get together and do it," he remembers. "Even my dad did it. I used to love to listen to them. I don't see any hope at all for that in this country."

BASQUE INSTRUMENTS

Accordion playing has probably accompanied Basques at their parties ever since the 1850s. Young Basques were encouraged to learn to play the instrument, and they were given many opportunities to show off their talent at picnics and dances. In fact, these opportunities probably encouraged a great number of young Basques to become musicians. Many were self-taught.

In the late 1980s the small diatonic accordion, which the talented Domingo Ansotegui of Boise once played, started making a reappearance. This instrument was introduced to the Basque Country in the late nineteenth century and is traditionally played along with a tambourine, or *pandareta,* in a combination known as *trikitixa.* The duet is referred to as *trikitilariak.* The art of the *trikitixa* was almost lost in the Basque Country, but it is experiencing a renaissance, with the support of a regional competition. Its growing popularity is also reflected in its reappearance in the United States. *Trikitixa* is usually

Boise accordionist Jim Jausoro, the champion of them all, (second from right), played in the Elko parade with the new generation of Boise musicians following in his footsteps. Pictured with him are (left to right) Janice Mainvil, Cindy Enrico, Juan Zulaika, and Cathy Clarkson. (Photo by Averie Cohen.)

performed by musicians from the Basque Country, but a few U.S.–born musicians are gradually taking up the instruments.

As a reflection of the changing times, Basque-American musicians are developing new Basque musical styles. In Boise Dan Ansotegi may have played drums with the late–traditional accordionist Jim Jausoro, but he also played with Ordago, a Basque rock group consisting of younger Boise musicians, who established quite a following throughout the West's Basque communities. A newer group that has replaced Ordago, Gaupasa (Overnighter), also plays rock. They play rock along with fandangos and other music the younger generation likes to hear. "We grew up with American music, and they play it," remarked Esther Bidaurreta, a native of Mountain Home, Idaho, referring to Ordago. "It gives a lot of people something to relate to. They really bridge a gap." Other modern Basque bands have come and gone in other Basque communities like San Francisco and Chino.

The accordion's importance in the Basque community continues, but other instruments have made inroads as well. Young Basque-Americans have learned the bugle, the French horn, the trombone, and the drums to play in local *klikas,* and they've learned to play the *txistu* (a flutelike instrument held straight up and down) as well. The *txistu* has maintained a small but continuous presence in the U.S. Basque colony. Instruction on the playing of this ancient flute, which originated in the Basque Country, was not readily available in previous years. But today it is enjoying a strong resurgence in the United States, primarily because it is taught at the annual NABO summer camp. Typically, the musician plays it one-handed, while playing a small drum or *ttun-ttun* with the other hand. A *txistu* player is called a *txistulari.*

The *klika*—a bugle corps that can also include drums, cymbals, and French horns—is one of several traditions that have developed in one region of Euskal Herria and not in others. The *klika* came from Iparralde where men learned to play the drum or bugle in the French army and went home and started village *klikas.* San Francisco had the first *klika* in the United States, but two others, in Chino and Bakersfield, which are also predominantly Iparralde communities, were to follow later.

Dance

The folk dance group started by the Southern California Basque Club in 1946 was possibly the first such group in the West. Boise, Idaho, started a dance group in 1948. In those early days, dance groups, just as the communities they lived in, evolved in complete isolation from each other. The dances from Iparralde were emphasized in California, where immigrants from Nafarroa Beherea were in the majority; while in Boise, where Bizkaitarrak dominated, the dances from that province were the best known. Over the years an individual group's proficiency and its repertoire was usually dependent on the teachers, who varied greatly in their level of ability. Many of them had learned the dances as members of a U.S. dance group, and as a result, the dances became standardized and simplified.

Since those early days, Basque folk dancing in the United States has been elevated to an art, with a great sense of competition existing among different dance groups. Costumes have come a long way from the white skirts and blouses with a red *lauburu* (Basque cross) on the breast pocket that Leonie Mocho remembers she used to wear in the Chino dance group during the 1950s. Every summer since at the different festivals, groups will introduce new dances with new costumes, evidence of their efforts to stay abreast of other groups. The competition is all in fun.

Johnny Curutchet, former president of the San Francisco Basque Cultural Center and an original member of San Francisco's Zazpiak Bat dance group back in the 1960s, said that he's glad to see the changing styles. "They do a dance that I haven't seen in forty-two years," said Curutchet, referring to a group that performed at the 1993 Elko festival. "They do it the old-fashioned way. When I see that, it touches my heart."

Dance groups everywhere have expanded significantly, and even the smallest Basque communities boast of a dance group. There's a Basque song that says that Basque children must learn to speak Basque, play pelota well, and dance well: "*Haurrak ikas zazue eskuaraz mintzatzen, ongi pilotan eta oneski dantzatzen.*"

Indeed, dancing has played a key role in youngsters identifying as Basque. You can ask any Basque-American who is active in his or her local Basque community and you'll probably find he or she participated in a dance group when young, at least long enough to learn the fandango (also referred to as the *jota*). This fast-stepping dance, probably the best known of Basque folk dances, was originally borrowed from the neighboring Spanish province of Aragon. The Basques adapted it and added the second half, called the *porrusalda* or *arin-arin*. Chino's John Ysursa, a cultural expert, has found evidence that modern ballet has borrowed from Basque dances. "Many of the steps in modern ballet have Basque names to them," he explains in his role as emcee at many festivals.

A U.S. Basque dance federation, the Ipar-Ameriketako Euskal Dantzarien Biltzarra, similar to a large federation in the Basque Country, was started in 1987 to increase communication between dance groups, to share information and videos on new dances, and to coordinate visits from dancers from the Basque Country. This federation was dissolved just a few years later, when the umbrella group North American Basque Organizations (see section in this chapter) agreed to establish a culture committee to accomplish a similar purpose. Among the projects of the NABO committee was to organize an exchange with a dance group in Argentina. In 1993 dancers from all over the Western states traveled to the city of Mar del Plata to participate in the annual Semana Vasca (Basque Week) celebration organized by a few of that country's many Basque clubs. The Argentinean dancers reciprocated the visit, performing at the NABO convention and festival in Bakersfield in 1994. Basque-American audiences marveled to see the same dances carried on in such distant parts of the globe. Other such cultural exchanges continue.

Old Country Reunions

Immigrants from several small Basque towns have started a new tradition. Several reunions have been organized for people or descendants of people from the towns of Esterenzubi and St. Martin, Osses, Bidarray, and Aldudes. The first of these reunions was the one for Esterenzubi and St. Martin, held in 1986 at the Chalet Basque, whose owners were from Esterenzubi.

The idea for the get-together came from Bay Area residents Jean Arambel and Dominique Arotzarena, who also come from that town. "We were afraid nobody would come," said Arambel. "Then we said, well if nobody comes, we'll celebrate by ourselves." But the party was a big success. The organizers made a mailing list of everyone they knew from those towns, and people just spread the word. Arambel's wife Monique decided to sponsor a similar reunion for her hometown of Aldudes, and the first one was in Los Banos in 1989; the second in 1993 at the Chateau Basque, whose owner, Yvonne Etcheveste is also from Aldudes, was also successful, attracting more than a hundred people from all over the West. A more recent reunion was held in 2001 at the Basque Cultural Center in San Francisco.

The valley of Aldudes, in Nafarroa Beherea, near the border, had one of the largest groups to immigrate to the United States. "There's no other town that had so many people here," said the late Henry Bidegain of Los Angeles, whose family also came from Aldudes. Bidegain said that for his many years he ran into Aldudes residents all over California, Nevada, Wyoming, Arizona, and Colorado. Although it may be true that Basques tended to follow neighbors and relatives and settle in the same areas, the far-reaching trails of Aldudarrak, considering the small size of the Old Country hometown population, are amazing. From Father Espelette, founder of the Southern California Eskualdun Club, one of the oldest Basque clubs in the United States, to John Etchart, in the northeasternmost corner of Montana, Aldudarrak settled throughout the West.

■ Basque Consciousness in the United States

Among American Basques, ethnicity created a natural bond. "The Basques over here, we're much closer to each other," said Frank Maitia Sr. "People who come from over there, they notice it right away." The closeness here was partly owed to the fact that the Basques had come from such a small region and because they socialized together a lot in the United States. The friendships led to so many marriages between Basques that the resulting interconnections between families in U.S. communities is astounding. Oddly there were a number of cases in which couples lived just one or two villages apart in the Basque Country but never met until they ran into each other in one of these tight-knit U.S. enclaves. But the earliest immigrants from different provinces had no sense of shared ethnicity. Many of them left their homeland before the nationalist movement lead by Sabino Arana took hold in Euskal Herria in the 1920s, bringing greater unity to the seven provinces.

Perhaps because of patterns established by the early immigrants, the regional differences in the Basque Country have been carried over here as well. The Nafarrak from Spain and France settled in California and western Nevada, but they hardly associated with the Bizkaitarrak in northern Nevada, eastern Oregon, and southern Idaho. They insisted they didn't understand each other—the Bizkaian dialect is significantly different from the Nafarroan dialect. (Yet a few say they can quickly understand general conversation themes.) The two groups interacted very little. Until the advent of the Basque clubs, they were only scarcely aware of each other.

In later years there were divisions among Basques over politics. American Basques did not support Franco, despite the U.S. government's recognition of the Spanish dictator. But most of them also did not support the separatist group ETA, which was fighting for the creation of a separate Basque nation independent from Spain. The violent ETA was seen as a Spanish Basque movement—and the Iparraldetarrak didn't want to be connected with it. Yet just as many Hegoaldetarrak were reluctant to claim any political affiliations with the ETA. "The newspapers, all they wrote about were the terrorists. They never told you what Franco did," said Marie Elu of San Francisco.

Idaho Secretary of State Pete Cenarrusa traveled to the Basque Country in 1971, where he met members of the Basque "underground," spoke to families of the prisoners sentenced to death, and heard stories of torture by Spanish police. Education officials told him of the obstacles they faced in teaching the Basque language. "I felt so intense about this and so sorry for them," said Cenarrusa. "If the Basques [in this country] had received the truth and known the facts, I think they would have acted in a different way."

Today Basque-Americans emphasize a unified Basque culture. Basques among Basques may highlight their regional differences, according to Father Eliçagaray, but put a group of them within a larger

American group and you'll see them present a solid front. Besides, for those who were born in the United States, the regional differences mean little. "There's no such thing as a Spanish Basque or a French Basque," said Marie Elu, expressing a commonly held, more modern view. "It's all Basque. It's just the way they divided the country." Much of this change of attitude can be attributed to the development of the North American Basque Organizations, which strengthened cultural pride among all Basque-Americans. Today the *ikurrina* (Basque flag) of red, green, and white is used in every Basque-American community to represent the culture as a whole; in Europe the flag is used officially to represent the semiautonomous community of Euskadi.

Basque Clubs and the North American Basque Organizations

In the early days, work or living situations naturally brought Basques together, serving to promote close social and ethnic ties. They socialized together at the boardinghouses. Sheepherders would reunite at the hotels usually in the fall, after the lambs were shipped to market. In rural areas they tended to settle in clusters around each other. Ranch families would get together to help each other with big jobs, like cattle roundups, and typically enjoyed big barbecues together. They would work for the same employer or join forces with other Basques as partners in businesses.

As the boardinghouses began disappearing, the Basque workforce diversified, and families spread out in urban settings, Basques realized that they needed to organize social activities to shore up the support system that had previously existed naturally. After an initial trickle during the 1940s and 1950s, many clubs were spawned in the 1960s or later. They organized dance groups and pelota competitions, among other activities.

Members of the social clubs eventually realized that there was a need for a network among the clubs, and they came up with the idea of creating a national organization. Much of the credit for saving the culture from extinction in this country belongs to the North American Basque Organizations, Inc. NABO, as it is usually called, has worked hard to promote activities and sports that are traditionally Basque.

One impetus for the umbrella organization came from the late Jon Bilbao, then a University of Nevada, Reno, professor, who traveled extensively in South America in the early 1970s, doing research for the book *Amerikanuak,* which he wrote with William Douglass. He became extremely enthusiastic about a federation of Basque clubs in Argentina, according to Douglass, and brought the idea back to the U.S. clubs.

Basques in Boise were eager to support the idea of an umbrella organization. They had organized their first big Basque festival, the Holiday Basque Festival, in 1972. As they worked on publicizing the event, they realized they lacked contacts with the clubs they knew were active in Nevada and California. "The only one that we had any way of contacting was Elko's, and that really upset us," said Al Erquiaga of Boise, one of the festival organizers. The Boise Basques jumped at the chance to break down some of the regionalism and unite with the other organizations.

The first NABO meetings organized in Reno in 1973 were attended by members of the clubs of San Francisco and Bakersfield, California; Elko, Ely, and Reno, Nevada; Boise, Idaho; and Grand Junction, Colorado.

Initially, the divisions between Bizkaitarrak and Nafarrak and Nafarro Behetarrak simmered under the surface. "We were afraid of each other," said the late Jean Leon Iribarren, a well-spoken insurance agent and Basque community leader from San Francisco. "They are from the other side—they must be different." Many were also fearful of politics. "We started NABO at a time when ETA was very forceful," said Janet Inda, another founding member. "Some of them thought we might be politically motivated."

After the initial suspicions were overcome, "we all realized we wanted the same things," said Iribarren. The group moved ahead quickly and established the nonprofit umbrella organization in 1974. The members wanted to keep Basque nationalism and politics out of NABO, so they forbade political activity. The delegates of the corporation have stood by this rule firmly. On more than one occasion, NABO has straddled a fence to avoid getting politically involved with issues in the Basque Country.

A real camaraderie developed among the original delegates. "I really think that we all got a good feeling from everyone at that first meeting," said Al Erquiaga. "The hard part was selling our members here [in Boise] on the idea." Many club members feared NABO would take too much control.

The original members agreed that NABO would do more than provide services to the different clubs—but it would not be a governing body. The idea behind NABO is to host events that are beyond the scope of the individual organizations without infringing on their autonomy. Delegates sent by each member club meet to make decisions. A legal technicality prevented the founders from calling it a federation, but in essence it is.

Al Erquiaga, NABO's first president, noted that the organization has far surpassed its original goal of opening the lines of communication among the clubs. "NABO has really brought a lot of clubs closer together," said Mary Gaztambide of Salt Lake City—a Basque community that few knew about until it joined NABO.

"NABO has accomplished exactly what our mission was," said Jim Ithurralde of Eureka, Nevada, NABO's second president. "They are keeping Basque culture alive. Now we don't have the California Basque, the Utah Basque, or the Elko Basque. We're all Basque."

Enhancing communication and exchange between the United States and the Basque Country has become an increasingly important goal of NABO. The regional Basque government, headquartered in Vitoria-Gasteiz, Araba, has taken greater and greater interest in satellite groups outside the Basque Country, and it has funded several events and programs in an effort to promote Basque culture abroad. In 1992 the Basque government offered grants for several individual cultural projects through NABO, as a spring board to the establishment of an annual grant program for NABO members' programs.

Since NABO started, the Grand Junction and Ely clubs have died, but many more clubs have been created and become members of NABO. The most recent clubs to join the umbrella organization were from the big cities of Seattle, Washington; Denver, Colorado; and New Orleans, Louisiana. Today NABO has thirty-six member clubs.

NABO conducts all its business at three annual meetings, which rotate among different Basque communities. Until recently, the fall meeting was held in Reno. The large summer convention is usually timed to coincide with the local festival of the hosting club, which rotates from year to year, and a lot of effort is made to sponsor special activities, bring together all the dance groups, and attract a larger crowd. New officers are selected during the summer convention. The third meeting, in February, also rotates.

The organization has also started its own newsletter, to inform clubs of the activities of the larger organization. John Ysursa is the current editor of the newsletter, *Hizketa*, which is published three times a year. In *Hizketa* he provides cultural information and brief news from the Basque Country, in addition to NABO news. NABO also publishes the annual Basque calendar, full of beautiful color photographs, with a listing of all major events throughout the year. You can usually obtain one through the local club or you can contact the NABO Web site (*www.basqueclubs.com*) to find the nearest club and e-mail contacts.

A summer culture camp for youth, and national *mus* (a Basque card game) and pelota tournaments have become the three most important events hosted by the federation. For the older generation, NABO's handball and *mus* tournaments are the most significant annual events. The summer camp has gone a long way toward developing young people's interest in their culture.

North American Basque Organizations, c/o Mary Gaztambide, 449 Shamrock Drive, Murray, UT, 84107 (801) 262-7673; *www.basqueclubs.com*

***Hizketa*—NABO Newsletter** *(Editor—John Ysursa)* 15180 Old Hickory Lane, Chino Hills, CA 91709 (909) 597-4526; *www.basqueclubs.com*

MUS

The first NABO *mus* tournament was held in 1977, and the event has continued to be held annually since then. The location rotates every year—the event is hosted by the club that sponsored the previous year's winning team. France and Spain hosted a regional tournament in 1978, and the following year, Pierre Etcharren suggested that NABO sponsor an international tournament as part of the summer NABO festival to be held in San Francisco. France, Spain, and other countries where Basque clubs were active (mostly in Latin America) were invited. Since that first competition in 1979, an international *mus* tournament has been held every year, rotating among the different participating countries. (It was held again in the United States in 1986 in Las Vegas.)

NABO sends the winners of its own annual *mus* tournament to the international one, and the host country pays for all the costs of the players' stay. Interest in learning and playing *mus* has multiplied since this practice started. Hoping for one more chance to win their way into the tournament, card players have pushed for new clubs where possible, such as San Francisco's Anaitasuna.

PELOTA

The NABO pelota competition also rotates to different communities, although it is naturally limited to those cities with adequate court facilities—San Francisco, Bakersfield, and Elko. Chino and Fresno also send participants, but their local courts are privately owned, making official competitions in those locations difficult.

NABO held its first national pelota tournament in 1976. There are men's categories and women's categories, different categories for different levels of playing ability, as well as *pala* competitions (*pala* is played with a wooden racket). To encourage playing among younger Basque-Americans, NABO has included several categories for youths in the competitions, including a peewee category for children as young as eight and nine, and for the same reason, in the 1990s, the organization hosted a summer pelota camp in San Francisco for a few years. Now pelota is taught as part of the summer youth camp.

YOUTH CULTURAL CAMP

NABO sponsors an annual summer cultural Udaleku camp that rotates to a different Basque community every year. It started with 40, and more recently attracted up to 100 youngsters. It used to be called music camp, but its offerings are so much broader than music that the name was changed to Udaleku (summer resort). During the two-week period teens and preteens are taught how to play the *txistu,* (an instrument similar to a recorder) and the *pandareta* (tambourine). They also learn how to do traditional dances as well as to cook typical Basque dishes. Euskara classes are held for two to four hours every day. They learn to play *mus* and pelota. Instructors from the Basque Country are invited to come and teach the youngsters. Father Tillous has been the regular *txistu* teacher for several years.

The NABO summer music camp plays an important role in maintaining the different arts and traditions among young Basque-Americans. "I think you really appreciate [the culture] more after," said Kristie Onaindia of Bakersfield, who attended camp three years in a row. Even more important, the camp has created friendships among teenagers from all over the West, and these relationships are renewed and strengthened at the festivals. In essence, the camp has established a Basque youth network. "It's like family," continued Onaindia. "You always have family whatever town you go to," she said, noting that she attends five or six different festivals every summer. "I have friends that I still write to now."

The camp first started in 1977, at which time three separate camps were organized in San Francisco, Reno, and Boise. The following year, the three groups combined to coordinate efforts and produce a better event. For several years a young energetic couple, John and Jenny Ysursa of Chino, organized the camp, and more recently Valerie Etcharren of San Francisco has taken charge. The children board with local families to keep costs down.

Survival of the Culture

The immigrant generation, despite its mostly successful efforts to assimilate into American life, has for years maintained the Basque culture through dinner dances, handball games, or afternoons of *mus*-playing, and, of course, the well-known annual Basque picnics. Each Basque community throughout the West tends to have a small but hard-core group who works hard to maintain the organizations. The larger cities that had a strong influx of immigrants during the 1950s and 1960s, are the strongest. They also benefited from added migration of Basques from surrounding rural areas. The desire to have a place where Basques could get together resulted in the establishment of Basque centers. Today the cities with large club membership—for instance, Boise, Idaho; Elko, Nevada; and San Francisco, Bakersfield, Fresno, and Chino, California—all have their own clubhouses, where social gatherings are held regularly. But many among the second generation have lost interest in participating in such events. As they married and had children, their integration into the American lifestyle seemed to leave less time for such activities.

Many Basque-Americans disassociated themselves from the culture a long time ago, especially if they grew up in a household where the traditions were not maintained. Such was often the case when one parent was not Basque. How many Americans fall into this category is hard to say. "It's pretty hard to count people who are not on the radar screen," Douglass said.

But the situation appears to be turning around. Basque-Americans are coming of age in an era of ethnic awareness. Many of them are rediscovering their Basque roots and throwing themselves wholeheartedly into Basque activities. Father Eliçagaray observed that tendency: "When they have children, they push them to the traditions, to the dance classes." A few are seeking leadership positions within the Basque organizations.

Yet the shift from the immigrant generation to the newer generations is not occurring without a struggle. "The generation that comes from over there must pass the baton to those born here," observed Father Eliçagaray, who had close contact with all the clubs. "But they want [the younger generation] to do everything the way they do," he said, trying to explain the tensions. Basque stubbornness doesn't help. In fact, almost every Basque club has been racked with internal feuds at one time or another. Unfortunately, members of the younger generation sometimes drop out rather than hang in there and work to overcome the problems. And the older Basques who worked hard to keep the traditions are troubled by their lack of participation. "You need a few people to keep the fire lit, to keep it going, so that later on somebody else can pick it up," said the late Jean Leon Iribarren, who worked hard to promote the culture.

Indeed, what makes Boise's Basque community stand out is the fact that an all-new all-American generation full of ambition and energy is already in charge. As the third generation, they are removed from the struggles of the early immigrants. They bring forward only the most positive characteristics of the Basques. "They don't have this problem of the passage [of the baton] in Boise," said Eliçagaray. "In California they are in the middle of it."

While some worry that Basque culture in this country may slowly disappear without the natural rejuvenation brought about by new immigration, active members of the Basque community disagree. They point to fairly recent developments, such as the creation of NABO, the cultural camp for youngsters, and the Basque Country study-abroad program (at the University of Nevada, Reno), all of which have strengthened ties among Basques both in this country and in the Old Country. In fact, some NABO delegates believe that the U.S. Basque colony is more united than it has ever been. Some find that the American Basques work harder at preserving the culture than do the Basques of the homeland, many of whom take their unique customs and language for granted. Linda Etcheverria of Penngrove, California, said that her two young daughters were surprised to find that they knew the Basque dances better than their cousins when they made a visit over there. "Here some of those traditions are carried on even better than in Europe," said Etcheverria.

Contact with the Old World has improved with better access to air travel and increased telephone communication. Whereas those among the earlier immigrant generations would not even consider making the costly return trip to the Basque Country unless it was to return for good, many members of the newer generations have already made the trip several times. Youngsters are often sent over to the Basque Country for the entire summer to get to know their cousins and attend some of the local Basque festivals. The historical tradition of not breaking up the family homestead has facilitated contact simply because immigrants' birthplaces and family are still in the same place. Some of the U.S.–born offspring feel a stronger connection to the land of their forefathers precisely because they have been able to return to their father or mother's house and observe their original lifestyle. "Until you go over there and see what a unique culture it is, you're not very interested in preserving it," said Shauna Cluck, a third-generation Basque-American who joined the leadership of the Susanville, California, club after she went to study for a year in the Basque Country.

For many, that first trip to their parents' homeland provided the key to many questions about their culture. "A lot of what you grow up with doesn't always make sense until you go back and see it," said J. B. Lekumberry, who at age ten traveled to his father's hometown. On that first trip to the Basque Country, he discovered that his name,

Jean Baptiste—so unusual among his American peers—was as common as Joe.

Will the Language Survive?

Basque culture in Spain was severely repressed under the rule of dictator Francisco Franco. Among the many prohibitions and restrictions placed on the Basques during his reign from 1939 to 1975 one of the most hated was the ban on speaking Euskara. Although the language continued to dominate in the rural areas, as industrialization brought people from other parts of Spain, Spanish became the predominant language in the Basque cities, and use of Euskara declined. A new cultural awareness took root in the 1960s, as people realized that the language was being lost. Language classes were offered clandestinely in cafés and restaurants. A unified Basque dialect, sometimes referred to as *Batua,* has been developed and is now used in the schools. This version of Euskara attempts to reflect the regional differences yet remain true to the origins of Euskara. The revival continues, so it is now fashionable and politically correct for Basque youth to regain their language. Today there is a new consciousness of the importance of the language, even in the cities. Young people who have attended *ikastolas* (schools taught in Basque) or the University of the Basque Country can be heard at cafés and on the streets speaking Euskara.

A completely different trend is taking place in the United States, unfortunately. English has become the predominant language among the majority of the Basque population here, and without the influx of new Basque immigrants, the loss of the Basque language here is a real threat.

In the early days of immigration to the United States, speaking English was the biggest obstacle to assimilation. In those times Basque families more often than not lived in small Basque enclaves or in isolated rural settings. Children were sent to live with Basque families in town, so they could go to school. Many, many second-generation Basques remember starting kindergarten without speaking a word of English. "I thought I would never get to first grade," remembers Emily Laucirica, who grew up in Golconda, Nevada. Her

Batua

A proliferation of dialects in the Basque Country stood in the way of greater cultural unity, as well as any hope of declaring Euskara as the official language of the region, so the Euskaltzaindia, or the Academy of the Basque Language, decided to unify the dialects in one Unified Basque, referred to as *Batua*. The unified language created many tensions, especially among regional groups who felt slighted, according to the reference booklet *Emendik Nora? (From Here to Where?)* from a 1990 symposium on Basque language in Boise. The model for verbs in Batua came from the dialects of Gipuzkoa and Iparralde. Spelling is being standardized, such as with the virtual elimination of the *H* used in Iparralde.

teacher wanted to keep her in kindergarten until she learned English. "My mother couldn't help me, and my father couldn't help me." There was no special help for non-English-speaking students like there is today, she noted. "In those days, you were on your own."

Euskara was particularly linked to the faith, especially for those who grew up in the Basque Country. The isolated herders hungered to hear the religious rituals in their own language. "They knew their prayers by heart, their songs by heart, and that is how they survived," said Father Jean Eliçagaray.

Many men married women from the Old Country, many of them even returning to the Basque Country to find a wife and bring her back. These couples taught their children Euskara. But, inevitably, Basques also married non-Basques. It was common for them to choose European or Latin American partners, with whom they share the Spanish or French language. The immigrant generation went from being bi- or trilingual to quadrilingual with the acquisition of English. The following generation was often bilingual, speaking English and one of their parents' other languages.

Today most families are spread out in populated urban areas, and their children are most comfortable with English. So the pendulum has swung around to the point where you can hear many parents who are fluent in the Basque language speaking English with their children. The likelihood that Euskara will continue to be spoken in the United States decreases with every wedding. "The language eventually is going to die" in this country, predicts Frank Maitia Sr., who has seen his own son, Frank Jr., lose his fluency in the language.

The fear that Euskara will eventually disappear in the American enclaves is actually nothing new. Basque journalist José Goytino was moved by this concern, and as editor of the Basque newspaper *California'ko Eskual Herria,* published out of Los Angeles during the 1890s, he worked hard to promote the language. (*California'ko Eskual Herria* was one of two Basque-language publications in this country. The other was *Escualdun Gazeta,* also published in Los Angeles for a short time during the 1880s by lawyer Martin Biscailuz. The only other Basque newspaper in the United States was *The Voice of the Basques,* published in English from 1973 to 1977 by a non-Basque, Brian Wardle.)

But there are a few, just a few, signs that weigh in on the other side of the balance. When Basques gather for special Catholic masses, Father Jean Eliçagaray said he heard from many young people that they wanted the Mass said in Basque even though they don't speak it. Simply the sound of the language imbues the ceremony with much more meaning for them. Other traditions continue to be carried out in Euskara, guaranteeing that youths growing up in the United States will at least be exposed to the language. Euskara is used at *bertsolari* (Basque poet-musician) contests at festivals and parties, and now at the annual Euskal Kantari Eguna, a celebration of Basque music and singing in Gardnerville, Nevada. In the small colony of Buffalo, Wyoming, a weekly radio program in Euskara was broadcast for years. Two places have consistently taught elementary Basque over the past years—the University of Nevada, Reno, and Boise's Basque Museum—and more recently Boise State University instituted a minor in Basque studies. Many students have traveled to the Basque Country to study the language through programs offered by these universities. Moreover, Boise has sponsored an Euskara preschool program, and clubs are promoting online classes.

In recent years, the Basque government has been avidly promoting efforts to teach Euskara abroad. It has developed a learning program called *Boga,* which it makes available on CDs and via an online Web site, *www.habe.org.* Currently, students can obtain the CDs to learn the language at home, but the program is administered through the local Basque clubs, which distribute them. In addition, many clubs are planning to offer classes to supplement the home learning. Each club is handling the program's administration differently. NABO is leading the efforts with a "Got Basque?" campaign. History professor John Ysursa created a superb Web site, *www.euskara.us,* linking Basque-language learners with pertinent links and providing much information as well.

As for the new unified Batua, Basques who speak Euskara in this country say it won't cross the Atlantic. "Who is going to teach Batua to those of us here? You have to go to Spain to learn that," said the late Juanita Hormaechea, a Boise native who grew up speaking the Bizkaian dialect. While the older generation may not learn Batua, perhaps the younger generation will.

The maintenance of the culture in South America, where Basques settled up to a hundred years earlier than they did in the United States, could be an indication of what the future holds for the U.S. Basque community. Aña Iriartborde of San Francisco was impressed when she traveled to Argentina in 1985 and visited a large Basque center that even included a retirement home for elderly Basques. "But the language isn't there," said Iriartborde, "and that is the most important. What is the Basque culture without the language?" But there, too, a possible revival of the language looms in the future. A growing number of university students in Argentina are traveling to the Basque Country to study the language, and Euskara classes are being offered at cultural centers.

Old Country Support for Basque Culture

Relations between the Basque Country and the U.S. Basque enclaves are stronger than ever. With the establishment of the regional Euskadi government in 1979, an expanding program of support for Basque cultural activities throughout the world was put into place. The Basque government has sponsored visits to the United States by professional dance groups and musicians, language teachers, and athletes, particularly for special events like the Jaialdi festival in Boise. Also financial support is offered to Americans to attend the World Basque Congress and other such events.

Basque President Jose Antonio Ardanza toured the United States in 1988 in an effort to strengthen ties between Basques and their homeland as well as promote trade between the Basque Country and the United States. He and several other Basque government officials visited Idaho, Nevada, and California, in addition to making a final stopover in Washington D.C., where they met with then President Ronald Reagan and trade officials to discuss improving trade relations. In 2003, President Juan Jose Ibarretxe came to the United States to visit with Basque Americans. He spoke at the Euzko Etxea of New York and made stopovers in Boston and Chicago. He returned in 2005 to attend Boise's Jaialdi festival.

The Basque government's campaign to strengthen ties with its people abroad is giving new life to such efforts by smaller private groups on both sides. In one development, officials in the Nafarroan towns of the Erro Valley sponsored a reunion celebration in the summer of 1994 for all those who had emigrated. Tony Espinal of San Francisco remarked that he and many Nafarrak from the Bay Area made the trip. "These days, they'll use any excuse to go to Europe at the drop of a hat," he noted, a far cry from earlier days when many Basques left for America never to return.

REFERENCES

Arrizabalaga, Marie Pierre. "A Statistical Study of Basque Immigration into California, Nevada, Idaho and Wyoming between 1900 and 1910." Masters thesis, University of Nevada, Reno, 1986.

Douglass, William A., and Jon Bilbao. *Amerikanuak: Basques in the New World.* Reno, Nev.: University of Nevada Press, 1975, pp. 117–76.

Eagle, Sonia. "Work and Play Among the Basques of Southern California." Diss., Purdue University, 1979, p. 36.

Edlefsen, John B. "A Sociological Study of the Basques of Southwest Idaho." Diss., State College of Washington, 1948.

Gachitéguy, Adrien. *Les Basques dans l'Ouest américain.* Bordeaux, France: Editions Ezkila, 1955.

Lane, Richard, and William A. Douglass. *Basque Sheepherders of the American West: A Photographic Documentary.* Reno, Nev.: University of Nevada Press, 1985, p. 4.

Llande, Pierre. *L'emigration basque.* Paris: Nouvelle Librairie National., 1910, p. 22.

Pagliarulo, Carol. "Basques in Stockton: A Study of Assimilation." Masters thesis, College of the Pacific, Stockton, California, 1948, p. 36.

Scott, Janny, "A Biting Analysis of Society." *Los Angeles Times,* November 18, 1993, p. A-1.

Wright, Alice. "Jean Urruty, Sheepman, American." *Colorado West,* December 3, 1972.

Xamurre. *Colonizadores de la epopeya americana.* Buenos Aires, Argentina: Editorial Vasca Ekin, 1966.

California

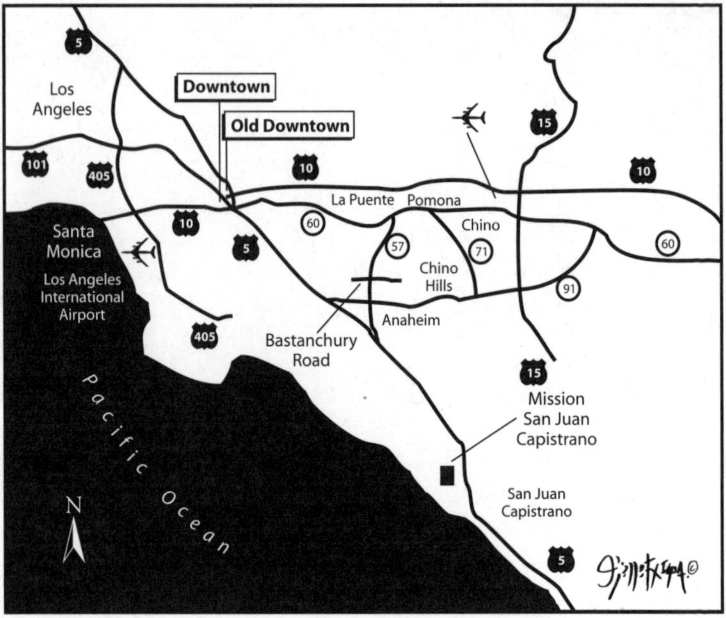
5
Los Angeles
Downtown
Old Downtown
15
101
405
10
10
La Puente
Pomona
Santa Monica
10
60
Chino
5
57
71
60
Los Angeles International Airport
Chino Hills
91
Anaheim
405
Bastanchury Road
15
Pacific Ocean
Mission San Juan Capistrano
San Juan Capistrano
N
5

Los Angeles.

■ Southern California

Los Angeles

The very first Basque community in the West was established in Los Angeles. Most of the early Basque settlers of the state had been living in South America and came to California by ship after hearing about the discovery of gold in 1848. Several of them quickly realized the potential to make money in the sheep- and cattle-raising industry on Southern California's vast, open ranges. They acquired or leased property and established sheep outfits beginning in the 1850s and 1860s around the southern part of the state, using the city of Los Angeles as a hub. Consequently, the Los Angeles area has some of the oldest historical vestiges of the early Basque immigrants to the United States.

The men who came in the gold rush years were not the first Basque arrivals. Some prominent Basques had been involved in the early settlement of the southwestern territory while it was ruled by Spain and then Mexico. The earlier arrivals had also found opportunity in California in military, religious, and commercial ventures. These immigrants tended to be few in number and more educated, and, although some of them became landowners, they did not get significantly involved in ranching.

After the territory was annexed to the United States in 1848, the number of Basque arrivals jumped. Some of them amassed huge ranching empires in Southern California, investing in sheep and cattle. Brothers Pedro and Bernardo Altube were among the most prominent Basque ranchers in California. But they are better known for the Spanish Ranch they established near Elko, Nevada. Others were Dominique Oxarart, Miguel Leonis, and Domingo Amestoy.

After 1848 Basques were among the ethnic groups that came to California in the largest numbers, reflected by the fact that early histories of California mention them specifically. There were Iparraldetarrak, from the region of Donibane-Garazi, as well as Hegoaldetarrak. California was still heavily influenced by the Spanish and Mexican eras, and Spanish was the most commonly spoken language. Many of the first Basque arrivals in California found that they could carry on business in Spanish. Basques with French names quickly adopted Spanish-sounding names. Thus Dominique became Domingo and Michel, Miguel.

The Los Angeles Basque community can be seen as a prime example of the Basques' ability to adapt and survive in the New World. Los Angeles has undergone a major transformation from those early days, changing from a primarily rural agricultural area to a sprawling urban center. Remarkably, Basques have found economic opportunity and success in the region throughout the past 150 years, changing occupations to suit the times. As industries sprouted in Los Angeles, Basques abandoned their traditional agricultural occupations and took urban jobs in bakeries, meat-packing plants, and construction projects. This diversification began earlier in Los Angeles than it did in other Basque communities. Yet the Basques in the surrounding area have continued in one land-based occupation, namely the dairy business. To establish their dairy farms, the Basques have been forced 40 miles east of Los Angeles, to the cities of Chino and Ontario, where dairy pursuits are still tolerated, although not for much longer. An active Basque population continues to maintain its ethnic identity through clubs and activities in Southern California.

BOARDINGHOUSES

In addition to being the first Basque community on the West Coast, Los Angeles was also the largest throughout the late 1800s. By 1886 two thousand Basques were living in the Los Angeles area, according to one of the two Basque newspapers of the time, *Escualdun Gazeta.* In those peak years, downtown Los Angeles had what could have been called a Basque "town." Between 1878 and 1888 some ten different boardinghouses had opened around the intersection of Alameda and Aliso Streets, according to Professor Jeronima Echeverria, who researched the state's boardinghouses in her Ph.D. dissertation, "California's Basque Ostatuak." Two or three handball courts, a pen behind one of the hotels for herders' sheepdogs, and a grocery store or two completed the picture. The creation of this Basque district coincided with the arrival of the railroad in Los Angeles and the opening of the first woolen mill. The neighborhood's Basque hotel business flourished through the turn of the century. Pascal Ballade was one of the hotel owners during those years, and he eventually became a councilman for the city. The Pyrenees Hotel, run for many years by Juan Ordoqui, was one of the most popular, particularly among handball players because of its big handball court.

In Los Angeles no remnants remain of the old Basque neighborhood, but it was located around the later-built Union Station, the city's train center. In Los Angeles and San Francisco, the hotels provided a nucleus for the larger Basque communities, which flourished.

A few locals remember that there was still at least one Basque hotel downtown during the 1940s. The French Taix brothers owned the building on Commercial Street and Los Angeles, and their elegant Taix restaurant was downstairs. The upper stories of the old building were the Commercial Hotel, which was apparently leased out for a while to Basque hotel keepers. A young Manuel Villanueva of Downey, California, stayed at the hotel during the 1940s, after sheepherding for a couple of years. Through contacts there he got his first city job, at a downtown bakery. He said that in those years a family called Lekumberry ran the hotel. The Taix family employed some of the Basques in their restaurant, and the restaurant and hotel were still there during the 1950s. The Taix restaurant moved to Sunset Boulevard, and before long the building was torn down. A large federal building was put up in its place.

During the 1930s the two places where Basques gathered in the Los Angeles area—the downtown Basque neighborhood and the Bastanchury Ranch in Fullerton—disappeared (see the Fullerton section). Most Basques had moved out of the city anyway, joining compatriots in rural outlying areas such as Fullerton, San Juan Capistrano, El Toro, Calabasas, and La Puente. Today the names of their descendants can be found in Orange County and Los Angeles County phone books.

CHURCH AND CEMETERY

In Los Angeles, Basque weddings and funerals were always held at the historic **La Placita Church,** where the city of Los Angeles started. Even ranching families living on the outskirts of Los Angeles would ride into town for such events. This church, first built in 1784, was the only Catholic church in Los Angeles for almost a hundred years. Today the church, located at the head of touristic Olvera Street, is all that remains to remind us of the old Basque town—which fell victim to urban renewal. By 1910 the San Francisco Basque colony had surpassed the Los Angeles one in size. In Los Angeles, older buildings were torn down to make way for wider roads. Eventually, construction of the Union Station railroad depot in 1930 and the influx of other ethnic groups, like the Chinese and Japanese, contributed to the demise of this first Basque town. Even the old Calvary Cemetery, where the early Basque settlers were buried, was moved, and Cathedral High School was eventually built on the spot.

A new **Calvary Cemetery** opened in East Los Angeles in 1896, and the remains of the dead were moved there gradually, over the next thirty years, as families were contacted. Among the prominent Basque pioneers whose names you will find there are Leonis, Oyharzabal, Salaberri, Bastanchury, and Amestoy.

La Placita Church (also known as Our Lady of Angels, Old Plaza, or Mission Church), 535 North Main Street (at Sunset Boulevard), Los Angeles, CA 90012 (213) 629-3101
Calvary Cemetery, 4201 Whittier Boulevard (at Downey Road), East Los Angeles, CA 90023 (323) 261-3106

RANCHING

Some men spent time in the mines in Northern California before they moved to the southern part of the state and became sheepherders. The most successful among the early Basques invested in sheep and cattle. Though sheep had brought little money on the market before the peak gold mining years, the demand—and the price—rose considerably once the state became filled with fortune hunters. The destruction of the South's cotton fields during the Civil War also upped the price of wool. Around 1865 there were 600,000 sheep in California. "By 1879, it was 6.3 million, and the biggest center was in Southern California," said longtime Bakersfield sheepman Martin Echamendy. Sheep adapted easily to the semidesert region.

Not all the Basques became big ranchers. More common were the stories of humbler men, such as San Martin Uharriet of Banca, France, who walked all the way from New Orleans to Los Angeles in the 1870s with a fellow Basque named Bidart. They came to work for one of Uharriet's first cousins who raised sheep.

Henry Bidegain and Early Los Angeles Dairies

Basques were running a dairy in Hollywood as early as 1900. Brothers Jean and Pete Bidegain both owned dairy farms in what is now south Los Angeles. The brothers spent a few years in Argentina before arriving here just after the turn of the century. Jean's son, the late Henry Bidegain, who was born in Los Angeles, remembered that his father's farm, Imperial Dairy, was located on Avalon Boulevard, and his uncle's was farther west at El Segundo and Main Street. Both locations are now smack in the middle of the city of Los Angeles.

In 1918 Bidegain's parents sold the dairy, which continued operating for many years under the same name, and they returned to their hometown of Aldudes, where the money they had made in America rendered them well-off. They could afford to send Henry to high school—a great luxury in those days. Urged by his parents, who assured him he could make money here, he eventually returned to Los Angeles, where he worked at dairies all over the region.

The late Bidegain, who passed away in 2003, was a much-beloved member of the Southern California Basque Community. Even into his eighties, the bachelor drove to almost all the local (and not so local) Basque functions. He was highly visible, either playing *mus* or visiting with friends at Basque dinners. "You have to keep up good habits," he joked.

They herded sheep from the ranch in the area that is now Culver City all the way to Ventura County, according to Uharriet's great nephew, Henry Bidegain, a longtime Los Angeles resident who heard many stories about those early days. Back then water in the semi-desert region was a big problem. "He would look for water and all he could find was black water, he used to tell us," said Bidegain. "It was oil, and he didn't know it." Uharriet and Bidart descendants continue to live in the Los Angeles area.

MUS AND A CLUB

Today most of Southern California's Basques live 30 miles east of Los Angeles, in La Puente and Chino. But a few of those scattered around Los Angeles decided to form a club during the early 1980s. They called it **Los Angeles Oberena,** after the small bands that play in the streets during the festival of San Fermín in Pamplona. "It's a real small club," said Manuel Villanueva. "When we started, the main reason was so we could play [the Basque card game] *mus* and play pelota, and that's the way it stayed." Villanueva and his two brothers, Martin and Jack, are avid *mus* players, and, in fact, their teams won first and second place in the national NABO *mus* tournament in 1993. "We practice enough," said Villanueva with a laugh, "but we don't win all the time."

When the club first started, many of the members also played in pelota competitions. But now their youngest member is over forty, and most have stopped playing the strenuous sport. But they make up for it with their *mus* time. They get together on Friday afternoons and Saturdays at the local Spanish clubhouse, **Salon de la Sociedad Española** (113 South 22nd Street) in Montebello. A regular group of about twenty-five card players gathers for the card game. They used to meet at the Chateau Briand restaurant in Pico Rivera. "We eat an early dinner together and then play all afternoon," Villanueva said. Sometimes the club members even drive out to the Centro Basco in Chino on Sundays and play *mus* there too. Many of them are hard-core players, paying for membership in other Basque clubs as well so that they can participate in other *mus* tournaments. And they aren't the only ones who make the rounds, according to Villanueva, who says that he recognizes many players at the different tournaments. From Los Angeles a few of them will even make the eight-hour drive to Gardnerville, Nevada, to play in that tournament every year. "When you play more places, you've got more chances to win," reasons Villanueva. The club waits until most of the other *mus* championships are over, in April or May, before it holds its own, usually attracting eighteen to twenty teams. Judging from the members' many wins over the years, the competition is serious. "My son, he likes to play," said Villanueva. "But he doesn't consider himself good enough to play in our tournament."

Los Angeles Oberena, c/o Manuel Villanueva, 9823 Parrot Avenue, Downey, CA 90240 (562) 927-2116

San Fernando Valley

RANCHO ENCINO

A limestone house, an eight-room adobe, and a blacksmith shop, all of which were part of a well-known Basque ranch during the late

1800s, have survived the passage of time and the urbanization of Los Angeles. Today the surviving ranch buildings are part of **Los Encinos State Historic Park,** a landmark that pays tribute to the early San Fernando Valley families that ran the ranch. Originally a 4,460-acre Mexican land grant given to three Indians, Rancho Encino was taken over by Don Vicente de la Ossa in 1849. He offered free overnight lodging to travelers on El Camino Real at his home, an eight-room adobe, which served as a ranch house for all the subsequent owners.

French brothers Phillippe and Eugene Garnier took over the ranch in 1869, turning it into a sheep ranch. In 1873 they built the limestone structure known as the Garnier House, which served as a bunkhouse, with a kitchen and dining room downstairs and rooms for the ranch hands upstairs. On the main road, now Ventura Boulevard, they built a roadhouse inn with a saloon and grocery. Basques in the area gathered here to talk business over a glass of wine or a beer, until the structure burned down in 1905. For many years the ranch was one of the few stops on the main stagecoach road from Los Angeles to Santa Barbara. Travelers along the way were terrorized by bandits, among them the well-known Joaquín Murrieta.

A big barn was built on the ranch, and according to Laura B. Gaye in her book *The Last of the Old West,* "Its sole purpose was to allow a stagecoach driver to drive his horses, coach, and passengers in to the barn, and pull a rope which would drop the big doors. This offered protection from bandits who had been in pursuit. When the danger had passed, they would go on their way."

The Garniers also built the surviving blacksmith shop, put a pitched roof on the old adobe, and capped a natural warm spring, creating a small lake in the shape of a guitar. (These springs were previously the center of a significant Indian village.)

But the Garniers' California dream soon faded away when they lost their investment in cattle and sheep owing to a big drop in wool prices and a serious drought in the 1870s. The two brothers went back to France, but their legacy lived on. "When we first started doing the tours, we called them French Basque," said park docent Lil Bauer, noting that the Garniers held big barbecues that were attended by many Basques in the area. Another Garnier brother, Leon, was married to Josephine Gless, who was part of an early Basque family. It's not surprising since there was much socializing among the early Southern California ranching families, regardless of where they were from.

Garnier family descendants who still live in the valley researched their ancestors and found that they were not from the Basque region of France, Bauer noted. There is no question, however, that the families who succeeded the Garniers as owners of the ranch were Basque.

Gaston Oxarart, who had come up to California by ship from Argentina in 1851, bought the bankrupt Rancho Encino in 1878. He continued raising sheep there, running as many as thirty-two thousand head. Oxarart's nephew, Simon Gless, took over in the 1880s after Oxarart died. "He was a wealthy man," said Bauer of Gless. "He had been at the gold mines when he heard what his uncle left him," she said. Gless replaced sheep raising with dry farming, introducing wheat, barley, and other grains, and he was also an early honey maker. But he was not a rancher at heart, and he quickly sold out to his wife Juanita's father, Domingo Amestoy.

The three ranch owners, Amestoy, Gless, and Oxarart had traveled to Argentina from the Basque Country, and they had all sailed to California on the same ship. Amestoy had worked as a shoemaker in Argentina, having immigrated there at the age of fourteen. In California he worked for a while in the mines and then as a herder for the wealthy American rancher Abel Stearns in Santa Barbara County. He eventually bought his own small band of sheep and moved down to Los Angeles, where he established himself as a sheep rancher even before he bought Rancho Encino. He was also one of the original stockholders of the Farmers and Merchants Bank and the German-American Savings Bank, and a charter member of the Los Angeles Chamber of Commerce. Amestoy was considered one of Southern California's biggest sheep ranchers.

After Amestoy died, his sons, Jean and Peter, took over the operation of the ranch, changing sheep ranching for wheat and barley production. They built a unique double-roofed storage house behind the limestone building, which is still standing. A street that starts near the old ranch and runs through several Valley cities is named Amestoy after this family. Although they were associated with Rancho Encino for many years, the family actually lived in Boyle Heights, a formerly well-to-do neighborhood on the east side of Los Angeles.

Los Encinos State Historic Park

By 1914 all but 100 acres of Rancho Encino had been sold off. Land was leased out, much of it used for poultry farms. The bunkhouse was later turned into a chicken restaurant and speakeasy. And for a while prostitutes entertained clients in the ranch hands' rooms upstairs. In 1945 a sign went up declaring the run-down property for sale, according to docent Lil Bauer. At that point a small group of local Encino women formed a historical group to save the property. They were able to acquire the 4.7 acres that make up the current park.

Later many improvements were made at the park, now maintained by the state. The women became Los Encinos Docent Association, a volunteer group that meticulously furnished the adobe house, known as De La Ossa Adobe, with curios and furnishings from the late 1800s. The group collected historical information about the property, dedicated each room to a different family that had lived and worked at the ranch, and hung portraits of family members on the walls.

Sadly, the January 17, 1994, earthquake, centered in nearby Northridge, severely damaged both the adobe house and the limestone-Garnier building. Damage was estimated at over $1 million. The Garnier building was the worst hit, despite the extensive work done earlier to make it earthquake resistant. "It would have come down, had it not been for that," said docent Virginia Cooley. The inside of the building had great gaping holes in it. State park officials are slowly restoring the buildings. The Garnier building has since been turned into a new visitors' center and is the only structure currently open to the public.

Nevertheless, the docent group continues its work. With a grant, the association obtained authentic costumes that reflect the ranch's early period and are used for monthly living-history events. The docents don the clothing of the nineteenth century and put on a program that includes music, traditional crafts like blacksmithing, children's games, and other activities. The living-history program is offered on the third Sunday of every month, from 1 P.M. to 3 P.M. The docent group also provides tours of the grounds when they are open, Wednesdays to Sundays from 10 A.M. to 5 P.M. Many visitors enjoy feeding the ducks that have made their home in the small lake fed by natural springs on the property.

This Franciscan monk is part of annual reenactments of Southern California ranching life in the 1870s at Los Encinos State Historic Park, a longtime Basque ranch.

The park's website, *www.historicparks.org,* is superb, with many easy-to-view historic photos of the Gless, Oxarart, and Amestoy families dating back to the 1800s, plus written chronicles of the Basque history of the ranch.

Los Encinos State Historic Park, 16756 Moorpark Street (and La Maida), Encino, CA 91436 (818) 784-4849; *www.historicparks.org*

Calabasas

One story of how Calabasas was first named has been repeated throughout the years, but the Basque who was supposedly behind it all is rarely mentioned. According to the tale, an early Southern California rancher in 1824 was taking home a load of pumpkins he had bought in Los Angeles. Arriving at the area that's now Calabasas, the horses reared upward, suddenly frightened by a rattlesnake. The wagonful of pumpkins toppled onto the road, and there were crushed pumpkins everywhere. The following spring, the seeds sprouted, and pumpkins were growing all over the place. Thereafter, this spot was referred to as Las Calabazas, which in Spanish means "the pumpkins."

Quoted in Laura Gaye's book, *The Last of the Old West,* longtime Calabasas resident Anna Yrigoyen claimed this rancher was her grandfather Antonio Jauregui, a native of the Basque Country who established his ranch in Oxnard. He reportedly walked across the country to reach Los Angeles in the 1820s, more than twenty years before the first big wave of Basques started arriving for the gold rush, when California was still part of Mexico. Yrigoyen, who said she frequently visited her grandfather in Oxnard and heard him tell this story, settled with her Basque husband in Calabasas where they became a well-known ranching family in the community.

Despite the Yrigoyen family's prominence here, the best-known Basque in Calabasas, and perhaps in the entire Los Angeles region in his day, was Miguel Leonis. Today his ranch home is a museum.

The old center of Calabasas has been granted architectural protection, and once you arrive in Old Calabasas, you will see why. Adobe buildings dating back to the last century are preserved here, giving one a feeling of what the Old West must have been like in the days when the feared Miguel Leonis had the run of the western end of the San Fernando Valley. The Leonis Adobe Museum, in the middle of old Calabasas, consists of his two-story 1844 Monterey-style mansion and surrounding property, which has been restored to its original state as a working California ranch from the late 1800s.

Miguel Leonis and El Escorpion Ranch

El Escorpion ranch, a 9,000-acre Mexican land grant, was originally owned by two brothers, leaders of a local Mexican tribe and former disciples of the San Fernando Mission fathers. Miguel Leonis took Espíritu Chijulla (also spelled *Chichuilla* or *Chijola*), the daughter of one of the men, as his common-law wife. Espíritu, one of the last of the Fernandeño Indians, inherited a portion of El Escorpion Ranch, which was about 2 miles north of the center of Calabasas. It stretched from where the Chatsworth Reservoir is now to about a mile south. Miguel acquired her portion and bought or manipulated his way into full ownership, according to a short history on the ranch, *El Escorpion.*

Miguel Leonis

As an old stagecoach stop between Los Angeles and Santa Barbara, Calabasas had a wild reputation, and rancher Miguel Leonis fit seamlessly into that milieu. He is considered one of the most colorful characters of the Los Angeles area's early days—a big man, six feet four inches tall, who was referred to as "el Vasco grande" (the big Basque).

Christened Michel, Leonis was called Miguel by his Mexican and Spanish acquaintances after he came to California via ship in the 1850s. According to Leonis's great-grandnephew Leonis Malburg, he came round the Horn, where he was almost shipwrecked, and jumped ship in the Los Angeles harbor. Leonis became a rancher in the Calabasas area north of Los Angeles.

"The sheriffs couldn't handle everything," said Malburg, "so they created vigilante forces, and Miguel was head of the Calabasas vigilante force." He was known to travel about with the likes of the famous Joaquín Murrieta, labeled a bandit by U.S. lawmen, and used a muzzle to keep settlers off public lands he claimed as his own. He was not afraid to back up his property claims with legal battles in the courtroom, which he often won. He was worth $300,000, a small fortune in those days. He dominated a wide swath of land called El Escorpion Ranch, bounded by the Chatsworth Reservoir on the north, Malibu to the south, and the Agoura Hills to the west. On the east his territory bordered on the Amestoys' Rancho Encino.

"He didn't actually own the lands on the perimeter of the ranch," said Malburg. "He controlled them by iron fist. Anybody who came in there and tried to homestead, they were forcefully run off, plain and simple."

The Leonis Valley, northeast of Calabasas, near Lancaster, where Leonis once had a house, was named after him, but the name was changed to Leona Valley under pressure from some local teachers. "He was such a mean man, they didn't want that name," said Malburg's wife, Leonie. Nevertheless, the man still garners prestige in some circles, since a school in nearby Woodland Hills bears his name.

Leonis died in 1889, when he fell from a wagon in Cahuenga Pass on his way home from Los Angeles. Rumors of a more sinister death by a gunshot to the head swirled about. "That theory is wrong," said Leonis Malburg. "He won a court case that day. He was elated, happy, maybe a little drunk," he said, explaining how the accident could have happened. Malburg heard about Leonis's death from his grandfather who was at his uncle's deathbed. Jean Leonis told him someone brought Miguel home, where he died within a couple of days. The gunshot rumors were squelched definitively when Jean Leonis's son-in-law, Raymond Malburg, an undertaker, exhumed his body years later and examined it, said Malburg. No evidence of any bullet wounds was found. However, docents at the association still believe that somehow, foul play was involved.

While they were at Rancho Escorpion, rowdy Frenchmen (probably some Basques as well) worked at the Simi Hills lime kilns and lived in the ranch's many adobe buildings, some built by Leonis himself. The Leonises' ownership of the house at El Escorpion was later challenged by lawyer Horace Bell, because it supposedly had been built on public land outside the ranch's boundaries.

It's possible that is what led the Leonises to move from the ranch to the adobe home at Calabasas in 1880. While the house is believed to have been built in the 1840s, its history seems to have become important only after the larger-than-life Miguel moved in with his wife. It is named after Leonis in recognition of his significant contributions to the house that exists today. He enclosed the patio areas, added a kitchen and the rooms upstairs, in addition to building up the ranch.

His descendants acknowledge that Leonis was a shrewd man. But the attorney Horace Bell, who both defended and fought against the Leonis family in court, was just as bad, said a distant relative, Leonie Malburg. "The other did it with a gun, and Bell did it with a pencil," she said, referring to the large amount of property the attorney acquired as payment for his services. Bell's family later acquired the Escorpion Ranch property.

Although Miguel and Espíritu lived their lives as a married couple and for all intents and purposes were man and wife by virtue of common law, no legal document was ever found to show that they were officially married. Local Basques despised Leonis for taking an indigenous wife, according to Leonie.

Espíritu and Miguel had only one daughter, named Marcelina after Espíritu's sister. Miguel was apparently very fond of his daughter, and he became severely depressed, even attempting suicide, when she died at age twenty of smallpox. He had been training her to take over the sheep ranching business when she died.

When Miguel sought to retire, he wrote a letter to his family in France to send someone to take over the ranch. His nephew Jean Baptiste Leonis, who had been slated for the priesthood, accepted the invitation. "The priests told him it was the chance of a lifetime to go to California," said Malburg about his grandfather Jean Baptiste Leonis. He was quickly introduced to the rough-and-tumble pace of life in Calabasas, when he saw his uncle shoot and kill one of his enemies on his first day in town (see sidebar on Jean Baptiste Leonis in the Vernon section).

His uncle Miguel died six months later, and Jean, because he was underage—he was seventeen—"got nothing," relates Jean's great-granddaughter, Linda Fletcher. As a result, the house was not passed down through the Leonis family but rather through Espíritu's side of the family. In his will, Miguel had only designated a small share of his estate for his wife, leaving most of it to relatives in the Basque Country. Espíritu had to wage a court battle for a wife's rightful share of the large estate. She was forced to prove that they were husband and wife, though there was no marriage certificate. She won her case eventually, with the help of several lawyers. Most of the land, however, went to Bell to pay for the legal costs.

In the end, Espíritu kept the house and the small plot of land it sat on, which is the museum property today. She continued living there with her son from an earlier marriage, Juan Menéndez, until her death in 1906.

Menéndez and his wife adopted several children, among them a daughter, Mary Johnson, who grew up in the house. She married Pedro Orsua and also lived with him on the ranch. The ranch eventually lapsed into ruins, and Menéndez sold it to a rancher, Lester Agoure, in 1921.

The families that lived there reported strange goings-on. Ghosts, said to be the spirits of Miguel and Espíritu, were seen in the house by later inhabitants. Two different families living in the house after Espíritu's son sold it reported hearing unexplainable noises and untraceable odors like soap and cigar. They often heard heavy footsteps on the stairs and on the second floor. The most remarkable event occurred one day when Mary Orsua was looking down the road, waiting for one of her daughters to return home. She leaned over the railing and felt a strong unseen force push her back. Later the family examined the railing and found it was weakened and on the verge of breaking away.

Leonis Adobe Museum

The adobe became run-down and it was slated to be razed to make way for a shopping center, until 1965, when the Leonis Adobe Association was created to save it. At the association's invitation, Pedro and Mary Orsua, poor parents of eighteen children, came back to live in the house. Based on the recollections of Mary Orsua, the association redecorated the house to resemble the days when her adopted grandmother Espíritu was alive. Floor coverings and wall paneling were removed to reveal the original adobe walls and dirt floors. The furnishings, photographs, costumes and tools all date back to the nineteenth century. Although Interstate 5 runs along the backside of the ranch, the state Department of Transportation recently built a sound wall to block the freeway noise from the museum grounds.

Jean Baptiste Leonis's great granddaughter Linda Fletcher became interested in the historic home and worked there for a while offering tours. She found that as the stories about Leonis have been retold, "they kept changing, and when I came here the stories were completely different from what I heard growing up." Fletcher acknowledges that she has learned that her great-great-great-uncle was much more ruthless than her family had ever revealed to her. But she

The adopted granddaughter of Espiritu Leonis, Mary Orsua, and her husband Pedro with their eighteen children were the last family to live in the Leonis Adobe near Los Angeles. This couple always had a baby in the house, who slept in a hammock over the couple's bed.

Linda Fletcher, great-grand-niece of the famed Miguel Leonis, gave tours showing off his 1840 home, before it was damaged in the January 1994 earthquake.

affirms that his reputation was largely due to his own personality and not to the Basque nature in general.

A grape arbor built by Leonis in front of the house and the original well have been restored. A brick beehive oven and a working windmill that existed during his time have been rebuilt. The grounds also include vineyards, an orchard, a garden, a wine vat, and a new water tank. One year the association made wine from the grapes growing on the property. Outbuildings, located beyond the six-hundred-year-old white oak that dominates the backyard, serve as home for some longhorn steers, horses, and assorted fowl. "A lot of the crops are just for show," says Fletcher, "because some of the city kids [who come to visit] have never seen a fruit tree."

The association offers living-history tours of the property, which are extremely popular among schoolchildren. Girls are taught how to spin wool, churn butter, grind corn, and make tortillas, and boys learn roping and branding. Horses are hitched to a wagon and driven around the property. The association sponsors group tours for twenty or more people, and they must be booked four to five months ahead of time, said director Phyllis Power, because they are so popular. Caretaker Jesus Puentes has been in charge of keeping up the grounds since 1981. When he first arrived, everything but the house was in ruins, he remembered. The proud caretaker said he's visited many a historic adobe home throughout the state, and "there aren't any like this, with gardens and animals."

As for stories of the house being haunted, Puentes, originally from Mexico, gives them credence. "These ladies say there aren't ghosts," Puentes said, referring to the women who run the association. "But there are." Puentes, who lives alone in the house, has left many times with lights blazing and inside doors open. When he returns, the lights are off and some doors are closed. "And the doors are heavy," he said. "They can't close with the wind." He's also heard noises coming from downstairs but has never found anything when he has investigated.

The 6.7 earthquake that struck the San Fernando Valley in January 1994 damaged the adobe, forcing the museum to close for several months. The most significant damage was the cracks that developed in the adobe brick walls. To preserve the house's historic authenticity, a meticulous reconstruction of the individual bricks has been undertaken. "For being 150 years old, it's miraculous that it even stood as well as it did," said Fletcher. The house was later reopened.

The visitors' center is located in the Plummer House, a historic mansion moved in 1983 from Hollywood where it stood for over a hundred years. Interestingly, around the turn of the century, long before the Leonis Adobe Association decided to save the Plummer home, the Leonises and the Plummers visited each others' ranches. Make sure you stop by the center to see additional exhibits including photographs from the ranch's early days. In addition, the association sells a wonderful assortment of books and other items, which sometimes include fruit grown on the grounds. An unauthorized biography of Leonis by attorney Horace Bell, *The Last of the Old West* by Laura Gaye and *El Escorpion* make for interesting reading.

The museum's visiting days are limited from Wednesday to Sunday, so make sure you take that into consideration when you plan your trip. To reach the site, take the 101 Ventura Freeway to the Parkway Calabasas or Valley Circle Boulevard exits. The adobe is located about midway between the two exits, on Calabasas Road, which runs parallel to the freeway on the west side. The house is set back off the road, in the middle of the town's cluster of Western-style buildings.

You might also want to stop for a picnic at the nearby Calabasas Creek, preserved in its natural state. It is located in a park just south of the adobe, on the other side of the Sagebrush Cantina, developed by the Leonis Association. This creek eventually turns into the Los Angeles River. You may also enjoy visiting the shops and restaurants located in some of the other old buildings nearby.

Leonis Adobe Museum, 23537 Calabasas Road, Calabasas, CA 91302 (818) 222-6511; *www.leonisadobemuseum.org.* Admission is free, although donations are encouraged.

Santa Barbara

The Santa Ynez Valley north of Los Angeles was first popular among Basque cattlemen, who established ranches there in the early 1850s and 1860s. Among the earliest families were the Yndarts, the Andonaeguis, the Ormarts, the Altubes, the Harispurus, and the Ypars. Double disasters—flooding and then drought—hit in the early 1860s, shattering the cattle market and sending many families fleeing. Ulpiano Yndart was among those who remained, and he entered local politics, serving as a local judge and city treasurer for Santa Barbara between the 1850s and the 1870s. Yndart was a member of an elite Basque family who came to California as part of its early colonization. Jose Antonio Aguirre and Cesareo Lataillade were other prominent Basques from the early 1800s who settled in this town. (Many of the historic buildings from the Spanish and Mexican era have been preserved, making Santa Barbara a popular stop among tourists.)

Sheep were an easy investment and in those early years, there was plenty of open land for grazing around Santa Barbara. Basque sheepmen herded throughout the area, and many a band of sheep was trailed down the main road of Santa Barbara, now known as State Street.

BOARDINGHOUSES

Eventually, Basque boardinghouses were established around Santa Barbara. The Borderre French Hotel, the most well known of Santa Barbara's Basque boardinghouses, stood in the historic De la Guerra Plaza, now property of the Santa Barbara *News Press.* "It wasn't French, but nobody knew what Basque was," explains local historian Frank Armendariz, who was born in the hotel. The hotel started around the turn of the century as the Borderre family home, and then Juanita Borderre began taking in sheepherders as boarders. In the boardinghouse's early years, husband José was away most of the time, tending to the many farms and ranches he owned.

The Borderres later expanded the hotel and added a handball court that attracted many players on the weekends. Basques were well known to be involved in bootlegging during Prohibition days, and the local police would stop by the Borderre hotel for drinks, according to Armendariz, godson of "Joe" Borderre. He remembered that the liquor came from a source in Los Angeles, and, apparently, Mrs. Borderre always kept a bottle of wine in her pocket. Eventually the building was torn down.

A taped interview with the Borderres' son Bernard, which provides some early history of the town, is on file at the Gledhill Library of the **Santa Barbara Historical Museum** (136 East De la Guerra St. [805] 966-1601), along with other information on some of the earliest Basque settlers. At least four other Basque boardinghouses existed in the old downtown for a time, some of which were simply Basque family homes where extra rooms were rented out. The Anchordoquys, a large family that lived in Santa Barbara in later years, operated a hotel or two, including the Borderre and a small third-rate establishment now known as the State Street Hotel. Antone Bastanchury, a cousin to the well-known Bastanchurys of Fullerton, took over the Borderre hotel in its later years. He was best known for cultivating and shipping lemons, and he developed the popular Carmelita lemon brand.

The coastal area's weather was not the best for raising sheep, and by the end of the 1930s, the boardinghouses had disappeared. By the mid-1940s, Santa Barbara's Basque colony, like that of downtown Los Angeles, was gone, and many Basques had moved to Bakersfield. A few of the old-timers remained.

In more recent years, an informal group of Basque immigrants in Santa Barbara held annual barbecues, but as they aged, there were no younger Basques willing to take on the responsibility, and the tradition died in the late 1980s.

RESTAURANTS

Because of the disappearance of the Basque community here, the presence of Basque restaurants has been sporadic. A Santa Barbara restaurant, E.J.'s Café on State Street, which had a bit of Basque history, closed in 2003.

Guadalupe, a tiny town north of Santa Barbara, boasted of the central coast's only Basque restaurant for many years. Set in a historic building at 992 Guadalupe Street, The Basque House was open from 1976 to 1990 but closed because of an explosion across the street. Today, San Luis Obispo offers the region's only Basque dining experience, and it's worth the drive. Locals love Michel Olaizola's cozy downtown café, Le Fandango Bistro, with its brick walls and black-and-white photographs of Basque scenes. Olaizola, who owned a restaurant in Paris before coming to the United States, serves many traditional dishes, as well as trendier variations. Before dinnertime, Olaizola enjoys having a drink at the front of the bar, near the door, to socialize with customers as they come in. Proud of his Basque ancestry, he displays a large Basque flag over the entrance to the kitchen, where he cooks and oversees the kitchen crew.

Le Fandango Bistro, 717 Higuera Street, San Luis Obispo, CA 93401 (805) 544-5515

AN ENDOWED ACADEMIC CHAIR

Additional focus in the field of Basque studies in the United States comes out of the University of California, Santa Barbara. Beginning in 1993 Basque culture and language classes are being sponsored through a chairmanship funded by the Basque government and the Federación de Cajas de Ahorros Vasco-Navarros. The position, the José Miguel de Barandiaran Chair, after the great Basque anthropologist and folklorist, was filled by Juan Bautista de Avalle-Arce, a long-time professor at U.C. Santa Barbara from 1993 to 2004. Basque studies classes are part of the larger Spanish and Portuguese Department. Catalan and Gallegan studies are also offered. With those five linguistic groups, the department was the first to offer "the cultural whole of the Iberian Peninsula," said Avalle-Arce. The focus on Basque studies from a larger perspective is what differentiates this program from the one offered at University of Nevada, Reno. It was unclear what would happen to the position after Avalle-Arce's retirement, but some classes continue to be offered.

Obtaining the Basque Country funding for the position was largely a result of the tireless efforts of the Basque American Foundation, a small group spearheaded by Professors Gloria Castresana Waid and Juan Mendizabal. The foundation, a nonprofit group, was created in 1983, basically as a result of a rift among members of the Society of Basque Studies in America (see the section on New York). The foundation published its own *Journal of Basque Studies* up through 1994, but had to cancel the publication because of lack of funds. The Basque-American Foundation had no activities at the time of publication.

Basque Studies, Spanish and Portuguese Department, University of California, Santa Barbara, Santa Barbara, CA 93106-4150 (805) 893-3162; *www.spanport.ucsb.edu*

Ventura County

RANCHING

Basque families have been ranching in Ventura County as long as they have in adjacent Santa Barbara and Los Angeles Counties, and many of their descendants remain here. In fact, at least one Basque, Antonio Jauregui, was in Oxnard as early as 1824. Back in the 1930s, Pete Etchechoury remembers, many of them would get together and roast a pig, or kill a few chickens and have a barbecue. "Every Sunday, there was a party somewhere," said Etchechoury, whose father managed a ranch on Gonzales Road near Oxnard. The Dufau brothers' ranch, also near Oxnard, was another popular gathering place. Today a local street is named after them. Robert Erburu, former longtime chairman and president of the Times-Mirror Company, which publishes the *Los Angeles Times,* came from an early ranching family here.

Few of the older families are ranching any longer, although the Jauregui family is still running cattle and sheep out of Wheeler Canyon. Nevertheless, the older Basque community was replenished by a more recent wave of immigrants who came during the 1960s and 1970s to work as sheepherders or milkers. "There are a lot more Basques now," said Etchechoury. The Basque community used to be centered in Oxnard, where a few Basques had bakeries or laundries. In recent years Jean Claude Etchegaray ran a restaurant called the Basque Café in Camarillo, but he finally closed it around 1990. Today Basque families are more likely to be found in upscale Fillmore and Santa Paula.

BASQUE CLUB

Three Basque women started a club in Ventura County in 1993 as a result of an odd coincidence. One day Cathy (Carricaburu) Foxhoven, whose license plate reads BASQ M I was driving around Camarillo, where she lives, when she spotted a woman in a car with the license plate BASQUE 1. "She honked at me and said, 'You're one of us,'" remembers Foxhoven. "Then she drove off, and I didn't know who she was." When Foxhoven happened to see the woman again a few days later, she flagged her down, and the two women exchanged phone numbers. When Foxhoven and Ellen (Etchechoury) Reser got together with a third woman, Arlene Burke, "We said we had to have a Basque club," said Foxhoven. They held an organizational meeting in May 1993. "Basically it was a get-together, get acquainted meeting," she said. The members, who named their club **Itxaso Alde** (By the Sea), jumped right in and started planning their first event—a picnic, for October 30, 1993.

Today the club has about 120 families as members.

Itxaso Alde (Ventura County Basque Club), P.O. Box 1872, Thousand Oaks, CA 91358-0906. Information: (805) 482-5289 (*Jeanne Etchechoury*)

FESTIVAL

At the first Itxaso Alde picnic, the club presented the typical offerings—the barbecued lamb, beans, and salad lunch—plus afternoon dancing and an evening dance. The folk dance group from Bakersfield was invited to perform, "and then they taught the rest of us some dances," said Foxhoven, with a laugh. The picnic attracted about a hundred people to Oak Grove Park in Camarillo. The picnics have continued annually at Oak Grove Park. Although the picnic is usually held in May or June, no regular date has been set, since the park site is not always available. The spring picnic attracts about 300 people. The club holds another smaller paella picnic in the fall just for its members.

Vernon

Jean Baptiste Leonis, better known as John, was one of the founders of the city of Vernon, a small industrial city in the middle of Los Angeles County. He owned land here, and in 1905 he joined with two brothers, James and Thomas Furlong, who were also local landowning ranchers, to found the city of Vernon. The founders campaigned hard to lure industry to their small city. Their campaign was successful, particularly their efforts to bring the railroads to Vernon. The town was right on the path from the Los Angeles Harbor to downtown.

Jean Baptiste Leonis

Before coming to America, Jean Baptiste "John" Leonis was a young, impressionable man who was studying to be a priest in France. He ended his life as a wealthy industrialist, banker, and civic leader whose presence is still felt today in the town he helped found—Vernon.

Leonis left the priesthood at the invitation of his uncle Miguel Leonis, who wrote to his family in France, hoping someone would take over his huge Calabasas estate. Because he was underage (seventeen) when his uncle died, Jean Baptiste received nothing of the inheritance. So the young Leonis took a job as a sheepherder in the Antelope Valley, where he met his wife, Adelina Clos. He later became a master vintner for a French wine maker in Los Angeles. In 1896 he bought some land in what is now the city of Vernon. Sonia Eagle wrote a lengthy history of the younger Leonis's achievements in her dissertation "Work and Play Among the Basques of Southern California." He planted crops and eventually opened a general store, winery, and distillery. He also managed the public weighing scales for the freight wagons heading down Downey Road to the Los Angeles Harbor in San Pedro.

In 1905 he and two ranchers in the area, James and Thomas Furlong, founded the city of Vernon. In the hopes of bringing more industry to the area, Leonis traveled to San Francisco, Chicago, and Omaha to persuade officials of the three main railroads to come to the Vernon area. "He was trying to peddle the city," said his grandson, Leonis Malburg. The campaign continued, as the civic leaders worked to lure industry to their small city.

Jean Baptiste Leonis was councilman of Vernon for forty-five years and served as its mayor several times. He started several small, independent banks around Los Angeles and served on their boards. The most successful was the First National Bank of Vernon, which lasted from 1916 to 1959 until it merged with the much larger Citizens National Bank, which later became Crocker Citizens Bank and then Wells Fargo. The small bank office where it began, at Thirty-eighth and Santa Fe, is still standing.

Grandson Malburg's wife Leonie remembers with amazement her first visit to the family ranch up north in Tujunga Canyon, now part of the Angeles National Forest. "He made his own little Basque Country there," she said, referring to her husband's grandfather. There were chestnut trees and sheep, and grapevines from which he made wine.

Today Jean Baptiste's grandson is carrying on his legacy, managing the family holdings and serving on Vernon's city council for more than thirty years.

Leonis never forgot his Basque roots, which he instilled in his grandson. It was Jean Baptiste Leonis and his wife who took Malburg to the Southern California Eskualdun Club picnics in La Puente, where their grandson eventually met his Basque wife, Leonie Mocho who danced in the club's group back then.

Throughout its history, the city has remained an industrial town. Railroad tracks run every which way through Vernon. Its nighttime population is 200, but 55,000 workers come into the 5.6-square-mile city every day. The establishment of two large stockyards in the city, one owned by Leonis, led to the city's development as a meat-butchering and meat-packing center. At one time there were twenty-five packing houses operating here. Many of them, particularly Farmer John's, which still operates, employed a number of Basques, most of them from Spain.

Leonis served on the city council for forty-five years and was a major financial and real estate power broker. His only grandson, named Leonis Malburg, stepped right into his grandfather's shoes, building a career in banking, real estate and Vernon politics. He has been on the city council continuously since 1956 and has been the mayor since 1974.

In an appropriate tribute to the Leonis-Malburg contribution to this city, there is a Leonis Boulevard and Malburg Way here. LEONIS MALBURG is spelled out in bold letters on the three-story office building where his office is located.

RESTAURANT

The Malburgs built a Basque restaurant, **Villa Basque,** smack in the middle of this industrial center. The restaurant was the pet project of Malburg's wife, Leonie, and she wanted to build it to resemble an elegant villa, but practicality won out over her artistic sense. So now the only thing that identifies the outside of the plain one-story building as a Basque restaurant is the sign on the corner. The interior, however, is another matter. A chimney warms the entryway, and above it a plaque honors the Basque people and John B. Leonis Sr. Coats-of-arms from every Basque province decorate the bar. A carpet decorated with *txisteras* (the basketlike extension worn on the hand in jai alai) and other Basque symbols was designed specially for the restaurant. Reproductions of works by Basque Country artist Ramiro Arrue liven the walls. At one time, according to Leonie, she displayed his originals, until they became invaluable after his death. "They were there for thirty years, and nobody knew who he was."

In the years after Villa Basque opened in 1960, the restaurant attracted big crowds from Los Angeles. "On Friday nights, people used to wait in line," said Leonie. "But this is all changed." Now the restaurant, run by Leonie's sister, Maite Mocho, is not open for dinner in the evenings nor on weekends, since most of the customers are businesspeople who come in during the week for lunch. Although the restaurant never intended to serve the large family-style portions, "we did have Basque dishes," stressed Leonie. But the customers seemed to prefer steak, so gradually the Basque dishes on the menu have dwindled. Nevertheless "*roti de veau Basquaise,*" cooked by longtime chef Jean Arhancet, is a popular special, and his exquisite *gateau Basque* (Basque cake) is always on the menu. If you drive here for lunch, you might enjoy viewing the colorful pig mural at the Farmer John Meats plant. The mural, begun in 1957, surrounds the building on Soto Street and East Vernon Avenue.

Villa Basque, 2801 Leonis Boulevard (at Soto Street), Vernon, CA 90058 (323) 583-1696

Venice

A BAKERY AND A BOULANGERIE

The **Pioneer French Baking Company** in Venice, which started its days as the National French Bakery, can probably be counted among the oldest Basque businesses in the West. Jean Baptiste Garacochea founded the bakery in 1908, at Fifth and Bicknell in Santa Monica. In 1917 he moved the business a few blocks away to nearby Venice. Today the bakery is at that same location on Rose Street, still churning out sourdough bread from the original recipe. The original brick building is still there, although it's been remodeled and expanded many times over since those early days, when "Mama" cooked and fed the help in the big dining room upstairs and raised her five children. Garacochea's grandchildren and great grandchildren are running the business now, carrying on a tradition of six generations that began back in the town of Aldudes, where J.B.'s grandfather started and ran a bakery for many years before it was sold out of the family.

When Edmund Garacochea's father started the bakery, "all there was in Southern California were dairies and farms," said Edmund. The Venice area had few if any Basque families besides the Garacocheas. The younger Garacochea started working in his father's bakery when he was seven and headed its production for many years before retiring in 1985. Edmund figures that his father settled here because urban Santa Monica and Venice provided lots of potential customers. While rural plains and hills surrounded them, the area west of Lincoln Boulevard was full of houses. "The red electric cars came all the way from Pomona to the beach back then," he said. Venice and Santa Monica both had amusement parks on their piers that attracted thousands as Los Angeles grew.

The bakery delivered bread three times a week directly to the farms, then later to stores, seeking an ever greater market share. "He worked eight days a week like they did in the Old Country," said

The National French Bakery in Venice, California, founded by Jean Baptiste Garacochea (in vest) in 1908 and moved to this location in 1917, is still at the same address. Now it's the Pioneer Bakery, and the original building has been expanded many times over. (Courtesy of Jack Garacochea.)

Edmund of his father. Jean Baptiste also grew his own vegetables and raised chickens and pigeons on the property around the bakery. He managed to enjoy some spare time, playing accordion at Basque affairs as far away as Norwalk or La Puente. Instead of money, payment was half a pig, or a whole pig for two days of playing, explained Edmund. "He lived in the hard times." To supplement the family's income from the bakery, Garacochea Sr. built an apartment building right across the street from the bakery in 1927 or 1928. The building, with a store downstairs and apartments upstairs, still belongs to the family. Garacochea Sr. died in 1940, and his oldest son, also J. B. Garacochea, took over the business, which he was already helping to guide. Edmund also took his turn alongside him. "I just never had any other job," he said. Wife Gloria boasts that Edmund was probably the last member of the family to load the loaves into the brick ovens on the old-fashioned spadelike wooden peels. It's his photo you'll see on the sides of Pioneer's delivery trucks. Today, J.B.'s sons Jack and Jay and grandson John are running the modern, automated business, and Edmund's children have also joined the family enterprise. "They all follow their own minds, but the business got so big that everyone got to do whatever they wanted to do," said Edmund.

After visiting the Basque Country with Edmund in 1973, Jack Garacochea came back fired up with the idea of making the family's Basque heritage a focal point and created the **Pioneer Boulangerie,** a self-contained cluster of shops—bakery, wine shop, coffee house, deli, outdoor and indoor cafeteria, and a fine restaurant—all emphasizing the Basque connaissance of food and wine. The girls dressed in the typical Basque costume, with red skirts, black vests, and aprons. "They had them special made, and all the fellows wore the berets," said Gloria Garacochea. The massive blockwide operation at 2012 Main Street in Santa Monica developed a loyal clientele, which was crushed when the Garacocheas closed it in 1993, after twenty years in business. A smaller version of the boulangerie, serving fresh bread, pastries, and coffee, opened at another location in Santa Monica that same year, continuing the company's presence in the city.

The company has big renovation plans for the original bakery in Venice, which include moving most of the primary baking operation to another location, rebuilding a small bakery and retail shop that will resemble the original historic building, plus adding some upscale apartments and shops, all on Rose Avenue.

The baking company continues to operate the Crunchy Crumb and Crouton Company in nearby El Segundo, which sells mostly day-old products, but it has sold another operation in Oxnard.

Pioneer French Baking Company, 512 Rose Avenue (at Fifth Street) Venice, CA 90291 (310) 392-3066
Pioneer Boulangerie, 804 Montana (at Lincoln), Santa Monica, CA 90403 (310) 451-4998

Famous Offspring

The Basques were prominent members of early Los Angeles, and their U.S.–born offspring also made names for themselves. Unfortunately, a couple of them were better remembered for bunglings in their later years than for their achievements.

Martin Aguirre, son of wealthy Basque merchant José Antonio Aguirre, was elected sheriff of Los Angeles County in the late 1800s. (For more information on the elder Aguirre, see the section on San Diego.) In 1886 Aguirre's courageous efforts in riding his horse into the rapidly flooding Los Angeles River to rescue up to twenty stranded people were splashed across the local papers. The college-educated man, who had lost his sight in one eye as a child, was a county constable at the time, and he used his moment in the spotlight to run for sheriff. Many years later, as warden of San Quentin State Prison, he was accused of mishandling government money. Nevertheless the county sheriff's department pays homage to Aguirre in a talking exhibit at their museum, the **L.A. County Sheriff's Department Museum,** which opened in 1989. His tattered saddle has also been preserved at the museum.

Martin Biscailuz was a prominent lawyer who published a Basque newspaper and stirred up controversy in his later years. Biscailuz was born on a Los Angeles ranch in 1860 and attended a private college in Los Angeles. He spent several years in Europe and spoke Basque and several other languages fluently. Biscailuz was the primary attorney for the Southern California Basque community, and for a short time he served as a member of the Los Angeles City Council. This ambitious man also published *Escualdun Gazeta,* the world's first exclusively Basque-language newspaper. But his reputation was dealt an irreversible blow when he was accused of mishandling the estate of Basque millionaire Simon Oxarart, who died in 1886. The successor paper, *California'ko Eskual Herria,* publicly criticized him. He was tried for defrauding clients, served a prison sentence, and ended his life as an alcoholic. He died at age thirty-nine.

His son, Eugene Warren Biscailuz, however, earned nothing but high praise for his twenty-six-year reign as Los Angeles County sheriff. He was responsible for some of the greatest changes in law enforcement in the Los Angeles area during his stint in office, from 1932 to 1958. "He took a small department that was still kind of old-fashioned, and turned it into the largest sheriff's department in the world," said Jack Kuner, a supervisor at the sheriff's museum. "He was really a legend in his own time."

Biscailuz studied law at the University of Southern California. He joined the sheriff's department in 1907 as a clerk, then left after a few years to help the state found the California Highway Patrol and served as its first supervisor. He came back to the sheriff's department as undersheriff and soon was elected sheriff. A great deal of memorabilia from his years as top sheriff can also be found in the L.A. County Sheriff's Department Museum, which is open Monday–Friday from 9 A.M. to 4 P.M. His Basque heritage was common knowledge. "Everyone just seemed to know he was Basque," said Kuner. Besides carrying out his duties as sheriff, Biscailuz became even more widely known in the Los Angeles area because of his many radio talks and public speaking engagements. He often related stories about the history of Southern California and was sometimes referred to by radio announcers as "the most popular man in the county." In fact, a biography was written about him, entitled *Biscailuz: Sheriff of the New West.*

L.A. County Sheriff's Department Museum, Sheriff's Training Academy Center, Building B, 11515 South Colima Road (at Telegraph Road), Whittier, CA 90604 (562) 946-7081. Admission free

Fullerton

SHEEP AND A CITRUS RANCH

Domingo Bastanchury, a native of Aldudes, France, was one of the few early Basques in the Orange County area who came directly from the Basque Country, sailing all the way around Cape Horn in 1860. After spending years as a sheepherder, he acquired his own bands, which numbered up to twenty thousand head and made him one of the biggest sheepmen in California. He bought thousands of acres of property in the area that is now Fullerton, which his four sons, Dominic (better known as D.J.), Joe, Gaston, and John, eventually developed into a huge citrus ranch. The ranch had its headquarters around what is now Harbor Boulevard and Bastanchury Road, and for a time it was the largest citrus ranch in Southern California. Citrus did not become an important crop until the refrigerated railroad car was developed, after the turn of the century. One of the orange brands the Bastanchurys grew was labeled the "Basque" brand. Highly regarded in the East, the brand logo featured a man in traditional Basque clothing on a hillside with sheep.

The Bastanchury ranch was a gathering place and source of employment for many Los Angeles Basques. It was conveniently located near Harbor Boulevard, which was once part of the historically important El Camino Real, and the railroad ran right by the ranch. Sonia Eagle interviewed many of the old-timers who worked there to give a history of the ranch in her 1979 dissertation, "Work and Play Among the Basques of Southern California." A regulation handball court was built on the ranch in 1913. The ranch workers themselves, most of them Basque, lived in boardinghouses on the ranch run by the foremen's wives. Large barbecues were common. Wine was made on the property from the ranch's grapes.

The Bastanchurys helped other Basques establish themselves as ranchers. One was José Sansiñena, who also became a big sheep rancher in the same area. The Bastanchury ranch operated from the late 1800s to 1932. The Great Depression seriously affected the price of oranges, and as a result the ranch went bankrupt. Until the 1940s,

Basques continued working for the ranch, which was put into receivership, under Union Oil Company, Bank of America, and the Times-Mirror Company.

Today the former orange orchards have been replaced by houses and oil derricks. Although the Bastanchurys did not exploit it, underground oil was plentiful on their land. (It's not clear whether the Bastanchurys knew about the oil when they declared bankruptcy. Norma Bastanchury, a relative by marriage, said that the Bastanchurys sued Union Oil over an oil lease and lost.)

Today Union Oil manages the land that is not covered with homes, but the open spaces are disappearing quickly. The street named after Bastanchury is a major Orange County thoroughfare. (There's also a smaller Basque Avenue and Domingo Road in Fullerton.)

After Domingo Sr. died in 1909, his widow Maria (Oxarart) Bastanchury held onto some land that was not part of the main ranch until 1942, when most of it was sold, according to Norma Bastanchury of Fullerton (who married a grandson of the pioneer couple). On this portion of land a house was built for Joe Bastanchury and his family in 1921—the only one of the family's many homes that is left today. Although it hasn't been designated a historic landmark, the subsequent owners have kept up the house's Spanish colonial-revival architecture. The white house with its red-tile roof is at 419 East Las Palmas Drive. To reach it from Bastanchury Road in Fullerton, head north on Harbor Boulevard. At Las Palmas, turn right and continue up the hill to the house. It's set back off the street and sits on 7/8ths of an acre.

HISTORICAL INTERVIEWS ON FILE

The center for Oral and Public History at Cal State, Fullerton has collected a series of interviews with many settlers in this region, including numerous Basques. Their insightful interviews are recorded on tape and available to the public. See their Web site, *www.coph.fullerton.edu*, to find their names.

Center for Oral and Public History, California State University, Fullerton, Pollak Library South, 363, 800 North State College Boulevard, Fullerton, CA (714) 278-3580; *www.coph.fullerton.edu*

San Juan Capistrano

Although this town is best known for the annual return of dozens of swallows to its mission, anyone looking for some Basque history will find it here.

In 1848, when California became part of the United States, San Juan Capistrano was a sleepy little pueblo of white-washed adobes with red-tile roofs, one of the privileged towns along El Camino Real where Father Junipero Serra and his friars decided to build a mission.

Basques played a small but important role in this town during the many years that it was primarily an agricultural center, from the 1880s through the 1950s. During the 1970s the Orange County Historical Society honored the Basques' contribution with a special festival for the county's Basque population at nearby Laguna Niguel Regional Park.

HOTEL

When Domingo Oyharzabal arrived in San Juan Capistrano, the town was already a cluster of adobe houses, with a few general stores, a stage line, and several saloons. Just down the street the mission had been abandoned and had fallen into ruins after the 1830s. Oyharzabal and a partner, Juan Salaberri, bought two existing adobe buildings on El Camino Real, or Main Street, in 1880. One was a hotel, probably the only one in town at the time. They renamed it the French Hotel, and Oyharzabal moved into the other building next door.

"They met on the boat coming over from Argentina," said Carmen Oyharzabal, Domingo's grand-niece, adding that the Oyharzabals and the Salaberris remained close all their lives. Oyharzabal was godfather to Juan's daughters, Felicitas and Juanita, and they cared for the bachelor before his death.

In 1840 Portuguese merchant Manuel Garcia had built the hotel structure that later became the French Hotel. It was the town's first hotel for travelers along El Camino Real and also served as the town's first American-era post office. In the original building the second story covered just half the building. When the Basque partners bought it,

The French Hotel around the turn of the century. Felicitas Salaberri is the woman on the balcony. The man second from left is hotel owner Domingo Oyharzabal. (Courtesy of Carmen Oyharzabal.)

they added the second half and built a balcony, whose lacelike, filigree design is noteworthy to this day. The hotel was the first and only two-story adobe house built in San Juan Capistrano. Known today as the Garcia Adobe, it is the only remaining Monterey-style adobe in all of Orange County (see the site description later in the chapter).

The French Hotel closed in 1903, but Salaberri's daughters continued to live in the rooms upstairs. The general store downstairs kept going for many years. A one-story addition was added in the 1930s, constructed to match the building's style. At one time, Oyharzabal also owned another prominent building in town, a two-story brick hotel across from the mission.

RANCHING AND FARMING

Domingo and his brother, Esteban, became significant ranchers in southern Orange County, and when they passed away, their nephews Esteban and Pedro Oyharzabal took over the sheep and cattle business and massive farming enterprise. Domingo died a bachelor, and

The Oyharzabal Family and Ranching

Domingo Oyharzabal and his descendants are the best-known Basque pioneer family in San Juan Capistrano. At age sixteen, Oyharzabal migrated first to Chile in 1863, like many of his compatriots of that era. Four years later, the native of Hasparren, Lapurdi, voyaged north to California. He was joined by his brothers, William and Esteban, and they worked in several different areas throughout California, saving their money, before eventually settling in San Juan Capistrano. "They thought Orange County was fertile for sheep," said their grand-niece Carmen Oyharzabal. William died a short time later, and the two remaining brothers began establishing a sheep business that eventually had up to twenty-five thousand head.

By 1910 the Oyharzabals had purchased 4,000 acres of land. They grazed their sheep and cattle and planted crops, for which they installed a state-of-the-art irrigation system that was the envy of all the farmers in the dry region. They had become significant landowners in the region. They planted crops—walnuts were a key crop here—and became big-time ranchers as well. The Oyharzabal brothers owned property as far out as Dana Point by the ocean. The land on which the Dana Point Ritz Carlton Hotel and Dana Point High School are now situated once belonged to them. Spaniard Juan Plaza managed the ranch for the Oyharzabal family for many years and was practically a member of the family. "He promised that if anything happened to my dad, he would come and take care of the ranch," remembers Carmen Oyharzabal. Plaza had been working for the Lacouagues when he joined the family. Plaza was buried in the same plot with Domingo Oyharzabal, Juan Salaberri, and Esteban Oyharzabal in Calvary Cemetery in Los Angeles. (For more on Calvary Cemetery, see the Los Angeles section.)

When Domingo died in 1913, his brother, Esteban Oyharzabal, took over the real estate and ranching businesses. Two nephews had come to work for them—brothers Esteban and Pedro Oyharzabal. They stopped first in South America, but in 1904 they decided to join their uncles who were already prominent Orange County ranchers. The nephews learned the cattle-ranching business, worked in the general store, and eventually took over the 4,000-acre ranch in 1920.

Esteban, although he married, had no children. Of the Oyharzabal nephews who took over the ranch, only Esteban had children.

"We used to have big barbecues," his daughter Carmen recalled of her childhood days. The barbecues, attended by several other local Basque ranching families, typically followed cattle roundups. "We would kill a pig and have a big dinner afterwards." Visiting the family of Basque rancher Pedro Changala and his twelve children was another major event during the early ranching days of the Oyharzabal family, Carmen Oyharzabal remembers. The Changalas lived in El Toro, now Mission Viejo, where Basque families often gathered together. The youths would ride horseback while the older family members played *mus.* Other Basque families in El Toro in those early days were the Etcheberrias, the Segouras, the Ustarizes, and the Daguerre sisters, all of them farming families.

Domingo Etcheberria started farming in San Juan Capistrano in the early 1900s, but he moved to the El Toro area so his children could attend school nearby. "My dad and Changala were neighbors in Spain," said Johnny Etcheberria, noting that they were from the same village of Luzaide (Valcarlos) in Nafarroa. "And here they were neighbors again." The Etcheberrias continued dry land farming and growing barley and black-eyed peas. "We always had milk cows too," said Etcheberria, a second-generation farmer. "Those were our chores. . . . We had to chase the cows down, bring them in and milk them."

"There weren't that many Basques in the area, but we all knew each other," said Etcheberria. Today all the ranches in San Juan Capistrano are gone, but some Basques have established ranches elsewhere. Some of the Changala siblings are farming in Porterville, California; Yakima, Washington; and even in Mexico.

Another Basque settler whose family is still in San Juan Capistrano was Pierre Lacouague, who arrived in 1910. Lacouague and his wife, Bonifacia Mojica, got their start locally working for Spanish Basque rancher Cornelio Etchenique. The rancher brought Bonifacia to the United States from the Basque Country after her sister Juanita left his employ to marry into another well-known Orange County Basque family, the Bastanchurys. "My father was one of the first citrus growers," said Julia (Lacouague) Pon of Saratoga.

The Oyharzabals followed Pierre Lacouague's example and planted orange trees as well, even though the primary local product was walnuts.

The Oyharzabal Family Home and the Old French Hotel

The fate of the Oyharzabal family's historic house remains to be written. Known as Domingo Yorba Adobe, it has undergone many additions since it was first built as a two-room structure in the 1830s by José Antonio Yorba II. The Esteban Oyharzabals were very community oriented, and they housed the town's first library in one room of their prominent home from 1936 to 1938. The two-story building, next to the old French Hotel, became a historic landmark in 1978. The two buildings are notable for having been kept in the Oyharzabal family since 1880. Esteban's widow, Eugenie, lived there until her death at age 106, and his daughter, Carmen, continues to live in the house at 31861 Camino Capistrano. She is the only descendant of the Oyharzabal family who bears the family name in the United States.

Since the ranch property was sold off in 1960, the former French Hotel building, now known as the Garcia Adobe, and the family home next door are all that remain of the once vast holdings of the Oyharzabals. Yet many of the barns and sheds built by the Oyharzabals in the 1800s in the yard behind the two buildings are still in use today. Carmen has the tough job of keeping up the historic buildings. Because of their age and simple construction, even the smallest maintenance job can turn into a major production. A marker outside the former hotel notes the building's status as a historical landmark, made official in 1978. The second floor has been converted to apartments, which are rented out, and the downstairs currently houses a western antique store.

Ghost stories also come with the territory. Martin Kaczmarek, who ran a store downstairs in the old French Hotel building, said that he felt spooked when working in the store alone after hours. "Sometimes I arrange things a certain way, and when I come back, they're arranged differently," he said. Then he admits, with a laugh, that it happened only once—"and it might have been my imagination." Meanwhile, Kaczmarek brings up a story that has been floating around this town for decades. "There supposedly was a buried treasure. We used to dig around here—needless to say, I never found it."

"I wouldn't be surprised if there were treasure buried around here," said Carmen. When an early German storekeeper was robbed and killed by the greatly feared bandit Juan Flores and his gang in 1857, the Yorbas, then owners of the hotel and general store, were believed to have hidden money away, according to Carmen.

Garcia Adobe, 31871 Camino Capistrano, San Juan Capistrano, CA 92675

The Capistrano Mission

The mission, located at the intersection of Camino Capistrano and Ortega Highway and founded by Basque Father Fermín Lasuen, is very much worth visiting. It is not only the state's oldest surviving mission, it is also home to the oldest structure still in use in California—the small Serra Chapel, built in 1777 and restored in the 1920s. It is also significant because it is the last remaining chapel in which founder Father Junipero Serra officiated. The mission has undergone several phases of reconstruction. The most recent was a 17-year-$9.6 million project to restore the Great Stone Church and to preserve the mission into the twenty-first century.

The mission, built in 1777 around a community of local Juaneño Indians, represented the first Spanish settlement in Orange County. Pirate raids in 1818 led to legends of buried treasure hidden for safekeeping by the friars, which Father John O'Sullivan propagated in the book *Capistrano Nights.* A local preservation group began restoring the run-down church in 1895, a job that was continued by O'Sullivan after his arrival in 1910 until his death in 1933.

The Great Stone Church, built in 1806 and partially ruined in a large 1812 earthquake, was the major focus of the latest restoration finished in 2004. Past attempts to rebuild it were finally abandoned, according to mission archivist Charles A. Bodnar, but the remaining walls have been stabilized so visitors can see the ruins up close. Already an outstanding cultural and historical landmark because of its age, the mission has become even more important now that the restoration is done.

If you stop by the mission's gift shop, you are likely to spot the Lacouague name. Renee Lacouague Bondi, granddaughter of Pierre Lacouague, has Christian music albums on sale, which are enjoying great success. The album contains her recordings of some of the songs that gave her strength after a minor fall at home in 1988 left the young Basque-American woman a quadriplegic at the age of twenty-nine. Bondi credits the Basque love for singing as being the source of her own interest. Inadvertently, she has become a popular motivational speaker, talking to groups about her recovery. Bondi and much of the Lacouague family remains in San Juan Capistrano, although they are no longer farming and have sold off most of the land that Pierre Lacouague had amassed.

Pelota at the Mission? One Basque expert on the history of Basque handball in the West, Frederic Fuldain, of Belmont, California, suggests an interesting theory about a wall with a rounded top at the mission. It resembles the ones built against churches in the Basque Country expressly for the playing of pelota. In a 1876 photo of the mission published in *California Missions,* the wall was not yet built. It is clearly visible, though, in a photo dated 1897, well after the time when Oyharzabal, and probably other Basques, had settled in San Juan Capistrano. "Nobody was building any walls at that time," said Fuldain. "The mission was going downhill. Why should they build a wall that shape?" he wondered. He concluded that the wall must have been built for handball.

No one alive today remembers anyone playing handball at the mission, according to archivist Bodnar. O'Sullivan, who provided some of the earliest recorded history of the mission, did not arrive until 1910. He made no mention of handball-playing against the

Could this wall at Mission San Juan Capistrano, resembling those built against the back wall of village churches in the Basque Country, have been built by Basques for handball?

wall, a practice that may have been forgotten by the time he came onboard. So the possibility exists that the wall was built for handball playing and abandoned once restoration of the mission started in 1895. Visit the mission and come to your own conclusions about this mystery.

Charles Saunders recorded much of the history of the mission, as told to him by Father O'Sullivan. In *Capistrano Nights,* O'Sullivan recounts hearing the sound of the ball bouncing as men played in "Handball Alley," down the street from the mission. This was probably at the handball court located behind the Oyharzabal buildings on the western side of El Camino Real, just a short way from the mission. The court, built specifically for handball, has long since been torn down, according to Carmen Oyharzabal, who remembers the days when Basques from all over Los Angeles came to play there. It's possible that the "Handball Alley" court was built to replace the wall that was once used at the church.

Mission San Juan Capistrano, 31882 Camino Capistrano (at Ortega Highway), San Juan Capistrano, CA 92675 (949) 234-1300; *www.missionsjc.com*

Other Sights to See

As you stroll south on Camino Capistrano, away from the mission, you'll spot the Franciscan Plaza Courtyard. Walk down the steps, and in a display on the right you will see photos of the town in the first half of the century, including a picture of some Basque men playing in "Handball Alley." Oyharzabal believes the men in the photo are Juan Plaza, Joe Malda, and Barney Ibargaray. Then, farther south, just beyond the Oyharzabal buildings, is El Adobe restaurant, built by José Antonio Yorba II in 1778. Stop in here to see a historic large black-and-white photograph showing the Oyharzabal and El Adobe buildings when El Camino Real was still a dirt road. It's in the foyer on the right.

The swallows leave on October 23 and return without fail every March 19, at which time annual celebrations are organized. (Their numbers have been decreasing yearly.) But if you can't visit this town on one of those days, you haven't missed out. Wednesdays from 3 to 6 P.M. are a good time to visit because of the nearby downtown farmers' market, a lively scene with entertainment, food, and fun. To reach the mission, take the Ortega Highway from Interstate 5 right into the center of town. The Amtrak train from Los Angeles to San Diego also stops in San Juan Capistrano, and the depot is just a short walk from the mission and the Oyharzabal family buildings.

CEMETERY

To find the graves of the early Basque pioneers, visit the **Mission Cemetery.** To reach it, travel east on Ortega Highway and cross the Interstate 5 freeway to the first street, Los Cerritos Road. Turn left here, and almost immediately on the right you will spot a road and a sign for the cemetery. Take that road up the hill to the cemetery.

La Puente

BOARDINGHOUSES

During the first half of this century, Basques settled in the La Puente area because there was plenty of open land and water for farming. "Almost all the Basques in Puente were from the little area of Banca, Urepel, and Aldudes," said Jean P. Nogues, who grew up in the area. Already, in the 1930s, there were apparently four Basque boardinghouses in La Puente, all in the vicinity of Second and Main Streets. In those days "Puente" was merely a small downtown surrounded by open space. One of the hotels was the Puente Hotel in the Bidart building built by Gratian Bidart, who later served as a La Puente constable. John and Alice Oxarart ran the Puente for many years, as well as the French Hotel and Restaurant in a building that still stands at First Street and Old Valley Boulevard.

Prohibition, between 1920 and 1933, did not keep the Basques from drinking their liquor. The Oxarart's son John said that they had moonshine-making stills in the San Jose Hills east of La Puente. They would bring it to the Puente Hotel, and from there large quantities were also secretly taken by Basques to other Los Angeles destinations, under the knowing eye of some local public officials. One such place was the Biminy Hotel, owned for many years by Frank Bidegain, according to Oxarart. It was one of three or four exclusive hotels on a knoll overlooking the Biminy Baths. "That was how I heard it," said Oxarart, adding that Prohibition may have worked in the East Coast, but not in rural California. "When you went downtown from Puente, you passed a lot of open country," he said. "It wasn't a big deal. There were speakeasies everywhere."

An anchor at the corner of Second and Main was the French-American Bakery, which opened in 1921 and employed many Basque workers through the years. It was known for its round three-pound, "king-size" loaf. "The herders would go there at two, three, four o'clock in the morning, when the loaves were just coming out of the oven, and take one to camp with them," said Oxarart, who worked there for over twenty years.

Another boardinghouse in the old downtown was the Valley Hotel, a beautiful Victorian building with a cupola, purchased by Jean Nogues in 1930. Nogues, with the help of other local Basques, built a small handball court behind the bakery in 1927, according to his son Jean P. Nogues. In those early days, the family that lived in a big house that stood next door to the court, where Le Chalet Basque restaurant is now (see Restaurant section), also rented out rooms. "Mart Martinez was born there when it was a room and board," said the Chalet's current owner Danielle Arretche Osowiecki, referring to a longtime local Basque. John Oxarart remembers a later era when the Garro family lived there, and there was a lot of carousing. "The Garros were the *kantxa*'s [handball court] keepers," he said. They sold liquor to all the Basques who were constantly dropping by, playing handball, and drinking around the kitchen table and in the living room.

The Basque community that revolved around the hotels was extremely close-knit, because they had come from such a small region and because they socialized together so much. Others even envied the clannishness. "They always had their picnics," noted Gloria Garacochea of Santa Monica, an Italian-American who grew up in La Puente and married a Basque. The family of her husband, Edmund Garacochea, often drove from Venice to La Puente for parties and picnics. The local Italians had no such annual events, she said. "I always ran with the Basque kids."

PELOTA AND A BASQUE CLUB

"As time went on, [the Basques] decided they wanted to have a real *kantxa*," said Jean Nogues's grandson, Joe. "So they got the idea to form a club." The founders had an obvious reason for creating the **La Puente Handball Club.** The group first formed in 1939, but with the war the project was put on hold. The members organized officially in 1947 and bought a condemned school, which they later sold for a profit. That money helped them buy a 10-acre property on Amar Road, part of the French Foure family ranch, and now part of the City of Industry.

The club started with about 120 members. The founders had not set out to create a Basque club per se, but because the club meant to build a fronton, it was natural that most of the members would be Basque handball players, though a few local Italian men joined in too.

Club members set about building the court in 1950. They worked slowly, putting in time on weekends. They dug deep holes for the eight or ten pillars that supported the *kantxa*'s 40-foot ceiling. "They built the building thinking they were going to play a little jai alai," said Oxarart. But the state prevented them from doing so because it was considered to be a gambling sport. Nevertheless, the court was still used for handball. In its day, it was one of the finest, with two side walls that could be raised or lowered with pulleys. Outside there were ample grounds planted with grass and trees. Barbecue pits were installed and a covered outdoor area with picnic tables was set up.

Club Activities. The club sponsored many of the typical activities: dinner dances, handball competitions with professional handball players from the Basque Country, and an annual picnic in June. The Southern California Eskualdun Club picnic was held there for many years as well. Although most of the initial members were Basques, the club quickly attracted many of the area's Italians, Spanish, and French, mostly from the longtime ranching families in the area. Basques living around Chino and El Toro came to La Puente for the monthly chicken dinners and the picnics. Johnny Etcheberria was one of those who would come from El Toro, along with his friend Joe Changala. Etcheberria ended up meeting his wife, Julie, at one of those dinner dances.

"Back then, that was one of the few social things available in what was primarily an agricultural area," said Joe Nogues, a longtime member of the board. Nogues's grandfather, Jean, one of the original founders of the club, died suddenly in 1947 before the facility was built. Joe Nogues can be counted as a rare third-generation Basque club member.

In 1960 the club sold the front portion of its property to a commercial developer to help pay the debt on the building and to make improvements. A market and a couple of stores were put up in front of the building on Amar Road. Use of the handball court had already decreased significantly. "The younger generation wasn't picking up on it," said Oxarart. So the members decided to tear down the bleachers and court walls. They put in a kitchen with a false ceiling, in effect closing down the *kantxa,* although the 40-foot-high walls are still there. To keep open the possibility of playing handball, they poured a cement slab floor outdoors, to allow play against the building's front wall. The building had been well planned, having been built for two-sided play. (The old court is directly opposite, in the interior.)

The improvements included a stage and a bar. "There was a great need for a place like that," said Oxarart, noting that local dances for years had been held in a couple of small clubhouses. During the 1960s the dinners attracted four hundred to five hundred people. "That was in its heyday," said Oxarart. "It was a hell of a place to go on Saturday night." The entire Puente Valley had been filling in with houses and people during the 1950s and 1960s, and the chicken dinners, as well as the bar, remained popular. Oxarart remembered that it would take club members into the early hours to get all the partygoers out the door. The club eventually decided that the annual June picnic was too much work, so it was canceled. In 1980 the Southern California Eskualdun Club moved its picnic to Chino. Handball playing continued to decline. Part of the problem, said Oxarart, was the lack of a staff person to open the gates to make the court available to players on a regular basis.

Today the monthly dinners at the handball club have been reduced to four times a year and attract an average of one hundred and fifty people. Membership in the club has dwindled as well. Despite the decline, the dinners are still lively. Local political leaders belong and frequently attend. Members cook the dinners themselves, varying the tradition of chicken with steak or lamb. The club sponsors the dinners in March, May, October, and November on the third Saturday of the month and a couple of members-only barbecues. The rest of the year, the hall is busy every weekend, and it's rented out for parties and picnics. "It's one of the few places where you can bring your own food and beverages," said Joe Nogues. In the past year, Argentineans, Chileans, and Cubans have held picnics there. And nine out of ten of the local Basque weddings or funerals are held there.

In 1997 the club celebrated its fiftieth anniversary. The facilities were recently renovated, outdoor bathrooms were added, and the outside was landscaped. The board members who meet regularly at the Chalet Basque restaurant are always talking about how to increase interest in the club's dinners.

Some say attendance at the monthly dinners has been on the rise, especially among Basques. "It's a real family affair," Oxarart commented noting that the younger Basques have married and now bring their children. But interest in handball has not been revived, and what was once the scene of lively pelota competitions has rarely seen a game in recent years. The members who used to play are too old to play now.

La Puente Handball Club, 15858 East Amar Road (opposite Greycliff Avenue) (626) 333-3709. Mailing address: P.O. Box 3024, City of Industry, CA 91744

RESTAURANTS

Jeanne and Peter Etchebarren bought the property next to the French-American Bakery in 1947 and tore down the old house where the Garros had lived. In its place they built a restaurant and called it the French and Basque. They improved the pelota court next to it, putting up side walls and fencing it in. Tournaments with players from other towns were held there frequently. Times were good, and the restaurant business thrived. In 1960 the bakery purchased the restaurant property, for expansion plans that eventually fell through, and the handball court walls were torn down.

In 1962 Danielle Arretche Osowiecki and her brother Jean Pierre "Pampi" Arretche bought the restaurant business, turned it into an elegant French Basque dinner house, and named it **Le Chalet Basque.** A colorful mural of a sheepherder tending his flock in the Basque Country, painted by a starving artist on one wall of the main dining room, portrays the simple country roots of the Arretche-Zubiri family, natives of Esnazu, Nafarroa Beherea. The restaurant has stayed in the hands the same family for over thirty years. Pampi Arretche, who started working there in 1959 under the Etchebarrens, was the bartender at the restaurant through all the changes, finally leaving his post after thirty-seven years.

Today the old downtown has lost its vitality. Many of the businesses are closed, and many locals do all their shopping at the big malls. Main Street isn't the main street any longer. Le Chalet Basque relies on its loyal, longtime clientele to stay open. It attracts big crowds every month for delicious barbecue lamb and chicken dinners. The barbecue—a bargain at $12 a plate—has been held without fail the first Saturday of every month for the last forty or so years. A favorite drink among the crowd is the Picon Punch. Known as the Basque drink of choice, Picon Punch is believed to have been developed in the American West. The picon liqueur comes from France, but it is typically served there in a different combination. In this country the picon liqueur is combined with soda and grenadine, to sweeten the bitter picon. You can get this drink in any Basque drinking establishment, but be careful. Its name is no joke. Typically topped with brandy, it definitely packs a punch.

Le Chalet Basque, 119 North Second Street (near Main Street) La Puente, CA 91744 (626) 330-9033

La Puente Today

Pastoral La Puente, with its orange and walnut groves, has long since disappeared. By the 1970s most of its former dairies, farms, and grazing land had been paved over and filled in with industrial buildings, houses, and shopping malls. Today the handball club and Le Chalet Basque restaurant are the only remnants of the once lively Basque community. The Puente Hotel was destroyed in an accidental explosion in the late 1940s. The Nogues family tore down the Valley Hotel, across from the Chalet, in 1948 and replaced it with the small shopping center that is still there today.

The Esquirre family sold the French-American Bakery in the 1980s, and today the building remains empty. Between the bakery and Le Chalet Basque, you can see the old home where the Esquirre family lived for years. What was left of the old handball court wall at the bakery was covered up years ago with storage buildings. The two-story brick building where the old French Hotel was located is still there today (123 First Street), and for several years it served as a used clothing store.

Chino

Chino is home to the newest and largest of Southern California's Basque communities. Basques first began settling here only about eighty years ago, much later than the first Basque community started growing in downtown Los Angeles. For many of the early years of this Basque community, social events were held at the Chilibolost Ranch in nearby Carbon Canyon. Pete and Joaquina Chilibolost had been among the first Basques to arrive in the Chino Valley. They had a huge barn where local Basques held dances and other reunions.

DAIRIES

If there ever was a cow town, Chino is it. Rows of elegant new homes abut fenced-in cattle pens, and the stench of cow manure pervades the air. In twenty-odd years, Chino has doubled its population to sixty thousand, changing from a rural, agricultural area to a more suburban area. Yet the dairy industry still plays an important role here. The Basque population throughout the Chino Valley is, and has been, heavily involved in the dairy industry. Fifteen to twenty Basque families have been owners of dairies or dairy-related businesses here. The Etcheverria brothers, Albert Goyenetche, and Jean Gastelluberry (with his "Basque-American Dairy") are among those who have figured prominently in Chino dairies.

Most of the Basque dairymen came to the Chino-Ontario area after World War II, when a major housing boom began in Los Angeles and pushed that city's former dairy farms farther and farther out to the rural fringes of the urban sprawl. Most of the dairies were owned by Basques, Portuguese, and Dutch. The farms employed Basques because they were among the few workers willing to put up with the difficult hours. Cows had to be milked twice a day, so workers had a split shift, six days a week, working both in the early morning and in the afternoon.

But even this far from the center of Los Angeles, land-intensive dairy farming has been affected by the region's continuous urbanization. Today land is much more expensive, and the cost in recent years has been a defining factor in Basque dairymen moving out of the area. During the 1970s several owners moved their operations to Oregon and Idaho, where land is cheaper. As more and more houses are built, land prices go up, and the exodus starts again. In 1991 the Petrissans Dairy, based just east of Chino in Mira Loma, sold its land for a small fortune and moved its operation to Bakersfield, where land prices are much lower. Others followed that example, as the pressure builds to convert agricultural land for residential purposes.

"Chino is overbuilt—there's too many people," said J. B. Aguerre, noting that as a consequence, more and more regulations are being applied to dairy businesses. "They're going to push the industries out. If all the dairies leave, then I gotta leave too," said the longtime Chino resident who raises calves for dairymen.

BASQUE CLUBS

Southern California Basque Club. The Southern California Eskualdun Club was started in 1946 by a Basque priest, Father Charles Espelette, from Aldudes, France, who served at the old Mt. Carmel Church in Montebello. (At least one other Basque priest, Father Leo Gariador, served at this church around 1910.) In addition to his mission duties, Espelette also ministered to the large Southern California Basque community, which was widely scattered throughout the region on various ranches. With the club, he hoped to bring the people together. Basques from Chino became the core of the group, and they began holding their meetings at the Chilibolost Ranch. *Mus* tournaments were sponsored by the club at Tito Chanchorena's ranch. The club they formed was responsible for starting the first folk dance group in the area.

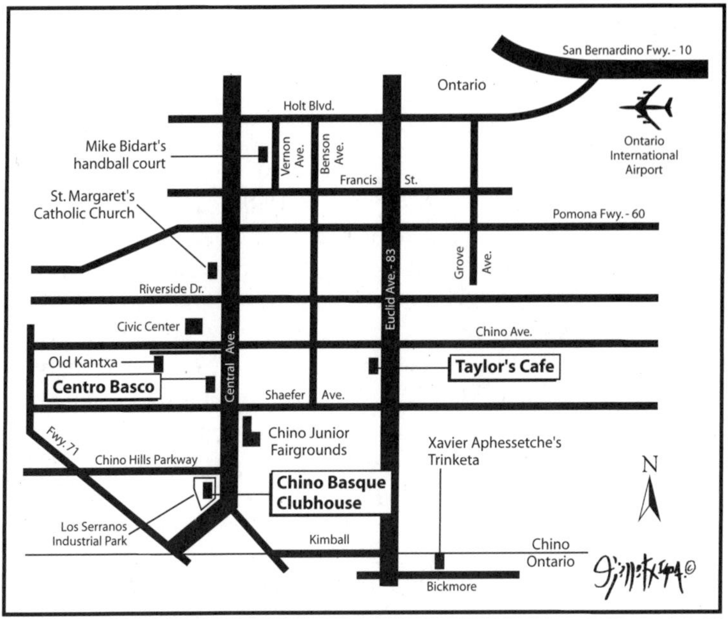

Chino.

Today the **Southern California Basque Club** (recently renamed) has a membership limited to approximately forty members. Dues are not collected, but every member is required to help in the planning and hosting of the annual picnic. "We found out we don't need more than thirty-five to forty people to run the picnic," said longtime member Dominic Etcheberria, explaining why the membership is limited to such a small number. Only when members quit or die are new ones invited to join. "All we want are workers," said Etcheberria. In exchange for their work, members and their families are provided free admission, meals, and drinks during the picnic. A second club, the **Chino Basque Club,** with no membership limitation, was organized here in 1967. In September 1996 the Southern California Basque Club celebrated its fiftieth anniversary. The two-day celebration was coordinated with NABO's fall meeting and included handball games among the old-timers, a barbecue lunch, a steak and chicken dinner, dance performances, and a historical review of the club. Among the highlights of the weekend festivities was the performance by some of the club's earliest dancers, from the 1950s and 1960s.

Southern California Basque Club, 1403 S. Dahlia Avenue, Ontario, CA 91762 (909) 986-6143 (Laurent Arretche)

Chino Basque Club. In its first years the **Chino Basque Club** members sponsored big dances in the dairy barn of Albert Goyenetche. Since then the members have managed to build a center large enough to accommodate the club's monthly dinner dances and dance practices.

The clubhouse, located in an industrial park off Central Avenue, was opened in 1986. Since then members completed major improvements to the building, adding a kitchen, finishing the interior's bare cement walls and floors, adding an elegant bar, wooden paneling, and paintings. The club holds a lunch or dinner every third Sunday of the month to help raise funds to maintain the building. The meal featuring traditional blood sausage is a particular favorite. The events attract between 100 and 250 people. In the afternoon, there's *mus* playing. And there's always dancing, which brings out the younger Basques. Second- and third-generation Basques actively participate in club activities. College professor and occasional chef Steve Gamboa started a *txoko* in 2004. Many younger members help cook the once-a-month feasts.

The Chino Basque Club has close to one hundred members, who with their families might number about five hundred. At least three hundred people have shown up in recent years for the annual Mass that the Basque priest offers the Sunday after Easter at St. Margaret's Church (Central Avenue at Mt. Vernon Avenue).

Chino Basque Club, 15181 Sierra Bonita Lane, (P.O. Box 1080), Chino, CA 91710. Information: (909) 597-4526 (*John Ysursa*)

FESTIVALS

Initially, the Southern California Basque Club picnics were held at Shell Park in Brea. When the La Puente Handball Club built its hall and picnic grounds in the early 1950s, the club moved its picnics there. (As a result the Basque club was often referred to as the La

Puente club.) Handball competitions were scheduled for the same weekend as the picnics, and busloads of enthusiastic players from Bakersfield made the trip south every year. Wood-chopping and weight-carrying competitions were also organized for a few years, especially when some serious wood choppers from Hegoalde could be counted on to attend. In the early 1980s the club decided to move its picnics to Chino, since most of its members lived there. The construction of the large Brinderson Hall at the county fairgrounds (Central and Edison Avenues) was the catalyst for the move, according to member Dominic Etcheberria.

There's no handball court at Brinderson Hall, but the club tries to schedule handball games before and after the picnic at courts nearby. The handball players no longer come from Bakersfield, because they prefer to attend the bigger Elko (Nevada) festival held on the same Fourth of July weekend. "We've talked about how we can make it more successful," said Etcheberria about the picnic, admitting that attendance at the Chino Basque Club's picnic on Labor Day weekend in September is much higher.

The format of the two picnics is pretty much the same, with performances by the Chino dance group at both. "You'd have a very difficult time telling the difference between the Chino picnic and our picnic," said Etcheberria. He claims that there is no competition between the two clubs. "What is there to compete about?"—besides trying to outdo each other in the food they serve at their picnics, he joked. Unlike all the other festivals, which offer just one big barbecue meal, both of the clubs here offer two. "We give a steak at noon and lamb at night," said longtime Chino club member Maite Petrissans.

A good indicator of the area's Basque population is the Chino Basque Club's annual picnic, which attracts up to two thousand people. The big festival is held on Sunday of Labor Day weekend at the county fairgrounds. Some say that the peak years are past. But others, like club president J. B. Aguerre, say that attendance is still as high as it's ever been. "In the 1970s we didn't have as many people as we have now," he said.

The picnic starts with a Mass, like every other Basque festival. Temperatures typically hit the nineties by midmorning. A big barbecued steak lunch is served in the cool main hall, where T-shirts, berets, *gateau Basque* (Basque cake), and other Basque souvenirs are on sale. A slow, hot afternoon, which many spend socializing around the bar or playing *mus,* is enlivened at about 3 P.M. when Chino's Gauden Bat Dancers show off their latest costumes and elegant dances. Picnic goers have an array of choices for dinner. They can have a full meal with barbecued lamb, but many choose to have a simple chorizo sandwich or to stop by the Centro Basco or the Pyrenees just down the street. The evening dance is the highlight of the day for the young people, replete with fandangos, line dances, and some rock and roll too.

To help cure residual hangovers and to send out-of-town visitors on their way with a full stomach, the Centro Basco restaurant offers a traditional Basque breakfast on Labor Day Monday. Don't expect to see a menu here. Make sure you're hungry, because you'll be served homemade sausage, ham, bacon, eggs, and French fries.

DANCE

The Chino dance group has evolved significantly through the years, formally incorporating as the nonprofit group **Gauden Bat** (We Are One) in 1992. Jean Louis Cihigoyenetche was one of the best early teachers of this group. John Ysursa was one of the Boise Oinkari dancers' most dedicated dancers, and he brought this energy with him when he joined Chino's group in 1986. Ysursa and his wife, Jenny, have been responsible for the continual expansion of the group's repertoire, regularly introducing new dances and new costumes from the Basque Country. "I have to give them credit," said Etcheberria, a former dancer in the group for many years. "They're doing some real tough dances." Many of the dancers are in their twenties and thirties and have been dancing for many years, so it is not surprising that this is one of the more talented dance groups.

The dancers host a popular raffle dinner annually in March to raise money for their many trips. In 2004, they traveled to Louisiana to perform for a new club.

Gauden Bat Dancers (Jenny and John Ysursa), P.O. Box 1329, Chino, CA 91708 (909) 597-4526; *www.gaudenbat.com/*

MUS

Both clubs sponsor an annual *mus* tournament. The Chino Basque Club holds theirs at the clubhouse; the Southern California Basque Club's is usually held at Tito Chanchorena's ranch.

MUSIC

Chino is one of only three Basque communities with a *klika* (bugle corps). Chino's *klika* is almost as old as San Francisco's. Started in 1962 by Jean Indart, the bugle corps was buoyed up by the Aphessetche brothers, who had played in their hometown *klika* in Donibane-Garazi, said Indart. The initial group of nine or ten members has grown to twenty-five. Indart, who has since moved to Madera, said he's happy to see teens filling the ranks.

Chino is also one of the few communities that has a choir—an unusual one at that, because, unlike San Francisco's and Boise's, the **Eskual Giroa** (Basque Ambiance) singers, who are all women, incorporate dancing into their songs. However, they perform only occasionally. More visible is Noka (*www.gaudenbat.com/noka/*), an a capella group of three local women—Andrea Bidart, Begoña Echeverria, and Cathy Petrissans—which has recorded two CDs.

RESTAURANTS

When the **Centro Basco** was built by Jean B. and Graciana Robidart in 1940, it replaced the Chilibolost ranch as the main gathering place for Basques in Chino. For many years Robidart had worked as a traveling insurance salesman. "My mother wanted to put down roots," explained his daughter Juliet Campos, of Carruthers, California. So the couple built the hotel. They sold it after seven years, and it was eventually bought by Ben and Melanie Sallaberry, who added the fronton during the early 1950s. (Melanie still owns the building.) On special occasions, the Sallaberrys would serve food at tables outside underneath the shade of a grape arbor and hold dances on the handball court. The restaurant and kitchen were expanded in 1970, the same year the Sallaberrys leased the business to the Berterretches, who still run it today.

Oxtail Stew, Monique Berterretche, Centro Basco

2 oxtails
4 carrots
1 onion
1 stalk celery
1 cup red wine
2 tablespoons beef base
Salt, pepper
2 tablespoons flour

Cut the oxtails into small pieces. (When you buy them at the store, they are usually already cut from the joints.) Fry them until brown. Dice the carrots, onion, and celery. Put in a pot with the oxtails and red wine, beef base, and salt and pepper. Add enough water to cover all the ingredients, plus a little more. Boil, covered, at low heat for three hours. Then mix the flour with one cup of water, and then add to the stew and stir until thick. Taste for salt and pepper and add if necessary.

The Centro Basco is Southern California's biggest Basque restaurant, and everything is still done the old-fashioned way. People still eat family-style, and handball is still played on the court out back. Centro Basco is one of the few Basque hotels left with a handball court still in active use. "There used to be somebody playing almost every evening," said the late owner Pierre Berterretche, remembering the days when he and his wife, Monique, first took over the business in 1970. Back then they had more than twenty boarders. "They used to come from the sheepherder camps, or they used to work milking the cows," he said.

For Jeronima Echeverria, provost of California State University, Fresno, her family's visits to the restaurant formed her fondest memories. She wrote in her dissertation, "California-ko Ostatuak: The History of California's Basque Hotels:"

> My childhood memories include regular Sunday visits to the Chino Centro Basco hotel with my family. I vividly remember my father and his compatriots playing handball at the *cancha* [court] while my mother sat in the bleachers and discussed the week's events with her friends. In the afternoon, we gathered for

supper at long picnic tables placed under dense grape arbors. After supper, the men sang folk songs in Basque, smoked thick cigars, and drank cognac while the rest of us visited or played in the area. I cannot remember anyone ever pointing out that we went to the hotels to see our Basque friends, to experience our heritage, or to strengthen our ties to one another. Despite the fact that the Chino hotel provided the setting for activities vital to my family, we never discussed its importance to us.

These days the outdoor court behind the restaurant gets the most use on Sundays, often from local Mexicans. And while the younger athletic types hit the ball in the hot sun, the old-timers play *mus* inside. Monique still does the cooking, and her three children, Joseph, Bernadette, and Jeanne, work there when they can.

Except for a very small percentage, the restaurants that advertise themselves as Basque continue to serve their hearty fare in what they term "family-style"—that is, in large portions to be shared by a group. These abundant servings—which diners can rarely finish—are what make Basque food so memorable.

While most restaurant owners have bucked the old tradition of long tables and created a more American individualized dining room, the Berterretches do both. They maintain the boardinghouse tradition, serving family-style lunch and dinners almost every day. They also have a large dining room where you can get a meal à la carte. If you want to soak in that old boardinghouse atmosphere, stop by on a Sunday for lunch, served only at noon. Lots of old-timers gather at this time, and everybody sits together at long tables the way the boarders always did. The restaurant sponsors a big New Year's Eve party every year that brings the local Basque community together.

During the 1950s, 1960s, and 1970s, there was another small concentration of Basque businesses in Chino. For nearly twenty years the late Martin Arrachea ran a bar called the Pyrenees at D Street and Central Avenue. "It was always full," said Arrachea's wife, Germaine. It was Basque-owned even before Arrachea bought it in 1957. Michel Irigoyen had been one of its original owners, and he built a restaurant called La Madelene nearby in 1969. And Juliet Campos remembers a Basque-owned grocery store in the vicinity as well. La Madelene suffered a fire in the early 1970s, according to one-time owner Joe

Almirantearena, and it was closed for a while. The city of Chino decided to locate its civic center there, so it bought the property from Almirantearena, as well as the Pyrenees property, and tore all the buildings down. Pyrenees owner Martin Arrachea decided to rebuild the Pyrenees as a restaurant next door to the Centro Basco in 1975.

Albert Gareste was chef at the Pyrenees Restaurant, which later became the Café du Midi. Although Arrachea passed away in 1992, his wife, Germaine, continued the family business, with the help of her children. It eventually closed in the 1990s.

There is another Basque eatery in the neighborhood, but there is nothing about the outside of this countryside truck stop to indicate the ethnic menu that you will find when you go through the door of **Taylor's Café.** This truckers' restaurant has a 70-foot public scale in the back. Its non-Basque name has been preserved since the restaurant opened in 1955. Dominique Reca has owned the business since 1989, but it was under Basque ownership for a long time before that. Local sheep and dairy workers like to come in for breakfast, because they know they'll get hearty Basque servings. As in many other Basque restaurants, the sausage, bacon, and *jambon* (or Basque ham) are made by Reca himself.

Luis Burusco Juanko and his wife Zuni opened a Basque restaurant in Chino, the Toki Ona, but it didn't last long.

Twenty minutes from Chino, the Sabarots family has been running a restaurant in Glendora for many years, with great success. The Basque logo at the entrance of the **Glendora Continental Restaurant** gives away the owners' birthplace, and there are many Basque items on the menu. Although the food is not exclusively Basque, groups can order banquets of Basque food, and the Sabarots will provide Basque cuisine for any event. They've catered many Basque weddings over the years.

Jean's Restaurant in Colton must be mentioned because even though the food is primarily French, the owner is from the Basque Country, and local Basques often come here to eat. The former husband-and-wife team of Gigi Harosteguy and Jean Irola opened the Colton restaurant in 1966. They opened a second restaurant, Gigi and Jean's, in nearby Redlands in 1976. When the couple split in 1988, each kept one restaurant. But Gigi and Jean's closed in 2003 after

Harosteguy passed away. Irola's restaurant dates back to 1957, when they opened the first Gigi and Jean's on Sixth Street and Western Avenue in Los Angeles. "I was only twenty-one when I started my business," said Irola. Although his restaurant does not have a Basque menu on a daily basis, they have a few Basque specialties and will serve family-style dinners to large groups by reservation.

Centro Basco, 13432 Central Avenue (near Shaefer), Chino, CA 91710 (909) 628-9014 or 628-1331
Glendora Continental Restaurant, 316 West Alosta Avenue, Glendora, CA 91740 (626) 914-1834; *www.glendoracontinental.net*
Jean's Restaurant, 592 North La Cadena Drive, Colton, CA 92324 (909) 825-0905
Taylor's Cafe, 7049 Chino Avenue (at Euclid Avenue), Ontario, CA 91761 (909) 628-3506

PELOTA

A handball court was built in Chino as early as 1927 or 1928 by Loran Arretche, according to Sonia Eagle, who wrote about Chino's early history. Although it only survived for a year before it was knocked down by a windstorm, the date of its construction provides a good idea of when Basques started arriving in Chino. After the court walls were blown away, Arretche gave the blocks to a Mexican, who constructed another handball court. This may have been the court purchased by Joaquín and Eduvigis Yzurdiaga in 1934, because it was in Chino's Mexican neighborhood, according to the Yzurdiaga's son Joe, although there was also another court in the vicinity.

For years the Yzurdiagas served lunch and dinner to all the handball players who gathered to play on Sundays. During the rest of the week local Mexicans often played at the court. The tradition of sharing a court among Basques and Mexicans continues to this day at the Centro Basco (see Restaurants section), where, oftentimes, the two groups will play against each other. Yzurdiaga said that his family's place was simply referred to as "la cancha," and even though his parents sold it in 1948, local Basques still refer to him as "*Kantxeraenea.*" Although it has deteriorated, this *kantxa,* next to a private home at 301 G Street, is still standing.

The Chino Basque Club is considering building a small court to keep up handball playing among youngsters. Chino has three other courts. For many years, local players had to make due with the court at the Centro Basco. But in 1981 two local Basques built courts on their property, and these are now used regularly by local players.

Xavier Aphessetche, a well-off Basque dairyman, built a magnificent *trinket* court (*trinket* is a form of pelota played against four walls instead of two) near his home on Bickmore Avenue, clearly visible from Euclid Avenue. The court is completely enclosed, with a metal roof and bleachers upstairs for spectators. "It's the only one of its kind in the United States," said Aphessetche. Aphessetche calls the fast-moving competition "spectacular." The retired dairyman, who plays himself, said he built the court simply for enjoyment and "the enrichment of the culture." *Trinket* is played mostly in Iparralde, where there are at least fifty such courts, according to Aphessetche.

Although professional players from the Basque Country come and play at Aphessetche's court every couple of years, only thirty to forty Basque-Americans in the area play, and of those, only a dozen could be considered decent players. They come from around the Los Angeles area on Sunday mornings or on weeknights for pick-up games. Classes for youngsters have been held there on and off during the years. There is a range of young and older players. Aphessetche says that the game will never acquire a big following in this country because there's no financial incentive. "We can't pay the players," he said, noting that a typical Sunday morning competition will attract only about twenty spectators.

Mike Bidart, a Chino lawyer, who in his early years was known for his singing and accordion playing, is also a handball aficionado, and he decided to build a traditional left-wall court on his property. "It was always his dream to have a handball court at home so he wouldn't have to go anywhere," said his wife, Jeanette. Bidart designed the court, and it is unusual in that it is sunk 10 feet into the ground. Unlike the court at Centro Basco, the Bidarts' meets the requirements for regulation play, so the local handball tournament is held there. Players typically stop by on Sundays for a game or two.

Xavier Aphessetche's Trinket, 7262 Bickmore Avenue (off Euclid Avenue), Chino, CA 91710 (909) 597-3259

Mike Bidart's Handball Court, 11566 Vernon Avenue (near Francis Street), Chino, CA 91710 (909) 627-8820

San Diego

San Diego has never had a significant Basque community, but there is a long history of Basques in the area, starting with the early Basque priests and merchants who were part of the Mexican colonization. They were known as Californios.

Casa de Pedrorena and Casa de Aguirre

One of the early Basques was Miguel de Pedrorena, who was born in Madrid and later settled in Lima, Perú, where he became a partner in a shipping company whose boats sailed often to California. Pedrorena eventually made his home in San Diego and married María Antonia Estudillo, daughter of Don José Antonio Estudillo, another prominent Californio who served as *alcalde* (mayor) of San Diego. Pedrorena, by virtue of his marriage, inherited two large Mexican land grants, El Cajón and San Jacinto Nuevo, a tract of land that covered a large part of what is San Diego today. One of the family's homes, **Casa de Pedrorena** has been preserved as a state-registered landmark. The house is believed to have been built in 1869 by Pedrorena's son, Miguel Jr., in order to establish residency to run for sheriff, according to state park historian Ron Quinn. When Miguel Jr. lost the race, he quickly lost interest in the house, and his sister, Ysabel Pedrorena de Altamirano, took it and lived there with her family for twenty-five years.

Another powerful don of early California, Jose Antonio Aguirre, of Donosti / San Sebastián, also married into the Estudillo family and had another home in Old Town that has been preserved. According to Mary Haggland, a historian of early San Diego, Aguirre married the oldest Estudillo daughter, Francisca, and built her a grand home in Santa Barbara. But soon after their marriage, she died in childbirth. The businessman sought solace for his grief with the Estudillos in San Diego and eventually married the youngest daughter, Maria del Rosario, with whom he had several children. He built her a house, Casa de Aguirre, near her parents' home, where they lived until he died at age sixty-one. He owned much property throughout California, helped develop early San Diego, and was in partnership in several ventures with his brother-in-law, Pedrorena. The Casa de Aguirre was rebuilt in the 1990s in the same location as the original house and is home to a gift shop and museum of early local history. The old adobe chapel that Aguirre built, and where he is buried, is nearby (3950 Conde Street).

These elegant adobe houses are among the original homes located in Old Town State Historical Park. The Pedrorena house had fallen into a state of disrepair and has been restored; most recently it housed a gem shop. (The San Diego Union started in the house next door, which was also owned by the Pedrorenas.) There is a marvelous and eclectic collection of shops at the Old Town Park (headquartered at 4002 Wallace Street), making it a highly recommended visit.

Casa de Pedrorena, 2616 San Diego Avenue, San Diego, CA 92110
Casa de Aguirre, 4008 Twiggs Street, San Diego, CA 92110 (619) 278-0955

PELOTARIAK

Today several ex-*pelotariak* (jai alai players) who retired from the Tijuana Jai Alai make their homes in San Diego, and a few of them get together for dinners and such at individual homes. Father José Mari Larrañaga, assigned to St. Anthony's Church in National City in recent years, often joins them. One former *pelotari,* José Tasende, opened his own art gallery, **Tasende Gallery** (820 Prospect Street, La Jolla), which promotes the works of the Basque artists Eduardo Chillida and Andres Nagel, among others. Tasende expanded his art business to the Los Angeles area in 1997, when he opened another Tasende Gallery in West Hollywood (8808 Melrose Avenue). Chillida's and Nagel's works are also exhibited there, said daughter Betina Tasende, the gallery's associate director.

RESTAURANT

J. B. and Joanie Arretche had the **Chateau Basque** restaurant for nearly twenty years in the city of Boulevard, outside of San Diego. In 1993 they moved the Chateau Basque 100 miles east to Yuma, Arizona, (4340 East Highway 80, Yuma, AZ [602] 341-9776). J.B. passed away in 2002, but Joanie has kept up the restaurant.

The Basque *pelotari* is immortalized in this statue, which has attracted thousands of sports fans, tourists, and gamblers to the Moroccan-Spanish–style Frontón Palacio in Tijuana, Mexico. (Courtesy of Raúl Lozano García.)

Mexico

Tijuana

JAI ALAI

The East Coast boasts of several professional jai alai courts, but for the last fifteen or so years, Tijuana's **Frontón Palacio** was the only one left in the West. Tijuana is just across the border in Mexico and consequently does not fall strictly within the purview of this book. But Tijuana's well-known Jai Alai palace imported Basque *pelotariak* since its founding in 1947 and had an interesting history. (For more information on the game of jai alai, see the section on Florida.)

The Frontón Palacio, with its Moorish-Spanish architecture, was first opened in 1947, after nearly twenty years of efforts by its founder, Mariano Escobedo González. Escobedo was a powerful Mexican businessman and one of Tijuana's greatest promoters. Over the years, his jai alai court has remained one of the city's top tourist attractions, employers, and moneymakers. Its continued popularity contributed to the development of the tourism industry of Tijuana, whose population now numbers over 2 million people. The statue of a jai alai player atop a globe in front of the club has become a well-known symbol of the city.

In 1957 a fire engulfed practically the entire building. Work to restore it began almost immediately, aided even by some of the *pelotariak,* according to a historical brochure about the fronton written by Raúl Lozano García. Modernized and enlarged, the new club reopened its doors later the same year.

Yet business began to decline after the fire and did not recover by the time Escobedo died in 1960. Reflecting on that era, Escobedo's son Mariano Escobedo Lavín said that the fronton should have been closed when he took over in 1966, at age twenty-one, but sentimentality kept him from making such a drastic move.

When several other frontons opened in the United States in the late 1960s, competition for good *pelotariak* from the Basque Country increased their cost beyond the means of the Tijuana fronton. That was when Escobedo decided to open his own *pelotari* school, which has produced many good players. After that 75 percent of the roster was Basque and the remaining 25 percent Mexican, with just a couple of U.S.–born players. In 1983 Escobedo began a major remodeling of the building and, the same year, the fronton sponsored by the MGM Hotel in Las Vegas closed down. Escobedo bought up all of its equipment, seats, and even the granite fronton wall, which he had transported in blocks by truck to Tijuana.

Jai alai was played at the fronton for several years after that, and spectators enjoyed many exciting evenings betting on the high-speed sport. Unfortunately, the building's owners suspended the game in 2000. According to one Mexican observer, it had become too expensive to import players from Miami and the Basque Country. The old fronton was remodeled and turned into a venue for concerts and theater groups. The outside of the building remains relatively unchanged.

For those who want to see or place bets on jai alai while in Tijuana, Caliente Race and Sports Books has several exciting venues where Miami jai alai games, along with many other international sporting events, are televised. The nearest location is at the Pueblo Amigo Hotel (Via Oriente 9211) about ten minutes from the border.

Caliente Race and Sports Books, For information in the United States: (619) 231-1910; *www.caliente.com.mx*
Frontón Palacio, Avenida Revolución (between Seventh and Eighth), Tijuana, Baja California

TRAVEL IN MEXICO

There are a few things you need to know before crossing into Mexico: for the 12-mile zone along the border, which includes Tijuana, U.S. residents need only a valid driver's license or a certified copy of their birth certificate. Western Europeans must bring their passports and visa documents with them. If you are traveling beyond the border area, your safest bet is to bring your passport or voter registration card, for proof of citizenship. If you are traveling with children under the age of eighteen, and one or both parents is absent, you will need a notarized letter of permission from the absent parents. This rule is strictly enforced, primarily to avoid parents in custody battles fleeing into Mexico. For this, and any other unusual travel needs, it is best to go through a travel agency, to be sure you have the appropriate paperwork.

There are numerous transportation options: From downtown San Diego, you can catch a trolley at the main station at Twelfth Street and Imperial for a forty-minute ride to the border. The station is conveniently located across the street from the Amtrak train depot. If you need to leave your car, there is public parking, but it is expensive. Instead, catch the trolley at 555 West Eighth Street in National City, where free parking is available. You can also drive right to the border, where there's plenty of parking. Park in a guarded lot for $5 to $10 a day. Then walk across the border to the taxi stand. Take a cab to the Frontón Palacio for about U.S. $5. If you decide to drive your car to Tijuana, be sure to pay to park in a lighted, supervised lot. Remember to bring your driver's license and car registration. U.S. auto insurance is not valid in Mexico, but you can easily obtain short-term insurance at any of the many agencies near the border (or check the insurance programs provided by your credit cards).

■ Central California

San Joaquin Valley

CATTLE RANCHING

The sprawling San Joaquin Valley was where the first wave of Basque immigrants realized the potential for making money in the livestock industry. As early as 1855 a group of Basque men created a partnership to buy herds of cattle from the Mexican land grant ranches down south, drive them up the valley, and fatten them up at the valley's northern end. They then herded them to the mining camps or to the bigger markets of San Francisco, Sacramento, and San Jose, where they sold the cattle for double the original price. According to Carol Hovey, who collected information about those early days, this early Basque partnership included Pedro and Bernardo Altube, Little John "Juan Chico" Indart, Big John "Juan Grande" Etcheverry, José Antonio Aguila, Salvador Ihitzaque, and Sequi Murrieta.

Rather than taking El Camino Real, the well-traveled route the Spanish friars used as they established their missions along the coast of California, the herders drove the cattle up the eastern side of the coastal range to the area of Rancho Centinela, later renamed Santa Nella, which in those days was all open land. They established a base for their cattle operations here. At Rancho Centinela during the 1860s John and Mary Indart established a hotel of sorts, an adobe house where Basques stocked up on supplies and sometimes spent the night. This two-story adobe, as well as an older one-story one, remained at the site for many years, until Miller and Lux (a large cattle company) tore them down in the 1890s and built a frame house in their place.

HOTELS

The **Plaza Hotel** in San Juan Bautista (see state park listing) holds a special place in the early history of Basques in California. In her dissertation on California Basque hotels, Professor Jeronima Echeverria wrote that Julián Ursua, believed to be of Basque descent, operated the hotel during the 1850s. His ownership, unfortunately, is not documented in the state Park Department's information on the hotel. The primary owner noted is an Italian, Angelo Zanetta, who bought the hotel in 1856. (Echeverria states that Zanetta's wife, María Laborda, was Basque. She is barely mentioned in books or other park information.) The Zanettas continued the business through the 1870s. Located as it was in San Juan Bautista, at an important junction of several major California roads, the hotel was a significant trading center. Butchers from San Francisco met with cattlemen at the Plaza's bar to negotiate prices and buy and sell beef. Among these visitors were Basque stockmen.

Among other hotels in the San Joaquin Valley was one built by John Etcheverry in Tres Pinos in 1874 that apparently continued to operate as a Basque boardinghouse until after 1900. Alfred Arnaudon built the Arnaudon Hotel in Mendota in 1893, which, along with its general store, was the town center for many years. Dominique Bordagaray, one of the first hotel owners in Fresno, moved to Coalinga and established a bar and hotel that survived until the mid-1980s. It catered mostly to oil-field workers. Arnaudon and Bordagaray established two of the most significant sheep shearing ranches in the valley during the first part of the 1900s. During those early years, other small Basque hotels opened in such towns as Chester, Lemoore, White's Bridge, Firebaugh, Volta, and Sonora.

SIGHTS TO SEE

San Juan Bautista, with its many historical buildings, antique shops, and a new Basque restaurant, makes for an interesting visit. Some stops for Basques should include the San Juan Bautista Mission, founded by Basque religious leader Fermín de Lasuen. It is one of the most significant missions in the California chain and is still in active use today. Another Basque priest, Father José Martín de Martiarena joined Lasuen in overseeing the mission's construction in 1797.

The names of some of the Plaza Hotel's past visitors have been preserved in a 1862–1863 registry exhibited in the office of the Plaza Hotel, which is now part of the **San Juan Bautista State Historical Park.** Julián Ursua, who was also a rancher in the region, signed his name as a hotel guest several times. Then there are other Basque names, such as Juan Salaberry, Pablo Loinaz, Francisco Chaportequi, Francisco Arachea, and someone who signed simply as "El Basco." There were other Basques who lived in the town, including a man named Dolleguy, who ran a general store.

Be sure to visit the bar and upstairs rooms of the old hotel, which have been decorated to re-create the 1870s era. The feast of St. John on June 24th was a big celebration in San Juan Bautista in those early days, and many Basques participated in the festivities. Today the celebration, "Early Days in San Juan Bautista," is celebrated annually on Father's Day weekend. The park also presents living history enactments on the first Saturday of every month.

Nearby is the former home of early California pioneer Rafael Pico, who some locals claim was Basque. Located on Fourth Street near Washington, it is one of only four original adobe houses in San Juan Bautista. The Native Daughters of the Golden West bought it, restored it in 1935, and use it today as their parlor. The local Chamber of Commerce office (410 Third Street) offers a walking tour map of this quaint historic city, which includes the above sites.

San Juan Bautista State Historical Park, Second and Franklin Streets, San Juan Bautista, CA 95045 (831) 623-4526

RESTAURANT

This town's historical connection with Basques was quite old, but a Basque family from Mexico has established a new connection. Brother-and-sister team Veronica Matchain Pirl and Luis Matchain opened the Matxain Etxea in San Juan Bautista in 2002. The family arrived in California from Mexico. The siblings' father immigrated to Mexico from the Basque Country and had a Basque restaurant in Tlaxcala, which was popular among local government officials. When Veronica and her husband, Bruce Pirl, decided to open a restaurant in California, according to husband Bruce, they brought brother Luis from Mexico to work as chef. In addition to traditional Basque dishes, they also serve paella and tapas. They chose the original spelling of the family name for the restaurant, which is located in the historic center of town.

Matxain Etxea, 206 Fourth Street, San Juan Bautista, CA 95045 (831) 623-4472; *www.matxainetxea.com*

RANCHING

More and more Basques settled in the San Joaquin Valley as they saw opportunities to buy land and establish livestock ranches, buying up land that had once made up the prestigious Spanish and Mexican land grants. Many of the Basque pioneer families knew each other and socialized together. Intermarriage was quite common among them, and they frequently traveled to San Francisco to be married at Notre Dame de Victoires Church and to celebrate at the nearby Basque hotels.

John Indart and John Etcheverry continued in the cattle business, in the 1850s and 1860s, moving out of the valley and west of the coastal range to the area around Hollister. Their ranch was divided by the Southern Pacific railroad line, which went through in 1873. The town of Tres Pinos grew up around the railroad line, and John Etcheverry became a leading citizen, according to scholar Carol Hovey. He donated land for the building of the **Church of the Immaculate Conception** (7290 Airline Highway), said Hovey, who reported that his name, as well as that of the Indarts and other early residents of the town, are noted on stained glass windows.

Also settled in the valley with their families were ranchers Juan Bautista Arambide, Miguel Goldaracena, Jean Garat, and José Aurrecochea. Henry Miller, of the Miller and Lux empire (built on sheep and cattle ranching), eventually pushed out some of the more ambitious Basques by grabbing up land throughout the valley. Garat and the Altube brothers took note of his actions and followed his example when they settled near Tuscarora, Nevada, to establish their own empires.

Eventually the cattle ranchers either sold out or went elsewhere, and Basques who settled in the valley chose sheep over cattle. They were concentrated most heavily around Los Banos, Stockton, Fresno, and Bakersfield. Some of the families have continued ranching in these areas to this day, thus maintaining some of the oldest Basque businesses in California.

Los Banos

Considering that Los Banos is such a small town, the **Los Banos Basque Club** (listed in a later section) is surprisingly large—two hundred and eighty members strong, in fact—and its picnic has been one of California's best attended for years. As with some of the other popular gatherings, the rural setting may give it greater authenticity and appeal. The proximity to San Francisco is an additional positive factor.

Until recently there was just one Catholic church, St. Joseph's, and one cemetery (Cardoza Road and Center Avenue) in this small town of about eighteen thousand people.

RANCHING

The history of Basques in the area around Los Banos extends back at least to the 1880s, when expansive ranches established on the huge Mexican land grants were still prominent. A few Basque families established sheep and cattle ranches in the area by acquiring land.

A Basque Mayor

As you're heading south on Interstate 5 towards Los Banos, you might be curious about the name Erreca posted at the rest stop between Santa Nella and Los Banos. Yes, John "Chuck" Erreca was Basque. Erreca served as mayor of Los Banos for seventeen years during the 1940s and 1950s. In 1962 he was appointed by Governor Pat Brown and later Governor Ronald Reagan, to head the state Department of Public Works, which later became the state Department of Transportation better known as CalTrans.

Erreca was the son of Martin Erreca of Aldudes, who established a large ranch in the Los Banos area. If you have time, stop in at one of the rest stops on either side of the freeway. You'll find a brief history of Erreca and the family's ME brand, in existence for nearly a hundred years, engraved at the bottom of a sun dial. The family is especially proud that it was CalTrans employees—not politicians—who initiated the legislation and pursued the red tape to put Erreca's name on the public rest stop. "It made us feel good to know that these were the people who actually worked for him," said son Bob Erreca. Today Bob Erreca runs the family's large ranching operation, although the farmland and sheep have been sold off and he deals strictly in cattle.

Among them was the Arburua family. In 1884 Miguel Arburua, who had emigrated from Nafarroa, bought a 22,000-acre grant known as the Rancho Panocha de San Juan y Los Carrizalitos from Julián Ursua. (According to a historical account written by descendant Joseph Arburua, Ursua, who was born in the United States, was granted the land in 1844 by then governor Manuel Micheltorena.) Numerous Basque families living nearby would gather at Arburua's sheep ranch, located 16 miles southwest of Los Banos, where he had established a handball court by painting lines on the wall of his barn and smoothing out the dirt floor. Today the five-hundred-head cattle ranch is still in the hands of the Arburuas, now the third and fourth generation.

Dr. John Arburua, the grandson of Miguel and a veterinarian by trade, has headed the ranch operation for the past forty years, most recently with the help of his children. The family represents the epitome of the American melting pot, since its Basque ancestry has been diluted by marriages with Irish and Danish. "But we do know our heritage, and we're very proud of it," said John Arburua.

Another significant ranching family here is the Errecas, who have also carried on a sheep and cattle business into the third generation. Like the Arburuas and the Errecas, most of the Basques in the Los Banos area are still primarily involved in sheep and cattle raising and farming. Sheep hooks, old wooden cattle and sheep brands, cooking pots used by sheepherders, and other tools of the livestock industry are exhibited at the **Milliken Museum** (925 Pacheco Boulevard [209] 826-5505). The displays, the names of Basque families who donated the items, as well as a short history of the Basques can be viewed there.

Elena Talbott, wife of Basque sheepman Ray Talbott, was very active in the community until her death in 1992, and a park on San Luis Street, just east of Highway 165, was named after her. (The family name was changed from Artari to Talbott when the family arrived in the United States, according to museum volunteer June Erreca.) She also was quite a historian and source of great information on the Basques in the valley during her lifetime.

RESTAURANTS

Unlike Stockton, further north, which had many hotels, Los Banos had only one long-term one. Anton and Josefa Lassart ran one hotel

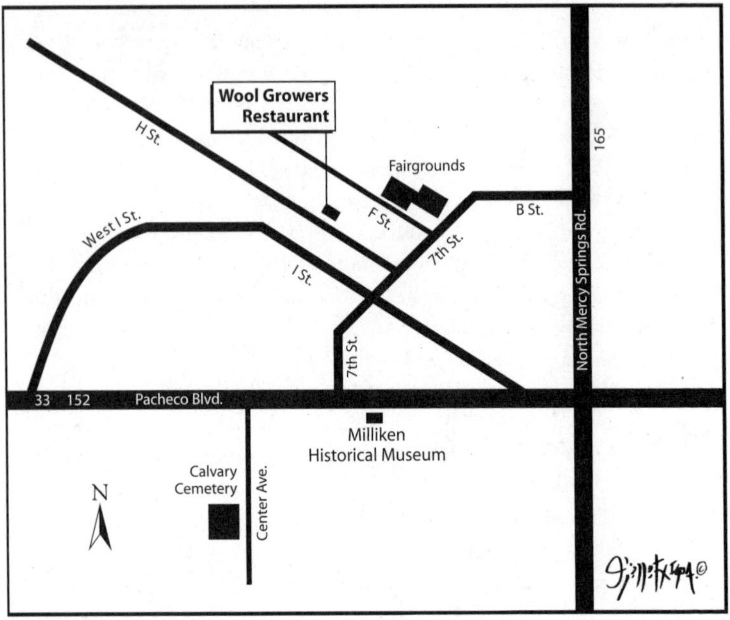

Los Banos.

for four years, but it burned down in 1918 and was never rebuilt. In 1925 or so, Joe Goñi came south from Alturas to open the Wool Growers' Hotel, which operated as a boardinghouse for more than half a century. The Wool Growers was well known for hosting a big "mountain oyster" (lamb testicles) dinner and dance every year around Valentine's Day.

Brothers Gabriel and Michel Iturbide bought the **Wool Growers' Restaurant** from Victor Arretche in 1974 and run a restaurant and bar there today. The Pyrenees Hotel in nearby Merced also operated from 1929 to 1968.

Ambroise Curutchague worked as the bartender at the Wool Growers for more than ten years before he opened the Chalet Basque restaurant (1639 Pacheco Boulevard) with his wife, Florence, in 1976. They ran the Basque restaurant in the traditional style for about twenty-five years before retiring. Curutchague tried to sell the restaurant to a Basque without success. It then became a barbecue place.

The Wool Growers serves Basque food in the traditional manner, with the family-style side dishes and only two or three entrées to select from.

Wool Growers' Restaurant, 609 H Street (and Sixth Street) Los Banos, CA 93635 (209) 826-4593

BASQUE CLUB

The **Los Banos Basque Club** brings together Basque families dispersed in such towns as Patterson, Turlock, Madera, Dos Palos, Chowchilla, and Firebaugh. The club was started in 1964, and its first picnic was organized that year as well.

Club Activities. In February the Los Banos Basque Club holds its annual *mus* tournament, coupled with the annual Ladies Night free dinner for members. The club's only other activity is a planning meeting the weekend before the picnic. That night they usually serve a chicken dinner. The club used to sponsor a New Year's Eve party, but it was canceled because of stricter drinking-and-driving laws, but also because the valley's foggy winter nights and lonely roads kept many away, Jean Pierre Petrissans noted.

The Basque population in Los Banos probably peaked during the 1960s and 1970s. In the 1960s the Basque club seriously considered building a handball court at the county fairgrounds. "Now it's too late," according to longtime club officer Ambroise Curutchague. Many new members come from as far away as San Francisco and Fresno mainly for the picnic and *mus* tournament. "Only a handful of us run the whole show," he said.

After the young people graduate from high school, they go away to college, said Jean Pierre's wife, Cathy Petrissans. Without any good colleges nearby, the youth tend to go to universities in the bigger cities—San Francisco, Fresno, Chico, and other places. "And then it all depends on where you get a job," she pointed out. Yet those who stay or come back to raise families tend to renew their interest, despite having ignored the cultural activities as teenagers. "Once they get married, somehow it changes," Petrissans said. They'll bring their small children to events and take them to dance lessons.

Los Banos Basque Club, P.O. Box 123, Los Banos, CA 93635-0123. Information: (209) 632-5158 (Jim Etchepare)

FESTIVAL

Picnics have been popular in this farming community for some time. Bob Erreca was well known for sponsoring a huge annual barbecue on Palm Sunday on the family ranch, along the Los Banos Creek, during the 1960s and 1970s. The barbecue started as a party for about twenty families, all you could eat and drink, for free, according to Erreca. Eventually the invitation-only affair turned into a community gathering of some three thousand people, more than half of them Basque. To cover the costs, organizers auctioned off bottles of wine, lambs, pigs, and even a car. In the barbecue's heyday, sky divers and acrobatic pilots put on shows for the crowd. The Erreca family finally stopped holding the picnic when they sold the property in the late 1970s.

Today the Los Banos Basque Club picnic is the premier endeavor of the local Basque community. Many San Francisco and Fresno Basques

San Francisco's *Klika* is not always greeted with the greatest enthusiasm. (Photo by Averie Cohen.)

come to this picnic, held on the third Sunday of May every year at the Merced County Fairgrounds (Fourth and F Streets). The festival attracts between twelve hundred and fifteen hundred people every year. Jeanette Bidart remembers playing accordion at picnics during the 1960s, when the Los Banos event was in its heyday. "It was *the* picnic," she said. The event was within easy driving distance for San Francisco's large population of single Basque men, who were always looking for a good time, as well as for potential wives. (Eventually, Bakersfield's festival surpassed the Los Banos picnic in popularity.)

The Mass at Los Banos, held in a covered pavilion, is one of the most beautiful. The San Francisco *klika* leads a procession of dancers ranging from four- or five-year-olds to college-age teens wearing Basque costumes. Sometimes the smallest ones will bring offerings, such as a tiny lamb, a potent Basque symbol for life and livelihood. Offerings have included items representing the many occupations of Basques—for example, bottles of wine to represent the bars and restaurants, vegetables and fruits to represent the ranches, a milking pail and stool to represent the dairy industry. All these items are offered to the priest for a blessing and to give thanks to God for success in these occupations.

Often the priest will hand out a song sheet so that everyone can sing along with the hymns "Gure Aita" (Our Father) and "Jainkoaren Bildotsa." Even for those who do not understand the language, listening to the Basque hymns can be a moving experience.

There's music after the Mass for anyone who wants to dance before the barbecue begins around 1 P.M. The afternoon is filled with dance performances by the Los Banos and San Francisco groups and weight-carrying and wood-chopping contests. The constant fear of a personal-injury lawsuit led the club to eliminate the *soka tira*, or tug-of-war, competition from the afternoon fun, according to club member Jean Pierre Petrissans. Weight-carrying attracts younger and older men alike. The wood chopping is usually performed by three or four Hegoaldetarrak from San Francisco who come every year.

No dinner is served, but hot chorizo sandwiches are available in the evening. The Wool Growers' Restaurant normally closes on picnic day. In the evening, a band plays dance music until 10:30 or 11 P.M., whenever the crowd decides it's time to go home.

Recently, club members have discussed changing the picnic's annual date to Saturday. Then visitors could spend the night and part of the next day rather than having to return home to work on Monday, according to Petrissans. Sunday has been the traditional day for picnics, because many of those in ranching occupations work Saturdays. Bakersfield and Chino have their picnics planned around three-day weekends, so picnic-goers can stay until Monday.

DANCE

The Los Banos Basque Club has maintained a dance group since its inception—not an easy feat in a small town like this. In fact, from the 1970s through 1985 the group could compete with the best. The group has missed the visits by professional dancers from the Basque Country, because of Los Banos' out-of-the-way location, and therefore their dancers have not been exposed to new or changing dances. But enthusiastic dance teachers keep up the dance tradition in Los Banos.

A RESTAURANT IN FIREBAUGH

Ramón and Cecilia Echeveste opened a Basque restaurant, the **Leku Ona,** in the tiny nearby town of Firebaugh in 1991. At the time, Ramón thought they could entice their married daughter, who lives in the Basque Country, to join them in running the business, but she declined, according to Cecilia Echeveste. Since they are off the beaten track, the Echevestes rarely get Basque customers, and they rely entirely on local clientele from the rural farming area. Consequently, they found the Basque family-style meals weren't that popular, so chef Jean Claude Lekumberry prepares the dishes à la carte. Meals are served up all day long here, and the Friday night dances with a D.J. attract quite a crowd.

Leku Ona Restaurant, 1641 North Street (and Satain) Firebaugh, CA 93622 (559) 659-3994

Fresno

Fresno is one of California's fastest growing cities, and with blocks of new homes spreading ever outward, its former Old West atmosphere is gone. The Basques, among the more significant immigrant populations here during the first half of the century, are hardly noticeable these days.

BAKERY

Thanks to François Pedeflous, founder of the **Basque French Bakery,** Basques have made their mark in Fresno. You can see bread delivery vans driving around town with the red Basque French Bakery logo—a loaf of bread, a slab of cheese, and a glass of red wine—painted on the sides. The bread is delivered to supermarkets and restaurants all over town, as well as establishments 50 miles to the north and south.

Basque French Bakery, 2625 Inyo Street, Fresno, CA 93721 (559) 268-7088

RESTAURANTS AND BOARDINGHOUSES

A small-town feeling still pervades the old downtown Fresno area that is home to the bakery and the nearby **Shepherd's Inn** (formerly the Santa Fe Hotel and Restaurant), just across from the Santa Fe Railroad Depot. Older brick buildings predominate in this longtime commercial neighborhood, once the core of the city and now designated a historic warehouse district. A couple of older Victorian residences, including the Meux Museum, distinguish the adjacent neighborhood, around St. John's Cathedral on R and Mariposa Streets, also designated a historic district.

In the old days many Basque establishments didn't have any special decor or other remarkable features to indicate that they were Basque. But the language, the celebrations, and the general lifestyle contained within their walls made non-Basque visitors feel they were in another country.

Two of Fresno's old boarding houses, the Basque Hotel and the Shepherd's Inn, are still operating, although today they serve as restaurants. They are among the oldest such businesses still operating in the West, dating from the 1920s. Yet the two hotels could be considered latecomers to Fresno's boardinghouse scene. Fresno was somewhat unusual in that the Basque hotels were concentrated around not one but two railroad depots, located several blocks apart. The Bascongado

Frank Pedeflous and His Basque Sourdough Bread

François "Frank" Pedeflous is the epitome of the self-made man. Orphaned at ten, Pedeflous went to live with his grandparents. To help the family out, he was sent to work for a family on another nearby farm. He left his village in Nafarroa Beherea at age nineteen to come to the United States.

He got his start the way many other Basque bakers did—working for other bakers. He spent nearly fourteen years at the Pyrenees French Bakery in Bakersfield, apprenticing with Pierre Laxague. He then moved to Fresno and opened his bakery in 1963 in what was once an old Safeway store. As the business grew, Pedeflous decided to relocate to the bakery's current location in 1969. The business required hard work, seven days a week, but his bakery enjoyed success for many years. But the recession hit the bakery hard, and Pedeflous found himself fighting a losing battle against corporate bakeries. "Everybody's knocking down the little guy," he said.

He would have loved to pass the bakery on to his children, but his son became an engineer, and his daughter moved away from Fresno with her family. But he was getting older, so he sold the business to a non-Basque. Today, the business continues exactly the same way Pedeflous ran it.

Basque Sourdough Bread,
François Pedeflous, Founder Basque French Bakery

½ cup sourdough starter
1 package active dry yeast
½ cup warm water
2 cups white flour
2½ teaspoons salt
½ to 1 cup water

Starter is a treasure that can be obtained any number of places, including the grocery store. Obtain your own special source, or learn how to make it yourself. ("I brought my sourdough starter from Bakersfield," said Pedeflous, referring to the Pyrenees Bakery where he worked for fifteen years.) *For starter:* Mix together 1½ cup flour and ¾ cup of sourdough starter with ¾ cup water (room temperature). Let it set for several hours. For real sour dough, let the starter set up at room temperature anywhere from 12 to 24 hours. Pedeflous likes his milder—7 to 8 hours. *To make the Dough:* Dissolve the yeast in warm water. Stir the flour and salt together, add the starter mixture and the water, and mix them all together to make a soft dough. Knead until supple and elastic. Mold it. Wait four to five hours for it to rise. Heat the oven to 400 degrees. For rolls, bake for 18 minutes; for baguettes, 25 minutes; and for a 1-pound loaf, 35 minutes. For crustier bread, cook longer.

Hotel opened around 1898. Fresno's second Basque hotel, the Hotel des Pyrenees, opened in 1901 near the second depot, the Santa Fe, which was then considered the other side of town. Also by the Santa Fe Railroad Depot, a third hotel, the Fresno "Sheepcamp" Hotel, was built in 1902 by the same man who built the Bascongado, Martin Yribarren.

The Bascongado Hotel had been doing business for about eight years when a young seventeen-year-old, Francisca Saragueta, got off the Southern Pacific train in Fresno in April 1906. Saragueta had first come to San Francisco to work for a doctor's family, but the devastating 1906 earthquake hit the evening of her arrival. The doctor decided to pack his family and head for New York, leaving Saragueta without a job, according to her granddaughter Jessie Zalba. So Saragueta took the train to Fresno, stepped across the dirt road to the doors of the hotel and asked for a job. "Grandma had heard that there were a lot of Basques here in Fresno," said Zalba, still amazed at the pioneer woman's courageousness. She married Juan B. Etcheverry, and the couple worked on different Basque ranches in the area, including that of John Bidegaray, who was probably the biggest Basque sheepman in Fresno in those early days. In later years, Saragueta served as midwife to many of Fresno's Basque mothers.

Bidegaray and Matías Erro were cofounders and president and vice president, respectively, of the Growers National Bank of Fresno. Other early families raising sheep around Fresno were the Etcheverrys, the Irolas, and the Yparreas.

The **Basque Hotel** was built in 1923, although it didn't acquire that name until several years later. Felix Esain, who had owned and operated the Santa Fe for several years, took it over in 1935. During the early 1940s he and his wife, Lyda, expanded the Basque Hotel's dining room and built a handball court that is still in use today. The Santa Fe also had a handball court next door, but Lyda claims that once they built theirs at the Basque Hotel, all the handball players preferred it, because Felix was an avid player and promoted lots of competitions. By the time Benita and Segundo Garcia bought the Santa Fe in 1961, the *kantxa* was long gone, its lot sold and the structure torn down.

The Yturri and the Vitoria Hotels, the Wool Growers Restaurant, and the Madrid Café were also popular gathering places for Basques

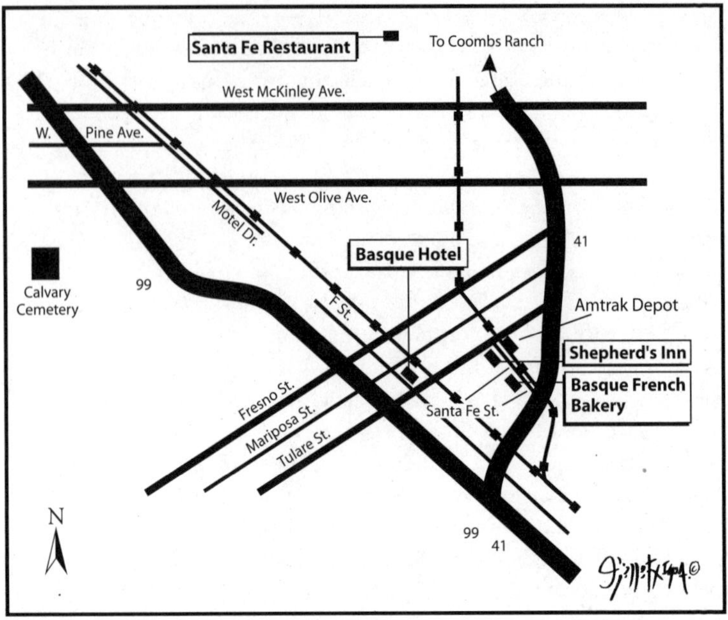

Fresno.

in the 1930s and 1940s. By the 1950s, though, only the Yturri, the Santa Fe, and the Basque Hotel remained. When Father Adrian Gachiteguy passed through during that era he remarked that the greatest number of Basques in Fresno were from the town of Esterenzubi.

The Esains sold the Basque Hotel in 1952 to Jean and Mary Nouqueret, who kept it until 1972. The Esains couldn't stay away from the business, and they were back in 1956, with the Villa Basque restaurant on Blackstone Avenue. They sold out in 1976, and the restaurant burned down later in a fire.

Benita Garcia, who like Esain was born in the United States, was another well-known figure in Fresno because of the motherly role she provided for dozens, perhaps hundreds, of sheepherders over the years. "They would come in for a week or two, spend all their money, and then go back to work," according to Benita, who with husband Pete Idiart ran the Yturri Hotel during the 1950s. Later, after Idiart passed away, she got back into the hotel business with Garcia, her

Surrogate Mothers

As a social institution, the boardinghouse played a significant role in maintaining the cohesiveness of the Basque community, as the boarders used it as a place to meet other Basques. Hotel owners typically shepherded the young non-English-speakers through the rigors of adapting to life in the United States. They served as translators and advisors in immigration and government-related paperwork and often acted as bankers for the immigrants too. "We took care of everybody," said Lyda Esain, who, with husband Felix, ran Fresno's Basque Hotel. "I chauffeured them around. I witnessed them for citizenship. I did everything." The large majority were single men, ages seventeen to twenty-five, who spoke little English and eventually intended to go back to the Basque Country. As the need for maids and waitresses in the boardinghouses grew, women made up greater numbers within the waves of Basque immigrants to the United States. Most of them married fairly soon after their arrival, as many of the male boarders anxious for family life whisked them away. There was a continual demand for more young women from Europe to fill their spots. The women came at a steady pace up through the 1950s.

Often the hotel keepers were a married couple. Men rarely if ever ran a place without a wife at their side. The husbands were often sheepmen. The capital they needed to open their business in the first place usually came from their lamb sales. Typically the woman was the one in charge at the boardinghouse, and if the husband passed away, the wife was likely to keep running the business on her own. Many of the boardinghouse matrons became surrogate mothers to the sheepherders who came through, like Esain, helping the men with any transactions that required fluency in English. "A lot of them treated them like the moms they left back home," said Leon Sorhondo, who grew up in San Francisco's Pyrenees Hotel. His mother, Amelie Sorhondo, as well as Esain and many others—Grace Elizalde of Noriega's in Bakersfield and Leandra Letemendi of Boise—are just a few that stand out.

second husband, and ran the Santa Fe from 1961 to 1975. Like the others, it was a family establishment. "My mom always referred to everyone who worked there as *la familia,*" said local attorney Mike Idiart, who spent his childhood at the Santa Fe and remembers eating at long tables with the boarders. "They kept the boardinghouse more out of a sense of duty, to give them a place to stay," said Idiart. During the 1960s, lawyers and judges from the nearby courthouse would pack the tables at noontime. "At that time we charged $1.25 for lunch, with wine," remembered Benita.

Jean Pierre and Manuela Etchechury operated the old Santa Fe for a few years and continued to rent rooms as a service to retired herders or herders passing through town. "It's more than anything else the upkeep of the tradition," said Manuela at the time. Built in 1926, the Santa Fe was designated a historic landmark in 1991 and bears a plaque on the front.

The Etchechurys were something of an anomaly in the Basque boardinghouse business. Whereas virtually every Basque hotel has been run by Basque immigrants, the Etchechurys are college-educated, U.S.–born Basques. "When we first took over [in 1991], people were confused," said Manuela. "They didn't understand why, with a college degree, we would choose to work so hard." But the Etchechurys, who studied small business and restaurant and hotel administration at California Polytechnic Pomona University, always had the intention of opening their own business one day.

In 2001, the Etchechurys had to move, so they opened a new restaurant two miles north. They did, however, keep their longtime business name, the *Santa Fe.* Meanwhile, the old place was purchased by non-Basques, who renamed it Shepherd's Inn, and hired Basque chef Manolo Moriano, who had cooked Basque cuisine at Fresno's Landmark Restaurant and at the Chalet Basque in Los Banos. They still serve a "boarders" lunch and dinner every day at 12:30 P.M. and 6:30 P.M. (with a fixed menu and low price) family style. Diners can also eat a la carte in the rest of the dining room.

The Yturri, a block away from the Santa Fe, was built by Paul and Marcelina Yturri in 1940. It finally closed in 1991, disappointing local Basques and downtown office workers who frequently lunched there. The city bought the building and tore it down in 1993, replacing it with a parking lot.

A futuristic city hall was built recently, just a block from the Basque French Bakery and the Shepherd's Inn, and a new federal building was to be completed in 2005, breathing life into the old downtown neighborhood but disappointing local historians who lament the disappearance of all the old buildings. The historic train depot, still in use by rail passengers who can catch a train north to Oakland or south to Bakersfield, was renovated in 2004. Today Amtrak provides passenger rail service to several old depot locations where Basque restaurants are located—Fresno, Reno, and Winnemucca are examples. Who knows? As train travel slowly grows in popularity, many of these restaurants may be strategically placed to take advantage of the business.

The **Basque Hotel,** unfortunately, doesn't benefit from the civic center foot traffic, since it is located several blocks away in the run-down part of downtown referred to as West Fresno, by the old Southern Pacific depot. At one time the area was known as Chinatown, but today it's primarily a Mexican neighborhood. In fact, a past Basque owner sold the hotel to Mexicans in 1970, and they ran it until 1978, when it returned to Basque hands. The historic establishment has its loyal clientele, and current owner Fermin Urroz said he does good business among Basques and Americans. Urroz took over in 1980 with partner Arnaud Ardans, who has since passed away. The boarders eat in the dining room at long tables, just like they always have. "They keep it up real nice and the food is very good," said former owner Lyda Esain. Do be careful in this neighborhood at night.

An American restaurant, the **Landmark** (644 East Olive), has been serving several Basque dishes for years.

Basque Hotel, 1102 F Street (at Mariposa) Fresno, CA 93706 (559) 233-2286
Santa Fe Hotel and Restaurant, 3110 North Maroa Avenue, Fresno, CA 93704 (559) 266-7499; *www.santafebasque.com*
Shepherd's Inn, 935 Santa Fe Avenue, Fresno, CA (559) 266-2228

PELOTA

The Basque Hotel is home to Fresno's only existing handball court. It's not a regulation-size court, so it can't be used for official competitions, and not many pelota players are left in Fresno, so the indoor court is rarely used.

BASQUE CLUB

François Pedeflous, the former bakery owner, is an enthusiastic promoter of Basque culture, and he was instrumental in starting the **Fresno Basque Club.** Anxious to launch a club like those in other cities, he called ten people with Basques names that he found in the phone book. Those initial calls led to a dinner of forty people at the Santa Fe Hotel in late 1977. Today with 230 members, the Fresno

Basque Club is still going strong, although members admit there's little, if any, involvement these days by the younger generation. For a while the club even had its own hall. It sponsors several events every year, in addition to its annual picnic. In February there's the annual *mus* tournament and the club's anniversary celebration—a dinner dance on the last Saturday of the month. December brings a winter brunch party.

Clubhouse. In its earliest days the club would rotate its gatherings among the Pedeflous's bakery office and the Basque hotels and restaurants. In 1991 the club purchased a building in which to hold its functions. "Initially, it was thought to build one from scratch," noted Mike Idiart, one of the club's former presidents. The club had purchased 10 acres outside of town to that end. But members realized that putting up a new building would be too expensive, so they opted instead to buy an Italian social hall in town when it was put up for sale. Pedeflous loaned the club a large portion of the money to buy the building. The debt was paid off when the surrounding acreage was later sold to a developer.

"Buying a club is important nowadays to keep up the culture," said Mike Idiart, "because you start to lose it if you don't." Unfortunately, the neighborhood in the vicinity of the hall at 1425 West Pine was not a good area of town, and rental of the location for parties was unsuccessful. So the club opted to sell the property. Today, most club events take place at the facilities of Tony and Juliet Campos' almond factory, Campos Brothers Farm (15516 South Walnut Avenue), in nearby Carruthers. The Camposes built a *kantxa* years ago, and handball tournaments have been held there. The national *mus* tournament, the 2004 Basque Hall of Fame festivities, and many weddings have been celebrated in the large warehouse building; dancers also gather there for practice.

Fresno Basque Club, P.O. Box 406, Fresno, CA 93708. Information: (559) 226-7499 (Jean Pierre and Manuela Etchechury)

FESTIVAL

Long before picnics were officially organized by the Fresno Basque Club, the Wool Growers Association in Fresno, as in other big sheep towns, would host picnics. Julia (Serrano) Jacobsen remembers events dating back as far as 1937, in the nearby cities of Huron, Mendota, and Tranquillity. Even then, the lamb was cooked over the open barbecue pits like it is today, according to Jacobsen. And while they didn't have the folk dance performances that the current picnics have, there was a lot of impromptu dancing. "Believe me, they had music out there, and those old-timers—they danced!" remembers Lyda Esain. Jessie Zalba was a young accordion player back then. "There would be ten to twelve accordionists playing, all young people," she said.

Fresno's annual picnic has traditionally been held in nearby Madera, at the Coombs Ranch. The picnic comes early, on the first Saturday in May. After one rainy picnic, they moved the date to Father's Day in June, but they changed it back when Fresno's searing summer heat came early one year, frying picnic goers. They also tried holding it at the Fresno County Fairgrounds, but that didn't last long. With its oak trees and the San Joaquin River running nearby, the scenic Coombs Ranch setting sets Fresno's festival apart from the others. Rancher Dennis Coombs offers his property for free to the club and other community groups. To get there, take Highway 41 out of Fresno to Twelfth Avenue and head east. The street turns into a gravel road and ends at the ranch.

Today's festival attracts an average of six to eight hundred people. It offers the traditional fare—the Mass, the barbecue lamb lunch, afternoon performances by the Fresno and Bakersfield dancers and the Bakersfield *klika,* hot chorizo sandwiches for dinner, and music for dancing. San Francisco accordionist Jean Flesher is invited to play dance music in the afternoon, and Joe Rebella has been a fixture on picnic night, playing his music until 10 or 11 P.M.

DANCE

Fresno's dance group was in a lull during the early 1990s, having lost many of its most enthusiastic dancers to college or marriage. "The group went downhill when [instructor Juliet Campos] retired several years ago," said Marsha Saragueta, whose daughter, a professional dancer, was once in the group. For years Campos led the dance group, which formed after the Basque club was organized in 1977. Campos taught students the dances she knew from the area of Valcarlos and Arnegi, dances that were emphasized when she was a young dancer in Chino. During the 1980s Fresno dancers expanded their repertoire with new routines from different parts of the Basque Country that they learned at the North American Basque Organizations' summer camp, according to Campos. In 1993 seven of the young women who had been the most dedicated dancers for many years were all living in the Basque Country, either to study or because they had married Basques. "It's almost ironic [that] all of the girls that were in the dance group are over there," said Campos. Today, though, some former dancers, including Campos's daughter, are teaching the group, which has regained its numbers and energy.

AREA RESTAURANTS

Although Basque families live in the suburbs and towns around Fresno, none of the latter have a restaurant. But in nearby Stratford, Mariana Irigaray is famous to this day for the Basque meals she once served at her home. "People say it was the best food they've eaten in their lives," said restaurateur Marsha Saragueta. From the 1930s through the 1960s Mariana and her daughter Alice Irigaray were serving California cuisine before the term was ever invented. Lyda Esain remembers the Irigarays as a place where you could stop anytime without a reservation and get a meal cooked with fresh vegetables and poultry raised right on the farm.

In 1986, Justo and Marsha Saragueta opened Justo's Basque Restaurant in Hanford. The restaurant was very popular and particularly known for its annual Lamb Balls and Tails Dinner. Prior to Justo's, the couple operated the New Rendez-Vous in Fresno for many years alongside Marsha's parents and Jessie and Antonio Zalba. After many years of hard work at Justo's, the couple decided to retire and closed the restaurant business in the 1990s.

Bakersfield

You can call Bakersfield the Basque gourmet capital of the United States. At last count this Central Valley city boasted six Basque

Early Basques in Monterey

While California was still under Spanish rule, military commander Gaspar de Portola founded Monterey in 1770, establishing a naval presidio and the mission San Carlos de Monterey. José Joaquín de Arrillaga came to live in Monterey when he was appointed acting governor in 1793. He was the first Basque administrator for Spain to actually reside in Alta California. Nothing is left of the Spanish naval presidio nor of Arrillaga. Nevertheless, one of the earliest historical reminders of the Basque presence in California is located in this city.

The elegant house of Basque merchant José Amesti, built in 1834, is a historic landmark open to the public. Born in Donostia/San Sebastián and educated as a lawyer, Amesti first traveled to Mexico, where he became a citizen, before arriving in Monterey in 1822. He married Prudenciana Vallejo, sister of then-governor Mariano Vallejo, and was given a 15,400-acre land grant, Rancho de Los Corralitos, east of the city of Santa Cruz, then known as Branciforte. After spending ten years on the cattle ranch, the Amestis retired to Monterey, where the *ayuntamiento,* or city government, gave him a lot in town on which to build a house. Amesti served as a justice of the peace and as mayor of Monterey for a short time during the 1840s.

Six or seven historic adobe homes remain in Monterey, and Casa Amesti is "one of the grandest," according to Esther Josi, a docent who has led tours through the house. The two-story home has two unsupported balconies, which are typical of Monterey architecture of that time, and an unusual center stairway. On the second floor there is a large parlor known as the *gran sala,* with a springy redwood floor that was built expressly for dancing. The dance floor was used often, because the Amestis were known for hosting large parties. José Amesti died in 1855, but his family continued to live in the house until 1912.

Frances Elkins, a lover of fine art, later bought and restored the place, filling it with elegant antique furniture and paintings that remain today. She willed the property to the National Trust for Historic Preservation, which opened the house to the public in 1965. During the week the house is the domain of the Old Capital Club, a men's social club, but it is open for tours on weekends. During 2004, the house and garden were undergoing a major remodeling. December will be a good time to visit after the house reopens in 2005 for the popular Christmas at the Adobes. Several local adobe homes are decorated at that time, and docents in period costumes give candlelight tours that include music and refreshments. As for the ranch, squatters took over much of the land, and houses were eventually developed there. The road from Watsonville to the town of Corralitos still bears the Amesti name.

Casa Amesti, 516 Polk Street (at Alvarado), Monterey, CA 93940. Information: (831) 372-8173 restaurants—and none seem the poorer for the competition. On weekends many of the diners tend to be visitors from the Los Angeles or Santa Barbara areas who consider stopping for Basque food as part and parcel of any trip to Bakersfield.

Bakersfield and the surrounding Kern County towns can probably be said to have the highest concentration of Basques in California. Estimates from knowledgeable local sources range from five thousand to ten thousand, although precise numbers are not available. The largest figure is not improbable, if second-, third- and fourth-generation descendants of the earliest Bakersfield settlers are counted. Through the years the Nafarroa Beherea region around Baigorri has been best represented here, but today a fair number also come from Nafarroa.

The first known Basque in Kern County was José Antonio Aguirre, who was born in Donostia/San Sebastián and migrated to Mexico, where he became a wealthy merchant and owner of several ships. He engaged in trade with California and ultimately settled there. He was granted the Rancho El Tejón, of nearly 98,000 acres, in 1843. Aguirre is credited with naming the grant, after seeing a *tejón,* or badger. But he quickly gave up his share. Much of this original land grant is still intact under the ownership of the Tejon Ranch Company. Aguirre, along with some other prominent Basque merchants who were active in California when it was under Spanish rule, had little connection with the waves of rural Basques who came after the gold rush.

Basques first settled around the Sumner railroad station just outside Bakersfield. The railroad had bypassed the bigger city because it refused to pay a subsidy. The town name was later changed from Sumner to Kern City, and then, for many years, it was East Bakersfield, before it was eventually incorporated into the growing city of Bakersfield. Many of the existing Basque restaurants remain in this old part of town, and Sumner Street is a reminder of the earlier era. Basque ranchers were concentrated in the Norris and Beardsley districts just north of the Kern River and in the Greenfield area to the south. Both areas eventually were covered with housing developments that were swallowed up by Bakersfield.

Basques were so numerous in Bakersfield that the *Bakersfield Daily Californian* printed occasional articles in Basque during the 1890s, according to Professor Mary Grace Paquette, who recounted those early days in her book *Basques to Bakersfield*. One of the most prominent marriages in Bakersfield's horse-and-buggy days was that of Marianne Laxague and Pablo Galtes, a well-known Bakersfield merchant who brought Laxague to Bakersfield from San Francisco in 1874. Galtes's family was Catalan, and Laxague's had immigrated from Aldudes, so she became the first of many Aldudarrak to settle in Bakersfield. The Galtes were responsible for some of the early influx of Basques to Bakersfield. Three of Marianne's nieces traveled from the Basque Country to join them and work in the Galteses' store and also in the couple's grand mansion on Truxtun Avenue. One of the three Inda sisters, Louise, married Faustino Noriega, a montañés (a native of Santander, Spain, just outside the Basque Country).

The Noriega family lived in a house that the prominent businessman had built between 1894 and 1900 at 1325 Baker Street. This magnificent old house—a mansion by the standards of the day—was renovated in the late 1990s and is a beautiful site, which is rented out for weddings and reunions. The family history is displayed at the home and on the Web site (*www.noriegahouse.com*). Call to arrange a tour of the house.

Noriega House, 1325 Baker Street, Bakersfield CA 93305 (661) 633-9016; *www.noriegahouse.com*

SHEEP

In the late 1800s many of these Basques who arrived after the gold rush worked in Kern County as herders and superintendents for the two local sheep companies, Miller and Lux and the Kern County Land Company. However, it wasn't until Faustino Noriega and Fernando Etcheverry built the Iberia Hotel in 1893 that Bakersfield's first Basque pioneers put down roots.

The Basques who came to Bakersfield found an already established French colony. Perhaps that strong French presence in the area explains why most of the initial Basques settlers were from the French side of the border. Many of them moved to the San Joaquin Valley from Los Angeles and Orange County in search of cheaper land prices. A few moved to the nearby Tehachapi Mountains. Other early Basque communities sprouted up in nearby McKittrick and Rosedale.

Businessman Faustino Noriega and his wife Louise (Inda) Noriega, two of the first Basque settlers in Bakersfield, lived in this mansion built in 1900. The house at the corner of Baker and Oregon Streets has been renovated and serves as a historic location for receptions.

Despite its transformation into a "big city" with an urban/suburban population of 350,000, Bakersfield can still be called a farm town. Its hot summer weather and mild winters are conducive to agriculture, and a significant portion of the economy still relies on crops and livestock. Many Basques here today are employed in such businesses. Perhaps that is why Bakersfield has maintained the most cohesive Basque colony in California. Almost every large sheep ranch here is owned by Basques. Kern County ranks second in the United States, and first in California, in the number of sheep it raises. Approximately 150,000 sheep are raised in the county, and 95 percent of them are owned by Basques, according to Paco Iturriria, past president of the Kern County Wool Growers Association. But the peak days for the industry are over in this country, and that change is reflected in the local sheep business. The biggest sheepmen, the Mendiburus, once ran up to 40,000 head in several states. Today the big outfits—the Iturriria brothers' I and M Sheep Company, the El Tejon Cattle and Sheep Company, and the Diamond Sheep Company, all Basque-owned—run only 10,000 to 12,000 sheep each. Local grazing land has become scarcer, pushing many sheep owners to buy land in nearby Nevada.

THE SHEEPMEN'S PICNIC

As in Fresno, the local Wool Growers Association began holding picnics in Bakersfield during the 1930s. Yet while that tradition fell by the wayside elsewhere, the Sheepmen's Picnic, as it is known, has continued in Bakersfield and become as much of a tradition as the Basque club picnic. The Sheepmen's Picnic was first held on St. John's Feast Day—June 24—and continues to be held around that date, on the last Sunday in June at the Kern County Basque Clubhouse. A popular event, the picnic attracted up to two thousand people as far back as the 1950s. But the large crowds became too rowdy, according to Iturriria. Organizers worked to limit attendance to sheepmen and their families, cutting back on publicity, and now the picnic crowd, which is predominantly Basque, averages between eight hundred and nine hundred people. The agenda is much the same as that of the Basque Club picnic that takes place a month earlier.

BOARDINGHOUSES

The Basque neighborhood near the railroad has had several hotels over the years. The oldest one of them is Noriega's and Etcheverry's Iberia Hotel, later renamed Noriega's (see listing under Restaurants). "The herders came in from New York, and the first place they came was here," recounted Gracianne Elizalde, who worked at the hotel for many years. "Their boss would pick them up here. This was the center point."

Several accounts name Etcheverry as the owner of a Pyrenees Hotel in 1894, but it's not clear whether this was a different building, or if Etcheverry simply renamed the place Iberia. The Hotel d'Europe, run in its beginning days by Jean and Jeanne Burubeltz, and the Metropole Hotel were also among the earliest, but these have since disappeared. St. Joseph's Church was just down the street, and many of the early families worshipped there. Great photos of the original

Noriega's, formerly the Iberia, built in 1873, is the oldest Basque hotel still in operation in the West. (Courtesy of Linda Elizalde.)

neighborhood hang on walls at the Wool Growers Restaurant (see Restaurants section).

Noriega's, the oldest Basque boardinghouse in the West still in operation, has appropriately held onto the traditional ways. Everyone sits down at the same time for lunch or dinner. "It's just like at home," said restaurant owner Janice Elizalde. "Dinner is at one time. That's the way it is here." That custom hasn't hindered business at all. In fact, it makes Noriega's stand out as a quaint anachronism. Reservations are a must, although a few free seats might be available on weekdays. Noriega's continues to house and feed men from the Basque Country, but these days they fill very few of the fifteen rooms upstairs. (See listing under Restaurants section.)

A couple associated with Noriega's in the years before Grace Elizalde and her husband took over was Francisco and Anselma "Chaparrita" Amestoy, who ran the hotel for eleven years before they left in 1928 to open their own hotel a block away, on East Twenty-first Street. Francisco Amestoy had arrived in California after having spent some time in the Philippines working in the sugar plantations. After they left Noriegas, the Amestoys ran the Amestoy Hotel until 1942, when their two sons-in-law took it over for a short time. In 1944 their son Frank Amestoy assumed the management. He finally sold the Amestoy in 1948 (today it's home to a club and restaurant, Narducci's) and moved out of the neighborhood to open **Frank Amestoy's Bar** (2303 River Boulevard), a popular eating and drinking establishment that is still open today. "We have some soups that are Basque, but we haven't gone the Basque way," said Frank's wife, Marie Amestoy. Frank Amestoy III is also involved in the operation.

Although it's not clear whether it was built at the same time as the hotel, a wooden handball court stood for many years in back of Noriega's. Apparently a fire in 1928 damaged the court, and a new one was built. A new addition was added to the western side of the hotel in 1940, and this newer section, which contains the bar and the dining area, is where most of the restaurant's activity takes place today.

Gracianne Elizalde, who ran the hotel practically single-handed for more than forty years, is closely linked with Noriega's history. She and her husband Jean took over its management in 1931, and Gracianne, or "Grace" as she liked to be called, was not daunted by the job of running the place when Jean died a short time later, although she had four children to raise. For years she played the role of substitute mother to dozens of herders who passed through the hotel, fretting over them and helping them with business matters as well. When Grace died in 1974, two sons, Louis and Albert, took over. When Louis died in 1977, behind the bar of the hotel where he lived his whole life, his non-Basque wife, Janice, decided to continue the tradition with the help of two of her daughters.

The Pyrenees Café on the corner of Sumner and Kern was once a boardinghouse just like the others (see Restaurants section). Jenny (Iribarne) Duns and Inocencio Juarena set up a room-and-board business there in 1935 and named the place the Pyrenees. "It used to be a house of ill repute, before it was a boardinghouse," said current restaurant owner Alvin Cerri, adding that liquor used to be made in the basement. Cerri estimates that the building dates back to the turn of the century, based on the age of the original bar inside. The beautiful long mahogany bar engraved with a drawing of a sheepherder in camp was probably built in the 1890s and brought from Europe by ship. A destructive earthquake in 1952 brought down many of the city's old brick buildings and damaged the building, forcing significant repairs. Cerri, who married Jenny Duns's daughter Catherine, has been associated with the business since 1949. "In the old days, the people didn't just come in. . . . You had to ask to eat here," he remembered. A pink neon *ALO, NOLA ZIRA* sign (Hello, how are you?) greets customers at the restaurant he runs today with daughter Susan Buck.

An interesting detail of life was that alcohol continued to be served in many of the Basque boardinghouses during Prohibition. Hotel keepers viewed serving alcohol as part of their contract with their boarders. Many of the hotel keepers during that era made their own wine and a type of whisky in their cellars and continued to discreetly serve it to their boarders.

In her book, on the subject of California's boardinghouses, Jeronima Echeverria describes how the owners of the Noriega Hotel in Bakersfield hid whisky in a teapot on the stove, where boarders and friends knew they could go in and help themselves and leave a fifty-cent donation. Boarders could even take swigs from bottles left in upstairs bathrooms. And everyone knows the story of how "Chaparrita" Amestoy even kept a flask in her bra. Stories like this were repeated in virtually every town with Basque boardinghouses.

A lively "Basque town" atmosphere prevailed in Bakersfield during the 1930s, 1940s, and 1950s, and Frank Maitia was one of its biggest promoters. The native of Donibane-Garazi herded sheep for twelve years before he came to Bakersfield, where he worked as manager of the Amestoy for three years and married one of the Amestoy's daughters, Louise. In 1945 he bought an old French hotel across from the Amestoy on East Twenty-first Street, renaming it the Basque Café. Located a block away from Noriega's and the Pyrenees, the Basque Café was the popular spot for sheepherders seeking entertainment. The crowd would cajole bartender Maitia into playing the accordion, while his wife and her sister Josephine would show off their wonderful dancing to get the crowd going. "You used to think it was a little Basque Country," remembered Maite Curutchague. "They used to shut the street down," said Janice Elizalde of Noriega's. In a throwback to those early dances, Noriega's has sponsored Basque dances occasionally on Saturday nights.

The historic Santa Fe Depot on Baker Street is still in use, although the only trains that rumble through now are freight trains. (Amtrak's passenger service stops at a depot built later at Fifteenth and F Streets.) A small park has been built across from the depot, near Noriega's and

The Basque hotels were usually located a short walk from the railroad station, which was typically the Basques' first view of the West after their cross-country trip. The Bakersfield depot is virtually unchanged.

the Pyrenees, where local transients hang out and food giveaways are sponsored. As a result, the area is not that safe, particularly at night. But there is ample parking nearby. If you park on the street, be sure not to leave valuables visible in your car.

BAKERY

Nearby, at 717 East Twenty-first Street, Pierre and Juanita Laxague opened the Parisian Bakery at Eighteenth and Kern, which they purchased from another Basque, Pete Borda, in 1945. Two years later they bought the Kern City French Bakery and eventually changed its name to the **Pyrenees French Bakery.** Today the family is still carrying on the sourdough-bread tradition in Bakersfield.

Pierre Laxague arrived from Aldudes when he was seventeen. "He came to herd sheep," Marianne Laxague said of her father, who died in 1993. "He didn't know what he was going to do after that." But relatives in La Puente got him a job at the French-American Bakery, where he learned the baking trade. Then he spent some years working under the supervision of his uncle Jean Baptiste Garacochea, founder of the Pioneer Bakery in Venice, California. In 1945 the Laxagues decided to move to Bakersfield, and soon they opened their own bakery. In addition to being good at the baking business, Pierre Laxague "was very sharp when it came to machinery," said Marianne, noting that it was her father who kept all the equipment in working order. Other Basque bakers, including François Pedeflous, founder of Fresno's successful Basque French Bakery, apprenticed with Laxague.

Today the Laxagues' bakery is still at the same location, but not in the same building. In 1961 the 1910 building that the Laxagues had first bought was moved to become part of a permanent display at the Pioneer Village of the Kern County Museum (more about this shortly).

When the Laxagues took over the bakery, they were using 200 to 300 pounds of flour a day. Today the business is using up to 7,000 pounds a day. The bread is delivered to almost all the local supermarkets, including Safeway, and all the Basque restaurants in the area, as well as other restaurants, serve it to their customers. Many walk-in customers still stop by the bakery shop—open every day—because "they still want it the old way," said Marianne. The old-timers prefer the crunchy crust, so they don't buy the bread packaged in plastic bags and sold in the supermarkets, she explained, because that bread takes on a sponginess they don't care for.

Marianne Laxague helped out in her parents' business all her life and ran the bakery for several years with her mother. "I'll continue as long as I can, but I'll probably sell it," said Marianne. "It takes a lot of time and hard work. You really have to be born into it. The way my folks ran the bakery—that was their life."

Pyrenees French Bakery, 717 East Twenty-first Street, Bakersfield, CA 93305 (661) 322-7159; *www.pyreneesbakery.com*

Kern County Museum

The popular historic town display at the **Kern County Museum** includes a railroad jail, a 1882 one-room schoolhouse, a log cabin, and a wooden oil derrick. The buildings are decorated with machinery and furnishings of the late 1800s. A sign on the old Pyrenees Bakery building gives the history of the business, which was first started in 1887.

Museum officials say they would love to set up the building as an old-fashioned bakery, but their plans are likely to remain on the drawing board for quite a while, because of the difficulty in acquiring old equipment.

Kern County Museum, 3801 Chester Avenue, Bakersfield, CA 93301 (661) 861-2132; *www.kcmuseum.org*

CEMETERY

The **Union Cemetery,** at King Street and Potomac Avenue, is the final resting ground for the most humble and the most prominent of this Basque colony.

RESTAURANTS

Almost all the owners of the existing Basque restaurants in and around Bakersfield have spent twenty years or more serving Basque food to the public, although many of them have moved their businesses to new locations or changed names.

Noriega's is the city's oldest existing Basque restaurant, and probably the oldest in California. The historic building, with its well-used original handball court, opened in 1893 as the Iberia Hotel, down the street from the Santa Fe Railroad Depot. "Any place you go, you find the railroad tracks and you'll find the Basque restaurants," said Mayie Maitia, owner of the Wool Growers Restaurant down the street. That's true in Bakersfield. Other hotels and restaurants have opened and closed since then, but Noriega's has remained. Its continued presence acts as an anchor for the Basque community, giving it a sense of history and permanence, even though many of the newer restaurants have moved away from the old depot area.

The **Pyrenees Café,** less than half a block away from Noriega's, was first owned by Basques in 1935 and has passed down through the hands of the same family through the years.

The **Wool Growers Restaurant** has existed since 1954, but the Maitias moved to a building a couple of blocks away in 1976 when they outgrew their former location. The adherence to a set, one-time-only family-style serving policy at Noriega's and the Pyrenees (the latter

A crowd rushes to the door to make the 7 P.M. dinner call at Noriega's. The hotel section on the left is the front of the original building; the bar and handball court (out of view to the right) were added later.

changed its procedure several years ago) is what prompted Jean Baptiste and Mayie Maitia to open the Wool Growers Restaurant in 1954. The two had worked at the Pyrenees and Noriega's for several years. "If you weren't there at 6:30, we would send you away," remembers Mayie Maitia. After they opened their restaurant down the street with a more flexible schedule, the two older restaurants would send latecomers to them. Sheepherders no longer arrived by train. But Americans already knew the neighborhood as

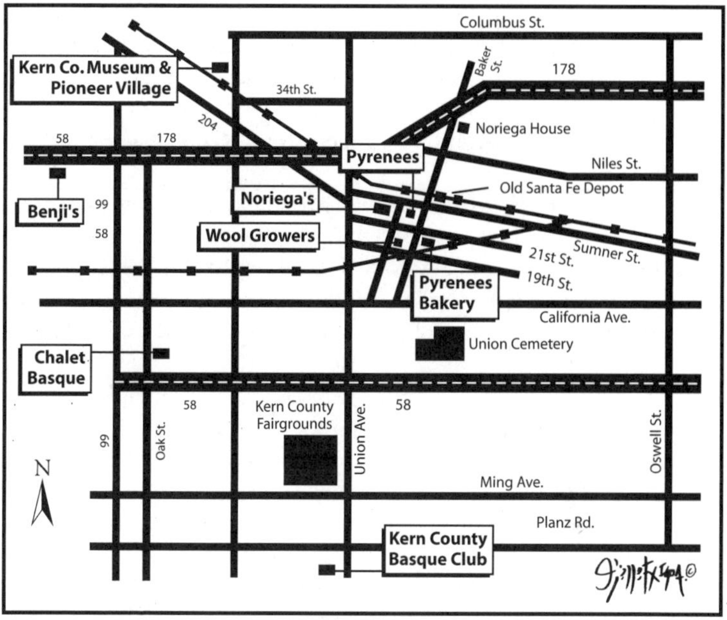

Bakersfield.

the place for Basque food, so the Maitias decided it was a good location. "We never advertised or anything," said Mayie. In fact, the business's popularity prompted them to buy a bigger restaurant just a short walk away. Although Jean Baptiste died several years ago, the Wool Growers is still going strong, and Mayie's son and daughter help her run the place.

The **Chalet Basque,** which opened in nearby Wasco in 1969, moved to its Oak Street site in Bakersfield two years later. Longtime owners Maite and J. B. Curutchague finally sold the place to new Asian owners who have kept all the Basque traditions.

Maitia's Basque Café, which recently relocated to Coffee Road from Union Avenue, was the offspring of the Basque Café, which Frank Maitia Sr. owned from 1945 to 1978. Later under the name Maitia's, the restaurant, created by Frank Senior and Frank Junior, was located at 3535 Union Avenue—one of the city's largest commercial buildings when it was built in 1979 and probably then ranked as the largest Basque restaurant in California. Unfortunately there was not enough business to fill the huge place, and it closed in 1997. The Maitias opened a new, smaller restaurant on the outskirts of town and took up their former name, Maitia's Basque Café, in 1997.

For many years, the elegant Chateau Basque on Union Avenue, was run by Yvonne Etcheveste and daughter Jacki. Etcheveste started in the restaurant business with her former husband, Raymond, leasing the Basque Café from Maitia for eleven years. In 1973 the Etchevestes took over a large nightclub and turned it into the successful Chateau Basque.

Although most of the Basque restaurants accommodate groups, the Chateau had a monopoly on most of the banquet business in town, catering business lunches or office parties throughout the year. It finally closed in 2000 after twenty-seven years in operation.

Benji's, only open since 1986, is a relative newcomer on the scene. But chef and owner Bernard Arduain was the chef at the Wool Growers Restaurant for fourteen years before he built a beautiful new restaurant just west of the Kern River, which he runs with his brother Rene. Despite its location apart from the rest of the restaurants, its popularity has grown steadily.

A good reputation, built over many years, appears to be the key to the Bakersfield restaurants' survival. Other restaurants that opened later, such as J and J's, opened by former Chateau Basque chef Joe Garde and Joe Coscarart in 1992, and Dominique's, operated for several years by Dominique Daramy near Highway 5, did not have staying power.

The Wool Growers Restaurant started a long-standing Memorial Day tradition of hosting a hearty Basque breakfast of home-cured ham, blood sausage, chorizo, and eggs. For those making the long drive home the day after the annual picnic, the Basque breakfast became de rigueur. For those who stuck around there was live music and dancing in the afternoon. Benji, who cooked up the breakfast for years at the Wool Growers, capitalized on its popularity. He now hosts a breakfast and dance at his own restaurant, Benji's. Sometimes Noriega's joins in the tradition. Mayie Maitia at the Wool Growers doesn't mind the competition, because the breakfast crowd had become too much to handle. "We were serving seven hundred to eight hundred people that day, starting at eight o'clock in the morning until two in the afternoon."

Benji's, 4001 Rosedale Highway (at Gibson), Bakersfield, CA 93308 (661) 328-0400
Chalet Basque, 200 Oak Street (near Stockdale Highway), Bakersfield, CA 93304 (661) 327-2915
Maitia's Basque Café, 4420 Coffee Road, Bakersfield, CA 93305 (661) 587-9055
Noriega's, 525 Sumner Street (near Kern), Bakersfield, CA 93305 (661) 322-8419
Pyrenees Café, 601 Sumner Street (at Kern), Bakersfield, CA 93305 (661) 323-0053
Wool Growers Restaurant, 620 East Nineteenth Street (at Baker), Bakersfield, CA 93305 (661) 327-9584; *www.woolgrowers.net*

A "Virtual" Mural

A longstanding mural at the Chateau Basque, *Gure Sor Lekuaren Orhoitzapenetan* (*In Remembrance of Our Homeland*) has gone into virtual existence. Since the restaurant's closure in 2000, the painting's fate remains unknown. However, the artist, Pierre Igoa, also a computer whiz, has put the six by twenty-six foot painting on the Internet for all to enjoy. Commissioned by former restaurant owner Yvonne Etcheveste, the painting presents a vibrant overview of the Basques, their activities, and their traditions. An enlarged globelike view of the Basque provinces dominates the middle of the mural, which melts into vignettes of Basque life. In one section the map turns topographical, and Etcheveste's village of Esnazu (in the valley of Aldudes) rises up to reveal its fields and houses, including the house "Lesaka" where she was born. One side is dominated by pictures of typical daily occupations: a fisherman carrying his day's catch, a man raking together a haystack, folks stuffing sausages, making cheese by hand, and sewing the rope soles of espadrilles. Cows are herded through the center of Donibane Garazi. Religious references are everywhere, such as the Biblical citation of Matthew 4:19 of Jesus calling to the fishermen, and two young girls taking communion.

Basque recreation is highlighted on the opposite side, with hunters catching pigeons in a net, dancers in brilliant costumes executing the dead-soldier's dance and the wineglass dance, men playing tug-of-war, and a musician playing with his drum or *ttun-ttun*. Bulls run through the streets of Pamplona, a group of men play *mus* amid bottles of liquor, and a weight-lifter shows off in front of a crowd in a Basque village. A sense of play permeates the painting. In the portrayal of the traditional Old Country marriage of Etcheveste's parents, Etienne and Jeanne Arretche, artist Igoa has posed them for the wedding photo in front of a village hotel. They are surrounded by contemporary guests, like daughter Etcheveste and granddaughter Jacqueline, and longtime Bakersfield baker Pierre Laxague and his wife Juanita. Igoa has also made fun, mysterious cameo references to himself in the painting. See it on the Internet by visiting Igoa's Web site, *www.pierrefx.com*, and clicking on the mural icon.

Vegetable Soup, Yvonne Etcheveste, Former Owner of the Chateau Basque

6 quarts of water
1 beef bone
Half a 6-ounce can of tomato paste
15-ounce can of whole tomatoes
1 head of cabbage
3 leeks
6 carrots
3–4 stalks of celery
2 potatoes
Salt, pepper to taste
A pinch of cayenne
1 tablespoon chopped parsley
2–3 cloves of garlic, chopped
1 tablespoon dried thyme

Place the water and the bone in a large pot and bring to a boil. Meanwhile peel and dice the vegetables. When the water boils, skim the foam off the top. Stir in the paste until it dissolves. Partially mash the tomatoes with a fork, then add them to the pot, along with the other vegetables and spices. Cover and simmer over a low heat until the vegetables are cooked.

BASQUE CLUB

The local Basque organization, the **Kern County Basque Club,** boasts the honor of being California's oldest, having been started in 1944. (Although the La Puente Handball Club founders got together in 1939, they did not officially form the association until 1947.) Today the Basque club has a healthy membership of about five hundred. "At the beginning, it was wartime," remembered Frank Maitia, one of the five people who founded the club. The Basques hosted an annual dinner, and frequently they would gather for monthly dances sponsored by the local Swiss club. "Everybody looked forward to the last Saturday of the month," he said. "Pretty soon the Swiss were decreasing, and the Basques were increasing. We thought we could do better, and that's when we decided to take it over," he said, referring to the hall out on Stine Road, purchased by the club in 1948. The monthly

Kern County Basque Club members are rightfully proud of accomplishing their dream—the park, clubhouse, and pelota court they built in Bakersfield.

dances, also attended by many Italians and Swiss, continued at the clubhouse for ten years before someone set it on fire and burned it down in 1958. (The history of the club was reported by Marie Jeanne Iribarren in the Kern County Basque Club 1986 festival handbook.)

Just like San Francisco's, Bakersfield's Basque community was reinvigorated with a stream of new immigrants during the late 1950s and 1960s. Handball playing at Noriega's picked up, and the younger crowd showed interest in keeping up the traditions. With greater participation, the club decided in 1974 to buy the current hall on South Union Avenue, known as Rainbow Gardens, which was built by a local Portuguese social club. That same year the club built a concession stand, a permanent white, red, and green-trimmed booth dubbed "Etchola" (the hut) at the fairgrounds, which since the beginning has served as an important fund-raiser for the club. Revenues from the food and drink sales during the annual fair have funded major improvements and maintenance of the clubhouse.

The Bakersfield club faces a bright future, with many young people involved in its activities and also participating in its leadership. Junior tournaments in *mus,* handball, and *pala* have been organized in recent years, to develop youths' interest in traditional Basque recreational activities.

Club Activities. The Kern County Basque Club celebrates the anniversary of its construction with an annual dinner dance on the first Sunday in November. The club also sponsors an annual Christmas dinner for the *klika,* the dancers, and people who help out at the Kern County Fair. There is an annual membership dinner in February, and a *mus* tournament is usually scheduled in March. Easter Sunday is also a special celebration at the clubhouse, with a visit from the Basque priest and handball games. Handball and *pala* tournaments are sponsored in the spring, although handball players have access to the court to practice all year long. You'll frequently find handball players there on weekends, and on Sundays many of the older members stop by for a game of *mus.* Otherwise the building is only open for special events. It's rented out quite frequently for weddings and other private parties.

During the two-week run of the **Kern County Fair** during the last week of September and the first of October, club members at the "Etchola" serve up lamb stew, beans, chorizo, pickled tongue or hot lamb sandwiches and drinks. (The fairgrounds are located at Ming and South Union Avenues.) The concession stand, open every day of the fair's operation from 11 A.M. through the evening, was the first to offer wine and beer at the fair, and it is a popular stop for local fairgoers.

The organization's by-laws feature a rule that differentiates the Kern County Basque Club from most other clubs. Non-Basques are allowed to be members, although they cannot vote or serve on the board of directors. Non-Basque membership has been growing in recent years, and some members say that the liberal, open-door policy is the reason for the club's continued success. "We all come together to put on the events," said club member Albert Etcheverry, noting that fifty to a hundred of the club's six hundred members are non-Basques. The only other club that has nonexclusive membership, the La Puente Handball Club, is fairly well mixed with Italians, French, and Basques.

Young people's attendance at the summer festival dances and their continued participation in their local folk dance groups buoy the optimism of the immigrant generation. "When you see all those kids in there, doing the *jota*, enjoying the culture . . . it's not dead," said former restaurant owner Maite Curutchague. "They still have enough pride that it will survive—even though the language may not. It's a good thing we still have the Basque picnics and the Basque gatherings, so that we might have a few Basque marriages still," she said. But as for her own adult children, she says, "There's only a slim chance that our kids will marry Basques."

Kern County Basque Club, 2301 South Union Avenue (near Planz Road) Bakersfield, CA; mailing address: P.O. Box 416, Bakersfield, CA 93302. Information: (661) 834-1326 (*Anne Marie Minaberri*); *www.kcbasqueclub.com*

FESTIVAL

The Kern County Basque Club started its own picnic tradition, on the Sunday of Memorial Day weekend, and sponsored the event at different locations, such as the golf course or the fairgrounds. When the members later acquired a few acres around the clubhouse property, they began holding the picnic there, where it continues to be held to this day. One of the club's proud early achievements was building a handball court next to the clubhouse, and the message emblazoned on the high court wall GURE AMENTSA (Our Dream), is testimony to that pride.

The Bakersfield picnic is probably the largest of California's Basque festivals, attracting about three thousand people regularly, sometimes more, sometimes less. Festivities get under way Saturday afternoon with men's and women's semifinal competitions of handball and *pala* (a variation of pelota played with a wooden racket on a handball court), and usually an evening dance, all at the clubhouse. Sunday morning starts with the traditional Mass. The line for the noon barbecue starts early and lasts late. But nobody complains, because the time spent waiting turns into a long social hour. The canopy of mature trees, planted several years ago by the club throughout the huge picnic area, provides refreshing relief from the valley's hot summer sun. Folk dances and the handball and *pala* finals follow lunch, all at the club. On Sunday night the young and old come together for a popular dance with Jean Flesher's band or the latest Basque rock group from Boise, Idaho. The Bakersfield festival has become more popular with each passing year, and visitors from San Francisco and Los Angeles regularly make the trip.

DANCE

The dance group, Dantzari Gazteak (Young Dancers), is strong, with twenty to thirty teenagers in the high school–age section and many more in the younger one. During 1991 and 1992 a former professional dancer from the Basque Country, Juan Montes, gave the club some direction, teaching the youngsters many new dances. "He was a beautiful dancer," said Kristie Onaindia who heads the older group and has been dancing since she was five. Many of the teens attend the NABO Basque summer camp, where they have been introduced to new dances every summer, which they bring back and teach to their groups.

Tehachapi and the Antelope Valley

A mini-colony of Basques existed for many years in the mountain town of Tehachapi, primarily sustained by mining. Miners converged here when gold was discovered in the late 1800s. Later a large lime kiln employed many Basques as wood choppers, and eventually their large numbers prompted the opening of at least seven Basque hotels: the Piute; the Cesmat; the Basses Pyrenees (later the Martinto) which had a handball court; the Bazko Hotel (later the Franco-American); the Hotel Capdeville; the Commercial Saloon and Hotel; and the Tehachapi Hotel. At the Martinto, Jean Pierre Martinto built his handball court of stone and cement, and lively competitions were held here during the early 1900s. Paquette's book *Basques to Bakersfield* is full of photos of the Tehachapi hotels. Most of the Basques here eventually left to find better jobs in Bakersfield or other nearby farm towns. Unfortunately the few hotels that survived the big Tehachapi earthquake of 1952 were eventually torn down to make way for other developments.

Mendiburu Canyon, at the southern end of Tehachapi, is probably named for one of Kern County's biggest sheepmen in the early days, Gregorio Mendiburu, who used to graze his sheep in the Tehachapi area.

The oldest home in Tehachapi, preserved by the Tehachapi Heritage League, belonged to a Basque family for many years. The Errea House is not a famous structure of architecture, but the historical group wanted to keep it from being torn down because of its status as the oldest house, said league member Mary Farrell. In fact, it looks like an elongated boxcar, she said. Martin Errea, who worked in the nearby quarry, bought the house around 1910 and lived there with his family for many years, occasionally taking in a boarder to make ends meet. He also worked in the local-lime kiln. Another Basque family, the Solas, had a barber shop in town. The Errea house is located across from the Tehachapi Museum at 311 South Green Street. It was built in the early 1870s in the nearby town of Williamsburg and moved on log rollers to its current location after the former town disappeared. It was designated a national historic place in 1997, and the league restored it and decorated it with historic photos of the Errea family. It serves as the league's headquarters.

Although the Antelope Valley, just south of the Tehachapi Mountains, may once have been home to many a Basque sheep band, few if any Basques live in the remote area today. Most of the business for a longtime Basque restaurant here was from local residents, including many from nearby Edwards Air Force Base. But a housing boom is overtaking the valley, as the town becomes one of the most popular choices among Angelenos looking to get out of their crowded city.

Henriette Ansolabehere ran a Basque restaurant for about twenty years in the town of Rosamond. She started the Villa Basque in 1975 with her late husband Jean, who sold his sheep ranch to get into the restaurant business. After he passed away, "I was just about ready to sell it," said Ansolabehere, but her children persuaded her not to. Finally, though, after a few more years they did.

Nearby is the Biscaichipy Ranch, where the Los Angeles family raises barley and alfalfa.

Bishop

Bishop is located in the Owens Valley, and sheepherders from Bakersfield regularly passed through town during their annual migration with the sheep. The lush valley, with its creeks and river, was a good source of fresh water.

SHEEPHERDER BREAD

Typically bread was baked by the camp tenders in stone ovens and then delivered fresh to the sheepherders. Some of the Basque camp tenders brought the bread to town, and a Viennese storekeeper named Schock agreed to sell it for them, according to Erick Schat. "He saw the quality of the product." That was in 1907, when Owens Valley was still an agricultural region. Despite its Dutch ownership, the extremely popular ERICK SCHAT'S BAKKERY in this town earned its fame from a bread recipe originally provided by Basque sheepherders. Although the ownership and the name of the bakery has changed over the years, the same recipe has been handed down and produced commercially on a continuous basis since then. The Schat family bought the bakery in 1962, and Schat said he learned to make the bread from bakers who had been taught by the Basques.

The bakery copyrighted the recipe and the Original Sheepherder Bread® name in 1938. "We're very flattered by the imitations," said Schat, "but they're not as good." The bread is still baked in stone ovens, which are in view of the customers. The round loaves are placed on the hot stone, and they pop open during baking. The bakery mills its own flour from wheat imported from Montana. The bakery's stone ovens are imported from Europe. Schat claims that all those factors, as well as the fresh local water used in baking, are what give the bread its unique flavor and appearance. "It's only available in Bishop," said Schat, explaining that the bread is not sold wholesale. He said his bakery is the largest retail bakery in the United States.

Busloads of tourists, particularly Europeans, stop at the bakery, and you're likely to find a crowd here any time of day. The bakery serves espresso, freshly squeezed orange juice, and innumerable wonderful pastries, but practically everyone goes away with a loaf of the sheepherder bread. “It’s our number one item,” said Schat. “It outsells everything we make.”

Erick Schat’s Bakkery, 763 North Main Street, Bishop, CA 93514 (760) 873-7156

The Owens Valley Today

The valley has changed drastically since sheepherder bread was first introduced there. After much of the valley’s water began being piped to Los Angeles, the farms began disappearing. Today the valley primarily serves as the doorway to skiing, fishing, and hiking areas. Tourism has become the primary business that feeds this town of about ten thousand, and the sheepherder bread has added to its fame.

A few of the old stone ovens that the Basques once used to bake their own bread can still be found in the Owens Valley. At least one is in plain view at the southernmost end of the valley, near Olancha. (For its location, see the section on Death Valley.)

Basque sheepherders provided the recipe for the trademark Sheepherder Bread that has made this Bishop bakery so popular.

Death Valley

Pete Aguereberry and His Gold Mine

One Basque gold miner reached such prominence in California's Death Valley region that a scenic point revealing the grand beauty of the desert was named after him. Yet few Basques know the story of Jean Pierre "Pete" Aguereberry, who came to this country from Maule, Zuberoa, in 1890 at the age of sixteen. After trying his hand at several different jobs, including sheepherding, he followed the gold mining boom to Death Valley in Southern California. After he nearly died trying to cross the desert by burro in 1905, he settled in the nearby Panamint Mountains. He prospected and staked numerous claims in the Emigrant Canyon area, which he mined for thirty-five years. The Eureka mine that belonged to Aguereberry, and the cabin he lived in, are now part of Death Valley National Park, and they provide a wonderful sense of the rugged life of the early California prospectors.

Death Valley has some magnificent vistas, but, according to park ranger Kari Coughlin, the one from Aguereberry Point "is the most

Gold miner Pete Aguerreberry's cabin is still standing, tucked into a hillside, at Death Valley National Park.

beautiful viewpoint in the valley." Coughlin, who works in the park's interpretation department and sometimes offers special walking tours, has taken a keen interest in Pete Aguereberry because "he was unusual as a Death Valley prospector." People typically associate prospectors with drinking and gambling, she said, but "Pete was completely different from that." He didn't squander his money on alcohol. Instead he lived a rather simple life there in the mountains. And whereas most prospectors sold their claims to mining companies, Aguereberry chose to work his mine. Work it he did, steadily, for the rest of his life. Coughlin attributes his dedication to his Basque heritage and its hard work ethic. She noted that mining required a whole range of skills such as blacksmithing, timbering, carpentry work, and dynamiting. Once he had dynamited the ore out of the hill, Aguereberry had to take it somewhere for processing. But in 1913 the Cashier Mining Company, which had been working some veins on the other side of the hill, abandoned the site, and Aguereberry took over its stamp mill and brought in a partner to work it.

Miner's Camp

The original cabin Aguereberry, built in 1907, is still standing, looking much as it did when he left it, although an old gas stove and refrigerator have been added. He added two other cabins later. Aguereberry lived in the small two-room building until he died in 1945. Author George Pipkin, who wrote a book about the miner's life, *Pete Aguereberry: Death Valley Prospector and Gold Miner,* spent much time there with him, listening to his stories. Coughlin said that if it weren't for Pipkin, little would be known about a man who was a major figure in Death Valley's mining history.

Aguereberry was very neat and apparently very conscientious about water. He had no natural water supply, so he had to truck it in. A gutter system is still visible at the cabins, and it apparently served to catch rain water and divert it into a small tank. The middle cabin was built in 1941 as a guest house. And a third cabin, on the left, was built around 1946. Coughlin said park officials don't know who built the third cabin or who put in the gas stove and refrigerator in Aguereberry's cabin, since they were not there when Aguereberry died in 1945.

If you enter the park by way of Highway 190, take Emigrant Canyon Road heading south to Aguereberry Point. But first you would be well advised to continue 10 miles north on 190 to the town of Stovepipe Wells, where a ranger station, gas station, and other services are available. You can pick up information on Aguereberry Point, hot weather hints, and a map of the park there. If approaching from the southeast entrance to the park, you'll find a visitors' center in the town of Furnace Creek. There are hotels in both of these Death Valley towns (and campsites throughout the park). Reservations are advised. (For information, call the Death Valley National Park at the phone number listed at the end of this section.) After stopping at the Stovepipe Wells ranger station, retrace your steps, back to Emigrant Canyon Road, which leads to Aguereberry Point and Wildrose Campground. Roughly 10 miles south on this winding road you'll see the sign for the turnoff to Aguereberry Point. Once you turn onto this dirt road, you will come across Aguereberry's old camp after about 1 mile.

Eureka Mine

The Eureka mine, from which Aguereberry was able to extract gold for most of his whole life, is accessible to the public. Park ranger Kari Coughlin described Pete's mine as "the best example of mining" in the park. The remarkable feature of this mine is that unlike most, which were excavated by dozens of men, Aguereberry dug this one out all by himself.

His mine is located just on the other end of the small hill next to the cabins. A wooden sign, EUREKA MINE, hangs over the entrance, and the rail lines once used to carry out the extracted ore are still there. The mine's tunnels have been stabilized with netting and are safe to enter. In 1992 an endangered bat species was found living in the mine, so during the wintertime, access to most of the mine is closed to the public. But the mine usually reopens in April or May. Take a flashlight—you won't see a thing without one—and visit an honest-to-goodness gold mine. It was a tourist attraction even when Aguereberry was still alive, and according to Pipkin, Aguereberry never tired of guiding people through it. Malvina Oyharçabal, who lived in California many years before returning to the Basque Country, visited the site three times, taking friends, after she first saw the sign for Aguereberry Point and discovered it for herself. "You feel the spirit of the country," she said of her visits. "The first prospectors, the pioneers. You really feel it because it's not developed. It's still authentic."

The gold mine that Pete Aguereberry carved out himself at Death Valley National Park is open to the public.

There are a number of mine shafts all over the hill, as well as the remains of the Cashier stamp mill. Pulley systems were used to enter vertical shafts, such as the one still visible above the old mill. The wooden structure reveals some of the risks miners took to get their gold. Give yourself at least a couple of hours to explore the cabins and the hill.

"The vein of gold that [Aguereberry] found has mostly been worked out," said park naturalist Charles Callagan. The U.S. Bureau of Mines estimated that $175,000 worth of gold was extracted from the mine. "That was over forty years of blood, sweat, and tears," said Coughlin, who suspects that Aguereberry barely broke even by the end. But the miner never gave up on his mine. From everything Aguereberry accomplished during his years at Death Valley, it appears he loved the natural desert beauty that surrounded him. For proof, you only have to drive to the end of the road, which he carved out by himself, to discover Aguereberry Point.

There are no regular guided tours of Aguereberry's camp or mine, but large groups can write and request one. If you'd like to visit Aguereberry's grave, you'll have to drive to the cemetery in the town

Pete Aguerreberry developed the road that leads to this point, which provides the most scenic view of Death Valley.

of Lone Pine, which is northwest of the park, on Highway 395. His epitaph is simple, like his lifestyle, giving just his name and dates of birth and death.

Aguereberry Point

In his book Pipkin said that Aguereberry carved out the 4½-mile road from his camp to the scenic point using a pick, shovel, wheelbarrow, and blasting powder, simply so others could see what he called "the Great View" of Death Valley. This he did long before the desert wonderland became a national park. Although signs indicate that four-wheel-drive vehicles must be used, unless there is snow on the road, it is usually accessible to normal passenger cars. Park ranger Coughlin suggests that cars need to have at least 7 inches of ground clearance, because the road is full of ruts. It's a bumpy ride, traversing the bottom of a gully and then proceeding up to a point where you should park your vehicle. (A portable toilet marks the spot.) The actual point, at an elevation of 6,433 feet, is about 200 yards farther along—an easy walk. You will see, spread out below, the vast desert valley. On a clear day, the lowest and highest points in the continental United States are visible from this point: the valley floor, at 282 feet below sea level, and California's highest mountain, Mt. Whitney, to the northwest at 14,495 feet.

Domingo Etcharren and the Keane Wonder Mine

Aguereberry was not the only Basque prospector in Death Valley, although he appears to be the only one who stayed in mining. Domingo Etcharren, known as "the one-eyed Basque butcher from Ballarat" (all of these descriptions are true), had been prospecting with Irishman Jack Keane for months when they discovered gold in 1904 and established the Keane Wonder Mine. Etcharren and Keane's discovery is significant in Death Valley lore for being the strike that launched the Bull Frog District and many of the valley's mining towns. The partners sold their claim to a mining company, and Etcharren used his money to buy property in nearby Darwin. The mine went on to become one of the two highest-producing gold mines in Death Valley, and a tramway to the mine operated for many years.

The Keane mine is east of Stovepipe Wells, and it's worth visiting. A dirt road takes you out to the old mill, where you can walk around and see the remains of the former tramway. Afterward, consider visiting the former mining town of Darwin, where Etcharren lived for many years.

Tips on Visiting Death Valley

If you plan a visit, don't plan on driving through the desert valley in the summer, when temperatures regularly top 120 degrees. The best months to visit are March, April, and May or October, although it may still be hot. Be sure you bring plenty of water with you. Take a jacket when traveling up to Aguereberry Point, which can be cool because of its high elevation. And be sure to fill your tank whenever you find a gas station, since you don't want to run out of gas in the desert.

If you plan to spend the night, the closest campground to Aguereberry's camp is Wildrose, which is open year-round. Located at an elevation of 5,000 feet, this campground can be very cold, and it is often snowed in during the winter. Remember, however, even at Wildrose, temperatures surpass 100 degrees during the summer, so be prepared when heading into the area. Call the park for additional information on traveling in Death Valley.

Death Valley National Park, Death Valley, CA 92328 (760) 786-3200; *www.nps.gov/deva/*

Darwin

If you leave the Death Valley National Park by way of Highway 190, you will want to take a short side trip to Darwin. Domingo Etcharren is buried in the town's cemetery, and his tombstone proudly bears the name of his hometown, St. Etienne de Baigorry. A picturesque wooden turn-of-the-century barn that he built is still standing behind the house at 211 South Main Street. Etcharren maintained an interest in the Keane Wonder Mine, and over the years he bought a great deal of property in Darwin with his earnings, including a general store. His history was researched by writer Bob Palazzo, who owns a house on Etcharren's former property. Most of Etcharren's buildings, except the barn, burned down in a fire in 1917. The clapboard family home, built after the fire, was later moved to Lone Pine and is still occupied by his descendants. (A nearby valley is also named after him, but today it is part of the inaccessible China Lake Naval Weapons Center.)

Seeing the town of Darwin is like taking a complete step back in time. As you enter the main road into town off Highway 190 you will see rows of empty cabins standing like sentinels on the hill. These were the former quarters of the miners. Old empty houses stand amid lived-in shacks, as well as one nice house or two. Most of the residents of the town are retired old folks who have moved to Darwin to get away from civilization. They care little for the incredible remainders of an old Western lifestyle that dot the landscape, such as the rooms dug out of the hills, where single miners once lived. If you're adventuresome, you'll want to see these dugouts, where old newspapers, a typewriter, and an old stove or two provide clues to an almost unbelievable lifestyle.

To reach the dugouts and the cemetery, turn right off the main paved road at the DMV sign. Take the next dirt road that veers off to the right and follow it to the cemetery. Etcharren's tombstone is not hard to find. Afterward, if you want to see Etcharren's old barn, go back and turn right onto Darwin's main road, and turn right again at the former post office, and you'll be on Main Street. Faded street signs are barely visible on old markers, but they're there if you look for them. Don't count on finding any services in this town. The only store is usually closed, as is the museum. (You can use the only pay phone in town, in front of the current post office, to call one of the numbers on the museum to have them open it. You won't find anything on Etcharren here.) To return to the main highway, take the same road you took to come in.

When you reach Highway 395, stop to take a look at the stone oven built by Basque sheepherders to bake bread. The oven was well used up through the 1960s. It is located close to the road, on the southeast corner of the intersection of highways 395 and 190.

Northern California

Stockton

Located at the head of the Stockton Channel and connected to San Francisco via rail, the city of Stockton has always been well situated. As early as 1870 Stockton was a major center for sheep raising and wool trading. Stockton was once a significant Basque colony and boasted dozens of boardinghouses. In this city a group of Basques made the first known attempt to start a Basque organization in the West in 1907 (although it failed).

BOARDINGHOUSES

The Basque Hotel, which opened in 1907, was the first one built, but others quickly followed. By the 1940s there were eight hotels—many of them with their own handball courts—all well patronized by herders. Though the turnover in ownership was high, there were a few exceptions, such as the Alustiza family, who ran the California Hotel for forty-five years, and the Artozqui family, who ran the Central Hotel for thirty years. (Maria and Santorino "Sam" Garamendi, grandparents of former California Senator John Garamendi, also ran the California Hotel for a few years.) The number of hotels gradually dwindled, and the last Basque hotel in that city closed in 1970. Between 1907 and 1970, a total of nineteen Basque hotels operated in Stockton.

"Stockton was an attraction at one time. The wool buyers would all come to the Stockton port," said John Ospital, recalling that Basque hotels were flourishing when he arrived in Stockton in 1955. There was the Wool Growers, the California, the La Coste, the Central, the Royal, and the Basconia. Ospital's father and uncle, both named John, ran the city's earliest hotel, the Basque Hotel, with its own *kantxa,* before they went back to the Basque Country in 1913. In a fitting ending, John Ospital and his brother Pete operated the last Basque hotel in Stockton.

Stockton was considered something of a wild town in the decades before World War II, so Basques, with their many hotels and handball courts, could be assured of a good time here. Almost every hotel was located on South Hunter or South San Joaquin Streets, near the port and railroad depot. Later this neighborhood became Stockton's Chinatown.

Many Basques in Stockton were from Baigorri and Donibane-Garazi, in Nafarroa Beherea, but there were enough from Bizkaia to be noted by Father Adrian Gachiteguy when he visited the city during the 1950s.

Ospital heard stories of Basques parading down the streets playing accordion music and drinking wine or whisky from their *zahakuas* (wine bags)—in the middle of Prohibition—"and no one ever stopped them!" They came from all over to spend a weekend. Ospital remembers that Basques from as far away as Colorado or Wyoming would show up in Stockton. "It was seasonal,"—the seasons relating, naturally, to the sheep. In the 1960s San Franciscans lost their only *kantxa,* so they would travel out to Stockton every Sunday to play at the Central Hotel, which had the last surviving court. (See the Pelota section in the San Francisco, California, chapter.)

But although additional waves of Basques continued to arrive in other communities after World War II, the Basque population in Stockton decreased. "I saw the tail end of it," said Ospital.

"We don't have a Basque club or any kind of organization here because there are hardly any Basques," said Ospital. Ospital and his brother Pete ran the Wool Grower's Hotel from 1955 to 1970, and toward the end they had only half a dozen boarders. By the time they finally gave up the hotel business, all the other Basque hotels had closed.

But the same year they closed the hotel the Ospital brothers opened Ospital's Villa Basque restaurant. Ironically, the restaurant, which they operated for years, was just one block away from the Ospital Hotel, which their father operated for a while at the corner of Hunter and Hazelton. Located among the city's oldest brick buildings, the restaurant was the only remnant of what was once one of California's most active Basque communities. Unfortunately, in 1994 the Ospitals decided to close Villa Basque. The neighborhood, once the center of this busy port town, had become too run-down, according to Ospital. A serious problem with drug-dealing and loiterers had developed. Business dwindled because people were afraid of the area, and property values were dropping. Yet longtime customers were devastated when the restaurant closed.

Today John Ospital works as a bartender at two other Stockton restaurants, including the El Rancho steakhouse, owned by his cousin, Ray Lacondegui. Your only chance to get Basque food today in Stockton is a few dishes at **El Rancho** (1457 East Mariposa Road).

CHURCH

Early Basque families also lived in this area and worshipped at nearby **St. Mary's** (203 East Washington Street), a historic Catholic church established in 1861.

CEMETERIES

The city's cemeteries, **Stockton Rural Cemetery** and **San Joaquin Cemetery,** both on Cemetery Lane off Harding Way, are landmarks of this town's early history, as well as of its Basque colony.

San Francisco

San Francisco has the oldest surviving Basque community in the American West. The city's port was bustling with activity even before the 1848 gold rush, and it was the most common debarkation point on the West Coast for foreigners arriving by ship. Before gold was discovered, the city had just a few hundred inhabitants, most clustered around Mission Dolores. But in the years following the discovery of gold, the city was booming, and at least one Basque entrepreneur saw the potential for making money from his fellow countrymen who were passing through the city, so he set up a boardinghouse in the neighborhood near the port, which became the North Beach area.

Pedro Altube was one of the very first known Basque pioneers to settle in the American West after the gold rush. Like many of his countrymen in those early years, he had first migrated to Argentina. He lived there with his brothers for five years before he caught the itch to come to California. According to one of his descendants, Carol Hovey, in a story repeated in her family for generations, Altube reportedly sailed north from South America, along with thirty-five Basques, and arrived at the port of San Francisco in 1850. His brother Bernardo arrived with more Basques the following year. The brothers represented the start of the first wave of Basque immigration to Northern California, which grew larger every year.

Scholar Jean Francis Decroos found evidence that Basques were working as gardeners at Mission Dolores as early as 1849. This was a portent of things to come, as gardening became, and still is, the primary occupation of Basque immigrants in the Bay Area. Many of those early Basque residents also worked in San Francisco's busy shipyards or ran laundries. But most left San Francisco for gold mines and later, sheep ranches.

CHURCHES

By the time the Basques started settling in this country, Catholicism was already well established here, so the immigrants were able to maintain their religious traditions. They did not have to create their own churches but could simply attend and participate in the existing Catholic church of their community.

Notre Dame des Victoires, the French Catholic Church in San Francisco, has some of the earliest records of Basques in California. St. Francis Xavier Catholic Church, named for an eminent Basque religious leader, served San Francisco's Basque community during its earliest days, but its books, dating back to 1849, were lost during the fires that consumed the city at the time of the 1906 earthquake, according to Father Etienne Siffert, the resident historian of Notre Dame des Victoires. At Notre Dame, however, the French Marist priests buried the church's registry in the courtyard garden when flames made their way toward the church on Bush Street, according to Siffert. The books were saved, and today they are among the only official records revealing the early presence of Basques in San Francisco. In fact, the first couple to marry at the church, less than three weeks after it was dedicated in 1856, was Basque—Bonaventure Dolheguy and Gracieuse Oyhamburu. Antonio Harispuru and Marie Amestoy, and Bernardo Altube and Marie Recart, were among the prominent Basque couples who were married there during the 1850s.

Notre Dame des Victoires Church, 566 Bush Street, San Francisco, CA 94108 rectory: (415) 397-0113; school: (415) 421-0069; *www.ndvsf.org*

HOTELS AND HOT SPOTS

Yesterday. Juan Miguel Aguirre built the city's first known Basque hotel in 1866 at 1312 Powell Street, just off Broadway. He also built the first handball court in the city on Post Street between Grant and Kearny Streets, which is now the city's Financial District. In those years, Montgomery Street, just one block north of Kearny, marked the water's edge. (Gradually, the city was extended another half-mile into the bay with landfill.) Aguirre was also reportedly the first person to supply water to San Francisco, transporting it by burro from a spring at the Presidio and selling it to businesses and residents downtown. He also helped establish Nuestra Señora de Guadalupe Church on Broadway, which served many of the city's Hegoaldetarrak with services in Spanish, according to Jean Francis Decroos in his book on Basques in San Francisco, *The Long Journey.* (The church is now closed). In San Francisco the old downtown was one of the closest neighborhoods to the port in the city's early days.

As for other hotels, the Yparraguirre family opened the Basque Hotel with a handball court at the corner of Broadway and Powell during the 1880s, and Basques also operated the Hotel de France, the Hotel des Alpes, and the Hotel de Basses Pyrenees before the turn of the century, according to Professor Jeronima Echeverria, an expert on Basque boardinghouses.

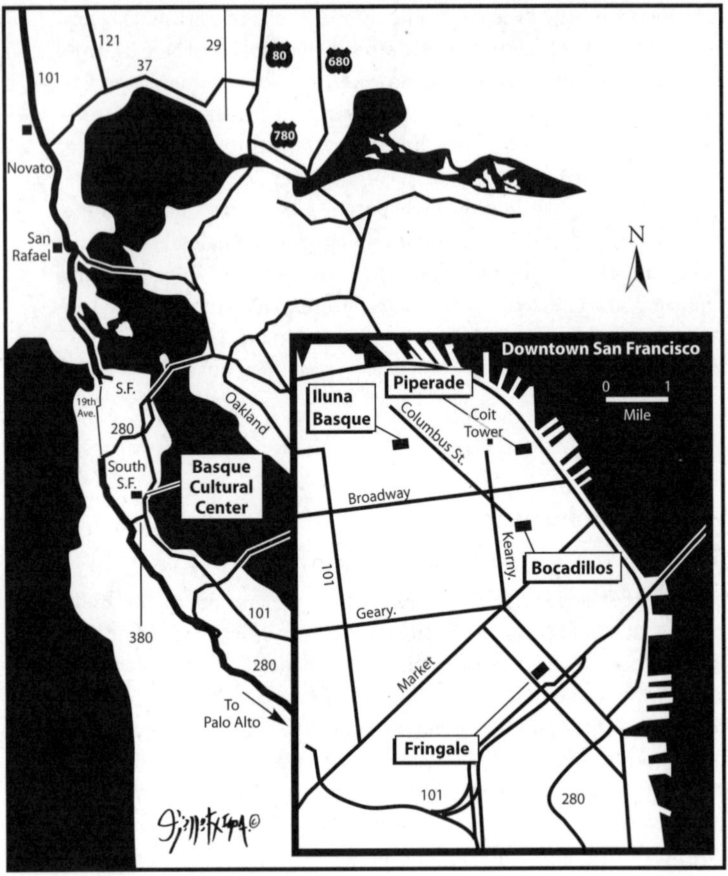

The San Francisco Bay Area.

Little else is known about the city's early Basque boardinghouses because the hotels, as well as the city's records on them, were consumed in the fires that raged after the 1906 earthquake. But it didn't take very long before a new cluster of Basque hotels and a handball court rose out of the ashes, still centered near the city's downtown around the intersection of Broadway and Columbus in the North Beach neighborhood. In the years that followed, San Francisco consistently had five to eight Basque boardinghouses operating at one time. Brothers José, Miguel, and Ramon Lugea built the Hotel de España at 785 Broadway in 1907, and it remained one of the city's most popular Basque hotels for years. Also on Broadway was the Hotel de Pyrenees and the Hotel Español. Stories from the early days of the Hotel Español, when it was operated by Martin and Angelita Abaurrea, were memorialized in 1968 in the book, *A Basque Story Cookbook.* Author Ann Rogers related the story of how the Abaurreas had teacups of wine and homemade whisky already waiting for their boarders at their table setting during Prohibition, while only fruit punch was served at the bar.

On the southeast corner of Powell and Pacific was the Hotel Iriarte. Leonor (Basabe) Taddeucci, who grew up in the hotel, estimated that it probably dated back to sometime around the earthquake. The Lugeas still had the Hotel de España when Taddeucci's father, Juan Basabe, bought the Iriarte in 1919. The 1920s and 1930s were "great years, fun years," said Taddeucci, remembering the dances every Saturday night. Her father remodeled the hotel and had beautiful Basque scenes handpainted on the walls. Juan Basabe, who was called "Gernika" after his hometown, was a big handball fan, so he renamed the hotel the Jai Alai. "The jai alai players would stop there on their way to the Philippines, to Florida, and to Mexico," she said. The Great Depression and the war brought hard times, according to Taddeucci, and the hotel was eventually torn down and replaced by a Chinese apartment building.

The boardinghouses, or *hotelak,* not only were home to single Basque men who worked in San Francisco, but frequently welcomed men and women from some of the outlying farm towns, such as Stockton or Tracy, when they had business in the city. Many of the more long-term boarders had left behind herding sheep or ranching for city jobs, the most common being gardening, but also bakery and janitorial work.

Both Los Angeles's and San Francisco's *hotelak* enjoyed many, many years of good business during the first half of the century. In other Basque communities, boardinghouses dwindled during the World War II era because of a drop in immigration. In San Francisco, however, the cluster of *hotelak* on Broadway remained a point of attraction for Basques from all over the West. In fact, one of the largest waves of migration from the Basque Country arrived after World

War II, and many of these immigrants came to San Francisco and took up rooms in its hotels. Jean Francis Decroos attributed part of this big migration to the city to the "occupational vacuum" in gardening created when Japanese workers were taken away to detention camps, since Japanese had filled most of the gardening jobs in San Francisco before the war.

"All the Basque hotels were lined up on Broadway," said Leon Sorhondo, who grew up in his parents' boardinghouse, the Pyrenees. Broadway was the boundary line between the Italian North Beach neighborhood and Chinatown to the south. The area was later engulfed by the local Chinatown, a phenomenon that was repeated around Basque boardinghouses in many other cities in the West, because so many Chinese came to work on the railroads. Luckily in San Francisco the Broadway neighborhood area has remained throughout the city's history as a thriving, culturally diverse commercial district that attracts city dwellers and tourists alike.

The city's best nightclubs were within walking distance—Bimbo's, which is still on Columbus Avenue, had the best floor show in town. The Bocce Ball had opera singers and flamenco dancers. There were the Jai Alai and Montmartre bars on Broadway. Many foreign languages swirled through the air. The Club Fugazi and the William Tell were popular dance halls, where groups of Basque, French, Spanish, Italian, and South American immigrants flocked to socialize on weekends. Sunday nights brought dances at several of the Basque hotels. Many couples, for example, the author's parents, Jean and Clara Zubiri, as well as Louis and Marie Elu met at these gatherings.

In 1957 the government came in and bought up a section of the block from Broadway to Pacific in order to put up a twelve-story low-income apartment building to accommodate Chinatown's many poor immigrants. The demolition ball the following year leveled the Hotel des Pyrenees, the Hotel Español, El Globo, and the city's prize handball court. It was an unfortunate blow for the Basque community. "If you had to think of any place in San Francisco that was Basque, that was it," said longtime Broadway resident Leon Sorhondo. But no one complained, and the government's offers to buy the properties were considered fair. "We didn't have all these lawsuits back in those days," he said. "The government made an offer, and everybody took it."

On the western end of the block, the Hotel de España at 785 Broadway and the Hotel du Midi around the corner on Pacific, which were connected, were spared the same fate because there was a newly remodeled firehouse next door. "They couldn't very well tear it down after spending so much city money," said Marie Elu, who with husband Louis later bought the two hotels.

But enough hotels remained to keep Basque business in the Broadway neighborhood. The Hotel des Alpes, the Hotel Cosmopolitan, the Hotel de France, and the Obrero were all still operating in full. The Basque Hotel opened in 1960. The same year their Pyrenees hotel was demolished, Amelie and Jean Sorhondo opened another hotel a couple blocks farther down on Broadway. The new Pyrenees Hotel was on the second and third floors of an older hotel building at 517 Broadway. It was among the most authentic boardinghouses to last into the 1990s.

Amelie was well known for taking off her apron at the drop of a hat to help many a young immigrant file for Social Security, find a job, or get medical attention. Like other longtime hotel keepers, the Sorhondos were something of an institution within the Bay Area Basque community. Unlike the hotels that turned their attention to their restaurants, modernizing and expanding them when the business of lodging single Basque immigrants fell off, the Sorhondos never really opened their dining room to the public. But without advertising, their tables were always full on the weekends. The local Basque community provided ample clientele. Old friends, many of them former boarders, now with families of their own, would stop by for a drink and stay to enjoy Amelie's plentiful dinners.

The hotels that remained did a booming business, as young men continued to pour in to the city by the bay. The core of today's San Francisco Basque community is made up of those later arrivals who came between 1948 and 1966. Franxoa Bidaurreta, who came in 1964, remembers the Hotel de France, now closed: "On Sundays, there were over a hundred people eating there, 95 percent of them single men. The bar would never let up. It used to be crazy in there sometimes."

Many of the young men found Basque brides, but inevitably, in this cosmopolitan city, they also married non-Basques. It was common for them to choose European or Latin American partners, with whom they shared the Spanish or French language.

In every Basque community, Sundays were the days when people got together at their favorite hotel for an afternoon of *mus* playing, drinking, dinner, and plain old socializing. Sundays were also for handball games. By the end of an evening filled with lots of red wine, some of the men would inevitably start singing traditional Basque songs. The nostalgia for their beloved Basque Country would come pouring out of their hearts, as they sang with vigor, their arms over each other's shoulders.

Ganix and Aña Iriartborde were another well-known couple in the San Francisco Basque community, because of the nearly twenty years they spent managing the Hotel des Alpes on Broadway. Theirs was a classic story. After buying into the hotel with a cousin in 1958, Ganix went back to the Basque Country in 1962, hoping to find a wife. He met and married Aña and brought her back to the States, and the two set about building up the restaurant and hotel business. The newly arrived Aña was somewhat disconcerted to find herself living among so many Chinese, but her life at the hotel was fairly self-contained. "I was happy because I was among the Basques who had come from the mountains. Everyone was so happy. It was all young people."

The Iriartbordes remained at the hotel until 1974, and they saw the changes in the neighborhood. During the 1960s a two- or three-block section around the prominent intersection of Broadway and Columbus was overtaken by a number of topless clubs and bars. Until recently the windows of the former Pyrenees Hotel overlooked a bright green and red ADAM AND EVE sign. Inside the hotel dining rooms and restaurants an enjoyable family atmosphere prevailed, but it was rather a jarring contrast to walk outside onto the wild scene of yelling barkers and bright neon signs of naked women. This area has never ceased to be one of the most popular among tourists. Today most of the topless clubs are gone, and busy cafés and restaurants are back.

Most of the city's hotels eventually became better known for their restaurants. One of the most popular was Elu's. Louis and Marie Elu had taken over the Hotel de España, with its downstairs restaurant, in 1959. "People thought we were going to serve enchiladas," joked Louis, former chef at the Palace Hotel (now the Sheraton). So the couple renamed the restaurant Elu's, and it became famous for Louis's paella. The highly popular eating spot among Basques and non-Basques alike was written up in the *New York Times* and touted by the

Lapin Chasseur, Ganix Iriartborde, former chef and manager of Des Alpes Restaurant and Hotel, San Francisco

1 rabbit, whole
3 tablespoons cooking oil
2 green peppers, chopped
1 chicken bouillon cube, optional, for taste
3–4 shallots, chopped
½ pound mushrooms, chopped
2–3 cloves garlic, chopped
Salt and pepper to taste
2 cups white wine

Preheat oven to 375 degrees. Cut the rabbit into pieces. Heat oil in frying pan. Sauté the rabbit until it browns, about 10–15 minutes. Add the peppers, shallots, mushrooms, garlic, salt and pepper. Continue frying for another 10 minutes. Then pour off the oil, place rabbit and vegetables in a baking pan. Pour 2 cups wine into frying pan. (Dissolve bouillon cube.) Heat liquid until it boils, then light the wine with a match. Let the flame die down, then pour wine over rabbit. Place the pan in the oven for just 5–10 min. Serves 4.

Michelin guides. Nevertheless, the hotel rooms were reserved for Basques, who filled them to overflowing. "They used to come just to get away from the intense heat in the valley," remembered Louis.

By 1983 the Elus decided to retire from the restaurant business. They could find no Basque buyers, so they leased their restaurant, the Hotel de España and Hotel Du Midi, to Chinese operators.

The End of the Boardinghouse Era. During the 1970s the souvenir shops and restaurants of Chinatown spilled over onto Broadway and beyond, with the few remaining Basque restaurants interspersed among them. Basque migration out of the city and the lack of immigration from the Basque Country forced most of the hotels in the heart of the city to close down.

The construction of the Basque Cultural Center in South San Francisco in 1982 and the resulting shift of focus away from downtown put the final nail in the neighborhood's coffin. Ironically, hotel owners had been among the biggest supporters of the construction of the center. Louis Elu was one. He spent part of almost every day helping out at the center during its construction, and he was on the first board of directors.

One of the more well-known establishments to close was the Obrero Hotel and Restaurant at 1208 Stockton Street, run for many years by the Yriartes, the Goyhenetches, the Mendiscos, and, finally, Bambi McDonald, an Irish-American. McDonald, who took over in 1978, was an anomaly in keeping the Basque menu that gave the restaurant its reputation. But she was not able to keep the Basque clientele, who had created much of the ambiance in the old days. "The Basques are very clannish, and they prefer to go where Basques are in charge," said McDonald just before she closed in 1993. She had been able to hang on for a while by catering to Americans looking for a unique ethnic dining experience. She also found a niche as a reasonably priced bed-and-breakfast hotel in the middle of one of San Francisco's top tourist attractions—Chinatown. But none of that was sufficient, so McDonald finally sold the hotel to people who were not interested in keeping up the Basque theme.

Today. The Basque presence on Broadway in San Francisco—once the heart of the this community—has finally ended. The Hotel des Alpes and the Basque Hotel and Restaurant, with their respective restaurants, were the last to carry on the cultural traditions in the neighborhood. The Pyrenees Hotel (517 Broadway) continued renting rooms to a few elderly longtime residents for years, but Amelie Sorhondo finally sold the business in 2000.

The Des Alpes Hotel on Broadway was probably the longest-standing Basque hotel, but the last Basque owners finally closed the business. During the early 1990s, Basilio Arraiz and Agustín Oroz, cousins from the Nafarroan town of Erro, managed it. Arraiz claimed it was a Basque hotel since 1908. According to Jeronima Echeverria's *Home Away from Home: A History of Basque Boardinghouses,* by 1907 Ambrosio Yriondo was operating a Basque hotel at 734 Broadway. The address of the Hotel des Alpes was 732 Broadway. It is possible that they are one and the same.

Single-Basque immigrants stopped coming to San Francisco in the 1960s, and eventually the Broadway hotels rented rooms to Americans. They operated essentially as residential hotels and had no problem finding tenants, considering the tough housing situation in

The Hotel des Alpes was the oldest surviving Basque hotel and restaurant in San Francisco, having been built soon after the 1906 earthquake that destroyed most of the buildings in this city. (Courtesy of Aña Iriartborde.)

this city. "If we had sixty rooms, we would rent sixty rooms," said Arraiz while he owned Des Alpes.

In addition to Hotel des Alpes, on a tiny street off Broadway was the Basque Hotel and Restaurant, which served Basque food through the 1990s. Even to this day, with its twenty-five rooms, the establishment continues its role as a residential hotel, and the Basque Hotel sign still hangs out front. Jean-Emile Idiart managed the Basque restaurant for many years. According to Idiart, this building also reportedly dates back to 1907, but it was only under Basque ownership since 1960.

The Broadway businesses were especially hard hit by the 7.0-magnitude earthquake in October 1989, which damaged the Broadway freeway exit just a few short blocks away. "It used to be real easy to get here," said Idiart, who finally closed the Basque Hotel's restaurant in 1996. Greg Lindgren, grandson of a Basque immigrant, bought the restaurant with a partner in 1997, renovated the hotel upstairs, and converted the restaurant into a trendy bar. Renamed **15 Romolo,** the place has just a few food items on the menu. The Basque Hotel sign still hangs out front. The pair later bought Des

Alpes and performed a similar transformation. The bar downstairs is known as Rosewood Bar (732 Broadway).

RESTAURANTS

As the last of the old boardinghouse-style eateries on Broadway were closing down, it seems logical that new sophisticated Basque restaurants would spring up to take their place in this cosmopolitan city. The new businesses, completely different from the old family-style menus, boast nouvelle-California cuisine. Well-known chef Gerald Hirigoyen and longtime restaurateur J. B. Lorda started the trend with the small **Fringale** in the SoMa district in 1991. The two also shared Pastis, a French bistro-style restaurant. More recently, Hirigoyen sold his share in Fringale and took over Pastis, remodeling the restaurant and reopening it as the very Basque **Piperade.** "It was time for me," said Hirigoyen, explaining his partnership break. In 2004, he opened a second business next to the world-famous Transamerica Pyramid, **Bocadillos,** specializing in tapas.

Despite his youth, Mattin Noblia, one of Hirigoyen's protégés, is already trying to make a name for himself with **Iluna Basque,** a small restaurant that attracts a young late-night crowd. He jumped into the restaurant business with less than a year's experience under his belt at Fringale. The restaurant's Web site (*www.ilunabasque.com*) is quite impressive. Noblia, born in the Basque Country, started his culinary training at age fourteen and worked in restaurants in France and Switzerland, according to the Web site. In the heart of North Beach, Iluna Basque looks out on Washington Square. It is walking distance to old Basque-stomping grounds—the nightclubs on Columbus, the boardinghouses down on Broadway, and the San Francisco Athletic Club facing the square on the opposite side, where Basque dinners were often held in the 1970s. For the daytime crowd, Noblia recently opened **Eguna Basque** (1657 Powell Street), a coffeehouse next door. **Cote Sud** (4238 18th Street; *www.cotesudsf.com*), a French bistro partly owned by a Basque, Raymond Arbelbide, opened to rave reviews in the Castro district in 2002.

Bocadillos, 710 Montgomery Street, San Francisco, CA 94101 (415) 982-2622; *www.bocasf.com*
Fringale, 570 Fourth Street, San Francisco, CA 94130 (415) 543-0573; *www.fringalerestaurant.com*

Iluna Basque, 701 Union Street (at Powell), San Francisco, CA 94133 (415) 402-0011; *www.ilunabasque.com*
Piperade, 1015 Battery Street, San Francisco, CA 94111 (415) 391-2555; *www.piperade.com*

Ties to the French Community

Many of San Francisco's Basques were from France, particularly from the province of Nafarroa Beherea, and some of them were very active in the city's large French community. They sent their children to the French Notre Dame des Victoires School to learn French; they subscribed to *Le Californienne* newspaper (which still publishes out of San Francisco today as *Journal Français*); they supported the construction of the city's French Hospital; and they belonged to some prominent French associations, such as the Ligue Henri Quatre and Alliance Française.

French Chefs and Bakers. The food business was another main attraction to San Francisco, long known for its fine restaurants. As a result of legislation passed in 1952, immigrants had to have an employer vouch that they had a job skill that was hard to fill from among American population. As a result many French-trained Basque chefs arrived in San Francisco in the years that followed. San Francisco has had a longtime reputation as being the home of some of the finest sourdough bread producers in the country. Basques had a hand in several sourdough bakeries, the most prominent among them being the Larraburu Brothers bakery, founded in 1896. The Larraburus sold their interest in 1945, but most workers continued to be Basque until the bakery closed in 1976. Brothers-in-law Pierre Saldubehere and Dominique Jambon were longtime partners in the Royal Baking Company, a San Francisco sourdough bakery, until they sold out their shares in 1987. They were the last Basques involved in baking in the city.

GARDENERS

In the San Francisco area, a large majority of Basque men work in the gardening business. Many opportunities were made available for Basque gardeners during World War II when the Japanese who did this work were sent to detention centers.

The Basques' familiarity with agriculture probably pushed them onto that career path, but there were other factors at play. Gardening was an ideal way for Basques to apply their farming expertise to the growing urban landscape. It was also a field in which they could start off working with another Basque owner and eventually go off and start their own business—always a goal for the Basque. Typically, established gardeners would sell clients' accounts to new gardeners to help them get their business off the ground. "You know how we got into gardening? We don't have any degrees, no school—but we know how to work with our hands," said Laurent Hardoy, who had a gardening business in Redwood City for many years.

SAN FRANCISCO BASQUE CLUB

For many years Basque gardeners formed the majority in a local French association for gardeners, Les Jardiniers, which held its own annual picnic. Frederic Fuldain said that a heated clash at one of these picnics led the Basques to form their own club in 1960.

Apparently two well-known *bertsolariak* (the Basque version of troubadours) who were visiting from the Basque Country, Xalbador of Urepel and Mattin of Ahetze, were invited to sing at the picnic that year, according to Fuldain. They had performed in Chino, La Puente, and Bakersfield, where Basque clubs were already organized. The singers were well into their to-and-fro when a few Frenchmen, irritated because they didn't understand any of the words, shut off the microphone, Fuldain reported. The Basques got hot under the collar. "A group of young Basques that afternoon swore that they were going to have a club for themselves and start their own picnic," he said. That very evening a group of them went to Claude Berhouet's Hotel de France and mapped out a plan.

The **San Francisco Basque Club** quickly attracted the membership of most of San Francisco's Basque immigrants—around seven hundred of them, as well as many of their sons, so the membership eventually reached nearly nine hundred. Joining the club was almost automatic for newly arrived immigrants. "I arrived here on a Friday night," said Johnny Curutchet, who came in 1966, "and I joined the following day." An immediate job tip showed him the value of this Basque network.

This wasn't the city's first Basque club. A Zazpiak Bat club formed in 1924 but lasted only about ten years, apparently because of schisms between Hegoaldetarrak and Iparraldetarrak. A mutual aid society, La Sociedad Vascongada de Beneficiencia Mutua, was formed in 1923 to provide financial help to Basques in need. Its name indicates a dominance by Hegoaldetarrak. Being such a cosmopolitan city, San Francisco always had a mix of Basques from all the provinces, but the large majority were from the two sides of Nafarroa and shared the same dialect.

Over the years, the San Francisco Basque Club organized dinner dances at the Italians' San Francisco Athletic Club or at the basement hall of Notre Dame de Victoires Church. A dance group, banquets, and the annual picnic kept the Basque community together. Today, most events are at the Basque Cultural Center in South San Francisco.

San Francisco Basque Club, P.O. Box 27021, San Francisco, CA 94127. Information: (415) 564-0900 *(Pierre Etcharren); www.basqueclub.com*

DANCE

Soon after it was organized, the new San Francisco Basque club organized a dance group, Zazpiak Bat (Seven are One), which performed at San Francisco's first Basque picnic in June 1961. The dancers' close connection to the French community was illustrated by their regular performance in the annual French Bastille Day presentation in Golden Gate Park. This dance group continues today.

MUSIC

A *klika,* or drum and bugle corps, was formed in 1963—the first official group in the United States, but two others, in Chino and Bakersfield, which are also predominantly Iparraldetarrak, were to follow later.

San Francisco is one of the few Basque communities with a choir, known as Elgarrekin (All Together). The majority of San Francisco's choir members were born in the Old Country, unlike the choir members in Boise, who are all born in the United States. Jeanne Mazeris, formerly the director for the Notre Dames de Victoires choir, gladly accepted the invitation to be choirmaster for the Elgarrekin when it was started in 1979. She headed the group through 1997. She calls it a folk choir—"It's just people who like to sing."

FESTIVAL

Starting with its first picnic in 1961 in Los Altos, the San Francisco Basque Club has rotated the annual event throughout the years to a number of different locations in the rural fringes of the Bay Area, although it always takes place on the first Sunday in June. For many years the picnic was held at a park in Walnut Creek, and most recently the members have settled upon the Sonoma County Fairgrounds (at Payran Street and Fairgrounds Drive) in Petaluma. In the early years, when San Francisco was full of eager young men just down from the sheep camps, its picnic was considered one of the best, attracting up to two thousand people. Many men found wives at these picnics. But in recent years, attendance has dwindled somewhat.

Go with a crowd of your own friends and enjoy a delicious barbecued lamb lunch. Bring a picnic dinner if you plan to stay late, although usually delicious hot chorizo sandwiches are sold in the evenings. You'll enjoy watching the dancing in the afternoon, particularly the group of little ones. If you want souvenirs, look for the Echeverrys' and the Foge-Jensens' tables. (For more information see the North Bay section.)

THE NABO CONVENTION

In 1979 the San Francisco Basque Club hosted the annual summer meeting for the North American Basque Organizations (NABO), putting on a grandiose Basque bash that attracted nearly twenty thousand people. For over a year beforehand a small committee developed the plans that ultimately created the largest Basque event up until that time. It became the model for NABO's subsequent summer conventions. It was the first time all the dance groups from California, Nevada, and Idaho performed together, and it was also the occasion of the first international *mus* competition, according to festival coordinator Pierre Etcharren. The club cleaned up Pier 2, which had been closed until then, and took over the Fort Mason parking lot in the Golden Gate National Recreation Area.

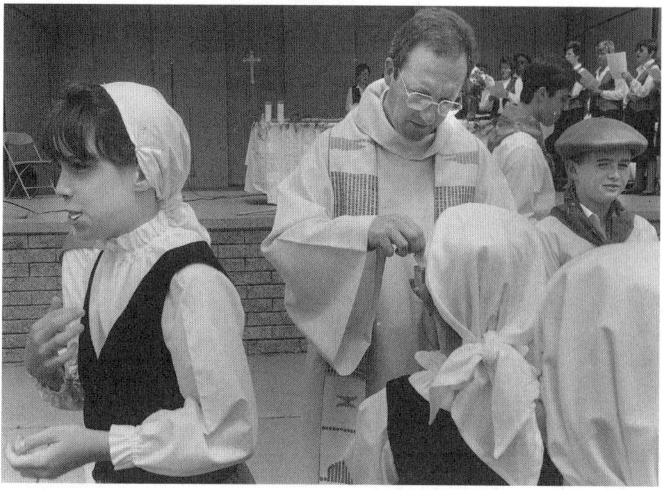

Father Eliçagaray, a former chaplain to the U.S. Basque community, serves communion to the younger set, while San Francisco's choir Elgarrinak sings in the background during Mass at the San Francisco picnic. (Photo by Averie Cohen.)

Johnny Curutchet during a moment of reflection at the San Francisco picnic Mass. (Photo by Averie Cohen.)

Odette Etcheverry and Her Basque Souvenirs

If you attend any of the festivals in California or Nevada, you are certain to see **Etcheverry's Basque Imports—** scarves, berets, music tapes, and other souvenirs, all imported from the Basque County. The business was founded by Odette Etcheverry of San Francisco. Later she was joined by Espen and Bernadette (Petotegui) Foge Jensen, who sell primarily T-shirts, cups, and other Basque mementos made locally. Odette started her business over thirty years ago. During those years, she has taught hundreds of Basque girls how to tie up their laces on the *espartinak* (espadrilles) she imports from France. She has provided the red scarves and berets for the men, many a young musician with a drum, and almost all the clubs with an *ikurrina* (the Basque flag) to display on special occasions.

With borrowed money and speaking little English, Odette initially opened a little gift shop selling Basque souvenirs in San Francisco's Sunset District. Her husband worked as a gardener. The couple, with their two small children, lived in the small living quarters behind the shop. At the time, her mother and sister in France bought items from stores at retail prices and sent them to her to sell. "They didn't know any better," she said, explaining that she now buys wholesale from twenty-two different companies in France and Spain. But bad luck struck the young family. A robber stole almost all of their inventory. "I lost my courage," said Odette, noting that she was ready to close shop. But a local Basque gardener, Auguste Garat of Hasparren, learned of the mishap and encouraged her to keep the shop open. He told his fellow gardeners, most of whom worked in the Sunset District, to buy items to help her out. "After that I saw all kinds of people I never saw before in my life in my shop. You see . . . the Vascos," she said, putting her fingertips together to demonstrate how the Basque community sticks together.

Her first experience traveling long-distance to a picnic in 1966 was very nearly disastrous, but she had some help from fellow Basques. "We went by air with two suitcases full," she said, but most of the merchandise was in three boxes she had mailed ahead of time. By the time of the picnic in La Puente, the boxes had not yet arrived. But some local Basque men contacted someone they knew at the post office and, despite it being a Sunday, they retrieved two of the three boxes. For years she did not sell at the Elko picnic, because it was too far. "It's like the Basque Country to Paris," Etcheverry said. But when Anita Anacabe became president of the Elko Basque club, she pleaded so much that Etcheverry finally made the trip with her merchandise in 1980. Etcheverry remembers her first Elko picnic vividly. People were grabbing up T-shirts right from the boxes, before she could even get them on the table. "I never sold anything so fast," Etcheverry exclaimed. "People were so happy to see us there."

Odette Etcheverry retired in 1996 after thirty-three years of doing business. She passed on her Basque import business to her daughter, Susie Etcheverry Fosse, who continues the business in the same manner.

Etcheverry Basque Imports, 765 San Felipe Ave., San Bruno, CA 94066 (650) 737-0332; *www.basqueimports.com*

In business for over thirty years, Odette Etcheverry of San Francisco became a permanent fixture at the West's picnics, selling imported Basque souvenirs, cassette tapes, and costumes. Today her daughter carries on the business. (Photo by Averie Cohen.)

In addition to the dance performances, there was wood-chopping and weight-lifting competitions, demonstrations of cheese making, bread making, and handball making, and sheep hooking and sheepdog trials. Card players from Mexico, Chile, Argentina, Venezuela, Spain, and France arrived for the *mus* tournament. Although such celebrations had been held before (in particular there was the large regional Basque festival that was organized in Reno in 1959), none had been on such a large scale. And certainly it was a first for the city of San Francisco. That two-day affair set the standard for the larger Jaialdi festivals that were first organized in 1987, according to Etcharren.

PELOTA

When La Cancha, the city's indoor court, was replaced by a government apartment building in 1958, San Francisco's hard-core handball players were not to be deterred. They would have a new place to play. During the 1960s San Francisco area Basques made an hour-long

Indoor handball courts have often served as banquet rooms for big Basque parties, like this one at San Francisco's "La Cancha," on Pacific Street, around 1917. Then-owner Antón Meabe is in forefront; former owner Ramon Elorrieta sits behind the small girl with the bow. (Courtesy of Juanita Meabe Fieldsoe.)

drive on Sundays to Stockton, where a court remained. Frederic Fuldain remembers the first trip out there after the San Francisco *kantxa* was torn down. No one had played on the court in years, and the place had served as a dog kennel, he said. It was dirty and full of junk. "We had to clean it up," he said. But that court too disappeared when the building was torn down in 1966. "Then we didn't have anything," remembers Fuldain.

But the resourceful handball players again found a way to keep playing. For years many of them played casually against walls in different playgrounds or in the American handball courts in Golden Gate Park. Eventually they began congregating at the Helen Wills Playground on Broadway at Larkin. But its wall wasn't high enough for regulation play, so in 1971 they sought permission and added another 10 feet to the height of the cement wall. On Sundays men and women would bring their own folding chairs and gather around to watch the men play, while children cavorted. Afterward they would

La Cancha

At the heart of the Broadway neighborhood was *La Cancha,* where everyone played handball. Despite the large Basque community here, it was San Francisco's only court for most of this century. Located on Pacific between Stockton and Powell, the court could be reached from Broadway by walking down an alley between the two streets. "It's the best one I've seen in California," said Frederic Fuldain, an expert on old handball courts, speaking, of course, of the time before the modern Cultural Center with its *kantxa* was built. Many of San Francisco's old-timers remember having a drink in the lounge while watching the action on the court. There were also a few rooms on the second floor. According to Elena Arralde, daughter of José and Expectacion Elizalde, early owners of La Cancha, it was in operation as a room-and-board place as early as 1907. When Jeronimo "Antón" Meabe bought the *kantxa* in the 1920s, or perhaps earlier, it was part wood and part cement, according to his daughter Juanita Fieldsoe. He remodeled the court and the rooms upstairs, where his family lived. He was known as "Antón"—"where he got that I'll never know," said Fieldsoe. "They never called them by their proper names," she said, referring to the Basque penchant for nicknames. In 1948, the Meabe family retired from the business and moved to Oakland. They leased it to different families during the remaining years, some of whom rented out the rooms upstairs to boarders. Unfortunately, the court was demolished in 1958 in the name of urban renewal.

all troop to the hotels on the other side of the Broadway tunnel for lunch. Inevitably, many of the pelota players and spectators would end up eating at the Hotel des Alpes, "because we would serve them all day," said Ganix Iriartborde, who was himself one of the best handball players around. "If they came in at three o'clock in the afternoon, we served them anyway." His wife, Aña, added with a smile: "Yes, we taught them a bad habit."

But development again frustrated the *pelotariak,* when their wall at the park was torn down in 1979 to build condominiums next to the playground. "*Adieu notre kantxa encore,*" said Aña in French. That was when the seed of the idea to build a cultural center finally germinated. It took the desire of the Bay Area's handball aficionados to bring it to fruition. The center had long been a dream, even before the last handball wall in San Francisco came down. "The idea was there for twenty years," said Aña, who along with husband Ganix was an ardent supporter of the idea.

A NEW HANDBALL COURT AND CENTER

Serious discussions by the San Francisco Basque Club about building such a facility had started in 1962. The city of San Francisco was offering a property at Geary and Webster Streets at a reasonable price ($30,000 for an entire city block, according to Jean Gorostiague) to any group willing to develop it. The Basque Club seriously looked into the possibility. Several members developed an official proposal and presented it to the club, suggesting a system of financing by the members themselves that proved to be similar to the one that was ultimately used when the cultural center was built, nearly twenty years later, in 1982. But the idea was voted down. Jean Gorostiague notes that the club was new, and many of its members had recently arrived and didn't have much money. Today Japantown, a shop-filled tourist attraction, stands at that spot.

Around 1970 the club bought property in Los Gatos, about an hour south of San Francisco, with the idea of developing it as a picnic site with a handball court. But neighbors and environmentalists were not happy about the possibility of having more traffic in the quiet wooded suburb, and the club's plans were blocked, according to Gorostiague. Besides, the site would have been too far for the handball players to travel every weekend. After many legal hassles, the property in Los Gatos was eventually sold. In the mid-1970s the club discussed the possibility of buying an existing clubhouse in Novato, but that idea was also voted down because many did not think the building was a good size. It could not have accommodated a handball court, in any case.

Finally, in 1979, when the handball wall at Helen Wills Playground was slated to be demolished, a group of Basques within the club decided they were not going to continue without their own building and handball court.

Many club members feared the financial risk, and others figured they would eventually return to the Basque Country and didn't want to make financial commitments. Attorney Marcel Biscay told them that as long as some members of the club were against the idea, it would always be a problem, and they should start a separate organization with the people who *wanted* to build the club. "Under the Basque club, it would never have been built," said Leon Sorhondo.

Franxoa Bidaurreta, who was president of the San Francisco Basque Club at the time, remembers vividly the evening when the cultural center plans officially got underway, after a regular club meeting at Notre Dame des Victoires. "I adjourned the meeting, and then I said I was going to talk about something that had nothing to do with the club. So if anyone wanted to leave, they could. Nobody left."

At the following meeting, about seventy people showed up, and almost all of them made a commitment to donate $1,000 each for the project. Not finding a suitable property in San Francisco, the club opted to buy 1½ acres in South San Francisco. Initially the idea was to build a handball court, but by the second or third meeting the concept had already grown to encompass a full-fledged center with meeting rooms and a banquet hall, according to Leon Sorhondo. The plans expanded to include a bigger kitchen and a restaurant. "We saw that the money was coming in, so we thought maybe we ought to make it bigger," said Jean Gorostiague, one of the main architects of the plan.

Under the arrangement, supporters became members of the center by donating $1,000. The group quickly incorporated. Once construction started, the cost of membership rose to $2,000. Anything above that amount was considered a loan to be paid back at a later date. Loans of $5,000, $10,000, and even one for $200,000, from Jean Pierre Elissondo, rolled in. Ultimately, the entire cost of $1.25 million came from the members. The names of all these founding members are on a plaque in the lobby of the Basque Cultural Center. (There was some hostility between the two groups for a while, but eventually most of the opposing Basque Club members became members of the Cultural Center, and now both groups are equally involved in hosting local activities, most of which are held at the center. The *klika*, the dance group, and the annual June picnic remain under the sponsorship of the San Francisco Basque Club. Both organizations host their own *mus* tournament.)

The Basques' strength and facility for labor-intensive jobs was evident as members set about building most of the complex themselves, under the watchful eye of supervisors Jean Gorostiague and Jean Jauretche. About 150 people pitched in over the ten-month period it took to complete the bulk of the work. That wouldn't have been possible if the majority of the Basques were not self-employed, Pierre Etcharren noted. "They could take the time off to work."

Franxoa Bidaurreta raises the Basque and U.S. flags at the inauguration of the Basque Cultural Center in South San Francisco, March 1982. (Courtesy of Jeannette Etchegoin.)

Gorostiague and Jauretche, both licensed contractors, worked with contacts in the building industry to help cut costs. Subcontractors lowered their prices or even donated their time. Materials were bought at wholesale prices. Counting all the discounts and free labor, Gorostiague estimated that the center probably saved about $700,000 or $800,000 on construction. Outside contractors were hired for the more technically demanding jobs such as the roof and the front wall, which required a special cement mixture to form the super-hard consistency that would withstand the abuse of professional jai alai. It was an amazing feat to watch as the cranes hoisted up the huge slabs of cement to form the walls of the *kantxa.*

Today the **Basque Cultural Center,** with its pelota court, large banquet hall, and restaurant, is the pride and joy of the Bay Area Basque community. Looking back, some members remark that the circumstances were ripe for such a monumental group undertaking. If it had not been done then, it might not ever have happened. "You have to dream the impossible and make it happen," said Pierre Etcharren. That first board was a reflection of the diverse groups who had come together—young American-born Basques in addition to the immigrants, and Hegoaldetarrak, who previously had been little involved, along with the Iparraldetarrak. (For a listing on the Basque Cultural Center, see the San Francisco Peninsula section.)

NAFARRAK BASQUE CLUB

Being such a cosmopolitan city, San Francisco had a healthy number of Nafarrak from Hegoalde, despite the predominance of those from Iparralde. A small contingent of the Hegoaldetarrak have always been members of the **Unión Española,** the city's Spanish organization, which was started as far back as 1923. For years the Unión Española had its own hall in North Beach, first on Pacific next to La Cancha and then on Broadway, where the Basque club's *klika* practiced in its early years. Following the lead of the Basques, in the mid-1980s the organization decided to sell that building and move to a bigger one. They remodeled a former commercial store, transforming it into a beautiful center, Union Española and restaurant (**Patio Español**) at 2850 Alemany Boulevard. Every year, on the Sunday closest to July 7, the date of the big San Fermín festival in Iruñea/Pamplona, the Basque members sponsor a big celebration. There are many parties throughout the year at the union, "but ours is the liveliest," claimed member Tony Espinal. "We all dress like Pamplonicos" with red berets and white pants and shirts. Recently, they started a fun Running of the Bulls with someone dressed up like a bull chasing the Pamplonico kids down the street. In 1991 group members decided they wanted to play in the NABO *mus* tournament, so they actually formed a separate club, **Anaitasuna.** They often gather at the Union Española to play *mus*. They sponsor occasional dinner dances there as well.

Anaitasuna Basque Club, 2850 Alemany Boulevard, San Francisco, CA 94112. Information: (415) 648-3476 *(Gina Espinal)*

San Francisco Peninsula

The Basque Cultural Center's location south of the big city is a reflection of the changing demographics in the Bay Area. Like the migration from Los Angeles to outlying suburbs, the Basque community in San Francisco has also shifted outward. The cost of housing in San Francisco has gone sky-high in the past three decades, and some young Basque families can no longer afford to settle in the city. Others simply prefer a quieter suburban setting.

Gardeners, who once lived and worked mostly in San Francisco's Sunset District, started moving out in the 1960s and 1970s. "They were all on top of each other," said Johnny Curutchet, who started his gardening business in the city and gradually transferred it to South San Francisco. Gardeners settled with their families in suburbs in the San Francisco Peninsula: Burlingame, South San Francisco, Millbrae, and Redwood City. Others chose the North Bay, moving to cities such as Novato, San Rafael, Petaluma, Sonoma, and Santa Rosa.

Consequently, the Bay Area Basque community has spread out extensively and has lost much of its cohesiveness. The one-hour drive from some cities to the Basque Cultural Center discourages many of the younger Basque-Americans who don't feel the same compulsion their immigrant parents feel to gather with other Basques. In fact, so many are living in the North Bay now, that they have started their own club, the Marin-Sonoma Basque Association, and dance group for their children (see listing in the North Bay section).

Nevertheless, the Basque Cultural Center is the hub of activity for Bay Area Basques, and some of the biggest events of the year—the February anniversary dinner, the annual September barbecue, and the New Year's Eve party—have been known to attract from five hundred to eight hundred people.

"If the Basque Cultural Center wasn't there, the only place a lot of those Basques would see each other is at the funerals," said Franxoa Bidaurreta.

BASQUE CULTURAL CENTER

The **Basque Cultural Center,** with its handball court, bleachers, restaurant, and banquet hall, opened in South San Francisco in 1982. The San Francisco Basque community now has the largest Basque center in the country, as well as the largest handball court in the West.

Fish in Piperade Sauce, Louis Marticorena, Basque Cultural Center Restaurant

⅓ cup olive oil
1 onion, chopped
3 red bell peppers, chopped
4–5 cups puréed tomatoes
1 tablespoon salt
5 tablespoons sugar
1 teaspoon cayenne pepper
4–5 cloves of garlic, sliced
Any type of fish fillets (chef's preference is halibut)

Lightly sauté onion in olive oil, then add bell peppers. Stir in tomatoes, salt, sugar, and pepper. Cook on low flame for one hour, stirring frequently to prevent sauce from sticking to the bottom of the pot. Fry garlic separately in a little bit of oil. Meanwhile, steam fish for 15 minutes in a steamer, or cook it in the oven at 350 degrees for 10 minutes. Pour piperade sauce onto platter, put fish on top, and sprinkle garlic over the dish. Serve with a couple of boiled potatoes on the side.

Restaurant. The *kantxa* is obviously the center's most prominent feature, although the restaurant and bar are probably more popular. Although small, the restaurant has proven to be an essential component in the success of the center, and it continues to be the gathering place for Basques in the Bay Area. Most recently headed by chef Michel Veron, the restaurant has earned a good reputation, and it has been favorably reviewed by national newspapers and magazines. The kitchen staff also serves banquets in the dining hall, which represent a significant percentage of the center's business. The overall success of the restaurant led the center to expand the parking lot in 1994, and in 1996 the popular restaurant was expanded to seat another fifty people.

A manager oversees all aspects of the center's restaurant and catering business. After a series of managers came and went, Louis Marticorena, who served as chef for fifteen years at the gourmet La Bourgogne restaurant in San Francisco, took over the reins in 1986. Under his stewardship the center thrived. Its restaurant and banquet business increased 75 percent, according to Marticorena. "You know what's the secret of that success?" he said. "Just putting in a lot of hours." The banquet hall is so popular for weddings and parties that it is fully booked a year in advance. After ten years, Marticorena decided to reduce his hours, and in March 1996 he left his position as manager. He was replaced by François Camou. The red-headed Camou, who received his master's degree in hotel administration, helped managed three gourmet French restaurants owned by the prestigious Pebble Beach company before he was hired to head up the cultural center restaurant. A small volunteer board of directors oversees the restaurant and banquet catering. Decisions regarding the entire center are made by a fifteen-member board, elected by the members.

Basque Cultural Center, 599 Railroad Avenue, South San Francisco, CA 94080. Restaurant: (650) 583-8091; event information: (650) 583-7018 *(Anita Arduain); www.BasqueCulturalCenter.com*

Other Facilities. The restaurant and its staff play a significant role in that they make it possible for the center to maintain regular hours. In La Puente, despite the existence of a professional-size court, interest in handball declined because there was not a regular staff person to keep the club open. The San Francisco center's restaurant is busy for lunch and dinner. Most evenings there are members at the center, playing handball, holding meetings, or attending *klika* or dance practice. The restaurant's bar is a warm gathering place.

The center also contains a large meeting room with a small library of Basque books and magazines, as well as a television and VCR. The library was established by the **Basque Educational Organization,** a nonprofit arm of the cultural center that has sponsored cultural programs and Euskara classes over the years.

A children's room with toys and playing equipment is also used for *klika* practice, the women's group meetings, and even aerobics classes. The women's club has, through the years, provided constant adult supervision in the children's room during club events. The handball court is used most evenings by the members, and on special occasions it accommodates Catholic Masses or extra-large banquet crowds. In the hallway there is a display case with changing exhibits of Basque artifacts and photos, and helpful information cards to inform non-Basque visitors about the culture. And outside, to the east of the entryway, there grows an oak tree sprouted from an acorn that came from the historic Tree of Gernika in Bizkaia.

Basque Educational Organization, P.O. Box 31861, San Francisco, CA 94131. Information: (707) 762-4644 *(Franxoa Bidaurreta); www.basqueed.org*

Center Activities. The center's biggest Basque celebrations are the anniversary weekend festivities in February and the Fall Festival in September, which attract from 900 to 1,000 people over the course of the two days. Each year the center tries to organize something special for the anniversary date, such as an accordion festival or a *joko garbi* (mini jai alai) competition with players from the Basque Country. The New Year's Eve party, and the members' annual free lunch and *mus* tournament in January are also popular. An awards dinner is usually sponsored in conjunction with the competitions. The cultural center board has begun a tradition of holding "Claim to Fame" dinners to honor some of the older esteemed Basques, such as hotel keeper Amelie Sorhondo, senior handball player Ganix Iriartborde, and handball historian Frederic Fuldain. The women's club sponsors a Santa party, a Christmas boutique, and parties on other special occasions to raise scholarship funds. The center has also hosted several Basque Cultural Days, which have featured lectures, films, dance, and cooking workshops. The event, sponsored by the Basque Educational Organization, has continued sporadically.

The Future of the Center. By 1997 the center had about five hundred members. Anyone who wants to play handball must join, but most of the center's facilities and social activities are open to the public.

Today the founding immigrants are getting older, and many are anxious to see the second and third generation get more involved in cultural activities to ensure that the magnificent center will carry on. Yet the shift from the immigrant generation to the younger generations is not occurring without a struggle. Basque-Americans inevitably battle with their elders over how to carry on the traditions. One battle is over the issue of having two organizations—the cultural center and the San Francisco Basque Club. Many think the two should be joined, because it seems appropriate that the center, which is more financially viable, should sponsor the dance and *klika* groups, which frequently travel to out-of-town events. But other old-timers refuse to let go of old animosities between the two groups and refuse to support the cultural activities, which involve mostly younger participants. "Sometimes they forget the basic reason we built this place," said Johnny Curutchet, who supports one united organization. "They put the business ahead of the culture."

Yet the future of the center looks bright. Although lifetime membership can be expensive, the number of young Basque-American members is growing, and more than half of the members of the board of directors are now U.S.–born. Discussions are under way to consider allowing non-Basques or children of non-members to participate in activities, and possibly to lower the cost of membership.

PELOTA

About once a year handball players from the Basque Country usually pass through the Bay Area, and exhibition games are organized. Handball competitions among young and old or among players from different U.S. Basque communities are regular events at the Basque Cultural Center as well.

Today handball is undergoing something of a revival, with the sponsorship of championship competitions. NABO's annual tournament, which has categories for all players, has been a motivating factor. Women and youth are taking up the sport of *pala* in greater numbers, and classes are being taught for youngsters. In an effort to develop their interest and also maintain participation in the sport, NABO organized summer handball camps for youngsters at the cultural center. Instructors from the Basque Country were regularly invited. Today, pelota lessons have been incorporated into NABO's Udaleku summer camp. (See earlier section on NABO.)

Several of the best handball players, most from San Francisco, have participated in the Amateur World Pelota Championship, held every four years. Front tennis (a version of *pala* played with different racquets) players from Arizona and Texas, jai alai players from the East Coast, and pelota and *pala* players from the West's Basque communities—all amateurs—make up the diverse group of U.S. athletes who participate in the games, which are attracting greater numbers of participants. A **U.S. Federation of Pelota** exists to help the

Enthusiasm for playing pelota (handball) is growing among young Basque-Americans, fueled by pelota lessons given at the annual NABO summer camp. Here youngsters play at the San Francisco Basque Cultural Center's fronton.

players who go to the competition. "But we're so far away from each other that we can't afford to have an elimination tournament," said François Pedeflous of Fresno, past president of the federation. The federation also has very little funding to help the players with travel expenses, so those who participate are usually the best players in each category who can afford to go. The games have been held in France, Spain, Uruguay, Brazil, the Philippines, Italy, Mexico, and Cuba.

U.S. Federation of Pelota. Information: (707) 762-4644 (Franxoa Bidaurreta)

MENLO PARK BASQUE CLUB

The many large homes with ample acreage in the communities of Atherton, Menlo Park, and Hillsborough in the San Francisco Peninsula made it a prime area to set up gardening businesses, according to Laurent Hardoy, who lived in Redwood City and ran his own gardening business from 1965 to 1993. While many of the gardeners worked in the wealthier suburbs, they lived in more middle class communities such as Redwood City, Millbrae, Burlingame, and South San Francisco. In fact, so many Basques settled on the peninsula to pursue gardening that a group of them got together and started a club. In 1964 seven Basques organized the Menlo Park Zazpiak-Bat Club, which at its peak had a membership of about sixty families.

The club sponsored a picnic for many years at Flood Park in the city of Menlo Park. Members held dinner dances three or four times a year at the Eagles Hall in Redwood City. Johnny Curutchet remembers them fondly. In the spring the dance was always scheduled for the weekend in which daylight saving time started, when the clock would be pushed forward an hour, extending the evening beyond the normal 2 A.M. closing time. "I thought it was great," said Curutchet. "Later somebody explained it to me."

The club members themselves, all men, were the ones in the kitchen cooking the dinners. "It was the same guys all the time," remembered Henri Bonzon, one of the cooks. So when the Basque Cultural Center project came along in 1979, practically in their neighborhood, it was easy to decide to merge, Bonzon said. The club dissolved and turned its funds of about $25,000 over to the construction project, and its members became members of the center.

RESTAURANTS

For many years you could find a row of pickups belonging to Basque gardeners lined up outside the **Garden Club** restaurant (1144 Old Mission Road near Chestnut, South San Francisco [650] 873-4910), just a few blocks away from the cultural center. Local Basques enjoyed this casual restaurant, headed by the late Arnaud Etcheto, and often hung out here, playing *mus.* Etcheto passed away in 1995, and the restaurant was sold to an Italian-American. A few Basques still stop by here, and when there's a group of them, the restaurant will serve Basque meals.

Another former Basque restaurant on the peninsula, the elegant Côte Basque in Millbrae headed by the late chef Jean Baptiste Larrateguy, closed down in 1995 as well. Larrateguy had named the restaurant after the famous Côte Basque in New York, and like that East Coast restaurant, Larrateguy served mostly French food. He and his wife Rose ran a restaurant of the same name for ten years in San Francisco's Sunset District before they moved it to the peninsula.

Annie (Mocho) Nunan whose parents, Gracien and Jeanne Mocho, ran the French TriColor Restaurant in San Francisco for many years, has introduced Basque cuisine at her **Nouveau Trattoria** in Palo Alto, and she has found an appreciative audience. Residents in this city, home to Stanford University, are seasoned travelers already familiar with Basque food, according to Nunan. "Now we don't have to go to San Francisco," they tell her. The Trattoria restaurant was already known for its Italian dishes when Nunan bought it in 1993, so she kept that part of the menu, added French food, and tacked "Nouveau" onto the name. She soon introduced the Basque family-style dinners and hired an accordionist to serenade the diners. "It's so popular," said Nunan, who does all the cooking. "We get a lot of professors here—sometimes they just get up and start singing." Even President Bill Clinton and his wife Hillary dined here when their daughter Chelsea attended Stanford. Nunan said she planned to rename her popular restaurant Chez Annie.

Nouveau Trattoria, (*Annie Nunan*) 541 Bryant Street (off University) Palo Alto, CA (650) 327-0132

CEMETERY

A large number of the Bay Area's Basques have chosen to be buried in **Holy Cross Catholic Cemetery** in the town of Colma, just a short distance from the Basque Cultural Center. Graves date back to at least 1905—and include that of pioneer rancher Pedro Altube, known as the Father of the Basques of the Far West. He made his fortune in northeastern Nevada, with the famous Spanish Ranch, but he came back to San Francisco at the end of his life and lived with his family in a luxurious home on Pacific Avenue. (For full history on Altube, see the section on the Spanish Ranch in Independence Valley, Nevada.) A glistening white statue of an angel, engraved with the Altube name, marks the family grave. The cemetery office provides information over the phone to confirm the names of people buried there and the location of their gravesites.

Holy Cross Catholic Cemetery, 1500 Mission Road, Colma, CA 94014 (650) 756-2060

North Bay

Although land has been most important to those in ranching, it is still held in great esteem by Basques in general, just as it was in their rural villages in their homeland. Many Basques are now scattered in cities, where owning large parcels is not possible. Yet you will often find them on the fringes of urban populations, like the North Bay, where it's still possible to own an acre or two and grow some produce. You will also find a large percentage of Basques up and down the economic ladder who own their own homes.

More and more Bay Area Basque families are moving to the North Bay counties, where there is still a lot of open space and a feeling of being in the country. Others have established second homes there.

BAKERY

The rural Sonoma Valley is among Basques' favorite choices for their weekend and summer retreats. Gratien Guerra and his wife Lili put the Basques on the map here when they opened the Sonoma French Bakery on this touristy town's historic central plaza in 1956. Guerra retired in the 1980s and sold the business to non-Basques. Sourdough and other breads sold at the Sonoma bakery continued to be popular, but the label was finally sold to the local competitor, the Franco American Bakery in Santa Rosa.

In 1994 the Guerras' daughter, Françoise Hodges, returned to the business in the same town, with her own bakery, **Basque Boulangerie,** which she runs with her husband, Ron, and baker Jack Montaldo. In addition to their own crusted bread, the café bakery serves salads, hearty soups, Basque omelettes, and pastries, including the cream-filled gateau Basque cake. Their bread production is expanding and is served at many local restaurants.

Basque Boulangerie, 460 First Street East, Sonoma, CA (707) 935-7687

RESTAURANTS

The Basque restaurants in the Bay Area have also followed the Basque community out of the city. Marin County to the north boasts of two: the **Chalet Basque** and **Chey Peyo,** although it has had others.

Jean Felix and Mayie Galzagorry served Basque cuisine at the Café Villa in San Rafael from 1988 to 1997, until the restaurant and the adjacent hotel were sold to non-Basques.

Opened in 1962, the **Chalet Basque** is the oldest Basque restaurant in Marin County. Raymond and Eugenie Coscarart ran the place for twenty-five years, slowly transforming it from a small hamburger joint to today's dinner house. Later owner Francisco Oroz started working there in 1973, then bought the restaurant with his wife, Antoinette, in 1986.

The Orozes, as well as Pierre Lagourgue, the owner of another restaurant farther north in Sonoma County, **Chez Peyo,** were all once part of the San Francisco restaurant scene. Antoinette Oroz, before she was married, had a small eatery on Polk called Izarra, and the Orozes ran the Basque Hotel and Restaurant on Romolo Place from 1978 to 1985.

Pierre Lagourgue, who once worked as the chef at the Ritz in Paris, operated Chez Leon in downtown San Francisco. In 1977 he and his wife Rose Marie took over a coffee shop in Sebastopol and remade it into an elegant restaurant, **Chez Peyo,** a reasonable French restaurant with a Basque touch, with the emphasis on "light" food. Even more ideal is its setting along a quaint country road amid rolling green hills.

Roger Minhondo is a longtime figure in the North Bay's Basque community. When he came to this country, he worked as a chef at San Rafael's Chalet Basque for a year and a half before he opened his own restaurant in Sausalito in 1974. Minhondo was "born and raised in the restaurant business," as he puts it. His family operated a restaurant in his hometown of Irisarri, Nafarroa Beherea. When he opened Guernica in Sausalito he broke with local tradition, opting to create the more intimate French bistro setting, rather than copying the boardinghouse atmosphere of San Francisco's Basque restaurants, with their family-style dining. Minhondo operated **Guernica** (2009 Bridgeway, Sausalito) for nearly thirty years, and he then returned to the Chalet Basque in San Rafael where he started. He bought the restaurant, which was much bigger than Guernica, from the Orozes, updated the menu with fresh seafood dishes, and remodeled the interior. Minhondo said the restaurant thrives on its longtime local clientele, including the civic center business community at lunchtime. Food is served family-style or à la carte. Even though the current owners are not Basque, Guernica kept its French bistro menu after Minhondo sold it.

Although many of the area's Basque restaurants are family-owned, not many of the U.S.–born offspring appear interested in taking over the business, according to their parents. The long hours and lost weekends that are part of the restaurant business are not appealing to a generation that has grown up middle class in a high-tech world, especially among those who are college-educated. Minhondo, who has dedicated a lifetime to the restaurant business, says with a big laugh: "I hope my children don't get into this business. It's a very demanding, very difficult business—even though it can be very rewarding."

Le Chalet Basque, 405 North San Pedro Road (1 mile past Civic Center), San Rafael, CA 94103 (415) 479-1070; *www.chaletbasque.com*
Chez Peyo, 2295 Gravenstein Highway South (near Bloomfield), Sebastopol, CA 95472 (707) 823-1262

BASQUE CLUB

The **Marin-Sonoma Basque Association,** founded in 1989, started after many former San Francisco Basques moved to the northern Bay Area counties of Marin, Sonoma, and Napa, preferring its greener, more rural setting. When she and her husband J. B. settled in Novato, Linda (Erdozainçy) Etcheverria, who was very active in the San Francisco Basque community growing up, was surprised to find many Basque families she had never met before. The distance to San Francisco probably kept them away, Etcheverria speculated. The Basque families here are much more spread out, living half an hour to an hour's drive outside of the city. There was a great deal of enthusiasm when the club was started, especially for a children's dance group.

Club Activities. The club sponsored less traditional activities, such as ski and camping trips. The highlight of camping excursions to the nearby Russian River were elaborate lamb bakes. The lamb, along with Dutch-oven homemade bread, was buried, covered with coals, and cooked slowly. "We've done a lot to try to keep the kids together," said Etcheverria, noting that the families with children are the most close-knit.

The club no longer has a dance group, because all the dancers Etcheverria once taught are now off to college. *Mus* caught on among the youngsters here, and now a group of them plays in the annual junior *mus* tournament that NABO recently started. For a short time handball lessons were offered on Sundays at Indian Valley College in San Rafael, but the teachers returned to France, and most of the young players have graduated to playing in tournaments at the Basque Cultural Center in South San Francisco, where they usually practice.

Marin-Sonoma Basque Association, 1824 William Drive, Penngrove, CA 94951. Information: (707) 792-9258 (*Linda Etcheverria*)

FESTIVAL

Besides hosting annual dinners, the club, composed of about eighty families, started its own picnic tradition on the second Sunday of September at Miwok Meadows in nearby China Camp. The successful picnic continues on the same date at Penngrove Community Park, where 120 people show up.

Basque Market. Espen and Bernadette (Petoteguy) Foge Jensen have become familiar faces at the Basque picnics since they started their gift mail-order business, **Basque Market,** out of their Napa County home in 1988. They primarily specialize in CDs, books, sweatshirts, T-shirts, and coffee mugs imprinted with Basque slogans or designs. They introduce new items every year and offer discount prices for large orders, which can be customized. More recently, they started selling food items, such as cheese, peppers, and chorizos.

Basque Market, P.O. Box 727, Napa, CA 94559 (800) 788-0409; *www.basquemarket.com*

Sacramento Valley

With the exception of San Francisco, Northern California did not attract Basques in the numbers that migrated to central and Southern California. But there were some Basque sheep outfits in the

Sacramento Valley, and small pockets of Basque families remain in towns like Marysville, Yuba City, Chico, Dixon, and Woodland. Marysville had three hotels at one time and even a couple of frontons. The **Uriz Hotel** (331 A Street) is still there, but Basques haven't spent a night there in decades. The other hotels have disappeared. Sacramento had at least one boardinghouse until 1965.

Farther north, Susanville had enough of a Basque population to start a Basque club that still functions. And in Woodland and Dixon Basque families continue running sheep. (Dixon, also home to one of the country's two lamb-packing companies, hosts an annual Lamb Town Festival during the last weekend of July. This popular festival [*www.lambtown.com*], which gets bigger every year, attracts Basques in the area.) A few of the Basques in the Sacramento Valley have assembled for some thirty years in Durham for an annual Mass offered by a Basque priest. And in the last ten years or so, a first-generation Basque-American, Fred Ithurburn of Yuba City, with the help of a few other Basques, has organized a Basque picnic in the Sutter County buttes.

Despite the scant settlement of Basques, a few Basque restaurants are tucked away here and there, enough to provide the traveler a place to eat while on the road to Reno or farther north.

RESTAURANTS

Arnaud and Marie Mendisco, once owners of San Francisco's Obrero Hotel, ran their own place, Arnaud's, from 1985 to 1998 in the small town of Winters, located at the base of the Vaca Mountains near Lake Berryessa. The Mendiscos said that they selected that spot for its scenic beauty. They left San Francisco because Arnaud was keen on running sheep, so they bought a small ranch in Dixon at the same time that they opened the restaurant. Since they closed the restaurant, the extent of this family's foray into Basque cuisine is son Philip's Basco Fiasco entry in the popular Lambtown Festival every year in Dixon.

Right now, Chico has a Basque restaurant owned by non-Basques and for many years had a full-fledged Basque running a non-Basque restaurant. How did that happen? Well, Stuart Allen explains that when his family lived in Spain for several years, they fell in love with Spanish and Basque food. Upon their return, his father

The Garamendi Family

One of the most prominent California Basques of recent years grew up within arm's reach of Sacramento, but not because of sheep ranching. Former state senator and gubernatorial candidate John Garamendi was raised in a family of seven children in the gold rush community of Mokelumne Hill, a small town in which his father Raymond became a prominent civic leader. The elder Garamendi was born in Bingham Canyon, Utah, where his father was a miner, and grew up in Ely, Nevada, where his parents ran the Ely Hotel. Unusually ambitious among early Basque-Americans, he graduated from the University of Nevada, Reno. There he met his Irish-Italian wife Mary Jane. Raymond Garamendi eventually settled in this rural part of California with his family to manage his in-laws' cattle ranch. In his later years, the elder Garamendi, by then a real estate developer, took on a project dear to his heart—the establishment of Maredda Park in Mokelumne Hill. "Someday, they hope to get enough funds to build an [outdoor] amphitheater and dedicate it to Ray," said his widow, Mary Jane.

Son John attended U.C. Berkeley and considered a professional football career, but gave up sports to join the Peace Corps and work in Ethiopia with wife, Patti. After a brief stint in the business world, he jumped into politics early, winning a seat in the state assembly representing his home district. After one term, he ran for the state senate. He spent fourteen years there, and meanwhile he ran for other state offices, losing for the most part. He finally won a state office in 1990, when he ran for the politicized job of insurance commissioner. That job's high visibility prompted him to try a second time for the Democratic nomination for governor in 1994. Despite a high-energy campaign, he lost to Kathleen Brown, who was later defeated by Governor Pete Wilson.

While raising their own large family of six children, the Garamendis bought a ranch in Mokelumne Hill, on Paloma Road, within walking distance of the still-existing Garamendi-McSorley cattle ranch where Garamendi had grown up. His property is located on a scenic ridge with a breathtaking view that reaches all the way to the coastal range.

The Garamendis have hosted an annual Basque barbecue at this location ever since 1973, when John first entered California politics with his race for the state assembly. Chino's Gauden Bat dancers have performed at the May event for years, and at least twenty lambs are roasted slowly on spits for the hundreds of guests who attend every year—primarily longtime supporters and family friends. It's not necessarily a Basque event, but for the Garamendi family, proud of its Basque heritage, it does a great deal for promoting the culture.

---

decided to open a Basque restaurant and filled it with artifacts from Spain. But the Allen family is not Basque, and, moreover, there's not a single Basque working at their restaurant. But that hasn't hindered the restaurant's business. If Chico's residents weren't familiar with Basque food or the traditional family-style dinners before the Allen family opened **Basque Norte** in 1975, "they are now," said Allen.

Furthermore, the Allen family has given the Basques greater fame by commercializing their popular steak sauce, "Basque Norte Marinade." Matriarch Barbara Allen developed the recipe, which is available at Costco, many local supermarkets, or via the Internet. She says the main reason people come back to the family's restaurant is because of the delicious steaks. Larry Juanarena, former owner of Pat and Larry's restaurant, is 100 percent Basque, and everyone knows it. But his bar and restaurant was known as a steak house. Still, Juanarena, the son of a sheepherder, couldn't give up cooking altogether after selling the restaurant and cooks Basque lamb and tri-tip steaks as part of a catering business ([530] 895-3663).

Except for the name, the **Español Restaurant** in Sacramento (5723 Folsom Boulevard) retains none of the flavor of a Basque boardinghouse, although the business was run as a boardinghouse in the past. Its advertising describes the menu as "Basque-style Italian," because of the large family-size platters the restaurant uses to serve its customers, reminiscent of the days when the Italian owners ran the boardinghouse. The original Español opened in 1923 at 114 J Street, which is now part of tourist-oriented Old Sacramento. In 1952 the Español was moved to the corner of Third and I Streets, and an Italian family, the Luigis, took over the restaurant and the hotel. "We had a Basque chef," remembers the Luigis' daughter, Karen Zita, and all the boarders were Basque sheepherders. In 1965 the whole building was torn down for redevelopment. When the Luigis reopened the restaurant at its current location, "we kept the name because it's seventy years old, and it's hard to change," said Zita. Photos of the old boardinghouse hang in the restaurant. Today, it's touted as the oldest restaurant in Sacramento.

Pierre and Olga Nogues served diners Basque cuisine, especially during hunting season, for many years at the Chateau Basque in Maxwell. Just west of Maxwell is prime duck and pheasant territory, and the countryside a few miles to the east is a deer hunter's delight. When the restaurant opened in 1976, the town had twelve hundred people, but it got busier during hunting season.

California politician John Garamendi flew the Basque flag along with the state and U.S. flag at his annual Basque barbecue fund-raiser, when he ran for state governor in 1994. (Photo by Paul J. Miller.)

No Basque festival is complete without chorizos, cooked up here by Raymond Lahargoue and Alain Falxa of San Francisco. (Photo by Averie Cohen.)

When her husband passed away, Olga ran the place practically single-handed, backed up by her right-hand man, chef Jean Carriquiry. But the town has dwindled to five hundred people, and the restaurant finally closed.

Basque Norte, 3355 Esplanade (at Eaton Avenue), Chico, CA 95973 (530) 891-5204

INFORMAL PICNIC

A local Basque barbecue has been held every spring at the Sutter County buttes since about 1980. Fred Ithurburn, a trial lawyer from Yuba City, said he started the picnic because he wanted to share the beauty of the local Buttes with his family. Ithurburn became familiar with this small mountain range while herding sheep for his father when he was young.

In 1992 and 1993 the event was held at a remote sheep ranch belonging to the McPherrin sheep family in the buttes near Sutter, and all the equipment had to be hauled in. It's a simple affair—just a barbecue and an afternoon for socializing. Eventually, however, it was combined with the annual Durham Mass.

DURHAM MASS

For at least the last thirty years, the Basque priest stationed in San Francisco has kept up an annual tradition of presiding over a Catholic Mass in Durham for Basques throughout the Sacramento Valley. For years, it was held at Durham's small wooden church. Fred Ithurburn remembers taking his small children, now all grown, to the annual Mass. "When we came outside afterward, there'd be glasses of whisky on the table—that was enough for us to spend the rest of the day there," he said, chuckling. Lunch would be an informal potluck affair. In 1994 at the suggestion of Father Jean Eliçagaray, the local picnic and the annual Durham Mass were combined and put on at Durham Park in April. Eliçagaray used the occasion to introduce the Basque priest Martxel Tillous who was to replace him. Father Tillous has faithfully carried on the tradition during the ten years he has been in the U.S. However, the location has changed numerous times, because unpredictable weather kept organizers on the look-out for the ideal setting. It has moved from the Buttes, to Durham, to a basement church hall in Chico, and back again.

The picturesque setting of recent years, Calvert and Begoña McPherrin's scenic ranch, has all but settled the matter, said Ithurburn. Their property is well equipped with a large barn in the event of inclement weather. In fact, in 2004, "we got a cloudburst right in the middle of the Mass," said Ithurburn. "We just picked up the altar and ran into the barn. After the cloudburst, it was a beautiful day."

The picnic, organized by a loose-knit group of Basques, has attracted from five hundred people to a hundred, which is more typical these days. The picnic organizers have shied away from starting a club, because the red tape makes it more trouble than it's worth, according to former restaurateur Larry Juanarena, who often cooked the meat for the barbecue. The organizers do send out announcement flyers for the April picnic, so if you're interested in receiving one, call Fred's son Bert Ithurburn at (530) 673-5637.

ANOTHER CLUB

More and more San Francisco residents are relocating to affordable rural/suburban areas of California. Noel Goyhenetche and his sister Allyn Terpstra are among them and are trying to start a club in the Rocklin area. Goyhenetche said many of the Basque-Americans in the area are younger families, and they would like to start a dance group for their children. The group, Iparreko Ibarra, was just getting organized in 2005 and was thinking of starting a *mus* tournament and dinner. They were also considering offering *klika* (trumpet) classes, so that area youngsters could join San Francisco's *klika* on special occasions.

Iparreko Ibarra, P.O. Box 3324, Rocklin, CA 95677. Information: (916) 435-8829 (Noel Goyhenetche)

CHORIZO COMPETITION

In earlier days, boardinghouse owners would butcher their own hogs to make the pork dishes they served in their dining rooms. Even today many Basque restaurants make their own chorizos and cure their own hams. When John Belza, grandson of the owners of the Uriz Hotel, noticed that the tradition of families making their own chorizo or *lukainka* (sausage) was disappearing, he spearheaded a unique revival—a *lukainka* contest. His goal: "to see if we can get the right flavors back." For years, he sponsored the competition every February at his ranch home in Yuba City for a small group of second- and third-generation Basque-Americans. "Most of them are connected with the old families that herded sheep around here," said Belza.

The late Richard Goñi of Susanville had just started a chorizo business when he entered his secret recipe—distinguished by Anaheim chili peppers—and won first place in the contest. When he put the trophy behind his former bar at the St. Francis Hotel, customers started flooding him with orders, and the business, G.L.&L. Smokehouse, was off and running. It is still in business today selling the same popular chorizo (See G.L.&L. Smokehouse under Susanville).

Recently, the competition moved into a permanent location, the Veteran's Hall in Sutter. Organizers collected donations as well, and the event was quite a success. To participate, you must be Basque and bring a chorizo for the contest, said Fred Ithurburn, although the first year they'll let you get by with just being a judge. In addition to the *lukainka* (chorizo in Euskara), everyone brings potluck dishes—traditional Basque recipes passed down from their grandmothers. Ithurburn's eight sons and daughters have won quite a few of the competitions in recent years, and people are starting to complain, he joked.

Lake Tahoe Region

Whiskey Creek Sheep Camp

In the earliest years of the itinerant sheepherders, once they headed into the mountains they were on their own with their sheepdog, donkey, and tent. But as the industry developed, sheep outfits established summer base camps, where camp tenders could store supplies and bake bread every few days. The camp tenders would use pack animals to deliver the bread and other supplies to their herders once or twice a week. The base camps usually consisted of a small cabin or two, corrals for the horses, and the all-important bread oven, built with

Log cabin hand-hewn by Basque herders at Whiskey Creek Sheep Camp, near Truckee, California. (Courtesy of U.S. Forest Service.)

Old World craftsmanship. Many of these camps were built by Basques throughout the western mountain ranges, but very few remain, most having been destroyed by the elements or razed by the U.S. Forest Service.

The survival of a sheepherders' base camp from the 1950s in the Granite Chief Wilderness in north central Sierra Nevada is unusual. Indeed, the two small log cabins and a Basque-style outdoor oven, built in the 1950s, were slated for demolition in 1992, because the area's wilderness designation does not allow for man-made structures. According to Richard Markley, U.S. Forest Service archeologist for the Tahoe National Forest, areas such as Granite Chief Wilderness are selected for wilderness designation precisely because of their remoteness, lack of roads, and absence of significant human intervention. That way, Markley explained, "the natural processes are allowed to dominate." Nonetheless Joxe Mallea, Basque historian at the University of Nevada, Reno, together with Markley and a couple of other Forest Service employees successfully argued for the protection of the three structures.

"We convinced them that it was a significant part of the Basque history," said Mallea. Markley commented, "This is an unusual case because of their [the structures'] value to Basque heritage."

The site, referred to as the Whiskey Creek Sheep Camp after the creek running nearby, served as home base for the Kuhn and Miller sheep company from at least 1925 probably through 1984, when the surrounding area was designated as wilderness, according to a 1993 report by Forest Service archeologists Carrie Smith and Michael Baldrica. The log cabins were built there by sheepherder Pete Bengoechea and camp tender Severino Ibarra during the summers of 1954 and 1955. The men had to cut and peel logs and drag them by mules or horses to the clearing—a laborious, time-consuming job. It was not a skill they had learned in the Basque Country, where logs are not used in construction, noted Mallea. Ibarra, who retired in Reno, told Mallea that he and Bengoechea learned to notch the logs and build walls merely by examining other log cabins in the mountains. The wood used on the inside of the cabins came from Squaw Valley, a good 2 miles away. Another sheepherder, Fausto Lavari, built the nearby granite and brick oven in 1954. The oven has a tin roof over it to protect it from the snow. It is still intact. Mallea said that the beehive-shaped ovens were usually built with brick and mortar, but this one makes rare use of granite.

In 1997 and 1999, in a project spearheaded by Mallea and Smith, many volunteers worked with the Forest Service to restore the camp structures to their original condition. Because of the wilderness designation, cars are not allowed into the area. Workers had to hike in, equipment and food had to be packed in by horse, and no power tools such as chain saws were allowed. A large tree that had fallen on the roof of the smaller building had to be sawed off, the bigger cabin had to be jacked up, and two or three logs had to be replaced. New logs were cut, peeled, and shaped by hand. Most of the work was done by volunteers from the North American Basque Organizations, and a few even came from the Basque Country to help with the restoration.

The Forest Service supports the preservation of the cabins and has left them open, despite concern over vandalism. "We want people to enjoy them," said Smith. Camping inside the cabins is prohibited.

To reach the site from Interstate 80, head south on Highway 89, which runs along the western border of Lake Tahoe. After about 10 miles, turn west, or right, onto Alpine Meadows Road, which leads to the Alpine Meadows ski resort. Drive another 2 miles and park at the trail head to the Five Lakes Trail and Granite Chief Wilderness. (You'll reach the trailhead before the ski resort.) The road, Deer Park Road, will be on your left, and you should see a sign that gives the mileage for several destinations, including Whiskey Creek. The hike to the sheep camp is approximately a two- to three-hour trek. For more information, call the Truckee Ranger District Office at (530) 587-3558.

Wheeler Sheep Camp

Carrie Smith, one of the U.S. Forest Service's archeologists, said it has only been since the mid-1970s and the passage of several significant environmental laws that the Forest Service has begun trying to preserve cultural resources such as the Whiskey Creek Camp. "As time goes on, the Forest Service gets more and more serious about it," she said.

More proof of that change in policy is the Forest Service's interest in the remains of the Wheeler Sheep Camp north of Truckee in the Tahoe National Forest, where sheepman Martin Gallues, originally from Nafarroa, spent many summers with his family. Around 1913 or 1914 Gallues became a working partner in the Wheeler sheep outfit, which grazed its sheep on land allotments in the area. Every summer the sheep were brought from Reno to the camp, and from there they trailed out to different ranges until the end of the summer. To serve the needs of the sheep and the herders, Gallues and his brother Felix built a base camp consisting of a three-room cabin, a horse barn, a chicken coop, and several other buildings that were in use well into the 1950s and 1960s.

According to stories from the Gallues family, sheepherders used to hone their wood-chopping techniques by splitting cedar posts for the corrals that are still there. The *kanperua,* or camp tender, would head out from the camp every five days, delivering food supplies, which included bread freshly baked in the outdoor brick oven at the camp. But the camp was abandoned after the outfit's owner retired in 1960, and the Forest Service eventually tore down the buildings. But the old outdoor bread oven, built in 1927 and thought to have historic value, was not touched.

Although the oven eventually collapsed during the 1980s, it has been restored, and today it is available for public use. With materials donated by the Forest Service, Basque historian Joxe Mallea coordinated its reconstruction with the help of several other people during the summer of 1992. A shed to protect it from the snow was rebuilt as well. The Gallues family was invited to christen the restored oven with an official bread-baking ceremony. Since then, several groups have used it. The Forest Service built a picnic area there with the oven as the centerpiece. In addition, signs are posted explaining the history of the camp and its day-to-day role in the sheep industry, with a map and photos of the Gallues family. District archeologist Michael Baldrica said people interested in using the oven need to make a reservation, so that people who drive from far away can be assured of the opportunity to use it. To reserve the site, call the Sierraville Ranger District Office at (530) 994-3401 and ask for Baldrica.

To reach Kyburz Flat, take Highway 89 north from Truckee for about 12 miles. You will turn onto the first road you reach on the right, a dirt road marked Road 450 (this is Henness Pass Road, but there are no signs). Drive 1 mile along this road until you reach an intersection, where you will turn left. Stay to the right, and about eight-tenths of a mile down this road you will reach the oven.

Kyburz Flat

The 1-mile area around Kyburz Flat is chock full of history, in addition to the sheep camp and aspen tree carvings left by Basque herders (for more information on carvings, see the Nevada chapter), according to archaeologist Michael Baldrica. Rock paintings, probably drawn by the ancestors of today's Washoe tribe, date back as far as A.D. 500. During the 1860s a hotel, stables, and other buildings were built in the area. When Henness Pass Road was the route from the Sacramento area to the Comstock Lode, Kyburz Flat served as a stage stop. Once the transcontinental railroad was completed, though, in 1867, the route, as well as the stage stop, were abandoned, and most of the buildings were torn down. Baldrica said that eventually all this history will be explained on interpretive signs to be posted in the area.

Susanville

SHEEP AND A LUMBER MILL

Susanville's Basque colony was probably in its heyday during the 1950s and 1960s, when Basques herded sheep in the surrounding mountains or worked in the nearby lumber mills. The sheepherders would come into town in the fall, after shipping out the lambs, and stay for three or four months, filling up the few boardinghouses in town. The lumber workers might choose to live permanently at one of the local boardinghouses. The men were employed by the Fruit Growers Supply Company, now Sierra-Pacific Lumber, and Lassen Lumber and Box, which is gone. Despite the fact that Basques no longer fill such jobs, a core of Basque families has remained in this town of ten thousand.

BOARDINGHOUSES

For many years, Basque businessman Richard Goñi and his wife, Angie, operated the St. Francis Hotel (830 Main Street), a former boardinghouse that Goñi's mother, Marie Jeanne, bought in 1947. The three-story-granite hotel was built as an American-style hotel, with a large lobby and coffee shop, and Marie Jeanne remodeled the restaurant and ran it for many years as a traditional room-and-board establishment. In spite of the fact that the Goñis sold it to non-Basques, the Basque coat of arms in faded red, green, and gold is still visible from afar on the outside wall of the hotel.

The St. Francis was the last of several Basque-owned hotels in this town, and it is one of the oldest businesses in town. In the 1930s there was John and Marie Beterbide's Pyrenees by the old Lassen Mill. Three generations of the Larrea family ran Marion's Hotel, but they finally sold it, and today it's a local bar. The Commercial Hotel served as a Basque boardinghouse during the 1940s. That was sold as well, and sometime during the 1960s the building burned down.

When young Basque men were plentiful here, the St. Francis sponsored a dance with accordion music at the end of every month. The St. Francis continued to serve boarders until the late 1980s, but by then there were only one or two. For years, the Goñis served Basque food family-style in the restaurant, with Angie as chef, until the Goñis decided they didn't have enough customers to justify the large servings that they had to prepare ahead of time.

The restaurant and bar continued to be the local Basque gathering place until the Goñis sold it in 2000.

CUSTOM MEAT AND GROCERY MARKET

Store owner Ignacio Urrutia was quite a story teller during the many years he ran Idaho Grocery in Susanville. Today, his sons and daughter carry on the legacy of their father who bought the store in 1968.

When he first arrived in this country in the 1930s, Urrutia jumped ship, and to escape detection he took the last name of a Basque friend, Idao. When he got to Boise for his first job as a sheepherder, the foreman thought Urrutia had misspelled *Idaho* "and put in the *h*," explained Urrutia, with a shrug and a laugh, adding that he used that name for twelve years.

He also had a tangled story of how he was denied entrance to the U.S. Army because he supposedly couldn't read English, yet he taught groups of immigrants about the U.S. Constitution so they could all become citizens. He was among those Basques who were specifically named in the series of Congressional "Sheepherder Bills" that granted them residency.

Besides herding sheep, Urrutia helped build railroads and did other odd jobs, but ultimately he returned to the grocery store business, following a family tradition. Urrutia's family still operates a store in his hometown of Galdakano, Bizkaia. Urrutia, who had worked at the Idaho Grocery since 1944 and took over twenty-two years later, remembered that when he started there were twenty-seven mom-and-pop stores in Susanville. Today Idaho Grocery is the only one left. His two sons, Robert and Joe Urrutia, provide a custom-slaughtering business for local ranchers, and the Urrutias provide custom-order meat. "We sell the best meat in town," said Urrutia's wife, Marceline. Urrutia's grocery store carries no specialty Basque items, except for the *lukainka,* or Basque sausages, produced by G.L.&L Smokehouse. The Urrutias also slaughter the lamb for the town's annual picnics. Marceline passed away in 1998, and Ignacio followed her in 1999.

Idaho Grocery, 2120 Main Street, Susanville, CA 96130 (530) 257-2194

BASQUE CLUB

Susanville's modest Basque club of about 150 members was organized in 1975. Shauna (Erreca) Cluck was just twenty years old when the local club elected her president in 1992. "Nobody wanted to be president," she said, by way of explanation. "Nobody wanted to put in the time. The older people who started this club want to relax. They want the younger people to take charge." Unfortunately, Cluck notes, most of Susanville's young Basques are not motivated to run the club either. A year of study in the Basque Country is what piqued her interest in preserving her unique culture.

As the club has gotten smaller, it has focused its energy on three events: the annual picnic, the *mus* tournament in March or April, and the annual stew feed on the first Saturday in May to raise funds for the dance group, Mendi Danzarriak. The *mus* tournament has helped beef up membership, with Basques from Reno showing up to try their luck. They also tend to show up at the August festival, said longtime member Michelle Zubillaga.

Festival. Even before Susanville's Basque Club was formed, local Basques were holding a picnic every year. That tradition continues annually on the first Saturday in August at the Lassen County Fairgrounds (195 Russell Avenue). It used to be just a dinner and dance, said Zubillaga, but now they start in the afternoon with weight-lifting relays and a performance by their dance group. They usually also have a wood-chopping exhibit, put on by a chopper from Reno.

Susanville Eskualdunak Club, P.O. Box 332, Susanville, CA 96130. Information: (530) 257-5367 (*Michelle Zubillaga*)

CHORIZO

G.L. & L. Smokehouse, a chorizo-making business in Susanville, was started by Richard Goñi and his partner, Ben Linschoteh. "Our chorizos are the real Basque chorizo," said Linschoteh's wife, Hedi. Basque people come from as far away as Elko, Nevada, to buy them, she noted. During the annual Lassen County Fair in July, they have sold as many as 3,200 chorizo sandwiches at their red-and-green wagon. While Goñi eventually left the business, his brother Jean helped out for years. At age seventy-three, he was still coming in daily, working for free just to keep busy, said Linschoteh. However, the mom-and-pop business grew bigger than the Linschotehs had ever expected, and they decided to retire and sold the business in 2004. The new owners, the Mallory family, continue to produce the chorizo and built a bigger meat-packing plant.

G.L. & L. Smokehouse, 1109 Riverside Drive, Susanville, CA 96130 (530) 257-2527

The quaint Sierra town of Susanville can experience considerable snow during the wintertime, making travel difficult unless you are prepared. If you plan to visit, the spring and summer months are best.

Alturas

SHEEP AND LUMBER MILLS

Basques had plenty of reason to come to Alturas in the first half of the century. Up to 100,000 sheep once grazed on the mountains surrounding this town at the southern end of the Cascade Range. And, as in Susanville, local lumber mills also provided plenty of employment.

Today, however, the mills are fighting a pitched battle with the government and conservation groups over the fate of the heavily forested mountains of Northern California, because they are home to the endangered spotted owl. And sheep grazing has diminished here as it has all over the West. Today there's only a handful of Basque families left in Alturas and nearby Cedarville. Nevertheless, there's definitely a historical Basque presence to be seen if you decide to make a trip to Alturas, now a town of 3,500. As a reminder of its former Basque population, Alturas also has a modern Basque restaurant.

BOARDINGHOUSES

It is believed that Pete and Mary Arena were the first Basques to open a boardinghouse in Alturas in 1929. The couple met in Gardnerville, Nevada, when Mary worked for John Etchemendy at the Overland Hotel and Pete boarded there while working at a blacksmith shop across the street. (Arena's son Al discovered his father's original name was Urbano Pedroarena, when he and his wife Shirley began researching the family's history. Arena suspects immigration officials may have written his father's name as Pedro Arena, and he never bothered to change it.) The couple married and eventually moved to Alturas to open their own business. The Arenas, along with Bartolo Goñi, salvaged the lumber from an old hotel torn down in Madeline, 35 miles away, and transported it to Alturas. The Arenas built the Buena Vista Hotel, and the Goñis built the Alturas Hotel. But their timing was bad.

The Pickering Lumber Company employed the earliest Basque boarders who stayed at the hotels. With the depression, the sawmill was bankrupted, many lumber workers lost their jobs, and the boardinghouse businesses were severely hurt. "They had quite a hard time," said Al Arena, who grew up in his parents' boardinghouse. In fact, he said, his parents were not able to pay off the building until the mid-1940s, when Mary Arena contracted with the U.S. Army to house and feed pilots who were training at the airport behind the hotel. The Goñis soon sold the Alturas Hotel to partner Benito "Benny" Apecechea and moved to Los Banos to operate another hotel.

After the war, Arena catered private parties and banquets at the hotel, in addition to feeding boarders, but she never opened her dining room to the public as a restaurant. Her place was popularly known simply as Mary's. Her son Al Arena relishes his childhood memories of the gourmet meals his mother cooked, adding that none of the modern Basque restaurants can compare. "She made her own raviolis, she made her own puddings and soups, and she made her own bread for a long time," he said. "We raised our own chickens and hogs, cured our own ham, and made our own chorizos."

The father-and-son team tried to keep up the bar business after Mary died in 1958, "but we couldn't make it work," said Arena, and they ended up selling out in 1965. Sadly, the barracklike structure built by Pete Arena himself, with the help of some men from the lumber mill, on the 1400 block of West Fourth deteriorated for many years and was finally torn down in 2004.

Nearby, however, at 1200 West Fourth, is the old Alturas Hotel building, now simply a bar, but still in operation. It's still called **Benny's,** even though "Benny" Apecechea sold out years ago.

Arena Blacksmith Shop

Although the Basque connection with the old hotels has been cut in Alturas, one historical setting here has been kept alive, the **Arena Blacksmith Shop.** While Mary Arena cooked at the boardinghouse, her husband Pete shod horses, made branding irons, and repaired tools in a nearby building, put up in 1909 from hand-hewn soft stone from a nearby quarry. Arena eventually bought the building in 1939, and his son Al carries on the trade there today, since he started helping his father in the shop when he was eight or nine years old. "To me it was just a lot of work. I didn't care about being a blacksmith," said Al Arena. They kept busy sharpening or repairing picks, sickle bars, plowshares, and other tools. But since that time, modern techniques have taken over, and "the blacksmith trade has died off," he said. "There's no demand for it whatsoever." The only custom iron work Al has done in recent years has mostly been to make wrought-iron decorations for his home, although he occasionally gets a request to make a branding iron or to sharpen some tools. Today Arena makes his living primarily by doing welding jobs and repairing big machinery using modern tools. But blacksmithing is gaining attention as a pre–twentieth-century trade, and hobbyists are learning it. Arena will heat up iron in the forge and work it on the anvil when an occasional group of tourists comes through and requests a demonstration.

There's no sign on the Arena Blacksmith Shop, which is across the street from city hall, and Arena frequently works elsewhere. So if you hope to catch a glimpse of him at the forge while you're in Alturas, call him ahead of time. The old building has hardly changed since it was built, and many of the original tools are still hanging on the

18-inch deep walls. You can see the original chisel markings on the exterior.

Arena Blacksmith Shop, 201 Howard Street (at North), Alturas, CA 96101 (530) 233-2947

RESTAURANT AND CAMPING

One sure thing you can count on in Alturas is a good Basque meal, at the **Brass Rail,** right on the outskirts of town. Owners Fernand and Joséfina Larrañaga took over the restaurant in 1973. At that time it was a small restaurant with nothing around it. In little more than two years the Larrañagas expanded the business, built a KOA campground for trailers, a gas station and small grocery store, a swimming pool, showers, and a self-service laundry. The Larrañagas cater to comfort-seeking campers, many of whom come to look for arrowheads made from the obsidian from nearby lava beds. If you spend the night, you can probably even fit in a game of handball on a one-wall court built by the pelota-playing Fernand. In 1980 the Larrañagas invested in the sheep business as well, and today they have about six thousand head that graze in the Modoc National Forest. They serve their own fresh lamb in the restaurant.

Banquets, weddings, and class reunions are popular at the large restaurant, which can seat up to four hundred. The Larrañagas, luckily, have profited from the nearby rail service, which normally doesn't make a stop there. Package tours for a scenic train ride north to Lakeview are organized by the local chamber of commerce, and the tour includes a special stop at the Brass Rail for a traditional Basque meal. The Larrañagas greatly expanded the restaurant to accommodate large banquets, and Joséfina said that conferences for groups from as far away as Colorado have been held there.

Every day Joséfina bakes twenty-two loaves of sheepherder's bread to serve fresh to the restaurant customers. She is pleased at her grown sons' interest in the family businesses, remarking of the U.S.–born Basques, "Very few keep up the traditions of the fathers." Larrañaga insisted that Basque be spoken at home, and when the family visited the Basque Country, her sons were surprised to find they spoke the language better than their cousins did.

Brass Rail, Lakeview Highway 395, Alturas, CA 96101 (530) 233-2906

Surprise Valley

SHEEP AND CATTLE

Near Alturas, nestled in fertile Surprise Valley, are the towns of Cedarville and Eagleville, homes to a few Basque families. At one time there were up to 150,000 sheep raised in this valley. Today John Espil is one of the few sheep operators left here, and another longtime Basque rancher, John Laxague, runs cattle.

Three Basque sheepherders allegedly killed by a family of Shoshones at Little High Rock Canyon in nearby Nevada in 1911—Pierre "Pete" Erramouspe, Jean Baptiste Laxague, and Bertrand Indiano—were from Eagleville, as were the men who went after the Indian family. (See the section on Winnemucca, Nevada, for more information.) "We knew all of them guys in the posse when I was a kid," said local Pete Ytçaina. "We used to hear some wild stories about all of that." The valley carries the sad legacy of that event. The rancher John Laxague, son of Jean Baptiste, was born after his father was killed.

Eagleville is practically deserted these days. In the middle of town, the old Ytçaina home, where Basques revved up the phonograph and played Basque songs during the 1930s, is empty now, right across from the old Eagleville store, also empty.

BOARDINGHOUSES

In picturesque Cedarville there were once three Basque boardinghouses. The largest of them was Valentine's, which had a handball court. "When the men worked up a sweat and had to go inside to have a drink, us kids would get out there to play," remembers Pete Ytçaina, who's now in his seventies. The court was torn down, and the hotel was moved across the street to be turned into a grocery store—now Page's.

CEMETERIES

Many tombstones at the cemeteries of Eagleville and Cedarville carry Basque names, including those of the men who were killed in Little High Rock Canyon. Cedarville's is on the west side of the highway between the two towns, as you head south out of town. Continue south about 15 miles, almost to Eagleville, and you'll find the Eagleville cemetery, on the same side of the road.

CHURCH

Stop by Cedarville's Catholic church, **St. James** (Garfield and Bonner), which has beautiful stained-glass windows etched with the names of some of the area's early Basque families who donated money to have them installed many years ago. Pete Ytçaina is one of the last Basques left here, and if you're lucky, you'll find him at the Surprise Valley truck "scale house" on the highway at the north end of town, which he owns, or you can even stop by his house, which serves as an office for his businesses, including the Cedarville Trailer Park, just off the main highway (650 Garfield [530] 279-2504). He has a lot of stories about the old days when there were many Basque families in town. He still speaks Basque, "but I'm losing it now, 'cause there's no one to talk it with anymore."

REFERENCES

Bynum, Lindley, and Idwal Jones. *Biscailuz: Sheriff of the New West.* New York: William Morrow and Company, 1950.

Castanchoa, Florence. *Gure Euskal Etxea: The House the Basques Built.* South San Francisco: Basque Cultural Center, 1992.

Cohen, Chester G. *El Escorpion: From Indian Village to Los Angeles Park.* Woodland Hills, Calif.: Periday Company, 1989.

Decroos, Jean Francis. *The Long Journey: Social Integration and Ethnicity Maintenance Among Urban Basques in the San Francisco Bay Region.* Reno, Nev.: Associated Faculty Press and Basque Studies Program, 1980.

Douglass, William A., and Jon Bilbao. *Amerikanuak: Basques in the New World.* Reno, Nev.: University of Nevada Press, 1975, pp. 117–76.

Eagle, Sonia. "Work and Play Among the Basques of Southern California." Diss., Purdue University, 1979, pp. 36.

Echeverria, Jeronima. "California-ko Ostatuak: A History of California's Basque Hotels." Diss., North Texas State University, 1988, pp. 4; 64–74; 136–69.

———. *Home Away From Home: A History of Basque Boardinghouses.* Reno: University of Nevada Press, 1999.

Gaye, Laura B. *Last of the Old West: A Book of Sketches about the Calabasas Area.* Encino, Calif.: Argold Press, 1965, pp. 68–75.

Hovey, Carol. "Altube Family: The California Years, Chapter II." *Journal of Basque Studies in America* 11–12 (1991–1992): 15–35.

Paquette, Mary Grace. *Basques to Bakersfield.* Bakersfield, Calif.: Kern County Historical Society, 1982.

Pipkin, George C. *Pete Aguereberry: Death Valley Prospector and Gold Miner.* Trona, Calif.: Murchison Publications, 1971.

Saunders, Charles Francis, and Father St. John O'Sullivan. *Capistrano Nights: Tales of a California Mission Town.* New York: Robert M. McBride and Company, 1930.

Nevada

When you speak of Basques in the American West, you probably conjure up the romantic image of a herder surrounded by thousands of sheep, leading them through the seasons from lonely mountain ranges to lowland plains and valleys, with his dog at his side.

You can easily imagine that scenario as you drive along Nevada's long desolate roads. Wide open spaces still prevail in this state, whether it is sagebrush flatlands or sparsely timbered mountains. One gets a keen sense of what life was like for those early sheepherders. Although the state's two biggest cities, Reno and Las Vegas, have grown into urban metropolises, most of Nevada seems to have changed little since the West was first settled. Indeed, the state, with its remote mountains, back roads, and ghost mining towns, offers the most realistic glimpse of the Old West lifestyle. Nevada is searing heat in the summer, snowy winters, and starry night skies.

Nevada is situated midway between the large Basque population centers of California and Idaho and is central to the Basque presence in the American West. Therefore it seems quite appropriate that a committee chose Reno as the location for a monument to the Basque sheepherder. The abstract figure of the herder with a sheep around his neck sits at the base of a hill that was once part of the sheep range of a Basque family.

Nevada was also the appropriate place for such a monument because of the contribution that Basques have made over the years to Nevada's livelihood. In the late 1800s and early 1900s, gold and silver strikes created booming mining towns in Nevada, which died almost as quickly as they sprang up. Sheep fed the early mining towns, and raising sheep provided jobs and continuity for many of the smaller communities. Mining has continued to play a significant role in the state's economy, and Basques have been among the most constant employees of the mines. Today tourism is the number one industry in the state, and Basques contribute by sponsoring their popular ethnic festivals and providing hearty Basque food at their restaurants across the state. In fact, more than one restaurant critic has touted the Basque restaurants along Highway 80 as oases in an otherwise bland culinary desert. A few also joined the popular casino business, which brings lots of money to Nevada because gambling is outlawed in many states.

The Basques are well known in this state, and Nevadans display a great deal of enthusiasm for Basque events. In fact, the Nevada festivals, especially Elko's, are probably the biggest of them all. Some say their popularity is owing to Nevada's location, smack in the middle of the Basque colonies, so that it is within relatively short travel time for Basques in California and Idaho. Maybe the competitive Basque games sponsored in Nevada attract a lot more people. Perhaps it is Nevada's rural setting that gives the festivals a more authentic feel. Or maybe Nevadans simply make a bigger fuss over these celebrations because there aren't as many ethnic celebrations in this sparsely populated state.

"Nevada loves the Basques because of how much tourism they bring to the state," said Dan Gaztambide of Salt Lake City, where the Mormon-dominated population barely takes note of its Basques. Over the years magazine writers have generously touted Nevada's Basque festivals and restaurants. Elko's National Basque Festival is the best, say visitors, with Winnemucca's taking a close second. But Ely, in its heyday, offered one of the best, as did Reno.

Nevada is also significant to the U.S. Basque population because of the strong Basque Studies Program and the rich Basque library at the University of Nevada at Reno. A collection of Basque books, begun in the mid-1960s, today overflows with materials on every Basque subject conceivable. Elementary Basque language classes are offered continually, and professors from the Basque Country teach at the university, giving lectures on their particular Basque subject of expertise and undertaking research projects. The University of Nevada Press publishes books in its Basque Series, which has gained a reputation as one of the most successful specialized book series among the country's university presses. The series now includes over forty-five books. The university also has an excellent Basque dance group.

Politicians in this state have always been keenly aware of the Basque population. The name McCarran is seen often in Nevada on everything from streets to airports, and its bearer, former U.S. Senator Patrick McCarran, offered significant help to the Basque sheepherders in this country. The powerful senator and chairman of the Senate Judiciary Committee was a sheep rancher himself and was instrumental in pushing through several pieces of legislation known as the Sheepherder Bills. When Basque attorney Peter Echeverria was chairman of the state Gaming Commission, a highly prestigious and influential position, he was instrumental in bringing the Basque game of jai alai to the big casino businesses in Reno and Las Vegas, although the venture did not last.

The first difference you'll notice upon entering Nevada's Basque restaurants are the slot machines by the door and the video black-jack machines inserted in the bars. The Basques, just like most other business owners, have cashed in on Nevada's legalized gambling. In fact, a Basque owns one of the state's larger casinos—John Ascuaga has the Nugget in Sparks. Ascuaga followed restaurateur Dick Graves from Idaho to Reno, working beside him as he built up the Nugget casino empire. He eventually bought the Sparks Nugget from Graves and turned it into a humongous complex, built under and around Interstate 80, which came through the area in the early 1970s. Ascuaga's Basque heritage is not overtly present here, although photographs of Basque scenes by Linda Dufurrena decorate every hotel room. But over the years, many Basque gatherings have been held at Ascuaga's Nugget, especially after he opened his Restaurante Orozko. At that time, he also installed a statue of a Basque sheepherder outside the casino.

Dan Bilbao recently sold the Stockmen's casino in Elko, after longtime ownership. Other Basques, such as Gene Gastanaga, have minority interests in the industry (the North Shore Club and the Crystal Bay Club at Lake Tahoe) or have been top executives (Roger Trounday of the Sparks Nugget and Tom Yturbide of Harvey's).

Interstate 80 traverses this state along the most direct route—meaning the most flat and boring territory. To see this state's real beauty, drive into any of Nevada's mountain ranges—most of them are open to the public as national forests. Few of the mountains here are accessible via paved roads, but with a four-wheel-drive vehicle or pickup you can easily navigate the dirt roads. And for adventurous hikers and backpackers, hiking any of Nevada's mountain ranges is well worth the trouble. The aspen groves scattered throughout the Western mountain ranges are littered with the scrawls and artistic renderings of the sheepherders who passed through the area.

ASPEN CARVINGS

Perhaps as a way to ensure that their presence here was remembered, and perhaps simply out of boredom, the Basque sheepherders left

Women's bodies were among the favorite subjects for Basque herder carvings. (Photo by Jorma L. Kaukonen.)

behind a legacy of carvings on the West's aspen trees. The historical value of these carvings has only lately been appreciated.

Professor Joxe Mallea of the University of Nevada, Reno, who has studied the carvings, estimates that there are at least 500,000 trees bearing Basque carvings throughout the thirteen Western states. That is a rough estimate based on the fact that the groves on Peavine Mountain outside Reno contain approximately five hundred carvings. "If there are that many on one little mountain, can you imagine [how many there are] in the West?" he remarked. As for how many sheepherders the carvings represent, Mallea responded, "There's no way of knowing because some of them came for three years and then they left, and there's no record of them anywhere. Nobody went up there to those mountains" to count them.

Typically, the herders simply engraved into the bark of saplings their initials or names and the date of their passage through a particular grove. The more creative ones wrote their thoughts, or even a poem, and drew pictures. Their most common subjects were women and sex, their homeland, or, more specifically, their *baserri* (farmhouse). Because of the particular nature of the aspen tree, over time scar tissue would grow around the knife marks, outlining the original carving. Herders also built small monuments of rocks—which the Basques call *harri mutillak,* or stone boys—usually on a high point that could be seen from miles around, as a marker for other herders. A few of these can still be found in the mountain ranges.

During the summer months they spent in the mountains, sheepherders sought out the aspen groves for their nightly campsites because they knew they would find grazing meadows and fresh water for their sheep nearby. Attracted by the smooth white bark, and for lack of anything better to do, they carved. The trees bear messages back and forth between herders, references to their homeland, province, or hometown; images of animals; criticisms of bosses or complaints about the job, peppered with swear words; pictures of

This herder marked every year he came through this grove near Lake Tahoe. (Photo by Jorma L. Kaukonen.)

local prostitutes, or nostalgic references to girlfriends back home—whatever came to mind. Many of the drawings are very detailed renderings of women and men (and their private parts), some in the act of making love.

One carver, who signed his name Borel, has left behind an artistic legacy in groves near Kyburz Flat in the Tahoe National Forest in California. "It appears he had some formal art training," said Michael Baldrica, the Forest Service's district archeologist. "The rest are primitive style, but Borel's are different. He knew how to draw," he said, adding that Borel's sketches, primarily of women's faces, were very proportional. "We dubbed it Borel's Grove," said Mallea, who takes groups to the site regularly. "He was an amazing carver." Other people call it Trini's Grove—in the name of a local prostitute named Trini whose image appears on many of the trees there. "I think Trini just went up there and made some money," chuckled Phil Earl, Nevada Historical Society museum curator.

This owl has grown more distinct with the passing years. (Photo by Jorma L. Kaukonen.)

Joxe Mallea and the Aspen Tree Carvings

When Joxe Mallea first came to the University of Nevada to begin his graduate studies in 1985, he was unaware of the existence of tree carvings in the area. He ran across them quite by accident when he decided to take a hike into Peavine Mountain, which was in plain view of his Reno home. The aspen trees were ablaze with fall colors. When he spotted the first name, he couldn't figure it out, because the writing is not always easy to decipher. But after the second or third, he recognized a Basque name among the scrawls. "We kept walking up the mountain and we kept finding more and more names," he said. Finally it dawned on him that these must have been done by sheepherders.

Hunters, backpackers, forest rangers, and archeologists have run across the tree carvings for decades, but only now are they being seriously researched and recorded. Dr. Mallea, now an adjunct history professor at the University of Nevada in Reno, is the first Basque scholar to launch an extensive study of the carvings. Students, photographers, and forest officials have done short studies. Former Nevada Historical Society museum curator Phil Earl spent twenty years creating rubbings of the carvings. But Mallea is the first to hone in on the historical significance of the carvings for the Basque people. Aside from the graphic renderings, most non-Basques were unable to fully interpret the writings, which are mostly in Euskara, French, or Spanish.

Because the carvings are located in high forested regions, they usually fall under the jurisdiction of the U.S. Forest Service or the Bureau of Land Management, particularly in Nevada, where more than 80 percent of the land is owned by the government. The two government agencies were well aware of the existence of the carvings, but their staff did little or nothing with them for years, according to Mallea. "They just didn't think they were valuable," he said. So Mallea embarked on a one-man mission to save the carvings, if possible, and to bring them to the attention of the public. He has spent several hundred hours videotaping as many carvings as he can and presenting slide shows and lectures. He has also launched a campaign to impress the importance of the carvings upon the two government agencies and gain their participation in the preservation efforts. "We have a whole new relationship with the federal government now," he said, noting that interested staff members are also studying them and seeking funds for their preservation. "This is the first time that the federal government is interested in the Basques."

Not every sheepherder knew how to carve on the tree so that his thought would become legible in future years. The best carvings were created with thin, light lines. In his attempt to document the history surrounding the art, Mallea has spoken with several former sheepherders. He found some who refused to acknowledge that they had even been to those locations, clearly embarrassed to be associated with any of the sexual carvings. One particular grove on Table Mountain in the Monitor Range of the Toiyabe National Forest southeast of Austin has been dubbed "Porno Grove" by Forest Service personnel because of the high concentration of erotic drawings found there. Mallea, who visited the grove, said the carvings are no more graphic than those at other locations. "I don't think it's pornographic. I think people just gave it that name."

Preservation. The most worrisome aspect of the carvings is that the aspen tree typically lives only eighty to a hundred years. Dead trees topple and rot, and living trees are prone to disease and have been victims of the tree-cutting work of beavers. Consequently, Mallea has found very few carvings that date back to the last century. But he has run across occasional carvings dating back to the 1890s in the California's Sierra Nevada and in northern Humboldt County in Nevada.

Considering that sheepherders abounded around the turn of the century, many of the trees they carved have already died, and Mallea is worried that more trees will disappear before their carvings are recorded. That is why the historian wants to both preserve a record of as many as possible and cut down at least a few for exhibition. "We can't preserve a whole forest," he said. Archeologist Michael Baldrica said that the Forest Service is primarily just taking inventory of the carvings, relying in large part on Mallea's research, but that they, too, would like to find some way to preserve the carvings. A few tree trunks have been cut for display, but it's not known how long they will last. Mallea said that some of these cut stumps have been kept a few years at the Basque studies library and in his office at the university, and they have suffered only minor cracking.

Phil Earl, former curator for the Nevada Historical Society Museum, calls the work erotic folk art. He's more interested in the drawings than the writings. Over the years, during their numerous camping trips into the Sierra, Earl and his wife Jean have perfected the art of capturing the drawings by doing tree rubbings. Imitating the methods used for taking tombstone rubbings in England, the Earls use rubbing wax to bring out a drawing on muslin cloth. They then spray the image to keep it from smearing. Earl has shown some of his rubbings as museum exhibits and has presented slide shows too. "We were hoping we could help in the preservation of Basque culture," Earl said. The Earls have also displayed their rubbings at Basque festivals, where they've found many interested second- or third-generation Basque-Americans. The immigrant sheepherders, though, "don't see this as art," said Earl. Some of the couple's early rubbings are now irreplaceable, because the trees have since died. The Earls have developed portfolios of ten reproductions, approximately eighteen by twenty-four inches, which are available for sale.

Park Service and Forest Service personnel worry about people mutilating the tree carvings. So did the Earls. "For a long time, we wanted to keep them secret, because we were worried people would take knives and chain saws up there," said Earl. "But we've never seen any of that." He did once find a drawing of a woman that had been scratched by what appears to have been a bear sharpening his claws.

"Our concern is making sure that vandalism doesn't increase," said Carrie Smith of the Forest Service. "Some people are offended by the nudity." There have been instances of people slashing or otherwise marring some of the drawings. But Smith feels that the public should be able to enjoy the carvings and appreciate their artistic appeal—she simply enjoins people to treat the carvings with the respect they deserve, since they are irreplaceable. "We don't have that much out there on the landscape that is a testament to the Basque experience and their contribution to the sheep industry. The carvings tell quite a story," she observed.

Some Forest Service officials are loath to reveal locations of carved trees for fear people will cut them down and take them home. Already, said Humboldt archeologist Fred Frampton, "our history is getting ripped off." He cites as examples that Nevada's ghost towns are disappearing bit by bit, as are the cliff dwellings in the Southwest, because people take pieces home with them. But because of the trees' short life spans, the Forest Service workers also feel compelled to make the carvings available to the public before they disappear.

Phil Earl, 700 Putnam Drive, Reno, NV 89503; (775) 323-2571. Portfolio of 10 reproductions, $100, plus $5 for postage.

Locations. Because the carvings are in high mountainous regions, they are not easy to find, and people who go in search of them often need the use of a pickup or four-wheel-drive vehicle. The roads leading to the groves are usually unpaved and unmarked, and often they are closed during winter and spring—and even if they aren't, they are likely to be muddy during those seasons. The best time to travel to the high country is between July and October. Leave your vehicle in clear areas by the road and do not attempt to drive off-road. Specific directions for just a few of the most accessible groves are provided here, but anyone venturing into these areas should be equipped with an emergency kit, maps, flashlights, water, a compass, and other necessities. It's also a good idea to check with the local Bureau of Land Management or ranger station. (Their phone numbers can be found in the local phone books.)

Kyburz Flat and Borel's Grove

Several areas around Kyburz Flat, which is a quick drive from Truckee, California, offer some of the most impressive carvings. Kyburz Flat is a big grassy meadow with a fresh water marsh at one end where ducks and geese nest in the winter. To reach Kyburz Flat, take Highway 89 north from Truckee approximately 12 miles to Road 450, a dirt road also known as Henness Pass Road, easily managed by car. Follow the road east for about 1 mile to an area of carvings. More groves of carved trees are located around the same road about 4 miles further east. You will be very near the site of the former Wheeler Sheep Camp, where a Basque bread oven has been restored and is available for public use. (For more information, see the section on Whiskey Creek Sheep Camp and Wheeler Sheep Camps in the Lake Tahoe Region, California, section.)

To reach Borel's Grove—or Trini's grove—you will continue north on Highway 89 for about 2 miles beyond Road 450 (approximately 15 miles from Truckee) to a paved road (Road 7) heading west to Jackson Meadows. Almost immediately upon turning left onto that road, you will spot a dirt road marked Treasure Mountain Road (Road 5) on the right. Follow it for a little more than a mile to a fork in the road. Take the left fork (Road 5-72) and continue for about half a mile. You will find a meadow with a large aspen grove on your right. For further information call the Sierraville Ranger District Office at (530) 994-3401.

Since there are obviously too many such groves to mention here, the other ones chosen are primarily well known in the centrally located

Lake Tahoe/Reno area and fairly easy to reach by car. Three other spots are the carvings along Pole Creek, on the northwest side of Lake Tahoe; the carvings near Genoa Peak, on the east side of the lake; and those on Peavine Mountain, just north of Reno.

Pole Creek

From Interstate 80 at Truckee, take Highway 89 south toward Tahoe City. Travel on this highway for 6.2 miles and you will see a dirt road on the right side (Road 8). Turn right, or west, and continue for 2.7 miles, where you will come to a bridge that crosses Pole Creek. After crossing it, follow the road to the left for ⅔ of a mile to a hairpin curve in the road. Stop here and park, and you can walk to an aspen grove full of carvings that is visible from the road.

Genoa Peak

To get to Genoa Peak (on the east side of Lake Tahoe) take Highway 50 (Spooner Summit Highway) south from Carson City, Nevada, just past the point where it meets State Highway 28, known as Spooner Junction. On the east side of the highway, you will spot a road next to the Spooner Guard maintenance station. This unimproved dirt road is usually closed until July, but it is fairly easy to travel by car during the summer. Drive up this road for approximately 2½ miles, until you reach a fork. Take the road going left, and stop about 100 yards further on. You will find carvings on either side of the road. You may also continue on the same road, and when you reach the next fork, take the road to the right. This will lead you to another extensively carved grove.

Peavine Mountain

Although carvings are located in the slopes of the mountain behind the Basque Sheepherder Monument in Reno, it would require a full day's hike to reach them from that point. They are much easier to reach from the north side of Peavine Mountain. To get there, take the Highway 395 business strip north out of the city. Exit at Stead Boulevard and turn left onto Stead traveling west under the freeway to North Virginia Street, where you will turn right. The first dirt road leading west, or left, will take you up the mountainside. You can drive partway up this road with a pickup or four-wheel-drive vehicle. Another option is to drive on Highway 395 one exit beyond Stead to

Red Rock and head west on Red Rock under the freeway to North Virginia. Turn right and follow the street until it turns into a dirt road, continuing until you spot an unmarked dirt road heading west up into the mountain. This road is partially driveable with a pickup but accessible also by foot. It's about a two-hour walk to the aspen groves.

Other Sites

These are just a few of the sites. "There are dozens and dozens of places," said Mallea. Some other groves where carvings have been studied or photographed are along the ridges of the Trident and Pine Forest ranges near Denio, just south of the Oregon/Nevada border and at the head of Lye Creek, near Hinkey Summit Road (this is the extension of Highway 290) north of Paradise Valley, Nevada. Richard Lane studied tree carvings on the western slope of the Ruby Mountains between Lamoille Canyon and Mitchell Creek, in the Red Rock area west of the town of Jiggs, and in the Mountain City and Gold Creek districts of the Humboldt National Forest near the Idaho border. Carvings can be found on trees lining the road to the town of Jarbidge, north of Elko, Nevada. (See the section on Independence Valley, Nevada, for more information.) Additional groves in this area, in the Mary's River Range in the Jarbidge Primitive Area, are referred to as "Bascoville."

It is highly likely that there are carvings in the mountains near just about every Basque colony, since the settlements typically cropped up near the common sheep trails, and the herders carved in nearly every significant aspen grove on the trails. So if you think there might be carvings in your area, look up some of the former sheepherders or local hunters and ask them where to look. There may be some carvings closer to you than you think. Although wildflowers bloom in the spring, the best times to visit the groves are during the summer, when the roads are dry, or the fall, when the aspen leaves turn brilliant colors.

ORGANIZED CARVING TRIPS AND INTERNET SITES

Over the years, several different groups have led trips to some local tree carvings. Passport in Time (PIT), a volunteer organization connected to the U.S. Forest Service, has led several such trips throughout the West. PIT has organized expeditions to record Basque tree carvings in California, Nevada, Wyoming, and most recently Idaho. PIT Idaho forest archeologist Susie Osgood plans to repeat the successful venture, probably in several different areas. "We're hoping to launch a national effort," said Osgood, who didn't realize how many carvings were in Idaho until an expedition in 2004. "This project opened our eyes to the magnitude of what we probably have." She noted that they found a tree carving dating as far back as 1899, which she is fairly certain is genuine. Information about the trips is available on their Web site, *www.passportintime.com.* Also of interest is Joxe Mallea's "Lertxun Marrak" page on the Center for Basque Studies Web site, *www.basque.unr.edu/trees/,* where you can view good photographs of about eighty carvings.

Reno

The First Big Basque Festival

Several years before Basque culture was pursued in Reno academically, the city was in the forefront of modern Basque cultural manifestations in Nevada. The Western Basque Festival was organized in nearby Sparks in 1959, and according to Professor William Douglass, it was a turning point for the U.S. Basque community.

Dick Graves, who was married to a Basque, owned the Nugget, a major Nevada gambling casino, managed by his right-hand man, John Ascuaga. The Nugget sponsored the big festival. In fact, Graves, a big booster of the Basques, was in large part responsible for initiating the idea. State senator and attorney Peter Echeverria and writer Robert Laxalt spearheaded the planning, which took more than a year. The team brought a larger group of Basques on board—immigrant and U.S. born, Hegoaldetarrak and Iparraldetarrak, in hopes of reaching a regional audience. "The obstacles were formidable, since the Basque populace of the American West was spread thinly over an enormous geographical expanse. Nor was it laced together by any kind of formal information network," wrote Douglass in an article entitled "Inventing a Basque Identity." There were few Basque clubs, and the formation of the North American Basque Organizations (NABO) was still fourteen years away.

Laxalt had published his book *Sweet Promised Land,* the story of his immigrant father's life in America and return visit to Europe. Most Basque families had similar experiences, and the author received many letters of gratitude from Basques throughout the American West. This correspondence provided the organizing committee with its initial mailing list. Laxalt used his journalism experience to get the media's attention, and the immigrants on the committee used their connections with many Old Country Basques throughout the West.

Basques in different communities had already been gathering for years at informal barbecues and picnics. At least four clubs that were already organized in Southern California and Boise, Idaho, were hosting events. But none was on the scale of the festival planned for Nevada.

The festival was the first time several folk dance groups, including one from New York, had come together to perform. The athletic competitions of weight-lifting, wood chopping, and weight carrying, now common at Nevada's festivals, were first organized for this event. A professional *txistulari* (a musician who plays an instrument similar to a flute, which is held straight up and down) traveled to Reno from New York. Among the crowd of five thousand to six thousand people who attended were the French and Spanish ambassadors from Washington D.C., as well as several state and local officials.

"It was fabulous," former Reno resident Mary (Laxague) Guerrica recalled. She was a teenager at the time. "It was completely different from what we have now." Her favorite part was the authentic sheepherder's camp that was set up complete with pitched tent and a campfire with cooking utensils next to it.

"Many elderly Basques who had lived through the difficult years of anti-Basque discrimination wept openly at this public display of their heritage," wrote Douglass. Many young Basque-Americans were introduced to aspects of their culture they were not familiar with. Being the first such event, it marked the beginning of public awareness of the Basque culture in this country and generated great pride within the Basque colony.

"It inspired all of Nevada," said Marie Ordoqui of Ely. "The Basque people didn't really do too much until that came along." It prompted

Basques in other Nevada cities to begin seriously organizing themselves and sponsoring their own local festivals.

Among the first to imitate the grand festival was Ely. Then Elko. And later came the Reno club in 1967. At that time, San Francisco's large population of young men who traveled to the Reno festival made it one of the most popular. "Years ago, when there weren't many festivals, Reno and Elko were the only ones that had games," said longtime Reno club member Janet Inda. Wood choppers and weight-lifters showed off, sheepdogs chased sheep into trailers, and contestants lined up for the weight-carrying contest.

RESTAURANTS

Food is an essential component of Basque community life in this country. Ask any Basque you know about his or her fondest memories, and you'll probably hear about family and friends together sitting at long tables at a local boardinghouse, serving themselves steaming bowls of vegetable soup, chomping on fresh French bread, eating crispy chicken and roasted lamb, and drinking wine. Those experiences also played a significant role in the lives of the U.S.–born generation. Because of the many Basque restaurants and barbecues that continue today, many can still enjoy this experience. In fact, it is this cultural experience that Americans have most commonly shared with the Basque community.

Although many Basque restaurants in other cities have given up the boardinghouse style of seating diners at long tables, in Reno the two long-time restaurants, **Louis' Basque Corner** and the **Santa Fe,** still do things the old-fashioned way. There is definitely something wonderful to be said for the interaction between diners that is part of eating together. What many diners most remember from these meals are the friendly chats with complete strangers. Martha and Mike Mahaffey of Reno are regulars at Louis' Basque Corner. "Invariably you spark up conversation with the people around you," said Martha Mahaffey, who has met long-time Renoites as well as tourists trying out Basque food. "We like to bring a whole table full of people. It's a great place to go with the family."

The old-timers in town accused Kent Mowry (Echevarria) of bucking tradition when he opened the elegant Pyrenees Bar and Grill

Poulet Basquaise, Louis Erreguible, Louis' Basque Corner

1 chicken (approximately 3½ pounds) cut up
Salt and pepper to taste
Cooking oil
1 medium onion, sliced in rings
4 tomatoes, blanched and peeled
6 green bell peppers, sliced
1 bay leaf, crushed
1 cup sliced mushrooms
2 pinches crushed thyme
2 slices jambon de Bayonne (Basque-style ham, can be replaced with smoked ham or prosciutto), cut in ½-inch cubes
¼ cup diced pimentos
1 sprig parsley, chopped
1½ cups dry white wine
1 cup chopped mushrooms (optional)

Season chicken pieces with salt and pepper. Heat small amount of oil in deep skillet. Add chicken pieces. Brown on all sides. Add onion, tomatoes, pepper slices, bay leaf, mushrooms, thyme, ham, and wine to skillet. Stir to mix. Cover. Cook over low heat for 30 minutes, until chicken is cooked. Stir in pimentos and parsley until warmed. Using a slotted spoon, transfer chicken and vegetables to warm platter. Spoon small amount of juice from skillet over chicken. Serves 6.

in a former French mansion in 1988. Tapas at the bar and individual tables were a far cry from the boardinghouse style. Nevertheless, Mowry was taking up a family tradition started by his maternal grandparents, who once ran the Paradise Hotel in Paradise Valley, and continued by his Zubillaga cousins who ran the Martin Hotel in Winnemucca. "The old-time Vascos—they're hardest to please," said Mowry. Unfortunately, business at the large "yuppie" restaurant was not sufficient to keep it going, and the restaurant closed in 1993.

Unlike some other long-time Basque restaurants, where the owners have hired younger men to do the cooking, at **Louis' Basque Corner** owner Louis Erreguible is still running his kitchen—more than forty years after he and his wife Lorraine opened the restaurant and hotel in 1967. At Louis' you know what day it is based on the four entrées you're served.

Erreguible corrects a couple of incorrect notions about Old Country home cooking: "We don't eat lamb over there like they think we do. People have gotten the idea that because we are Basque, we eat lamb," he said. Pork is eaten frequently in homes in the Old Country, since most farming families raise a few pigs specifically for their own consumption. But lamb is more of a delicacy. In the average family, lamb stew might be a common dish, but only because it can be made with cheaper cuts. Also in the Basque Country they don't know the pinto bean that the U.S. Basque restaurants serve up regularly, according to Erreguible; in the Old Country they use the white or navy bean.

Son Mark Moberly manages the restaurant, and Louis's wife, Lorraine, handles public relations. Her efforts have probably made Louis' Basque Corner one of the best-known Basque restaurants in the country. But the couple attributes the restaurant's success to authenticity. "We keep so many things that are really true Basque," said Louis, who is from Maule, Zuberoa. "We keep the old recipes." But he also admits that advertising helps. "We advertise *and* we keep the tradition." The Erreguibles still run the hotel upstairs, but American guests have replaced the old Basque sheepherders.

The city is renovating the old downtown, which is sure to bring more business to Reno's two longtime restaurants. A new convention center opened down the street from Louis', and the train tracks that run near the Santa Fe are now underground.

When the original **Santa Fe** burned down in 1948, then-owner Martin Esain rebuilt it and reopened it in the same spot one year to the day later. Aurelie, Anita, and Joe Zubillaga inherited the business from Esain, their uncle, and they ran the hotel and the restaurant in much the same manner. They serve big tureens of soup, french fries, meat, and other side dishes family-style on long tables. As at Louis', the hotel guests there are American. The Zubillagas have a legend attached to their name because they stood up to the gambling giant Harrah's. The big casino tried to buy up the property in the late 1970s as part of its expansion plans, but the family refused a generous offer for the building. Today the small brick building sits surrounded by Harrah's. Joe's son Phil Zubillaga is mostly running the show these days.

Louis' Basque Corner Restaurant (Courtesy of Lorraine Erreguible)

John Ascuaga, Basque owner of the massive John Ascuaga's Nugget casino-resort in Sparks, introduced the cuisine of his forefathers in 1998 with the opening of Orozko Restaurante. It is the eighth restaurant in his gambling complex on Victorian Square, next to the City of Reno. The opening of the restaurant coincided with the unveiling of *The Shepherd,* a seventeen-foot sculpture that stands outside the 275-seat restaurant on the street corner of the Nugget. According to Professor Carmelo Urza, in an article that appeared in the Basque Studies newsletter in 1999, the sculpture was one of the pieces of competing artwork for the National Basque Monument in Reno. The bronze sculpture depicts a herder picking up a lamb to protect it from the cold wind. Restaurante Orozko is a favorite with casino visitors, who arrive early for a breakfast of bakery goods or throughout the evening for a leisurely dinner. Some traditional Basque dishes are on the menu, but its cuisine reflects a broader Iberian influence, and it is described as Mediterranean in many tour books. The once-a-week wine tasting is popular.

Louis' Basque Corner, 301 East Fourth Street (at Evans), Reno, NV 89512 (775) 323-7203
Santa Fe Hotel, 235 Lake Street (next to Harrah's), Reno, NV 89501 (775) 323-1891
Restaurante Orozko, John Ascuaga's Nugget, 1100 Nugget Avenue, Sparks, NV 89431 (775) 356-3000 ext. 4232; *www.janugget.com/restaurants/orozko.cfm*

BOARDINGHOUSES

Until 1998 the Santa Fe was the only surviving hotel still owned by Basques among several that operated during the first half of the century. Because of declining business, most of Reno's Basque hotel keepers sold out during the 1940s and 1950s. Located as they were in the downtown area, the hotel properties became prime locations as gaming establishments spread.

In 1917 Sol Silen published a collection of biographies of successful Basques in the West, and his book, *Historia de los Vascongados en el oeste de los Estados Unidos*, recorded some of the earliest hotel owners. According to Silen, Reno's earliest known Basque hotel was the Commercial Hotel, built around 1900 and run by Jean Etchebarren and J. P. Aldaz. The fate of this establishment is not known.

There may have been others that followed, but the Basque hotel business in Reno really flourished between 1920 and the mid-1940s, according to Irene Arbeloa, whose parents, Josephine and Martin Orriaga, were the enterprising couple behind four Basque hotels in town. "Dances on Sunday nights were a regular thing," remembers Arbeloa. Reno had at least eight or nine boardinghouses during those years, most of them just a few rooms above other independent businesses on the ground floor. Arbeloa theorized that being on the second floor gave them added protection during the Prohibition days, when Basque moonshiners snuck alcohol into the hotels in suitcases, because being upstairs they had a little more time to hide their goods.

The word would quickly get around when federal agents were in town. Nevertheless, "a couple of Basques got caught in the action—they had to spend six months or a year in jail," she said. But that didn't stop the Basques from making and drinking their alcohol. "That was part of the life." After Prohibition, hotels often expanded to include a bar and dining room downstairs, according to Arbeloa, like the Santa Fe, the Indart, the Toscano, and the Martin. The hotels were next to Reno's red-light district, centered on Lake Street, up until World War II, when prostitution was outlawed in the county.

Irene Arbeloa and her sister Lucy grew up in several different hotels, as her parents moved from one operation to another. "When dates came to pick me up, I just wished we could have had a house with a living room," said Irene. Looking back now, she realizes that the hotel dining rooms, where dozens of men ages seventeen to twenty-five gathered every day to eat, offered more than she could have asked for. "There'd be singing at the table, or we'd put records on the phonograph and have impromptu dances after dinner."

The focal points of the Basque community were the Indart Hotel on Lake Street and the Hotel Español on Plaza Street, because they had handball courts. According to Arbeloa, Francisca Elia and her first husband built the Español near the railroad tracks in 1916 or 1917. After Elia's husband was killed by a train, Francisca married Eusebio Barcos, and the couple ran the hotel for many years. The old Hotel Español, on Plaza at Evans Avenue, still stands much as it was, although it has not been Basque or had a handball court for over fifty years. The Santa Fe and the former Hotel Español buildings are the only ones left in Reno that were actually built by Basques, according to Arbeloa.

The Alturas Hotel, the French Hotel, the Star, the Altona, and the Santa Fe were all on one square block bounded by Lake, Center, and Commercial Streets. Today the entire block, with the exception of the Santa Fe, is taken up by Harrah's casino. Across the street on Lake, the Indart and the Toscano, the latter being among those that survived the longest, were razed to create parking lots. Harold's Club now occupies the spot where the Martin Hotel stood on East Commercial Row, and the Pyrenees, near the Español on the other side of the railroad tracks, is also gone.

BASQUE CLUB

One of the Catholic traditions enthusiastically upheld by the Basques in this country was the celebration of the feast days of their patron saints. The very first event sponsored by Reno's **Zazpiak Bat Basque Club** when it organized in 1967 was a St. Martin's Day dinner dance. The idea for the date may have had its roots in the annual celebration at the Santa Fe by hotel keeper Martin Esain of the feast day of his patron saint on November 11.

Today the St. Martin's feast tradition continues to be a well-attended celebration, and is usually held, appropriately, at its original spot, the Santa Fe. For many years it was also the site of the NABO fall meeting.

In 1973 the Zazpiak Bat Basque Club published its own cookbook, *From the Basque Kitchen,* with over a hundred classic recipes from the Basque Country and a short, interesting introduction on Basque food written by the late Jon Bilbao. After selling about 10,000 copies over the years, the club finally decided to stop printing the book.

The St. Martin's Day dinner dance and the two picnics are the main events put on by the Reno Basque club, although there's a fourth popular party for the members.

The current Basque club was the second one to organize in Reno, after an earlier group, the Basque-American Club, which was organized in 1950. It sponsored an annual picnic for six years before dissolving.

Zazpiak Bat Basque Club, P.O. Box 7771, Reno, NV 89501. Information: (775) 329-1476 (*Mary Lou Urrutia*)

FESTIVAL

Reno, like Susanville, California, has two picnics. In addition to the big July one, which aims to attract a larger public, there's also a smaller one primarily for the members of Zazpiak Bat Basque Club. The membership picnic is held in June, at the Sparks Recreation Center, and resembles a Fourth of July picnic, according to Inda. Corn on the cob is served, and horseshoes and other all-American components are featured.

The big Reno Basque festival is held on the third weekend of July, and for the past few years it has been held at Wingfield Park in downtown Reno, a beautiful setting with a nearby rushing river. The competitions, which include wood-chopping, weight-carrying, and bota-bag drinking, are sometimes extended to two days, with the Mass and typical Basque barbecue on Sunday.

MUS

The *mus* tournament with its potluck dinner on the first Sunday in March is the first event of the year. The day starts off early at 8 A.M. for the cardplayers at the Sparks Recreation Center. The tournament usually ends in time for lunch, and afterward the local dance group puts on a performance. The potluck dinner, attended by about 150 people, is orchestrated so everyone brings a little of everything. Several women cook up a large batch of *bakailo* (codfish), and chef Louis Erreguible dishes up his special tripe recipe for the crowd. Basque musicians, often Jean Louis Curutchet and Jean Flesher of San Francisco, are invited to play for the evening dance.

DANCE

Reno's dance group has always been small, although in 2004 it boasted having about thirty dancers led by Kate Camino. "Reno's always had a hard time reaching them in junior high and high school," said member Janet Inda. Students are continually coming from the Basque Country to study at Reno, "but 90 percent of them go back after a year or two," Inda said. Hence they are rarely involved in club activities, except to enjoy themselves at the celebrations.

Sister City

In view of the many features that link Reno with the Basques, Reno established a sister-city relationship with Donostia/San Sebastián in 1989. The relationship was formalized when Reno officials hosted a ceremony for Basque Country representatives, who came for the unveiling of the Sheepherder Monument in August 1989. A reciprocal ceremony was carried out in San Sebastián for Reno officials in January 1990.

The relationship has been maintained primarily through the university's study abroad program in which Reno students go to the Basque Country, but San Sebastián students have also visited Reno. Another project is a public sculpture by the renowned Old World Basque artist Mikel Anjel Lertxundi, in front of Reno's City Hall (490 South Center Street). The abstract piece of stone, steel, and wood was completed by Lertxundi on location in 1994.

The Basque Sheepherder Monument

The dedication of the Basque Sheepherder Monument at the foot of Peavine Mountain in August 1989 was a significant milestone in the history of the U.S. Basque colony.

"It is the first time that we did something together, and for the Basques that's not very easy," said José Ramón Cengotitabengoa, who spearheaded the project. "It was very successful because [we] raised money from all sides." The organizing committee, sponsored by the Society of Basque Studies in America, sought support in Europe, where government agencies from the French and Spanish sides of the Basque Country joined to contribute about half of the $350,000 needed for the project. (For more information on the Society of Basque Studies in America, see the section on New York.) Stateside all the money came in small checks from individuals across the country.

The inspiration for the monument initially arose during a discussion between Cengotitabengoa and three modern Basque artists—Nestor Basterretxea, Vicente Larrea, and Remigio Mendiburu—who had been invited to show their works at Chicago's annual contemporary art exhibit in 1984. Cengotitabengoa took the men to visit Mt. Rushmore. While there, someone suggested the idea of a monument to the Basques, and "José Ramón ran with it," said Professor Emilia Doyaga of the Society of Basque Studies. From that brainstorm to the monument's unveiling, the project took five years. The project was fraught with obstacles even up to the end. The actual construction, using a labor-intensive process known as *lost wax,* took longer than expected. Toward the end it looked like the long-awaited inauguration would have to be canceled because the transportation of the statue from Mexico was delayed by red tape.

Nonetheless, the unveiling ceremony took place on August 27, 1989. It was a momentous occasion, bringing together over a

The modern Basque Sheepherder Monument in Reno, Nevada.

thousand Basques from all over the United States, in addition to local officials and officials from the Basque Country. The event was also covered by local and Basque Country media. Official proclamations honoring the contribution of the Basque sheepherder to the development of the American West had been signed by the governors of California, Nevada, and Idaho in anticipation of the event.

The five-ton green piece, which stands 22 feet high, was sculpted from bronze by acclaimed Basque artist Nestor Basterretxea. Named *Bakardade,* or *Solitude,* his work represents a sheepherder carrying a lamb in his shoulders under a full moon.

Controversy. A project of this magnitude carried out by Basques was naturally not without controversy. Many of the former sheepherders that it was supposed to represent and their families did not like the statue because it is abstract, a criticism that is still repeated today. Many would have preferred something more figurative. Basterretxea defended his work. "I wanted it to look as though it was a stone carved from the wind," he told newspaper reporters a few days before the ceremony. "I wanted the sheepherder to be part of the elements."

Professor Carmelo Urza of University of Nevada, Reno, a member of the original design committee, admits that the committee anticipated controversy over the abstractness of the statue. The monument was intended for the twenty-first century, according to Urza, and consequently a more modern artistic language was needed to represent the herders—"something that is going to bear witness to their history."

The abstract design was chosen by the committee after an international competition in which several European and American artists participated. Even for the committee, whose members were not experts in art, the choice between the figurative and abstract proposals was difficult, according to Cengotitabengoa. "But it is the artists who should tell us what to do," he said, not the other way around. "It's the artists who are the messengers of what's going to happen in the future—if they are great artists," he said.

When a miniature model of the committee's final choice was shown to Basques around the country, horror and disdain were among the reactions. "But the committee decided that they [the herders] didn't need to have a sculpture up there showing them what they looked like. The last thing we wanted was to create something that was boring and easy," said Urza—something that people would view and forget about. "What is appealing is that it creates a question in their mind—'What does this mean?' And maybe they are stimulated to ask who the Basques are and why that monument represents them." (Urza later wrote a book, *Solitude: Art and Symbolism in the Basque Monument,* interpreting the statue.)

Memorial Plaque. At first there were to be three sculptures, one by each of the three artists, but eventually the group agreed that there should be just one sculpture, for practical and budgetary reasons. To solicit support in the U.S. Basque community, the committee decided to include a memorial plaque on which the names of donors or their ancestors would be engraved, expecting that families would contribute to honor their fathers' sacrifices. "The Basques respect the dead," said Cengotitabengoa. So even though they would have preferred a statue that looked like their fathers, ultimately the Basque

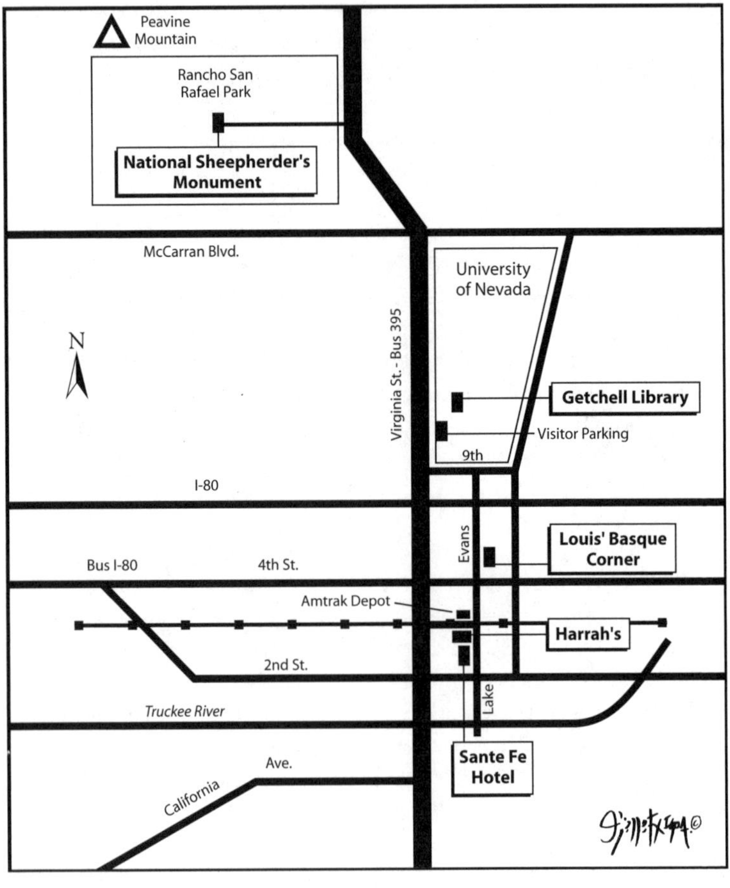

Reno.

Americans gave in. "They were doing it for their husbands and for their grandfathers who were sheepherders—or for the concept," he said.

Today the hundreds of names engraved on the memorial are testimony to the many families who made contributions to the development of the West over the past 150 years. Nearby a bronze map of the United States indicates the regions where the early Basques settled. At the foot of the monument is a poem, entitled "Solitude," written by Basterretxea in homage to the sheepherder. "Sometimes people leave flowers and such," said Urza, "so you know people are visiting it." But there's no record of how many visitors have come to see the monolith.

Location

The road to the monument is marked by a sign at the entrance to the Rancho San Rafael Park on Virginia Street, just north of North McCarran Boulevard. You can park close by. The monument is located on the Great Basin nature trail, which leads to a glen that was previously used as a campsite by many Basque sheepherders. Once upon a time this land belonged to a Basque family—the Landas. Today it is part of the county-maintained Rancho San Rafael Park. Follow the trail behind the monument and you'll find four large bronze plaques that explain the immigration of the Basques into the United States.

Basque Sheepherder Monument, 2975 North Virginia Street, Reno, NV 89557

THE UNIVERSITY OF NEVADA AT RENO

The Center Basque for Studies. The Basque Studies Program at the University of Nevada, Reno, is a good indicator of how far the Basques have come in the United States. The program is the only one of its kind in the country. Its Web site has become a major clearing house for Basque news (*www.basque.unr.edu*).

The Basque Studies Program was started in 1967 after a committee of professors decided that Basque studies should be part of a planned research institute focusing on the study of local geography. They concluded that the Basques' presence throughout the region and their close identification with the sheep industry made them a key human factor in the study of the ecology of the Great Basin.

Professor William A. Douglass, who had conducted social anthropological research in the Basque Country, was chosen to coordinate the program, and he continued as director until he retired in 1999. The late professor Jon Bilbao soon became a key staff member. The program was initially part of the university's independent Desert Research Institute, but in 1972 it was moved onto the university campus. By then the Basque Studies Program was well on its way to developing its world-class collection of Basque books, particularly on the subject of Basques in the New World. The program offered classes on different Basque subjects and coordinated a Basque book series for the University of Nevada Press and a summer program in the Basque Country—areas in which the program has continued to expand. Professor Joseba Zulaika became the program's director in 2000, and it was renamed the Center for Basque Studies. In 2006 professor Gloria P. Totoricagüena took over the directorship, when Zulaika stepped down to continue his research. The University began construction of a new library in 2005, and the center is scheduled to relocate when the building is available.

Euskara Classes. Two levels of elementary-Basque-language classes are taught every semester at the university, in addition to various less frequently offered courses on Basque history, literature, and culture, which are taught in English. Undergraduate students may minor in Basque Studies, and a special Ph.D. program in Basque Studies is available.

The Basque Library Collection. The Basque library is the cornerstone of the Center for Basque Studies. Now including more than 50,000 books, it includes the personal collections of several Basque scholars including Phillipe Veyrin, Ramón Goñi, Rodney Gallop, Eloy Placer, and William Douglass. It also contains hundreds of magazines, journals, videos, films, tapes, musical recordings, manuscripts, newspapers, and a collection of thousands of photographs and slides. Jon Bilbao compiled one of the most significant reference works on Basque studies, *Eusko-Bibliographia,* which has more than 300,000 entries.

In one of the library's cabinets is a growing collection of rare and fascinating treasures. The *Larramendi Diccionario Trilingüe, en*

Castellano, Vascuence y Latín, from 1745 is one. Others are Pierre Lhande's *Dictionnaire Basque Français*, Larramendi's *Arte de la Lengua Bascongada,* and an original 1930 edition of *Book of the Basques* signed by author Rodney Gallop. (When it was published, Gallop's book was the most significant treatise on the Basques written in English.) The library's physical space has become too small to house all the materials, so many of them are stored at other locations, but they are available upon request. Most of the books in the collection are available through interlibrary loan from local universities or public libraries.

Every year dozens of visitors pass through the Center and its library collection, both of which are currently located in the back of the second floor of the university's main library but which will eventually move to the new building.

Newsletter/Web site. The Center for Basque Studies publishes a newsletter twice a year on its activities, the staff, and the results of scholarly research. This newsletter, published since 1968, has proven to be the longest-standing publication disseminating Basque information in the United States. It is free to anyone who is interested, and it is currently distributed to nearly ten thousand people. To receive a copy, write to the Center, or view it online at *www.basque.unr.edu* by clicking on the publication link.

The Center's Web site is one of the most important Internet sources of information on Basques in English. Efforts to acquire as many Basque resources as possible have been extended to the Web site, which offers a huge list of the books, journals, and magazines in its collection as well as Basque newspapers and other news sources, dance clubs, and other information. The *news* link on its home page provides frequent updates on a broad spectrum of academic topics.

Center for Basque Studies, Getchell Library/322, University of Nevada, Reno, Reno, NV 89557-0012 (775) 784-4854; *www.basque.unr.edu*

Basque Art. In the lobby of Getchell Library, the university's main library, to your immediate right you will see *Orreaga,* a significant wooden-abstract sculpture by Nestor Basterretxea, which was named in Basque after the site of a famous battle otherwise known as Roncevaux (or Roncesvalles). Its plaque explains that in A.D. 778

Orreaga sculpture by Nestor Basterretxea, now located in the lobby of University of Nevada Reno library. (Courtesy of the Basque Studies Library, University of Nevada, Reno.)

Basques attacked the rearguard of Charlemagne's army as it passed through the Pyrenees Mountains. This epic event in Basque and European history prompted the ballad "Song of Roland" to commemorate the death of the commander of Charlemagne's troops. The U-shape, formed by the side panes, represents the canyon in which the troops were ambushed. The lower circle is the doomed army, and the out-thrusting pegs represent the cries of its dying men. The suspended circle is the avenging Basques, and the descending figure, a bird of death.

In the Basque Studies library, despite its cramped quarters, several smaller pieces of Basque artwork are on display, including a maquette of the Basque sheepherder monument and aspen tree trunks with carvings done decades ago by passing sheepherders. And don't miss the painting *Buruaste* hung on the back staircase leading to the library. Basque artist Enrique Linatza, of Léon, Spain, has captured in this piece the sense of isolation and homesickness of the Basque sheepherder. Portrayed with a cigarette in hand and his loyal dog at his side, the sheepherder watches over his band of sheep, separated from the rest of the world by a wide ocean. A typical small Basque town with its white houses and shuttered windows, set on a hill in the distance, and a farmer in his beret cutting hay are reminders of the homeland the sheepherder left behind. A big gray ship fills the center of the painting, depicting the all-important voyage, and a clump of skyscrapers represents the foreignness of America.

Basque Book Series. In the years since the **University of Nevada Press** began publishing books on Basque themes, the series has acquired a large and faithful readership, and there are now more than forty-five titles in print.

Basque-American novelist Robert Laxalt, who founded the press and served as its first director, started the series with anthropologist William A. Douglas, the former coordinator of the Basque Studies Program at the University of Nevada, Reno. A reprint of *The Book of the Basques*, by Rodney Gallop, first published in Great Britain in 1930, was their first publication. The two thousand copies sold out in a matter of three weeks, astonishing the press staff.

The idea for the Basque series, as Douglass and Laxalt initially conceived it, was to translate books on Basque subjects that had been published in Europe. "We figured that every few years there might be a book good enough to be worth publishing," said Douglass. "But it was the Franco era, and the whole Basque-academic scene was repressed." As it turned out, several of the first publications were generated by Laxalt and Douglass themselves, and others were written by scholars associated with the Basque Studies Program.

The series has accumulated a fair number of awards and distinctions throughout the years. Laxalt's award-winning novels about the Basque-American experience, published as part of the Basque Book Series, gave the program greater prominence. The *Basque-English Dictionary*, published in 1989, and the *English-Basque Dictionary*, published in 1990, were "the crowning achievements of the [Basque Studies] program and of the series," according to Douglass. Scholar and author Gorka Aulestia, with the help of several collaborators, primarily Linda White, spent eight years preparing the *Basque-English/English-Basque Dictionary*, a 1,100-page, two-volume edition.

Call their toll-free number or write the Press for the latest catalog.

University of Nevada Press, MS 166, University of Nevada, Reno, NV 89557-0076 (775) 784-6573; toll free (877) 682-6657; *www.unpress.nevada.edu*

Studying in the Basque Country. In 1969 the Basque Studies Program started a summer study program that has evolved into probably the most significant program helping to perpetuate Basque culture in this country—the **University Studies Abroad Consortium.** This effort began because the university wanted to create a way for American students to study in the Basque Country. In the beginning, it was limited to an annual summer program. When, in the mid-1970s, Boise State University began its year-long course of study in the Basque town of Oñati, UNR suspended its summer offerings. But after a few years, the Boise State program was discontinued. In 1979 UNR invited Boise State University and the University of Nevada, Las Vegas, to form a consortium that would initiate semester- and year-long courses at the campus of the University of the Basque Country in the city of Donostia/San Sebastián. The University Studies Abroad Consortium is coordinated by Professor Carmelo Urza.

Today, thirty U.S. universities are members of the University Studies Abroad Consortium, which offers academic credit for programs in such varied countries as Spain, France, Italy, Germany, England, Chile, Costa Rica, Thailand, Japan, and Australia. The program's strength still lies with its numerous offerings on both the French and Spanish sides of the Basque Country. Thousands of students have studied abroad since the consortium began, and of that number a majority have chosen to study in the Basque Country. Many concentrated on learning Euskara.

Urza has found that many of the students are third- and fourth-generation Basques who travel to the Old Country "to recoup what has been lost." Commonly in the first-generation immigrant family, children were encouraged to learn English and to fit into American culture. Hence second-generation Basques often forgot or never learned some of the traditions unique to their heritage. "I think that a lot of them want to learn Basque because it's the language of their fathers and their grandfathers, and they want to be able to communicate with family members," said Urza. "And they often already have a background in Spanish or French. We also have any number of students who aren't Basque who take [Euskara] because of a linguistic interest."

By the 1970s, with the end of Basque immigration to the United States, Basque traditions practiced here began losing steam, and Basque-Americans faced the possibility that their culture would die out. Without the influx of new ideas and renewed energy, "this generation could have remained here and repeated the same archetypes that have gone on here for years," said Urza. Because they have been able to study abroad, students of all ages have been exposed to a modern, much more urbanized view of the Basque Country. And with that new perception, they are replacing the nostalgic image of rural life (Old World and New) from forty or fifty years ago, which Basque-Americans attempted to re-create for so many years, with dances, songs, and festivals.

The program has inspired its alumni, giving them greater understanding of the culture and infusing them with the energy and the desire to promote Basque studies. Today many of the Basque-Americans in their thirties and forties who are actively involved in Basque organizations in the Reno area are alumni of the University Studies Abroad program. Many of those who are teaching or have taught Basque subjects today, including Urza and the late professor Pat Bieter of Boise State University, are graduates of the program, according to Urza.

The program plays a very important role "of reestablishing ties with the Basque Country more on a professional level than a personal one, and these relationships have taken on a life of their own," said Urza. In addition to professional contacts, however, long-term friendships have developed, and some of the students have even married Basques.

The dance class offered through the program by members of the professional Basque-dance group Argia has had influences on the Basque-American dance scene. "There is no question that it has affected the evolution of dance here," said Urza. He pointed to Lisa Corcostegui as an example. The folk dance classes she took abroad inspired her to start a group at the university when she returned to pursue graduate studies at UNR in 1989, and which she completed in 2005 when she received her Ph.D.

The program offers intensive language classes, as well as culture and history classes in English. Short trips to important local sites are included in the package, whether participants go for a summer, a semester, or an academic year. Arrangements are made for students to stay in group housing or with families in private homes. For more information on the University Studies Abroad program, write for their booklet.

University Studies Abroad Consortium, University of Nevada Reno, MS 323, Reno, NV 89557-0093 (775) 784-6569; *www.usac.unr.edu*

Dance. The university's Basque dance group, **Zenbat Gara Euskal Dantzari Taldea** (How Many Are We? Basque Folk Dance Ensemble) has raised the standards of Basque folk dance in the United States to new heights. The group focuses on a different region or period of the Basque Country every year, introducing its unique dances and costumes. One year it was the horn-shaped headdresses of the Medieval period; another time it was Lapurdi Province's Karnaval dance with its bright-flowered hats and pleated white skirts. "Our mission is to educate ourselves and the community," said director Lisa Corcostegui.

Corcostegui, who began dancing at the age of five with the Basque group in her hometown of Ontario, Oregon, founded the university dance group with her husband, Enrike, after she spent two years studying in the Basque Country. But it wasn't until her dance group saw the professional Basque dance group Argia during its tour of the United States in 1990 that Zenbat Gara got serious about its presentation. "That's when we really started to do things right," she said. With an apprenticeship grant she received, Corcostegui brought two members of Argia, master dancer Jexux Larrea and his wife, costume designer Ane

Zenbat Gara of the University of Nevada, Reno, continues to break new ground introducing old dances (*Imotzeko Esku Dantza*) and performing them to perfection. (Photo by Averie Cohen.)

Albisu, to Reno. The couple worked with the dance group for three weeks in 1991, and the impressive results are evident today. Zenbat Gara members produce elaborate and authentic costumes, right down to such details as embroidered landscapes on their rope-soled *espartinak* (espadrilles), all sewn by the members themselves—even the men!

The group is always looking for new members, since students come and go every year. Nevada's many Basque-Americans have few in-state choices for college, and consequently many of them attend the university at Reno. Inevitably a good number of Basque-Americans have made forays into the dance group. But at least one Japanese and several other non-Basque students have done stints in the group as well. Originally, all the dancers were UNR students. After seventeen years in existence, the student-dancers are few, points out Enrike Corcostegui. Referring to the meaning of the group's name "How many are we?" he notes, "there's not a definitive answer." Today, Zenbat Gara is more likely to get help from expert Basque-American dancers from other communities who join them for special performances, such as Jean Escoz from Seattle or Jenny and John Ysursa from Chino. "It's a lot of fun" bringing the dancers together, says Lisa Corcostegui, adding that the only tricky part is getting a chance to practice and make choreographic adjustments beforehand, because dancers sometimes know different variations of a particular dance.

Lisa and Enrike Corcostegui's personal commitment to the group and their dedication have raised the group's performance to a level that easily rivals that of Boise's Oinkari dancers. With their attention to costuming, they go far beyond what any Basque dance group has attempted before in this country. Nevertheless, their repertoire has still only scratched the surface of the rich Basque dance traditions. "There are over four hundred dances catalogued in the Basque Country," said Lisa Corcostegui.

In addition to performing at Nevada's Basque festivals, Zenbat Gara appears year-round at university events, local schools, and multiethnic celebrations. The group often travels to perform at important Basque events in the United States.

Zenbat Gara, c/o Center for Basque Studies, University of Nevada Reno, MS 322, Reno, NV 89557-0012. Information: (775) 852-7885 *(Lisa and Enrike Corcostegui)*; *www.dantzariak.net*

Carson Valley

As recently as 1970 Douglas County, whose main towns are Gardnerville and Minden, had less than seven thousand people. Today the county is home to some thirty thousand, and the population is still growing—fast. Basque families are spread throughout the valley. More and more Basques are choosing to live just north of the valley, in Carson City, the state capital. It was once home to the Laxalt family's French Hotel. Former Senator Paul Laxalt later built the elegant Ormsby House hotel and casino in Carson City.

BASQUE CHORIZO

Pete Coscarart, who became famous for his chorizos in the small town of Battle Mountain, decided to find bigger horizons for his chorizos and his children. The native of Azpilcueta, Nafarroa, opened the **Villa Basque Cafe and Deli** in Carson City in 1997. His special chorizo recipe is his main attraction.

Villa Basque Deli, 730 Basque Way, Carson City, NV 89706 (775) 884-4451

FESTIVAL

During the 1990s, John Borda helped start the St. Teresa of Avila Basque Festival in Carson City to benefit the church's Catholic school; for information on the festival call (775) 882-2079. The successful event, on the third Sunday in September, attracts 1,500 people and includes performances by a *bertsolari,* wood choppers, Basque dancers from Reno, as well as a Basque lunch with barbecued lamb and turkey. Most recently it was held at Fuji Park. "It's a family day," said Jeanette Blanco, one of the organizers, noting that kids under sixteen have free admission, and the event includes snow cones, face painting, and children's games.

Besides the deli and the annual festival, there is not much else in Carson City that reveals its Basque population. But nearby, in Gardnerville, several longtime Basque businesses are still in operation, and the Basques continue to gather there in large numbers.

Gardnerville

Gardnerville, set in the Carson Valley just an hour south of Reno, has an impressive view of the Carson Range of the Sierra Nevada, rising sharply to the south and west and the Pine Nut Mountains to the east. There are no foothills here to block your view. Job's Peak, Job's

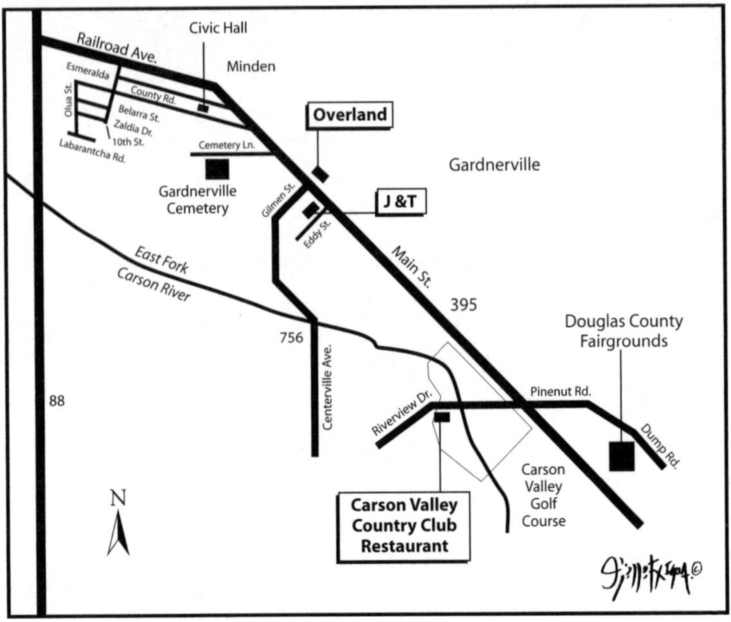

Gardnerville.

Sister, and Freel Peak jut more than 5,000 feet straight up from the valley floor.

A funny thing has started to happen within the last few years. Basques in the big cities, mostly from the San Francisco and Los Angeles area, have been moving to Gardnerville. “In the last five years, a lot of San Francisco people have been buying property up here,” said former restaurant owner Jesus Rey. He can understand why others are attracted to the valley. “Give me the big open spaces,” he said. Annie Guecamburu, recent Basque club president, is a transplant from the Bay Area.

Gardnerville’s older Basques who have helped keep the culture alive for so long are dying. “I’m sure you’re going to find more Basques in the cemetery than in town,” said restaurateur Elvira Cenoz. Without the interchange with the older generation who came from the Old Country, some worry that the younger Basques are losing the traditions.

SHEEP AND RANCHING

Gardnerville, founded in 1879, was an important sheep center in Nevada, and Basques first came here to raise sheep around the turn of the century. Today there are still a couple of sheep ranchers, but they're quickly being crowded out. Gardnerville and Minden, once separate towns, are now practically joined, with four thousand residents between them. Housing developments with hundreds of homes are springing up practically overnight in the surrounding valley. Nevertheless, Basques from urban areas still find the setting rustic.

The Bordas, former hotel owners in town, are probably the last of the Basque families that still run sheep in the valley. If you're driving around Carson Valley in search of Basque memorabilia, someone is bound to tell you about the cluster of streets in Minden—recently built—all of which have Basque names. It seems a local developer decided to give a Basque theme to one of his subdivisions.

RESTAURANTS

The heart of this Basque community is Gardnerville's Main Street, where Basque food is still served in the old style. The two remaining old-style Basque restaurants are the **Overland Hotel** and the **J and T Bar and Restaurant,** which may be over 130 years old, according to its owners. There is also a lovely restaurant by the golf course, the **Carson Valley Country Club Bar and Restaurant.**

The **Overland Hotel,** built in 1906, has been in Basque hands since 1921 when John Etchemendy became a partner in the business. He was involved in its operation until Eusebio Cenoz, after a short stint as cook at the nearby J and T, took over the Overland in 1967. Cenoz presided over the place alone until he married Elvira in 1980, and then she became a fixture there alongside him. The two were featured in numerous magazine articles highlighting their cooking and the fact that they butchered their own lambs. When her husband died, Elvira decided to continue on her own. "After it costs so much to build it up, you can't let it go," she explained. She still butchers the USDA-approved meat herself. According to Elvira, preparation is half the art of cooking. It's a lot of work, but she claims to get six different cuts from one lamb at less than half the precut price. "You put your shoulder to it when it's your own business."

Elvira Cenoz has run the Overland Hotel single-handed since her husband Eusebio passed away in 1989. She's no exception, since Basque women are known for their strength and determination. They often took over family businesses when their husbands passed away. Cenoz' buoyant, outgoing personality, expressed in a thick accent, is at least half of the reason customers enjoy this place so much. She has a delightful habit of sprinkling sayings throughout her conversation.

"Never say that you won't drink from this water," she says in Spanish, grinning, as she explains the irony of ending up in the hotel and restaurant business. She and her sister turned their backs on the family's former summer pension hotel in Saturraran, near Motriko, during their youth, promising they would never get involved in the business again. Her sister runs the Brass Rail restaurant in Alturas! Cenoz doesn't believe in leaving a business to anyone else, and consequently she has not taken a day off in five years. "If the roof has a hole, water is going to get in," she explains. In fact, when she and her husband went for a monthlong vacation to Spain during the 1980s, they closed the restaurant.

Asked if she ever thinks about retiring to the Basque Country, Cenoz replied: "You sacrifice everything to come here. How am I go-

Basque Lamb Shanks, Elvira Cenoz, Overland Hotel

- 6 lamb shanks
- 1 red pepper
- 1 green pepper
- 1 medium-size onion
- 2 to 3 cloves of garlic
- 1 shot of good-quality cognac
- 1½ cups of white wine

Put the lamb shanks in a covered pan in the oven at 350 degrees for 60 to 90 minutes. This initial cooking serves to get rid of some of the fat. Meanwhile, cut the peppers, onions, and mushrooms lengthwise. Sauté them together with the garlic in a covered pan, over a low heat, adding the mushrooms last. Set aside. Take the shanks out of the oven and pour as much of the grease out as possible. Sprinkle with salt, then pour the cooked vegetables into the pan with the shanks. Pour in the cognac and wine. Cover again and place back in the oven, set at 350 degrees, for another 90 minutes.

ing to go back when I have my last and final house here next to my husband?"

Cenoz is one of the few hotel owners who still provides food for the boarders. "On Mondays we're closed, but the boarders are still served," she said. The hotel's fourteen rooms are usually full, but only one resident is Basque today. Some are long-term residents, others are tourists passing through.

Much of the life of this Basque community takes place at the Overland. With its large banquet room with a podium and microphone system, the Overland hosts many of the local Basque club's meetings. Beautiful photographs of award-winning Basque floats from local parades and other memorabilia line the walls, along with a large painted portrait of Cenoz's husband.

The food at the Overland and the J and T is still served the traditional Basque family-style. At the Overland, Cenoz herself might even come to your table to ask which of the five entrées interests you. Beware of lots of luscious garlic.

Across the street at the **J and T Bar and Restaurant,** "we don't have menus," said bartender J.B. Lekumberry. In fact, J and T's main entrée every night since 1971 has been sirloin steak, although the second entrée changes every weeknight. The restaurant has added individual seating to the long tables in the back. A dated newspaper article on former Nevada governor Paul Laxalt cites the J and T as his favorite restaurant.

The origins of the Lekumberrys' building are not known for sure. It was brought to Gardnerville from Gold Hill or Silver City around 1895, which makes it over a hundred years old, according to J.B. Lekumberry, but he adds that the building may even be 130 years old.

J.B. is the son of longtime owner Jean Lekumberry, who died unexpectedly of cardiac arrest sitting right at his bar one night after closing in 1993. The elder Lekumberry, who had run the J and T since 1960, left his imprint on the place. A hat collection that has been growing since 1967, when a local cowboy forgot his hat and never got it back, decorates the walls here, and the ceiling is covered with dollar bills that Lekumberry tossed up there as part of a special trick. The elder Lekumberry was the guy to know in this town if you wanted to talk about the news of the day. For years the bar has sold polo shirts emblazoned with a design of Lekumberry in his beret with his trademark cigar in his mouth. The elder Lekumberry always intended to leave the business to his three children, who were interested in it and worked beside him. "My dad ran the place for thirty-three years, so we'll have to run it at least thirty-three more," said his daughter Marie Louise Lekumberry.

Carlos Iribarren and Jesus Rey both worked as bartenders once upon a time at the Centro Basco in Chino. For years, they operated the **Carson Valley Country Club Bar and Restaurant,** which sits upon the resplendent greenery of the Carson Valley Golf Course. Windows all around the restaurant provide a wonderful view. "All the trees, all the green makes it pretty. It beats the heck out of looking at the cars in the street," joked Rey.

The two bought the restaurant in 1974 from Dick and Helen Chapell, also Basque, who had run the restaurant for five years. In 2002, three non-Basques bought it but have kept the Basque cuisine. "It's a successful concept, and we want to keep it the same," said Heinz Blaum, one of the owners.

Several Basque dishes made with more unusual meat cuts have been eliminated from many restaurants' menus because Americans just won't go for them. "You tell them to eat *txipirrones en su tinta* (squid in its own ink)—never!" exclaimed Jesus Rey. The same is true for pigs feet, blood sausage, and tripe dishes. "With the American people, as long as you stay away from the innards, you're okay," said Rey. As for *koskolak,* or lamb testicles, the very idea seems repulsive to most diners. But Gardnerville hotel owner Elvira Cenoz claims that as soon as any red-blooded American tastes this delicacy—they're hooked! And Ramon Zugazaga of the Biltoki in Elko says that his customers would cry out if he cut the beef tongue appetizer from the menu.

While Basques come into town in droves for special events, the Basque restaurants primarily earn their livelihood with Americans.

The Carson Valley Country Club Bar and Restaurant's beautiful setting, and its location just an hour south of Reno, attracts a fair number of celebrities too. They come for a golf game or two and a meal at the restaurant. Clint Eastwood, Neil Diamond, and Perry Como have been among the visitors. Country singer Willie Nelson stops by about once a year, according to Rey. The restaurant sells white polo shirts with the Basque coat of arms and the restaurant's name in the front left-hand corner for $20.

The local Basques hold their restaurants dear. The owners here greet all their regular Basque patrons by name. And during any significant Basque event in town, such as the annual festivals, the local restaurant owners can be assured that Basques will eat in their restaurants in large numbers on those nights. Restaurant owners say Basques are loyal, spreading their patronage among the local hotels or restaurants.

Juan and Michele Leonis opened the Pyrenees Bar in town in 1997. Juan Leonis's brother, Miguel, is the most recent owner of the well-known Star Hotel in Elko. This couple gave a twist to the Western bar atmosphere by serving Spanish tapas. However, the venture didn't last long.

Carson Valley Country Club Bar and Restaurant, 1029 Riverview, Gardnerville, NV 89410 (775) 265-3715
J and T Bar and Restaurant, 760 South Main Street, Gardnerville, NV 89410 (775) 782-2074
Overland Hotel, 691 South Main Street, Gardnerville, NV 89410 (775) 782-2138

BOARDINGHOUSES

Besides the Overland Hotel, Gardnerville had at least three other Basque hotels in its earlier days, and remnants of them all are still visible. Next to the Overland was the East Fork Hotel, run by Ramón and "Mama" Borda. And next to the East Fork, a cousin, Baptiste Borda, ran the French Hotel for a while. Then from 1937 to 1947 the Bordas leased the French Hotel to Joe and Jeanne Micheo, until the Micheos decided to buy their own place, the Pyrenees, across the street. Local Basques used to play handball on the court in back of the French Hotel until the court was torn down in the 1950s. The Micheos' daughter, Mary Abbott, remembers those early days, when all the children from the boardinghouse families played together. "It was a good place to grow up when the town was small," she said.

The Borda families eventually eliminated the boardinghouse operations and ran the French and the East Fork as bars. The French Bar still exists, although it is no longer owned by Basques. The East Fork was seriously damaged in a fire in the late 1980s and has stood empty ever since, its sign still hanging above the door. Joe Micheo died in 1968, and his widow finally sold the Pyrenees in 1972. The building is still there, although today it houses the Aladdin Flower Shop.

Basques have continued in the hotel/motel business in Carson Valley, owning and running at least five motels between Minden and Gardnerville, but the modern-day versions are a far cry from the old boardinghouse establishments.

BASQUE CLUBS

The Carson Valley Nut Club. Before the town's official Basque club, Mendiko Eskualdun Cluba, was organized, another club of sorts was sponsored by Basques in Gardnerville, according to local historian Raymond Smith. The organization was called the Carson Valley Nut Club, and the idea behind the group was to bring the boys together once a year to enjoy a wild evening of eating *koskolak,* or mountain oysters—young lamb testicles, that is. According to Smith, the tradition started in the 1930s at the old Pyrenees Hotel when it was run by Joe Micheo. When Micheo died and the hotel closed in 1972, the club moved its annual dinner to the Overland, because owner Eusebio Cenoz had access to the main course. Cenoz would go out to the ranches and help out with the castration "because you had to thank them in some way," said his wife, Elvira. Today Cenoz gets the testicles from one of the last sheep ranchers in the valley, Fred Fulstone, as well as from the Iturriria brothers in Bakersfield.

Elvira hosts the festivities for the wild and crazy crew of 100 to 120, which includes politicians, lawyers, and doctors, some of whom travel to Gardnerville from Las Vegas for the annual event on the first Friday in June. In fact, according to Elvira, the elderly men now bring their sons with them, to keep up the tradition. The evening, as always, is full of a lot of joking and drinking, and members show a video of the castration technique commonly used by Basques, which is still in use on many sheep ranches today, in which men pull the testicles out with their teeth. As Smith put it, "The Nut Club is pure Nevada, a faint recollection of an earlier day when the state seemed to have more gusto and more fun."

Basque Club. Gardnerville's **Mendiko Eskualdun Cluba** started in 1981, primarily because the Basques here felt they lived too far from Reno's club to be involved in its activities. The Gardnerville club has a whopping membership of about 320 members, although the large number of members is somewhat misleading, according to member Mary Abbott, because it includes Basques from San Francisco, Fresno, and cities even farther away. "The people who really helped us start the club were from South San Francisco," she said. Gardnerville is within easy driving distance of several Basque communities, and as a result its events are usually well attended.

The Basque club contributed $1,000 toward renovating the Carson Valley Improvement Club Hall, in view of the many events it holds there. Basques also helped establish the first Catholic church in Gardnerville, St. Gall, and when church officials recently decided to replace the old building (now real estate offices) and put up a new one, Basques were right there too, providing financial support for the new **St. Gall** (1343 Centerville Lane).

On Christmas Eve for several years local Basque children traveled down the usually snow-lined main street of Gardnerville in hay wagons, displaying the Nativity scene, singing *gabon kantak* (Christmas carols) and playing instruments—an Old Country tradition. Their procession would end at the Overland, where they received gifts and Cenoz served them the traditional hot chocolate. But the custom ended when the number of children participating dwindled. The club has participated in the town's Christmas Parade of Lights during recent years, even winning first prize once.

Club member Jesus Pedroarena explained the popularity of the club's events to out-of-town visitors: they can drive up Friday night in time to attend a Saturday event. In the evening they can go gambling in South Lake Tahoe's casinos, just an hour away, and the next morning they can go have breakfast at the Overland or J and T. "It's still a good time of day to return to San Francisco or wherever," said Pedroarena. Besides, say the residents, the mountain scenery is beautiful. "People say it reminds them of Euskal Herria," said club member Annie Guecamburu.

Mendiko Eskualdun Cluba, P.O. Box 2168, Gardnerville, NV 89410. Information: (775) 782-2898 (Jesus Pedroarena)

FESTIVAL

As for the Gardnerville picnic, "it's the best-kept secret here," said Jesus Pedroarena. Without any advertising whatsoever, the picnic, held on the second Saturday of August, regularly attracts five hundred to six hundred people. "We get people sometimes all the way from Chino," said Pedroarena. For the past few years, it's been held at the CVIC Hall in Minden, adjacent to Gardnerville. People who attend Gardnerville's picnic say they enjoy the rural setting. Cenoz generously prepares big vats of lamb stew, red beans, and salad every year for the picnic, and she also provides the lamb for barbecuing. The popular picnic seems to get bigger every year. A highlight for the youngsters is the *jota* (fandango) contest, which attracts dancers as young as five, six, and seven years old. Small cash prizes are offered. The contest and some other activities are held outdoors in Minden Park, which is adjacent to the hall.

Another specialty of this festival is the garlic soup that is served for free at the end of the evening. Club members cook it up early, while the dance is in full swing, and the aroma of garlic permeates the hall. This practice is reminiscent of the tradition in the Basque Country, and also preserved here by a few restaurants or families, of getting together for garlic soup after an evening of drinking and partying. Late in the evening the bowls of hot soup are passed around. You'll be amazed—although you might be wickedly tantalized with the wonderful smell all evening, the soup itself has only a slight taste of garlic.

MUS

The club's *mus* tournament has the largest turnouts of all the U.S. club tournaments, with up to seventy teams competing some years. Participation in the tournament is limited to club members, so many players from other towns and cities pay their dues with the club every year just to be able to compete.

The Mendiko Eskualdun Cluba's annual *mus* tournament is held in adjoining Minden, at the Carson Valley Improvement Club Hall on Esmeralda between Fifth and Sixth Streets. This street is part of the town's historic business district. Several buildings here, including the CVIC Hall, were built in the first decade of this century, when Minden was the county seat. Nevada's last bandstand is located in the park near the hall.

EUSKAL KANTARI EGUNA

A special event has been organized during the past few years in Gardnerville to showcase the *bertsolariak* (Basque troubadours) as well as many other types of Basque singing and music practiced in the United States—and help keep them alive. The Day of the Basque Singer, better known as the Euskal Kantari Eguna, sponsored by NABO, was spawned from a similar annual competition of amateur singers in the Basque Country, where singers, *bertsolariak,* musicians, and choirs compete for top prizes.

The enthusiastic crowd at the musical festival snaps photographs and records the performances on videotape. The festival has attracted soloists as well as choirs, *txistulariak* as well as duets and bands, and, of course, the local *bertsolariak*—a luscious panoply of the culture's wealth of musical offerings. "We need a day like this to renew the roots," said Jesus Pedroarena, one of the biggest fans of the musical fête.

For the first festival in April 1988, participants competed in categories of old and new songs, both with musical accompaniment and

Euskal Kantari Eguna, a new tradition to celebrate the Basques' love of music and singing, is celebrated in Gardnerville.

a cappella. Gorka Aulestia, then a professor at the University of Nevada, Reno, was asked to be one of the judges. "Gorka, who had been in this country for thirteen years, said the *Eguna* was one of the best days that he experienced in the United States," remembered Pedroarena. The following year Boise was supposed to host the Kantari Eguna, but Boise's NABO members proposed that the event remain in Gardnerville permanently because it was centrally located for all the clubs. "Gardnerville is where it was born, and this is where it needs to be," said Elvira Cenoz.

But without enough time for Gardnerville to organize the event that year, the event had to be canceled. The Gardnerville club surveyed the first year's participants—the responses overwhelmingly favored a singing festival rather than a competition—in the spring, before the picnics. For three years, the Eguna was held successfully around the beginning of May. One summer, for comparison's sake, Pedroarena attended the competition in the Basque Country. "I saw that the caliber of our singers was just as good as over there," he said. In fact, at least one U.S. Basque resident, Anne Marie Minaberri of Bakersfield, participated in the Basque Country's Kantaldi Eguna in 1992 and won a prize in the a cappella category for a song she composed herself, "Garaziko Mendian."

The festival moved to Boise in 2003 and 2004, because club directors wanted a break. It returned to Gardnerville in 2005. The Nevada border town is much closer to California Basques, who enjoy participating in and watching the event, which was held along with the August picnic.

Winnemucca

A big bright red, white, and green Basque flag (*ikurrina*) greets you as you enter Winnemucca, leaving no doubt about the Basque presence in this town. Although Basques have never been the majority here, possibly one fourth of the population—maybe more—has Basque roots.

"If you counted people who were at least one quarter Basque, you could count two thousand to three thousand people," said Lyle Davis (Sarasua), a Winnemucca insurance agent who is half Basque.

After some of the California colonies, Winnemucca was probably the earliest and most significant Basque settlement. After Basques began arriving in Nevada in the 1870s, the greater Winnemucca area quickly became the number one destination. Through the years, Basques have maintained their influence and status here despite, or perhaps because, Winnemucca has grown to a town of ten thousand people. Active gold mines in the area have spurred population growth more recently.

About half of Winnemucca's current population has arrived in the last twenty years, after the majority of Basques settled here, and as a result the newer residents know very little about the Basques' significant contribution to Nevada history, according to Davis. But the local Basque club, Euskaldunak Danak Bat, educates the locals with its popular Winnemucca festival, held during the second weekend of June. Here, as in Elko, the local community wholeheartedly supports the ethnic festival, which brings in lots of outsiders, and their business, to this Nevada town.

The *ikurrina* you see on your left as you drive into town along Winnemucca Boulevard from Highway 80 belongs to the Pyrenees Motel, built in 1985 by local Basque real estate developer Tony Mendieta, a lifelong miner who eventually bought his own small gold mine. This modern-day motel has nothing of the boardinghouse ambiance, but the lobby is replete with all sorts of Basque memorabilia, including beautiful color photos of what else? Sheep.

Early Basques

Among the first Basques known to have applied for citizenship in this country were three men in Winnemucca: José Erquiaga, Juan Aldamiz, and Diego Ferraro. Their applications, dated 1873, are some of the first official documents to show the presence of Basques in Nevada. Some of the earliest Basque ranchers who were successful in the sheep business—Erquiaga, Aldamiz, "Spanish Joe" Ugarriza, and Mateo Badiola—all traveled back to the Basque Country during the 1880s, according to newspaper reports, and returned with many more Basques, promoting the area as a prime destination for immigrants.

The settlers would arrive in town by train, the Central Pacific, which had first reached Winnemucca from San Francisco in 1868. From Winnemucca, many would then travel north to the town of

McDermitt, at the Nevada-Oregon border, one of the primary launching points for Basques heading further north into Oregon and Idaho. From the turn of the century when mining was reaching its peak in the area and through to the 1950s or 1960s, McDermitt was heavily populated with Basques. But today no Basque social institution remains from earlier times, although the town once had Basque hotels. In the hills 11 miles southwest of Winnemucca, you can see the colored mine tailings left from the Cordero mine, now closed. In 1931 Basque Tomás Alcorta discovered the ore that led to the establishment of the mine, which was the richest mercury-producing mine in the country at the time.

The quaint farming community of Paradise Valley was also another important early Basque settlement. The old Paradise Hotel, run by the Echevarrias, was torn down in the 1950s, and the Basques have left little else behind. Paradise and McDermitt, as well as Golconda and Lovelock, on either side of Winnemucca along Interstate 80, had Basque hotels once upon a time. In Golconda both hotels, the Arrascada and the Star, with its handball court, burned down, just like so many other old wooden buildings in Nevada. "We didn't have fire departments in those days," said Emily Laucirica of Winnemucca, who was born in the Arrascada. All these towns have shrunk in size, and most of their Basque populations went elsewhere.

Winnemucca, on the other hand, grew into a fair-sized town, and its Basque community grew as well. Many of the newcomers were transplants from the smaller towns. Located on the banks of the Humboldt River, Winnemucca was supported primarily by farming and ranching. Several mines of gold, silver, copper, and tungsten brought many immigrants to the region. But in surrounding Humboldt County towns the mostly wide-open ranges with adequate greenery were an attractive starting point for Basques hoping to establish their own sheep band.

Ranching and a revived mining industry are still important in Humboldt County, but today tourism has taken a prominent place on the list. Summer is the time when the town's Basque restaurants enjoy most of their business and motel rooms are hard to come by. Both Winnemucca and Elko were hurt in the 1970s when Interstate 80 was turned into a superhighway that bypassed their towns. Up until then, cross-country traffic drove right down their main streets. Nevertheless, their locations midway between San Francisco and Salt Lake City, make them natural stopping points. Travelers will inevitably stop here for lunch, dinner, or to spend a night. People planning to attend Winnemucca's Basque Festival are advised to make motel reservations well ahead of time.

CEMETERY

As you drive into town on Winnemucca Boulevard you'll also pass the town's picturesque Winnemucca cemetery on the south side. This is where the town's pioneers, many of them Basque, are buried. If you stop here, signs direct you to the Catholic section, on the east side of the cemetery, where you'll find the Basque names.

SHEEP

In the summers Winnemucca-based outfits trailed their sheep into the Santa Rosa Mountains, the Pine Forest Range, and the mountains around Summit Lake. UNR researcher Joxe Mallea describes the northeast corner of Humboldt County as one of the "richest data banks" of Basque aspen carvings, with a large number dating back to the early part of the twentieth century and deriving from carvers from both sides of Nafarroa and Bizkaia. A majority of the earliest names were not reflected in the national censuses of 1900 and 1910, indicating that many of these early herders came for a few years to make some money and then left, according to Mallea.

One of the grisliest episodes in sheepherding history occurred in this desolate region. Four men, including three Basque sheepmen (Pierre "Pete" Erramouspe, Jean Baptiste Laxague, and Bertrand Indiano) from Eagleville, California, were shot to death in 1911 at Little High Rock Canyon, northwest of Winnemucca, near the border of Humboldt and Washoe Counties. Some people still have doubts about the contention that a band of Nevada Shoshones killed the four men; instead they blame the killings on a cowboy-sheepherder feud—despite the fact that two books have been written about the subject. (Dayton O. Hyde, *The Last Free Man: The True Story behind the Massacre of Shoshone Mike and His Band of Indians,* and Frank

Bergon's *Shoshone Mike.*) The true story of their slayings continues to be contested. "There ain't no cowboys out there when there's four feet of snow, and that was the way it was that year," said Pete Ytçaina of nearby Cedarville, California. Whoever killed the sheepherders, a group of about twenty local vigilantes took the law into their hands and pursued the Shoshone family east beyond Winnemucca, killing eight Shoshones. Historian Joxe Mallea has recently found tree carvings in the canyons at the edge of the Black Rock Desert made by a herder with the initials P.E.—very possibly Pete Erramouspe—dating from between 1895 and 1909.

In 1911 the Santa Rosa Mountains were placed within the National Forest system, locking out the landless sheepherders. But there was ample pasturage in other parts of the county where woodlands were not dense enough to qualify for the forest designation. In addition, many Basques in the Winnemucca region filed for citizenship to buy property and thereby acquire additional grazing rights on public lands.

BOARDINGHOUSES AND RESTAURANTS

According to Emily Laucirica, her mother, Estebana Sololuce, was on her way to California when the train stopped in Winnemucca, and hotel keeper Ignacio Arrascada boarded, asking if there were any Basques interested in working for him. "He must have given a good sales pitch," she said, "because my mother decided to get off." Arrascada ran a hotel in the town of Gold Creek and also in Elko before he got into the hotel business in Winnemucca around 1908. He was managing the Busch Hotel across from the railroad depot when Estebana Sololuce joined his staff, according to Laucirica, and Estebana later followed him to Golconda, where the two of them, as husband and wife, opened their own place, the Arrascada Hotel.

Basques in Winnemucca also stayed at a Hotel Lafayette sometime after the turn of the century, but it's believed that this was not a Basque boardinghouse. The Busch, near the Martin, was consumed by a Christmas Eve fire in 1924.

The **Winnemucca Hotel,** built in 1863 and run by the Olano family since 1965, is the oldest hotel still in operation in Nevada, according to its longtime owner "Big Mike" Olano. Olano is practically a

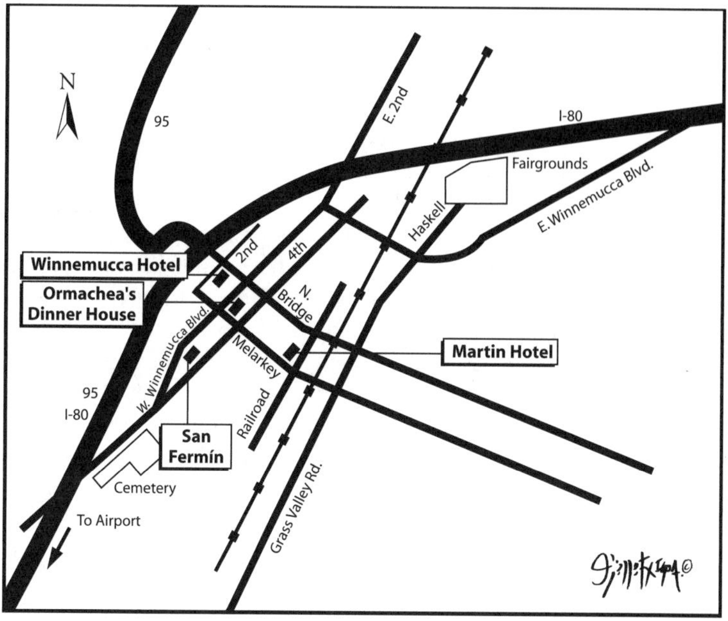

Winnemucca.

Basque institution by himself. With his thick eyebrows and tall stature, Mike, who arrived stateside in 1948 from Busturia, Bizkaia, is an imposing figure. Sit at his bar for any length of time, and Mike, in his heavily accented English, is likely to tell you the story of how the beautifully carved wooden back bar (estimated 1887) behind him was shipped from Europe "round the Horn" of South America. In its earliest days the Winnemucca Hotel was owned by Frenchmen, who added the two-story wood-frame addition on Bridge Street to the original adobe structure. The first Basque owners, as far as Olano knows, were three brothers, John, Epifanio, and Daniel Esparza, who ran the business during the 1930s and probably back to the 1920s.

Mike Olano first acquired the Winnemucca Hotel with partner Claudio Yzaguirre and then bought it from Yzaguirre outright in 1971. Olano's wife, Margaret, and his son Mike Jr. are integral parts of the institution. Mike Jr. has been cooking here for the past twenty years.

During the 1920s and 1930s, there was a handball court at the back of the hotel, but it was torn down at some point. According to Olano, children used to play on the court walls, and the owner at the time was told that the hotel needed to close off the court to avoid liability problems. Instead that owner tore the walls down. The floor was later ruined for future handball use when that owner put in horseshoe pits. The back wall is still there, and painted on it is the slogan WINNEMUCCA HOTEL, HOME OF THE PICON PUNCH. Olano and local club members considered putting the left wall back up, but the idea died when they found out the cost involved. Because the hotel is so old, building codes would require a new separate structure, which the small club could not afford, said member Isidro Etcheto.

According to the tradition of this place, diners tell Mike they're here and then sit down at the bar for a Picon Punch or two. When dinner is served, someone will ring the cowbell to let everyone know it's time to eat. If you'd rather not have the full-course meal, you can order up a chorizo or steak sandwich for $5 and eat it right at the bar.

The author's father, Jean B. Zubiri (in cap), plays handball at the old court in Winnemucca in 1931, just a few years before the court walls were torn down. The back wall is still there, with the words WINNEMUCCA HOTEL—HOME OF THE PICON PUNCH now painted over the plaster patch.

The boardinghouse's thirty-six rooms are rented out on a daily, weekly, or monthly basis, mostly to local miners, who still take their meals in the hotel dining room.

Bill Arant, owner of the **Martin Hotel,** realizes the value of preserving the Basque culture and the need to keep up the old traditions at his hotel. He bought the business in 1972 with Tom Ruddy, who was half Basque. Ruddy has since died. The two men didn't change a thing about the hotel and restaurant's long-standing Basque traditions. Actually, according to Arant, the Basque boardinghouse tradition was started by a Frenchman in 1914, although every owner since then has been Basque. The Martin Hotel building itself dates back to 1880, although a portion of it had to be rebuilt after a fire in 1919 burned down practically the entire block. The hitching posts lined up outside may make the place look more authentic, but Arant admits that they were put in only about twenty years ago. His nephew John Arant runs the place now.

You'll find that many of the waitresses, and usually the bartenders, who tend to be women at this place, are of Basque parentage. If you dine in you'll sit at long tables, and waitresses will serve you the traditional side dishes on big platters—although you can also pick your own entrée. You may buy a bottle of the house salad dressing to take home.

The hotel no longer has boarders, although it rents out hotel rooms once in a while, when friends are in town. Although the hotel was once part of the town's hustle and bustle of travelers coming in at the former Central Pacific Railroad station, today this place is off the beaten track. It is located three blocks from the main thoroughfare that brings tourist traffic to Winnemucca—Winnemucca Boulevard, also known as Highway 95. Even though the depot is now just a plastic shelter, continental passenger train service still stops there daily, across from the Martin.

Ormachea's Dinner House is one of two modern additions to the town's Basque restaurant scene. Tom Ormachea, whose family ran sheep and cattle in the area around Fallon, built this restaurant in 1978—and it was one of the city's major commercial projects at that time. Unlike the older two Basque restaurants in town, Ormachea's has individual seating and a choice of entrées, although the soup and side dishes are still served family-style. A large fireplace, with hearths on either side, and antique oak furniture make this Spanish-style stucco building a cozy gathering place. Framed works by Winnemucca photographer Linda Dufurrena, who has specialized in capturing Basque life with her camera, line the walls here. Many diners have bought her photographs over the years.

In May 1995, husband-and-wife team Alicia Garijo and Jesus Flamarigue opened the newest eatery in Winnemucca—**Restaurante San Fermín**—giving this small city its fourth Basque restaurant. Its upscale flavor breaks ranks with the other restaurants in town. Garijo felt that it was not necessary to serve the typical side dishes from the boardinghouse era, but the demand from customers seeking the traditional Basque-American setting won out. Tourists traveling on I-80 make up the majority of the restaurant's clientele, and Alicia finds most are very familiar with Basque cuisine.

Garijo and Flamarigue, who hail from Pamplona, decided to return to the Basque Country, but they still own the restaurant, which continues to be managed exactly the same as before. Garijo's family brought her to Winnemucca when she was small, but as an adult she returned to Pamplona, where she met her husband. The walls of this locale are decorated with photographs of the annual running of the bulls in the couple's hometown, for which their restaurant is named.

Martin Hotel, Railroad and Melarkey Streets, Winnemucca, NV 89445 (775) 623-3197
Ormachea's Dinner House, 180 Melarkey (U.S. 95 at Second), Winnemucca, NV 89445 (775) 623-3455
Restaurante San Fermín, 485 West Winnemucca Boulevard Winnemucca, NV 89445 (775) 625-4900
Winnemucca Hotel and Bar, 95 Bridge Street (at First), Winnemucca, NV 89445 (775) 623-2908

FESTIVAL

Dancers in their red skirts twirl down Winnemucca's main street to kick off the annual Basque festival on the second weekend of June. The two-day affair is a favorite among Basques, offering competitions galore. The festival shows off the best of Basque traditions: dance demonstrations, wood chopping, wood tossing, and *soka tira* (tug-of-war) competitions, and weight-carrying relays. Between Saturday and Sunday there's also bota drinking, bread making, *jota* (another term for *fandango*) and *irrintzi* (Basque yodel-like cry) competitions.

Most of the competitions are broken down by age groups, so teens and even six- to twelve-year-olds compete in carrying weights. The games on Saturday are held at the Humboldt County Fairgrounds, and the Saturday night dance and Sunday's events take place at the Humboldt County Convention Center (50 West Winemucca Boulevard). One of the teens' favorite events is the *jota* competition Sunday afternoon. Sunday's barbecue lunch is served indoors and includes a delicious lamb stew in addition to New York steak.

Jim Ithurralde of Eureka, Nevada, master of ceremonies for several festivals for many years, had his favorite picnics sorted out according to their specialties. "It was Elko for their steaks, Ely for their lamb, and Winnemucca for the lamb stew." Watch the men do the cooking here, as they do at most of the picnics.

Signs directing you to the Humboldt County Fairgrounds are posted all over town at festival time. From Winnemucca Boulevard, head south on Bridge Street just past the railroad tracks to Haskell Street. Turn left on Haskell and follow that road all the way to the festival. In good years the festival has attracted up to three thousand people, but that number has dropped to an average of twelve hundred. Conflicts over end-of-school schedules keep away many families from distant places.

BASQUE CLUB

The Basque club in Winnemucca, **Euskaldunak Danak Bat** (Basques Are All One), is about 250-members strong, with about an equal mix of Nafarroa Behereans and Bizkaitarrak. Longtime member Emily Laucirica believes the club started around 1947, although she could only find documents dating back to 1952. In any case, it is Nevada's oldest Basque club.

In its earliest days the club would hold a dance once a year at the Sonoma Inn (now the Winners Hotel). The restaurant hosted a free buffet dinner at midnight, but because the Basques would buy so many drinks, the restaurant "used to make a killing on us," joked Laucirica. Band leader Jim Jausoro remembered playing his accordion for those all-night dances. "We would end at five o'clock in the morning, and it was just two of us in those days," he said. During the 1950s the Winnemucca and Martin Hotels also hosted dances.

The Euskaldunak Danak Bat's energy is primarily concentrated on organizing the festival. Yet, as in Reno, the Basque club holds a modest members' picnic in August as well as a Christmas party and *mus* tournament and dinner in the spring, all at the convention center. The high priority the club places on maintaining the culture is reflected in its sponsorship of its young members' participation in the annual NABO summer camp. College scholarships for high school seniors of Basque descent are also offered.

In 1993 the club seriously considered buying an older house and renovating it as a clubhouse, but members ultimately decided it was unnecessary. The issue has come up before. "Our first president [Julio Laucirica] was all gung ho about getting a center, but we didn't have any money," said Laucirica. Club members decided that they were perfectly content with the existing community facilities, including the new convention center. The spacious 4-H building at the fairgrounds was built in the early 1980s with some help from the Basque club. And for years the club meetings have been held in the basement hall of St. Paul's Church (350 Melarkey). This elegant church was built in 1924 with donations from the local Basque community.

The Basque club is in the midst of passing its leadership to younger Basque-Americans, and clashes between the Old World and New World are typical here as the new generation seeks its own way of carrying on the traditions. In fact, at one point, some Basque-Americans thought of starting a second club. Tensions sometimes result when some of the old-timers worry that the new generation won't do things right. But Laucirica, who is training a younger member for her longtime job as festival program coordinator, views the situation more positively: "You have to give them a chance. They'll learn, just like we did."

Euskaldunak Danak Bat, P.O. Box 3560, Winnemucca, NV 89446. Information: (775) 623-3706 (*Isidro and Muriel Echeto*); festival information and accommodations: (775) 623-5071

Cultural Identity

Despite the early formation of a club, the Basque community of Winnemucca didn't do much more until 1978, when it started hosting its big annual festival. Interest in public expression of ethnicity developed slowly among Basque-Americans. With the exception of Boise, Idaho, and La Puente and Bakersfield, California, where Basque clubs and dance groups were organized during the 1940s, there was little in terms of cultural expression elsewhere.

Bob Echeverria, a Winnemucca native who now lives in Elko, is one of the biggest promoters of the Basque culture in the area today. He grew up in Winnemucca before there was a festival. Indeed, during the 1940s, 1950s, and 1960s, his hometown provided Echeverria with no hint of the richness of his cultural background. And at home a defensiveness against discrimination had built up. "My father, my aunts and uncles—none of them wanted to be Basque," he said. "They wanted us to be American." Having heard one too many jokes about Basques, Echeverria's father Pablo refused to speak Basque at home with his family. "His college education was the sheep camp, and he didn't want that for his sons," said Echeverria.

Up until the 1960s, most Basques were even unaware of the Basque activities going on in other parts of the West, primarily because of their geographic isolation. A few did know—those who had relatives in the largest Basque communities. "We used to think the Basques in the (San Joaquin) Valley were so united," said Irene Arbeloa of Reno, who often visited Bakersfield with her family in the 1940s.

Intermarriage with other ethnic groups also eroded ethnic awareness among second-, third-, and fourth-generation descendants of Basques. "There's not much purity left," admitted Bill Arant, who's one-quarter Basque himself. The family of his Basque grandmother, Ermelinda Arana, settled first in nearby Unionville to work in the mines.

But in Winnemucca later migrations strengthened Old Country ties and revived customs. A national wave of ethnic consciousness overtook the Winnemucca Basque colony during the 1970s. A Basque radio program was broadcast on Sundays, and in 1978 the town put on its first Basque festival.

DANCE

As early as the 1950s, according to Emily Laucirica, Winnemucca had a dance group. The Irrintzi Dancers practiced in the basement church hall and performed at the hotel dances. Winnemucca's dance group nurtured the ethnic awareness of the young Basque-Americans over the years. In 1992 there was no teacher, and the teenage group began to disintegrate. But a new teacher has taken up the job, and a whole slew of young dancers is primed to move into the older group's slots in a couple of years.

National Antelope Refuge Headquartered at Old Basque Ranch

Highway 140, which heads north to Denio and on into Oregon, is the only paved road in the northwest corner of Nevada. There is one significant reason to take a trip on this lonely road. Just west of Denio, you'll find the **Sheldon National Wildlife Refuge,** established when antelope seemed to be a vanishing species. (Today, antelope exist by the thousands in Wyoming and are proliferating in many states, including Nevada.) The refuge's subheadquarters are located at the former Dufurrena family ranch, just off Highway 140. The old stone buildings and willow corrals built by this Basque family are worth seeing. "There are probably more pictures taken of the willow corrals and barn than anything on the refuge," said former field station manager Lane Slover, who lived here for several years. The buildings, which date back to the 1910s and 1920s, were made with what's called Dufurrena sandstone, quarried right on the property. The barn and a couple of other buildings are in active use by refuge employees. "We don't allow anybody in there, because they're starting to deteriorate," said Slover, adding that the stone is very soft and crumbling. "We've done some work to try to preserve them, but it's almost impossible." It is a constant job to maintain the corrals, and visitors are asked not to take pieces away.

Although the refuge's main headquarters are in Lakeview, Oregon, the former Dufurrena ranch and refuge subheadquarters are located 30 miles west of Denio, Nevada. Make sure you pick up a map at the subheadquarters if you plan to wander about the 573,000-acre refuge. "It's a long way to anywhere," said Slover, and you don't want to get lost. Although the subheadquarters is accessible all year long, snow makes the rest of the refuge inaccessible from November 1 through April. According to Slover, the best time and place to see the antelope is off Refuge Road 34, at Swan Reservoir, in August. Bring your binoculars. In addition to antelope, there are also quite a few wild burros and horses roaming around this expanse, offspring of domestic stock turned loose around the turn of the century. "The burros really tick off the ecology-minded people," said Oregon museum curator Bob

Boyd, because they are not native to the region. "Most people who go there, though, think the burros are the coolest part of the place." If you decide to cross into Oregon via Highway 140, look for the "stone boy," possibly built by Basque herders on a rim rock, on the south side of the road, about 5 miles before the border.

Sheldon National Wildlife Refuge, Mailing address: P.O. Box 111, Lakeview, OR 97630 (541) 947-3315; *www.refuges.fws.org*

Battle Mountain

BASQUE LANDMARK

The town of Battle Mountain was created in 1870 to serve several mining camps to the south, and it never grew very large. A small contingent of Basque families has survived throughout the years in this town of 3,000. At the east end of town, you'll see a Basque sheep wagon in front of Etcheverry's Food Town (424 East Front St.), owned for years by Ray Etcheverry, a major Basque supporter. Pete Coscarart popularized his homemade chorizo during the 1980s at a deli in historic Lemaire's general store, and he eventually moved the business to Carson City.

DANCE AND A NEW CLUB

The Basque group formed in Battle Mountain is one of the newer clubs sprouting up in the West. At least three families were driving an hour one-way to Elko to carpool nearly twenty children to Basque dance practices there, and finally they decided to start their own club and dance group in 1997. "We put an ad in the paper to see if there was interest, and the response was overwhelming," said Kris Itza. Soon after, thirty-eight children were regularly attending dance practices.

Battle Mountain has always had a contingent of Basque families, and today anywhere from fifty to a hundred families—first-, second-, and third-generation Basques—are involved in the **Oberenak Basque Club.** The group's first picnic on the last Saturday in August of 1997 attracted about a hundred people and raised $2,000 in profits, primarily through the successful auction of such items as wine, cheese, and bread. The picnic continues on the same date at the Lions' Club park with a steak barbecue and afternoon competitions. They also hold a big sit-down dinner on the third Saturday in January at the Civic Center. "We thought we were going to keep it low-key," said club president Shirley Shepherd of the Winter Fest fund-raiser, but three hundred people regularly show up for the Basque food and dancing.

Oberenak Basque Club, P.O. Box 1595, Battle Mountain, NV 89820. Information: (702) 635-3302 (*Kris Itza*)

Elko

It seems appropriate that the largest annual Basque celebration is held in Elko, midway between the large Basque populations of California and Idaho. Elko was once an insignificant Nevada city, its only importance being its location on the railroad line and later along the interstate highway. The discovery of some large gold mines nearby has turned Elko into Nevada's fourth largest city. The city's longtime dependence on the livestock industry, which dominates the economy in the northeastern corner of the state, and its distance from any major urban center has turned Elko into the state's "western" capital, a reputation that the locals work hard to maintain with their Cowboy Poetry Gathering every January. The Basques are also considered part of that tradition, because they have raised beef and lamb in the area since at least the 1870s.

Elko, like Winnemucca, was for many years a small Nevada town. Original train service came to Elko in 1868, and a second line bringing passenger traffic was completed in 1907. Cross-country automobile traffic began coming through on Idaho Street in the 1920s. Elko, Winnemucca, and Battle Mountain all benefited from being smack dab on these major lifelines across the country.

Many of the Basques who have come to Elko more recently came for mining jobs. Some were able to establish businesses, and those who went into construction did very well for themselves. Many of them are now men in their forties, fifties, and sixties. They make up the core of Elko's Basque community, and they work hard every year to put on the festival.

MINING

With the resurgence of gold mining during the 1980s, Elko has mushroomed. Mining accounts for 54 percent of the economy here, even though the two biggest employers, the Newmont and Barrick mines, are across the line in Eureka County, just west of Elko. Nevada's population has been growing by leaps and bounds in the last twenty years, and Elko has been part of the boom. Passenger rail service still serves Elko, but today more of the city's visitors arrive via the municipal airport, which has plane service to Reno and Salt Lake City.

Winnemucca and Elko have both grown, but during the 1950s, 1960s, and the 1970s Elko appeared to have received a much larger influx of Basque immigrants than Winnemucca did. Most did not come directly from the Basque Country, but rather drifted in from other smaller towns, or simply down from the mountains. Thirty years ago, Elko had five hundred Basques from the Old Country, maybe more, Jess Lopategui estimated. Today these immigrants (less than two hundred) with their children and grandchildren constitute a strong Basque community.

FESTIVAL

The Elko Basque club, **Elko Euzkaldunak Club** (see later section), sponsors the biggest of Nevada's Basque festivals—and probably the best in all of the West, surpassed in size only by the occasional Jaialdi festivals in Boise and San Francisco's 1979 Basque festival. In Elko the festival is a two-day-long show of all that is Basque, and it attracts all the locals, decked out in their cowboy hats and other Western regalia. The Basques of Elko definitely extend a hearty welcome to the non-Basque community during the festivities held the first weekend in July.

In the wake of the enthusiasm generated by the regional Basque festival in Sparks in the summer of 1959, Basques in Elko organized the Elko Euzkaldunak Club later that same year. A dance group, Elko Ariñak, was quickly organized as well, attracting between fifty and eighty youngsters. The club sponsored small dances and picnics until 1964, when it decided to gear up and put on the bash to beat all bashes as part of the Nevada state centennial commemorations. Elko's annual National Basque Festival was born. The organizers named the event after the very first such festival that had been organized three years earlier in Sparks. "We just took the name—it wasn't being used," said Bob Echeverria, one of the most active and longtime members of the local Basque club. And it has lived up to its name year after year.

"We've made a concerted effort to bring over Old Country talent consistently," said Echeverria, "to have something a little bit different every year." Club members bring down big tree trunks from nearby mountains for the *aizkolariak* (wood choppers), who are regularly showcased along with champion weight-lifters. In 1993 the famed Saralegui brothers wowed the crowd with a trick never before seen at a U.S. Basque festival. The wood choppers cut a slit about 6 feet up an upright trunk, slipped a board into it, and climbed on top of the board, where they began chopping a slit another 6 feet up. They continued in that fashion almost to the top before proceeding to chop the trunk in two from a height of about 15 feet up. "If there's anything different to do for the sake of challenge, the Basques will find it," remarked Jess Lopategui, the picnic's master of ceremonies, as the Saralegui brothers clambered up the pole.

Champion wood choppers from Spain, Gabriel and Esteban Saralegi, wowed the crowd that came for the Elko festival's thirtieth anniversary in 1993. (Photo by Averie Cohen.)

Young Elko residents dress the part just to watch the parade that precedes the annual Basque festival. (Photo by Averie Cohen.)

Festival emcee John Ysursa (right) introduces Roberto Echeverria and Kepa Arrizabalaga, a *trikitrixa* duet playing the diatonic (button) accordion and the pandareta at the National Basque Festival in Elko. The *trikitrixa* is making a comeback in the Basque Country and the United States. (Photo by Averie Cohen.)

The Elko Basques have come up with a wild and crazy event to kick off their festival. A "Running from the Bulls," imitating the real thing in Spain, attracts twenty-five to thirty participants who pay to get chased by the bulls. High excitement marks the atmosphere at this Friday-night event in front of Stockman's, with musicians and people dancing in the streets afterward. "It was really like being in Europe," recalls Gina Espinal of San Francisco. See a video clip of the the craziness on the Elko club Web site, *www.elkobasque.com*. Anna Urrizaga, who spearheaded the running of the bulls, said she had a hard time convincing local officials to "let Mexican fighting bulls loose in downtown Elko." Just as hard was finding the bulls, because American bulls won't chase people, but she tracked some down at an Idaho ranch.

Elko's Ariñak dancers, out-of-town dance groups, musicians, as well as a local official or two partake in the Saturday morning parade along Idaho Street, the city's main thoroughfare, which attracts two to three thousand spectators. A group of older dancers often adds to the party atmosphere by running around squirting the crowd with wine from their *zahakuak*. This spirited squad is made up of former Ariñak who reunite every year to help put on the summer festival. Marchers eventually proceed over railroad tracks to the Elko County Fairgrounds (Thirteenth and Cedar Streets). Sizzling sausages await the crowd. The schedule for the afternoon is nonstop, with demonstrations of folk dancing, sheep hooking, athletic competitions and contests, including a sheepherder's bread-baking competition, an *irrintzi* (yelling) contest, and sheepdog trials. Hefty cash prizes are offered in many of the contests, making them even more popular. The fairgrounds' bleachers fill up with a capacity crowd of up to four thousand spectators. In the evening Elko's youth gather at Elko's Basque clubhouse for a big dance, with Basque music. The dance attracts an immense crowd of young Basques and probably even more non-Basque teens, who look forward to the dance all year. It's one of the town's biggest parties.

The second day of the festival is more laid-back and includes the Mass, the big barbecue lunch, and some dancing. On both days handball games are held at nearby courts, and outside handball players compete against the locals. Elko is one of the few Basque communities with a fronton that qualifies for serious competition.

BASQUE CLUB

The **Elko Euzkaldunak Club** built its own clubhouse in 1977, on 2½ acres. Designed to resemble an Old Country *baserri* (farmhouse), the structure has flagstone set in the corners and around the doors, and a stucco effect was created for the walls. To raise the money for construction, club members sold life memberships, and two Basque contractors built the clubhouse at the lowest possible cost. "When we built it and opened the doors, it was paid for," said club officer Bob Echeverria. Today the club has about three hundred members.

In 1998, the Elko club saved an old bread oven at a sheep camp, which was going to be razed by the Yellow Jacket Gold Mine. Today, this oven sits near the clubhouse and is used to cook bread and stews for club functions. These days, besides the *mus* tournament every March, the club's only real activity is the festival. But that project takes an army to organize, and as soon as one festival is over, preparations for the next one begin. "It requires a lot of attention," said Echeverria.

Elko Euzkaldunak Club, P.O. Box 1321, Elko, NV 89803. Clubhouse: 1601 Flagview Drive, Elko, NV. For festival information, call the Elko Chamber of Commerce (775) 738-7135; *www.elkobasque.com*

Elko built its clubhouse to resemble a Basque Country *baserri.*

SHEEP

Basques ran sheep north and south of Elko in the late 1800s and well into the 1900s. Before 1900 there were more cattle than sheep owners in the area, and many Basques were buckaroos. A lot of them had started working for Pedro and Bernard Altube's large cattle operation, established in 1871 in the Independence Valley near Tuscarora (for more on the Altubes and the Spanish Ranch, see the Independence Valley section). In those days, Tuscarora was bigger than Elko because of its gold mines. The Altube brothers and Jean Garat had migrated from California, where both families had extensive ranch holdings, because unlike California, where open land was quickly occupied before the end of the 1800s, Nevada still had a great deal of unused public land around the turn of the century. These men had the first known livestock interests in the Great Basin.

Nevada sheepman John G. Taylor hired some of the earliest Basque herders to trail his sheep into Elko County, and by 1900 Basque herders outnumbered herders from other ethnic groups. Many of the herders were hired in the Winnemucca area before World War I, because that was where most of them alighted from the train. But as the job opportunities around Elko expanded, it became the economic hub of this vast rangeland. In 1907 passenger trains began stopping in Elko. Basques trailed the sheep to the north, where they had ample summer range in the Jarbidge Mountains and Mary's River Range, in Nevada's northeastern-most reaches, and into the Ruby Mountains to the east.

Today the sheepdog trials, which are traditional at the biggest affairs such as Elko's annual National Basque Festival, are as close to sheep as many second- and third-generation Basque-Americans will get. (Photo by Averie Cohen.)

The biggest Basque festivals, like this one in Elko, always feature wood-chopping competitions. (Photo by Averie Cohen.)

When sheepherders discovered the northeastern corner of the state, they quickly overran it with sheep, locking horns with cattlemen over grazing turf. According to Richard Lane, who wrote his Ph.D. dissertation on sheep nomadism in northeastern Nevada, in 1905, 392,000 sheep crowded the summer range in the Bruneau country between White Rock and the Jarbidge Mountains, of which only 14 percent was owned by Elko County taxpayers—landowners, that is. In fact, herders viewed the Bruneau territory as such valuable grazing land that they raced to get their flocks across the river first, ignoring the abundant pastures along the way. In 1906 small local cattle ranchers banded together as a political force to claim their rights and decided to petition the government to control grazing.

Arpanan: Logging, the old-fashioned way. (Photo by Averie Cohen.)

Dozens of sheep outfitters, a majority of them Basque, were driving their sheep into the higher ranges of northern Nevada "to the point where the whole countryside was being denuded," said Fred Frampton, a U.S. Forest Service archeologist based in Elko. "We were actually requested to come in," said Frampton. (In contrast to those early days, Frampton points out, "Now we're seen as the bad guys" because the government imposes too many restrictions on grazing.) The Bruneau area was designated part of the National Forest system in 1909, and that same year, in a significant move, U.S. Forest Service officials decided to limit access to the highest pastures to landowners, blocking the entry of transient Basque sheepherders. At that time, not all the desirable grazing land fell within the controlled districts, so in the summer of 1911 there were still more than a million sheep in the county. Basques who brought their sheep into contested areas were harassed, and a couple were even killed in turf battles.

Prejudice against Basque sheepherders is documented in newspaper editorials, forest ranger reports, and even in congressional records, in which Nevada ranchers complained about the overgrazing problems caused by the sheep. The tensions were evident throughout the West. According to one comprehensive book by Bill O'Neal on the war between cattlemen and sheepmen that spanned from the 1870s to 1921, twenty-eight sheepmen were killed. In *Cattlemen vs. Sheepherders* O'Neal identified only one fatality specifically as a Basque sheepherder, but the number is likely to be somewhere between half a dozen and a dozen. Several were roped and dragged by their feet to intimidate them, and at least one was dragged to his death in northwestern Nevada; another died in a similar manner in North Fork, in northeastern Nevada. Scholar Richard Lane found reports of sheepherder deaths that led him to believe that several were the result of the range troubles. Douglass and Bilbao also cite evidence of a fatal shooting of a Basque sheepherder in northern Nevada in 1924 and another in western Utah in the early 1930s. (The fatal shooting of one Basque sheepherder, Felix Jesui, by black cowboy Charlie Glass in 1921 actually went to trial in Maob, Utah, but Glass was acquitted.)

All-American—or all "Western" kids—get a kick out of the Basque feats in Elko. (Photo by Averie Cohen.)

Mikel Saralegi, champion weight-lifter in the Basque Country in 1993, shows off his strength at Elko's National Basque Festival. (Photo by Averie Cohen.)

RANCHING

Inevitably, Basques began acquiring property throughout northeast Nevada, becoming established ranchers around towns such as Mountain City, Jack Creek, Gold Creek, and Charleston, acquiring their forest grazing permits at the same time. With the exception of Mountain City, the rest of these old mining towns don't exist anymore. At Jack Creek in Independence Valley, at least one Basque, Felix Plaza, had a hotel and general store around 1915, and Joe and John Saval were successful longtime ranchers nearby. Basques settled to the east and south of the area too, in the Starr and Lamoille Valleys, down to Jiggs, as well as in Clover Valley, on the other side of the Ruby Mountains. Nick Goicoa, a partner in the Clover Livestock Company during the 1920s and 1930s, sponsored annual lamb barbecues on the Fourth of July at his sheep camp in Clover Valley, south of Wells. Pete Elia and Celso Madarieta hosted extravagant barbecues at "Buckaroo" Pete Barinaga's ranch in Lee. These

Bob Echeverria and emcee Jess Lopategui (right), the locomotives behind the National Basque Festival, auction off the best part of the annual sheepherder's bread-baking contest—the bread. (Photo by Averie Cohen.)

and other prominent Basque ranchers are all described in a comprehensive book on the region, *Northeast Nevada Frontier.* Sheep-raising continued to be a prominent business through the 1950s, when it began a gradual decline.

Basque immigrants living in the United States today often remark that their children will never be able to build up economic wealth the way the earlier generations could. The times in which immigrants to America could amass property and wealth—at least within one lifetime—are over, they say. "I feel sorry for the young generation because it's going to be hard to make a living in this world," said Cruz Bilbao of Elko, who made a small fortune during a lifetime of ranching. "You have to be educated, educated, educated to get a job." Yet the generation that came before them to America might have said the exact same thing about success. The early Basque pioneers, in the late 1800s and early 1900s, built up vast ranching empires with sheep and cattle. And land—lots of it.

Northeastern Nevada Museum

Elko's **Northeastern Nevada Museum** is one of the state's best local museums. An electronic slide show gives a quick history of the Basques, and there is a small display case with typical Basque items. Many of the longtime Basque families are featured in a photo display. The museum has a good selection of books for sale on Western history, travel, and Native American and Basque subjects, plus handcrafted Basque jewelry.

Northeastern Nevada Museum, 1515 Idaho Street, Elko, NV 89801 (775) 738-3418; *www.museum-elko.us*

BOARDINGHOUSES

Basques were running businesses in the colorful neighborhood around the old railroad depot at least as early as 1904, when the first "Basco saloon" was reported to have opened. Hotels soon followed. Unlike some other cities where the original boardinghouses have been torn down, most of Elko's are still standing, and, fortunately, still in business. In fact, Elko's old downtown is probably the closest thing you'll find to a "Basque town" in the West today.

Of all the businesses here, the **Star Hotel** takes the prize as the Basque hotel in longest continuous operation in Nevada (see listing in the Restaurants section). Pete Jauregui was partners in the nearby Telescope Hotel with Guy Saval, another important early Basque rancher and businessman, before he built the Star Hotel with his wife, Matilde. The story of her marriage to Pete was the classic tale of so many Basque women who came to this country. She arrived in 1908 with plans to join two siblings in Elko and work at the Overland, another Basque hotel. Pete, who was bartender at the Telescope at the time, sent two men to pick her up from the train station because he was told she was arriving late at night. Four months later, she and Pete were married. In 1910 they built the Star.

The Jaureguis quickly found that they needed to double the size of the hotel, because so many sheepherders were stopping there. The Star sponsored the early forerunner of the Sheepherder's Ball, a winter dance that became an Elko tradition. Many a wedding celebration was held at the Star, and the Jaureguis would offer the wedding dinner and dance as a gift to the newlyweds. What the Jaureguis' daughter Theresa Comish remembers most is all the babies. According to her, women from outlying ranches would come to the Star to have their babies. "The doctor would be called to the hotel," and her

The Star Hotel in Elko, Nevada, soon after it was built in 1910. (Courtesy of the Northeast Nevada Historical Society and Museum Collection.)

mother Matilde would act as nurse, she said. Matilde Jauregui, who lived with Comish in Elko, was most likely the oldest Basque in the country when she died at the age of 105 in 1995.

The Telescope Hotel, built in 1908 at 346 Silver Street, preceded the Star (see listing in the Restaurants section). Although it hasn't been run as a boardinghouse for at least twenty-five years, it's still Elko's oldest Basque-owned business. The hotel and bar was owned by the Samper family since 1936 through the 1990s. (The Samper family also had the Amistad, before they bought the Telescope. The Amistad building was eventually bought by non-Basques, who reopened it as the Cloud Nine bar.) Handball was played at the old hotel at its inception. First there was an indoor handball court, which was converted to a dance hall in 1911, when an outdoor court was built. The court was finally torn down in 1954, and Henry Samper added six bowling lanes to two existing ones and created a legitimate bowling alley in its place. When his wife, Jeanne Samper, who did all the cooking, became ill, the hotel stopped serving boarders. "You know how these Bascos are," commented the Sampers' son Albert. "If you can't do it yourself, you just don't do it." Eventually Albert and brother Adrian, and their three other siblings, took over from patriarch Henry Samper.

The Overland, at the southeast corner of Fourth and Idaho Streets, was also built in 1908, by Domingo and Gregoria Sabala, and this building also had a handball court. Interstate handball matches in Elko were being played as early as 1907. (The old Overland was finally razed to make way for a parking lot in the 1970s.)

The **Clifton Hotel** at 516 Commercial Street deserves credit for having been around longer than any of the others (see listing under the Restaurants section). It's known to have been operating in 1888, possibly earlier, although Basques did not own it in its earliest years. The Plaza family ran it during the 1930s and 1940s, when it was always full of herders. Jack Errecart bought the small nine-room hotel in 1960.

"One wet winter, we lost our pickup," related Jack's wife, Barbara Errecart. "It just sank right through the ground into a hole." After they winched out the truck, they found a tunnel that went underneath the railroad tracks, according to Barbara Errecart. Opium bottles were among the loot of vintage items they found in the old subterranean chambers. At one time the building was in the heart of the old Chinese enclave and housed Chinese opium dens and bordellos.

The Nevada Hotel was first built in 1927 as a bar by Anastasio and Jeanne Viscarret. Rooms were added later. In 1949 the Aguirre family moved the entire building across the street to its present location, next to the Telescope. Anita Anacabe Franzoia, a current owner of the building, tells the story of the move—they placed the building on the railroad tracks, turned it around, and set it on the new foundation—"all without closing the bar." The boardinghouse was popular for another forty years. Today it is operated as a restaurant, the **Nevada Dinner House** (see Restaurants section).

The Pioneer Hotel, one of the town's largest, and the site of the popular annual Cowboy Poetry Gathering, was owned by a Basque named Marticorena at one time. Joe Marisquirena, who owned the old Amistad hotel a few doors down from the Star, was in the newspapers all the time during the 1920s and 1930s. "He got busted on a weekly basis during the Prohibition because of a still he had in the backyard," said Janet Petersen, researcher at the Northeastern Nevada Museum. The Arrascadas, who had the Elk Hotel on Commercial Street during those years, also made moonshine and stored it in a tunnel underneath their hotel, which was later torn down.

The Basques were somewhat territorial about which hotels they would stay in. For instance, sheepman Beltran Paris spoke, in the book *Beltran: Basque Sheepman of the American West,* about the boardinghouses of the 1920s: "The owners of the Star and Overland were Vizcainos, and all the Vizcaino guys stayed there," said Paris, who was from Lasse, Nafarroa Beherea. "Martin Inda owned the Telescope, and he was a Navarro from Valcarlos. So that was my place. I always stayed there when I was in Elko." (Inda was in partnership with Pedro Goicoechea and Pedro Orbe. He also owned the Spanish Hotel in Eureka in the late 1920s, although it's not known when he first began operating it.) Although a political boundary separated the Nafarrak from the Nafarroa-Behetarrak, their dialect was the same. Elko has always had a good cross-mixture of Basques from different provinces, from both sides. The small Nafarroan town of Lesaka is one of the best represented here. Hotel ownership easily crossed from Basques of one province to those of another.

HISTORIC BARS

The train tracks ran right by most of these hotels, going east on Silver Street and west on Commercial. "The trains would bing and bang," remembers Jess Lopategui, but it didn't much bother the herders who stayed in the hotels. "We weren't interested in sleeping much when we only spent three days a year in town." (The train tracks were moved down to Water Street around 1980, and the new depot is now located a good distance away, at Twelfth Street and Water.) After dinner they would walk to one of the nearby saloons or casinos that were open all night long. In addition to the hotels and restaurants, Basques owned many of these watering places through the years. There was the Blue Jay bar at 238 Third Street, owned by Basques for eighty-odd years. Tony Leniz, the last Basque owner, ran the bar for thirteen years before selling it in 1989 to Americans who changed the name to Miner's Camp. Before the **Biltoki** opened at the corner of Silver and Fourth (see listing in the Restaurants section), Basques ran the Corner Bar there for many years. Between the Pioneer and the Commercial hotels on Railroad Street was Shorty's club, named after the Italian owner, who was married to a Basque woman. It was one of the Basques' favorite places. (Today it's called Goldie's.) And then there's the Silver Dollar Bar (400 Commercial Street)—not the casino—owned by Ralph Fagoaga.

RESTAURANTS

Elko's strong Basque community supports four different Basque restaurants—two fairly recent additions, the **Toki Ona** and the **Biltoki,** and two historic establishments, the **Star Hotel** and the **Nevada Dinner House.**

The **Toki Ona** is across the street from the Northeastern Nevada Museum, on Elko's main thoroughfare. (The name means "the good place"; it is a common name for bars in the Old Country.) The town's other Basque restaurants are located in the old downtown.

Toki Ona is the most recent addition to Elko's Basque dining scene. Tony and Ruth Leniz, in partnership with Ignacio Iriondo, took over the American eatery in 1990. Unlike the town's other three Basque restaurant's, Toki Ona serves food all day, starting with breakfast—usually the most popular meal of the day here, replete with all kinds of chorizo dishes—chorizo omelette, chorizo sandwiches, or just plain chorizo. Tony Leniz, who does a lot of the cooking, decided to serve breakfast because the restaurant was already known as a popular breakfast stop when he took it over. For eight months Leniz was there at dawn when it opened and at night when it closed. "Nobody knows what my life was like," said Leniz, who had had no restaurant experience prior to working at Toki Ona. The breakfast and lunch crowds help him compete with the other Basque eateries, with their longtime faithful clientele, as well as with the casinos, which can afford to offer inexpensive food.

Ramon Zugazaga's **Biltoki** is the newest addition to the old downtown neighborhood, having opened in 1983. Zugazaga has run the gamut in the restaurant business, starting at his family restaurant, Madariaga's, in Gernika, Gipuzkoa. He herded sheep for a while upon his arrival in the United States, but he got back into the business by cooking at Elko's Star Hotel for ten years. Then he went to Boise, where he worked as chef at the Boardinghouse restaurant before opening his own place, Biltoki, in Gooding, Idaho. But Elko beckoned him. "I feel like Elko is my home," he said, so he came back and opened the Biltoki, just down the street from the Star.

Stop in at the bar at the **Star Hotel** for a drink. This place is proof of the saying "The more things change, the more they stay the same." The Star still has boarders and has fed its customers at the same dining room tables for years. Posted on the wall here is a list of the many Basque families who have owned the place since it opened in 1910: Jauregui, Corta, Arrascada, Garamendi, Bengoa, Ozamis, Jauristi, Esnoz, Yanci, Aldazabal and Sarasua. Most recently, owners Miguel and Teresa Leonis and Severiano Lazcano sold the place to Scott and Tricia Ygoa in 2004. Scott, an Elko native, said he plans to keep all the same traditions. Once upon a time you sat down at the table of the restaurant and ate what they served you. Now you can pick your entrée from the menu.

Leo and Leonie Morandi added to the neighborhood's well-entrenched reputation for good Basque food when they bought the Nevada Hotel from the Aguirres in 1985 and turned it into a restaurant, the **Nevada Dinner House.** Anita Anacabe Franzoia bought the restaurant with a group of partners. "We still have the best salad in town," she said, and they added a fourteen-layer lasagna "to die for."

There are several bordellos still in operation in Elko, red lights and all, on River Street behind the Nevada and the Star. Elko County is one of the counties in the state where prostitution is still legal.

Biltoki, 405 Silver Street (at Fourth Street), Elko, NV 89801 (775) 738-9691
Nevada Dinner House, 351 Silver Street (near Third Street) Elko, NV 89801 (775) 738-8485
Star Hotel, 246 Silver Street (at Third Street), Elko, NV 89801 (775) 738-9925
Toki Ona, 1550 Idaho Street (across from the city park), Elko, NV 89801 (775) 738-3214

BASQUE HANGOUTS

Over at the Clifton Hotel, tiny "Papa" Jack Errecart used to pop into the downstairs bar at least once a day, despite his eighty-plus years. The high ceilings and antique backbar with silver mirrors denote the age of the place; today it is the oldest bar in Elko. For years, Errecart used to cook a free Basque lunch every Sunday with all the trimmings for family and friends. Papa Errecart died in 1997, and his son Jacques inherited the hotel. For a while, Jacques Jr. moved his architectural

Pete Itçaina and the Silver Dollar Bar

The Silver Dollar bar carries a Basque legend that it will never live down. Jess Lopategui relates the story that so many locals have heard about Pete Itçaina, who was probably the region's wealthiest Basque sheepman: "Pete Itçaina came to town one time. . . . He used to drink and raise a little hell and gamble." He went into the Silver Dollar, which at the time was the most popular place in town. Some say Itçaina had just finished a day of sheep dipping and came in dusty, dirty, and stinking like roses. "He didn't look like a wealthy man, but he sure was," said longtime Elko resident Adelita Viscarret. Well, the bartender apparently made him wait with his money on the counter—he went so far as to tell Itçaina he would get to him when he was ready. "Pete took it pretty hard," said Lopategui. He knew the bar's owner, went to his house and woke him up and convinced him to sell the place, said Lopategui. "He bought the bar that same night and went back and fired the guy," he said.

Itçaina, who ran sheep in Elko County from 1910 to 1958, is one of Elko's more colorful characters from its early days. He became a millionaire from the sheep business and was known for taking over land right and left in early homesteading days. He also participated in range wars in three northern Nevada counties.

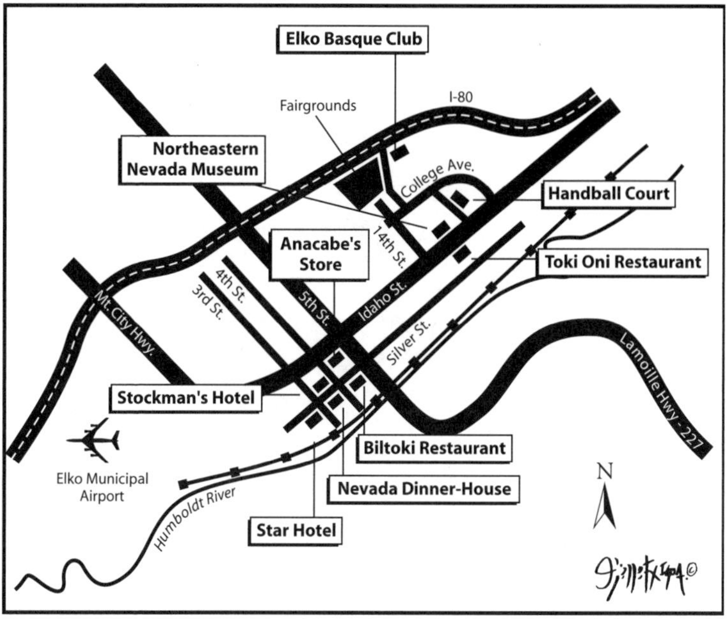

Elko.

office to the historic bar. But with some partners, he later turned the place into an art gallery, with the elegant, remodeled Gallery Bar featured prominently in its midst. Up to forty wines and other specialty drinks are served, and artwork, including Basque-themed paintings by Errecart and his partner Joan Anderson, surround customers in this renamed Duncan LittleCreek Gallery. The hotel rooms are being renovated, too.

At the old Telescope Hotel, little has changed besides the addition of the bowling alley. The old backbar and tin ceiling are the originals. The Sampers put the building up for sale in 1990. "We've been here a long time, and we've all hit that sixty mark," said Albert Samper. "It's time to go fishing." Phil Kemmish bought it from the Samper family and runs it solely as a bowling alley now, but you can still get a drink at the old bar.

Beef Tongue, Ramon Zugazaga, Biltoki Restaurant

1 beef tongue (approximately 3 pounds)
1 onion, chopped
2 tablespoons tomato paste
1 tablespoon chicken broth
4 tablespoons cracker meal or dried bread crumbs
4 cloves garlic
White wine
Salt and black pepper to taste

Fill a pot with water and a teaspoon of salt and boil the tongue until tender—about 1½ hours. (Check with a fork for tenderness.) Peel skin off the tongue (running the boiled tongue under cold water makes the peeling process easier). Cut the meat into thin slices and set aside. In a frying pan, saute chopped onion, finely sliced garlic cloves, salt, pepper, a little white wine, and the dried bread crumbs. Add the tomato paste and chicken broth and stir until it thickens. Pour sauce into a baking pan, place the tongue on top. Cook in the oven at 350 degrees for 45 minutes to 1 hour.

Clifton Hotel and Duncan LittleCreek Gallery, 516 Commercial Street (at Fifth Street), Elko, NV 89801 (775) 738-3426; *www.dlcgallery.com*
Telescope Lanes, 346 Silver Street, Elko, NV 89801 (775) 738-3926

OTHER LONGTIME BASQUE BUSINESSES

Anacabe's General Merchandise Store is another longtime Basque business in this neighborhood and the de facto Basque clearinghouse in town. Leaving behind the life of a buckaroo, Joe Anacabe opened the business in the town of McDermitt in 1924, moving it to Elko in 1936. His store provided all the supplies a sheepherder would need out on the sheep trails—work clothes, boots, and camping gear. In the old days his store even made the herders' bedrolls. "They would come into town to our store, buy our clothes," remembers Joe's daughter Anita Anacabe Franzoia, then they'd walk over to Julio Arostegui's Paloma Barber Shop (now the Downtown Barber Shop), across from the Star Hotel, which had showers. "They'd shower, shave, put their new clothes on, and they were set," she said.

Anacabe's store still fills outfitting needs even today, for buckaroos, miners, hunters, and the Peruvian and Mexicans who do most of the herding these days. The original old-fashioned decor of hardwood floors and rolling ladders along the wall haven't changed, and the store still offers a good all-around selection of work clothes and Western wear, with a fair price spectrum. If you want a *txapel* (a Basque beret), a *zahakua* (wine bag) for your wine, or a postcard to show you've been to this Basque town, stop in. You'll find the knowledgeable Anita Franzoia completely fluent in Basque and English. She is often called on to translate for new arrivals or visitors, and she is also very active in the Basque club. Because she has four children at home, she is not always at the store. You can call ahead to find out about her availability.

The **Stockman's Hotel and Casino,** (340 Commercial) a major player in Elko, is also in the neighborhood and was Basque owned for many years. Dan Bilbao Sr. became a partner in the business in 1953 and acquired full ownership after a major fire in 1957 forced a breakup of the partnership and reconstruction of the business. The elder Bilbao, along with Dick Graves, founder of Nuggets casino in Sparks, were part of the exodus of business owners from Idaho during the 1950s, after gambling was outlawed in that state, according to Dan Bilbao Jr. Bilbao Sr. had owned the Boise Club in Boise, and he then moved to Winnemucca, where he owned the Winners Hotel for a short while before establishing himself in Elko. Bilbao Jr., one of the biggest boosters of Basque activities, ran the Stockman's for several years after his father died.

Anacabe's General Merchandise Store (also known as Elko General Merchandise Co.), 416 Idaho Street, Elko, NV 89801 (775) 738-3295
Stockman's Hotel and Casino, 340 Commercial, Elko, NV 89801 (775) 738-5141

CHURCH

Almost every town the Basques settled in had at least one Catholic Church where they could worship, and if it didn't, they helped build one, as they did in Jordan Valley, Oregon. In the early 1900s Elko did not have a Catholic church, so the Basque hotels typically offered their facilities for weddings, baptisms, and funerals. **St. Joseph's**

Catholic Church (986 Highland Drive) was first built on Court Street (where the library is now) with the support of local Basques.

PELOTA

In addition to keeping up the Basque restaurant tradition here, Biltoki's Ramón Zugazaga and Miguel Leonis, former co-owner of the Star, also do their fair share of work to keep up the Basque sports of choice—handball and *mus*. Zugazaga hosts *mus* tournaments at his restaurant, where the locals often come to play. Almost every year, on Memorial Day weekend, he invites the club champions from all around, from places such as Gooding, Salt Lake City, Boise, and so forth, for an unofficial tournament. The two men are among the most ardent *pelotariak* (handball players) in town—when Leonis was young, he was invited to join Spain's national team.

Up through 1950 the Telescope Hotel had a fronton, but after the Sampers tore it down and built a bowling alley in its place, Elko had no court for twenty-five years. During the 1970s local handball players sought support to build a new court, and the Spanish government, via a supportive consul general in San Francisco, offered $25,000. The city donated the land, and two local Basque contractors, Nick Fagoaga and Pete Ormaza, donated their labor toward the construction of the **City Park Fronton** in 1975. Today local Basque businesses provide support for the upkeep of the outdoor court.

With its own handball court, Elko joined the circuit for Western handball competitions—it had the only such court outside California until recently. Although Elko has one of the West's few good courts, it's used less and less. The Basque club has had a hard time getting youngsters interested in the tough sport, and older players are retiring from it. Because of Northern Nevada's fierce winters, it is too cold to play most of the year. And in the summer—prime playing weather—the youngsters have a myriad of other sports to pick from. Besides, playing handball is painful, admits Zugazaga, adding with a chuckle, "Maybe they have more brains than we do."

Pala, played with a wooden racquet, is the preferred version of the sport these days because it's easier, but Elko's court is too short for good *pala* competition. The club has discussed converting the court into an indoor facility, but the high cost has deterred the project so far, according to Zugazaga. The club is also reluctant to make such an effort on what is, in reality, public property. Even now roller-blade hockey players are chipping and ruining the court floor with their hockey sticks, but there's nothing the club can do to stop them, lamented Bob Echeverria.

The fronton was enhanced during the 1990s with the addition of a black-and-white mural of a man saluting the Tree of Gernika. This famous tree, located in front of the Assembly House in Gernika, Bizkaia, is the historic gathering place for the early lawmakers of Bizkaia and is considered a sacred place for the Basque people. Anna Urrizaga designed the mural on the backside of the fronton, based on a photograph of the original site. She oversaw its painting and gave quick art lessons to the local people, so they could participate in the actual painting. These individuals then signed their names on the side of the mural. "The town loves it," said Urrizaga, "it's a little treasure here in Elko." A bronze plaque in front of the mural, titled "Our Roots Run Deep," gives a quick explanation of Basque migration to America. An oak tree representing the Tree of Gernika was planted nearby.

The old-timers, like Pettan Urruty (front), love to watch a good game of pelota. (Photo by Averie Cohen.)

The fronton in Elko gets the greatest use during the annual festival. All the local supporters, many of them prominent Basque businesses, are named on the wall. (Photo by Averie Cohen.)

Also at the Elko City Park is a rose garden with a Basque sheepherder statue in its midst. The herder in the middle of the Horizon Hospice Rose Garden represented a Nevada pioneer, but when it came time to restore it, the Basque club took over the project and turned the statue into "The Watchful Shepherd."

City Park Fronton, Chris Sheerin Way near Idaho Street, Elko, NV 89801

BASQUE RADIO AND LANGUAGE CLASSES

During the 1970s the herders in the mountains, as well as the Basques in town, listened to the local Basque KELK radio program broadcast every Sunday at noon. There were easily thirty men herding sheep in northeastern Nevada. Jess Lopategui started the program, which ran from 1968 to 1980. Music, news, birthdays, and other messages were broadcast, as well as the Mass, all in Basque. It was the only radio station with commercials in Basque, Lopategui reported with a chuckle. Other manifestations of the culture include Basque language classes taught by Anita Anacabe Franzoia for the past few years at Great Basin College.

Independence Valley

Two Basque ranching families, the Altubes and the Garats, came to Nevada from California looking for open range in the 1870s and found it in the Independence Valley north of Elko. They were among the first big cattle ranchers in this region and Nevada's most significant Basque ranchers during the 1800s. Their adjoining ranches, the Spanish Ranch and the Y-Par Ranch, are still intact, and some of the older buildings, although on private land, can be viewed by those interested in an enjoyable scenic side trip.

RANCHING

Brothers Pedro and Bernardo Altube made a name for the Basques in Nevada when they established a cattle ranching empire in northeastern Nevada about 1871. Jean Garat, also a cattle rancher and close friend of the Altubes in California, joined the brothers in this part of the country with his family and established his own cattle operation nearby, the Y-Par.

Neither severe financial losses caused by winter blizzards nor the premature deaths of some of their children prevented the Altubes from leaving a legacy that continues to this day. Although the ranch has not been owned by Basques since 1907, dozens of Basques have worked there over the years, and the current owner maintains a relationship with the local Basque community to this day.

"You can drive from Idaho to Highway 50 and never leave our land, if you know how to go," said DeLoyd Satterthwaite, until recently head of the Ellison Ranching Company, which owns all of the land that used to constitute the Spanish Ranch. According to the *National Cattlemen's Yearly*, for 1992, in terms of land, the Ellison Ranching Company was the largest land-holding cattle ranch in the United States. Satterthwaite downplays the figures, noting that because of Nevada's dry desertlike geography, much more land is needed to support a head of cattle. In addition to the Spanish Ranch, the ranching operation owns the Squaw Valley, Upper Clover, Lower Clover, White Horse, Cottonwood, and Fish Creek ranches. Today, as in the Altube era, the operation includes sheep as well as cattle.

The Spanish Ranch

Unfortunately, few if any of the buildings on the Spanish Ranch property today appear to have been constructed during the Altubes' time. Yet because of the Ellison company's deliberate intent to maintain the old ranching traditions, the ranch today nearly resembles what the Altubes' ranch probably looked like in earlier times.

With the help of Native Americans from the nearby Duck Valley Reservation, the Altubes had dragged logs from the mountains surrounding the valley and built a bunkhouse, blacksmith shop, storehouse, and a spacious home. The oldest buildings on the ranch today appear to have served these purposes, although the Ellison Ranching Company does not have records to show when the existing structures were built or which original structures are still standing. The Ellisons purchased the ranch in 1925, many years after the Altubes had sold it.

For decades this sign has identified the Spanish Ranch, started by two Basque brothers, the Altubes, in 1871 near Tuscarora, Nevada, and still going strong today as part of a larger ranch. (Photo by Averie Cohen.)

Pedro and Bernardo Altube and the Spanish Ranch

Pedro Altube, who joined his brothers in South America, sailed to San Francisco in 1850 to take a stab at gold mining. But he quickly abandoned mining when another brother, Bernardo, also sailed from Chile to join him. They ran a dairy just south of San Francisco in the San Mateo area for a short time. The two decided there was more success to be had by supplying San Francisco and the mining camps in the Sierra foothills with meat, so they joined several other Basques in a partnership, running cattle from southern California north to the markets. The two brothers were Hegoaldetarrak, from Oñati, Gipuzkoa, but in California they established many friendships with Iparraldetarrak, like the Garats. Bernard's wife, Marie, was from Iparralde as well. In the 1860s Pedro with his family headed south to Santa Barbara, while Bernardo settled in the San Joaquin Valley, both to raise cattle.

California's crowded range pushed them to try their luck in the wide-open expanses of northeastern Nevada. They bought 3,000 head of cattle in Mexico and drove them north. It was 1871, and they aimed for the Independence Valley beyond the town of Tuscarora, which was already booming because of its gold and silver strikes. They established their cattle operation as the Palo Alto Land and Livestock Company and called the property the Spanish Ranch, a name it maintains to this day. Pedro Altube was nicknamed Palo Alto (Tall Pole), an appropriate moniker since he stood a tall six feet eight inches and had resided for some years in the town of Palo Alto, south of San Francisco.

The Altubes encouraged their employees to homestead, a practice that was common among early cattlemen in that region. The workers would fraudulently file for range land, but the land would be folded in with their employer's holdings. The steers raised on their property commanded some of the highest prices on the market. The Altubes added sheep to their stock, almost as a property marker. The sheep would graze down the ranch's outside boundaries, discouraging competing sheepman John G. Taylor from running his herds on their lands.

The brothers' later years at Spanish Ranch were not without their misfortunes. In the harsh winter of 1889–1890, the Altubes, along with other ranchers, lost most of their cattle. Bernardo became disheartened, not eager to start again at his late age. Pedro encouraged him to keep on, and they built up their herds again. Bernardo lost his wife and then a twenty-four-year-old son. His remaining son, Jules, married one of Pedro's daughters, Amelia, and the couple had twins, whom they named Pedro and Bernardo after their grandfathers. Pedro Altube eventually returned to the Bay Area where he died in 1905.

The Altubes sold most of their property by 1907, although Jules and his family stayed on at the Taylor Canyon Horse Ranch, just south of Spanish Ranch, until 1918. Basques continued their involvement in the Palo Alto Land and Livestock Company Ranch. Partner and longtime manager Peter Garat was Basque, as were many ranch workers through the years. Many Basques in the Elko area found their first job at Spanish Ranch. The Altube brothers' historic P-Bench brand is still in use today, registered to Frank Arregui, who runs some cattle in the county.

This 1917 bunkhouse on the Spanish Ranch near Tuscarora, Nevada, looks like a Basque Country farmhouse. There is a chance that Basques built it. (Photo by Averie Cohen.)

Edna Patterson, one of the authors of the book *Northeastern Nevada's Frontier,* said that there's only one building left that appears to have existed during the Altube era. It is the tiny one behind the bunkhouse, with iron bars on its windows; it may have served as a storage room.

In the 1990s, a deteriorated wooden blacksmith shop still stood with a rusty press and old forge inside, leftover from the Altube era. By 2004, this building was gone. A large storehouse and a bunkhouse, both still in use today, resemble the stone houses of the Pyrenees countryside, with their thick walls, and they could very well have been built by Basques. A sign over the door of the bunkhouse reads PALO ALTO LIVESTOCK CO., a name the Altubes used, and the year carved on the plaque is 1917.

As you drive into the ranch, you'll see a beautifully kept house. Partly made of stone, it was probably built about the same time as the bunkhouses. The ranch manager lives here. As for the storeroom, its stone and mortar building materials indicate it is old, but Satterthwaite doesn't know its age. Part of it was used for many years as the ranch company office, the rest for storage. The thick walls prevent freezing in the winter and keep the building cool in the summer. The building survived a serious fire sometime after 1935, although the roof had to be rebuilt. A tiny rickety wooden building near the modern cookhouse served as the ranch schoolhouse from 1932 to 1961. Before then it was a pump house, and it may well have served that purpose for the Altubes.

Corrals were built with branches of the willows that grew in the area—"that was all they had," said Satterthwaite. Today at least two round corrals made of willow, possibly first put up during the Altube's time, are still kept up, renewed every so often with new branches.

On the site is the original old slaughterhouse, in the south corner of the yard, behind the bunkhouse. Thick timbers support the pulley, which hangs over a tiny channel built into the cement floor. Satterthwaite said that it was designed to be flushed out by a natural spring that runs three to four months a year.

Today strains of Mexican *ranchera* music waft across the ranch.

Satterthwaite retired from the business, but basically the old ranch is still the same. Visitors who would like to wander around the old ranch buildings need to call the ranch office ahead of time to see if a visit is possible. To reach the ranch, take Highway 225 north out of Elko for about 25 miles until you see Highway 226 on your left. Follow 226 past the road leading to Tuscarora, until you see the Spanish Ranch sign. You'll follow the road that curves into the ranch for about a mile before you see the main yard, buildings, and the ranch office.

Spanish Ranch, (HC 32, Box 240) Highway 226, Tuscarora, NV 89834 (775) 756-6542

Trips for the Adventurous

If you are feeling adventurous and want to view some of the scenic countryside around northern Nevada, you can continue north on Highway 226 all the way to Owyhee and then loop back to Elko along Highway 225. You'll pass through a lot of sagebrush country, but it is beautifully green in the spring. You will also drive through the aspen-covered Bull Run Mountains as well as the former Garat family holdings, which are still part of an active, prosperous cattle outfit, the Petan Ranch (formerly the Y-Par Ranch). But be warned—you will face 17 miles of graded dirt road before you hit pavement again just south of Owyhee, where Highway 226 meets up again with the main road, Highway 225.

As you head north from Spanish Ranch, you'll drive through the former bustling town of Jack Creek, where Basques ran a store and a hotel around the turn of the century (now just a cluster of mostly empty buildings). The graveled section starts after Jack Creek, about 11 miles north of Spanish Ranch, just beyond Deep Creek, where the main road veers sharply to the west. The dirt road straight ahead travels over high mountains, although it too winds back to meet Highway 225. After about 6 miles, you'll pass the Wilson Creek Reservoir turnoff. Continue north, up and over the hill, and as you come down the slope you'll see the Petan Ranch headquarters off to the left. This ranch was under Garat ownership until 1939, when C. H. "Pete" and Ann Jackson bought the ranch. Today their son Pete Jackson runs the cattle ranch and maintains ownership of the Garats' Y-P brand, which the Garats established in 1852 in California. It is believed to be the third oldest brand in the country.

A large tin-roofed barn put up by the Garats looms over the rest of the buildings a mile away from the road. Although the paint is seriously faded, the name Garat is still visible on the barn roof, according to Jackson. "If you know it's there and have a little imagination, you can see it." That barn, along with the former Garat home that you'll see next to the road about 5 miles farther north, are all that is left of the original Garat structures. The old Garat home was moved from its original location to its current spot on Jackson ranch land that never belonged to the Garats. (The overall operation has expanded significantly since the Garat days.) Jackson family members live there now.

ASPEN CARVINGS

While you're in Elko, you might also consider taking a very different side trip to the "high country" near Jarbidge to view aspen carvings and *harri mutillak*, the stone boys that Basque sheepherders left on hillsides as markers. The journey from Elko to Jarbidge is approximately 100 miles one way, so be prepared for a long but beautiful drive. The Jarbidge Mountains are the only heavily forested area in this corner of Nevada. Before setting out, it's a good idea to check in at the Forest Service's Elko office, at 2035 Last Chance Road, to pick up a map of the region.

The road to Jarbidge leaves Highway 224 about 55 miles north of Elko. On the Forest Service map, it's County Road 746. This is a dirt road easily traveled in a passenger car, but keep in mind that this whole region is heavily snowed in during the cold months. The highest reaches of the road are typically closed until July 1, opening just in time for a Fourth of July celebration in the quaint mining town of Jarbidge—one of the most remote on earth. The narrow, winding road is definitely prohibitive for trailers or motor homes.

At Charleston Reservoir the road turns north (Road 748). You won't find any carvings until you've been driving on the Jarbidge road for about 35 to 40 miles. As you approach Coon Creek Summit, however, you'll easily find aspen groves all along the road. A *harri mutil,* poised on a nearby peak, is also visible from the road. The road leads north through incredible gorges, steep rocky outcrops, and thick groves of trees. You'll bump into Jarbidge right after you cross the Jarbidge River bridge. There you'll find bars to quench the thirst you've developed on the long trip, along with services and overnight accommodations.

For a while, the U.S. Forest Service offered campers the ability to rent the "76 Creek Cabin" located in an aspen grove about halfway along the road north to Jarbidge from Elko. Spruced up by the Forest Service and painted white with a green roof, it is just barely big enough for the two cots and wood stove you'll find inside. There is an outdoor toilet, and right in front of the cabin is an old Basque bread oven. Although it was closed in 2004, the Forest Service office was considering reopening the place. To find out if it's available, call the Forest Service at (775) 738-5171.

About 2 miles before you reach the town of Jarbidge, you'll see signs for the Jarbidge Wilderness Area, a primitive zone where no cars are allowed. Hikers and horseback riders love this region. Sheepman Pete Itçaina used to run many of his sheep through an area here dubbed "Bascoville," which is part of the Mary's River Range and full of sheepherders' carvings.

Ely

Ely no longer has any significant Basque activities, but it deserves mention because it was once home to a number of Basque boardinghouses, and its Basque club had a reputation for sponsoring the best annual Basque festival in the state for many years.

FORMER FESTIVAL

The two-day Ely festival used to be the most popular of Nevada's annual gatherings. Up to fifteen hundred people, including Basques from all over Nevada as well as Utah and California, would show up in this small town for the annual festivities, always held on the third weekend of July. Senator Paul Laxalt and other prominent state dignitaries, including Governor O'Callahan, would drop by occasionally, particularly in election years. The picnic was touted as the oldest Basque party in Nevada.

As soon as a group of young Ely Basques returned home from the 1959 Basque festival extraordinaire in Sparks, they asked themselves, "Why can't we do something like that?" said Marie Ordoqui of Ely. By 1960 a small group of Basque-Americans had organized the Ely Basque Club with a great deal of encouragement from the older generation. Mining work in Ely had attracted a number of different ethnic groups such as Greeks, Italians, and Serbs, along with Basques. Several of them had their own ethnic gatherings, and the Basques did not want to be left out, according to Ordoqui.

The Basques started out by holding a few dinners at the church hall, and a year later they organized their first picnic. The Ely Basques were proud of their picnic, and they worked hard to keep it traditional. Marie Ordoqui's husband, Gilbert, as well as other club members, often took their vacations the week before picnic time, just to get ready. The Ciscar brothers were among the main organizers.

On Saturday musicians, dancers, and athletes would strut down Aultman Street, along with a float or two, in the annual parade from City Park across from the high school to Broadbent Park, where the afternoon's program was held. The club charged admission to see a show of dancing, wood-chopping, weight-lifting, and *soka tira* (tug-of-war) competitions—with champions from all over the West. For a while, Ely even had its own dance group. Jim Ithurralde of Eureka was master of ceremonies at the Ely festival for many years. A lamb was always auctioned, and in a charitable gesture, winners would give up the lamb to be raffled off again and again, to help raise more money. Accordionist Jim Jausoro of Boise was always invited to play for the evening dance at the National Armory in the park.

The most appealing feature of the Ely picnic was the unique setting for the Sunday Mass and barbecue. The Berry Creek Grove picnic site was as authentic as they come, located up in a former sheep camp in the mountains, on land that belonged to Basque rancher Alfred Uhalde, about 30 miles outside Ely. Everything about the barbecue was primitive, especially in its earliest days. Organizers had to haul up generators and chairs. Club members would hand-turn the lambs roasting over the open pits. The local paper lauded the picnic's authenticity. Eventually the organizers rigged up the roasting spits to operate by generator, but they continued the practice of roasting whole lambs until 1989, when the festival was finally canceled. For those who didn't like barbecued lamb, there was turkey or chorizo. "A lot of people would sit by the creek and eat chorizos," said Marie Ordoqui.

There were no picnic tables or dance floor, but that didn't discourage anyone. When the club finally did have money to buy a dance platform, everyone still danced on the ground around it anyway, remembered Ordoqui. Often in the evenings it would rain, and the ground would get muddy. Then the dance would be moved back to the armory in town.

The picnic was enhanced by a sense of exclusivity. "You had to know a Basque to get a ticket," remembers Janet Inda of Reno. Of course, it wasn't hard to track one down in Ely.

SHEEP

Basques first summered their herds in the Cherry Creek Mountains in 1909, and by the 1920s many Basque sheep outfits had established themselves in White Pine County. They supported a vital Basque community in Ely through the 1970s. For many years there was a big ram sale in Ely, and because the local sheep industry was predominantly Basque, the two-day affair was always a good excuse for a

Basque celebration. There was a lot of interaction between Basques in Ely and Eureka. Nafarrak from both sides of the border dominated in this area.

Winters were harsh, so the northern sheepmen would often trail their sheep to the desert country of northern Nye and Lincoln Counties. Even then there were no guarantees. The winter of 1948–1949 was among the coldest and snowiest ever recorded in Nevada, leading to Operation Haylift, in which feed was dropped to stranded animals on the southern deserts. Only the toughest outfits survived. Some of these stories are recorded in *Beltran: Basque Sheepman of the American West.*

Beltran Paris built up a healthy sheep and cattle ranching business based in Butte Valley north of Ely, which has been carried on by his sons. Paris also helped his nephew, Paul Inchauspe, set himself up in the sheep business north of Austin. The Paris brothers and the Uhalde family continue to ranch in White Pine County today.

Up through the 1940s Ely was one of Nevada's biggest towns. "It was a company town," said Bob Ithurralde. Most of its residents worked for the Kennecott Copper Mine in Ruth, one of the largest copper pits in the world, which first opened in 1902. (Kennecott also owned a large copper mine that employed some Basques near Salt Lake City, Utah.)

BOARDINGHOUSES

At the heart of the Basque community was the Ely Hotel, owned by Basques from the early part of century. The Nafarroan Sebastián Irigaray held it around 1920, according to Beltran Paris. It housed the town's only Basque restaurant, most recently run for many years by Marianna Goyhenetche.

Goyhenetche's mother, Gregoria Cordana, ran several Basque boardinghouses in the Ely area. She and her first husband, Pete Mariluch, ran the Currie Ranch in southern Elko County, where they also had the Currie Hotel, which catered primarily to railroad workers. When her children were teenagers, Cordana moved south to Ely so the children could go to high school, and she took over the Spokane Hotel, turning it into a Basque boardinghouse. "She worked like a man—in the Old Country and here," her daughter remembered.

The Spokane burned down—"nobody really knows why," said Goyhenetche. Pete Mariluch died, and Gregoria eventually married Charlie Cordana, a rancher. She took over the Ely Hotel sometime during the 1920s or 1930s. The Plaza Hotel next door belonged to the family too, although it had no dining room. All its boarders would

The Ely Hotel isn't Basque anymore, but the old sign, familiar to hundreds of Basques who spent some time there over the years, still appears on the hotel.

walk over to the Ely to eat. During the Great Depression, the Parises bought a rooming house, Scott Rooms, in town, to bring in some extra income, and completely refurbished it. Beltran Paris's wife, Marie, ran it. A few years later, they sold it to Joe Gamboa. It closed down years ago.

Ely women appear to fit the tough frontierswoman mold, even well into the second half of the twentieth century, and Basque women were part of that scene. "Mostly Basque women owned the bars in town during the Kennecott era," said Ely native Jeanie Boundy, adding that one woman bar owner also ran a couple of bordellos.

Cordana's daughter, Marianna Goyhenetche, is one of those wiry independent women. After she married sheepherder Johnny Goyhenetche, Marianna worked as his camp tender, delivering his supplies—a job usually held by men. In 1972 she divorced him, and she made it on her own afterward, running the Ely and Plaza Hotels and tending bar. Her brother William Mariluch manned the Ely Hotel kitchen, but Marianna was the one everyone knew. "She had the best business in town, but she got sick," said local bar owner Eusebio "Jimmy" Zubizarreta. Goyhenetche sold the business to non-Basques in 1991, because of ill health.

Other Basque women who worked in hotels and bars were Dora Olareaga, a partner in the Club Rio, who tended bar until she died at age eighty-nine; and Mary Asena, who ran the Mystery Bar.

The Plaza and Ely Hotels, which are still in existence but have not been run by Basques for many years, were part of a row of Basque businesses on the 700 block of Aultman Street. Right next door was Greg's Club, belonging to Greg and Wanda Etchegaray. In recent years, the club was run for a while by the couple's granddaughter Jan and her husband, Dave Grubic. "At one time, Greg owned the whole block," said Dave Grubic. One wall of the place is full of Basque memorabilia. During the 1940s Eusebio "Jimmy" Zubizarreta leased Greg's bar along with partners Olareaga and Candido Batis. The other Basque boardinghouse in town, the Commercial Hotel next door, run for many years by Jean and Eva Orrueta, burned down in 1952 in a fire that killed two people. Zubizarreta bought the property, and in 1954 he built a hotel and bar, the **Club Rio** (751 Aultman Street), in its place. In its best days, the hotel, which provided no meals, had so many herders that Zubizarreta had to put them up on cots in the basement. "We never had steady ones," he said. "They would come from the mountains for two or three days, or a week." Non-Basques bought the club after Zubizarreta passed away in 1997.

BASQUE SIGHTS

The Ely Renaissance Society, a group dedicated to creating employment independent of the boom-and-bust mining industry, is bringing life and the arts to Ely through a series of murals around town. As part of the project, artists Don and Jared Gray put up a commemorative Basque mural on the street side of Joe Ciscar's Cruise In Car Wash (1603 Aultman Street), in which Ciscar's dad, Antonio Ciscar, is depicted as a sheepherder with his sheep wagon. Paul Ygartua, an internationally famous Basque artist from Canada, painted the murals, *United by Our Children,* at Aultman and Great Basin Boulevard and the *Ghost Signage* at 740 Aultman Street. While the Ely Hotel sat empty and boarded up, the group also painted the front to look like the inside of the hotel lobby, with curtains, "like it used to be when Marianna [Goyhenetche] had it," said Basque club member Kerri Pintar. This painting and the old Ely Hotel sign were still up in 2005, and no plans were yet in place for the former hotel. See the murals online at *www.elynevadamurals.com.*

BASQUE CLUB

When the NABO federation was created in 1974, the **Ely Basque Club** was still going strong and became one of the charter members. But in 1979 Kennecott closed the copper mine, disrupting the economy and triggering unemployment. "When the mine closed, everything went with it," said Jean Flesher, a Salt Lake native who often attended the Ely festival. "There's no money in Ely anymore." Ely's population has remained fairly stable since then, at around six thousand, because many who moved away were replaced by unemployed workers from the mine in Ruth or from the smelter in nearby McGill. Now a local state prison and small mines are among the few employers. The biggest attraction in Ely now is the Nevada Northern Railway Museum on the northeast side of town, which houses a historic 1909 depot and working railroad stock and offers steam engine rides in the summer.

The Ely Basque Club is still in existence. It had been reduced to twenty to thirty members and an annual Christmas dinner. The festival was canceled in 1989 because the club could no longer afford to hold the event.

In 1996 Chickie Schroeder, then club president, assembled the troops, and a big festival was organized anew, on the third weekend of August. "The initial concept was to revive it and to break even," said Schroeder. Although the turnout was much smaller than in earlier years—approximately five hundred people—the club made money, surprising the naysayers. However, that was the club's last big hurrah. These days, the few Basques in town sponsor a small club picnic for themselves. Most of the younger Basque-American generation has moved to larger urban areas.

Ely Basque Club, P.O. Box 151014, Ely, NV 89305. Information: (775) 289-6314 (Kerri Pintar)

CEMETERY

If you do go to Ely, you might want to stop at the **Ely Cemetery,** right on Aultman Street. It's one of the most picturesque cemeteries around, and you'll be sure to spot a few Basque names. Before he died, Zubizarreta dropped by every so often and put flowers on the many graves of the old Basque sheepherders. "Marianna used to do that too," he said. "They were good customers at one time."

Eureka

A few years ago a magazine writer branded Highway 50 through Nevada "the loneliest road in America," and the name stuck. Despite initial resistance to that claim, towns along the state highway are finding some commercial value in touting it themselves. Eureka has the dubious honor of being "The Loneliest Town on the Loneliest Road in America," a title you'll see splashed in big letters on a sign as you enter town.

Today Eureka is the only place with a population deserving of the label "town" in all of Eureka County. Once a booming mining camp with a population of 10,000 after the discovery of silver in 1864, it shrank to a mere 950 in 1970. Yet the town refuses to die and is experiencing a revival of sorts for two reasons—because mining is undergoing a comeback throughout the state, and because the town is cashing in on its importance as a historical outpost left over from the nineteenth century. The entire town is on the National Register of Historic Places because of the abundance of turn-of-the century buildings. All of these sites are recorded on a public tour map of the town, so be sure to pick up a copy at the courthouse, museum, or at other businesses around town. At least three of the buildings on the list—the **Nevada Club Bar,** the **Eureka Café,** and the **Colonnade Hotel**—were owned, or are still owned, by Basques, and other places probably were as well.

The county renovated the 1880 Eureka Opera House as a small convention center, but with the original architecture intact. The County Courthouse, built in 1879, has been beautifully restored. Make a visit to the town's Catholic cemetery, where you'll find the names of all the old Basque families that lived here. This is one of seven in Eureka, all located on a hillside known as Graveyard Flat or Death Valley—number 37 on the map.

The town could use at least one Basque restaurant to cater to the tourists that come through, but unfortunately it has none.

SHEEP

Basques first started trailing sheep in the Diamond Mountain region in 1907, moving south into the area from Elko. Probably the last big sheepman here that employed Basque herders was Johnny Laxague, owner of the Eureka Livestock Company, who ran thousands of sheep and cattle before he sold out during the mid-1950s. He would sponsor a big barbecue for the Basque workers and local families every year, according to Mary Jean Labarry. "After Johnny sold it, things changed a lot," she said. But the operation is still Basque owned, although the owner lives in Bakersfield.

Up through the 1950s a majority of the area's ranching families were French Basque—such as the Arambels, the Etcheverrys, the Goyhenetches, the Labarrys, the Sallaberrys, and the Etchegarays. "I think Eureka didn't have a [Basque] club because there was such a large group of them in such a small town—there wasn't a need for one," said Bob Ithurralde, a Eureka native who now lives in Salt Lake City. Today quite a bit of the county's rangeland is still controlled by Basque ranchers from California who graze their sheep and cattle here.

The Fourth of July is celebrated with great fervor in Nevada. Each town has its own special celebration. In the smaller towns, the holiday has always been one of the biggest events of the year. Janet Inda, who lived in Eureka as a child, remembers Independence Day barbecues at a Basque ranch in nearby mountains. The high school rodeo was another big to-do. "It wasn't necessarily Basque things that brought us together," she said.

But today the situation has completely turned around. In the 1960s a few Hegoaldetarrak arrived looking for mining jobs, but most of them have since relocated to Elko. And by the 1970s most of the ranching families had sold out, and their descendants had moved away, to Reno or other bigger cities. "Since I came back in 1973, there are no more Basques," said Labarry.

MINING

Gold mining declined in Eureka County by the late 1800s, although it has never ceased completely and has experienced minor booms over the years. Today a new way to process gold has brought mining operations back to life. The county's two main employers, the Barrick and Newmont gold mines, are at the northern end of the county, and most of their employees live in nearby Elko County. The Atlas Gold Mine employs two hundred people locally. Consequently, the county's population wavers around a mere sixteen hundred, while its daytime labor force is about five thousand. The money brought in from mining makes Eureka County one of the richest in the United States per capita, according to Jim Ithurralde, who has reigned as the county's assessor since 1978. Considering the mining taxes pouring into the county's coffers, his job carries considerable weight here—as well as pressure from state and Elko County officials, who Ithurralde says would love to cash in on some of that money.

"We're the hidden Virginia City of Nevada," claims Ithurralde proudly. But he's not just referring to Eureka's wealth. The town's historic past is just as important, and a museum, once home to the town's former newspaper, the *Eureka Sentinel*, houses the original presses and memorabilia from the early years. (Unfortunately, you won't find any mention of the Basques here.)

BOARDINGHOUSES

The existence of three early Basque hotels is recorded for posterity via advertisements on the historic Eureka Opera House theater curtain, which dates back to 1924. One of the establishments advertised on the curtain is the Eureka Hotel and Café, owned by Ed Herrera in those days and purchased in the 1930s by Pete Laborde. (Town elder Norman Rebaleati said that Herrera also owned the Colonnade during the 1930s.) Laborde and his wife, Mary, ran the business through the 1940s. The Eureka Hotel, made of locally quarried volcanic rock, is still standing on Main Street.

Martin Inda, who was also owner of the Telescope Hotel in Elko, publicized his Spanish Hotel on the opera house curtain, and John Landa touted his "Store & first class Rooming House, fresh meats and

This 1924 theater curtain still hangs at the restored Eureka (Nevada) Opera House, advertising the hotels of the day that belonged to three Basques—John Landa, Martin Inda, and Ed Herrera.

bakery." The location of these establishments is unknown, since they no longer exist. Rebaleati said that Landa's place was near the Opera House. And according to Eureka-born Jim Ithurralde, the Alpine Lodge, which was earlier known as the Star, and the Lincoln Hotel were also Basque owned at one time. Most of these hotels catered to Basque miners or sheepherders who worked for local sheep ranches. The town also had a significant number of Italian residents, most of whom worked in the charcoal furnaces.

The last Basque establishment from earlier days that continued to operate into the 1990s was the **Colonnade Hotel,** one block south of Main Street at Clark and Monroe Streets. The Colonnade was a Basque hotel since 1947, when Gracieuse and Jean Sallaberry bought it. Built in 1880 by the Italian Benevolent Society, the solid brick building with 1½-foot walls, was remodeled in 1926, and it remained relatively unchanged from that early era, thankfully with the exception of a few extra bathrooms and hot water.

The Sallaberrys' daughter, Mary Jean, married Ely-born Basque rancher Raymond Labarry, and for years they ran the Cottonwood and Circle ranches, which straddled Diamond Mountain. But in 1973 Mary Jean's father became ill, and Raymond and Mary Jean came to town to help her mother run the hotel. "I came here with two suitcases, and I'm still here," said Labarry in the 1990s. Mary Jean Labarry's father died that same year, and her husband died four years later. After that, Labarry, aided by her elderly mother, continued to run the place until 1999. The year her husband died, Grace stopped serving food in the hotel dining room. The women converted the dining room into their living room and a cozy hotel lobby with its old dining table, complete with lion's paw feet, a reminder of the days when Basque boarders filled the place. "They used to have a good time here," remembers Labarry. "They used to sing and play accordion."

Tourists driving along Highway 50 love the quaint town of Eureka, which often becomes an unexpected stop. Mary Jean Labarry, who now lives across the street from the old Colonnade, kept the Colonnade Hotel's guest registers dating back to 1947, when her family bought the hotel. The registers tell an interesting story, reflecting the changes from days when her guests were mostly Basque sheepherders to recent times, when guests were welcomed from all over the United States and from all over the world. The man who bought the historic building from Labarry planned to restore it and convert it into his private home. He generously offered to give tours to anyone who might stop by.

PELOTA

The Nevada Club Bar on Main Street is notable because it once housed a handball court, and the walls are still there. The current building was put up in 1930, at which time the indoor court was probably built. Will and Jeanne Etchegaray operated this club as a Basque bar and restaurant in the 1940s, and perhaps even earlier, according to Etchegaray's niece, Mary Jean Labarry, former owner of the Colonnade. Pete Laborde ran the club during the 1960s and 1970s.

Old-timers in town remember that Basques played handball at the indoor court during the 1930s, but the Basque population and handball playing declined considerably during the war years, and the court became the town's only dance floor. Since then the court has been completely hidden by renovations, including a phony ceiling. But step back into the street a bit and you can still see the high wall. Walk inside, and at the back of the dance floor you can see the angled right corner.

Austin

Austin, west of Eureka on Highway 50, once had a Basque hotel and a small Basque community—primarily because the herders used mountain ranges nearby as summer feeding grounds for their sheep. Frank Aldape ran the Silver State Bar and Hotel for thirty-one years, until a fire destroyed it in 1968. The solid rock walls and the front verandah of the old building are still standing on Main Street, just down the street from the historic International Café. Aldape's daughter, Elisa Gandolfo, who still lives in Austin, said that there were never very many Basque sheepherders in the area, and the hotel catered to a diverse crowd. Today the town of Austin has dwindled to a mere three hundred residents. Rancher Paul Inchauspe, who lives north of Austin with his family, is the most prominent Basque in this part of the state, running three ranches, mostly cattle these days.

ASPEN CARVINGS

Roberta McGonagle, archeologist for the Bureau of Land Management, investigated Bates Mountain in the Simpson Park Range near Austin, where she found numerous aspen groves and hundreds of carvings. The most prolific writers there happened to be three Mexican herders competing with each other during the 1920s. The Basques mostly just signed their names, according to McGonagle. But the numerous carvings make the site worth a visit if you are in the Austin area. Heading east from Austin on Highway 50, follow Grass Valley Road to the north. Take the first dirt road on your right. You can continue on this road with a four-wheel-drive vehicle for a good 5 or 10 miles. Park your car and follow any of several roads crisscrossing the top of the mountain. Information on specific locations is not available, so make sure you bring a good map if you go exploring in the area.

Las Vegas

Las Vegas is home to the newest of the Nevada Basque communities. Most of the Basques who live in this city arrived after the 1960s. And sheep were not the attraction.

Despite the large presence of Basques in Nevada since the 1800s, few or none settled in Las Vegas until recently. The southern Nevada desert conditions were not conducive to raising sheep. "You can't herd sheep in Las Vegas," said resident Mary Guerrica. "It's too hot." There's no vegetation either. "You can run sheep in the desert only one time of year—in the spring, right after the rain," added her husband, Jess. There also aren't any high mountain ranges nearby offering summertime feed, as there are farther north in Nevada. At any rate, the big open desert spaces just north of Las Vegas have been monopolized by the federal government for years, for use as missile test sites.

Despite the hundreds of restaurants that cater to the 12 million visitors who come to this lively gambling town every year, there isn't a single Basque restaurant here. "Two or three tried, but they didn't make it," said business owner José Mari Beristain. Basques here say it's impossible in this town to compete with the moneymaking casinos that can offer meals for practically nothing. "For $3.50 you can eat all you want. . . . How can you compete with that?" remarked Las Vegas resident Jesus Belaustegui, who once owned a Basque restaurant near San Diego.

Job opportunities brought a few Basques to Las Vegas, such as construction business owner Beristain, who headed the local Basque club for almost ten years, and member Jess Guerrica, whose company transferred him here from Reno in 1987. New members keep appearing as the metropolis grows, bringing more Basques from northern Nevada.

JAI ALAI

This Basque community has a number of former jai alai players who were brought to the city to play at the former MGM fronton, which operated from 1973 until 1983. The fronton was opened by the MGM Las Vegas in December 1973, and jai alai was played in the club until financial concerns and a players' strike prompted MGM to close it. "MGM thought they could use the space better as convention space, so they shut it down," said Jose Mari Beristain. (For more information on jai alai, see the section on Florida in the East Coast and South chapter.) Today, the MGM is Bally's.

BASQUE CLUB

The **Lagun Onak Las Vegas Basque Club,** formed in 1984, has only about sixty members, but for years it sponsored a fairly successful annual festival that raised thousands of dollars for Catholic Community Services (CCS), a local Catholic charity. In fact, the fund-raising event was the impetus for founding the club. Sister Suzanne Laxalt, who worked with CCS, first proposed the idea of a benefit dinner with a Basque theme, and the group of Basques who got together to organize the event later decided to form an official club, **Lagun Onak** (Good Friends). The members have also managed to organize a small dance group for their young people, Ibar Izarrak.

Ines Yturri Park, a retired lawyer and one of the founders of the local club, said her family lived in Las Vegas for many years without knowing a single other Basque. "My folks were probably the first Basque family to come to Las Vegas," she said, noting that they arrived in the city in 1932. Her parents had run the old Bengoechea Hotel in Mountain Home, Idaho, for many years, but her father, Victor Yturri, suffered from asthma, so his doctor sent him south to seek a drier climate. Yturri said that it was hard for her parents, moving from an area of so many Basques to one with none, especially for her mother who spoke very little English. The young Pete Echeverria, who went on to become a state senator and a well-known trial attorney in Reno, worked at a Las Vegas grocery store for a time, according to Yturri. "He used to come and visit," remembered Yturri. These days the Basque communities are much more organized than they were when she was young. "They've got Basque clubs all over the West," said Yturri, adding that she was glad to see so much interchange between the different groups.

The club sponsors a *mus* tournament, usually on the first Saturday in February, and also participates in Las Vegas's International Food and Folklife Festival in April. It hosts an Aberri Eguna celebration, too, the week after Easter.

Lagun Onak Las Vegas Basque Club, 3467 Beam Drive, Las Vegas, NV 89118. Information: (702) 361-6834 (Jose Mari Beristain).

FESTIVAL

The Lagun Onak Las Vegas Basque Club sponsors one of the last Basque festivals of the year—the Las Vegas Basque Festival on the second Sunday in October.

For years the festivities started on Saturday night with the fundraising dinner to benefit the Catholic Community Services. Tickets for the dinner were $100 apiece, and Beristain said that during the ten-year period that he was president, the event raised a total of about $400,000. Most of the tickets were purchased by local hotels and casinos, which passed them out to their employees.

Some of the chefs came down from Ely. The club also entertained the crowd with Basque weight-lifters and dancing. The dinner was canceled in the late 1990s.

Now the club focuses on its Sunday picnic for members. It used to take place indoors at St. Viator's Community Center, but in recent years, it has been held at the Sammy Davis Jr. Festival Plaza in Lorenzi Park (720 Twin Lakes Drive). "It's the best place to perform," said Chino dancer Jenny Ysursa, because it is shaded and has wooden floors. A crowd of three hundred to four hundred people typically shows up, many from Ely and Chino, which are a few short hours away by car. The local club does things a little bit differently at their picnics. They get a late start, with Mass, usually led by the Basque priest, starting at 11A.M. Then lunch is your pick. Instead of getting a pre-served plate of barbecued lamb, beans, and salad, you can choose from among several courses such as paella, lomo sandwiches, roast lamb, or chorizo, cooked up by the members themselves. Then the Las Vegas and Chino dance performances follow.

REFERENCES

Bergon, Frank. *Shoshone Mike.* Reprint, Reno, Nev.: University of Nevada Press, 1994.

Douglass, William A. "Inventing a Basque Identity: The First Basque Festival." *Halcyon: Journal of the Humanities* 115–130 (1980): 123, 129.

Douglass, William A., and Jon Bilbao. *Amerikanuak: Basques in the New World.* Reno, Nev.: University of Nevada Press, 1975, pp. 117–76.

Hovey, Carol. Article taken from Chapter 4, "The Spanish Ranch." In *From the Pyrenees to the Pampas to the Pacific Coast.* Reprinted in *Journal of Basque Studies in America* 5 (1984) 87–101.

———. "The Altube Family: The California Years, Chapter II." *Journal of the Society of Basque Studies in America* 11–12 (1991–1992): 15–35.

Hyde, Dayton O. *The Last Free Man: The True Story behind the Massacre of Shoshone Mike and His Band of Indians.* New York: Dial Press, 1973.

Lane, Richard. "The Cultural Ecology of Sheep Nomadism: Northeastern Nevada, 1870–1972." Ph.D. diss., Yale University, 1974.

Mallea-Olaetxe, Joxe. *Speaking Through the Aspens: Basque Tree Carvings in California and Nevada.* Reno, Nev.: University of Nevada Press, 2000.

O'Neal, Bill. *Cattlemen vs. Sheepherders,* Austin, Texas: Eakin Press: 1989.

Paris, Beltran, as told to William A. Douglass. *Beltran: Basque Sheepman of the American West.* Reno, Nev.: University of Nevada Press, 1979.

Patterson, Edna B., Louise Ulph, and Victor Goodwin. *Nevada's Northeast Frontier.* Sparks, Nev.: Western Printing and Publishing Company, 1969.

Silen, Sol. *La historia de los Vascongados en el oeste de los Estados Unidos.* New York: Las Novedades, 1917.

Smith, Raymond M. *Untold Tales of Carson, Eagle and Smith Valleys, Nevada, Circa 1865 to 1915.* Minden, Nev.: Silver State Printing, 1991, p.110.

Urza, Carmelo. *Solitude: Art and Symbolism in the National Basque Monument.* Reno, Nev.: University of Nevada Press, 1993.

Wyman, Walker D., and John D. Hart. "The Legend of Charlie Glass." *Colorado Magazine* 46, no. 1 (Winter 1969).

Idaho

In a search of early census records, researcher Julio Bilbao found a few pioneers bearing Basque surnames who first arrived in Idaho Territory after the gold strikes in the 1860s. He surmised that these were miners who had come east from California after the 1849 gold rush, and who had probably spent some time in South America or Mexico before moving on to the United States.

But greater evidence puts the first large influx of Basques to Idaho in the late 1880s. Historian John Edlefsen claims to have spoken with the first Basque who entered southwest Idaho—Antonio Azcuenaga, who immigrated from Bizkaia to McDermitt, Nevada, in 1887, then trailed his sheep throughout the area, reaching as far north as the Idaho Territory in 1889. Azcuenaga eventually settled in Jordan Valley, Oregon, where he claimed he was the only Basque for many years.

A few Basque settlers came to Idaho following the discoveries of silver in 1889 and 1890 in De Lamar and Silver City, both in the southwest corner of Idaho. They quickly left mining to enter the sheep business. Following the typical immigration pattern, they wrote home to family and neighbors from their hometowns and asked that they join them. Hundreds arrived between 1900 and the start of World War I in 1915. Although the largest number came to Boise, Basques also settled in significant numbers throughout southwestern Idaho, particularly in such cities as Mountain Home, Emmett, Shoshone, Gooding, Jerome, Twin Falls, Nampa, Marsing, Caldwell, Hailey, and Ketchum. As elsewhere, they worked as sheepherders and eventually bought property, establishing livestock ranches and sometimes dairies. A few worked in mines or as laborers on public construction projects such as irrigation canals and the Arrowrock Dam.

Juan Archabal was one of the successful early Basque pioneers in the Boise Valley. Arriving in the late 1880s, Archabal built up a large sheep outfit, bringing in several other Basques as partners.

The largest influx of Bizkaitarrak to Idaho appears to have occurred between 1900 and 1920. Because so many of Idaho's Basques came from Spain, the low immigration quota set for Spanish nationals in 1924 affected Idaho's Basque communities more than those in other states. For years thereafter, however, hundreds entered the country illegally by jumping ship on the East Coast.

When they first arrived, immigrants to Idaho worked for American sheepmen. But following Archabal's example they would go on to establish their own outfits. And before long Basques were the big sheepmen, and the fresh arrivals set to work for them. Juan Domingo Aldecoa, of Motriko, Gipuzkoa, eventually joined his brother-in-law, Juan Archabal, as a partner. Eventually he broke away and with his son Basil started what is now J. D. Aldecoa and Sons. The company sold the sheep portion of the business during the 1970s and converted to raising cattle. Today with their extensive livestock and ranch holdings, the Aldecoas are one of the wealthiest families in Idaho.

Social Security and unemployment benefits programs were unknown in this country when Basques first arrived here, so they developed their own insurance programs to help each other out. As early as 1908 mutual aid groups were created here. Members paid into the Sociedad de Socorros Mutuos or the Fraternidad Vasco-Americano, which provided sick or unemployed Basques with money to tide them over. Apparently, one of these organizations, the Organización Independiente Social, which was exclusively for women, continues to exist, and the families of some longtime members have even recently received reimbursement of the funeral expenses of their elderly relatives.

Descendants of Bizkaia

The most remarkable feature about the large Idaho Basque community is that 90 percent or more of its members can be traced back to the Basque province of Bizkaia. In fact, the majority came from a 20-mile stretch of coastline between Bermeo and Ondarroa and approximately 12 miles inland. The quaint fishing village of Lekeitio, the bustling Basque metropolis of Bilbao, and the historic Basque capitol of Gernika, all in Bizkaia, hold a special place in the hearts of Idaho's Basques. Although the Nafarrak from both sides of the political border who immigrated to the United States were primarily inland, mountain folk, the Bizkaitarrak were part of a coastal zone whose lifestyle was oriented toward the ocean and fishing. These Basques were likely to sit down to a meal of rice with clams or *bakailo* (codfish). The dialect of Bizkaia is so different from that of Nafarroa that a Basque who is not from Bizkaia is hard-pressed to understand it. In Boise the Bizkaitarrak were a clannish bunch, and some say they even developed their own version of the Bizkaian dialect.

Up until the 1960s or so, you could visit southwestern Idaho and probably count on one hand the Basques who were not from Bizkaia.

Those who weren't were probably "Giputxes," or Giputzak, who were also from the Cantabrian coast. In the last twenty to thirty years, however, a few Basques from other Old Country regions, as well as some from California, have relocated to southwestern Idaho. Some of them have been dairy or sheep owners looking for open land, which is less expensive in Idaho.

The Basque population of the state, estimated at about twenty thousand Basque immigrants and Basque-Americans, constitutes 2 percent of the population of Idaho. Estimates of the Basque-American population of the state go as high as thirty thousand, taking in the area just across the Oregon border, around Ontario and Burns. If census takers were to reach back to count all those who came for a short stay and returned to Europe, as well as those who have died, the percentage would be much higher. Although the greater Boise area has the largest concentrated colony of Basques in the United States, as a state, California has nearly four times more Basques than Idaho has. Yet the concentration of Basques within Boise proper is probably much greater than that of any California city. According to newspaper reports, Boise itself is said to have about seven thousand to ten thousand Basques. Unlike California, where the Basques are quite spread out among several communities that are hundreds of miles apart, in Idaho the large majority reside in the southwestern corner of the state. The phone books of every town and city along Interstate 84 contain dozens of Basque names. The Basque language is still spoken by perhaps a thousand or more people in Idaho.

Another factor making Idaho's Basque community stand out within the U.S. Basque population is the large number of Boise Basques who are active in local cultural activities, and the fact that many are second- and third-generation Basque-Americans. The Euzkaldunak Club is supported by some 850 members. It is probably the largest Basque club in the United States, and new members are joining every day. The Boise Basque community, with a great deal of support from other clubs and the Basque government, has hosted the five largest Basque festivals held to date in this country—Jaialdi 1987, 1990, 1995, 2000, and 2005 ("*jaialdi*" is Basque for "festival"). For more details on Jaialdi, see the section on festivals later in this chapter.

Boise also boasts the only Basque museum in the country, a large Basque center, built by the Boise Basque club, and a first-rate Basque folk dancing group that has performed around the country and abroad. All of these institutions were developed with the efforts of many people. Ironically, there were times in recent decades when Boise did not have a single Basque restaurant or a pelota court.

Many of those who participate in the local activities are several generations removed from their immigrant origins. "Boise, for the most part, is a third-generation Basque town, or fourth even," said Dan Ansotegi, the young owner of Bar Gernika whose grandparents came from the Basque Country. Many of the young dancers in the prestigious Oinkari dance group—products of mixed marriages—don't have Basque last names, yet their cultural identification with Basque traditions is very strong. In many cases the third-generation Basque-Americans are rediscovering their roots, after the second generation pulled away from the culture.

Prejudice and Pride

During the first half of the century, some of the American-born Basque population were ambivalent about identifying themselves as Basque. The late Juanita Hormaechea, a native Boisean, said that Basque-Americans suffered a great deal of discrimination. She clearly remembered the era when they were called "dirty black Bascos." The sheepherders had a terrible reputation among the non-Basque townspeople, Hormaechea explained, because when they came into town for the winter, many of them would get drunk and chase after the local women. Their behavior, although perhaps not acceptable, was understandable considering the many lonely months they spent without female company. In addition, parents who themselves experienced difficulties, mainly because of lack of proficiency in English, didn't want their children to have the same problems. It was easier simply to try to be more American.

John Edlefsen, who wrote about the Basques of southwestern Idaho in his 1948 Ph.D. dissertation, argued that denigratory comments were made in isolated incidents and that Basques suffered little prejudice compared to other ethnic groups. He wrote off the sometimes significant problems between sheepherders and cattle ranchers to occupational—not ethnic—conflicts, misunderstandings that were mostly a result of Basques' poor English skills.

But the many newspaper reports uncovered by the authors of *Amerikanuak* suggest otherwise. The tension between cattle ranchers and sheepherders was a grave problem that resulted in several deaths. Even greater antipathy appears to have been reserved for Basques because they saved their money, invested little in their communities, and then returned to the Basque Country with their savings. Ultimately the Basques were able to offset any negative reactions by gaining a reputation for having a strong work ethic and being dependable, a reputation that has stood them in good stead through today.

Edlefsen noted that during the mid-1940s Idaho's Basques appeared to be losing their customs and cultural patterns as they became assimilated. Except for the Basque Girls' Club of Boise, which maintained an active membership of second-generation Basque women, attempts to organize Basque recreational activities met mostly with failure. A growing number of second- and third-generation Basques were unfamiliar with the folk dances of the Old Country. Edlefsen wrote: "Basque costumes are seldom worn. No longer are the colorful Basque street dances held in Boise and other communities as was formerly done. The young Basques have become thoroughly American in their thought processes and in their habit patterns, and it seems apparent that in a comparatively short time, most, if not all, overt signs of Basque recreational patterns will have disappeared in southwest Idaho."

Fortunately Edlefsen's prediction of the Basque culture's demise in the state has been proven wholly wrong. With the coming of age of the third generation, the name-calling was in the distant past, and the situation had turned around. Young Basque dancers became cultural ambassadors, answering lots of questions from curious Americans during their many public performances, including at their dancing engagement at the state Capitol Rotunda. "Wherever they went, people asked them, 'Who are the Basques?' They didn't know anything about them," said Hormaechea. "They [the dancers] had a real strong feeling that there was something different about the Basques." That, she concluded, was when they began discovering that they had a special cultural heritage worth preserving.

The expression of Basque ethnic awareness created a long love affair between the Basques and the Idaho media. The unique customs and colorful costumes of the Basques made them ideal subjects for journalists, and to this day Basque events in Idaho receive extensive coverage from local television stations and newspapers.

Boise

Like the Irish in New York City and the Chinese in San Francisco, the Basques in Boise have managed to bring the rest of their city's population into their fold when celebrating their ethnicity. The annual San Inazio celebration in July regularly attracts large crowds. The first Jaialdi festivals of 1987 and 1990 had phenomenal attendance—up to twenty-five thousand people—putting Boise on the map specifically because of its Basque population.

Boise's Basque colony has accomplished what no other colonies have. Despite the fact that most of the immigrant generation has passed away, second-, third-, fourth-, and even fifth-generation Basque-Americans have joined en masse to carry on the customs of their forefathers' homeland.

Despite the loss of almost all of its many boardinghouses, the Basque community had the foresight to realize that it needed to save some of its history before it was all gone. As a result, the community controls a city block of properties that have served it in one way or another since at least 1910. Among the structures that are still intact is a boardinghouse that is part of the country's only Basque museum; it is the city's oldest brick building.

Between 1900 and 1920 almost all of Boise's Basques were concentrated in the neighborhood around Grove Street in the old downtown. "There were enough of them early in the century that they formed a cohesive cultural group, politically and economically," said Basque supporter Linda Alzaa of Gooding. Married couples came to Boise from Europe. The tight-knit community produced many Basque marriages. Elsewhere in Idaho, the number of Basque marriages was not nearly as high.

During the early years there were enough Basques in Boise to warrant sending over a priest from the Basque Country. Father Bernardo Arregui arrived in 1911 to minister to the needs of Basques in Idaho and Oregon. In 1918 the Boise Bishop decided that the local Basque congregation needed its own church, and two apartment buildings at

Boise's Basques had their own church for a couple of years around 1911. Now the former Church of the Good Shepherd serves as law offices.

the corner of Fifth and Idaho Streets (420 West Idaho Street) were purchased for that purpose. In March of the following year the converted Church of the Good Shepherd was dedicated. Arregui presided over the marriages, baptisms, and funerals that were conducted there. Because of financial troubles, the church closed in 1921, and Basques began attending services at the **Cathedral of St. John the Evangelist** (807 North Eighth Street), which had been dedicated that same year.

They continue to patronize the cathedral today. The building that housed the Church of the Good Shepherd now serves as law offices.

BOARDINGHOUSES

Yesterday. The city's many Basque boardinghouses—there were up to twenty or so at one time—were all within fairly close proximity of one another. Some of them were simply homes converted into boardinghouses; others housed other boarders before Basques took over. The Letemendis' and Jayos' boardinghouses were among the most popular.

The Hotel Oregon at Ninth and Front Streets is believed to be one of the earliest Basque hotels, built by Antonio Azcuenaga around

Basques, Liquor, and Prohibition

As in every Basque community, hotel keepers in Boise and other Idaho towns sold liquor during the Prohibition days, and federal agents knew it. But they rarely nabbed anyone. "They would raid the boardinghouses, but the liquor was always well hidden," said Jay Hormaechea.

Eating was so intertwined with drinking wine and whisky, that it was unlikely that a Basque would consider doing without alcohol, laws or no laws. "Can you imagine the Basque people thinking it was wrong to serve wine and whisky?" said Marie Galdos Landeen, whose parents ran "Charcha's" hotel in Emmett. Sometimes Basques were involved in cooking up the moonshine, hidden away in big stills in the countryside. In Idaho most people said theirs came from Canada, although according to the stories that were told, there were Basque moonshiners just across the border, in Ontario, Oregon. The liquor was circulated within a tight-knit circle of Basques. While Basques did not always make the moonshine, "everybody bootlegged," said Al Arena.

Some say that the Basques weren't really in the business to make money—they were just making it available to each other for social use. Others argue that the profits were the main incentive. "They didn't make any money on the food," said history professor Paquita Garatea, who studied the boardinghouses of Burns, Oregon. "It was the shots of whisky where they would make the money." Despite their reputation for making wine and whisky during the Prohibition, Basques did not get involved in the wine industry, now a billion-dollar industry. In one very rare instance, AL Arena remembered it was a Basque winemaker in Redding who made the moonshine that his parents Pete and Mary hauled up in kegs to serve in their hotel in Alturas, California. "They were just trying to survive," Arena said.

1900, when he lived in Boise for a few years. Mateo and Adriana Arregui were among the earliest Basque hotel keepers. They ran the Capitol Boardinghouse, on the second floor of 706½ Idaho Street from 1905 to 1912. Then Crusa Arostequi operated the business for nearly fifty years, through the early 1960s, although a partner, Maria Epeldi, helped her run it until 1942. Between their two families, they raised a total of eleven children at the boardinghouse. The building was finally torn down in 1965.

For a short time, starting in 1911, Jay Hormaechea's parents, Juan "Saracondi" and Juana Uberuaga, ran Saracondi's Boarding House, at 211 South Sixth Street. In a pattern repeated throughout the West, families running room-and-board establishments were related. "Saracondi" Uberuaga was the brother of José Uberuaga, who ran Uberuagas'. The Saracondi Uberuagas did not stay long, moving in the 1920s to 614 Grove Street to raise their seven children. The old building where they offered room and board, across the alley that runs behind the Basque Center, still exists, and most recently, a catering business was located there. (Local Luis Arrizabala collected much of the history on the old Boise boardinghouses and published it in the 1990 Jaialdi program.)

Barbero's, better known as the Modern Hotel, at 613 West Idaho Street, was a Basque boardinghouse that started around 1912. Benito and Asunción Ysursa and Tomás and Antonia Ysursa ran the popular hotel from 1927 to 1940. The Modern was eventually replaced by the new city hall, built in the 1970s. The Del Rio, at 716½ Main Street, was run by several Basque families. Hipólito and María Sabala were running the Del Rio when Falk's Department Store took over the property during the 1950s and tore it down to enlarge their building. So the Sabalas moved their business to 910 Grove Street and ran it until 1969 when the city took that location over and tore down the building. Next door on Grove Street was the Blue Bird Rooms. These, along with several other boardinghouses on Grove and Front Streets, succumbed to the wrecking ball when the city decided to widen the streets in the late 1960s.

Built in 1864, the house at 607 Grove Street is the oldest brick house in the city and served as a Basque boardinghouse. Local merchant Cyrus Jacobs built the house, considered quite modern for its time, installing a bathtub and a piano. Simón and Josefa Galdos were the first Basques to operate it as a boardinghouse in 1910. José and Hermenegilda Uberuaga took it over in 1918, bought the building outright from the Jacobs' heirs in 1928, and kept up the business known simply as Uberuaga's for another fifty years.

Antonio and Leandra Letemendi converted a house at 521 Grove Street into a hotel in 1939. Sadly the building, located a short walk from the current Basque Center, was demolished and turned into a parking lot in 1972. Leandra was known as the mother of all Boise Basques and lived to be ninety-nine years old. The Letemendis, who had come to the United States in 1901, got into the boardinghouse business in 1912 with the DeLamar. Built in the late 1800s, the DeLamar, at 807 Grove Street, was in Basque hands from 1912 to 1973. The most recent Basque owners were Hilario and Laura Arguinchona, who operated the boardinghouse for its last twenty-eight years. It, too, was torn down as part of the city's expansion projects. "It was a beautiful building," said Luis Arrizabala. "They wanted to save it," he said, but the walls were several feet thick, making relocation all but impossible. A small piece of this historic brick building has endured, as part of a parlor setting at the **Idaho Historical Museum** (610 North Julia Davis Drive), which has an exhibit on the Basques.

Anastasio and Anunciación Jayo provided room and board at six different locations, all known as "Jayo's," in the old downtown. All of these places have been torn down too. Anunci, who lived into her nineties, ran the last one at 612½ Main Street for many years by herself. This popular spot was eventually torn down to make way for the new city and county public building. There were others that came and went, such as the Iberia Hotel, later known as the Overland, on Ninth Street between Front and Grove; and Arego's on Front Street across from the old train depot. One of the last boardinghouses was the Vizcaya, run by Juan and Cristina Uscola in the old Sears building on Jefferson Street. Even though it wasn't a restaurant, everyone acted like it was, stopping by to eat regularly.

Today. Unfortunately, by the end of the 1960s, most of the older homes that had served as boardinghouses had been razed, with little thought given to their historic past, and, shamefully, parking lots were poured in their place in many instances. Luckily, a few of the Basque hotels, although they no longer serve that purpose, do remain in use in some fashion—namely the Valencia, the Star, Anduiza's (with its fronton), and, of course, the Uberuaga boardinghouse, which is now part of the Basque Museum. Another one is the old **Chico Club,** run by Agustín and Francisca Belaustegui at the corner of Sixth and Grove Streets, across from the Basque Center. The old hotel, still Basque-owned, served as an office building and today is a restaurant.

Ysursa brothers Tomás and Benito, who had been leasing the Modern Hotel, wanted their own place, so they ordered the construction of the **Valencia Hotel** across the street in 1941. This large, staunch brick building at 620 West Idaho still stands today, relatively unchanged. The rooms and boarders' dining room were downstairs, and the second floor was a restaurant. Among the Basque hotels, "the Valencia broke ground because it was open to the public," said Benito's grandson John Ysursa. But the restaurant, along with its cooks, was more American than Basque, according to Ysursa, who lived there as a young boy. The Ysursas operated the hotel from 1941 to the 1970s, during which time the talented musical family hosted many a lively party. In the 1980s the Valencia building housed two Basque restaurants—Oñati's and the Old Basque Inn, neither of which lasted very long. These two eateries, along with the short-lived Boardinghouse Restaurant at Sixth and Main Streets, were among the city's only Basque restaurants during the last thirty years. Today the Valencia houses Louie's Italian Restaurant.

A block away from the Valencia was the **Star Rooming House** at 512 West Idaho Street, which was first operated by Basques as early as 1903. During its earliest years, José and Felipa Uberuaga operated this popular hotel, which had a handball court in the back. (About that time, José Uberuaga—not related to the José Uberuaga who ran the Uberuaga boardinghouse on Grove Street—also ran a restaurant called Vasco for eight years, according to author Sol Silen.) Then around 1915 the Uberuagas sold the hotel to Francisco and Gabina Aguirre, who set up a shoe store and shoe repair shop in the front and ran the hotel for about sixty years. Gabina gave up the business when Francisco, better known as Zapatero (shoemaker), died in 1975. But she went on to live to the age of one hundred, finally passing away in 1990. Aguirre was one of several veteran Basque immigrants, mostly women, who joined the centenarian circle.

Businessman Gary Mullard of Northern Stone Company in Oakley, Idaho, bought the old Star building in 1982 to use for business offices. "I enjoy old buildings," said Mullard. "There's a lot of character to them." The interior was remodeled and most recently accommodated law offices, a souvenir shop, and a travel agency. The exterior of the beautiful building, which dates back to 1895, is completely unchanged except for a sprucing up. "It looks like it did when I was a kid," said longtime Boise resident Luis Arrizabala. The handball court floor in back of the building was covered with flagstone, but the cement walls are still visible. Because it is on the National Register of Historic Places, the outside of the building cannot be changed architecturally. "The way downtown is going, I think it will be a nice permanent part of the history here," said Mullard.

PELOTA

Boise had its fair share of pelota courts in its day. A small court, possibly the first one in Boise, run by a man known as Panadero (baker), was built around 1903 on Thirteenth Street off Grove. Then there was the court at the Star and another one at the Iberia hotel (later known as the Overland) on Ninth Street between Front and Grove Streets. A fourth court, the largest of all of them, and one that has survived until today intact, is **Anduiza's** at 619 Grove Street. (For more information, see the entry for the Basque Museum.) This indoor court was also the largest in the Northwest when it was built in 1912 as part of a boardinghouse by Juan Cruz and Juana Anduiza.

But the courts fell into disuse and were eventually torn down. Even the one at Anduiza's place was abandoned. When the Anduiza building became vacant in 1948, Raymond Briggs bought it and turned it into offices for his engineering firm. But Briggs essentially left the court untouched, using it for storage and locating the offices in the rooms in front and along the side of the court. Finally, in the 1970s, local Basques used some federal grant money to fix up the court and lease it from the Briggs family, and Boise had a fronton again. Basques played handball there through the mid-1980s, until a break-in raised the Briggs family's fears about security, according to Adelia Garro Simplot. For six years, the community again had no handball court.

This fronton in Boise, Idaho, built in 1912, is the oldest indoor fronton in the country. (Photo by David Reyes.)

The story has a happy ending, however, because the court has reverted back to its original use. Simplot and Richard Hormaechea acquired the building in 1992. The purchase came after some heartache. At least two years prior to the purchase, the Basque club had begun serious fund-raising efforts to acquire the building. Chris Bieter, a handball player and one of the project organizers, said that supporters pledged up to $120,000. But negotiations with the building owners broke down when they refused to allow a structural inspection of the building. The club, not wanting to risk buying a building that might have serious problems, backed out. But Simplot, an avid preservationist, did not want to risk losing the historic building and fronton, so she and Hormaechea bought it privately. Except for minor changes, the building remains relatively faithful to the 1912 original and currently has the oldest Basque pelota court in the United States. A group of local Basque handball players formed a Fronton Association and lease it and collect annual dues to pay for insurance and lights. The owners renovated and painted the building. "It's a group effort," said Simplot. "It's to everyone's benefit to see that it stands." Other than the fronton at the Basque Cultural Center in South San Francisco, it's the West's only indoor handball court in use.

A Grand Social Life

Music, dancing, and having fun were the focus of many Basque activities in Boise through the years. Basques began participating in Boise's annual Music Week as early as 1921. With their talent and interest in music and dancing, they became more involved with each passing year. In 1934 they put up a model Basque Village on Grove Street for the statewide celebration of Fort Boise Centennial Days. The open-air garden, complete with a balcony from which accordionists, guitarists, and other musicians entertained the crowd in a round-the-clock schedule of music, was rated the celebration's top attraction by hundreds of celebrants. This should give one an indication of the Boise Basque community's flair for organizing large events—which is still evident today with the success of the Jaialdi festivals. The large Basque colony gained so much notoriety that in 1938 and 1939, a local newspaper, *Boise Capital News*, published a weekly section on its activities in English, Spanish, and Basque.

Sheepherders Ball. Juan Archabal began the first of many longtime Basque traditions in Boise. In 1928, or thereabouts, the sheepman organized a Christmastime dance for the herders when they returned to town for the winter after several lonely months on the range. The event was called the Sheepherder's Ball, and in the early days a strict dress code was enforced. The Basques wore their traditional costumes; other men had to wear overalls and the women, cotton dresses. A sheep wagon was parked at the front of the Riverside Pavilion dance hall, selling Levi's to those who didn't have any. This popular event attracted Basques and non-Basques and marked the beginning of Boise's introduction to Basque culture. The proceeds from the traditional lamb auction and raffles were donated to local charities. Boise's annual Sheepherder's Ball was later copied throughout southwestern Idaho's smaller Basque communities. The dance is still held today, just before Christmas, at the Euzkaldunak Club's Basque Center.

Early Picnics. By the early 1930s, Boise's Basques were already organizing large potluck picnics. In the early years, the picnics were held at the Mode Country Club, out at Dry Creek, or on Apple Street. Basques from hundreds of miles around attended. "It was done so different from today," said Irene Anderson, whose family would travel from Emmett for the picnic. "There was nothing commercial. You couldn't buy anything there. Everybody brought their own food and drink and blankets to sit on the ground." Unlike every other Basque picnic today, where many people come solely for the barbecue, as long as Basques have gathered in Boise, the picnic has remained a "bring your own" affair. For a while, the club offered a steak and hamburger barbecue, but that did not seem to make a difference. "Even though we tell them there's food there, they still bring their own," said Basque club officer Michele Alzola. "It's a strong tradition."

Basque Girls' Club and a Military Regiment. Some of the young Boise women formed the Basque Girls' Club in 1936, and, amazingly, its members—all of whom speak Euskara—were still getting together sixty years later when some were in their eighties. "It started as a knitting club," admits member Marie Galdos Landeen. The women would meet at Anderson's department store to buy yarn and have lunch. Their aims became more serious during the war, when they helped out the Red Cross in the war effort. They also enjoyed good times at dances for servicemen. After the war they continued their civic work.

The Idaho Basque communities lost a few of their young sons in World War II. Most of the immigrants came here during the 1910s and 1920s and married and started families soon afterward. A great number of their sons were of draft age when the United States got involved in the war in 1941. Men who were not inducted organized their own civil defense regiment in Boise as part of the volunteer reserves, in case they should be needed—the Basque Company, Ada County Volunteers. They were never called up.

Juanita "Jay" Hormaechea and Basque Cultural Performances. In 1948 Juanita "Jay" Hormaechea decided to teach some of the Basque dances to youngsters before the dances were forgotten. In 1949 city officials asked the Basques to organize a special performance for Boise's Music Week, so Hormaechea spearheaded a major production of traditional dance and song at the Boise High School auditorium, using over a hundred members of the Basque community, both adults and children. That production, called "The Song of the Basques," was one of the first public displays of Basque culture in this country and created the good reputation that Basque dancing has earned in Idaho. The following year, in 1950, Hormaechea organized an even larger production, using 180 people for "The Basque Festival." The performance was held outdoors, at the school's athletic field, to accommodate the expected overflow crowd. The show attracted the attention of several newspapers, including the *Christian Science Monitor*, which gave the group a glowing review.

BASQUE CLUB AND BASQUE CENTER

Buoyed by the success of Juanita Hormaechea's "Song of the Basques" performance at the Boise Music Week and their children's enjoyment

Juanita Hormaechea and Basque Folk Dancing

Most of the original Oinkari dancers would agree that the late Juanita "Jay" (Uberuaga) Hormaechea deserves the credit for regenerating Basque folk dancing in Boise when she organized the first group of dancers in 1948.

Hormachea's parents ran a boardinghouse known as "Saracondi's" just off of Grove Street for a short time when she was young. Their cousins lived around the corner at another boardinghouse, "Uberuaga's" (now the Basque Museum). Her parents gave up the business but stayed in the neighborhood, at 614 Grove Street, to raise Juanita and her six brothers and sisters. Hormaechea had fond memories of New Year's Eves spent running through the boardinghouses with other young Basque women, dancing the *jota* during the 1920s and 1930s. Afterward they would close off a block for a public dance. When she realized young Basque-Americans were growing up without knowing the *jota* or any other Basque dances, she set out to teach them in 1948. She organized two major dramatic performances that were open to the public. The response to the shows was tremendous, and the Basque community, particularly the youngsters who learned the dances, regained pride in their traditions. "I taught them the love of being an American *and* being a Basque," she said.

Hormaechea led the dance group for many years, until the Oinkari dance group was established. During those years, the American-born Hormaechea, who was fluent in Basque, also acted as a community spokesperson, responding to phone calls and requests for information from the press. She became the community's historian, collecting newspaper clippings, business cards, and literature on anything written about the Basques. She collected dozens of scrapbooks filled with such information, which she donated to the Basque Museum. Hormaechea was honored by the Society of Basque Studies in America in 1985. Hear Hormaechea tell the story of her life at *www.basquemuseum.com/oral history/*.

Basque culture was first put on public display in Boise. This float appeared in the Boise Music Week parade in 1949. (Courtesy of Juanita Uberuaga Hormaechea Collection, Basque Museum and Cultural Center.)

of the dances, members of the Basque community decided to organize a club as a way of keeping their community together. In 1949 five hundred members formed **Euzkaldunak Club.** To be a member you had to be Basque or married to a Basque. That same year the club broke ground on its own building, in the old neighborhood, at Sixth and Grove Streets. The clubhouse opened a year later.

The Basque Center, at 601 Grove Street, forms the cornerstone of a block of properties that hold great significance for the U.S. Basque community. Inaugurated in 1950, the center probably represents the first joint effort by a group of Basques to build a place for the community to carry on its cultural traditions. (The La Puente Handball Club in California built its own facility, with a court, around the same time, but its members were not exclusively Basque.) Although Basques had owned many hotels, restaurants, and bars in the past, those had all been privately owned. The club issued bonds to finance the construction, and, in addition to the Basques, other community supporters bought bonds as well. When it came time to pay off the

These women are dancing the fandango in the 1948 performance of "The Song of the Basques" in Boise, probably the first Basque play presented publicly. (Courtesy of Juanita Uberuaga Hormaechea Collection, Basque Museum and Cultural Center.)

bonds ten years later, about 25 percent of the purchasers donated their share to the center, according to John Bastida, one of the early organizers.

The center first opened with just the bar and upstairs card room. In 1951 the facility was expanded to include a dance hall and kitchen. Once most of the boardinghouses were closed, the center became the only place where the Boise Basque community could gather for card playing, dinners, and dances. In 1972 the club completed a significant renovation of the building.

Besides the huge festival the club sponsors in July (for more information, see the section on festivals), today the club, with its eight-hundred-plus members, sponsors events all year long. A monthly dinner is held at the center, attended by two hundred to four hundred people. In March and April the annual card game tournaments of *mus* and *briska* (Spanish card game similar to hearts) are held. In late October or early November it's the annual Holiday bazaar and *morcilla* (blood sausage) dinner, an event originated in 1957 by the Girls' Club. "It's one of the events that we really try to share with the public," said member Miren Artiach. Christmas gifts are on sale during the event, and people play bingo, but the biggest draw is the *morcillas.* "People come to the dinner and buy tons of them," said club officer Michelle Alzola. Members grow the leeks used in the *morcillas,* and they spend the week before the event making hundreds of them, to eat and to sell.

The December calendar is busy. The Sheepherders' Ball, on the third Saturday of the month, is a classic. Right after the club was organized, it took the long-standing Boise tradition of the Sheepherders' Ball and turned it into its first charity fund-raiser. The general public is also heartily welcome to attend this event. Today the lamb, which is paraded around the room halfway through the dance, is no longer auctioned off. Corporate donations are sought instead to benefit local charities. The Oinkari dancers put on a special performance during the evening.

The club also hosts a Christmas party with a visit from Santa for the children. Then Boise's Bihotzetik (From the Heart) Basque Choir performs at the regular December dinner (see the Music section). On another night, the choir rents a bus and goes out Christmas caroling, driving all over the valley, making stops at nursing homes. The carolers also visit the homes of elderly Basques who love to hear the old songs. "That's the most touching thing we do," said Alzola. On December 31 there is a big New Year's Eve Dance at the center.

In addition to all the significant club events that take place at the Basque Center, the building serves as the headquarters for all the local Basque groups—the dance groups, the choir, the Euzkaldunak Club. Check out their Web site, *www.basquecenter.com,* for lots of information.

Most afternoons you can find the old-timers playing *mus* at the card tables upstairs. Julián Lete is the longtime bartender, and Flora Ysursa has become nearly a fixture at the center, where she has tended bar and managed the kitchen for years. At least five kinds of wine from the Rioja region in Spain are served.

Basque Center, 601 Grove Street, Boise, ID 83702 (208) 342-9983; *www.basquecenter.com*
Euzkaldunak, Inc. P.O. Box 2613, Boise, ID 83701 (208) 342-9983 (If no answer, wait for recording.)

DANCE

One of the U.S. Basque colony's most venerable institutions is the **Oinkari Basque Dancers** group. Through the more than thirty years they have been in existence, the Boise dancers have developed a reputation that is unrivaled, despite concerted efforts by other U.S. Basque dance groups to match it. The Oinkariak have represented the state of Idaho at events across the country. More important, a solidarity formed among Oinkari members strengthens and preserves the Basque culture in the Boise area. "I really think that is the backbone of what's going on here," said Gina Urquidi, a former Oinkari dancer who heads the young dance group, Boiseko Gasteak (Boise Youth). Most of the dance teachers who work with her are former Oinkariak, as are the teachers of the Caldwell and Ontario dance groups.

The Oinkari group was created after seven members of that first young dance group organized by Juanita Hormaechea made a now well-known trip to their ancestral homeland for the first time in 1960. While there, the group, which included Al Erquiaga and Diana Urresti, were taken under the wing of the Oinkari dance troupe in San Sebastián and learned some of the old dances. Before their departure, the dancers from the Old Country gave the Basque-Americans a message: "The biggest honor you could pay us would be to go home and start a group and call it the Oinkaris," Erquiaga said their hosts told them. The youths warmed to the idea, but they did not think themselves capable of meeting the challenge. The young dancers performed that winter at the Sheepherder's Ball, but the group really did not get off the ground, according to Erquiaga, "until we got a call from the State of Idaho to dance at the World's Fair" in 1962 in Seattle, Washington. The young adults were excited about representing their state, so they recruited dancers for the performance and began raising funds to pay for their transportation to the fair.

The state's biggest newspaper, the locally owned *Idaho Statesman,* took up the group's cause and gave great publicity to their fundraising efforts, which included performances in towns all around Boise. Local bars sponsored Basque nights and turned over a portion of their profits to the dance group. "The community support . . . was phenomenal," said Erquiaga.

In Seattle during the World's Fair, the Oinkari dancers' twirls and hoops caught the eye of many a fairgoer, and afterward invitations to perform abounded. The group was invited to be part of the World's Fair in New York in 1964, as well as later ones in Montreal, Canada, in 1971 and Spokane, Washington, in 1974. The public attention and interest in Basque culture that the Oinkariak generated had repercussions in Basque communities throughout Idaho. "A lot of these towns had an annual Basque dance after that," said Erquiaga. Many also started their own dance groups.

The Oinkariak were responsible for initiating the first Basque language classes in Boise in 1963. "People would ask them to say a few words in Basque, and they couldn't," said Hormaechea. So the dancers recruited Joe Eiguren to teach them Euskara. Eiguren had to develop his own instructional materials, because there were none. He went on to teach language classes off and on for several years. Eiguren became something of an amateur historian and language expert as a result.

The Oinkariak have continuously maintained very high standards for themselves. John Ysursa, a longtime member of the group, said that part of Oinkariak's success was able leadership and the fact that "we had a lot of dedicated people who were willing to work hard." The dancers have choreographed their own dances, as well as expanded their repertoire by adding some of the centuries-old folk dances still performed in the Basque Country. Once a year, for the feast of Basque patron San Inazio de Loyola at the end of July, the Oinkariak perform an ancient religious dance in Boise's St. John's Cathedral as part of the festival celebration. Out of respect, the Oinkari dancers asked for permission from the dance group in the town of its origin, Oñati, Gipuzkoa, to perform the liturgical dance. Oinkari is one of very few Basque dance groups in the world that has been taught the steps. Since the dance is limited to eight, present and former male Oinkari dancers rotate every year, to give everyone a chance to perform. A history and photos of the dance are available at *www.ysursa.com /onati.htm.*

In 1972 the Oinkariak went on a six-state tour. In 1985, for their twenty-fifth anniversary, they decided to travel to Europe to perform. To raise funds, the Oinkari wrote, directed, and performed a play about the immigrant experience, "*Nundik Nora?*" (From Where to Where?). The play followed the format of Hormaechea's first "Song of the Basques," in which traditional dances were interwoven with a story line. The first performance was held at the Morrison Center for Performing Arts in Boise. "It was magical," remembers former Oinkari John Ysursa. The dancers had never performed the play all the way through until that first night. "We didn't even know if the costume changes were going to work." The show was very successful and was performed in several Basque communities.

Under then twenty-four-year-old president Patty Miller, the group raised $70,000, chartered a plane for sixty-five dancers, and flew to the Basque Country, where they performed in several towns in Hegoalde during a three-week tour. "It was a marvelous trip," said former Oinkari Chris Bieter. "Some of the performances were spur of the moment. . . . A lot of the people couldn't believe we were from the States, because a lot of the kids spoke Basque. I think people were pretty impressed."

Unlike other dance groups, the Oinkariak have always had plenty of male dancers. The group, which numbers between forty-five and sixty at any one time, is primarily made up of young people in their teens and twenties, many of them second-generation Oinkari. To be eligible to participate, at least one parent must be of Basque descent and belong to the Euzkaldunak Club.

Since it incorporated in 1964, the dance group has been led by an elected board of directors, mostly Basque-Americans in their twenties, which oversees the Oinkari's far-reaching fund-raising efforts. The Oinkariak have done much toward popularizing the Basque chorizo in Idaho, which they sell as a fund-raiser at numerous events, including the annual Western Idaho Fair at the end of August at the Western Idaho Fairgrounds, a short drive from downtown Boise.

The Oinkariak have seen their numbers go up and down since they first started, but they needn't worry about their future. By example, they have kindled interest in Basque heritage among even the youngest Basque-Americans, who have joined dance groups in small Idaho towns and in Boise by the dozens. One such group, Boiseko Gasteak, had some 150 children participating in 2004. Many of these youngsters are children of former Oinkari dancers. Today, their impressive Web site provides the latest news on the group.

Oinkari Basque Dancers, P.O. Box 1011, Boise, ID 83701 (208) 336-8219 (*Miren Artiach*); *www.oinkari.org*

MUSIC

In addition to a professional dance group, Boise also has a respectable Basque choir, known as the **Bihotzetik Basque Choir,** one of only three choirs among the many Basque clubs. The singers are of a wide range of ages and are first-generation Basques as well as third- or fourth-generation ones. Started in 1986, Bihotzetik is at least the second Basque choir in Boise, because another existed briefly in the 1970s. Choir members do not have to be Basque.

Jim Jausoro: Premier Accordion Player

Accordionist Jim Jausoro and his partner, Domingo Ansotegui, embodied the Basque love for the accordion. Jausoro played for Boise's Oinkari dancers week in and week out since their formation in 1960. During the 1940s Jausoro and Ansotegui played a variety of instruments including the accordion, the diatonic (or button) accordion, and the *pandareta* (tambourine) for Basque dances organized here and there, in Winnemucca and McDermitt, Nevada, and at boardinghouses around Boise. In the beginning, Jausoro remembered, "We would fill in when the band would take a break." The talented musicians formed a four-man band in 1957, and as Basque dances became more frequent during the 1960s, the group of musicians became well known. "The band was booked almost every single weekend through the winter," said Al Erquiaga, who went to many of those dances when he was young.

In 1985 Jausoro received the highest recognition for his musical contribution when he was chosen as one of twelve master traditional artists across the country for the National Heritage Award, conferred by the National Endowment for the Arts. The Oinkari dancers accompanied Jausoro to Washington, D.C., where they all performed for an audience of government officials. The North American Basque Organizations also gave him a lifetime achievement award in February 1994 at the San Francisco Basque Cultural Center during the first Basque Accordion Festival held in the United States.

Jausoro passed away at age eighty-three in 2004. But even a month before his death, he was playing for Oinkari's weekly practices. When his band was invited to play for a party, Domingo Ansotegui's son Dan accompanied him on drums, while Dick Lenhardt played trumpet. But sadly, noted Jausoro during his later years, there's not much call for the polkas, waltzes, tangos, and rumba that made him popular, and the requests for his music had dwindled. "The young people don't dance to our music today," he said. Nevertheless, during his lifetime his family said he had played at some four hundred weddings. Hear Jausoro tell the story of his life as part of the oral history project on the Basque Museum Web site (*www.basquemuseum.com*).

Boise Basques have had many musical performers over the years, not the least of which was well-loved accordionist Jim Jausoro and his band. Ordago, a Basque rock band, existed for a few years, and later its spot was filled by Gaupasa, which continued to play at Basque events in 2005. Dan Anchustegui, whose father, Domingo, played button accordion alongside Jausoro, decided he wanted others to carry on the tradition, so in 2000 he started Txantxangorriak, a group at the Basque Center for young people interested in playing accordion and tambourine. The youngsters joined Basque musicians at numerous performances in 2004, including the famous Tapia eta Leturia, a *trikitilariak* (button accordion and *pandareta)* duo in Elko.

RADIO STATION AND BASQUE NEWSPAPER

Other Basque cultural manifestations have surfaced in Boise over the years. Julián Lachiondo and later Espectación Alegria produced a weekly Basque radio program that was aired for many years, playing records and providing news from Spain. Juanita Hormaechea said that the program began sometime during the 1930s or 1940s, and it continued, every Sunday night, through the 1950s. "The boys in the sheep camp used to wait and listen for that," she said.

A non-Basque closely linked to the Basque community, Brian Wardle, published the newspaper *Voice of the Basques* (in English) in Boise from 1973 to 1977.

A GRANT FOR BASQUE CULTURE

In 1971 Idaho's Office of Higher Education received a federal grant specifically to promote the Basque culture. That grant, from the National Endowment for the Humanities, proved to be the impetus for an amazing number of projects and programs whose effects are still felt today. A group of Boise Basques, under the name Idaho'ko Eusko Zaleak, (Basque Fans of Idaho) formed a nonprofit group with a board of directors to oversee the handling of the money. With the organization of the board, a choir was started and language classes were organized. The Holiday Basque Festival was also organized. The group also funded the restoration of the fronton at the former Anduiza boardinghouse, which had been unused for years.

Basque Studies Abroad. Also under sponsorship of an NEH grant, professor Pat Bieter and four other Boiseans traveled to the Basque Country for a summer of studies offered by the University of Nevada, Reno, a trip that had great repercussions. While there, Bieter met with professor Jon Bilbao, who suggested that they work together to start a yearlong study-abroad program at a seminary building that was available in the Gipuzkoan town of Oñati, the Colegio San Lorenzo. The program was coordinated by Boise State University in 1974 and was a great success from the beginning. The first year, eighty students, including Bieter and his family, traveled to Oñati, where they took part in language, history, and culture classes. "It was the perfect place to study," said Bieter, partly because the dialect spoken in Oñati is similar to the Bizkaian dialect spoken predominantly by Basque-Americans in the Idaho-Oregon region. In addition, because Franco's repressive regime was still in power, the residents of the small town were eager to keep the language alive, according to Bieter.

The classes and dormitories were all in one building, but the setup did not prevent students from getting involved in the local community. Indeed, thirty-five marriages between students and Oñati residents have resulted, according to Bieter. There were many other benefits as well. "It was responsible for a real renewal among the second and third generation to learn Basque again," said Bieter's son, Chris. The number of Euskara speakers in Boise, which had been on the wane, was increased by about a hundred people, Pat Bieter reported. "My five children speak Basque as a result of that program," he said. Exposure and contacts with dance groups in the Basque Country spurred the local Oinkari dance group to try to make their dances more authentic.

The Oñati program continued for five years, and more than two hundred students participated before the program was discontinued. Then in 1979 Boise State University was one of the founders of the University Studies Abroad Consortium (the other founders were the University of Nevada, Reno, and the University of Nevada, Las Vegas), which offers a year-round program in Donostia/San Sebastián. (For more information, see the section on the University of Nevada, Reno.) Euskara continues to be taught and learned in Boise. At Boise State University one can take elementary language classes in Batua, the

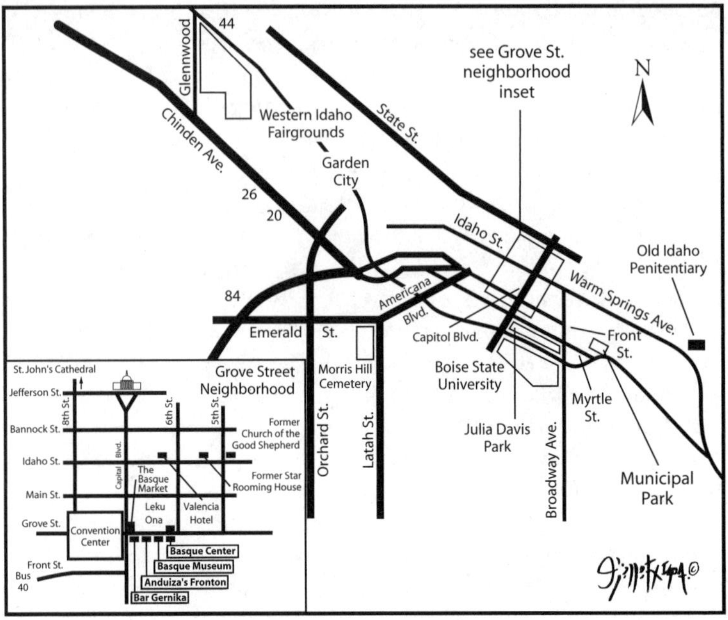

Boise.

unified version of Basque, or join the evening language classes offered at the Basque Museum.

THE BASQUE MUSEUM AND CULTURAL CENTER

Today almost an entire block of Grove Street properties from the early era of Basque settlement have been reclaimed as Boise's Basque stomping grounds. With the exception of the building that currently houses the museum's permanent exhibits, "everything else on the block was Basque," remembered the late Juanita "Jay" Hormaechea, who grew up in the neighborhood. The block is part of the old downtown, an area that has undergone a major revitalization beginning in the late 1960s.

As with many urban downtowns, Old Boise had become rundown. Yet the renewal has been slow. Older structures were torn down, and nothing was built in their place. "For many, many years, people complained that there were more parking lots than buildings," said Basque Museum director Patty Miller. "There wasn't a tree in sight," said Adelia Simplot, noting that Grove Street was originally named "because of the wonderful grove of trees all along it." Even the original city hall, a large brick Victorian building with turrets, was torn down in the fury of urban renewal. Luis Arrizabala described the old municipal headquarters as "fantastic" and "unbelievable." "Now people are just sick about it," he said, adding that a Kmart store was put up in its place. Today, however, the area has been turned around, and, on one block, the thanks is due to the Basques.

Along with the Basque Center at 601 Grove Street, the **Basque Museum and Cultural Center,** in the heart of Boise's downtown, holds great promise for the future of Basque cultural awareness in this country. While the Basque Center provides the community with a venue for its own events, the museum exposes the rest of the community to Basque culture. It is the only Basque museum in the country, and it was inaugurated in 1987, during the first Jaialdi celebration. Curious visitors stop by every day, and volunteers offer tours and field dozens of questions about who the Basques are and where they come from.

Adelia Garro Simplot, Helping to Preserve Basque Heritage

Adelia Garro Simplot has been a key figure in acquiring and preserving much of the historic property on Grove Street. "I'm really happy about the way it turned out when I see that wonderful old block," said Simplot, widow of Richard Simplot, son of Idaho ranching tycoon J. R. Simplot.

In 1983, fearing that the former Uberuaga boardinghouse would be torn down, she purchased it from the family. "I didn't want anything to happen to it," she said. Three years later, she proceeded to form a nonprofit organization with several other Basques and preservationists, in order to turn the building into a Basque museum. "That was my husband's and my sister's idea. They said it should be something for the Basques." (For more information, see Basque Museum and Cultural Center section above.) Simplot later joined with another local Basque, Richard Hormaechea, to buy Anduiza's fronton before it was lost. "All I wanted was for the place to be saved," said Simplot, who would have also been happy if the Basque club had purchased the court and land around it.

The building housing the only Basque museum in the United States once served as a boardinghouse. (Photo by David Reyes.)

For the first several years the museum was housed solely in the former Uberuagas' boardinghouse, at 607 Grove Street, which was run for many years by José and Hermenegilda Uberuaga. This 1864 brick house, with its white picket fence, is a remarkable structure for a museum. "It's a time piece," said Adelia Simplot. Although the structure was built by a non-Basque merchant, Cyrus Jacobs, it stands as a monument to the Basques' presence in this city. As noted previously, it was a boardinghouse from 1910 to 1969. After both Uberuagas died, the couple's children remained in the house until 1984, when they sold the building to Adelia Garro Simplot to be saved as a historic building. "We didn't want to just sell it to anyone and have them tear it down," said the couple's grandson, Tom Mendiguren.

When Basque president José Antonio Ardanza visited the United States in 1989, he planted a small oak tree, grown from an acorn of a tree in Gernika, in front of the historic building.

While the museum was housed in the old boardinghouse, very few changes were made to the Uberuaga house, because the board of directors planned to turn it into a living-history museum. In 1988, the board bought the building next door, 611 Grove Street, with the idea of using it as the main museum building. That part of the museum was opened to the public in 1993. (Meanwhile, the Uberuaga house next door continued to be open to visitors and rented out to groups for luncheons and dinners.) The original portion of 611 Grove was built in 1910, and it, too, had served as an old rooming house for many years. Although its owner, a man named Parker, was not Basque, many of his boarders may have been. The small structure was later incorporated into a larger building that served as a credit union office. The museum purchased the building after it had been vacant for several years, and most of its interior has been significantly remodeled since then, except for the library and meeting room, which were a part of the old house. The main room has been transformed into an exhibit hall for Basque artifacts and paintings. The sheepherder's life, folk dance, musical instruments, boardinghouses, the church, and Basque cuisine have all been subjects of displays. In 2005, *Amerikanuak,* an exhibit on the Basques of the Great Basin organized by Robert Boyd of the High Desert Museum in Bend, Oregon, was at the museum and expected to continue for at least two more years.

Patty Miller, an energetic young pillar of the Basque community, was chosen to head up the museum and cultural center in 1993. She managed it for years as the only paid staff member with a slew of volunteers. In 2002, Jeff Johns was hired as the museum's first curator. The two headed the campaign to restore the boardinghouse and in 2003 were rewarded with a $200,000 challenge grant from the E. L. Wiegand Foundation. Staff and volunteers worked for eighteen months to successfully raise the matching funds. About half of the money came from other foundations and corporations, and the other half came from individual donations.

In 2004, the museum began the painstaking process of bringing back to its original state the Cyrus Jacobs–Uberuaga Boarding House. Part of the job entailed contacting family members of both families for advice. Once the restoration began, the team of workers made fascinating discoveries. While uncovering boards to reveal the original floor in the front parlor, workers found evidence of a fire. It appears the fire was sufficiently extensive that four rooms had to be replastered, said Miller. More flooring was pulled up and another grand discovery resulted. "There was a fireplace in the parlor that no one knew about," said Miller. After lifting up several layers of flooring, a number of old items were discovered underneath. Archeologists were consulted to help identify the hidden artifacts. Some of the items they found in covered spaces gave clear clues to different eras in the house, such as marbles, which were not mass produced until 1908.

The décor in the two front rooms of the house reflects the late-1800s era in which Cyrus Jacobs' family lived. The rest of the rooms reflect furnishings and accessories from the heyday of the Basque boardinghouse era, around 1928, Miller said. Museum staffers worked hard to finish and re-open the Uberuaga house for the Jaialdi festival in July 2005.

Library. The museum's library, the Joseph V. Eiguren Memorial Library, houses an extensive collection of books in Basque, Spanish, and English and includes a children's section. Basque-language classes have been held in the library.

Oral History Project. Interviews with more than 150 Boise Basques, many of them now deceased, are available via the Internet. This monumental project, the Oroitzapenak (memories) Basque Oral History Project, was carried out by museum volunteers over many years. It was recently put on the web, via a link on the museum's Web site, (*www.basquemuseum.com /oralhistory.asp*) with the help of a grant from the Basque government. This collection of interviews is also available on tape in the museum library.

Basque Museum and Cultural Center Activities. The directors, as well as a crew of volunteers, are always pitching in to help with fund-raisers and other events at the museum, such as the annual September Wine Fest—the museum's biggest fund-raiser. Volunteer efforts have sustained and kept the museum growing. Anyone interested in helping the museum can become a member by making an annual donation of $25 or more. Members receive a quarterly newsletter chock-full of information on Basque community events and updates on museum activities.

The museum was also responsible for erecting a number of interpretive signs on the Basque block that describe the historical richness of all the buildings. The area around the block is alive with the city's business, much of it the result of recent urban redevelopment in the area, including the new convention center across the street from Bar

Gernika. "Not ten years ago, that place [the convention center] was on its last legs," said Simplot.

Basque Museum and Cultural Center, 611 Grove Street, Boise, Idaho 83702 (208) 343-2671; *www.basquemuseum.com*

ACADEMIC ORGANIZATION

In 2004, the **Cenarrusa Center for Basque Studies,** an academic and research program to promote Basque culture, was created in Boise. The brainchild of local history professor John Bieter, the organization seeks to promote Basque studies in Idaho's three main universities and also to provide academic presentations linked to the Basque Museum. The center is named for Pete and Freda Cenarrusa, who have promoted Basque culture in Idaho for years. Pete Cenarrusa, who served as Idaho's secretary of state from 1967 to 2002, is a major contributor to the center.

In 2004, Bieter was the center's only staff person. A full-time professor was hired in fall 2005 to teach Basque-related courses at Boise State University. The Basque government provided $150,000 for the new program at the university, which includes the establishment of a Basque studies minor. Programs hosted by the center in 2004 and 2005 included lectures on Basque themes such as dance and Basque tree carvings. The best place to get information on the center's activities is through its Web site, *www.cenarrusa.org.*

Cenarrusa Center for Basque Studies, 611 Grove Street, Boise, Idaho 83702 (208) 426-5332; *www.cenarrusa.org.*

BASQUE PRESCHOOL

Many Basque-American communities would like to have a school where children can learn Basque, but so far only Boise has had the concentration of Basques necessary to sustain such a project. Since 1998, the Boise Basque community has supported a full-time Basque preschool, Boise'ko Ikastola, where children are fully immersed in the Basque language. The curriculum is identical to that of *ikastolak,* or Basque schools, in the Basque Country, where children learn the language through immersion. The popular preschool is run at St. Paul's Catholic Student Center, across from Boise State University. Interest in the language-immersion program even extends to non-Basque families. After starting with just eight children, in 2005, the school had twenty-one, three of whom were not Basque. School director Geneva Ayarra noted that she has an American boy "who speaks Basque perfectly."

Ayarra did not speak Euskara when she first began working at the *ikastola,* but she said she studied the language intensively for ten months in Gernika before taking the job as director. The primary-language teachers have all come from the Basque Country, rotating every year or so, because of work-permit restrictions. The school accepts children from the ages of three to five, and now offers an after-school kindergarten program for the oldest ones.

Boiseko Ikastola, St. Paul's Catholic Student Center, 1915 University Drive, Boise, ID 83706 (208) 343-4234
Basque Museum and Cultural Center, 611 Grove Street, Boise, ID 83702 (208) 343-2671; *www.basque museum.com*

RESTAURANTS

Despite Boise's reputation as the Basque stronghold in the United States, this city has offered the public very little in the way of the Basque culinary experience. Unlike California and Nevada, where many of the old room-and-board places survived into the 1980s and 1990s by switching to restaurant businesses, none of Idaho's made that transition. After the last of Boise's boardinghouses closed down, Basque food lovers were lucky to find one Basque restaurant in the city. One of these short-lived ventures was called, appropriately enough, the Basque Boardinghouse, but it closed in 1985. For several years during the 1980s the city had none. The problem was not necessarily that Basque restaurants were unpopular. "There were way too many restaurants in Boise for the population," said John Ysursa. "Very few lasted very long."

Restaurateur and chef Jesús Alcelay filled the void when he opened **Oñati** in 1987 in the former boardinghouse known as the Valencia on Idaho Street. "The people who know how to cook are the ones who come from the Basque Country, and I am one of the last [in Boise]," said Alcelay, giving his own theory about the reason for the scarcity of Basque restaurants.

In 1990 the Bizkaian chef moved his restaurant to Garden City, just a five-minute drive from downtown Boise. Alcelay did more than his share to expose the community to Basque cuisine by catering civic events and offering his food at many local Basque activities. Typical dishes from the Basque Country's coastal region that were served at Oñati are *txipiroi* (squid), *bakailo* (codfish), and paella.

In a novel twist, Alcelay decided in 1996 to open a restaurant in the Basque town of Oñati called Bar Boise. Fried chicken, hamburgers, and other typical American fare is served there. Eventually, Alcelay decided to return to the Basque Country and closed Oñati.

Alcelay's restaurant was located in the Ranch Club, a bar and dance club that was run by the Arana family since 1950. The Ranch Club deserves mention as a Basque institution. Tony Arana bought the gambling club in Garden City in 1950 because gambling had already been banned in surrounding Boise. His brother Pete soon became his partner, but the two were faced with a dilemma when gambling was banned altogether in Idaho three or four years later. All the clubs faced closure the day the law went into effect, but the Aranas loaded their slot machines onto hay wagons and hauled them away. "This was the only place that got opened," said Pete's daughter, Trina Arana, meaning that because they were able to eliminate the gaming features, their club could open. Before Oñati came in, the Ranch Club was the twenty-five-year home of the Chateau Briand restaurant, one of the best steak houses in town. "We've had live music and dancing six days a week since day one," said Arana. The Aranas finally sold the business, which continues in much the same manner.

Dan Ansotegi, a Boise native, added to this city's Basque dining fare in 1991 when he opened a small pub and eatery, **Bar Gernika,** named in honor of the historical city in the province where many of Boise's Basques originated. It can't really be called a Basque restaurant, because the eatery and its unique menu are a complete departure from what is offered at the traditional Basque eating establishments, but it does represent a slice of life from Euskal Herria. "That is the talk of the town here, because he did capture the essence of the bars in Bizkaia," said Boise writer Juan Oleaga. "They're small, they're packed and decorated in that same way." Hamburgers and sandwiches are the

The novel tapas bar in Boise, Bar Gernika, is located in the old Basque neighborhood, within site of the state capitol building.

main offerings, along with a healthy selection of microbrews and imported beers. But tapas are the real treat here. Small chorizo or *solomo* (pork loin) sandwiches, slices of *tortilla de patatas* (potato omelette), and *croketas* (fried creamed chicken snacks) fill the appetizer menu, just as they do in Basque Country bars.

Bar Gernika is located in a remodeled brick building that dates back to the 1910s and has served as a working-class bar for most of its existence. Basques have run the place on and off since the 1940s, and the old corner bar would have taken its place as another historic building on the block, but Bank of America took over the building and drew up plans to tear it down in 1990, threatening to turn the spot into yet another parking lot. The Basque Museum three doors down saved it, obtaining a twenty-five-year lease from Bank of America and working out a deal with Ansotegi to open the eatery. The outside tables at the restaurant, located on the corner of Capitol Boulevard (once Seventh Street) and Main, command a view of the state capitol building, just four blocks away. Bar Gernika has joined the growing list of historic buildings in the city's old downtown that have been refurbished and are contributing to a major rebirth of the area.

Ansotegui's two sisters, Chris Ansotegui and Gina Urquidi, joined the culinary fray when they opened **Epi's Restaurant** in nearby Meridian in 1999. With the restaurant, they realized a longtime dream to recreate the dining-room environment of their grandmother's boardinghouse in Hailey, Idaho. The restaurant came after much thought. While they were still in the planning stage, Ansotegui would drive by a house everyday that reminded her of her grandmother's house. "I would always say—'we need a house just like that one.'" One day she drove by the house and saw a "For Sale" sign. They pounced on the old home and restored it, infusing it with the warm atmosphere that enveloped their grandmother Epi Inchausti's kitchen. (For the story on Epi, see the sidebar in the Hailey, Idaho, section). Business at Epi's in 2005 was booming, a far cry from some of the earliest days, remembered Ansotegui, when they had a mere twenty customers in an entire evening. The coziness of the stylish bungalow, replete with Basque folk art and photographs, creates a homey atmosphere. The place only seats forty-six diners at a time, and Ansotegui said the restaurant's smallness is part of the appeal. The food is commendable and abundant, and the staff's friendliness is lauded by every culinary reviewer who comes through Epi's. Chef Alberto Bereziartua from the Basque Country has managed the kitchen since day one. The town of Meridian is a suburb of Boise, a mere 20 minutes from downtown.

In November 2005, a full-service restaurant opened on the Basque block, giving Basque-cuisine fans another place to eat in Boise, in addition to Bar Gernika. The former Chico Club, a historical building, which was once a Basque boardinghouse and had served as offices in recent years, has been remodeled by owners Miren and Jose Mari Artiach. The new eatery, **Leku Ona,** has been designed to provide a "total Basque experience," said Miren. One chef is from the Basque Country, the other trained there. The restaurant has sandstone on the walls, and the ambiance is reminiscent of many eating places in the Basque Country, she said. The restaurant will initially serve only dinner, and eventually serve lunch, too. The Artiachs have other ambitious plans to turn a second building next to the restaurant into a small five-room bed-and-breakfast inn. Although blueprints were drawn up in 2005, Miren did not have an expected opening date.

Bar Gernika, 202 South Capitol Boulevard (at Grove), Boise, ID 83702 (208) 344-2175
Epi's Basque Restaurant, 1115 North Main Street, Meridian, ID 83642 (208) 884-0412
Leku Ona, 117 South 6th Street, Boise, ID 83702 (208) 345-6665

FOOD AND WINE IMPORTS

A Boise businessman decided just a few years ago to start importing gourmet food items and wine from his homeland to sell to retailers when he realized that no one else was doing it. Arabese wines, asparagus, tuna, anchovies, olive oil, peppers, marmalade, and *turrón* (bars of nougat and almonds) are among the choice products from the Basque Country that entrepreneur Justo Sarria has been trying to introduce to the U.S. market through his wholesale business, **Basque Country Imports.**

A few years later, another Boise Basque, Dan Ansotegui, followed his example by opening a retail store, **The Basque Market.** Part of these entrepreneurs' work naturally entails educating American buyers about what is special about Basque products. "First of all, they have to understand where they're coming from," Sarria said. The fish products are good because of the rich feeding grounds of the Bay of Biscay, he explains. The anchovies he sells are from Motriko and Bermeo, areas that have been fished for centuries, and the fish do not tend to be as salty as many on the market, "because they know how to cure the fish," he said.

Sarria's sales of the Rioja wines are doing fairly well, he said. He makes sure to emphasize the fact that his wines come from the Araba Province—the upland part of Spain's renowned grape-growing Rioja region, which, because of its higher elevation, produces a different-tasting wine. The marmalades have no added sugar. As for the *piquillo* peppers—"the only place they have *piquillo* pepper is Navarra," he said. The products cost more than comparable American products, but Sarria stresses that they are of higher quality, and not mass-produced: "Over there, everything is handmade or hand-handled." Sarria believes his business is doing well, because "the American people, like everybody else, are trying to buy better products." His products can be purchased in individual quantities. Call or write for a list of his products.

Ansotegui's store, The Basque Market, is located on the Basque block across the street from his longtime restaurant, Bar Gernika. For many years, Ansotegui received requests to cater events, but his small restaurant-kitchen could not accommodate them. He finally decided to answer the catering calls by opening a store-and-catering kitchen across the street from Bar Gernika. The location was a vacant warehouse before Ansotegui took it over and renovated it. The Basque Market carries cheeses, chorizos and other meats, tuna and anchovies, wine, and other food items not just from the Basque Country, but from the Iberian Peninsula. Since The Basque Market's opening in December 2000, Ansotegui has catered everything from a tapas party for fifteen people to weddings with up to five hundred guests. The store has a full kitchen in the back. One of the most popular events sponsored by the market is the cooking classes, which include wine tasting and sell out weeks ahead of time.

Basque Country Imports, 6929 Supply Way, Boise, ID 83716 (208) 343-5308
The Basque Market, 608 West Grove Street, Boise, ID 83702; *www.thebasquemarket.com*

FESTIVALS

San Inazio Celebration. The annual picnic started in the 1930s and lost some of its momentum during the 1940s. But after the organization of the Euzkaldunak Club in 1950, the club sponsored the event, and it regained a fervent following. It was held at the end of July in honor of the feast day of San Inazio de Loyola, patron saint of the Basques. Races and egg-throwing contests were held for the children, and weight-lifting and log-chopping, both popular in Bizkaia, became regular competitions. Benito Goitiandia and José Luís Arrieta were among the premier weight-lifters for many years.

For years, Boise Basques had their picnics and participated in the city's annual Music Week celebration, but with the celebration of 1972 the city's Basque gatherings were transformed into the humongous events they are today. That was the first year that the Holiday Basque Festival was held at the Western Idaho Fairgrounds. It was the biggest Basque festival of its time. Even without advertising the event among most of California's or Nevada's Basque communities, hundreds came to enjoy the celebration of music, dance, and food. It was a portent of bigger things to come.

The original San Inazio de Loyola celebration—Boise's annual festival—has expanded into three days of unique cultural offerings. Friday evening is Family and Friends Night, with tapas and music at the center and pala games at the fronton. For a couple of years concerts were held at the Boise State amphitheater, a beautiful setting with the Boise River in the background. On Saturday afternoon there's a showcase of Basque traditions, known as Basqueing on Grove Street. The lineup includes musicians, the Oinkari dancers, weight-lifting, and other performances. The street is filled with booths selling chorizos, *croketas,* and other goodies. The festival is a popular event that attracts hundreds of non-Basques.

At 6:30 P.M. on Saturday a group of dancers carrying a four-foot statue of St. Inazio leads a procession from the state capitol building to the front of the cathedral, where a special evening Mass is held. "Because it's the feast day of San Inazio, and San Inazio is the patron saint of the Basques, that Mass is the central point of the weekend," said Patty Miller. To give the service more solemnity and to focus the public's attention on the Mass, it was moved from an outdoor location to St. John's Cathedral. Church rules required that the nontraditional Mass could not be held on Sunday morning, so it was changed to Saturday evening. Eight male Oinkari dancers, wearing short red skirts over white pants and shirt, perform the Oñati liturgical dance at the altar during the consecration (see *www.ysursa.com/onati.htm*). The dancers genuflect to the host and clack their castanets. "In St. John's, it just rings in there because of the marble," said Miller. Later in the evening a public dance is always held at the Basque Center, for many years animated by the Basque rock group Ordago and accordionist Jimmy Jausoro's band.

On Sunday, at Boise's Municipal Park on Riverwood Drive, there are *txinga* (weight-carrying) competitions, games for children, and the traditional afternoon picnic. This event primarily attracts the Basque community. Despite a full weekend, the festival finishes with a bang. "We close down Grove Street at night for a dance in the street" in front of the Basque Center, said Miller, just like the Basque neighborhood used to do more than fifty years ago.

Jaialdi. The idea of organizing the first Jaialdi (festival), held in June 1987, came about during discussions among Boise NABO delegates and an official from the Basque Country. The conversation took place after a NABO meeting in Salt Lake City, according to Gerri Achurra, who was there and has been a codirector of every Jaialdi since then. The Basque official "encouraged everyone to think about doing something on a larger scale," said Achurra. By the time the event rolled around, two years later, as many as nine hundred people had been involved in its organization in some way or other. "We reached out to the community and used a lot of non-Basques. We got them from everywhere," said Achurra. Everyone helped on a volunteer basis. "It's strictly one of those things you do because you love it," said Achurra. More than fifty committees organized different aspects of the festival. Every club in the West was called upon to send dance groups, *klikas,* or singers. The inauguration of the Basque Museum kicked off the 1987 Jaialdi.

The Basque government also supported the event, sending dancers, athletes, and musicians. Organizers didn't have a good grasp on the attendance at the first Jaialdi, according to Achurra. "We were too busy trying to stay ahead of this speeding train," she said. But Al Erquiaga, who notes that they were originally hoping for at least ten thousand, estimated that the first festival probably attracted from twenty to thirty thousand people.

With the Idaho Centennial celebration scheduled for 1990, state officials asked the Basques to sponsor another Jaialdi. "The first one was the only one we intended to do," remarked Achurra, laughing.

For Jaialdi 1990 there was a weeklong series of events leading up to the weekend festivities, which included a Basque film festival and an open forum with scholars speaking on Basque topics. The first two Jaialdis started with parades down Warm Springs Road, an elegant street of old homes. Homeowners joined in the spirit of the day by displaying Basque flags. The historic former Idaho State Penitentiary at the eastern end of town was chosen as headquarters for the Jaialdi festivals. "The old Pen lends itself to the Old Country look," said Achurra.

Despite all the work involved in putting on the festival, Boise's Basques realized they had created a momentous regional event of great cultural value that had taken on a life of its own. The community decided to make the Jaialdi a regular event, once every five years. The third Jaialdi was organized in July 1995, and the subsequent festivals took place in the summers of 2000 and 2005. Having outgrown the Old Pen location, the festivals were held at the Western Idaho Fairgrounds. At that event dancers from all over the West, along with dance groups from the Basque Country, entertained crowds throughout the weekend.

POLITICS AND TIES TO THE HOMELAND

Despite Francisco Franco's blatantly anti-Basque policies, Basques in the West took a reserved approach and did nothing when he came to power during the Spanish Civil War, which broke out in 1936. Franco was not expected to stay in power after the United States joined the Allies in World War II, but the U.S. government preserved its military bases in Spain and maintained relations with Franco. Since news of the bombings and other violent acts carried out by the separatist group Euskadi 'Ta Askatasuna (ETA) were among the only reports about the situation in the Basque Country publicized in U.S. papers, Basques in this country feared that if they expressed their nationalism they would be labeled communists. They also feared for family members back home. As a group, they eschewed any political stand.

Probably the only political group among the West's Basques was Anaiak Danok, a short-lived nationalist group based in Boise during the 1970s. It was organized as a reaction to the Burgos trials, an internationally publicized series of trials in which several Basques were accused of terrorism and sentenced to death. "We wanted to help people that were affected by the Guardia Civil's activity," said the late Joe Eiguren, a former member, to explain the purpose for Anaiak Danok.

Idaho Secretary of State Pete Cenarrusa was a member of the group, and he was an outspoken critic of Franco's repressive tactics. After a trip to the Basque Country in 1971, he wrote a strongly worded statement criticizing Franco's treatment of the Basques, which Idaho Senator Frank Church included in the Congressional Record. Meanwhile, other Anaiok Danok members were misquoted in newspapers, found little support among a suspicious Basque-American community, and quickly disbanded. Cenarrusa attributed the U.S. Basques' reticence to the barrage of negative media attention on ETA's activities.

Today, the ties between Basque Country officials and American Basques seem to be strongest in Idaho, and over the years they have been strengthened by political gestures. In recognition of the Basques' contribution to Idaho, Governor Robert Smylie pronounced May 23 Basque Day in Idaho in 1964. In 1971 State Senator Pete Cenarrusa made a visit to the Basque Country. It was followed in 1973 by Idaho Senator Frank Church's visit to the Basque Country to show the support of the Idaho Basques and the U.S. government for the Basque Country. In 1989 Boise was an important stop for Lehendakari (President) José Antonio Ardanza, during his short visit to the United States. The bond was further strengthened in May 1992 when Idaho governor Cecil Andrus became the first foreign statesman to address the Basque parliament.

In 2005 Lehendakari Juan José Ibanretxe spoke at Boise's Jaialdi festival. A sister-city relationship has also been established between Boise and the city of Gernika. In October 1993 a small delegation of Boise officials visited Gernika, and documents were signed by the two cities in an official ceremony in the historic Basque headquarters, Batzar Etxe. In July 1994 a delegation came from Gernika to Boise for a visit to enjoy the San Inazio celebration. Officials exchanged gifts, and a showcase of the gifts was unveiled at City Hall (150 North Capitol Boulevard). The showcase, displaying commemorative items and memorabilia, along with the Gernika flag, is on permanent display in front of the council chambers.

In 1975 and 1976 Governor Cecil Andrus chose Basque Aberri Eguna, or Day of the Motherland (celebrated on Easter Sunday), as Basque Day. In 1990 Andrus declared the week of the Jaialdi as "Basque Cultural Week" in Idaho. Among state and local officials in Idaho,

"Basques do enjoy a lot of great favoritism," said Gerri Achurra. "And only because they work hard at organizing," she said.

CHURCH AND CEMETERY

Throughout the city's history, the local Basques have been closely linked with St. John the Evangelist Cathedral (807 North Eighth Street) in the city's oldest neighborhood. But every Catholic Church in Boise has Basque parishioners. During a remodeling in 1985, **Sacred Heart Church** at South Latah and Cassia Streets recognized its Basque members by establishing a Basque chapel with a statue of St. Inazio and a beautiful dark wood carving of Our Lady of Begoña. The **Morris Hill Cemetery,** at 317 North Latah, is not far away. Many of Boise's Basques are buried there.

IDAHO STATE HISTORICAL MUSEUM

The **Idaho State Historical Museum** at nearby Julia Davis Park is not a priority for the traveler with just a couple days to soak in Boise's Basque culture, but if you have the time you might want to stop by. Probably because the Basque Museum is located just a few blocks away, this museum devotes little space to the Basques. One wall panel downstairs gives a short history of the Basque community, part of the larger story of Idaho represented on this floor. A few Basque items, such as a *txistera* (jai alai wicker basket) are on display. A sense of fun imbues the second floor, where rooms have been decorated in different settings to give a sense of earlier days in Boise. The DeLamar Hotel's bay window sets the scene for a turn-of-the-century parlor, and a gorgeous antique back bar that was part of the Merino bar and pool hall, once owned by Anastasio Jayo and son-in-law Antonio Murelaga, provides the backdrop for a bar from the early 1900s.

Idaho State Historical Museum, 610 Julia Davis Drive, Boise, ID 83702 (208) 334-2120

Rural Southern Idaho

During the first half of this century, small towns throughout southern Idaho had boardinghouses filled to capacity with sheepherders.

The largest concentrations of Basques were in the Treasure Valley around Boise, in towns such as Marsing and Nampa, but Basques also settled in towns all along the Snake River Plain, from Ontario, Oregon, all the way east to Pocatello, and including the towns of Mountain Home, Shoshone, Gooding, Twin Falls, and Rupert. A bit farther north, in the Wood River Valley, Hailey had Basques families too. Mining in the northern part of the state attracted a few Basques to Mullan, which stood out as one of the only towns in that region with a Basque boardinghouse, but the establishment lasted just a short while, from 1925 to 1939. More recently a lumber mill in Spokane, Washington, drew Basques to the northern reaches of Idaho around Coeur d'Alene.

Social Life

In the decades before World War II the boardinghouses held monthly dances for the herders, and they were the venues for every holiday celebration. Three Kings Day, on January 6, was typically a bigger celebration than Christmas, just as in the Basque Country. Few unmarried Basque women immigrated to small towns outside of Boise, so in these places Basque men were more likely to marry non-Basques. But many of the men never married and returned as bachelors to the Basque Country. The exception was the boardinghouse families, whose children grew up in tight cultural enclaves and usually married fellow Basques. "Great marriages came out of them," said Marie Galdos Landeen, who herself grew up in a hotel in Emmett.

Social gatherings dwindled when many of the young Basque-Americans went off to World War II, but a revival of the culture in the small towns started during the 1950s. A women's group, the Organización Independiente Social, sponsored dances for the herders at the boardinghouses. "They would send out flyers to the sheep camps so [the men] would get the message," said musician Jimmy Jausoro, who was called upon to play at most of the dances. Someone would dig a costume or two out of a closet, and some of the herders would don white pants and shirts and put on a show for the crowd. "Many of those fellows could do the *aurresku,*" said Jausoro, referring to the men's dance where they kick their legs as high as they can.

In the 1960s a cultural awakening sparked by publicity of Boise's Oinkari dancers prompted Southern Idaho communities to organize their own clubs and winter dances, modeled after Boise's Sheepherders' Ball. The most popular among them attracted up to two thousand people.

By the 1970s most of the dances had disappeared. "With the fall of the sheep industry, there were no herders to patronize those dances," said Jausoro. Today most of the Basque communities in these smaller towns have faded. Many of those who came to make money went back to the Basque Country, and the children of those who stayed and married are now more American than anything else. "Of my generation, less than half married Basques," said Basque-American Helen Berria, who grew up in Gooding. Gradually, many of the Basque-Americans moved to Boise in search of jobs.

Of the many towns outside Boise that once had significant Basque colonies, today only Gooding and Mountain Home have Basque clubs that host annual social events. In Hailey, Gooding, Rupert, and Hagerman, Basque dinners are still held every year to raise funds for local Catholic churches and schools.

SHEEP

Fifty years ago, Idaho had 2 million sheep. Today they number fewer than 200,000. The bigger sheep outfits shifted to cattle, and the smaller ones got out of the business. Trucking and crop farming became a viable alternative for many. There are still a few Basque sheep outfits spread along the Snake River plain. Today they hire Peruvians, Chileans, and Mexicans to herd their sheep.

BASQUE PRIESTS

During the late 1960s and early 1970s, Idaho had two Basque priests who circulated among the sheep camps during lambing season. Fathers Santos Recalde and Juan Garatea served as chaplains to the Basques. Unlike the traveling French Basque priest in California, the Idaho priests were assigned to specific parishes, according to Garatea, who currently works for Little Flower Church in Burley, Idaho. Recalde left for Venezuela in 1970, but Garatea continued on the job for a few more years. Eventually Basques stopped immigrating here. "When I came, all the Basque funerals, weddings, and baptisms, everything they wanted in Basque," said Garatea. "But not anymore," he said, noting that fewer and fewer of the Euskara-speaking immigrants are still alive.

Emmett

LUMBER MILL

The Basque population in the town of Emmett was supported for many years by the Boise Payette lumber mill, part of the larger lumber company now known as Boise Cascade Corporation. The mill was originally located in the small town of Barber, which was in essence owned by the lumber company, according to Luis Arrizabala. At least 20 of the 110 families that lived there were Basque, and most of them moved to Emmett when the mill relocated there in 1936. "They were loyal to the mill," said Arrizabala, whose father, Ereño, was a mill employee. In its early years, first- and second-generation Basques filled the blue-collar ranks of the company. Today Basque-Americans work in administrative positions at the corporation headquartered in Boise.

CULTURAL OBSERVANCES

Around 1940 professor Jon Bilbao came to Emmett and prepared a group of young Basque-Americans to perform folk dances at the Idaho State Fair, according to Irene Bicandi Anderson. "We studied all summer," she said. Bilbao was a delegate to the exiled Basque government during those years. "He brought over a *txistulari* (*txistu* player)." (A *txistu* is an instrument like a flute that is held straight up and down.) That was even before Boise had a dance group. During those years the immigrant folk had kept more of their traditions in the rural towns than the citified Basques in Boise had. Nevertheless, the summer picnic in Boise was "the event of the year" for families in all the surrounding small towns.

During the 1960s Emmett's Basques organized their own Sheepherder's Ball in March. Their youngsters learned the traditional dances and performed at the ball and at summer picnics, which continued into the early 1980s. But in Emmett today Basque cultural practices have all but disappeared. Agriculture continues to be important in the larger Emmett Valley, located next to the Payette River.

BOARDINGHOUSES

Simón Galdos, better known as Charcha, and his wife, Josefa, who once operated the boardinghouse (later known as Uberuagas') in Boise that is now the home of the Basque Museum and Cultural Center, came to Emmett in 1917 and opened a boardinghouse. "There had been sheepherders going through Emmett, but none of them had settled there," until the Galdoses came, said the couple's daughter, Marie Galdos Landeen. In 1921 the family bought a rooming house at 109 South Commercial, which they ran until 1967. Eugenio and María Dolores Bicandi ran a boardinghouse in their home at 327 Main Street from 1925 to 1957.

The rooming houses were known simply by the name of the family that owned them. "They didn't really have a name," said Irene Bicandi Anderson, whose parents' place was known as "Bicandi's." Most of the boarders were sheepherders, and many worked for Idaho's sheep king, Andrew Little. "He was an awful big name even in 1930," said Anderson. For many years, there was a sign on Highway 16 between Emmett and Boise that read SHEEPHERDERS HEADED FOR TOWN HAVE THE RIGHT OF WAY.

Irene Bicandi Anderson, who grew up in one of Emmett's two boardinghouses, recalls those early days with fondness. The Basque hotel keepers in Emmett, just like those elsewhere, engaged in bootlegging and suffered for it, according to Anderson. Her father was fined on numerous occasions. "You could see that stuff in the movies, but it was happening right there in Emmett," she said, remembering her uncle Pete driving into town to deliver moonshine in his Lincoln Zephyr, in custom-made shirts with gold cufflinks. "We were picked on a bit," said Anderson, who remembers being called a bootlegger's daughter.

The Bicandi family suffered more than its share of sad moments, but the Basque community lent its support. Anderson's brother Lucio at age eleven drowned after being knocked unconscious when he jumped into the mill pond to save a younger boy who had fallen in as they played on some logs. "That was the biggest funeral they ever had in Emmett," said Anderson, who remembers dozens of families driving into town from Boise. "That is how close those people were with each other."

But most of those early days were happy ones. How could they not be, especially for the girls growing up in the boardinghouses filled with young good-looking men, with music and dancing every weekend. "I'm sure the people in Emmett wondered what was going on in those houses where all that music was going on," said Galdos Landeen. In retrospect, Anderson said, "It was the time to live."

The Galdos' boardinghouse—the town's last building with a false front, which dated back to 1905—was torn down in 1973. The Bicandis' old boardinghouse is now the private home of one of the daughters, Margaret Foruri. Except for a paint job, it hasn't changed at all since its earlier boardinghouse days. "It looks so small to me now," said Anderson. "When I was young, it looked so big because it was always full of people."

Caldwell and Nampa

SHEEP

The area around Marsing, Nampa, Homedale, and Caldwell was sheep country, and Basques settled in all these towns from the early 1900s onward. From the Treasure Valley, herders would trail the sheep north to areas that now are part of the Boise and Payette National Forests. Most of the sheep business was primarily dominated in the early years by sheepman Andrew Little, who trailed over 100,000 sheep in the area and shipped most of his lambs out of Smiths Ferry. But gradually Basques made inroads into sheepherding in the region, the Aldecoa and Aldape families standing out in particular.

The passage of the sheep and the wintertime layoffs of herders supported a few boardinghouses, including a couple in nearby Cascade. But most of the boardinghouses were in Nampa, because that was where the railroad was. Basques also owned several bars in Homedale over the years.

LUMBER MILLS

Sawmills and construction in the area sustained the Basque community in later years. The Boise Cascade sawmill is still in operation, although another mill in nearby McCall has closed.

NAMPA'S BOARDINGHOUSES AND BUSINESSES

In Nampa, sheepman Luis Bermensolo ran a magnificent hotel around the 1910s and 1920s, the Spanish Hotel. In his book, *Los Vascongados en el oeste de los Estados Unidos,* Sol Silen wrote that the hotel had a candy shop, barber shop, and billiard tables. The Spanish Hotel at 119 Twelfth Avenue North was a boardinghouse and home to Tomás and Tomasa Jausoro's family of eight children, including the renowned musician Jim Jausoro, from 1920 until the 1950s. The building is still there, between First and Second Streets, although today it is empty and run-down.

The Modern Hotel was another one, built over the Eleventh Street Subway at 16½ Eleventh Avenue South. It was run by the Bastida and Arana families. Later it was torn down and replaced by a bank.

"The Echeverria and Onaindia families had boardinghouses before we got here," said Frances Bilbao, who operated the Valley Club and Emery Hotel on Main Street with husband Frank from 1945 to 1972. The old Emery has since burnt down, and a bar went up in its place. Bilbao said that the former Onaindia place at 121 Main Street is now a law office, and the Echeverrias' is a private home.

In 1912 Candido Mendiguren started a shoe repair shop in Nampa, and in 1918 he built his own place, the Nampa Shoe Shop, at 10 Thirteenth Avenue South, which he ran until 1959. Today his grandson Tom Mendiguren carries on the family's shoe repair business in Ontario, Oregon, but the stone building where Candido worked is still in Nampa and now serves as a bar called the **19 18 Club.**

During the 1950s and 1960s, while other Basque communities became more unified as they rallied around their annual winter dance, Nampa's disintegrated. The town didn't have a hall big enough to sponsor a big dance, and its boardinghouses had closed down. "After the war, Nampa dwindled as far as the Basques were concerned," said

Jim Jausoro. More recently Basques from Jordan Valley and other smaller towns have moved into Nampa and Caldwell.

EUZKALDUNAK CHARITIES GROUP

In Caldwell a loose-knit group of Basques organized a big charity ball in 1970, prompted by news of the success of Basque dances in other towns. The annual benefit dance raised $500,000 over the following twenty-three years, according to one of the longtime organizers, John Beitia. The first year the dance was organized for a simple cause—to raise money for a scoreboard for the Catholic church's new school gym. Over the years the organizers raised money for a number of lesser-known charities, particularly children's groups—"the ones that fell through the cracks," said Beitia. Caldwell's Basque Charity Ball was probably the biggest of the Basque dances in Idaho, attracting anywhere from two thousand to thirty-five hundred people regularly. "We stacked them in there," said Mark Araquistain.

Today, the event is a dinner and dance. Always held on the third Saturday of January, it included the auction of a fat lamb, which would often raise $10,000 to $15,000 alone (since many of the successful bidders donated it back for more auctioning). And locals, especially older folks, loved watching the weight-lifting pros show off their prowess by lifting the cylinder or rolling the granite *bola* around their necks. Some of them joined in for the weight-carrying contest. "We had a couple of non-Basques who were bound and determined to win it," said Beitia. "They would build their own weights and practice all year." The local dance group—Caldwell'ko Euzko Dantzariak—has always performed at the ball.

For a few years, the party became a rowdy affair, and fears about liability and skyrocketing insurance costs pushed the Basque group to cancel the event in 1993. The group of about twenty-five members, officially incorporated as the Euzkaldunak Charities, began sponsoring an annual benefit golf tournament.

The following year, however, the group decided to reinstate the event, but on a much smaller scale. Today the tickets for the January event are limited to five hundred. It still resembles the earlier version, with the lamb auction, weight-lifting competitions, performances by Caldwell and Boise dancers, and a big auction of interesting items, including Basque and Western art, to raise funds. The event is still held at the O'Connor Fieldhouse in Caldwell, but the evening is a much more relaxed family event. The organization has continued its golf tournament as well, raising a lot of money between the two events. Many groups have been helped by Euzkaldunak Charities, which prefers to pay for airplane tickets and hotel rooms for families with children undergoing medical treatment and sponsor holiday food baskets or bags of groceries instead of cash donations.

Euzkaldunak Charities, 307 Badiola Street, Caldwell, ID 83605. Information: (208) 459-8277 (*Mark Araquistain*)

DANCE

Despite the lack of a social club, the local dance group, Caldwelleko Euzko Dantzariak, has thrived here, and in 2004 it had about forty young members. "So many times the program takes off because of the person in charge, and that is the case there," said Weiser resident Grace Mainvil of the Caldwell dancers, taught by former Oinkari Gloria Lejardi. The five- to thirteen-year-olds come from towns all around Caldwell and often graduate to the Oinkaris in Boise.

Homedale

CLUB AND DANCE

Homedale is one of many southwestern Idaho towns with a longtime Basque population. Several Basque bars have existed in Homedale, and some forty years ago the Basques held dances, too. Nearby Marsing was home to a few Basque boardinghouses. In 2000, local Basques decided to start their own club, and it quickly attracted about 160 members. "We are far enough away from Boise that people felt they needed their own group," said Tony Uranga, an officer in the club, noting it is at least an hour drive to Boise. The Homedale group, named **Txoko Ona,** attracts members from the entire region, including Caldwell, and Jordan Valley and Ontario in nearby Oregon. Most of the children dance in the Caldwelleko Euzko Dantzariak. The concentration of Basques here has lent success to the club's main event, its dance on the first Saturday in March. Held annually at the Homedale Armory since 2001, the dance and auction earn a hefty profit for the club, which is already making plans to build a center. Next to the Armory, the club sets up a tent where people can participate in a silent auction or bid on hundreds of items in the live auction. The club publishes a schedule of the auction so people can plan their evening, and they tend to go back and forth between the dance and the auction, said Uranga. More than seven hundred people arrive for the popular event, which also includes performances by the Caldwelleko and Oinkari Basque dancers. Txoko Ona holds a fall picnic for its members in September.

BASQUE CENTER

When the railroad, located in the middle of town, was being dismantled and the property sold off, Txoko Ona decided to buy a chunk of it, said club member Tony Uranga. The club bought ten acres in January 2005 and made ambitious plans to break ground on a cultural center by 2006 or 2007. The plans for the center have generated a great deal of excitement among the membership.

Txoko Ona, P.O. Box 1163, Homedale, ID 83628. Information: (208) 898-0160 (Tony Uranga)

Mountain Home

In the early part of this century, Mountain Home was just a dot on the map, a tiny railroad town of two hundred to three hundred residents about 40 miles southeast of Boise. Cattle and sheep grazing were the primary industries. Eventually the town became one of the largest wool shipping points in the country.

The Basque children who grew up in small towns and rural areas had a strong sense of their ethnic community. All of them had close relatives in the Basque Country, many of whom joined them in Mountain Home. "I grew up very aware of where my roots were," said Esther Bidaurreta, a Mountain Home native who spoke Basque at home with her Bizkaian parents, Paula and George Anchustegui. "All my parents' friends were Basque, and until I went to first grade, I had no American friends," she recalled. Mountain Home, Grand View, and Bruneau sponsored wintertime dances. "Those were the only events that we had," recalled Bidaurreta, who now lives in Petaluma, California, with her husband, Franxoa, and their two children. The yearly Christmas dance at the town's Basque Hotel, built by her great-uncle Pedro Anchustegui in 1907, drew Basques from miles around.

The sheep industry reached its peak in Idaho around 1910 and began a slow decline in the 1940s. So did the Basque population in many of the small towns of southwestern Idaho. Cattle are still raised in the area, but the sheep business is gone.

The establishment of a military base next to Mountain Home supported the town's continued growth. Today the town's population is eleven thousand, and the nearby Mountain Home Air Force Base is home to another ten thousand people. Today less than two thousand people in Mountain Home are Basques. Nevertheless, the descendants of many pioneering Basque families continue to live in the area, and their influence is very much in evidence here. A wrought-iron sign boasting the very distinct Basque name of Bengoechea still stands atop the landmark hotel, although the building has been transformed into a shopping complex. An old fronton nearby was restored in 2003, and a park was added. And in the middle of town, a former Basque boardinghouse still stands, restored to its former state as a beautiful stone gingerbread-style house.

SHEEP

Basques settled in Mountain Home because of the many sheep camps in the area. The winter sheep camps were in nearby Grand View, and most of the sheepherders stayed in town during that time. The herders' annual trek took them up to Stanley in the summertime.

The Bruneau Sheep Company was one of the big Basque enterprises that developed in the region. It was eventually purchased by non-Basque J. R. "Jack" Simplot and forms the basis for his large company's land and livestock division. Simplot was referred to as an honorary Basque. His company is one of Idaho's biggest, with significant mining, chemicals, and food divisions. The late John Basabe, a Basque, headed the division for forty years, and today his

This old Basque boardinghouse in Mountain Home, Idaho, was a bed-and-breakfast for a while.

son Thomas is running it. The Basabes were among the many Basques who worked for Simplot over the years.

BOARDINGHOUSES

The Basque Hotel was built by Pedro Anchustegui in 1907 and stood behind the Bengoechea Hotel on North Third West, until the Basque Hotel burned down in 1984. Yet the old hotel's pelota court, which Anchustegui had built of stone, withstood the test of time and was recently restored. It's a remarkable remnant of the architecture of its time (1908) and has been placed on the National Register of Historic Places.

Another Basque, Agapito Bideganeta, owned several Basque boardinghouses in town over the years, some that his family operated, and others that he leased out, but the best known was the Royal Hotel on the 100 block of South Second East, which had a handball court on the side of the building. Carmen (Oñederra) Arruti ran the Royal from 1945 to 1956. The old Royal was eventually demolished to make way for a new fire station. Arruti bought her own boardinghouse at 395 East Second South, which was known as Carmen's, and ran it for almost thirty years. The family still owns the lovely two-story house, built between 1905 and 1910.

Bideganeta also owned a boardinghouse at 495 North Third East (on Fifth North), which was restored in the 1990s by two women who ran it for a short time as a bed-and-breakfast inn. He bought the house in 1917 and converted the upstairs into a boardinghouse with six small rooms. Later it served as the private home of two Basque families, but it is best remembered as a stopping place for Basque sheepherders. A local doctor had it built as his home in 1907 on a corner that was once at the edge of town, adjacent to a dairy on one side. The stones used for the exterior of the historic home were hand-hewn onsite from a cement-like mixture. Two non-Basque women turned the quaint gingerbread-style house into the Rose Stone Inn in the 1990s, re-creating the interior décor from the first half of the century. While the inn did not last long, the restoration remains. The owner of the beauty salon that occupied the home in 2005 said she enjoyed the historical Basque building and did not mind having visitors.

The region's most elegant hotel in its day was the old **Bengoechea Hotel,** a three-story brick building constructed in 1910 by wealthy sheepman José "Joe" Bengoechea. The small town already had a big hotel, which is now named the Mellon, but, according to Marjorie Streeter, who currently owns the Bengoechea Hotel building with her husband, Jack, Bengoechea built his own because "he knew his sheepmen weren't welcome [at the Mellon]. There were a lot of cattlemen and wealthy people who stayed there who looked down on the sheepmen because they didn't speak English, they were foreigners, and they wore dirty clothes." Richard Urquidi, a Mountain Home schoolteacher who researched the town's history, said that Bengoechea built the hotel because "he thought he could make that place a showcase for the people who got off the train." In any case, Bengoechea built the fine hotel near the railroad tracks, next to the small Basque Hotel. Bengoechea asked Ignacio Berriochoa, a stonemason from Shoshone, to come down and cut the corners for the building, according to the stonemason's son, Luis Berrio-Ochoa (see the sidebar on the elder Berriochoa in the Shoshone section).

"It was one of the most modern ones that was produced for its time," said Urquidi, noting that the hotel even had running water. Bengoechea, who began as a herder for the Altube brothers in

The old Bengoechea Hotel in Mountain Home (circa 1920) was the finest hotel in the region in its day. (Courtesy of the Idaho State Historical Society.)

northeast Nevada, acquired twenty-five to thirty thousand sheep at one time. One of the wealthiest sheepmen of his era, he also served as vice president and board member of the Mountain Home Bank. The Bengoechea family eventually sold the hotel to the Bideganeta family, and it was later leased to numerous hotel operators, who changed its name over the years. In 1982 the building was placed on the National Register Historic Places, and a plaque at the door announces it as THE SHEEPHERDER'S HOME.

The Streeters took over ownership of the Bengoechea Hotel in 1988 and attempted to turn the building into a mini-mall with little success. They had better luck renting out rooms for longterm use. The upstairs remains similar to the original state, with old-fashioned bathrooms down the hall. The exterior of the historic building remains relatively unchanged. The Streeters, who run an antique store and real estate business downstairs, were ready to retire in 2005 and hoped to sell the building to the Basque community. "That's who should have it . . . the Basques," said Marjorie Streeter.

The Towne Square (formerly the Bengoechea Hotel), 195 North Second West (at West Second North), Mountain Home, ID 83647 (208) 587-4698

WINTER DANCE

The annual Sheepherder's Ball, held in the winter, was the main Basque event in Mountain Home for many years. The tradition got started after the Boise Eskualdunak Club came to Mountain Home in 1959 and sponsored a winter dance, prompting a group of Mountain Home Basques to organize their own ball the following year. According to newspaper reports uncovered by Richard Urquidi, the first Basque fiesta turned into a near riot when fifteen hundred people tried to jam in the small Mountain Home Legion Hall. But in later years the event's success prompted the local Basques to form an association and sponsor the dance. In the 1990s, attendance had been dropping, and the club canceled the event in 1995. However, the Sheepherder's Ball, just like the annual picnic, is enjoying a renaissance. Finding a good location was originally a problem, but organizers settled on the Elk's club (325 South Third West) even though the Elks are in charge of the liquor sales. A couple of days before the event, club members hitch a sheep wagon to a pick-up truck and drive through town, cooking chorizos on the wagon's stove and handing them out to promote the dance on the fourth Saturday of March.

BASQUE CLUB

In its most active days, during the 1960s and 1970s, the **Euskal Lagunak,** also known as the Elmore County Basque Association, was one of the town's most important civic organizations. With profits from the dance, over the years the group bought an organ for the Our Lady of Good Council Catholic Church and equipment for the local hospital. The club contributed to other community projects and nonprofit groups and also sponsored small scholarships for college-bound high school seniors for many years.

For years the association members were all male, but David Knox said that no one ever complained. "It's a working club rather than a social club," he explained. But that rule was finally changed in mid-1992, according to Knox, partially in hopes of increasing the group's membership. The club was fizzling out, and the few members who were still involved didn't want to see it die. A local dance group waxed and waned over the last few years. But recent events, such as the renewal of the annual festival and the restoration of the fronton, have revitalized the club.

More energy has been infused into the club with a new children's group that has been performing at local Basque events. To promote the culture, club member Jose Ibaibarriaga received a grant from the Idaho Arts Council to work with master Basque teacher Jill Aldape and a group of youngers, to teach them not only Basque dance, but also songs, cooking, pelota, and the language. "The kids need to learn everything about the culture," he noted, not just the dances. In 2003 the group, Etxeko Gazteak, had ten children, and the following year twelve. And as the kids get more involved, "that brings the parents in," said club member Jo Anne Hoffman. Some club members even created a couple of giant puppets, like those used in the Basque Country, dressed in Basque costumes for local parades and events. Today, with the help of some dedicated members, Mountain Home Basques have lots of activities to instill pride in their culture.

Euskal Lagunak, c/o Elmore County Basque Association, P.O. Box 88, Mountain Home, ID 83647. Information: (208) 587-3760 (*Lisa and David Knox*)

Festival. For many years the club held a picnic in August. All kinds of competitions were sponsored—foot and sack races for the kids and athletic contests for the men, such as iron bar throwing, weight tossing, weight carrying, wood cutting, weight-lifting, and weight pulling. Lambs for the barbecue were always donated by local sheep ranchers, until 1974, when the last of the sheep outfits in Mountain Home disappeared. The picnic was canceled in 1990, because so few Basques attended. But the event was revived in 1996, and up to fifteen hundred people have shown up since then, surprising organizers. It continues, most recently on the first Sunday in August, at the new Basque Park, invigorated by all the recent activities of the club.

Fronton and Park. The town's historic fronton was built in 1912 by the owner of the Basque Hotel, Pedro Anchustegui, and other local Basques. It was restored and inaugurated at a big Basque festival in August 2001. Father Martxel Tillous, the Basque priest from San Francisco, came to bless the new court, and Basques from all over came for the festivities, which included friendly competition between handball players from San Francisco, Elko, and Boise.

In the 1990s, the Basque club decided to preserve the fronton, which had fallen into disrepair, particularly in light of the fact that the stone structure survived while the adjacent hotel burned down in a 1983 fire. Club members were inspired by the restoration of the historic fronton in Jordan Valley, Oregon. With the help of a grant from the Idaho Historical Trust, the club successfully raised matching funds primarily by selling memorial tiles. The tiles, engraved with the names of the contributors, became part of a beautiful tile representation of the red, white, and green *ikurrina* on a large free-standing wall in a park across from the fronton. The backside of the wall displays a wrought-iron map of the Basque Country made by a local artisan. The *ikurrina* wall is located on the lot where the Basque Hotel once stood, on the corner adjacent to the fronton property. Another grant from the Basque government covered the rest of the restoration, carried out by local contractor Claude Bermensolo. Both properties have been planted with grass and trees by the Basque club and are referred to as the "Basque Park." In 2004, with the help of the Mountain Home Arts Council, the club had a mural painted at the end of the left fronton wall, highlighting themes of the Basque community such as Basque dancers, sheep and a sheep wagon, and the face of longtime Basque resident John Lasuen. Another attractive addition is the installation of an authentic sheep wagon, which was inaugurated during the August 2004 picnic. Donated by a local ranching family, the wagon was completely restored by the club and set on a cement pad in the park, where people driving by can see it. Although it is enclosed inside a gate for security purposes, the club opens the gates for the annual festival and sets up the wagon to look authentic, with clothing, food, and even a fire in the stove. The club also takes the wagon out to show it off at other events, such as the Sheepherder's Ball in March.

Next to the fronton and park is the old Bengoechea Hotel, adding historic charm to this Basque Block in Mountain Home and giving visitors a feel for the old Basque neighborhood that once thrived here. The club is seeking ways to promote pelota locally, to make better use of the court. They approached a local school within walking distance about offering physical education classes there and have obtained instruction booklets in English from the Basque Country on how to play the sport. A group of Basque children is learning the game as well, but teacher Jose Ibaibarriaga admits they play with tennis balls, rather than the hard pelota ball that regular players use, which are so tough on the hands.

Basque Block, North Third West at West Second North, Mountain Home, ID

RICHARD AGUIRRE PARK

Domingo Aguirre was a relative of Joe's who played a significant role in Mountain Home's history. He arrived in this country in 1905 and built up a significant sheep and cattle grazing business in the area, buying up several homesteads, which became known as the Basque Ranches. **Richard Aguirre Park** at East Tenth (between Ninth and Tenth) is named after the oldest of Aguirre's three sons, who volunteered for the U.S. Air Force and was declared missing in action in the South Pacific in 1943.

BASQUE BARS

If you're in the mood for a drink while you're in Mountain Home, stop by **Adrian's Club** at 240 South Main. In 1943 the late Adrián Berriochoa opened the bar, which he converted from an old laundry. It was a favorite drinking hole, and for years the Basque association has often held its meetings there, even after Adrián passed away. According to Richard Urquidi, during World War II Berriochoa agreed to be the one bar in town that provided drinks to black soldiers. Another popular Basque hangout in the 1940s was Pete's Pastime, a bar owned by Peter Monasterio. For many years, you could get Basque food at Joe's restaurant (185 South Second East), which was first run by Joe Aguirre and later by his daughter Jo Anne Hoffman.

CEMETERY

As for Domingo and his wife Juanita Urquidi Aguirre, they are buried, along with most other local Basques, close together in a small section of the town's **Mountain View Cemetery** (East Eighth North and North Eighteenth East). Richard Urquidi explained that in the early part of the century, the Basques were discriminated against just as

This colorful billboard in downtown Mountain Home, Idaho, painted by a local high school class, was a testament to the Basque presence in the area during the 1980s and 1990s before it was removed.

Chinese and African-Americans were. "They put us over to the far (north) side of the cemetery," he said.

Mural

A bright-colored mural of a Basque man in a beret, with a map of the Basque Country and the Basque flag, was displayed for years in the center of town at South Main and East Jackson at the former location of the Corner Cigar Store, and owned for many years by Basque John Cristobal. When Cristobal sold the building, the deteriorated mural came down.

Shoshone

Shoshone, one of the oldest towns in Idaho, developed around the turn of the twentieth century as a railroad center. It was one of the first stops for Basques coming to Idaho from the East Coast. Four rail lines traversed its main street. At one time the town had at least five Basque boardinghouses, where herders often stayed during the winter through lambing time, which starts in January. There were "hundreds and hundreds" of Basques in Shoshone during the first three decades of the twentieth century, according to Gooding resident Andy Lejardi. In those days all the sheepmen in the area came to the bustling town to recruit their herders.

At one time Shoshone also had a small close-knit Basque community. In fact, it was so close-knit that when Margaret Gray studied the Basque community in 1955, she found 83 percent of Basques were interrelated.

Gooding, meanwhile, was just a speck of a town in the desert for many years. "Now it's just the opposite," said Lejardi, estimating Gooding's population to be about three thousand, whereas Shoshone's has dropped from a high of eighteen hundred to about twelve hundred.

While the strong Basque community is gone, a few Basque are still here, and they often participate in Gooding's Basque event. This picturesque historic town, located at the crossroads of four state highways (24, 26, 75, 93), still attracts quite a few tourists. Shoshone continues to be a rail thoroughfare between Portland and Salt Lake City for freight and passenger service, and its historic train depot is quite picturesque—but the train rarely stops in Shoshone these days.

SHEEP

In the first half of the century, there were many sheep outfits in the area. Twin Falls, Jerome, and Hagerman had a few as well. These towns were the winter stopping places. The sheep owners typically owned large farms in the area, where they grew hay and grain for feed and put up big sheds for lambing time in January. The sheepherders typically would help the ewes through lambing.

The desert-like southwestern corner of Idaho was a warmer setting for the young lambs. When they were strong enough to go outside, they would pasture along the Snake River Plain. In the summertime, Hailey got the Basque business as the herders with their sheep stopped over there on their way up into the Pioneer Mountains around Sun Valley or the Sawtooth Range. Many of the hotel keepers would follow them. It was not unusual for a family to run a boardinghouse in Shoshone during winter, then close it and open another one in Hailey in the summer.

BOARDINGHOUSES

Three of the town's boardinghouses—the Pagoagas', the Soloagas', and the Oneidas'—were clustered at South Rail and Alta Streets, a few blocks from the big train depot. Between his place and the Oneidas', Domingo Soloaga also had a small bowling alley. On the other side of the tracks, on North Rail Street, was Beitia's boardinghouse. On North Greenwood Street by the bridge was Pete Mendiola's boardinghouse. On North Alta Street, Soloaga had a fronton, and José and Gertrude Ansola ran a room-and-board place for a short time across the street. Joe Oneida, now in his eighties, said that he heard that a small café in town made of stone also used to be a Basque boardinghouse, "but that was before my time."

One or two boardinghouses survived outside Boise beyond the 1960s. But only one, in Shoshone, continued operating up through the 1980s and 1990s, and in 1995—Oneida's—was probably the last authentic boardinghouse in Idaho to close.

Francisco and Benita Onaindia were already married and had children when they arrived in Idaho in 1916 and decided to open their own boardinghouse. They changed their name to Oneida when they came to this country, according to their son Joe, because it was easier to pronounce. Frank Oneida built his wooden boardinghouse with help from Basque carpenter friends in 1917 or 1918. During those same years, in the midst of World War I, the boardinghouses filled up with herders felled by an epidemic of Rocky Mountain spotted fever and influenza that was sweeping the country. A few died, "but they saved a lot of them," said Joe.

Frank's wife, Benita, whom everyone called Amuma (Grandmother), operated the boardinghouse and was known as one of the best cooks around. She ran a second place in Hailey during the summertime, according to Dollie Oneida, Benita's daughter-in-law, who ended up taking Amuma's place in the kitchen. Dollie, who is not Basque, learned to cook pig's feet, tripe, codfish, potato soup, and other typical Basque dishes by watching her mother-in-law.

Dollie and Pete Oneida moved into the boardinghouse at 120 South Rail Street in 1968 and took over the business when Frank and Benita passed away. "It was sort of a hand-me-down deal," said Dollie. As long as there were older Basques who needed a place to

This former Basque boardinghouse, Soloaga's, is part of a walking tour of Shoshone, Idaho. The inner walls were built of indigenous lava rock by stonemason Ignacio Berriochoa. (Photo by David Reyes.)

live, Dollie kept up the business while Pete continued the sheep business his father started south of Shoshone. "Work never hurt anybody," said Dollie. "I love the people. And it's hard to say no." But by 1995, according to Dollie, they were ready to say good-bye to their last boarders and retire from the business on South Rail Street. But single Basque men who needed a place to stay inevitably found their way to the Oneidas' door, and Dollie was still renting to a couple of boarders in 1995 before it closed.

During the 1920s the Mendiolas moved to Hailey, where they had another boardinghouse, and Ramón Urrutia took over their place in Shoshone for a few years, before he sold it to Carlos Berriochoa in 1929. Berriochoa's wife, Ramona, ran things in Shoshone, while Carlos often spent time in Ketchum, where he also owned the Rio Club.

Frank Oneida, Domingo Soloaga, and Mitch Lecertua became some of the area's more important sheepmen. Today Frank Oneida's son Pete continues to run sheep as does a cousin, Lewis Oneida, out of Jerome.

Manuel and Fernanda Beitia operated a boardinghouse with a pool hall from 1910 to 1938. The Beitias' building was constructed from local lava rock by Basque stonemason Ignacio Berriochoa. Berriochoa also built Domingo Soloaga's boardinghouse on East A Street and the fronton and attached house on North Alta Street, and he installed the corners on the Bengoecheas' hotel in Mountain Home.

The boardinghouses were in their glory days during the 1920s and 1930s, hosting dances for all the young sheepherders. "I used

Ignacio Berriochoa, Stonemason

Ignacio Berriochoa was one of several Basques who brought their skills as stonemasons from the Old Country. He lived 6 miles outside of Shoshone, near the town of Dietrich, in the early part of the twentieth century. He built many homes, including his own, out of local rock. Miles of lava beds stretch east from Shoshone across Idaho, the result of volcanic activity thousands of years ago. Berriochoa's grandson, Luis Berrio-Ochoa, joked about his grandfather's "rock farm." Berrio-Ochoa and his siblings were asked to help dig up the rocks in his fields. "It seemed like every year there was a new crop," he said chuckling.

Several of Berriochoa's structures served as Basque boardinghouses for many years. Today a few monuments of his stone handiwork remain. In Shoshone, unfortunately, Beitia's was razed in 1967. Domingo Soloaga's boardinghouse at 201 East A Street is in fine shape, but the stone walls were covered with plaster. However, the fence around the back reveals Berriochoa's stonework. At the old fronton at 123 North Alta Street, current resident Tom Jackson built his living quarters in the former court space after he moved in in 1978. But the court's cement wall juts up above his home, and you can still tell it was once a fronton. In later years, Berriochoa put up an L-shaped building of stone around the court, which Jackson has left unchanged. Although the stone walls are still intact, the wooden interior of the former two-story boardinghouse is in ruins. Jackson also owned the old Ansola place across the street. Built by Berriochoa in 1913, during an era when fire was the only heat source, the house's chimney had four openings. Illness forced Jackson to sell the historic building and the current owner remodeled it, covering up the old stone walls.

As for Berriochoa's own stone house in Dietrich, it's still there. It remained in the family for many years but was finally sold. It's an empty building now, according to his grandson. Lava rocks were piled up to create a fence around the farm's property line, a fence that is still there and visible from the road. To see the house and the fence, drive east from Shoshone on Highway 24 for about 6 miles until you see a road heading north across the railroad tracks. The rock house will be about 2 miles down, on the left.

to go to all the parties in Shoshone and Gooding," said Joe Oneida. Shoshone's church didn't have a hall, so the Basques organized their winter dances at the brick schoolhouse, Lincoln Elementary, which is still on Fourth Street at the northwest end of town. Basques in the town of Jerome hosted occasional dances as well.

In Shoshone, weddings and funerals were held at St. Peter's Church, established in 1905 on West B Street. Basques also got together at the pool hall that was part of the Beitias' boardinghouse.

By the time World War II was over, the majority of the boardinghouses in rural south Idaho were closed, and Basque gatherings were a thing of the past. The sheep business began declining, and many turned to farming the fertile fields of the Snake River Plain.

Today. If you want to see any of the old boardinghouses in this part of Idaho, probably Shoshone is your best bet. **Soloaga's** place at 201 East A Street is probably the most remarkable, with its bold white star and two pillars in the front. It was a children's home for a while and is now a private residence. It's listed on a historic walking tour of Shoshone. (Pick up a brochure for the walking tour at city hall or the town library.) The current resident is attempting to restore the building, which is still in fine shape.

Dollie and Pete Oneida still live at the boardinghouse at 120 South Rail Street, known as **Oneida's,** and still had boarders in 1995. The exterior of the house, with its tin roof, is shabby, but the big warm kitchen still serves its purpose quite well. A collapsed wooden structure attached to Oneida's is apparently all that is left of Soloaga's former bowling alley. None of the Pagoaga family, which ran a boardinghouse in the first half of the century, is left in Shoshone. But the wood-frame house, which was a retirement home for a while, is still there, now full of apartments, across the street from Oneida's.

Across the railroad tracks is the **Berriochoas'** room-and-board house, with its picturesque setting next to a grove of trees and the creek. The Berriochoas quit the business in 1953, when Ramona Berriochoa died. But Carlos Berriochoa remained at the house on North Greenwood Street (Highway 93) on the edge of the Little Wood River until 1987, when he sold the place. It's now a private home. The current owner is considering remodeling and reopening the big old house. It is definitely worth stopping to see Soloaga's former fronton nearby, at 123 North Alta Street on the other side of the railroad tracks.

CEMETERY

If you're heading east out of town, you might want to stop by the picturesque **Shoshone Cemetery,** located on Highway 93 (also Highway 26) about a mile outside of town.

Gooding

In recent years not only has Gooding's population grown, but its Basque population has become highly organized. Gooding has a Basque club, the Gooding Basque Association, which hosts the largest Basque picnic in Idaho on the third Sunday in July—an event that attracts so many Basques and Americans from throughout the southern part of Idaho that the population of this small town practically doubles. In recent years, the club has raised enough money to build its own clubhouse, the Gooding Basque Cultural Center.

DANCE

For several years on the second or third Saturday in March, Gooding held its annual winter dance, attracting up to five hundred people at the War Memorial Hall on Third Avenue West. For years, Jim Jausoro's band provided music for dancing, and then it was the younger Ordago rock group's turn to perform. But dwindling attendance pushed the club to change the date to the Saturday before the annual picnic, when many people come to town. Boise's Oinkari dancers rent a bus and come en masse for their performance, given midway through the dance. They usually stay for the evening, livening the atmosphere. There are hot chorizo sandwiches for sale.

The change in date has made the weekend events even more popular, and out-of-towners from as far away as Canada travel to Gooding for the two-day festivities.

FESTIVAL

Gooding has put on a good, old-fashioned picnic on the third Sunday in July since 1982, the same year the Gooding Basque Association was organized. By then the Boise picnic, which had been popular for many years, had lost some of its pizzazz. But once the Gooding Basque Association started running their own picnic, the event picked up where the Boise one left off. Today Boise's Basques come to Gooding for the annual picnic at the Gooding County Fairgrounds (201 Lucy Lane on Highway 46).

The festivities start Saturday night with a dance at the cultural center. On Sunday, after an 11 A.M. Mass, usually celebrated by a local American priest, everybody eats the traditional lunch of pinto beans or garbanzos, Basque rice, and lamb chops off the grill. "We still kill our own pigs and make our own chorizos," said Linda Alzaa, emphasizing the authenticity of the meal. Many of those who come are American. Everybody loves the food and the beer. The Oinkariak, as well as Gooding's dancers or other nearby dance groups, perform. Kids compete in running races. Then there's weight-lifting, sheep hooking, and weight carrying, and there are chorizos to eat while you're watching. "It's usually 8:30 or 9:00 before we finish," said Andy Lejardi. By then it's time to go home, because many who come have a long drive home. The local club works hard to put on the picnic, but once it's over the members and their families get together again at West Park, on the third Sunday in August, to enjoy a smaller members-only picnic.

BASQUE CLUB

The **Gooding Basque Association,** organized in 1982, finally raised enough money to build its own clubhouse. Located at the junction of state highways 26 and 46, the **Gooding Basque Cultural Center** is 6,400 square feet. The building was completed at the end of 2002, and it is where the club holds its monthly dinner and dance practices. During the annual Basque festival, on the third Sunday of July, most activities are held at the Gooding County Fairgrounds, but the evening dance is held the night before at the center. The facility has been a popular location for weddings and parties, and it is rented out almost every weekend, said Andy Lejardi.

Lejardi is a pillar of the Gooding Basque Association; he was president for sixteen years. Lejardi says he doesn't mind shouldering the responsibility. He's worried because he sees the membership getting older every year. "That's our problem," he said. He was encouraged when Jud Astorquia, a young local rancher, served on the board of directors. The lack of young blood is reflected in other ways. The club's dance group lost its teacher in 1993. However, Julie Osarungo organized a dance group in 2004.

Mus. Ten or twelve teams get together for the club's annual *mus* tournament, which lasts for six weekends, from the first Sunday in December to the middle of January. "Wintertime there's not much going on," said Lejardi. "We like it to last. We play everybody against everybody." On the last Saturday of January there's a membership dinner to honor the winners.

Monthly Dinners. Now that the Gooding club has its own center, it puts on a monthly Basque dinner that is open to the public. The popular event, usually held on the first Friday of the month, attracts two to four hundred people.

Gooding Basque Association, Box 517, Gooding, ID 83330. Information: (208) 934-5905 (*Andy Lejardi*).
Basque Cultural Center, 285 Euskadi Lane (at junction of Highways 46 and 26), Gooding, ID 83330. Information: (208) 934-5577 (Julian Legarreta).

BASQUE FUND-RAISING DINNERS

In Gooding, Twin Falls, and Hagerman, local Basques, in conjunction with their Catholic churches, sponsored Basque dinners as fundraisers for years. The dinners were always held at the end of winter, when the men were in town for lambing, according to Father Juan Garatea. "The lamb was tastier then," he added. In Twin Falls and Hagerman, the dinners were always at the end of February. During the twelve years that Garatea was assigned to Our Lady of Guadalupe in Twin Falls, he helped organize the dinner. "Everything was for the church," he said. "The Basques donated food and time." When Garatea was transferred to Burley in 1992, the dinner tradition in Twin Falls died.

The roast lamb dinner and auction put on by **St. Catherine's Church** in Hagerman continues to be held on the first Saturday of April, at the Legion Hall on Main Street across from Hagerman High School. The tradition in Hagerman was started by longtime Basque resident María Larragan, possibly forty years ago. "Ours is getting bigger and bigger every year," said Carmen Zabala, adding that they served more than five hundred people at the dinner in 1994. In 2004, the dinner tradition continued.

In Gooding **St. Elizabeth's Catholic Church** sponsored a Basque dinner for years. When the Gooding Basque Association was formed, it took over the springtime event and turned it into a dance, according to club president Andy Lejardi. The church then picked the third Sunday in October for its annual Basque dinner, which features roast beef instead of lamb and continues at the Gooding Basque Cultural Center. That date is the opening day of pheasant hunting season, and the hunters who descend on the Gooding-Shoshone area have come to count on the hearty dinner, which attracts up to a thousand people.

BOARDINGHOUSES

There were at least two boardinghouses in Gooding in the first half of the century. The Casa Española was built by Claudio Ascuena in 1907. Ascuena and his wife, Gregoria, raised eight children in the house, which also served as the local hospital in the days before the small town of Gooding had an official hospital. The old house, originally located by the railroad station, was later moved outside town and is still standing today.

Antonia and Florencio Uriaguereca ran a hotel in a large brick building at 121 Second Avenue East from 1922 to 1935. Of those days, their daughter Lucia Osa remembers, "We were forever playing *mus*, *briska*, casino, and the stakes were either hot chocolate, chorizos, or dried sardines, real salty. Mother would put them on the hot coal stove to grill them, the ones that lost at cards would do the paying. She used to get the sardines from the Basque fish market in Boise." Osa still gets together with some of the older Basque women in town every month to play cards.

Osa's brother Luciano started a family grocery store, Uria's, downstairs, which remained open until 1978. (Like other families with long Basque names, they shortened theirs for easier pronunciation.) They sold Basque items such as dried codfish, pimentos, and Basque bread, remembers Andy Lejardi, who always shopped there. The building is still standing, but a second-hand store replaced the grocery store.

Henrietta and Felix Gamboa entered the hotel business in later years with a place on Fourteenth Avenue West, according to Osa. "It was a big beautiful old house," remembers Carmen Luther, who used to visit there with her family when she was young. But by the mid-1960s the Gamboas had closed down the business, and today it's the private residence of a local dentist. During the years when the hotel was open, boarders were sheepherders and employees at a local meat-packing plant. Lejardi was one of about twenty or so Basques who worked at the plant until it went bankrupt and closed in 1983. Perhaps this employer helped keep a local concentration of Basques in Gooding into the 1980s.

RESTAURANTS

Gooding had two Basque restaurants, the Biltoki and the Toki Ona, during the 1980s. The Toki Ona burned to the ground in 1986. The Biltoki's owner, Ramon Zugazaga, left Gooding and reopened a restaurant in Elko, Nevada. The former Biltoki, at 530 Main Street, remained in Basque hands for several years, under different names, but today it's the Wood River Inn, and there's nothing Basque about it. There is a bar in town that has been owned by Basques for many years. It's officially called T and J's Jai Alai Bar (*T* and *J* stand for Tina and Julian Legarreta), but townsfolk refer to the place by its longtime name, the Miramar. You're likely to find a few Basques there after work any day of the week.

CEMETERY

Early Basque settlers in this town are buried at the **Elmwood Cemetery** on Elmwood Road.

HARRI MUTILLAK AND A SWINGING BRIDGE

If you drive to Hailey from the Gooding-Shoshone area, there are a couple of roadside attractions that will make your hour-long trip more enjoyable. As you head north on Highway 75, look for the *harri mutillak*—stone boys—composed of piles of lava rock. You'll see them off to the west, in the flat, desertlike Snake River Plain, which is full of lava beds.

When you reach the intersection of Highways 75 and 20, take Highway 20 west toward Fairfield for about 4 miles. Take the turnoff for the Sheep Bridge, and one tenth of a mile south of the highway you'll find it: a quaint wooden-plank bridge suspended by cables over the Wood River. The narrow old-fashioned bridge is at least forty years old, probably older, and is still used by herders when they trail their sheep toward the summer pastures north of Ketchum. "When the sheep cross it, it starts swinging," said Bureau of Land Management livestock monitor Dean Brown. If you want to get a picture of the bridge in action, plan to be at the bridge in May or in late October or early November, when the sheep make the return trip. At those times you're also likely to run into sheep on the highways. The once wide-open Wood River Valley is now filling up with homes, and, sadly, herders are forced to trail their sheep more often along the highways for short stretches to get around housing developments. Sheep have always created traffic jams on Idaho's roads, and many newcomers to this state resent the inconvenience. "People have to realize that is the way life is here in Idaho," said Brown, who's heard his share of complaints. A big festival in Hailey, Idaho, The Trailing of the Sheep celebrates this lifestyle in recognition of the importance of the sheep industry in Idaho's history (see the Hailey section for more information on the festival.)

Twin Falls

BOARDINGHOUSES

In Twin Falls, Florentina and Francisco Sabala opened the town's first Basque boardinghouse in 1920. Located at 214 Second Street South, the boardinghouse once served as the town's hospital. The building was demolished in 1952. In 1925 Lorenzo and Benita Selaya opened a boardinghouse at 564 Main Avenue South, which they ran until 1946, when they sold the building. This beautiful house, built in 1908, stood until the 1990s, when a fire destroyed it.

Santa Bilbao opened the town's third hotel on Main Avenue South. In 1937 she left that building to build her own, which she operated until 1949. A few years later Aniceto and Alma Bengoechea bought the business from the Bilbao family and continued operating it until 1976, when they sold it to the city. Today the nicely kept building at 302 Second Avenue South is a refuge for abused women and their children.

Adela Olavarria ran a room-and-board place at 461 Second Avenue East about the same time that the Bengoecheas ran their business. The house is still in the family and has been well maintained over the years. Both the Olavarrias and the Bengoecheas ran bars in town as well.

RESTAURANT

During the 1990s, Twin Falls had a Basque restaurant for a couple of years, called The Basque Kitchen.

Jerome

BOARDINGHOUSES

In Jerome Mercedes Gogenola and her daughter Julie offered room and board at 220 North Lincoln from 1939 to 1955. There weren't too many Basques in Jerome, so the Gogenolas started serving dinners to outside groups at their hotel, a building that has now been remodeled into commercial offices. A couple of other Basque families in Jerome had boarders as well.

Rupert

SHEEP

Basques still own sheep outfits in Rupert and continue to host an annual Basque dinner there. In 2005, Henry Etcheverry, Robert Oxarango, and Larry Basterrechea were running some of the few sheep outfits left here. They spend the summers in Lava Hot Springs or Soda Springs, where the sheep pasture on Caribou National Forest lands. There's a close connection between these ranching families and those from Rock Springs, who summer with their sheep just on the other side of the Idaho-Wyoming border.

BOARDINGHOUSES

Louise Etcheverry ran a hotel in Pocatello for a few years, then moved to Rupert where she opened another one. In Rupert the best-known boardinghouse was La Chata's. Everyone knew the woman who ran it as Tia Chata, according to Father Juan Garatea, who often stopped by the place on the corner of Eighth and J Streets for a game of *mus* on Sunday evenings.

"She was a terrific cook," said Rupert resident John Treviño. "Even if you came in late, she could have a banquet on the table in twenty minutes." There were a couple other rooming houses nearby, but the men would all go down to Chata's to eat. Her old place, although a bit run-down, is now a private residence, painted a bright blue.

Basque dinners once held in nearby Pocatello died out, and its beautiful longtime boardinghouse burned down.

ANNUAL DINNER

Father Garatea arrived in Idaho in 1966, and at that time the annual Basque dinner for St. Nicholas Church in Rupert was already in full swing. It has always been held on the third Saturday of March, in celebration of the Feast of St. Joseph—patron saint of the "*hombres honrados*"—the good men. The proceeds of the dinner, known as the **St. Nicholas Basque Festival,** as well as an auction of a lamb and other donated items go to the Catholic school. The event outgrew the parish hall, so for the past few years it's been held at the Elks Lodge, a mile west of Rupert (at 200 West and 100 South Streets). Many of the older ladies who were once involved are gone, and John Treviño has been doing the cooking for the last few years.

Hailey

Hailey has continued to expand in recent years, partly as a the result of the growth of the resort town of Sun Valley. "Bellevue used to be five miles south of Hailey," said Pilar (Arriaga) Harris. "Now it's two miles." With forty-two hundred inhabitants, Hailey is the largest town in the region of ten thousand people.

Sun Valley has been growing by leaps and bounds, suffering growing pains as Californians and other urban escapees settle there, raising property values beyond the reach of working-class citizens. Hailey and Bellevue, on the other hand, have remained more blue-collar communities, where most of the resort employees live. Harris is none too happy about the growth. "I guess I don't take to change very well. People come from cities to small towns to get away from the big city, and they promptly bring their problems with them."

BOARDINGHOUSES AND BARS

Eusebio Arriaga and Pia Unamuno got married and established their hotel in Hailey in 1911. "And since then there's always been an Arriaga in Hailey," said Pilar (Arriaga) Harris. In addition to the Arriagas' place, there were the houses of the Mendiolas and the Menchacas, who had a handball court. They were five blocks west of the train depot, all around the intersection of River and West Bullion Streets, with a row of brothels smack in the middle. "Mother absolutely would not allow us to go down Bullion Street through the red-light district," remembers Harris. The Mendiola children had to come to the Arriagas if they wanted to play. Why did the Basques settle there? "That's the million-dollar question," chuckled Harris.

Eusebio Arriaga died fairly young, and Pia, unwilling to bring up three young girls in that atmosphere, left the boardinghouse business.

During those years, except for the Arriagas, most of the Basque families in Hailey only stayed through the summer. Then Julio and María Astorquia arrived and took over the Arriagas' business. The old Arriaga place served as a private residence until several years later, when a fire burned it down, killing two young children, according to Harris. The Urresti family had a boardinghouse in nearby Mackay during those years too.

In addition to the boardinghouses, there were at least two Basque bars in town. Pete Gesuraga had the Mint bar and restaurant and Boni Rementeria owned Boni's bar across the street, according to Andy Lejardi, who tended bar for his aunt at the Rialto for years.

In 1934 the Astorquia family decided to build their own hotel, the Rialto Hotel and Bar, on South Main Street. Many of the town's Basque dances and celebrations took place there. Soon after the Rialto opened, David and Epi Inchausti added to the lively social scene when they opened a bar and dining room known as the Gem Bar in what had been a Chinese laundry on West Bullion.

Epi Inchausti and Her Famous Home Cooking

Epi Inchausti got into the restaurant business without even trying. Word spread about Epi's exceptional cooking, and "it got so people would be sitting with the boarders," said Dorothy Ansotegui, one of Epi's daughters. Before long, she was cooking banquets for large groups. When a 1950 fire burned part of the Gem Bar where the boarders and guests were served, the whole dining room operation was moved to the family's big house across the street, at 19 West Bullion Street, which had once been a brothel.

Epi's popularity continued until well into the 1960s. Movie stars staying at the Sun Valley resort would drop by to eat. Once Clark Gable, Bing Crosby and Gary Cooper all came by on the same night, with a big party of people, according to Ansotegui. Much as the daughters loathed working in the dining room, they were all eager to help out that night, she remembered. Colonel Sanders, founder of Kentucky Fried Chicken, ate there once and praised Epi's fried chicken for being almost as good as his. Author Ernest Hemingway, who had a great fondness for the Basque Country, lived on a ranch in Ketchum for many years, and he reportedly came by fairly often. "He loved to go to Epi's just to visit and talk with the old sheepherders," said Carmen Luther, of Jerome, whose family stopped there often as well. For the visitors, the dining room was a unique place to have dinner. Ansotegui said that she and her sisters asked their mother where she learned to cook, and the former seamstress said she learned it all from cookbooks. Today, two of her grandchildren run successful Basque restaurants in the Boise area.

The family rented another building around the corner on River Street for boarders, and at meal time they all strolled into Epi's dining room to eat. This place became quite popular and gave the Basques a name in the region.

Although part of the old Gem Bar building is still there, it's a repair shop now and doesn't resemble its earlier self in the least. Except for the Rialto, all the other Basque hotels were torn down years ago. The Rialto stopped serving Basque food after the Astorquias sold it. Today, it is the **Hailey Hotel,** (208) 788-3140, and although it was modernized in 1982, the place's European Victorian style is relatively unchanged. In 2005, new owners were refurbishing the place, but the chandeliers and other such décor would remain in the historic building. The upstairs hotel rooms were possibly going to be converted into offices. The area's growth has spelled continued success for the small hotel and bar at 201 South Main Street, although less so since the restaurant downstairs became a bar in 1993. But it still gets quite a bit of business from Sun Valley tourists. "It's a nice well-kept place," said Joe Astorquia, who grew up there.

CEMETERY

The **Hailey Cemetery** (700 Fifth Avenue South), where many Basques are buried, was once surrounded by sheep corrals and farmland. Today it's in the middle of a subdivision of homes and a high school.

SHEEP

Sheep have always been a vital part of life in the Wood River Valley. Mining played a significant role in the establishment of the towns of Hailey, Bellevue, and Ketchum. But when mining faded, sheep ranching took its place. Basques found lots of work here. On their annual trek north to summer mountain pastures, the sheep always spent the night in the Hailey corrals, on the other side of the Big Wood River bridge. That was always a night of celebration for the herders, remembered Andy Lejardi: "We'd go downtown to visit all the bars and restaurants." In the fall the sheepherders would come through town to send their sheep off to market. Nearby Ketchum was among the biggest sheep shipping stations in the country, and every year thousands of sheep were herded onto stock cars there to be delivered to Chicago, Kansas City, and other points farther east.

Longtime Secretary of State Pete Cenarrusa is from Carey, just south of Hailey, and through 2000 his family's company continued running the sheep operation started by Pete's father, José María Cenarrusabeitia. Pete Cenarrusa has enjoyed a long political career, having been elected to the state legislature in 1950, where he served as speaker of the house for three terms. He was elected secretary of state in 1967, a job he held until 2002. He has held public office longer than any other elected official in the state.

SHEEP FESTIVAL

Today, a huge festival pays tribute to the local sheep industry. The **Trailing of the Sheep Festival,** which started in 1997, attracts about 10,000 visitors. The three-day event, usually held on the second weekend of October, includes sheep-dog trials, story-telling, sheep-shearing, spinning and weaving, along with dozens of other activities. St. Charles Church puts on an outdoor Basque dinner to raise funds (see page 432 for more information). Local restaurants feature lamb dishes, the local libraries and museums put on special exhibits, and a Dutch-oven bread-cooking class is offered. The Basques, who herded sheep here, too, are an integral part of the festivities. The Oinkari Dancers and Basque musicians perform annually at the Sheep Folklife Fair on Saturday, and event participants can take tours of the local aspen groves to see Basque tree carvings. Basque sheep rancher and longtime Idaho politician Pete Cenarrusa is a sponsor of the event. The 2006 festival is scheduled to highlight the Basques. Excellent photographs of Basque dancers are displayed on the festival's Web site, *www.trailingofthesheep.com.*

The weekend's events all lead up to Sunday's trailing of the sheep through downtown Ketchum, which highlights a practice that has become familiar in recent years as urbanization of the region has forced herders to trail their sheep along main thoroughfares. A parade of historic sheep wagons, dancers and musicians, along with spectators, join the hundreds of sheep on their trek through town. Dogs are not allowed on the trek.

Trailing of the Sheep Festival, P.O. Box 3692, Hailey, ID 83333 (800) 634-3347; *www.trailingofthesheep.org*

Picnics and Dinners

Back in the 1940s there was at least one Basque summer picnic up at Trail Creek Summit, near the summer sheep trail. During the 1970s the Sun Valley resort attempted to capitalize on the popularity of Basque food and sponsored a similar picnic at Trail Creek, but it apparently did not last more than a couple of years.

Parishioners from Hailey's Catholic church, many of them Basque, have organized an annual Basque dinner over fifty years. The **St. Charles Annual Basque Dinner** started merely as a way to raise some money for the church. It turned into the social event of the year in Hailey, surpassed only by the Fourth of July rodeo.

"We really have a name," said Pilar Arriaga Harris, who was one of the main cooks for the dinner. "People come from all over." She knew of people who came for a good fifteen years from as far away as Pocatello. The dinner was held on the last Saturday in September at the church hall for more than forty years. After the Trailing of the Sheep Festival began in 1997, the dinner was combined with that event.

St. Charles Church held its first Basque dinner in 1946 or 1947 at the Rialto Hotel, according to Harris. An annual St. Patrick's Day dance had not proven too successful, so a priest suggested hosting a Basque dinner to raise money for the church, since Basque food was popular. Epi Inchausti and María Astorquia cooked for those first benefits. They served the meals at the two boardinghouses until a new church hall was built that could accommodate the big crowds. Harris has remained involved in the organization for many years, but other Basque and non-Basque parishioners have gradually learned the recipes for cooking lamb, beans, and other dishes and have taken leadership roles. "It's good food, and it's such fun," said Harris.

Today, the dinner is served on Saturday and is part of the continual entertainment at the Sheep Folklife Fair at Roberta McKercher Park on Highway 75 in Hailey (see page 431 for more information). The meal, served from 11 A.M. to 4 P.M. includes lamb, Spanish rice, Basque beans, a glass of red wine, coffee, and dessert. People can also choose lamb or chorizo sandwiches. The church still serves about

1,000 people over the course of the afternoon, said Sister Regina Burrichter. For more information, call St. Charles Church (208) 788-3024.

REFERENCES

Douglass, William A., and Jon Bilbao. *Amerikanuak: Basques in the New World.* Reno, Nev.: University of Nevada Press, 1975, pp. 117–76.

Edlefsen, John B. *A Sociological Study of the Basques of Southwest Idaho.* Diss., State College of Washington, 1948, pp. 133–34.

———. *Emendik Nora? (From Here to Where?).* Boise, Idaho: Idaho Humanities Council, 1990.

———. *Jaialdi 90.* Boise, Idaho: Euzkaldunak, Inc., 1990.

Silen, Sol. *La historia de los Vascongados en el oeste de los Estados Unidos.* New York: Las Novedades, 1917.

Oregon and Washington

Oregon

Jordan Valley

For anyone driving from Winnemucca to Boise, Jordan Valley is a must-see. Up through the 1960s, three quarters of a mile up the hill north of town a sign announced to Highway 95 motorists that Jordan Valley was HOME OF THE BASQUES. The high concentration of Basques in this rural outpost was so unusual that it became the focus of several academic studies. Set aside a few hours to spend in this quaint little town, where Basques played an influential role at the beginning of the twentieth century and where several vestiges of their influence still remain.

Many buildings in Jordan Valley—the Elorriaga home, the Jordan Valley Hotel, the church, and the bank—were built of sandstone brought from a quarry two miles outside town, the stone blocks hewn by hand. Around 1915 Ambrosio Elorriaga, Domingo Yturri, and several other Basque stonemasons built a fronton on Bassett Street between the Yellow House and the Jordan Valley Hotel. It was to be Oregon's only handball court. Today it still stands, recently restored after many years of abandonment, just across the way from the Old Basque Inn restaurant, formerly a Basque boardinghouse.

Jordan Valley was originally a stage stop along a north-south route. Basques probably first passed through here in the 1860s and 1870s, when early discoveries of gold along the Jordan Creek brought fortune hunters. But Basques did not begin settling here until 1889. Antonio Azcuenaga and José Navarro are believed to have been the first to arrive and settle here in 1889. They set out from the thriving mining town of McDermitt at the Nevada border on foot with a pack horse, heading north across the desert to the Jordan Valley, where they had heard of the opportunities for raising sheep. They got lost and ran out of water during the harrowing trip, which took them almost a week.

Despite the fact that there were no Basques in Jordan Valley before Navarro and Azcuenaga started raising sheep in the area, it was a mere twenty to thirty years before Basques dominated the local population. Jordan Valley was referred to as "the Basque settlement."

This sign announced the Basque settlement of Jordan Valley, Oregon, for many years until it finally fell down during the 1960s. (Courtesy of the Basque Studies Library, University of Nevada Reno.)

In addition to the Azcuenagas and Navarros, who were joined by other relatives, other big or prominent families in the area were the Eigurens, the Elorriagas, the Yturris, and the Elordis. Azcuenaga and his brother Agustín built up a significant sheep operation in the area, Cow Creek Ranch. They were instrumental in initiating the Jordan Valley Irrigation District, a series of dams and feeder canals to divert flood water for irrigation of the semiarid valley.

The Basque migration in the West followed other migrant groups who headed in a northeasterly direction. From Winnemucca, they had moved to McDermitt, which was primarily a mining town, and from there into Oregon, to Jordan Valley and Ontario. At the same time some were settling in Jordan Valley, others were trekking into Boise and other towns in southwestern Idaho. The largest Basque migration into these areas occurred between 1900 and 1920. Basques could also be found in other smaller nearby settlements: Andrews and Fields in Oregon; Paradise Valley and Denio in Nevada; De Lamar and Silver City in Idaho. Many first came to mine silver in these latter two early boomtowns but soon made their way into the prospering sheep business.

Basque immigration into Jordan Valley probably peaked in 1920, although it continued steadily into the 1930s. The town never grew very large, numbering perhaps six hundred families in the entire Jordan Creek Valley. Basque families represented about two thirds of the population. Scholar Joseph Gaiser who studied the rural area in the 1940s estimated that at that time Basques owned 50 percent of the local farms and represented about 90 percent of the area's sheep owners. They also filled the posts of mayor and council members at different times.

Second-generation Basques own most of the town's commercial businesses, such as its second restaurant, the two motels and gas stations, and the grocery store, all of which are located right on the main drag, Highway 95. Basques helped build the town's stone Catholic church, and their complex names dominate the hand-hewn headstones in the old cemetery.

Despite the small size of this town, it generated two state leaders—first cousins John Elorriaga and the late Anthony Yturri. Law school–educated Yturri, son of Domingo and María Yturri, became a five-term state senator who considered running for governor. He headed the Oregon Transportation Commission for many years and retired in Ontario, Oregon. Elorriaga, also an attorney, was CEO of the powerful U.S. Bank Corporation for many years.

The Sheep Ranch Fort and the Eiguren Ranch

The Sheep Ranch Fort in Arock, located on the Eiguren Ranch, is the oldest building in Malheur County. This stone building served as a refuge for travelers on the stage line between California and Silver City. Later it harbored U.S. Cavalry soldiers sent to protect local settlers from attacks by local Indian tribes. According to Fred J. Eiguren, the first story of the fort was built in 1863, and the second was added in 1873, when the soldiers were stationed there. Eight portholes were built into its walls, which are three feet thick and made from local sandstone and mud. The fort's name, purportedly given in 1864, indicated that sheep were being raised in this area long before the Basques arrived here.

Cousins Pascual Eiguren and Manuel Navarro bought the large ranch on which the fort was located in 1914, with money loaned to them from their uncle, José Navarro. The Eiguren family lived in the old fort for more than forty years. During the 1950s Catholic Mass was celebrated for the local community in the old fort, until the Holy Family Catholic Church was built in Arock in 1958. In 1959 Eiguren's son, Fred, moved his family to a house built nearby. The fort now stands empty, but it's still part of the Eiguren Ranch, which is now run by Fred's two sons; it is probably the oldest ranch in the area, having been established in 1860. Today the Eigurens raise cattle, hay, and grain.

Although the ranch and historic fort are located way off the beaten path, anyone going through the area can easily find them. "You can't miss it," said Fred J. Eiguren, explaining that it's on Highway 95, known locally as the old ION (Idaho–Oregon–Nevada) Highway, 2 miles west of Arock. The fort is in disrepair, according to Eiguren. He cautions visitors to stay out of the building. The family hopes to restore the structure eventually.

Hazel Fretwell-Johnson, a longtime writer for the *Owyhee Outpost* who wrote a history of the lower Jordan Creek communities like Arock, highlighted the historic stone fort as well as a landmark sheep bridge, built by ranchers Lázaro Urquiaga and John Acarregui in 1909. The bridge was needed to allow sheep to cross the Jordan Creek when it was swollen from winter rains. "It took ingenuity and proficiency to build a bridge of this length with so little support to hold its weight," she wrote in her book *In Times Past: A History of the Lower Jordan Creek Communities*. The bridge, moored to lava rock on either side, became useless when the Antelope Reservoir dam and other smaller dams were built on the creek, and it finally collapsed in the 1930s.

BOARDINGHOUSES

In Jordan Valley just after the turn of the century Basques built homes and boardinghouses, turning the town into a thriving center. José Navarro had the Monopole Hotel and livery stables. Agustín Azcuenaga was an early owner of the Jordan Valley Hotel, established in 1880 and rebuilt in 1912. The hotel was part of a large brick commercial complex located at the northwest corner of Yturri Boulevard and Highway 95 that also had a bar and a theater. There were also boardinghouses belonging to the Yturris, the Madariagas, and the Elorriagas.

Domingo Yturri came to Jordan Valley in 1908 after working in the mines at De Lamar, Idaho, for several years. On Bassett next to the handball court he built a boardinghouse that was referred to as "the Yellow House," remembered his son Anthony Yturri. Domingo Yturri quickly sold his place to his sister Eustaquia Marquina and her husband, who continued to run the boardinghouse for many years. Yturri then became a partner in the Helm and Yturri general store, opposite the Jordan Valley Hotel. Eventually he took over the popular grocery store and ran it for forty years, until he sold it to the Elordi family.

Ambrosio Elorriaga left his wife and two daughters back in the Basque Country and came to America in 1911. He, like Yturri, his brother-in-law, mined in De Lamar. When he had built up a little nest egg, he wrote and asked his wife and family to join him. But she told him she wasn't about to bring her children to Indian country, recounted her son John Elorriaga. So to entice his wife to join him, Ambrosio Elorriaga built an exact replica of her family home in Sondika near Bilbao. When it was done, the two-story stone Elorriaga house was one of the finest in town. The house, with its 18-inch walls and sleeping porches, slept seventeen people. Elorriaga, who was injured in the mines, died fairly young, and the boardinghouse provided his wife with a livelihood so that she could raise her four children. The big stone Elorriaga house is still standing, less than 50 yards from the town's handball court. For many years, it sat overgrown with trees and shrubs, with a mystery-house appeal. It was eventually donated to serve as a museum (see the museum section in Jordan Valley).

Many Basque couples, such as Eulogio and Trinidad Madariaga, got married in Boise before they came to live in Jordan Valley. The Madariagas, both of whom immigrated from Bizkaia, ran the Overland Hotel in Boise for a few years before moving to Jordan Valley. Eulogio took a job tending bar at the Jordan Valley Hotel for a short time, then the Madariagas bought the house at 308 Wroten Street, expanded it, and ran it as a boardinghouse for many years. They raised their own hogs and cows, which they slaughtered to feed the family and the boarders. Sunday nights were dedicated to dancing to a player piano and accordion. Many of the town's babies were born at the house, with Trinidad serving as midwife. The Madariagas raised eleven children in the house before they finally sold it in the late 1940s.

The Ebb and Flow of the Basque Community

In the early days Basque ranching families got together in Jordan Valley to celebrate religious holidays, and the festivities rotated among the boardinghouses, with Christmas at Marquina's, New Year's at the Madariagas', and the Three Kings Day at the Elorriagas', according to Aiden Madariaga. These celebrations often made up for the lack of church services, when there was no priest in residence at St. Bernard's. Within this tight-knit Basque community, the immigrant generation was able to maintain a strong cultural identity. In fact, Basques were so isolated within their own community that most of their offspring spoke only Basque when they started school, but their teachers reportedly forbade them to speak Euskara in school.

Sarah Baker in her thesis "Basque-American Folklore in Eastern Oregon," documented evidence of local traditions from the Basque Country that were not really practiced anywhere else in the West, except in Jordan Valley and perhaps in Boise. On New Year's Day the men, most probably the young Basque herders, trekked from house to house singing a ditty called "Urte Barri Ekarri," ("Bringing in the New Year") hoping to be offered a drink in return. On St. Agatha's Day (February 5), referred to in Basque as Santa Agueda, the children would imitate the pattern, singing a "Santa Agueda" song. They expected bacon and sausages in return, which they skewered onto sticks that they carried along until they had collected enough for a feast, hosted by one of the boardinghouses. The concentration of Basque homes in Jordan Valley probably allowed the Basque youngsters to carouse with one another easily.

The series of events that sounded the death knell for Jordan Valley's sheep business, and as a result, that of the Basque community here, were aptly described by Sarah Baker in her dissertation. Immigration quotas imposed in 1924 severely restricted the arrival of Bizkaitarrak, who had filled the local demand for herders. Disease, drought, and then the depression forced many sheepmen into bankruptcy. The Bank of Jordan Valley closed in the crash of 1929. The last straw was the Taylor Grazing Act, passed in 1934, restricting public grazing lands to land-owning ranchers who had applied for citizenship. A town that was already small soon became smaller.

Assimilation was not long in coming. Basque families began

intermarrying with others, Irish in particular, and the language was lost. The pelota court probably fell into disuse by the 1940s. "After the war, people started settling down to different lifestyles," said Jordan Valley native Aiden Madariaga. Younger family members moved to Ontario, Nampa, Caldwell, and Boise in search of jobs. The Basque population shrank. Already in 1972 Baker found that only 14 of the town's 196 residents had actually migrated from the Basque Country. Today probably very few (if any) of them remain. The Basques who do live here are descendants of families who once lived on isolated ranches nearby. Old-timers from Jordan Valley isolated themselves, rarely participating in Basque events in Boise. Some families have kept their properties, and family members and friends regularly return on Memorial Day weekend to visit the cemetery.

Much of the old Basque heritage disappeared in this town. Under the weight of time, the handball court all but collapsed. The Yturri store is gone. The hotel Domingo Yturri built next to the handball court was torn down over twenty years ago. The HOME OF THE BASQUES sign by the highway disappeared by the wayside. The roof of the dance hall and movie theater that were part of the Jordan Valley Hotel complex collapsed in 1951, and the building was never repaired. The restaurant in the complex was restored by Jimmy Elordi as a big bar in the 1970s, and locals gathered for parties there. But in the end the building could not be saved. "It would have cost too much to fix it," said Madariaga, noting that there was not enough business in town to support the cost of rebuilding. There are barely four hundred people in Jordan Valley.

Today modern commercial buildings have replaced the old ones, and some people worry that Jordan Valley will fade into the landscape as just another colorless small town. After the early silver boom at De Lamar, Jordan Valley quickly became a ghost town. But for the past twenty years, an open pit ore mine has been in operation in De Lamar, attracting a new population of miners to Jordan Valley. Many of these newcomers are oblivious of the town's Basque history.

PELOTA

Basques hope to revive some of the town's history with the restoration of the old fronton, the only court in the state. "We would

The handmade stone fronton in Jordan Valley, Oregon, built circa 1910, endured without repairs until 1997, when it was restored to its original state. The restoration was celebrated with a huge Basque party. (Photo by David Reyes.)

hope to have Basque tournaments there, but our primary goal was to preserve it," said City Recorder Ila Harnar, who was on the restoration committee. Plans to repair the court had been discussed since 1970, when the Elorriaga family donated the property to the Oregon Historical Society, which pledged to repair the court and collected $700 in donations. After years of dragging its feet, the society finally deeded the property to the city in 1990. The city was working jointly with the Malheur Historical Project out of Vale, which received a corporate grant that funded an architectural study. When the court began crumbling through neglect, the city took over the project and established a sixteen-member restoration committee. Then a large tractor-trailer crashed into the corner of the court, tearing a big chunk out of the corner and making restoration plans even more urgent, according to Harnar.

Despite years of delays and inaction, serious efforts to restore the fronton were begun in the 1990s. A thermometer citing incoming donations was posted on the court, and the money came in slowly, in small sums, to the Fronton Committee. When one of the court's biggest advocates Jordan Valley–born Pete Araquistain died in 1994, many memorial contributions were sent in his name. With the help of grant money, nearly $70,000 was collected, and the court was restored to its original splendor in 1997. A small park surrounded by wrought iron was built around it, and a brick memorial with names requested by contributors was included. Harner said that the memorial bricks became the most successful moneymaker, and after people saw how beautiful the memorial was, they continued to send in contributions to have names added. The bricks were inlaid by locals, who showed up in great numbers to help out.

The fronton was inaugurated in September 1997 with a party bigger than Jordan Valley had seen in many years. Nearly fifteen hundred people, many of them descendants of Jordan Valley Basques, came from all over for the festival. "It was like a great big reunion," said lifelong resident Mitzi Elordi. Out-of-town handball players gave the crowd a show, and Boise's Oinkari dancers and other dance groups performed. At least six hundred people enjoyed the evening barbecue. The festivities were repeated in September 2003, and Elordi said they will probably organize such an event every few years.

The manager of the Pelota RV Park (Highway 95, Jordan Valley; [541] 586-2477) next to the fronton said people occasionally stop and play a game. Spaces are available for travelers to pitch a tent or park their trailer next to the historic site.

MUSEUM

The Elorriaga family, who donated the pelota court for its eventual restoration in 1997, more recently donated the longtime family home (see section on boardinghouses) next to the court so that it can be converted into a museum. The two-story stone house with its porches and veranda had been empty for a few years and was hidden by overgrowth when the Jordan Valley Owyhee Heritage Council approached its owner, John Elorriaga, about a museum idea, said council member Jennifer Trautman. The house was full of such historical items as antique furniture, clothing from Spain, and musical instruments when the Elorriagas donated it in 2003.

The council auctioned some of the historical items to raise funds for the restoration and creation of the museum, but kept representational pieces for the museum's collection. It will not be an exclusively Basque museum, said Trautman, but rather a regional museum with exhibits on mining and cattle and sheep ranching, as well as on cultural and ethnic groups, including the Basques, Chinese, and Native Americans. The house's history as a Basque boardinghouse will definitely be reflected in the new museum, to be named ION Heritage Museum (Idaho, Oregon, and Nevada). "The original rock structure has been added onto over the years," noted Trautman, and some of the additions need to be restored. Opening of the museum was expected in 2006.

ION Heritage Museum, 502 Swisher Avenue, Jordan Valley, OR 97910. Information: (541) 586-2233 (Bob Skinner) or (541) 586-2216 (Mike Hanley)

RESTAURANT

The focal point of any visit to Jordan Valley will be the fronton and before long, the museum. But for those who pause in search of the town's rich Basque history, there are other treasures as well. The Madariaga boardinghouse is now a restaurant called the **Old Basque Inn,** and the place looks much like it did in its early days. The restaurant serves Basque dishes, although not family-style, and its menu contains an equal number of American dishes, including several hamburger plates. After longtime local resident Gary Moran bought the place in the early 1980s, Aiden Madariaga, who grew up in the house, kept trying to convince him to turn it into a restaurant—so he did in 1983. The current owners continue the Basque traditions.

Because of the state's strict laws prohibiting the serving of alcohol, you can't get beer or wine in this restaurant—a far cry from Prohibition years, when some Basques were known to make moonshine in the hills along the Owyhee River and served it regularly at the boardinghouses. Old-timers remembered with fondness those days of hidden stills and bootleggers delivering the stuff in fancy cars. Any worries they may have experienced are forgotten in the storytelling.

Old Basque Inn, 308 Wroten Street, Jordan Valley, OR 97910 (541) 586-2800

CHURCH

The Basques in this town joined with the few Irish Catholic families to build a Catholic church, **St. Bernard's,** on Main Street in 1914. The church, on the east end of town, is still well maintained. According to Sarah Baker, the names of Yturri, Marquina, and Chertudi are among those of local builders etched on the Catholic Church's high tower.

BASQUE BUSINESSES

For years, if you stopped by the **Sahara Motel** or Chevron gas station at 607 Main Street (541) 586-2500, you might have been lucky enough to run into owner Aiden Madariaga, who was full of stories about the old days in Jordan Valley. "I get quite a few Basques going through here on their way to Boise," said Madariaga, who loved to tell the stories. They don't take me for a Basque. I surprise the hell out of them when I start speaking Basque to them." Today, his son Johnny Madariaga runs the businesses. Basque-Americans also own the other motel and gas station in town—Jim (Zatica)'s Shell Station and the **Basque Station Motel** at 801 Main St., (541) 586-2244—and the only bar, **J. V. Club and Café,** (541) 586-7982, also on Main

Street. Brother and sister Jim and Mitzi Elordi own the bar, which also has a restaurant that serves American food. For years, the Telleria family ran Telleria's market located in the original 1919 building, but Robert Telleria admits it is unremarkable, having been remodeled and modernized many times over the years. The family sold the building in 2005, and it was boarded up.

Old Jail and Pony Express Building

Take a peak behind the old market at 603 Main Street to find a delightful hidden relic from earlier days—the town's original two-room jail. "Just the way you picture the old West—that's what it looks like," said Robert Telleria. The original Pony Express building is also still standing.

CEMETERY

To really get a sense of the great number of early Basque pioneers who once populated the area, stop at the **Jordan Valley Cemetery** on Highway 95, half a mile north of town. "It's the first thing you see as you approach Jordan Valley from Boise," said Aiden Madariaga in 1994. "That is where most of the Basque population is right now." Two Basques in Jordan Valley carved several of the headstones by hand from stone. The cemetery has been kept up nicely, with newly planted grass and fir trees. "They really flock in here on Memorial Day," said Madariaga.

HARRI MUTILLAK

If you are driving from Jordan Valley to Burns via Highway 78, make sure you look for the *harri mutillak* (stone boys) that the herders built out of the region's abundant lava rock. These are some of the best preserved and easiest to see. You'll spot them among the sagebrush about halfway between Burns Junction and New Princeton, near the intersection with the road that leads to Crowley. "They're about six feet from the road," said Bob Boyd, curator of the High Desert Museum in Bend, Oregon. Boyd has traveled the Great Basin in search of artifacts for an outstanding Basque exhibit for the museum (see the section on Bend, Oregon). "There's some that must be eight feet tall out there," Boyd reported. The *harri mutillak* guided the herders to their winter campsites around Saddle Butte year after year and served as markers in the fog that sometimes covered the wide open expanses. "The lava made great stacking rock because it was flat," said Boyd.

Basque Station

If you intend to drive south on Highway 95 into Nevada, you're likely to spot the name Basque Station on your map. You won't see anything remarkable when you pass through this location. The name supposedly was coined because of the dominance of Basques among the crew at the highway maintenance station.

Burns

Burns probably has had the longest-running Basque colony in Oregon. Starting in the 1920s Basques have herded sheep here, summering on nearby Steens Mountain or in the Pueblo Mountains near Denio, Nevada. And when the sheep industry slackened, many found employment in the successful Hines lumber mill. New immigrants were arriving in Burns as recently as the 1960s, and Euskara is still spoken by their children today.

BOARDINGHOUSES

There were really only two boardinghouses in Burns—the Star and the Plaza Hotels—and both were in operation for many years. Basques also ran the Commercial Hotel, now a derelict building on Egan Street, but it was strictly a rooming house; no meals were served.

The Star Hotel, built in 1911, first served as a maternity house and only began offering room and board to Basques in 1926, under Felix and Cecilia Urizar. The couple ran the hotel for twenty years before the business was taken over by Pedro and Elvira Zabala, who had the place for years and years.

The Plaza Hotel operated from 1939 to 1981, changing hands many times before Lucy Garatea took it over in 1948. Lucy Garatea came to the United States at age fifteen in 1920 to work for her aunt, Gabina Aguirre, at the Star Rooming House in Boise. In 1948 the widowed Garatea came to Burns and took over the Plaza Hotel. "I ran it all by myself," said the eighty-nine-year-old woman in 1994, "washing, ironing, and taking care of the guys." "I've never seen women work so hard," said Garatea's granddaughter, Paquita Garatea, who remembers seeing her grandmother soaking sheets in the bathtub with bluing. Her place was so clean you could eat off the floor, according to the younger Garatea. Garatea finally retired from the business in 1965 and moved to Boise. María Lete later took over the business until 1981, when she finally sold it to a non-Basque.

Paquita Garatea was the granddaughter of Lucy Garatea and of Marcelino and Margarita Osa, earlier owners of the Plaza. Now a history professor, Garatea thinks that the important role Basque women have played in maintaining the culture in this country has been overlooked. In a master's thesis entitled "Etxeko Andreak: Women Boarding House Keepers," Garatea focused on the fact that her grandmothers, along with many other Basque women, were the ones running the hotels—not the men. You can listen to Garatea's taped interviews with the boardinghouse women of Burns, including Zabala, Lete, and Osa, which are on file at the **Harney County Library** (80 West D Street), many of them in Basque with English translations. "I wanted to get the language down so it would be preserved," said Garatea.

The old Plaza on Madison Street finally burned down in 1991, but the **Star Hotel** at 537 North Alder is still perfectly preserved and surrounded by a beautiful flower garden. Drive by and take a look. "It's incredible," Garatea said, noting that the eighty-year-old house has not been changed one iota. Even through 1992, when Pedro Zabala passed away, Elvira was using a coal furnace and hanging the clothes out to dry. The Oregon Historical Society has approached the family about putting the house on the National Register of Historic Places. The Zabalas stopped housing boarders in the 1970s, but for years the local Basques continued to stop by to chat and drink their coffee royals or to play a game of cards. "When you'd go in there, you felt like you were still in a boardinghouse," said Garatea. "You wouldn't hear English being spoken."

SHEEP AND A LUMBER MILL

Basques first came to Burns, probably in the 1920s and 1930s, to herd for American sheepmen, but eventually a few established their own outfits. Tom Zabala and Joe Madarieta had some of the largest flocks. But as the industry declined, Basques increasingly looked for jobs at the lumber mill, built in nearby Hines in the 1930s. The owners closed the mill during the 1980s for a major modernization, breaking the union at the same time. Many longtime Basque workers lost their jobs, but when the new, slimmed-down operation reopened, just as many were rehired. "Everything changed then," said Juanita Andueza, whose husband Agustín was one of those who were rehired.

BASQUE CLUB

For many years there was an informal organization among the Basques in Burns, and social gatherings were held at the boardinghouses. In the 1960s and 1970s the group, officially known as the Harney County Eskualdunak, sponsored picnics at Veterans Memorial Park and held Christmas and New Year's parties. But a quarrel led to the dissolution of the club.

Through the years, the Basques in the West have lent very little support to the cause of nationalism in the Basque Country. But there were occasional offers of aid, namely from Boise, particularly after the highly publicized 1970 Burgos trials, which put the Basque cause in the spotlight worldwide. But in Burns, when some club members offered club money to help, a major controversy ensued.

A group of Boise Basques, including Idaho Secretary of State Pete Cenarrusa, had decided to send money to the Basque Country for the families of the political prisoners. According to Cenarrusa, the Basque community of Burns was approached for donations. A group of Burns Basques called an informal meeting at the Star Hotel and agreed to use some money from the club's coffers to make a donation. Other club members, including the president, were left out of the meeting, and when they found out about the decision, they were furious, Cenarrusa reported. The members who had been left out sued the others for reimbursement of the money and refused to talk to them. Cenarrusa played mediator. "I just wrote my own check to pay it off," he said—but to no avail. The lines were drawn according to which of the two hotels Basques frequented, and the women and children were involuntarily drawn into the feud. It continued for years, and as a result the club was dissolved.

During the 1980s Basque culture in the community faded. After more than a decade of silence between the two groups, the women finally decided it was time to set aside their differences and form a new club to revive the traditions. They established **Danak Bat** in 1991. They revived the picnic, and for a few years organized a young dance group.

Responding to frequent requests for Basque food, the group of about twenty women decided to cook dinners for private groups as a way of making money. The proceeds were used for scholarships for young people. Legislators from the area have had Basque meals catered from the women's group at the state capitol in Salem. The catering came to an end, however. "Everybody has moved away from Burns," said Maria Iturriaga.

A few of the women still clean up the Basque grave markers in anticipation of Memorial Day. "There are some really old ones here that nobody takes care of," said Iturriaga, who headed the club for a while. Members bought dozens of miniature Basque flags to post at the seventy or so graves in the Burns Cemetery.

In 1994 the group jumped at the chance to showcase the Basque culture when the city asked the Basques to sponsor its summer Diversity Festival. Underground cooking, sheep-shearing, and dancing were among the traditions demonstrated at the event.

For the past few years the group has focused its energy on putting on an annual picnic, held the last Saturday in June at Hines Park. A small dance group composed of young children has performed at the picnic, as well as in the Harney County Fair Parade. Local Basque Avel Diaz reigned as grand marshal of the Fair Parade in 1996.

Basques have made their mark in this county, where the last three elected county clerks have been full-blooded Basques—Avel Diaz, Dolores Swisher, and in 1996, Maria Iturriaga.

CEMETERY

If you are in the Burns area around Memorial Day, be sure to stop by the **Burns Cemetery,** on West Monroe Street (Highway 20), to see the Basque flags at the grave sites. The older graves are on the hillside, and the more recent ones are around the Catholic altar on the north side of the cemetery.

RESTAURANT

After several years in the restaurant business, Tony Diaz decided in 1994 to open a Basque restaurant in Burns. He called it the Steens Mountain Café, in tribute to the many Basque men, including his father, Avel Diaz, who spent so many years on the mountain. Tony learned to cook from his father, whose first job was as a scrub in the sheep camp. At the time, it was probably the only Basque restaurant in Oregon, but unfortunately the business didn't last long.

ASPEN CARVINGS

Evidence of the time the Basque men spent in the mountains is in plain view in an aspen grove referred to as "Whorehouse Meadow." This place is well known by area residents. The carvings depict women with or without their clothes, names and dates, most of them from the 1920s, 1930s, and the 1940s. The carvings marked a camp of prostitution that was apparently well used during those years. "It was a place where in the summer, the entrepreneurs would bring ladies in there to sell themselves," said Bruce Crespin, archaeologist for the Bureau of Land Management.

Some of the carvings are so old they have deteriorated and can no longer be deciphered. Nevertheless, the grove, close to the popular Fish Lake resort, is the highlight of many visitors' trips up into Steens Mountain, according to Crespin. "Given the age of them, I have no doubt that they are Basque," said Crespin. And at least one Basque in Burns admits authorship.

The grove is located on private property belonging to a local realtor, who bought it as a retreat but who has long since resigned himself to sharing his piece of paradise with the world. To get there, take Highway 205 south from Burns for about 50 miles to the town of Frenchglen. From there, take the North Loop Road east to Fish Lake. Continue for 2 miles beyond the Fish Lake campground until you see the sign for Honeymoon Lake. The meadow is on the north side of the road, opposite the sign. This road is best traveled in a pickup or four-wheel-drive vehicle, and, remember, it is only clear of snow between July and October.

Locals describe the Fish Lake setting as spectacular, so if you're interested in camping, this might be the place for you. The North Loop Road makes a 66-mile circle around the mountain, so if you continue on, it will eventually bring you back to Frenchglen. If you're interested in exploring the mountain's more remote roads to seek out other carvings, be sure to stop by the Bureau of Land Management office in Hines (HC74, 12533 Highway 20 West) for a map of the southern half of the BLM's Burns District.

Antelope Refuges

If you're on the lookout for other things to do in the area, you might want to visit the Hart Mountain National Antelope Refuge to the east and the Sheldon Antelope Refuge just across the border in Nevada. (For more information on the Sheldon refuge, headquartered at an old Basque ranch, see the section on Winnemucca, Nevada.)

Ontario

Ontario is located on the western fringe of the Treasure Valley, which overlaps the Idaho-Oregon border, and it is home to many Basques. A lot of Basques who came to the area were herders. Over time they left the range and took permanent city jobs. Several worked as bartenders, and a few got jobs as janitors. While the sheep industry around Jordan Valley declined, agriculture prospered around Ontario. The construction of dams and reservoirs increased the productivity of the Snake River Plain, and Ontario became the center of an economy fueled by irrigated row crops and dairy farms. As time went by Ontario grew into a city offering greater job possibilities, which attracted more Basques. Not many went into farming, which was dominated by the Japanese locally. In the last twenty years, a few Basques, particularly from California, have gotten into the dairy business, settling around Nyssa, Vale, and New Plymouth, and also in Idaho around Weiser and Payette.

Jack and María Echanis—The Root of the Basque Colony

María Echanis cooked for the herders who worked for the sheep outfit owned by her husband Jack and his brothers, and the men persuaded her to move from Burns to Ontario to provide them with room and board. By then the town had two thousand residents. The first house in which they opened the boardinghouse burned down in 1930. The fire started when a pot-bellied stove exploded, according to the Echanis' daughter Josephine Keim. An older brother was burned, although not seriously, and everyone else got out safely. Not to be deterred, the Echanises built another large beautiful house at the same location. The family had a bountiful garden, and in addition to cooking for all the boarders and her five children and keeping her house spic-and-span, María canned about a thousand jars of fruits and vegetables every year, Keim reported. "How she did it, we don't understand." Maria would also cook dinners for groups, such as the friends of attorney Anthony Yturri, who was a regular there. The strong-willed woman continued cooking until she was ninety-two, when the last boarder passed away. "She buried seventeen of them who never married and never went back to the Basque Country," said Keim.

BOARDINGHOUSES

Ontario was a small town when eastern Oregon's biggest stockyards were built in the area in 1890. Basque herders accompanying their sheep often stopped over in Ontario. But it wasn't until María Echanis opened the Echanis Boarding House (115 North Oregon Street) in 1922 that a Basque community took hold here. In fact, María and Jack Echanis were probably the first Basques to set down roots here.

The Echanises were largely responsible for the early development of a Basque colony in Ontario. The railroad didn't come through Ontario; it was in nearby Vale. That's where Francisco and Angela Unamuno opened the Spanish Rooming House in 1912, which they operated for several years. That hotel disappeared beneath state buildings that went up in the neighborhood.

The Mingo family, which had run a hotel up north in the mining town of Mullan, tried to run a boardinghouse in Ontario, but it didn't last, according to Josephine (Echanis) Keim. So most of the herders ended up at the Echanises'.

Through the years, the Echanises' hotel was really the only Basque gathering place in Ontario. After Maria Echanis died in 1990, her daughter Josephine Keim remained in the former boardinghouse with her family, keeping up the beautiful house with its immaculate gardens.

BASQUE CLUB

Up until recently, the city boasted of one of very few all-women Basque clubs. Although the gentlemen helped out with the club events in the past, the ladies ran the show.

A group of local women led by Serafina Mendiguren, who had come to Ontario from Boise with her husband John, started the Ontario Basque Ladies Society as early as 1948; it is one of the oldest Basque clubs. The following year the women held their first winter dance, and soon they began organizing potluck picnics on Father's Day.

When the North American Basque Organizations started in 1973, the Ontario Basque Ladies Society was one of the first to join up. About that same time it had officially incorporated as the **Ontario Basque Club.**

More recently the women reached a crossroads, realizing that without bringing in men and younger women and their families, the club would die. Membership was down to forty, and the youth dance group had been shrinking. Half of the members were over sixty years of age, and, tired of carrying the load for so many years, they decided in 1994 to open up membership to men and families in hopes of reenergizing the club. Club members conducted a survey of the local Basque community and found that the majority wanted such a change. Today, membership has increased to ninety. After many requests for recipes, the women published a cookbook, *Basque Recipes,* in 1966 (available by mail for $6.00 plus $1.50 shipping and handling). It includes a hundred favorite recipes of the members, although only about half are Basque; the rest reflect typical ingredients of the region, such as onions and pheasant.

Club Activities. Outside of Boise, the Ontario club's annual dinner dance fund-raiser and live lamb auction on the last Saturday of February are among the longest-running Basque celebrations in the region. Every year, in anticipation of the dance, local clothes shops dressed up their mannequins in Basque costumes provided by the club members. The club members and their husbands wore Basque costumes to the dance, and other women were encouraged to wear cotton dresses and aprons and the men overalls. A lamb was auctioned off to raise money. Over the years, the club has donated the proceeds of the dance to many local charities. The toughening of state liquor laws a few years ago changed the club's practice of opening the event to old and young alike. Grace Mainvil said that the new laws put club members in the difficult position of admitting youths and not selling alcohol at the event, or simply excluding those under the drinking age, which tends to discourage their general participation in Basque activities. Finally, in 1994, the group decided to cancel the event for a year. But the club kept the winter tradition alive and it continues at the Four Rivers Cultural Center; local businesses help advertise the event. The profits have been used for local charity needs —to provide full one-year tuition for Basque students at Treasure Valley Community College and also to help local youngsters attend the annual NABO music camp. "We've raised a lot of money in years gone by," said Martina Echanis.

In 2004, the club celebrated its fifty-eighth annual winter dance. The local dance group, Beti Alai, led by Maria Tipton, was a highlight of the celebration. The Japanese chef/owner of Matsy's restaurant has learned to cook Basque cuisine and cooks the annual dinner, which serves five hundred people. He hosts occasional Basque dinners at **Matsy's** (1241 Southwest Fourth Avenue). The annual Basque dinner includes lamb, paella, salad, a vegetable dish, a glass of wine, and desserts made by club members. In 2005, dinner tickets were only $15. However, the event is a big charity money-maker because of the lamb auction, which has been held since the dance first started. Local business owners receive free tickets to the event, and during the auction they bid on the lamb, then the winner re-donates it to the club. By the end of the bidding, everyone has won and made a contribution to the club.

In addition to the winter dance, the club holds a June picnic and participates in the Global Village, a local international festival at the local Lion's Park, also conducted in June. Members sell chorizos as well as other Basque items, and the children's Beti Alai dance group performs.

Club member Lisa Corcostegui, who has become a web expert, is responsible for making the Ontario Basque Club Web site, *www.ontariobasqueclub.dantzariak.net,* the best of all Basque clubs, with lessons on *mus*, a children's page, and many historical photos.

Ontario Basque Club, P.O. Box 1233, Ontario, OR 97914. Information: (208) 938-4297 (*Grace Mainvil*); *www.ontariobasqueclub.dantzariak.net*

FOUR RIVERS CULTURAL CENTER

Basque culture is on display in a big way in Ontario at the **Four Rivers Cultural Center.** Despite Ontario's small size, this spacious site includes Japanese gardens, a theater, conference rooms, as well as museum exhibits. The center is located on the Treasure Valley Community College campus (at the corner of South West Fifth Avenue and South West Fifth Street). The region's significant ethnic groups—namely Japanese, Paiute Indians, Basques, and Latinos—are represented in permanent museum exhibits. A display on the Basques includes a realistic sheep camp, the mock front façade of a Basque boardinghouse, and a table setting with typical Basque Food. In the past few years, the annual dinner-dance fundraiser has been held here. For more information, call or write the center.

Four Rivers Cultural Center, 676 Southwest Fifth Avenue, Ontario, OR 97914 (541) 889-8191; *www.4rcc.com*

Pendleton

A BASQUE BBQ CATERING BUSINESS

Mariano Zubiria is making up for the scarcity of Basque dining in this state by offering a unique Basque-style barbecue catering service. Zubiria came to the northeastern corner of Oregon in 1959 to work for the Cunningham sheep company. Basques did not herd sheep in this area until the mid-1950s, when they were recruited from other sheep outfits in Oregon and Washington. Mariano Zubiria was one of just a few Basques who settled in Pendleton. Most of the herders eventually left herding and took logging jobs.

There never was a Basque club in Pendleton, but during the 1960s Zubiria and a few of the other Basques in the area would barbecue lamb for a community picnic in the nearby town of Ukiah. In the beginning, two hundred people came to the Fourth of July celebration, but by the late 1960s it was more like two thousand. It had become too commercial, according to Zubiria, so he and his buddies dropped out of the picture. Then for several years they barbecued lamb for an Elks picnic in Pendleton. "But we got tired of doing it just for fun and decided to go into the catering business," he said.

Zubiria, who describes himself as semiretired, never imagined his business would become so popular. Today the catering service is booked for two or three events every weekend and employs fifteen to eighteen people. In the summer, it's picnics; in the winter, company parties. People always ask Zubiria where his restaurant is, but he is strictly a caterer-on-wheels. He rolls up to party locations in his trailer, and he and his team set up the portable grills outdoors—"rain or snow, a hundred degrees or five below." His specialty, of course, is lamb, which he slaughters himself, and it's served with all the traditional trimmings, such as salad with vinaigrette dressing, beans, and paella. He mostly sticks to the northeast corner of the state—"We've got all the business we want locally," he reports.

Mario's Basque BBQ, 43419 Boylen Lane, Pendleton, OR 97801 (541) 276-1665

Bend

BASQUE CLUB

Several families in Central Oregon, in such communities as Bend, Redmond, Madras, Crescent, and Prineville, joined the Portland Basque Club when it was organized a few years ago. Eventually someone in the Portland group pointed out, "There's a lot of you there—why don't you form your own group?" said Bend resident Anita Hasert. The area doesn't have a historical Basque presence, and, hence, many of the families had not associated much. Since they formed the **Central Oregon Basque Club** in 1995, twenty families have become members. It is one of the few active clubs that is not a member of the North American Basque Organizations. Hasert maintains they are too small to go to all the effort.

Numerous activities have quickly caught on here. A Basque dance group, made up of children and adults, has performed at local events, including the Deschutes County Fair, on the last weekend in July, where the group won a blue ribbon in 1996. "We danced all the way down the street and just about killed ourselves," laughed Hasart, a former Boise Oinkari who leads the group. Since Basques are little known here, the club is seeking to expose the local community to the Basque culture, by staging dance performances and selling chorizos at local events.

The members also get together once a month at someone's home for potluck dinners. Learning *mus* and how to cook different Basque dishes, such as Gateau Basque, has also been part of these social evenings. An annual picnic tradition has begun, on the third Sunday in September at Sam Johnson Park in Redmond. The group always celebrates New Year's Day at a member's home, and they host occasional Basque-cooking demonstrations.

Central Oregon Basque Club, 20505 Bowery Lane, Bend, OR 97701. Information: (*Anita Hasart*) (541) 382-6023

High Desert Museum

The **High Desert Museum** in this city chose the Basques as one of three ethnic groups from the Great Basin's high desert regions to highlight in a permanent traveling exhibit, *Amerikanuak.* Exhibit items include photos, historic and current, and many artifacts of sheepherding, aspen carvings, boardinghouses, pelota courts, and other historic spots, all belonging to prominent Basques of the past. The exhibit opened at the High Desert Museum in May 1995. It traveled to Idaho and Nevada. The exhibit was most recently stationed at the Basque Museum in Boise and was expected to continue there through 2006. To find out where the exhibit is, or where it will be in the future, call or write the High Desert Museum. Be sure to purchase one of the museum's brilliantly photographed catalogs on the *Amerikanuak* exhibit from the museum store.

High Desert Museum, 59800 South Highway 97, Bend, OR 97702 (541) 382-4754; *www.highdesertmuseum.org*

Portland

Historically Portland and Seattle have not had Basque colonies, but Basque-Americans have migrated there in recent years from other parts of Oregon and Washington. "Half the population of the state lives in the Portland metropolitan area," said Patricia Ayerza, founder of the Portland Basque club.

The number of Basque-Americans in Portland is not very large. It's probably a mere one hundred to two hundred people, and there is no single occupation that has drawn them to the city. Professionals from the Basque Country have also immigrated to Portland for different reasons. In recent years, the number of Basques has grown sufficiently that they are aware of one another. "There were starting to be more and more of us," said Pilar Echanove. In 1990 a small group of them gathered for dinners, establishing friendships that continued to grow.

BASQUE CLUB

In 1992 the Basques organized their first picnic, and Patricia Ayerza spearheaded efforts to organize a club. By 1994 membership was up to fifty and climbing, and the third picnic was in the works. In 1994 the potluck picnic was held at a private ranch on the picturesque Sauvie Island, where the Willamette River meets the Columbia River. The club hoped to continue the event there.

"We're growing all the time," said Ayerza soon after the group started. Basques from all around Portland, and as far away as Bend, joined. Banker John Elorriaga and his large family became big boosters. But busy urban lives kept people away from the events, and "by the time we whittled down to the last one [the fourth picnic], there wasn't hardly anybody there," said Anita Peterson. The club's last events were held in 2001. They are maintaining a mailing list in case they decide to start up again.

RESTAURANTS

Two sisters, Pilar Echanove and Carmen Lotina, and their husbands put Basques on the map in Portland with their **Basco's Burgers** eateries. "We wanted to bring in the name to show that there are Basques in the area," said Echanove. Lotina and her husband José Mari first opened their place at 1880 South East Baseline in Cornelius, a suburb of Portland, in 1981, and Pilar and Angelo Echanove later opened theirs just 4 miles away at 807 South East Baseline in Hillsboro. The two families sold both restaurants, but in 2005, Carmen Lotina reappropriated Basco's Burgers in Cornelius, with its basic all-American fast-food menu, and planned to keep the restaurant ([503]359-0447) at least three more years.

■ Washington

Yakima Valley

The area around the small town of Yakima had the only Basque community of note in the state of Washington. There were not large expanses of public domain land in Washington State where Basque sheepmen could gain a foothold, and possibly that is why not many Basques migrated to Washington. Nevertheless, Basques still ran some sheep throughout the Columbia River Basin, summering near Mt. Rainier or Mt. Adams or other peaks in the Cascade Range. A few families also settled around Ellensburg, Sunnyside, and Quincy. Sheepman Sebastián Etulain established his outfit in Ellensberg, which is famous in the state for its lamb, and his brother Juan Miguel Etulain established his in Sunnyside. The Etulains, along with other friends and relatives who came to the Yakima Valley for sheepherding, hailed from the town of Eugi, near Iruñea/Pamplona, or the towns around it.

Today there's only one sheep outfit—not Basque—in the entire valley, and most of the Basque families left are isolated on farms or ranches. Some of the Basques in this area get together at an annual picnic put on by a Spanish group. Recently there has been talk of forming their own Basque club, according to farmer Mike Etulain.

BOARDINGHOUSES

José and Expectación Elizalde, who had run La Cancha hotel in San Francisco, came to Yakima and opened El Hotel Bascongado in 1912. This boardinghouse proved to be the only establishment of its kind in the region, although a few Yakima families offered room and board in their homes over the years. Expectación ran the place alone after her husband died, and she hired a contractor to turn the small four-room house at 105 South Fourth Street into a grand two-story, twenty-five-room house. During those early years, Basques came to the area to work as herders, and a few of them ran their own outfits. "We were filled to overflowing, packed like sardines, yet they wouldn't go to the hotels downtown," said the couple's daughter, Elena Arralde, when she was in her seventies. There was one feature of this place that set it apart from every other Basque hotel. "My mother refused to serve liquor," Arralde said. "So our men, when they wanted to drink, all they had to do was walk a block and a half to Yakima Avenue, where they could go to the taverns." When Expectación died in 1937, Elena and her husband Joe took over the hotel and renamed it Hotel Arralde.

The young couple fretted over the liquor ban but decided to continue it, according to Elena Arralde. "We did not lose a one," she said. Arralde and her daughter Isabel were in a serious car accident in 1961, in which Isabel was killed and Elena was confined to a wheelchair for many weeks. She stopped cooking meals for the boarders after that, although she said the men insisted she come with them to the local restaurants to help them order, because of their poor English. "The only thing they knew how to say in English was 'beer' and 'whisky,'" she said.

Unlike most of the other Basque boardinghouse owners, who closed their businesses once Basque immigration ceased, Arralde took in the Peruvian and Chileans who came in to herd sheep. Arralde stayed at the boardinghouse until December 31, 1993, when the city took over the property by eminent domain. All the buildings on the block were quickly torn down, and a bus transit center was built in their place. "It just broke my heart," said Arralde.

Seattle

Seattle has no original Basque community, but Basques inevitably have migrated to this city of 900,000 people.

BASQUE CLUB

The Seattle Basque club has come a long way from the small nucleus of young Basque professionals who started it in 1993. Andoni Diego, an engineer who grew up in Washington State and in the Basque Country, was the main driving force behind the creation of the early club, called the Washington State Basque Club. In 1993 he organized a picnic at his ranch in Monroe, which attracted about eighty people—the largest gathering of Basques in the state outside of the Yakima area. However, the early club, like other new clubs in metropolitan areas, later fizzled because of lack of support. But a few years later in 1997, another group of energetic Basques, spearheaded by Blas Uberuaga, creator and designer of Buber's Basque Page, helped restart the group. Uberuaga was attending the University of Washington and has since moved away, but the club, **Seattle Euskal Etxea,** continues today with the help of other supporters, such as Toni Sabarots, originally from Chino, California, and her husband, John Etulain, related to the Yakima ranching families. The distance between Basque families in this state, however, makes it difficult to sponsor successful events. "Even though we have two thousand Basques in the state of Washington, which is the fourth largest Basque population in the country, we are really spread out," said Sabarots, who was president of the club in 2005. The picnic on the first Saturday in August is the most popular event. While it has been held in the small town of Carnation outside of Seattle fairly regularly since 1997, the current board of directors is considering moving it to different locations, to reach the Basques in those areas, such as the Yakima Valley or the Olympic Peninsula. Sabarots, who spent her childhood in the tight-knit Chino Basque community, notes that Seattle's group has few of the activities of Chino's. "We're lucky we have events," she noted. However, the club leadership's connections to other clubs have helped them attract the ballet group Kukai and accordionist Kepa Junkera from the Basque Country. But planning such events is tricky. "There's a real fragile balance between how much [money] you are going to collect and how much you are going to spend," she said. The Seattle club sometimes puts on events with the highly active Basque club in Vancouver, Canada, (*www.bcbasque.com*), a mere two hours away. In 2005, the club had about forty-five member families, but membership fluctuates as people come and go. Many of them find out about the club from the club's excellent Web site, *www.seattleeuskal.org.*

Seattle Euskal Etxea, 2802 East Union Street, Seattle, WA 98122. Information: (509) 750-6254 (John Etulain); *www.seattleeuskal.org*

RESTAURANTS AND FOOD

Harvest Vine is a fancy tapas restaurant headed by renowned Basque chef and owner Jose Jimenez de Jimenez. His wife, Carolin Messier de Jimenez is the pastry chef. This small restaurant, which specializes in Basque and Spanish tapas, is a popular eatery. Its reputation is perhaps more enhanced because of the no-reservation policy that makes long-waiting time inevitable. Part of the appeal is the cozy setting and the copper bar in front of the open kitchen where you can see the chefs at work. Good wine accompanies the food. Jimenez helps out the local Basque club and occasionally sponsors cooking classes in different Basque communities. See their Web site, *www.thescarletmacaw.com/harvest_vine.htm,* to find out about the classes and to read the interesting story on how the concept of "tapas" evolved.

Two local stores, **The Spanish Table** and **Big John's PFI,** also cater to the Basque palate and give Seattle food aficionados two great places to buy specialty items. At The Spanish Table you'll find an abundance of food items and wines from Spain. You can also buy ready-to-eat food, such as *tortilla de patatas, bocadillos,* and soup. This store opened in 1995, and two others, in Berkeley, California, and Santa Fe, New Mexico, have followed. This store offers so many tempting food items that you'll probably buy lots more than you need. Seattle cooks love Big John's PFI (Pacific Food Importers). Starting with oils and olives from Greece and Italy, in 1971 owner John Croce expanded his import business to include items from many other countries and had to expand his store as well. A small portion of his warehouse inventory is sold at this retail store near the downtown sports arena. Toni Sabarots said it's a great place to buy Basque cheese rounds, and there are many other imported items at great discounted prices. Plan to spend some time at this store perusing the aisles. Much of their merchandise can also be purchased online at *www.pacificfoodimporters.com.*

Harvest Vine, 2701 E. Madison, Seattle, WA (206) 320-9771; *www.thescarletmacaw.com/harvest_vine.htm*
The Spanish Table, 1427 Western Avenue, Seattle, WA 98101 (206) 682.2827; *www.spanishtable.com*
Big John's PFI, 1001 6th. Avenue South, Level B, Seattle, WA 98134 (206) 682-2022; *www.pacificfoodimporters.com*

TOURS TO THE BASQUE COUNTRY

The Scarlet Macaw is a Seattle travel agency that offers many tours to France and Spain, and its specialty is trips to the San Fermín festival in Iruñea/Pamplona. Its 2005 calendar included a gastronomic tour to Gipuzkoa and another trip was geared around the Tour de France bike race, but it seems to be best at guiding people to Iruñea/Pamplona and all of the San Fermín festivities. The company's lively Web site provides information on the history of *los encierros,* where the running of the bulls takes place.

The Scarlet Macaw, 2145 North 115th Street, Seattle, WA 98133 (206)364.6723; *www.thescarletmacaw.com*

Spokane

Jobs in mining were the reason a small unnoticed Basque community grew up in the Idaho towns of Kellogg, Wallace, and Mullan, east of Spokane, during the early 1900s. Today descendants of these Basques, as well as Basques from other communities, have migrated to Spokane, a city of 400,000, because of increased urban job opportunities.

BASQUE CLUB

In 1994 a small group of Basques joined together to create the Northwest Inland Basque Club. The group grew slowly and met casually in people's homes once a month for potluck dinners. The club attracted about forty people. Nevertheless, it was not enough to create a cohesive group to organize events, and by 2001 the club had disbanded. "It got to be more work than we could handle," said Jo Dickinson, who moved to the Spokane area from Boise. "In Boise, you have the generations to back you up," she noted. Spokane, unfortunately, does not have that history.

Northern Washington State

A small number of Basques live in the Bellingham area north of Seattle, and at one time a Basque hotel operated on the San Juan Islands. Basques have been attracted to this region by jobs in the region's large shipping industry. A small cluster of Basques also settled in the Clallum Bay area, at the northwestern tip of the Olympic Peninsula, because there was a lumber mill there. The Seattle Euskal Etxea occasionally rotates its annual picnic to this region (see the Basque club listing under Seattle).

REFERENCES

Baker Monroe, Sarah. "Basque American Folklore in Eastern Oregon." Ph.D. diss., University of California, Berkeley, 1972.

Gaiser, Joseph Harold. "The Basques of the Jordan Valley Area, A Study in Social Process and Social Change." Ph.D. diss., University of Southern California, 1944.

Utah, Colorado, New Mexico, Wyoming, and Montana

Utah

SHEEP

The state of Utah is unlike the other Great Basin states in the West in which Basque communities developed and were supported for many years by involvement in the sheep industry, because few if any of the Basques who came to Utah ever became owners of sheep outfits. This appears to be in large part because of a lack of opportunity. Mormons, members of the Church of Jesus Christ of Latter-day Saints, developed most of this state after their arrival from the East in 1847. They dominated the sheep business, just as they did most every other industry in Utah, and they discouraged participation by non-Mormons. They hired Basque sheepherders to work for them through the years, but according to local Basques, the Mormons gave Basques little chance to break into the business as owners and operators. Since the greatest incentive to most Basque herders in the United States was the prospect of eventually owning their own band, and this was not possible in the Mormon-dominated state, Utah held little appeal for them.

In the early part of the century some Basque herders did graze sheep over the winter in southeastern Utah, in the desert lowlands between Grand Junction, Colorado, and Price, Utah. Price had at least two large Basque boardinghouses, the French and the Allies, and a fronton in the days before the Great Depression, according to Father Adrien Gachiteguy, who traveled through the West in the early 1950s. There were many Greek sheepherders in that part of the state as well as Basques, and dark-haired Basques were often referred to by Utah's Mormons as "Greeks," and usually in a derogatory sense. By the 1930s and 1940s the few Basques who were grazing sheep in southeastern Utah were owners of their own flocks, based out of nearby Colorado.

Probably the largest number of Basque herders came during the war years, between 1941 and 1956, when young Mormon men tending their father's flocks were called to service and the older men entered the defense plants in large numbers. In those days most of the Basques were from Nafarroa Beherea; the majority of those who came later for mining jobs were Bizkaitarrak.

MINING

A larger number of Basque immigrants came to Utah to work in the mining industry, which, like sheepherding, did not require a proficiency in English. The miners were predominantly Italians, Greeks, Basques, Slavs, and Swedes. Among the significant employers were the Kennecott mine in Bingham Canyon and the Silver King mine near Park City, to the east, both within an hour's drive of Salt Lake City. Typically Basques stayed in such jobs only long enough to learn English or make enough money to open their own business. "Most of them left with good money," said Rose (Zabala) Hoover, who grew up in Highland Boy, a small mining town that has since disappeared.

"There was a big gap between those people (the early herders) and the modern [Basque] immigrant," said Salt Lake City native Jean Flesher. The largest numbers of Basque immigrants who came looking for mining jobs arrived during the 1950s and 1960s. Basques in Salt Lake City interviewed by scholar Louise Brown Dunn during the early 1970s said that Utah was a second or third choice, after they had already looked for work without success in other Western states. "Originally, the immigrants had the [mining] jobs because they were among the 'low' jobs," said Pilar (Sangroniz) Shortsleeve, whose father, Jaime Sangroniz, worked for the biggest of the mines, Kennecott Copper Corporation. According to Shortsleeve, the Mormons looked down on people who worked in the mines. "They were the jobs that nobody else wanted. Then the unions came along, and everybody wanted their jobs," because of the wage increases the unions brought.

Highland Boy, Copperton, and Bingham were all small towns that sprang up around the Bingham copper mine. Rose Hoover grew up in Highland Boy, where her stepfather, Pete Zabala, worked at the mine as a "powder monkey"—so called because he packed the explosive powder into the pit's walls when the company was blasting for ore.

Matilda Zabala, Rose Hoover's mother, ran one of several small room-and-board places from the 1920s to the mid-1950s. Matilda's food was so good that the local schoolteachers came to eat there every night, according to Hoover.

"In our little town we had every nationality and creed," remembers Hoover, adding that racial or religious conflicts were nonexistent then. "If I could live my childhood over," she said, "I would do it again in Highland Boy." But the towns got in the way of progress, and by the 1950s the mine company had bought out all the towns and razed them to allow for expansion of the mine. "I can still see my mom sobbing," Hoover said, when a landmark bridge was blown up.

Copperton, a bit farther away, was once the home of the rich mine officials. Acres of farmland used to separate Copperton from Salt Lake City, but today the urban ring around Salt Lake has extended all the way to Copperton. The miners live in Copperton today, and the mine, bigger than ever (2 miles across and twice as deep as the Empire State Building) continues to operate. Unionized miners went on strike at the Copperton mine during the late 1970s, but the company retaliated by closing the mine and breaking the union. The mine reopened in the late 1980s.

Ogden

Salt Lake City Basques knew there were Basques in Ogden. "You would see them at funerals and things like that," said Tony Barrutia of Salt Lake City. Yet isolated within the vast Mormon population, the pockets of Basques in Ogden, in southeast Utah, and later in the Salt Lake City area developed almost unbeknownst to one another. When the current Basque club, based in Salt Lake City, filed its application with the state for incorporation in 1973, the group was surprised to learn that a Utah Basque club had previously existed in Ogden. "Nobody alive knew anything about it," said Mary Gaztambide—not even the oldest Basques in the community. Her husband Jean kept a copy of the incorporation application of the earlier group, which had been filed in 1914. Judging by the first names of the original club founders—among them Aniceto Varelo, Santiago Sapelana, Ignacio Botino, José Erquiaga, and José Laucirica—most of them were probably Hegoaldetarrak. Laucirica was an owner of one of the early Ogden hotels.

BOARDINGHOUSES

In the northern part of Utah a few Basque hotels were known to be operating in Ogden as early as the 1890s and continued at least through 1916. These hotels were probably home to the earliest Basques in

The old Hogar Hotel in Salt Lake City was home to Utah Basques for fifty years. Today it is home to an antique store.

Utah. Since few if any Basques were involved in sheepherding around Ogden, it's most likely that the hotels opened there because the town was an important stopover on the transcontinental railroad. After spending the night in Ogden, Bizkaitarrak changed trains to travel north into southern Idaho or continued west to Nevada and California. Many sheepmen sent back to Europe for brides and met their wives-to-be in Ogden upon the women's arrival from the Basque Country. The couples were married and honeymooned in the city's hotels. Father Gachiteguy found a handful of Basques in Ogden when he traveled there in the 1950s.

The history of a former Basque boardinghouse in Ogden, the Royal Hotel, is described in detail on a Utah governmental Web site, Utah History to Go, *www.historytogo.utah.gov/royalhotel.html.* You will learn that John H. Maitia and John Etcheverry were the first owners of this historical hotel, which was built in 1914. The Royal Hotel at 2522 Wall Avenue was like many boardinghouses located near the Union Station railroad depot, and several other hotels were built around it at about the same time. It has been placed on the National Register of Historic Places as part of the Lower 25th Street Historic

District. According to the Web site, the three-story masonry hotel had a fronton. The subsequent owner, Sam Maruri, was another Basque. In 1943, Basque ownership of the building ended about the same time that trucks took over the transportation of sheep, diminishing the importance of Union Station. Interestingly, afterward the hotel became one of the few places where blacks who worked as porters and waiters on trains could reside in an era of discrimination. In 2005, the Royal Hotel sign still hung on the hotel advertising rooms on a weekly basis.

Salt Lake City

HOTELS AND BARS

For fifty years the Hogar Hotel in downtown Salt Lake City was where most of the recent history of the Salt Lake Basque community transpired. Two blocks away on the same street was La Fonda Española, another Basque hotel, but it was torn down during the 1970s. Up through the 1940s, there were at least one or two other Basque hotels in the area, and apparently some Basque families also lived in the neighborhood at one time. Most Basque families have since moved to Salt Lake Valley suburbs. But their nostalgia for the old days at the Hogar lives on.

The late Jean Leon Iribarren, a prominent member of San Francisco's French and Basque communities, was among those who herded sheep in Utah during the 1950s and stayed at the Hogar. "There were a couple of hundred bedrolls there from Basques who had gone to California or back to the Old Country and never told anyone," he related during a 1992 interview. The sight of retired herders whose lives were reduced to waiting for the lunch or dinner bell made him sad and pushed him to aim higher. (He later opened his own insurance agency and made significant contributions to many community groups, including NABO.)

At many Basque hotels anyone who wasn't Basque was simply not allowed to come in. This restriction was well known at Salt Lake City's Hogar Hotel. "Nobody could get in there unless they were Basque," remembered Jean Gaztambide. But if you were Basque, Hogar Hotel owner John Landa would bend over backwards to help you.

All the big events were celebrated at the Hogar—Christmas, New Year's, funerals, and marriages. There was a close-knit group of Basques. Basque families who didn't live at the Hogar came to join in the celebrations. Anything that happened in the Basque community was quickly news at the Hogar.

For many who had once lived there, like the Gaztambides, their social life revolved around the Hogar. Even after the Gaztambides had settled in their own home and were raising a family, their adult daughter Denise remembers that the Hogar was like a second home. "We'd be down there every weekend just about."

A block and a half away from the Hogar was the Barrutia family's bar, the Downtowner Lounge. In the evenings, herders staying at the Hogar would walk down there to shoot dice and drink beer. "That's all we could do," said former bar owner Tony Barrutia, referring to the liquor laws that restricted the sale of anything but beer. Tony's parents, Pascual and María Barrutia, left Bingham during the Great Depression and bought and refurbished the Realty Hotel in downtown Salt Lake City. It was never a boardinghouse, according to Barrutia. The bar was downstairs, at 225–227 Southwest Temple Street. In 1973, when the city moved forward with redevelopment plans, the building was condemned and torn down. Today the Red Lion Hotel sits in its place.

During the late 1960s and 1970s, the Landas leased the Hogar Hotel to two other Basque couples, Milagros and Gracian Etchepar and Pete and Kathy Urquidi. The sale of the historic building in 1977, after John Landa's death, marked the end of that era.

The Hogar Hotel—Hill's House Antique Gallery

An antique dealer, Jonathan Sweet, bought the Hogar Hotel in 1977 and was very interested in restoring the building to its original condition. He received a federal grant to redo the exterior woodwork on the building—a painstaking process. Except for removing layers of white paint on the facade to reveal the original brick, the renovation left the exterior of the building looking virtually as it did in the era in which the Landas ran it as a boardinghouse.

Sweet's antique shop, **Hills' House Antique Gallery,** is open to the public, and Sweet is very knowledgeable about the building's Basque history and is usually delighted to show it off. "They [the

John Landa and the Hogar Hotel

Bob Ithurralde, a resident at the Hogar for eight years, described longtime hotel keeper John Landa as "a tiny man with a powerful voice. He had all the connections. He was like the Basque ambassador." Landa was well known within the Salt Lake community, and occasionally he hosted dinners for local dignitaries. He knew the state politicians, who called on him to bring herders to Utah. Landa, in association with the Western Range Association, would make all the arrangements and even pick up the herders from the airport.

Landa and his wife Claudia took over the Hogar in 1927, after having run a boardinghouse in Pocatello, Idaho. "They were like second parents," remembers Mary Gaztambide, who came from nearby Wells, Nevada, to attend college in Salt Lake City and lived at the Hogar from 1954 to 1963. She met her husband, Jean, at the Hogar.

Despite the Mormons' restrictive laws against alcohol throughout most of the state, Landa sold drinks at the Hogar just like almost every other Basque hotel keeper. "If the doorbell rang, the bottles and everything were hidden," remembers Mary. "But he was well known in the city, and I think people knew what was going on," she said, noting that Landa bought a large supply of liquor at the state-controlled liquor stores every week.

Landas] obviously had a lot of pride in the building and really took care of it," said Sweet, pointing to a couple of repair jobs in which great care had been taken to restore moldings and to paint walls to match the existing woodwork. Except for partitioning the upstairs rooms to make more rooms for boarders, the Landas essentially kept the house in its original condition, according to Sweet.

Part of Sweet's restoration work involved removing the divisions in the upstairs rooms and replacing the wood shingle roof. "It took six years to restore this place," said Sweet, emphasizing that most of the time-consuming work is not visible to visitors.

"We found a stash of Prohibition whisky in the wall," related Sweet, adding that some bottles, dated 1924, were still full. He suspects they were hidden away and forgotten during the boardinghouse era. When Sweet bought the place, he allowed one longtime resident of the home, José Ariastegui, to remain on for several years.

The Hogar Hotel building, originally a Victorian house built for banker Louis Hills in 1877, is on the National Register of Historic Places. Located in the midst of some huge structures—a high-rise apartment building to the back, a large parking structure (for the Salt Palace Convention Center) in front, and parking lots or big stores on either side, it stands like an island, reminiscent of an earlier era. "It's the only one of its kind left in Salt Lake," Sweet contends.

Inside the building you'll find remnants of days gone by. Sweet still uses the original steam heaters, built in 1874, to heat the building. One of the house's original sinks is still in place on the second floor. The hanging light fixture in the foyer is also original. Outside the building you'll find other reminders of the Landas' era. An old mulberry tree, two pear trees, and one of the city's only almond trees still bear fruit. Along one side of the building Sweet restored a grape arbor, which was probably built and planted by the Landas. A horse chestnut tree decorates the front yard. Sweet has also placed some old farm equipment in front, but the wrought-iron fence is original.

The old Hogar Hotel, like most historic Basque hotels, was within walking distance of the Salt Lake City depot. While you're visiting the city, you might hear the train whistle blow, tipping you off to the proximity of the depot, also known as Union Pacific station. You might want to drop by the elegant train station, which today houses a popular Mexican restaurant.

Hills' House Antique Gallery (Old Hogar Hotel) (*Jonathan Sweet*) 126 South 200 West, Salt Lake City, UT (801) 359-4852

Family History Library

Salt Lake City's downtown is completely planned around a central point—the main Temple of the Church of Jesus Christ of Latter-day Saints. If you go downtown to see the old Hogar, you might set aside time for a visit to the **Family History Library,** the world's largest repository of personal records and documents, just a block away from the temple. The Mormon church emphasizes the importance of the family and knowing the family tree, as do Basques and other ethnic groups. To that end, the Mormons have established the Family History Library, with branches all over the world, to provide church members access to genealogical information. Fortunately, the Mormons consider this information valuable to everyone, and their libraries are open to the public.

The Family History Library is an incredible accomplishment, spanning four stories and filled with books and information on heraldry, genealogy, and onomastic information from around the world.

The basement floor is dedicated to Europe and South America. There you will find several thick books on Basque family names, Basque coats of arms, Basque emigration to South America, and other such subjects, enough to keep you busy for several hours. The library's computer system contains millions of names, birthdates, and birthplaces from thousands of family trees, all of which are accessible to the public, although most of the information is inputted by individual family members and thus is mostly Mormon. Everyone is encouraged to input their own family data into the computer system, so others can find relevant information. Much of the library's documentation, in the form of old registers, manuscripts, censuses; birth, death, and marriage certificates; and court, property, and church records, from cities and towns in every country, is stored on computer and on microfiche. The library maintains records on over 1.5 billion deceased people from around the world. The library is open every day except Sunday. Today, much of its information is available through its Web site, *www.familysearch.org*, and family history centers are located throughout the country where anyone is welcome to do research.

Family History Library, 35 Northwest Temple Street, Salt Lake City, UT 84150 (801) 240-2331; *www.familysearch.org*

RESTAURANT

Salt Lake City has no Basque restaurants to the chagrin of its Basques. "Every one of them would like to have a restaurant," said Mary Gaztambide, referring to the area's Basque families. One Basque restaurant, the Celebrity House, opened up in the downtown area, but it didn't even last a year, according to Gaztambide. Locals say the most feasible place for such a restaurant is probably the touristy Park City, because of the many visitors it attracts.

BASQUE CLUB

Throughout most of the Hogar Hotel's existence, the Basques who frequented the hotel felt little need for a Basque club. But as the Landas got older, local Basques realized that the hotel was likely to close down, and they might be left without a gathering place. "After that ceased to exist, we felt it was time to organize a Basque club so we could stay together," said one of the current club's founders, Bob Ithurralde. In 1973 he and Rose Hoover organized the first meetings, which were held at her former restaurant, La Casa Supper Club in Lehi.

Today the **Basque Club of Utah** has about a hundred members living in Salt Lake and its suburbs, such as Lehi, Herriman, Sandy, Midvale, Murray, Kearns, Holladay, and North Salt Lake. Locals estimate that the greater Salt Lake Valley area probably has some three hundred to four hundred Basque families.

The active members in the Utah club are all first- and second-generation Basques. By the third generation, Basques in Salt Lake have mostly drifted away from the culture. "We're not concentrated enough," said Pilar (Sangroniz) Shortsleeve, a U.S.–born Basque. So the later generations tend to be more American than anything else. She noted that in Boise, third-generation Basques are heavily involved in Basque events—"because they have such a concentration [of Basques]."

Club Activities. The Basque Club has developed its own traditions and specialties to expose the wider population to the Basque culture. Members host one big dinner dance yearly in February to raise funds, and the club participates in several other large community-wide events, such as the Living Traditions Fair, an ethnic festival held in the latter part of May at Heritage Park on the grounds of the City and County Building (451 South State Street) downtown. The club sells chorizos and *churros* (fried pastry) at this event to raise funds for the club.

"Our *churros* sell like crazy," said Mary Gaztambide, emphasizing that the *churros* they prepare are the fat European-style *churros,* not the more common skinny Mexican kind. Just getting a machine to make the pastries was an ordeal initially. Gaztambide called dozens of companies in the United States but was unable to track one down. Finally the club had to order one from Spain, and it was very expensive. "But it's paid for itself time and time again," said Gaztambide, who is surprised that other clubs have not jumped into the *churro* market. The club also sells *churros* and the dancers perform at the annual Carmelite Fair in September, a benefit for the Carmelite Sisters at their convent on Holladay Boulevard in Holladay.

The only other place to taste Basque food in Utah is at the club's annual Basque dinner dance on the second Saturday in February at St. Ambrose Hall (1975 South 2300 East) in the Sugarhouse area. "It's gotten so popular that people come year to year, and we don't even have to advertise," said Gaztambide. The fund-raising dinner inevitably starts off with the typical leek soup known as *porrusalda.* "The public won't let us change that because they love it," said Gaztambide. Typical Basque dishes such as lamb or clams and rice are served.

Several other events are held expressly for the enjoyment of the Basque community—the annual picnic on the second Sunday in June, a Halloween party, a Christmas party, a New Year's party, a *morcilla* dinner in March, and the annual *mus* tournament in the spring. The Christmas party is on the second Saturday of December at St. Vincent's Hall in the Holladay area. The Utah'ko Triskalareak dancers perform at the picnic, at the Christmas party, and at the fund-raising dinner dance. The Halloween, New Year's, and *morcilla* dinners are all at the Lion's Club Hall at 530 East 73rd South. Club meetings are held at the Gaztambide home.

Basques in the closest communities—Boise, Elko, and Buffalo—were aware of the Salt Lake Basque group's existence because the dance group participated in their festivals. But among the more remote Basque colonies, the existence of a Basque group in Salt Lake was not well known until after NABO was formed and the Salt Lake club joined about fifteen years ago. The club, then headed by a nineteen-year-old club president, Jean Flesher, hosted the NABO convention in the summer of 1982, and the NABO music camp the following summer. Mary Gaztambide was elected president of NABO in 2004, bringing more attention to the Utah Basques. "We need all the exposure we can get," said Gaztambide, noting that few in the Mormon-dominated state know about the Basques.

Basque Club of Utah, c/o Jean and Mary Gaztambide, 449 Shamrock Drive, Murray, UT 84107
(801) 262-7673; *www.members.aol.com/utahbasq/*

FESTIVAL

The annual picnic is held on the second Sunday of June at the Cottonwood Complex Park, which is a baseball park with pavilions and picnic grounds at 4302 South 1300 East, in the Murray area. After a morning Mass, competitive games such as *soka tira* (tug-of-war), horseshoes, and weight-carrying competitions, as well as *mus* playing, fill the afternoon.

A steak or chorizo lunch is served and *churros* are sold. For many years, people brought their own lunch to the picnic. Attendance, which has never been high, hovers around a hundred.

DANCE

Utah'ko Triskalareak was started in the mid-1970s when ex-Oinkari Delfina Arnold of Boise came to Salt Lake City and started a formal dance group. For the first year or two after the club began, it had just five or six young dancers, children of Basques who frequented the hotel. "All we knew were the *jotas* and *porrusaldas* [the second half of the *jota*] that my mother taught me," said Rose Hoover. Pilar Shortsleeve was in that initial group, and her involvement continued until she became the group's leader, a position she still maintains today. With influence from the Oinkariak, the help of a professional dancer from the European group Oldarra, and videos filmed at dance festivals in the Basque Country, the Utah dancers have kept up with the modernizing trend among the Basque-American dance groups, which ironically consists of reviving ancient dances.

Probably in no other Basque community have the club and the dance group been so closely linked as in Salt Lake City. "One kept the other going," said Mary Gaztambide, whose three children, along with children from the Sangroniz and Cendagorta families, kept the dance group together for many years. The dance practices were always held at the Gaztambide home in Murray, which, for all practical purposes, has served as the club's headquarters through the years. The Gaztambides' daughter, Denise, who participated for many years in the Utah'ko Triskalareak, said that frequent requests for the Salt Lake City group to dance "kept us in the public eye, and it kept us together." In fact, she added, the dance groups "were kind of the glue for most clubs." Buried as they are within Utah's large Mormon population, Utah's Basques would have probably been obscured if not for the dance group, according to Mary Gaztambide. "They have promoted the Basques in Salt Lake."

Park City

Underground silver veins, discovered in the late 1860s, turned Park City into a booming town and kept it alive well into the mid-1900s. Originally a raucous camp of soldiers who had been sent to keep watch on the Mormon settlers, Park City later gained a reputation as a wild town. The strict Mormon laws that prevailed in most Utah cities were unknown in this town, since most of the residents were foreigners who worked at the mines.

Today the town has been reincarnated as a chic ski resort town, and the number of vacation homes constructed in recent years has been phenomenal, raising property values by leaps and bounds. "If we only knew a long time ago, we could have bought some property," said Rose Hoover, who remembers skiing in Park City as a young girl and being towed up the hill on a primitive t-bar. In tribute to the town's early mining era, many of the older buildings have been preserved. Main Street is now a historic district, and two old Basque boardinghouses have taken on new life as bed-and-breakfasts.

BOARDINGHOUSES

Make a visit to this historic district and you'll take a delightful trip back in time. There were at least four Basque boardinghouses in Park City that rented to the miners, the biggest of them being the Imperial and the Star on Main Street. Frank and Teodora Allende ran the Star for some fifty years, until approximately 1960, according to Tony Barrutia, the couple's nephew. In 1929 the Allendes hired miners to expand the existing building, adding on the entire front of the hotel with its beautiful arches framing the front porch. Eventually, the silver was played out, and Park City became a shadow of its former self. The Allendes as well as other hotel owners went out of business. "They sold [the Star] for a pittance," said Barrutia.

Today the **Star Hotel** at 227 Main Street, (435) 649-8333, maintains its 1929 appearance. Current owner Carol Rixey, a non-Basque, said that since she bought the place in 1975, she has merely glassed in the arches, expanded the upstairs rooms, and added a fourth floor to the building. Everything else remains virtually the same, including the bathrooms, which are down the hall from the guest rooms. Rixey even kept the original dressers furnished by the Allendes, as well as the long dining room table, where she feeds the inn's guests breakfast *and* dinner. "We have tried very hard to keep it as authentic as possible," said Rixey, who offers some of the more reasonable winter prices in town.

Next door the **Imperial Hotel** at 221 Main Street, (435) 649-1904 or (800) 669-8824, was built in 1904 for John Bogan, the original owner of the Silver King mine, and it appears to have been Basque only in its final years of operation as a boardinghouse, during the 1950s or 1960s. According to town historian Bea Kummer, Justo Unamuno bought the business in the late 1950s. Only the front of this luxury ski lodge is original, the entire interior having been gutted and rebuilt in the 1980s. Step into the lobby to see the old photos of the building.

Main Street runs into Daly Avenue, once known as Empire Canyon, another street with several historic homes that rented out rooms to miners. In 1924 a Basque sheepman, Arsenio Treviño, built the house that Kummer now lives in, at 166 Daly Avenue, and rented rooms out to Basques for many years. Today Kummer rents out those same rooms to young resort employees. Basques also boarded at the house across the street from hers, at 167 Daly Avenue, she reported. In Park City it was not just the Basques who lived in boardinghouses. In fact, before 1901, the town had a law obligating all single men working at the mines to live in boardinghouses. Most of these boardinghouses were simply private homes that rented out extra rooms to the miners, usually along ethnic lines. At one time there were twenty-three bars in town that catered to the different ethnic groups. Kummer said that of the Basques who lived in Park City, most have died or returned to the Old Country many years ago.

Colorado

SHEEP

The Rocky Mountains, which slice Colorado in half, form the Continental Divide. To the west is the Great Basin stretching across several states. The western slope of the Rockies became the state's main sheep range, and it was in this area of Colorado that many Basques

Jean Urruty and Emmett Elizondo

Sheepman Jean Urruty, who was partners for many years with John Lamicq, eventually became a wealthy man, primarily from oil discovered on his ranch property. During the 1960s and 1970s he led a one-man campaign to promote Basque culture in Colorado. He single-handedly organized a performance of a professional Basque singing and dance troupe on tour in the United States at a local high school. He and his wife, Benny, essentially represented the state in the initial efforts to launch NABO. He starred as himself in an independently made movie *The Basque Sheepherder.*

He was instrumental in organizing a local Basque club. He built a handball court on his property in Grand Junction and invited a group of Iparralde ball players to put on an exhibition during their visit to the United States in 1979. He equipped one of his barns with a kitchen so it could be used as a clubhouse of sorts for barbecues.

Urruty was an expert blacksmith, and he spent his life decorating his longtime home at 465 Mesa Court with wrought iron. If you drive by the house (please don't disturb the occupants), you can see his ironwork, including Basque mementos and his well-known 101 brand.

Emmett Elizondo was probably the wealthiest rancher in this state. He herded sheep around Buffalo, Wyoming, and Ogden, Utah, before settling in western Colorado to begin building his empire in 1922. At the peak of his sheep business, he ran thirty thousand head. Later he invested in cattle too.

As a businessman, Elizondo helped organize the Fruita State Bank and served as its president for many years. (It has since merged with other banks and is now Bank One.) "He started the bank just because it was needed in the area," said Emmett's sister, María Elizondo, who worked side by side with her brother in his ranching business starting in the 1950s. If you're interested in reading some old history of the bank and Elizondo, ask a bank employee if you can see the bank's scrapbook. Emmett's only son, an engineer, was never involved in the business. When Emmett died in 1992, the livestock and much of the property holdings were sold to non-Basque Texan ranchers. In 1994, the Elizondo estate still had a small office in Grand Junction, to oversee the final disposition of his property holdings.

Both Elizondo and Urruty maintained homes in Grand Junction, and they interacted quite a bit, but they weren't the greatest of friends, according to Benny Urruty. After all, she explained, her husband was from Iparralde, and Elizondo was from the other side. Her comment is one example of the internal tensions that characterized relations among Basque-Americans.

---

settled. Sheepmen would winter their bands in Utah's southern deserts, around Price, then trail them to the forest reserves of western Colorado's high mountains each summer. The best-known Basque sheepmen in Colorado, Emmett Elizondo and Jean Urruty, followed this pattern. Grand Junction and Fruita, on the fertile plains of the Colorado River, became outposts for sheepherders, and eventually a few of the Basque families in the area took up farming. They also settled further south in Montrose, as well as to the north in Rifle, Meeker, and Craig. According to Father Gachiteguy, who traveled through the Western states in the 1950s, the Basques in Colorado were much more spread out, a few here or there in communities easily 50 miles apart.

URBAN CLUBS

In recent years, Basque groups have sprung up in Portland, Seattle, Denver, Sante Fe, and New Orleans, places that were not known for any significant concentration of Basques. The natural migration to urban areas is in large part responsible for bringing together enough Basques to make them aware of each other. In hopes of developing a cohesive group, a number of Basques in these cities have decided to organize their own clubs and sponsor events. In Washington, Colorado, and New Mexico, the creation of Web sites has helped bring in more people. In the course of getting to know the local Basques, people have also learned more about the historical presence of the ethnic group in their areas. (For more information on New Orleans, see The East Coast and the South chapter.)

Colorado had a Basque sheepherding and mining community in Grand Junction and Montrose on the Western Slope up through the 1970s. But most of the members of the current Colorado group are in the Denver/Boulder area. (See the Denver, Colorado, section.)

Denver

BASQUE CLUB

"We have an incredible diversity of Basque connections," notes President Mike Matassa about the membership in the new **Colorado Euskal Etxea** club. That is the challenge of being a new urban club. "All of us have a different view of what Basque is," he said. There are second- and first-generation Basques who are connected to the Grand Junction community that developed during the sheepherding and mining era. The club also includes a few who came from other places in the West with tight-knit Basque communities, like Matassa's mother, Mary Anne Carricaburu Matassa, who is from Rock Springs, Wyoming. There are recent Basque immigrants who came for jobs or to study at the University of Colorado. The membership includes a woman from the Basque Country, whose young son speaks Euskara, as well as a Basque priest who works in Denver. The Colorado club applied and was accepted for membership in the North American Basque Organizations in 2004. Even though the group is centered in Denver, it chose Colorado for its name in order to bring together Basques from all over the state. In 2005, the club had almost fifty members, which Matassa noted is more than some of the older clubs in NABO.

Club Activities. The club held a successful picnic in 2004 and plans to continue to hold the event on the last Saturday in June. However, other events have not attracted as many people. The group is still searching for a clear identity by scheduling different types of activities to see which are the most successful. The physical distance between its members, however, is a hindrance. "We may serve a different purpose," admitted Matassa, than some of [the] clubs in older, established Basque communities. "We may be more of a resource," he said, adding that they hope to offset part of the low attendance with their Web site, *www.coloradoeuskaletxea.com*. Members want to provide educational opportunities so that local Basques can learn more about the culture, said Matassa, and with that in mind they have already established a relationship with a Basque *ikastola* in Iruñea/Pamplona and have a grant from the Basque government to promote the exchange of people in both communities. The club has sent members to the Iruñea school to teach English. In return, in July 2005 the club received several young people from the school and planned a Basque week of events in Denver and Grand Junction at the time of their visit, which included music, dance and cooking classes, and dance performances.

Colorado Euskal Etxea, 11114 West 78th Avenue, Arvada, CO 80005. Information: (303) 665-2910 (Mike Matassa); *www.coloradoeuskaletxea.com*

Grand Junction

Grand Junction, the largest city (population of 40,125 in 1995) on the western slope of the Rockies, was named for its location at the junction of the Colorado and Gunnison Rivers. Herders with their sheep would cross the Colorado River and come right through town, over the Main Street bridge in Grand Junction, or through Fruita, on their annual trek to the mountains. Grand Junction probably had Colorado's most significant Basque population, based on the fact that there were two Basque hotels here, along with several small Basque rooming businesses in private homes.

As elsewhere in the West, tensions between sheepmen and cattlemen were high in the area surrounding Grand Junction. Cowboys often played dirty tricks on herders, who were considered lowly characters. Benny Urruty told the story of the death of one Basque man, whom her husband Jean had to bury himself because no one else was willing to do the job. "Even the mortuary people wouldn't accept him," she said. "That's how barbaric people used to be."

BOARDINGHOUSES

Tony and Margarita Retolaza were the longtime owners of a big boardinghouse, the Cantebarria, in downtown Grand Junction at 224 Colorado Avenue. Tony's uncle, Tony Coscorrozza, opened the boardinghouse in 1919, and the Retolazas took over the following year. Their place was a combination grocery store, pool hall, and boardinghouse, according to their son Louie Retolaza, who still lives in Grand Junction. The Retolazas had a player piano that they bought for $2,000 in 1920—a small fortune in those days.

Louie and Isadora Eisaguirre came from Salt Lake City and ran a boardinghouse at 234 Ute Avenue from 1936 to 1946. Jean Urruty and his wife Benny had a motel, the La Salle, on the corner of Colorado and Second Streets, but all the men went to the Retolazas' boardinghouse, a couple of buildings away, to eat.

The Retolazas' place finally closed in 1946. In later years a few families rented out rooms to the few herders who spent time in town, but any sense of a Basque community was gone. Both boarding-

Basques commonly had pool tables in their saloons. Antonio Retolaza (left), here with sons Johnnie and Louie and some regular patrons, at their "Cantebarria Pool Hall" in Grand Junction, Colorado. The player piano in the background was an expensive luxury piece, and the drawing on the wall shows the ship that brought Retolaza to America. (Courtesy of Louie Retolaza.)

houses have been torn down, and the La Salle is likely to disappear soon, as the city's modern convention center expands.

BASQUE CLUB AND PELOTA

After the boardinghouses disappeared, Jean Urruty was primarily responsible for unifying the Basque community in the 1960s and 1970s. The wealthy sheepman donated 2 or 3 acres on a corner of his farm property for use by the Basque club, which he was instrumental in organizing—the Western Slopes Basque Association. He built a fronton on the property and invited a group of Iparralde ball players to put on an exhibition during their visit to the United States in 1979. He equipped one of his barns with a kitchen so it could be used as a clubhouse of sorts for barbecues. The club organized parties and pelota tournaments for a few years. The pelota tournaments were typically broken down along Old World regional lines. Unfortunately, all the activity ceased after Urruty died in 1983. The fronton property was sold to the city, but Basques continued to play handball there.

However, during the early 1990s, the city put a NO TRESPASSING sign on it that remained for several years and the court became rundown, said local resident Maggie Doyhenard. In 1999, the city announced it was going to raze the court to create a parking lot for a park, and the local Basque community rose up in arms over its destruction. Doyhenard said the agitated group found out about the plan through an article in the newspaper. "My husband [Jean Pierre] said if they tear that down, nobody will know that the Basque people were in this area," said Doyhenard. Local court backers raised $50,000 in donations and in-kind services to support their cause, and city officials finally agreed to save the court. The court walls were reinforced, and a new floor was poured. A bronze plaque honoring the Basques was posted on the fronton. Volunteers planted donated trees and shrubs and created a picnic area. The Doyhenards donated an oak tree, to represent the Tree of Gernika. In October 2003, the ribbon on **Plaza Urrutia,** at the newly named Basque Cultural Corner, was cut. Today, Basque and non-Basque locals use the court, which is part of the larger Canyon View Park, to practice tennis, handball, and racquetball. Doyhenard said the fronton proved a rallying point for the local group of about thirty Basques. They gather for a potluck picnic and to play on the court on the first Sunday of every month. In July 2005, a group from Denver, which included Basque Country visitors, celebrated at the fronton with the local Basques. It was the first time in many years that Basque dancers had performed in Grand Junction, noted Colorado club president Michael Matassa.

Plaza Urrutia fronton, intersection of 24 and G Roads, Grand Junction

Montrose

Although a small Basque community has existed in Montrose over the years, very few of the Basques who came to the area to herd sheep stayed. There was never a Basque boardinghouse, a place to get Basque food, a Basque club, or a fronton. In the 1960s and 1970s the Colorado Basques had frequent get-togethers, but they were always held in

Grand Junction, either at Urruty's place or at the Café Caravan. Many Basques did herd sheep in the mountains around Montrose, though, or worked in the mines in Ouray and Silverton. And a few established sheep operations in the area, including Emmett Elizondo, whose long-time ranch headquarters were in Cimarron, just outside Montrose. The Etcharts, the Chuchurros, and the Allies also ran sheep.

Montrose, which has about twelve thousand people today, is experiencing growth, many of the newcomers being retired Californians looking for tranquility.

BOARDINGHOUSES

Starting in 1952 Martín and Rosalie Arruabarrena at the Mesa Hotel welcomed herders who came to town. When he was still herding sheep, before opening his own place, Martín Arruabarrena had gotten room and board at Pia (Olarain) Ansa's big house. There were also a few other families who rented rooms to the herders during the fall months. But none of these places could be considered a Basque boardinghouse in the true sense; that is, none of these places was a hotel where the herders were all fed in a big dining room. Even the Mesa Hotel could not be considered a boardinghouse, because it didn't serve meals to tenants on a regular basis. "[Preparing meals is] where all the work is, and there's no money," said Rosalie Arruabarrena. But often on weekends, some of the regulars, aching for some homemade food, would talk Rosalie into cooking for them. A majority of the Arruabarrenas' business was Basque herders. "In the fall we were always filled up," she said. But there were also truck drivers and lots of Basque and non-Basque miners who frequented the Mesa Hotel.

In 1971 the couple bought the building at 10 North Townsend that currently houses the **Mesa Hotel** in the center of town at the corner of Highways 50 and 550. The historic brick building, with a bookstore and barbershop downstairs, was built in 1904. The Arruabarrenas renovated the two-story building and touted it as a "multilingual" hotel. They were written up in two travel guides, *Penny-wise Travel* and *Let's Go USA* as a comfy inexpensive place to stay in Montrose—"and with that, I didn't need any other advertising," said Rosalie. So when the herders disappeared and the mines closed down, tourists became the Arruabarrenas' mainstay. The Arruabarrenas ran the hotel until

1990, and when they finally sold out and retired, it wasn't because business was bad. In fact, Rosalie said that she sometimes regretted the decision later. Had her adult children been around to oversee the hotel so that she and her husband could take occasional vacations, she might not have sold it. "I don't miss the work," she said. "I miss the life." She fondly remembers baking cakes for birthday celebrations and other parties held in the big lobby with the hotel regulars.

The new owners of the historic building, with its neon MESA HOTEL sign, are now renting out efficiency apartments with kitchens, yet the longtime advertisements put up by the Arruabarrenas at the small Montrose airport are still evident.

The house where Pia Ansa once rented rooms at 500 North First is also still standing. Very little else marks the Basque presence here. Even the longtime ranchers have disappeared, their children having gone into other businesses. The one exception is Martin and Marie Etchart, who still run a ranch in the area with their children.

■ New Mexico

Santa Fe/Albuquerque

CLUB

In New Mexico, the arrival of her cousin Blas Uberuaga, webmaster of Buber's Basque Page, was the catalyst that inspired Suzanne Uberuaga to start a Basque group in the Santa Fe/Albuquerque area. The **New Mexico Euskal Etxea** started off with a couple of potluck dinners, said Blas Uberuaga, so people could get to know each other. Originally from Homedale, Idaho, Uberuaga helped found a Basque club in Seattle while he was a student at the university there. Now, working at Los Alamos National Laboratory, Uberuaga is the first president of the New Mexico club. In 2005, members were organizing their first picnic and a small formal dinner for their first official year as a club. Uberuaga said he would like to eventually sponsor performances by such Basque Country artists as Kepa Junkera to expose the local community to Basque culture.

New Mexico Euskal Etxea, 2307 Camino Artista, Santa Fe, NM 87505. Information: (505) 670-9642 (Blas Uberuaga); *www.buber.net/NMEE/*

HISTORY

Most of the Basques in the current group are first- or second-generation Basques connected to the sheepherding industry in the West. Club members have learned of a Basque boardinghouse that existed in Grants, west of Albuquerque. However, Basque history in the Santa Fe area extends back to the founding of the state in the late 1500s. As part of the Spanish colonial expansion from Mexican territory into what is now the southwestern United States, Basque leader Juan de Oñate, with a group of colonizers that included other Basques, began the settlement of New Mexico in 1598. He served as its first governor from 1601 to 1609 before returning to Mexico. Some credit him with the founding of Santa Fe, although the capital during his leadership was located in San Juan Pueblo, 25 miles north of Santa Fe. It was not until Oñate retired and Governor Pedro de Peralta took over in 1610 that the capital was moved to its current location of Santa Fe. As a result, the city is considered the oldest capital city in North America and the oldest European community west of the Mississippi. Descendents of this historic Spanish expansion into the Southwest have always proudly traced their lineage all the way back to Spain, not Mexico. And of course, many of those early Spanish colonizers were Basques, including wealthy businessmen, politicians, and religious leaders. Some of these early colonizers also went to California.

BASQUE SOUVENIRS

The Spanish Table, which opened in Santa Fe in 2002, is a relatively new store selling gifts, imported food items, and wine from Spain and many items from the Basque Country. The store is the third Spanish Table—the original being in Seattle (see the Seattle section for more information). It is located in the city's historic plaza near the Hilton Hotel.

The Spanish Table, 109 North Guadalpe Street, Santa Fe, NM 87501 (505) 986-0243; *www.spanishtable.com*

■ Wyoming

Wyoming is the country's least populous state, with less than half a million people. Its harsh winters, which last more than half the year, keep the frontier spirit alive. The state straddles the Continental Divide. More than half of its tax revenue comes from oil and gas wells. But sheep and mining, the two traditional industries that attracted Basques elsewhere, supported two significant Basque communities in the state—at Buffalo and Rock Springs.

As in Utah and Colorado, the Wyoming Basque colonies are small and isolated. In Buffalo, where Basques have been a predominant group for many years, the larger community is knowledgeable about the culture. But in Rock Springs, as in Salt Lake City, the Basques struggle to pass on the traditions to their children and to make others aware of their culture.

SHEEP

In California and Nevada most sheepmen have converted their operations to cattle in recent years. Not in Wyoming. Here most Basque ranchers are still predominantly dedicated to sheep, although the transition to cattle has begun. In Buffalo sheep ranchers don't even need herders, because all their grazing land is privately owned and fenced in. The most significant Basque ranchers in this state are probably John Iberlin, in Buffalo, and Paul Etchepare, once a partner of the late Emmett Elizondo of Colorado, and currently CEO of the huge Warren Livestock operation. Etchepare is based out of Cheyenne, where few other Basques migrated.

Rock Springs and Green River

SHEEP AND MINING

Rock Springs has always been an industrial town, its economy based primarily on different kinds of mining. In the first half of the century, coal mining jobs brought the earliest Basques to the area. They were among several immigrant groups that made this town quite a melting pot. That diversity is still celebrated today in this city of twenty thousand with its annual festival, International Day, held in June.

Four or five families, who were among the earliest Basque settlers in Rock Springs, started sheep-ranching operations that continue today. Ask anyone who they are and you'll hear their names: the Arambels, the Erramouspes, the Carricaburus, and the Jaureguis.

If you ask people about Rock Springs in its early days, they'll probably say that it was an Iparralde colony, because most of the ranching families came from the towns of Baigorri and Banka, in Nafarroa Beherea. But just as many of the longtime families in town—the Larrabasters, the Aguirres, the Loisates, the Zabalas, and the Jaureguis—were from Bizkaia.

Coal mining ceased in the 1950s, just about the time that local trona mines went into high gear. Two thirds of the world's supply of trona, the ore from which soda ash is derived, comes from this area. (Baking soda, glass, and crystal are made from soda ash.) So when a herder's contract was up, Rock Springs had another industry to employ him. When the word got out, Basques also came from Nevada and Idaho in search of mining jobs, and many of them settled 15 miles from Rock Springs, in Green River, because it was closer to the mines. Basques who arrived in Rock Springs from the 1950s to the 1970s to work as herders—mostly Bizkaitarrak—eventually secured jobs in the soda ash (trona) mining business. Today, most of the soda ash workers have retired, and younger Basques work in many different businesses.

BOARDINGHOUSES

Casimiro Larrabaster was an early coal miner, and he and his wife Aniseta were the first known Basque settlers in Rock Springs. Shortly after arriving, the couple established the town's first Basque boardinghouse, around 1909. The two-story building was downtown at 416 Blair Avenue. The house is still standing, behind the Superior Lumber company, although being empty and run-down and having had a storage addition built in the front of the building, the house is hardly recognizable. "Our streets are very funny, because they built anywhere they wanted to at that time," said Felicia (Aguirre) Hatt, explaining that part of Blair Avenue was closed off, so now it is merely an alley behind C Street.

Cecilia Tayo opened a second boardinghouse on the other side of the railroad tracks, a big building on the western corner of M and North Front Streets. Today a large tree shades the side of the tall old green house. Mary Loisate came a little later, in 1921, and offered room and board for many years at her home at 209 K Street, where the perky woman lived with her family into her nineties. Another early family, Juana and Eusevio Aguirre, built a house of local sandstone in which to raise their seven children. Off the road 6 miles south of Rock Springs, the house was the location of many parties of the early Basque community.

RANCHING

Brothers Miguel and Luís Jauregui were probably the first Basques to establish a sheep ranch in Sweetwater County, having first herded sheep in Nevada. In 1905 they came to Rock Springs, where they went into business with Gaston and John Erramouspe. John Arambel, who had run sheep in Montana, as well as John and Jean Inchauspe, Pete and Domingo Etcheverry, and Pete Minhondo soon followed with their own outfits. The Jaureguis eventually sold their ranch to the Erramouspe brothers and went back to Europe. Gaston Erramouspe ended up with his own outfit, and Gaston Carricaburu eventually bought out Gaston's brother, John Erramouspe, in 1949.

Today Carricaburu's outfit is in the hands of his daughter Josie and her husband, Leon Jauregui. Ironically, Leon is the son of Miguel Jauregui, who nearly ninety years ago founded the operation now known as Carricaburu and Jauregui Livestock. "He ended up with the same sheep outfit that his father had originally," said Josie. The ranching families, all of whom had several children, have remained close through the years—and the relationships have been tightened along the way by several marriages.

But all the sheep and cattle ranchers are fighting for their livelihoods these days, as the federal government continues to restrict the use of public lands for grazing. The local ranchers, organized as the Rock Springs Grazing Association, have long had a formal cooperative partnership with the Bureau of Land Management and Union Pacific that gives them complete access to a huge 400-square-mile range along both sides of the railroad tracks to the east of Rock

Springs. They've been suffering, though, because the Red Desert region has offered little feed after several years of drought. The ranches still use herders—in fact, the Red Desert is so desolate that state law forced ranchers here to assign a herder *and* a camp tender to each herd. But the ranchers comply, realizing that the harsh climate, with its severe winters and the endless desert stretches, can be deadly. They take respite from the summer heat by heading west to the Bridger Teton National Forest.

BASQUE CLUB

Despite the longtime presence of Basques here, this small colony did not establish any Basque traditions until recently, and their club is less than ten years old. The descendants of the pioneer ranching families, mostly Iparraldetarrak, started joining the newer immigrants from Bizkaia during the 1970s at annual get-togethers. In the mid-1970s the ranching families began organizing dinner dances at the end of lambing, usually in April, and the event quickly became very popular. The invitation-only event started with a 6 P.M. Mass. "We always drew a big crowd for the Mass," said Josie Jauregui. Afterward dinner was served in the hall of St. Cyril Methodius church, followed by folk dance performances and social dancing until the wee hours. The annual dinner dance continued until locals decided to form a club in 1989, the **Alkartasuna Southwestern Wyoming Basque Club.**

Families in Rock Springs and Green River form the core of the group of about seventy members, but their events draw families living in outlying towns such as Kemmerer, Cokeville, Lander, and Rawlings. The union between the fewer, older Basque-American ranching families and the more numerous, more recent Bizkaian immigrants has not been the most congenial one, as has been borne out by early differences of opinion among club members. Under the leadership of Tomás Lejardi, the club changed the April dinner dance to a May festival and then to a big festival held in September that is open to the public, and a small members picnic was scheduled for June. More recently, the big public festival was switched to June and the membership picnic to August. The changes prompted more than one ranching family to drop out. "They're set at a time when none of us can go," said Josie Jauregui, noting that in the summer, the ranching families move west, close to the Bridger-Teton National Forest where their sheep spend the hot dry months, and then the ranchers are busy with shipping in the fall. Those who have worked hard to buoy up the club say that the switch to September was made at the request of a rancher who said that the festival, first held in May, interfered with lambing. Some say that the American-born Basques and the immigrant group are simply working at cross-purposes. "It would be nice if everybody could get together," said active club member Felicia (Aguirre) Hatt, whose family has lived in Rock Springs since 1910. In 2005, the group had around eighty members.

Club Activities. In the years that the club has existed, it has made significant strides in promoting Basque culture locally.

In July 2005, the club sponsored the annual NABO convention for the first time. This weekend of festivities, which included performances by U.S. and Basque Country musicians and dancers, as well as homages to Wyoming's Basque sheepherders, brought many U.S. Basques to Rock Springs for the first time.

For the members the club holds a picnic in August at the Sweetwater County Picnic Grounds west of Green River. The club serves grilled lamb chops, and families bring salad and dessert. It's a laid-back afternoon with lots of games for the kids, such as watermelon-eating contests and water-balloon fights. The club holds its *mus* tournament at a local hotel in March, and Santa Claus or the Basque Olentzero makes a visit with gifts for the kids at the yearly Christmas party. The Christmas party and a recent Thanksgiving dinner have been held at the **St. Cyril Methodius Church** hall (633 Bridger Avenue). A small dance group here was short-lived, mainly because there are no older Basque dancers to teach the young ones. "We're not like California and Nevada and Idaho, where they have taught their kids since they were little," said club officer Tomás Lejardi. Instructors have come and gone over the years. A group of dancers was revived for the big NABO convention in July 2005, which was Rock Springs' first hosting of such a big event.

The club is also involved in several longstanding community events. In the past, members have built floats with Basque themes for the Flaming Gorge Days parade in Green River, usually held on the last weekend in June, and the Red Desert Rodeo parade in Rock Springs, part of the bigger Red Desert RoundUp that occurs in early August. One year group members decorated the float as a sheep camp; another time it was a fishing boat.

To raise money for the club, members sell chorizos during Flaming Gorge Days and at the Sweetwater County Fair in Rock Springs, which follows the Red Desert RoundUp in August. "People didn't even know what a chorizo was until we started selling them in 1989," said Felicia Hatt. "Now they can't wait until the festivals come around to buy them." The proceeds are used to sponsor scholarships for young Basque-Americans and to help some local charities.

Alkartasuna Southwestern Wyoming Basque Club, P.O. Box 6157, Rock Springs, WY 82901. Information: 1-800-772-5990 (*Martín Goicoechea*) or (307) 875-5814 (*Tomás Lejardi*); *www.alkartasuna.us*

MUSIC

The close-knit Basque ranching families have put together a choir—the Rock Springs Family Choir—which seems a natural outcome of years of singing together at family gatherings. The group gets requests to perform from different organizations. They don't practice regularly, but round up the choir members for occasional performances.

FESTIVAL

The annual Rock Springs Basque festival, usually held in June, receives the most publicity of any Basque event year-round. In 2000, the event was renamed Kultura Jaia. Held at the Sweetwater County Events Complex, north of town at 3320 Yellowstone Road, Kultura Jaia includes a Basque dinner and an evening of performances from such out-of-town groups as Salt Lake City's Triskalariak dancers, or Boise's Oinkari. Rock Springs resident Martin Goicoechea, an award-winning *bertsolari*, has also performed his Basque poetry at the festivities. In addition to Wyoming Basques, the event attracts families from Boise and Salt Lake City.

Red Desert

Green River is a bit prettier than Rock Springs, but the expansive surrounding Red Desert has to be one of the most desolate areas in the state, or maybe the whole country for that matter. Coal mining and oil derricks decorated the landscape around Rock Springs for years. Today the big industries are strip-mining and power plants. A tourist attraction it's not. The desert, part of the gigantic, treeless Great Divide where all the streams disappear into the ground, is where the Rock Springs ranchers graze their sheep during the spring. Interstate 80 stretches east of Rock Springs, crossing flat terrain for 110 miles. "You can fall asleep at the wheel," said Josie Jauregui with a grin. But, she adds, "There's beauty in that desert—and it's very good for livestock." The region is also home to game animals, and one of the largest herds of wild horses in the country. So if you love wide open spaces, you might not mind seeing the Red Desert.

The Powder River Basin

If you're looking for a more scenic route to Wyoming's other Basque settlement—Buffalo—from Rock Springs, and you are willing to spend a little extra time on the road, consider making this trip: From Rock Springs head north on 191. By taking this route, you don't have to miss the wild horses. A good viewing spot is on the west side of 191, about 30 miles north of Rock Springs. To reach Buffalo, continue on 191, then 28, to Lander, where you'll take 789, then 26 to Shoshone. Here you will run into U.S. Highway 20, which traverses the awe-inspiring Wind River Canyon. From Worland, head east on Highway 16, which goes through the small town of Ten Sleep, where the cattlemen-sheepmen war reached its bloody climax in 1909. The highway will take you through the southern end of the Big Horn Mountains, through the Powder River Pass, then down into Buffalo. This route provides an introduction to the beautiful mountain scenery that has shaped the lives of the long-established Basque families here.

Several defining moments in the history of the Old West were played out in the Powder River Basin, all duly identified with markers and signs or at local museums. The Bozeman Trail leading from the North Platte to Virginia City was first blazed by white explorers through the middle of Sioux country in 1863, triggering warfare with the local tribe that lasted until 1877. The Native Americans did not view boundaries the way the white settlers did, yet the Sioux considered the river basin their chief hunting and camping grounds to be defended from other invaders, be they the neighboring Crow tribe or American and European invaders.

The United States built Forts Reno and Kearny along the trail to show the Sioux that the white settlers intended to stand their ground in the region. In 1867, near the town of Story, soldiers stationed at Fort Kearny got into a battle with the Sioux. Now referred to as the Wagon Box Fight, it resulted in the deaths of nearly two hundred Sioux. Although initially there was a reconciliation between the Sioux and the government, eventually the tribespeople were forced onto reservations in the Dakotas.

In the ten years that followed the Indian wars, large cattle ranchers set up ranches in the basin, creating an ideal setting for the glorification of the cowboy, which continues to this day in the area. But rebellious small ranchers also squeezed their way onto the range, and the ensuing tension between the big and small outfits resulted in the Johnson County War in 1892. In the end, the small homesteaders earned their place among the big cattle barons.

Buffalo

Located at the foot of the Bighorn Mountains, Buffalo is the Johnson County seat. Several features distinguish the Basque community here today. Ever since they first arrived after the turn of the twentieth century, Basques have owned more land than any other ethnic group in the county. They are still heavily into ranching, and, unlike in California and Nevada, where Basque ranchers have switched to cattle, ranchers here still specialize in sheep, although the business is getting tougher every day.

Esponda: First Basque in Buffalo

How is it that the small community of Buffalo in the northern reaches of this state—with no railroad in its early days—came to attract such a significant Basque population? It reportedly started with one man named Jean Esponda, from the town of Baigorri, who ran into sheepman Patsy Healy on the train as he was heading west. The year was 1902. The sheepman was an owner of the Healy-Patterson Ranch in Buffalo, the largest sheep raisers in northern Wyoming at the time, and he convinced the Basque traveler to come work for him. "He was needing help and needing help bad," said Buffalo rancher Simon Iberlin.

Most histories about this Basque colony tell the story this way, but the late Grayce (Esponda) Miller claimed that they all got it wrong. It was Jean's brother, John Esponda, who first arrived in Buffalo, not Jean, she insisted in a 1995 interview. Jean was the oldest of the family, and he first traveled to California in 1888, where he herded sheep around Bakersfield for Jean Burubeltz and eventually established his own band of sheep. After that is where the story goes awry, according to Esponda Miller. Supposedly, Jean Esponda sold his flock and went home to the Basque Country, and he met Patsy Healy on the train going back to California several months later. Esponda Miller said it was her father John, or *Joanes,* who was headed to California to meet his brother Jean when he ran into the Buffalo sheepman on the train. The confusion likely stems from the common family practice of giving the sons names that are all different versions of John. According to Esponda Miller, Jean did soon arrive in Buffalo to join his brother, and was there long enough for Pete Harriet, another early Buffalo arrival, to court and marry Jean's daughter Catherine in 1907.

Jean Esponda eventually sold out and went back to France, but his brother John stayed and continued to expand his operation, until it was the largest in the region. He brought Basques over to work for him, often going into partnership with them until they could get on their feet with their own business, according to another daughter, Jeanette Maxwell. He helped them out when they were in trouble. "He wouldn't let anybody go on welfare," she said. "He'd take care of them rather than have the government take care of them."

John married late in life and brought up his family in a big house on Main Street. He built a pelota court behind the house that was heavily used for many years. Because of his economic power, Esponda became known as the "King of the Basques." And after his death in 1936, it was the late John Camino who replaced him in that role.

Despite its isolation from other Basque communities, and its small size, this proud Basque population has managed to keep its culture alive. You could probably say that Buffalo started the Basque "community picnic" tradition more than seventy-five years ago, and it continues to sponsor its annual celebration on August 15. In 1988 Buffalo hosted the annual NABO convention, which attracted some four thousand people, essentially doubling the town's population. This Basque community has also maintained the longest-running Basque radio program in the United States, which continued for forty years through 1994.

Brothers Jean and John Esponda were the first Basques to arrive in this small town, far removed from any of the major transportation routes. By chance they encountered an owner of the Healy and Patterson sheep ranch, who convinced them to come work for him. Within three or four years, several Basques from the Espondas' hometown of Baigorri and neighboring Arnegi in Nafarroa Beherea had arrived in Buffalo. They in turn encouraged relatives and neighbors from their hometowns to join them at Healy and Patterson, the largest sheep ranch in northern Wyoming.

When the Espondas first arrived in Buffalo, the majority of the sheep outfits were owned by Scots. But the Basques eventually replaced them. The two Esponda brothers gradually gained control of most of the Healy and Patterson range, and they continued to recruit sheepmen from Nafarroa Beherea. Many of the Basque families who live in Buffalo today, such as the Espondas, the Harriets, the Caminos, the Martons, the Iberlins, the Etchemendys, and the Falxas, are descendants of the earliest Basque settlers in Johnson County, all of whom were originally from the same two or three adjoining villages in the Old Country. Dollie Iberlin, who helps husband Simon keep up his ranch, wrote a book, *The Basque Web,* about the Buffalo community. In it she details how all the existing families can be traced back to a connection with pioneers Jean and John Esponda, showing how tightly interconnected the Buffalo Basque community was.

Hundreds of herders have made their way to Buffalo over the years, although most of them did not stay. Despite Buffalo's isolation, Basques still found ways to get to the town. During a visit to New York a while back, Simon Iberlin said that he visited Ellis Island, where immigration officials had processed the majority of those who arrived here. Iberlin checked a computer listing for Wyoming. He said that 499 Basque names showed up on the list, "and I'm guessing 490 of them came through Buffalo." Some arrived here just before World War II and enlisted in the U.S. Army, since that was a guaranteed way to get U.S. citizenship. Later many soldiers returned to Buffalo after the war. The earliest herders were all from Nafarroa Beherea, but later it was mostly Bizkaitarrak who immigrated, and many settled in Buffalo.

Unlike in other states where ranchers ran their herds on public lands, most of the sheep walks in Johnson County are privately owned by the ranchers. During the 1950s and 1960s the ranchers began fencing in their land. Consequently, they could put the sheep out to pasture and check on them once a week or so. As a result, the need for herders evaporated, and Basque immigration slowed down.

RANCHING

Basques began arriving in Wyoming around 1900, but life was not necessarily peaceful. They introduced sheep into the region at a time when competition between cattle and sheep ranchers for public grazing land was fierce. But whereas serious cattle-sheep feuds raged on the other side of the Big Horns, in the Buffalo area the competition was resolved without bloodshed. Basques simply proceeded to buy up the land from the Scots sheepmen, from the winter plains to their summer mountain ranges, without any problem—sometimes just for the price of unpaid taxes. "The Basques of Buffalo have been, from the outset, land-oriented, a fact that makes their early pattern of settlement unique when compared to that of Basques of other areas," wrote William Douglass and Jon Bilbao in *Amerikanuak*.

The pattern started with the Esponda brothers and two cousins who formed a partnership and began purchasing land in Buffalo in 1904. In fact, Douglass and Bilbao suggest that it was Jean Esponda's experience in California, where competition for open land was fierce, that prompted the first purchase. The ownership of land and the operation of sheep ranches held the Johnson County Basque community together for many years, according to scholar Joseph Roy Castelli, in his 1970 Ph.D. dissertation "Basques in the Western United States." "The purchase of land indicates the change in goals and the change from being transitory herders to becoming Basque-Americans," he wrote. Castelli made an interesting comparison between the price of lambs and the purchase of land in Johnson County. When lamb and wool prices went up, so did the rates at which the Basque ranchers bought land.

The largest purchase of land by Basques occurred during the 1940s, when they bought over 100,000 acres of land throughout the county. Castelli noted that the Basques owned more than 250,000 acres in the county at that time. The local availability of land dropped off significantly in the late 1960s. According to Castelli, while Basque immigration in the United States in general slowed down in the 1960s, the decline was even more significant in Buffalo because there were fewer opportunities to buy land.

Although their numbers are shrinking, Basques continue to be the largest individual land owners in Johnson County. The region is still primarily grazing country, and ranching continues among members of the younger generations of the same families. Johnson County currently has the largest number of sheep in the state.

Simon Iberlin, his brother John Iberlin, Charles and John Marton, Simon U. Harriet, and Pete Camino all worked hard to keep their families' longtime ranches in operation. Gladys Esponda, widow of John Esponda's son, Art, and her sons kept up the historic Esponda ranch.

"Everyone who is here has been here thirty to forty years," said Joe Reculusa of Kaycee, who inherited his business from his father.

SHEEP

The business of sheepherding is getting more and more difficult. One problem that has always plagued the herders in northwestern Wyoming is the weather. Lack of rain and blizzards exist within the same territory. The conditions are poor for cattle, which explains the predominance of sheep here. But the extremes are hard on sheep ranchers as well. Large numbers of sheep are lost every year to coyotes, especially ever since controlling them with poison bait was outlawed. Mountain lions pose the same threat. Gates to private ranches are left open by hikers or hunters tromping through federal lands. And recently public officials have been talking about raising grazing fees. "Everything is against us," said Madeline Harriet. "Everything we have to buy goes up, up, up. Everything we have to sell keeps going down." Madeline and Simon U. Harriet sold their business at the end of 1994, as did the Charles Marton family. "It has been a wonderful way of life, but not anymore," Madeline said. Slowly some ranchers

Sheep Wagons

The wagon had a significant place in Buffalo's ranching life, perhaps because it was part of everyone's life, not just the herders'. Even families would ride up to the annual parties in wagons. "I can remember when I was six or seven and coming [to the picnic] in a chuck wagon and having it rain," said Florence Camino, in a 1994 interview, before she passed away. Men didn't always wait until they had a nest egg to get married. More than one young couple spent a few years living in the wagons, while the husband got a foothold in the business. Entire families lived in them in the summers, when they went up to the mountains. Almost everywhere else in the West, mountain ranges were too steep to allow herders to use their wagons. Most brought tents and everything else they needed on the back of pack animals. But in Johnson County, roads were built on the private range land where the sheep spent the summers. "We used the wagon year-round," said rancher Simon Iberlin. Indeed, wagons were used in Johnson County until fairly recently. Although most of the ranchers have switched to camper-trailers, with gas stoves and refrigerators, more than one rancher has refused to give up the old wagons. They've converted them, though, to be hauled behind a pickup. "Sheep wagons are still easier to pull in rough country," said Iberlin.

are switching to cattle. Others are opting to sell their land. No one can predict what will happen to the sheep businesses they have worked so long to build. In 2005, John Iberlin was sheep ranching, but he had moved to the area near Gillette. Pete Camino still had sheep, but his cousin's son John Camino sold his after working for twelve years to keep up his father's business. The Curutchets were among the few Basque families still raising sheep in Johnson County. Most other longtime Basque families retired from the business. "There aren't too many left, and that's the sad truth," said Alberta Escoz.

Filmakers Tim and Ben Kahn and Scott Carroll made a feature film about the end of sheep ranching, highlighting Buffalo rancher Pete Camino. The film's Web site (*www.thelastlink.org*) provides lots of information about this disappearing lifestyle. (In 2005, copies of the film were being sold by NABO, with a portion of the proceeds going to the group's educational fund.)

Simon Iberlin's daughter was not the least interested in his cattle business, but his two young grandsons enjoyed playing on his farm equipment. The seventy-two-year-old rancher hoped that one day the boys would take over, but he ended up selling, too. Iberlin went into local politics, serving as county commissioner for twelve years and as a state highway commissioner for six. (This small Basque community has been well-represented in politics. In 1995 native son John Marton was starting his fifteenth year in the state House of Representatives. He has also served as speaker of the house.)

BOARDINGHOUSES

The **Occidental Hotel** was the biggest commercial building in town, and up until 1972 many of the locals, including the Basques, stopped in at the bar and dining room to while away an afternoon or evening, having a drink and playing cards (see site listing later in the chapter). "It was a place where they could catch up on the news," said Joan Smith, whose family owned the historic hotel for eighty years. Over the years, many Basque herders stayed there too.

The 21 Club (4 South Main) directly across the creek—a small bar with a pool table and card tables that was once a brothel—was also a Basque hangout. Madeline Ardans rented a few rooms upstairs and cooked meals for the men. Joe Lawrence, son-in-law of Gaston Irigaray, owned the club for at least ten years. This icon was finally sold and renamed.

Unlike most of the other Basque communities that quickly established boardinghouses, "there was nowhere for [Basques] to stay in Buffalo," said Simon Iberlin. Most of the herders stayed with their employers in their homes. During the short periods when they weren't on the trail in their wagons, that is. There were a couple of boardinghouses in town over the years. The one most people knew best was John and María Bilbao's place, a big house in the 400 block of South Main that the Bilbaos operated during the 1930s and 1940s. It was right across from the Espondas' house. The Bilbaos' place was mainly just a big two-story family home where a few herders got room and board. But some wonderful parties spontaneously erupted around the beautiful player piano in the dining room.

Madeline Ardans also offered the men room and board for a few years at a couple of different locations while she raised five children. In 1950 Madeline and Simon U. Harriet opened the **Hotel Idlewild,** to give the herders someplace to stay in town, but they never served meals, Madeline emphasized. The hotel on Main Street is part of Buffalo's historic downtown.

Despite the absence of big boardinghouses, the Basques weren't about to skip their parties. Their festivities were held in the garages and barns of the Espondas and the Irigarays, or at Celestina Curutchet's or Joe Bejino's place.

A great number of the herders moved on to Nevada and California. San Francisco and Chino are full of gardeners and milkers who started out herding in Buffalo. Herders who stayed but did not marry eventually retired to the Occidental Hotel or the Idlewild. Anna Michelena, widow of Sebastian and mother of twelve children, was one of those who retired to the Occidental. Her room had a big window overlooking Main Street, where for years she kept an eye on everything happening below.

Occidental Hotel

In the early 1980s Buffalo's Main Street was dead. A few years later the town's economic development committee decided that the reopening of the historic sixty-room Occidental Hotel, which had closed in 1984, was key to the revival of the city center. A civic group of fifty to sixty local people cleaned and painted the south end of the Occidental from top to bottom, and part of the building was reopened in 1990 for tours. One of the upstairs rooms was dedicated to a Basque exhibit, organized by Dollie Iberlin, with a six-foot replica of a sheep wagon and early photos of the local Basque community.

The hotel was purchased in 1997, and the owners restored the historical landmark to its former splendor, and rooms furnished with antiques are now available.

The economic recovery plan was successful, and nearly every business on Main Street is now open. But where once there was a hardware store, market, or other service that the local ranching families needed, today there are art galleries and antique stores to cater to the tourists. For more information, contact the Buffalo Chamber of Commerce (55 North Main Street) at (307) 684-5544.

Occidental Hotel, 10 North Main Street, Buffalo, WY 82834 (307) 684-0451; *www.occidentalwyoming.com*

WALKING TOUR

Main Street, a picturesque crooked street, complete with its bridge and creek, has remained the center of this small town. The entire street has been declared a historic district, and all the businesses have signs in their windows explaining their building's history. Take your own walking tour down Main Street to see the houses and businesses that shaped daily life for the Basques. Walk by the Occidental, the Idlewild, and the former 21 Club, which is still a bar. You might enjoy seeing the Espondas' old place at 511 South Main Street. Imagine young Basque men playing pelota in a court against a barn in the back of the property. The pelota court on the Esponda ranch fell into disuse by the 1950s and was torn down.

The old Bilbao place, which was across the street, has been moved to the back of the property, facing High Street, but it's still there, now a private home that has been nicely spruced up. Check out the big house with the long stairway at 472 South Main, where Madeline Ardans used to offer room and board. All the homes of these early pioneers, including the Espondas', are in fine shape and currently inhabited.

Visit the beautiful brick building at 390 South Main Street that was once the Marton family home. A British count and countess lived there once, and later it belonged to the Catholic church, which hosted potlucks and parties there. A parish priest traded houses with Charles and Pat Marton, who raised their seven children there.

You can't miss the historic Rothwell house, a Victorian home with lots of turrets, right across the street, at 341 South Main. Former Basque radio station owner Jeanette Maxwell lives there today.

Walk a few blocks to the other end of the street, at 513 North Main, to see the longtime home of Bernard and Catherine Marton, Charles's parents. The oldest Basque home in town is probably that of early pioneers Peter and Catherine Harriet, just a block away from Main, at 290 North Adams Street, and it hasn't changed a bit despite the passage of time. Theirs was probably the first Basque marriage in Buffalo, and their home was a gathering place for many years. Later the couple sold their sheep and went back to France, where they built a beautiful house in Uhart-Cize, just outside Donibane-Garazi.

Drop in at **St. John's Catholic Church** at 532 North Lobban, which John Esponda collected money to help build. More than half of its parishioners over the years have been Basque. See **Willow Grove Cemetery** at the south end of town, at the junction of Main Street and Highway 196, for a real view of this town's past. You might also want to walk the hiking trail that has been developed along Clear Creek, which starts at South Bypass Road behind the Super-8 Motel and winds through town all the way to Mosier Gulch Picnic Area.

BASQUE CLUB

Dennis Lawrence, grandson of Gaston Irigaray and the late Mary Camino, daughter of Florence and Martin Camino, collaborated in 1983 to start a Basque club in Buffalo, the **Big Horn Basque Club.** "It hasn't really changed anything else that we do around Buffalo," said Lawrence. The first year the group received a state arts and humanities grant and asked Janet Inda and William Douglass of Reno to come to Buffalo to provide some information about other clubs. For the following August 15 celebration, the club invited the Salt Lake and Boise dancers to perform. This tradition continued, but the club also organized its own dance group, an annual meeting and dinner in January, and a *mus* tournament in the spring. For a while members got together once a month in people's homes for a covered-dish supper and *mus* playing, but those gatherings have petered out. "We're not that many any more," said Madeline Harriet. The *mus* tournament is also getting smaller, because young people are not learning the game, said Alberta Escoz.

Except for the dancers, Lawrence noted that it's mainly the older generation that is working hard to maintain the club. "The third and fourth generations have been remiss in keeping it up," said Lawrence, noting that he, too, is less involved these days.

Big Horn Basque Club, P.O. Box 308, Buffalo, WY 82834. Information: (307) 684-5472 (*Alberta Escoz*)

NABO CONVENTIONS

When Buffalo hosted the NABO summer convention in 1988, the businesses in town were not ready for the more than four thousand people who showed up. "They ran out of wine. They ran out of eggs," said Simon Iberlin. "They couldn't believe it." The whole town got into the spirit of the event. "Everyone wanted to be Basque then," said Iberlin's sister, Madeline Harriet. "All the clerks downtown wore berets." The town sponsored another NABO convention in August 1995, which was just as successful.

The Buffalo Basque community was gearing up to host the 2006 NABO festival as well. "We have great support from the whole community," said Alberta Escoz.

FESTIVAL

Buffalo's Basque people took to celebrating the church holiday of the Feast of the Assumption of the Virgin Mary (Andra Mari) on August 15 in honor of the feast day celebrations held in Arnegi and other towns in the Old Country where they were from. So August 15 became the date of the annual Buffalo picnic. The first known celebration was organized in 1918, and John Esponda invited Father Leo Gariador of California to say a Mass before the party. Some estimate that picnic did not become a fixed celebration until much later, and once it got going it was probably the largest of the early Basque picnics—a real community affair. It started as a big party up in the Big Horn Mountains. "To thank the owners and their wives, the Basque herders would put on the party," said Simon Iberlin. The men would buy the booze, and the women would bring the food. The earliest parties would be held at John Esponda's mountain cabin in Hazelton, where his family stayed in the summer. Wooden planks were set up on wooden boxes to seat people for the outdoor Mass that has always started the festivities. The priest would come up on horseback. The herders would park their wagons on the mountainside. By nightfall the herders usually had to rush back to their bands, before the sheep began mixing together. Separating them was a big headache.

The dance floor was a portable affair set down on the ground. If it was cold or raining, everybody would crowd into the cabin to dance, and there was always a musician or two—usually an accordionist or a trumpet player. In cowboy country, even a Basque fiddler or two was not unusual. Despite the fact that there was no formal dance group in Buffalo until the 1980s, everyone knew the fandango. There were no folk costumes either, but the crowd put on berets and red scarves for the occasion. Through the years, the party moved to different mountain cabins—the Espondas', the Falxas', the Irigarays'. For a while, the event was so popular that it attracted more non-Basques than Basques, and it was canceled for a few years because of too much drinking and rowdiness.

The annual August 15 celebration is still a popular event, especially the dance, although a big crowd here is 200 to 250. "Now we go in cars, have the food catered, and hire an orchestra," joked Madeline Harriet, pointing out the changes time has wrought. Basques from Billings, Montana, and from Rock Springs show up like clockwork for the party, no matter what day of the week it falls on. Young people who don't get together all year long show up for the dance. It's still set in the mountains at the Johnson County youth camp in the heart of the Big Horn Mountains. Signs all over town point the way to the lamb barbecue and dance, twenty miles west of Buffalo on Highway 16.

In 1994 the club sponsored a Basque Day, the Saturday before August 15, featuring lambs above all—sheep shearing, lambs to pet, and lamb burgers. It took place at Buffalo's city park on Main Street. Iberlin said that the event at Buffalo's city park on Main Street drew quite a crowd and may well be repeated in future years.

DANCE

The **Zaharrer Segi Dancers** are in great demand and get constant invitations to perform. If you want to be sure of seeing the dancers, you can catch them at the annual picnic and at the Johnson County Fair and Rodeo parade through town on the first Saturday of August. The dancers also perform at the Sheepherders Rodeo in Kaycee in July.

BASQUE RADIO PROGRAM

For more than forty years, Basques throughout Johnson County were able to tune in to a local radio station and hear Euskara. The weekly radio program was inaugurated in 1956, soon after Jeanette (Esponda) Maxwell bought a local radio station, KBBS, the call letters standing for "Buffalo's Basque Station." Originally a young Basque approached Maxwell about announcing that he had some sheep for sale. According to Maxwell, that spurred the idea of putting together a regular program. But the Basques didn't want to be beholden to any sponsors and decided to raise money to fund the program themselves. As a result the Basque community contributed money every year to keep the program on the air. It was broadcast every Sunday at noon for one hour on 1450 AM on the dial.

Domingo Martirena was the program's first announcer; later there was Martin Camino; and for the past few years Grayce (Esponda) Miller was the announcer. Most of the program was in Euskara, although a few of the announcements were in English for the sake of the non-Euskara speakers who listened regularly. "They wouldn't miss it for the world," Miller said in 1995. The program played many different kinds of Basque music, from records and tapes that have been donated over the years, and sometimes live music was aired too—mostly performed by singers or accordion players. The announcements were somewhat provincial, consisting primarily of news about local Basque families, but the program covered local Buffalo news as well, and it had a faithful following.

Esponda Miller passed away in March 1996. She asked to be buried on the mountain, on land that had been in her family since the 1910s. The beautiful mountain service was attended by almost the entire Basque community.

Several other local Basques took over Miller's job as announcer on the Sunday Basque program. Unfortunately, Miller's sister, Jeanette Maxwell, finally decided to sell the radio station after forty years. "It's time to do other things," said Maxwell, adding that a trip to the Basque Country was among her plans. The non-Basques who bought the station indicated they would keep the popular program, but their interest faded and the program ended. The nine Basques who had broadcast the radio program through the years were honored by induction into the Hall of Fame by the Society of Basque Studies in America in 1997. At the same time, to honor the Basques of Buffalo, the city named one of their streets "Euskaldun Kalea." It is located next to the BLM offices at 1425 Fort Street.

LIVING HISTORY DAYS AND OTHER ATTRACTIONS

Located at the junction of two interstate highways (90 and 25), and midway between Yellowstone National Park and the Black Hills of South Dakota, Buffalo attracts quite a few tourists. Many of them come to see the battle sites, museums, and historic buildings. If you can't make it here for the August 15th picnic, you might try the Thursday, Friday, and Saturday following the Fourth of July, when the **Jim Gatchell Museum** sponsors Living History Days, a major community affair. There are all kinds of demonstrations of early Western life, and that includes the herder's life. Domingo Martirena and a couple of other men always volunteer to talk about their experiences. They dress up in berets and red scarves and carry sheep hooks and their leather *zahakuak* (wine bags). "They usually give the tourists a little shot of wine from the wine bag," said museum curator Gary Anderson. Sometimes the dates change, so call the museum.

The Jim Gatchell Museum, which highlights America's frontier history, has an authentic, restored sheep wagon on display, complete with bedroll, pots, and pans. The history of the Basque sheep ranchers is chronicled in an exhibit that includes photographs. Museum educator Bob Edwards said the wagon is the museum's most photographed item. The museum closes during the freezing winter months.

On the second weekend of July there's also a "Sheepherders' Rodeo" in Kaycee, with sheepdog trials, sheep hooking, and sheep roping. Also in Kaycee at the **Hoofprints of the Past Museum** (344 Nowlan Avenue), which opened in 1990, among the exhibits of early settlers, outlaws, and the range wars, photos of the Basques and a sheep wagon are on display.

Jim Gatchell Museum, 100 Fort Street, Buffalo, WY (307) 684-9331; *www.jimgatchell.com*

BASQUE RANCHES IN HISTORIC SETTINGS

It was inevitable that the far-reaching lands of the Basques in Wyoming would overlap with some of the historic places in the Powder Basin. Gaston Irigaray's former ranch was one setting where the Johnson County War took place, although nothing on the ranch ever marked the site.

The old Bozeman Trail goes right through the Reculusa ranch. The trail was first established in 1864, but because of all the trouble it caused, it was hardly used after a couple of years. "That was ancient history by the time we bought the ranch," said Joe Reculusa whose father first purchased the property in 1943. Fort Reno was built in 1865, half a mile from where the Reculusa ranch is now located, supposedly as a show of military force in the Powder River Basin.

It is beautiful countryside, should you decide to drive through it, but be sure to have a detailed map of the roads here. Reculusa cautions travelers to be aware that there's nothing left of the old fort or the Bozeman Trail, and that the road is gravel for a great part of the way. A monument marks the old fort site, and a few signs indicate where the old trail once was. If you're interested in following the early pioneers' trek, take Highway 192 east from Kaycee for 19 miles, where you'll see the road heading north toward the Fort Reno site, paralleling the Powder River that gave this region its name. The road splits, and the Bozeman Trail heads northwest, while the old fort lies to the northeast. If you head to Fort Reno, another northwest road there eventually meets with the Bozeman Trail road, which will take you back to Interstate 25 and Buffalo.

While you're here, you'll enjoy visiting the many sites that commemorate the historic events of the area. In addition to the museums in Buffalo and Kaycee, Fort Kearny, 17 miles north of Buffalo, has a visitors center and museum. The TA Ranch, between Buffalo and Kaycee, is where the main battle of the Johnson County War took place. It has been restored to its original bare walls, and bullet holes from the main battle are still visible. Tall tales of vigilante gangs and rustlers roaming the countryside make the rounds here. One of the most famous of these gangs was "the Wild Bunch," headed by Butch Cassidy and Harvey Logan, whose favorite saloons were in Buffalo. Local companies take tour groups into their most famous hideout—Hole-in-the-Wall, a valley reached via a narrow gorge, west of the town of Kaycee in the southwest corner of Johnson County.

And if you're driving through the town of Casper, you might stop to see the replica of a *harri mutil* (stone boy) in front of the office of the Wyoming Wool Growers Association (811 North Glenn Road across the interstate from the Hilton).

■ Montana

The Basque settlements in this state have been so small that they are almost not worth mentioning, except for the fact that their presence has continued from the early part of the century until today. Basques have herded sheep in Montana since at least 1910. When Father Adrien Gachiteguy visited Miles City in the 1950s, there was a small Basque community there, several of the residents being Basque ranchers who had relocated from Buffalo, Wyoming. When Father Martxel Tillous traveled to the town during 2004, Basques were still getting together. Basque families were spread out mostly in the eastern third of the state. In addition to Miles City, they live in Billings, Glasgow, Sidney, Plentywood, and other towns along the Missouri and Yellowstone Rivers.

In the early part of the 1900s the Etchart, Etchepare, and Oronoz families were among the first Basques in Montana, and they were followed by several others. Among the best known was John Etchart, who arrived in 1910, when Montana had the largest sheep population in the country. Etchart and his brother had started a sheep business in Elko, Nevada, but when he was on a return visit to the Basque Country, a friend advised him to seek out the open ranges of Valley County. In 1914 Etchart built a beautiful stone house for his wife Catherine near Glasgow and raised sheep on the rich grasslands along the Missouri River. Their home became the heart of a tiny Basque community, many of whose residents were from Etchart's hometown of Aldudes. Basque ranchers had a hard time with Montana's severe winters—another possible reason why fewer Basque sheepmen settled in the state.

Today the Basque families of Montana are few and far between, but they continue to ranch and keep in close touch with each other. The West's Basque chaplain makes an annual visit to the area in the summer, and word of his visit is quickly circulated. "I would say to someone that I'm coming, and they would organize a picnic," said Father Jean Eliçagaray. Father Tillous, who has served U.S. Basques for over ten years after Eliçagaray, visited the Montana community numerous times. A small group reunites at Fort Peck, near Fort Peck Lake, on the first Sunday of June. Father Tillous makes his appearance on the last Sunday of August at a picnic on a private Basque ranch, which attracts nearly all the Basques in Montana. "The priest doesn't just come to say the Mass but to bring the culture, too," said Father Tillous.

REFERENCES

Castelli, Joseph Roy. "Basques in the Western United States: A Functional Approach to Determination of Cultural Presence in the Geographic Landscape." Diss., University of Colorado, 1970, p. 120.

Douglass, William A., and Jon Bilbao. *Amerikanuak: Basques in the New World.* Reno, Nev.: University of Nevada Press, 1975, p. 334.

Dunn, Louise Brown. "The Salt Lake City Basque Community: Atypical in the American West." Master's thesis, University of Utah, 1972.

Gachitéguy, Adrien. *Les Basques dans l'ouest Américain.* Bordeaux, France: Editions Ezila, 1955.

Iberlin, Dollie. *The Basque Web.* Buffalo, Wyo.: The Buffalo Bulletin, 1981.

Iberlin, Dollie, and David Romtvedt. *Buffalotarrak.* Buffalo, Wyo.: Red Hills Publications, 1995.

The East Coast and the South

New York

New York City

Unlike the American West Basque colony that saw its beginning in the California Gold Rush of 1848, Basque settlement in New York was closely linked to the construction of the transcontinental railroad. Until the railroad was built, most Basques who yearned to reach the Golden State traveled by ship and landed on the Pacific Coast, since the central and western United States was still mostly unexplored territory and very difficult to traverse by land.

Once the transcontinental railroad's last spike was driven in Promontory Point, Utah, in 1869, Basques could sail from their homeland to New York and take a train across the country. Almost all of them arrived with the intention of joining their fellow countrymen in the West, but some never made it. They became the first residents of a longtime Basque colony in this giant city. There were also those who never planned to go beyond New York, especially seafaring men who came to work in the bustling maritime industry of the New York and New Jersey ports.

New York's Basques were a close-knit group living in the neighborhood at the foot of the Brooklyn Bridge, along Cherry and Water Streets. Several Basque couples operated boardinghouses there. The neighborhood was also home to Italian, Greek, and Irish immigrants, according to Mary Toja, who grew up there. Basques worshipped at the nearby St. Joachim and St. Joseph's Churches, but they often traveled to the West Side, to Nuestra Señora de Guadalupe Church on Fourteenth Street (between Seventh and Eighth Streets) on the northern border of Greenwich Village, established in 1906, because it was a predominantly Spanish church and had a Basque priest. Many of the neighborhood's Basque couples were married there. Across the street from the church, Carmen Moneo had a store where she sold all sorts of imported Spanish and Basque goods. "To go to Moneo's or that church, you had to take the trolley or the subway," said Toja, who remembers making the trip often on Sundays. Moneo's Store endured for over seventy-five years, carried on by Carmen's son and grandsons up through the 1980s.

A Founder of the New York Basque Colony

The most prominent of the group's founders was Valentín Aguirre, who became a successful businessman and had a profound effect on the New York City Basque colony. Aguirre also worked as a boatman when he arrived here, ambitiously learning English and passing the civil servant test in 1897 in order to work on New York City boats. Aguirre and his wife Benita ran a boardinghouse that became quite well known. Immigrants sought out the Aguirres' boardinghouse as soon as they arrived. The couple's business thrived, and they moved several times before settling in the famed Greenwich Village neighborhood, where they opened the Santa Lucia Hotel at 82 Bank Street. The Basque community continued to gravitate around it.

Aguirre began helping Basque immigrants with their travel plans, and opened his own travel agency, along with the well-known Jai Alai Restaurant next door to the hotel. He went out of his way to seek out Basques coming through New York to assist them on their trip west. Many an immigrant remembers docking at the New York harbor, frightened because he or she knew no English, only to hear a voice asking in Basque if there were any Basques on board. Aguirre himself escorted them to his hotel, and, in later years, sent one of his eight children, all of whom spoke some Spanish and Basque, to do the job. The new arrivals would inevitably spend the night at the Santa Lucia, and Aguirre would make their travel arrangements for them. Professor Emilia Doyaga, who wrote about the early New York colony, related how he would send them on their way, with a sign of their final destination tucked in their hat or pocket.

Today the Alfred Smith Housing Project covers the old Basque neighborhood. The nearest church to the neighborhood, **St. Joseph's** (5 Monroe at Catherine), now has the documents of the old St. Joachim Church, which was torn down. The building that once housed Aguirre's Santa Lucia Hotel and Jai Alai restaurant at 82 Bank Street is still there.

CEMETERIES

A number of Basques from the early years of this colony are buried at Calvary Cemetery in Brooklyn, and also in St. John's Cemetery in the Middle Village section of Long Island. During the last fifty years, however, they've been buried all over, and most any Catholic cemetery throughout New York City and its suburbs is likely to yield Basque names.

BASQUE CLUBS

Centro Vasco-Americano and Euzko Etxea. In 1905 a group of Basque men began meeting regularly at a house on Water Street in lower Manhattan to talk about starting a Basque organization, according to a history of New York's Basque club written by professor Emilia Doyaga.

Encouraged by Italian friends who had started their own social club, the men formally organized the Centro Vasco-Americano in 1913. The charter was drafted by a young Italian-American attorney, Fiorello LaGuardia, who would later become the mayor of New York. Today this is the oldest Basque organization in existence in the United States. Initially it served as a mutual aid society for the Basque community. Only immigrant men and their sons were allowed to be members of the club, and they had to get a medical exam first. Dues were collected, and money was paid out to men who were sick or had lost their jobs, or to the family when a club member died. Very few of the industrious immigrants ever applied for the sick benefits.

In 1928 the Centro Vasco-Americano bought a building at 48 Cherry Street for social gatherings. Basques bought bonds at an interest rate of 2 percent to finance the purchase. The Centro Vasco, as it was known, was a narrow four- or five-story building with a store on the ground floor, and a bar, kitchen, card tables, a few rooms, and even a small *kantxa* (ball court) upstairs. "We would hold monthly dances there," said Mary Toja. Even back then the club had a dance group that performed publicly. Toja, who was in the group, remembers dancing at Carnegie Hall and Town Hall in 1928 and 1930. The Basques also sponsored big annual picnics at Ulmer Park at Brooklyn's Coney Island.

After World War II the city razed the buildings in the Cherry Street area, including the Centro Vasco-Americano, to build housing projects. The city bought the property from the organization, which opted to pay off the bondholders. But after they had sold off the property the members realized they didn't have the money to buy into a new location, according to longtime member Irene Aguirre. The Centro Vasco-Americano relocated to Madison Street, and later to two locations on East Broadway in Chinatown, always renting. The next twenty-odd years were unsettled years for the organization. Albert Uriarte became president and shouldered the burden of keeping the club together. Most of the Basques had moved away from the old neighborhood and lost touch.

Finally, in 1973, the Centro Vasco-Americano members became tired of renting a facility for their gatherings and decided to buy a building. They chose a two-story brick building at 307 Eckford Street, in the Greenpoint section of Brooklyn, a heavily Polish and Italian neighborhood. The members themselves renovated the building, and in 1980 they changed the club's name to **Euzko Etxea (Basque House) of New York.** In the years since, the building has been modernized. It has a European-style bar, a dining room, a meeting room, a library, named after Jon Oñatibia (mentioned later in the section on Juventud), and upstairs it has a stage and hall for presentations.

Juventud In the late 1940s and early 1950s a group of young Basques, dissatisfied with the way the older generation was running things, broke away and formed their own group, Juventud. Jon Oñatibia, a virtuoso *txistulari* (someone who plays the *txistu,* a flutelike instrument), was another Basque who made a great contribution to the New York Basque community during those years. The talented musician joined the youth group and instructed its dance troupe from 1950 to 1963. The Basque dancers were well known by then and participated in city events, including a big city parade down Fifth Avenue. Oñatibia led them on a tour of North and South America. (Oñatibia taught Euskara and music classes and was a guest instructor for the University of Nevada's summer program in the Basque Country until he was killed in 1979, at the age of sixty-nine, in a car accident over there.)

Feast Day Celebration When Father José Mari Larrañaga arrived at St. James Church in 1962, he found a Basque colony greatly in need of revitalization. "I realized that it was dying," Larrañaga said. At that time a group of only five or six older Basques were getting together to play cards at the hall the club rented on East Broadway, in a run-down neighborhood under the Manhattan bridge overpass. Meanwhile the younger generation maintained a dance group and regularly celebrated the feast of San Inazio at the Nuestra Señora de Guadalupe Church on Fourteenth Street. In creating their own organization, the young Basque-Americans had completely disassociated themselves from the older immigrants. So Larrañaga worked to reunite them, calling the young people to start a choir and organize a celebration at his church, **St. James** (23 Oliver Street), near the old Cherry Street neighborhood.

Every year the festivities were slated for Aberri Eguna, the Basques' Day of the Homeland, which is always celebrated on Easter Sunday. The decision to establish Aberri Eguna, on Easter, politicized a holiday that had long been celebrated by the Basques for religious reasons. All the East Coast Basque communities celebrate Aberri Eguna, while most of the older communities in the West continue to celebrate Easter. Father Larrañaga would celebrate the Mass in Euskara, and then everyone would troop down to the basement hall for a big meal and dancing. Larrañaga, who later relocated to St. Anthony's Church in National City, California, remembered that they always ran out of food, because every year more people came for the celebration. In the beginning, about 150 people attended. By the time Larrañaga left New York City in 1970, 500 to 600 people were showing up. St. James Church was also the venue for a performance by Boise's Oinkari dancers when they came to New York representing Idaho for the 1964 World's Fair, and a big party was organized for them. Some of the young people who became involved in those years have continued to be active in Euzko Etxeak.

Club Activities Basque women had formed their own group, Andrak, in 1966, when they were not allowed to join the Centro Vasco. Today, however, women and men are members of Euzko Etxeak. Some are descendants of early immigrants, but many are immigrants themselves, a majority from Bizkaia. The newspaper *Voice of the Basques,* published out of Boise during the 1970s, carried reports filed by the New York Basque community. For many Basques in the West, it was the first time they had heard of the large community in New York. In 1993, eighty years after it was first started, Euzko Etxeak became a member of NABO, forging a definite link with the Basques of the West.

Today few of New York's Basques live close together in a neighborhood as they once did near the Brooklyn Bridge in Lower Manhattan. Back then the center was open every day, and there was always somebody who lived in the building. Now nobody lives near the center, and it's only open for special events and sometimes on weekends. The Basques are scattered throughout New York's five boroughs and beyond. Many who live in New Jersey, and even in Connecticut, make the trip to the center for the club dinners. Many came together for the annual picnic, most recently held at Willow Brook Park on Staten Island. But since 2001, only one picnic has been held, because attendance has been low as the result of vacationing Basques. The community reflects a diverse group, ranging from construction workers to doctors and lawyers, as well as young university students who come over to study and often end up staying. Euzko Etxeak serves as a point of contact for about five thousand to ten thousand Basques throughout the East Coast. Because of the large number of immigrants from Hegoalde during the last twenty years, this community, just as those in Florida, is influenced by newer and, in some cases, more nationalistic, traditions from the Basque Country.

For years, the center sponsored a dinner on the third Saturday of every month, which attracted about a hundred people. More recently, the dinners have included a speaker, concert, or presentation, such as Mark Kurlansky, author of *Basque History of the World,* or a film by Basque filmmaker Begoña Plaza. The date of the dinners is picked to accommodate the guests, noted club officer Koitz Foncillas Etxeberria. Aberri Eguna is probably the year's biggest celebration. For years, Auxiliary Bishop Patxi Garmendia of New York said the Mass for Aberri Eguna, and more recently the Mass has been celebrated by Auxiliary Bishop Josu Iriondo. Basque Country officials sometimes stop over in New York, and events are organized around their visits. The Basque Lehendakari, Juan José Ibarretxe, came to the center in 2003, and his trip was celebrated at the center with dancers and festivities. "People were very happy with his visit," said Foncillas, who was club president at the time. Ibarretxe spoke very informally and proved easy to talk to, Foncillas said. The center also celebrated its ninetieth anniversary in 2003.

Karlos Iturralde has taught Basque-language classes at the center to a group of eight to fifteen students every Sunday for more than two years, and the local dance group rehearses there as well.

Webmaster Foncillas Etxeberria has contributed greatly to the center's reputation by establishing a professional Web site, *www.eeny.org*. The site, maintained with the help of Basque Country grants, presents top news about Basques around the world and is perhaps the most extensive news site on the subject in English. Even though it's Euskal

Etxeak's Web site, in fact, it's more of a news bureau than a club site. Inaugurated in 2003, it was the brainstorm of Foncillas Etxeberria, a journalist and former president of the club, and media businessman Mikel Amigot, president of IBL News, which is a competitor to CNN News in Spanish. The Web site reflects the latest Internet and marketing innovations, which makes it easy to navigate, and has three main categories—Basque America, with news on U.S. Basques from many different sources; New York News, with information for N.Y. fans who might want some interesting tidbits on the Big Apple; and Front Page News, which reports news on Basques from many different publications. It also has a fourth smaller category dedicated just to news from the Eusko Etxea.

Eusko Etxeak of New York, 307 Eckford Street, Brooklyn, NY 11222 (718) 383-1974. Information: (718) 782-1205 (Koitz Foncillas Etxeberria); *www.eeny.org*

POLITICS AND BASQUE NATIONALISM

Whereas the Basque communities in the West largely ignored politics in their homeland, the New York Basque community took a completely different stance. Basque politicians and intellectuals were attracted to this international city, and through them the colony maintained stronger ties to the Basque Country and took up its political causes. As early as 1926 a group of young political Basques in New York broke away from the Centro Vasco and started their own group, Aberria. They sent funds to the Basque Nationalist Party and put out a publication, *Aberri.* (Other publications that came out of New York included a nationalist periodical *Basques,* published by the Basque government in exile in 1943 and 1944, and a cultural review, *Argia,* published from 1946 to 1948.)

During the years of the Spanish Civil War and World War II, New York had a special relationship with the beleaguered Basques back home. The Spanish Republic had granted the Basque region autonomy in 1936, a gesture that lasted a mere six months. The charismatic, nationalistic José Antonio de Aguirre was then chosen as *lehendakari* (president) of the Basque government, and he hastily organized a military defense of the new Euskadi. After severe bombing, the Basques were subdued, and the government was forced to flee to Paris. Its leaders sought support abroad, in Latin America and the United

States, where they felt there might be strength in the numbers of their countrymen who had preceded them. They dispatched delegates to established Basque colonies to campaign for the nationalist cause. A delegation was established in New York City in 1938. Jon Bilbao was sent as delegate to Boise. But there the efforts to seek support for the exiled government failed miserably. "Basques were torn between a fear of being identified as procommunist and a concern for their relatives in Europe. Consequently, little or no aid for the Basque military cause was forthcoming from the American West, although war relief was provided," wrote William Douglass and Jon Bilbao in their book *Amerikanuak*.

In New York, however, there were numbers of Basques who supported the nationalistic cause. More than two hundred Basques formed a short-lived group, Comité Pro-Euskadi, in 1937 to collect funds for the Basque government. In a humanistic gesture, Albert Uriarte, an apparel maker who served as spokesman and president of the New York Basque organization Centro Vasco-Americano at the time, helped many Basque refugees find sponsors in the United States. The supporters of refugees, however, did not represent the majority; most Basques waited to see what the U.S. government would do vis-à-vis General Francisco Franco. The United States government never openly opposed Franco.

When Germany invaded France in 1940, the Basque leader Aguirre and his associates were forced to flee Europe. He sought refuge in New York City in 1941 and opened an office at 10 Fifth Avenue, which remained open even after he left seven years later. The authors of *Amerikanuak* summed up Aguirre's view:

> As the United States was drawn into the Second World War, Franco's identification with Hitler and Mussolini prompted United States government support for exiled Spanish opposition groups like the Basque government.
>
> Aguirre believed that the shape of postwar Europe after an allied victory would be heavily influenced by the United States. He felt that his presence in this country was imperative if the Basques were to obtain autonomy through negotiations.

Aguirre's expectations that Franco would be removed by the victorious Allies were not realized. But the creation of the United Nations

Basque Country Representative Jesús de Galíndez Disappears

Basque delegate Jesús de Galíndez, an attorney and professor at Columbia University, disappeared off the streets of New York in March 1956 and was never seen again. It was one of the most talked about and publicized events in New York during the 1950s.

Born in Madrid and exiled during the Spanish Civil War, he ended up in a French concentration camp from which he managed to escape. He traveled to the Dominican Republic, in the Caribbean, where he was allowed entry by dictator Rafael Leonidas Trujillo. He took over the position of delegate of the Basque government there. In a 1990 article looking back on the event, the magazine *Euskal Etxeak* wrote: "He was eternally grateful to the country, but it was there that he discovered at [*sic*] first hand, the methods which Trujillo used [to stay in power] and especially those which were used against his enemies."

Galíndez came to New York when President Aguirre asked him to join the exiled government headquartered there, and he was appointed as a Basque observer to the United Nations. He also taught as an associate professor at Columbia University, while he obtained his Ph.D. He was a poet and a prolific correspondent for Basque Country publications. Galíndez worked for the cause of Basque nationalism while in New York, but he also became very close to the Dominican colony there. He was about to present his dissertation, in which he analyzed the government of Trujillo, when he disappeared one evening, after leaving a class he taught at the university. Reporters and the general public concluded that Trujillo had ordered Galíndez killed because the dictator was afraid of what the Basque professor's dissertation would reveal, but the specific motive in Galíndez's disappearance was hotly debated. "There does not seem to exist any implication about Trujillo which had not already come to light one way or another," wrote *Euskal Etxeak* about Galíndez's dissertation. The mystery remains unresolved, and his body was never found. Jon Oñatibia replaced Galíndez as the New York delegate of the Basque government-in-exile.

headquarters in New York City justified the maintenance of a Basque delegation there in order to plead the Basque case in an international forum. Aguirre stayed until 1948. He appointed Jesús de Galíndez to take his place after he left. (For more on Galíndez, see side bar.)

RESTAURANTS

Between New York and adjacent New Jersey just a few Basque restaurants have endured. In New York City, many Basque restaurants have come and gone. One restaurant that has endured a long time is La Côte Basque. While the restaurant's name probably did the most to raise

New Yorkers' awareness of the Basque Country, the food served here is actually French, not Basque. The elegant restaurant, originally established by a Basque chef, has figured prominently for many years among the city's finest places to eat. An average meal here can easily cost over $100 for two. In 2004, the name and décor were changed to Brasserie LCB (La Cote Basque). Much of the menu remained the same, as did the chef and owner. The restaurants serving authentic Basque food in New York City are **Pintxos** and **Euskadi.** Pintxos is owned by Donosti chef Javier Ortega and his wife, Debra, a Texan who has put some Tex-Mex food on the menu. However *pintxos,* or tapas, are the main attraction here, although Ortega also likes to cook paella. The couple has an interesting background, having owned a fish market and bar in Antigua, Guatemala. Initially, the restaurant was off the beaten path, on the edge of Greenwich Village, "but we've made ourselves a destination location," said Debra Ortega. They have quite a few regular customers, many of them from the Eusko Etxea. The owners of Euskadi are not Basque, but Basques here enjoy the food. Customers have praised Euskadi for its cozy atmosphere and excellent food. Until recently, there was also another popular Basque restaurant. Several years ago, chef Teresa Barrenechea and her husband, Raynold von Samson, opened Marichu's north of the city, in upscale Westchester County. Barrenechea, who wrote a popular cookbook, *The Basque Table,* served traditional Basque cuisine, although not in the family-style familiar to the West. It did so well that they opened a second Marichu's in Manhattan, next to the United Nations building, in 1994. They closed the suburban restaurant and kept the Manhattan location. It was a popular restaurant that catered to diplomats and tourists, but the couple finally decided to get out of the restaurant business in 2004. Marichu's has been replaced by a Spanish restaurant, **Alcala** (342 East 46th Street).

Just across the Hudson River, in Newark, New Jersey, you will find the longtime Basque restaurant, **La Casa Vasca,** run by Maria Gema Aurre. **Manolo's,** a Spanish restaurant in nearby Elizabeth, has served some Basque dishes in the past.

Euskadi, 108 East 4th Street, New York, NY 10003 (212) 982-9788
Brasserie LCB, 60 West Fifty-fifth Street, New York, NY 10019 (212) 688-6526
La Casa Vasca, 141 Elm, Newark, NJ 07105 (973) 465-1350

Manolo's, 91 Elizabeth Avenue, Elizabeth, NJ 07201 (908) 353-7674; *www.manolos.com*
Pintxos, 510 Greenwich Street, New York, NY 10013 (212) 343-9923

ELLIS ISLAND IMMIGRATION MUSEUM

If you are visiting New York City, you should make time to visit Ellis Island, home of the Statue of Liberty and the **Ellis Island Immigration Museum.** After a $140 million renovation, the museum reopened in 1990. Seventeen million men, women, and children were processed here between 1892 and 1954. They represent the ancestors of approximately 40 percent of Americans. The museum has computerized the names of all the immigrants, and they are available through their Web site, *www.ellisisland.org*. The museum has a fascinating collection of personal belongings, documents, and processing paraphernalia. With a $100 contribution, you can have your ancestor's name placed on the Immigrant Wall of Honor, which already lists the names of some 500,000 people.

Ellis Island Immigration Museum, Ellis Island, NY (212) 363-3206. Catch the ferry from Battery Park in Manhattan. For information on the immigration checkpoint: *www.ellisisland.org;* for museum information: *www.ellisisland.com*

SOCIETY OF BASQUE STUDIES IN AMERICA

An official national organization whose sole purpose is to promote the Basques and their works, the **Society of Basque Studies in America,** started in California in 1979. Professors Emilia Doyaga, Juan Mendizabal, and Gloria Castresana Waid ran into each other at a national language conference and talked about the need for more Basque studies and communication among Basque-Americans. They decided to form a scholarly society. Doyaga, based in New York, became the focal point for the organization, and José Ramón Cengotitabengoa of Chicago has served as its president for several years. The society has two major projects that are worthy of recognition: it publishes an annual journal, *Journal of the Society of Basque Studies in America,* with articles on a variety of Basque subjects in different languages, and it sponsors an annual Basque Hall of Fame awards banquet. The journal is distributed to society members, professors, and university libraries across the country. (Membership in the organization is very inexpensive.)

The Basque Hall of Fame awards banquet rotates among different Basque communities every year and has slowly gained prominence as an important symbolic gesture of recognition of Basques and others who have made significant contributions to Basque culture in America. A wide range of people, from former Basque president José Antonio de Aguirre to boardinghouse "mothers" and outstanding *pelotariak* have been honored at the banquet. Plaques describing the stories of these "Hall of Famers" are available at the Basque Museum and Cultural Center in Boise. Biographies of the award recipients are usually included in the annual *Journal of the Society of Basque Studies in America*. In 2003, the society honored five New Yorkers, Rosa, Gloria and Iñaki Aberasturi, former president Juan Ángel Landaburu and writer Mario Salegi, at a banquet also celebrating the 90th anniversary of the Eusko Etxea.

In May 1984 the Society of Basque Studies in America brought three prominent sculptors—Nestor Basterrechea, Remigio Mendiburu, and Vicente Larrea—from the Basque Country to display their work at an important annual art exhibit in Chicago. This was the first exhibition of renowned Basque artists at a national level. Informal conversations between the artists and Cengotitabengoa led to the idea of creating a national monument to the Basques in Nevada. The result was the Basque Sheepherder Monument, a monumental effort that was spearheaded by the Society. (For more information on the monument, see the section under Reno, Nevada.)

In the mid-1980s a rift developed within the group over objectives, and the Basque-American Foundation was created. This latter organization published its own journal until 1994. (See the section on Santa Barbara, California, for more information.)

Professor John Ysursa is current editor of the Society's journal. He welcomes contributions on almost any subject pertaining to the Basques—popular history, literature, family stories, and so forth. Articles can be of any length, and submissions can be made in English, Spanish, French, or Basque. Send your contributions to his address below, or by e-mail to the Web site by December 1 for the annual issue.

Society of Basque Studies in America, 19 Colonial Gardens, Brooklyn, NY 11209. Information: (718) 745-1141 (*Emilia Doyaga*); *www.basque.ws*

Journal of the Society of Basque Studies in America, c/o Professor John Ysursa, 15850 Old Hickory Lane, Chino Hills, CA 91709.

An International Cultural Center. Professor Emilia Doyaga, one of the Basque community's biggest promoters, is also behind one of the most ambitious Basque projects to date. She believes the United States needs an international center to educate the public about Basque culture and that New York is the best place for it. She feels the current Basque building on Eckford Street, hidden away in a residential Brooklyn neighborhood, is an inadequate location for such an endeavor. She would like to see a new center in a prominent location, such as the South Street Seaport, a touristy location in Manhattan.

Fund-raising for the center started in 2002. Numerous Basques have enlisted as supporters, including banker John Elorriaga and businessman José Ramón Cengotitabengoa. Author Mark Kurlansky is on the project's board of directors and brings up the subject whenever he is invited to speak. Fund-raising dinners have been hosted in New York, and now the primary efforts are aimed at seeking contributors whose names will be engraved on a Tree of Gernika and Town Hall and displayed on a donors' wall.

The center is projected to include a restaurant and bar, a meeting hall, a museum, a library, a gift shop, and offices. Its activities will include classes of Basque language, dance, singing, cooking, as well as lectures on Basque history and art.

In 2004, a bank building in Manhattan became available that would have been ideal, said Doyaga. However, the organization did not have enough funds at the time for the down payment. The group is not discouraged by the missed opportunity, as "location is very important to ensure the success of this kind of place," she said. She added that in New York, finding a good location will take time. "It won't be done in a day."

Basque International Cultural Center, 67 Wall Street, 22 Floor #8284, New York, NY 10005-3198. Information: (212) 709-8284

Washington, D.C.

This gigantic megalopolis and all its suburbs attracts such a range of Basques of all levels and types of professions that any attempt to categorize them is both impossible and inappropriate. As a result of the variety and the small numbers, Basques in the area have not managed to create a club that has survived for any significant length of time.

A few Basques who lived in the Washington D.C. area established a club in 1981. However, their small numbers and the relatively transitory nature of this community, governed by the ebb and flow of this capital city, led to its dissolution by the late 1980s. The club remained together long enough to organize a reception for the Basque president José Antonio Ardanza when he came to the United States in 1988, according to Basque journalist Joseba Etxarri.

A former representative of the exiled Basque government, Pedro Beitia, lived in D.C. here for many years.

For years, Basque chef Josu Zubikarai headed the kitchen at the elegant **Taberna del Alabardero,** a Spanish restaurant in downtown Washington since 1989. He returned to Spain in 2002, but current chef Santi Zabaleta is earning praise for his cooking. Numerous Basque dishes are on the menu of this elegant Old World restaurant, which caters to diplomats, executives, and even members of Congress. Another elegant restaurant just across the Potomac River in Alexandria is **La Bergerie** (218 North Lee Street), known for its French and Basque cuisine.

Taberna del Alabardero, 1776 I Street, NW, Washington D.C. 20006 (202) 429-2200; *www.alabardero.com*

■ Connecticut and Rhode Island

JAI ALAI FRONTONS

Three professional jai alai courts opened up in Connecticut after legislators approved the playing of professional jai alai and pari-mutuel betting in the early 1970s as a way to raise state revenues, and another court opened a few years later next door in Newport, Rhode Island. The biggest fronton, or court, was the one in Milford (Connecticut), a huge facility with five thousand seats and a bar and lounge with room for hundreds more to watch the sport via video. Milford also had the only training facility for jai alai players in the region. (For more information on jai alai, see the Florida section.)

The jai alai frontons on the East Coast have employed hundreds of Basque *pelotariak* since the 1920s. (Courtesy of Newport Jai Alai.)

However, professional jai alai in these two New England states was not destined to last. Foxwoods, a large gambling casino, opened in 1992 near New London, Connecticut, and the Mohegan Sun started in 1996 nearby, both part of a new trend across the country for Native American tribes to develop casinos on their land.

The casinos created stiff competition for jai alai. "People who gamble will be attracted to a casino first," said Bob Heussler, former spokesman for the Milford Jai Alai. The casinos played a significant role in the closure of the Bridgeport and Hartford jai alai facilities in 1995. A major players' strike that lasted from 1988 to 1991 was also a contributing factor, as was a new law that prohibited minors in the frontons. Jai alai business owners had no way to attract new fans. While the Milford fronton did well during its initial years, expanding its season from six months to year-round, the owners ended up canceling jai alai games at the end of 2001. "There's a real good reason why there's no live horse racing, no live jai alai, and no greyhound racing in Las Vegas—because they can't compete against casino gambling," Heussler told the *Fairfield Weekly* after the Milford fronton closed. "That said, we did compete. We hung in there for a while."

The sport at Newport Grand Jai Alai in Rhode Island lasted the longest, partly because of the introduction of video slot machines in 1992, which brought more money to the court. Unfortunately, the slot machines continued while the game of jai alai was canceled in 2003, and the fronton was closed. In 2005, the only jai alai left at the facility was on TV screens, simulcast from the Miami and Dania frontons. The facility continues to operate, with simulcast thoroughbred and greyhound racing, jai alai, and the slot machines as the main attractions. A large resort hotel was to be built at the location in 2006, eliminating the fronton altogether.

Newport Grand, 150 Admiral Kalbfus Road, Newport, RI 02840 (401) 849-5000; *www.newportgrand.com*

AMATEUR JAI ALAI

American Amateur Jai Alai in Milford, Connecticut, was a recreational jai alai facility where amateurs could learn to play. After the Milford fronton closed, it disappeared as well. However, near Hartford, Connecticut, a few diehard players have created their own little jai alai court. They formed a group, **Jai Alai Heaven,** and they play in a court they built at a Bloomfield seminary. Group member Bob DiScipio admits their interest in the sport is highly unusual. They are simply a group of guys who like to play jai alai for exercise and fun. None of them is Basque. DiScipio initially saw the game in Florida and Las Vegas and became interested in it. He found a few friends who were willing to play with him, but their problem was always where to play. They played on makeshift outdoor courts, but finally hit pay dirt when they worked out a deal with the seminary to lease an unused space in the basement of its athletic building. That was in 1986. The members had to tear down tile walls and oak and steel basketball courts to create the jai alai fronton. At a mere 90 feet long, the court is not of professional size—and it's taken them years to find the right ball to use on the court, said DiScipio. These days they order their balls, used for baseball pitching machines, online.

Twenty or so professional Basque players have stopped in over the years. The game was not always easy for them, noted DiScipio, because it is played differently on the shorter court. "There's a lot more kill shots," he said. Izpa was the one who played there the most, but after the heyday of jai alai in the 1980s and 1990s, most players moved away from New England. Visitors are not allowed except as guests of the current members.

Jai Alai Heaven. Information: (860) 633-0783 (Bob DiScipio)

NO BASQUE CLUB

The community of Basques who have chosen to live in the New England states of Rhode Island and Connecticut permanently is not very large, and their numbers decreased with the cancellation of jai alai in those states. There have never been any efforts to start a Basque club in the area. Those who do yearn for a taste of home drive down to New York City, just a few hours away, to participate in social activities sponsored by the Euzko Etxea Basque club there.

Florida

JAI ALAI

Professional Sport. Jai alai is a complex game, played with a *txistera,* a basket-like extension tied to the wrist, and a very hard ball made by hand. The sport requires a larger, stronger indoor *kantxa* (court) than does pelota or handball, as well as lots of training. The covering of these small balls, which are harder than golf balls, typically has to be resewn after about fifteen minutes of play. Just try to keep your eye on these balls during the game, as they zip by at an average speed of 150 miles per hour. In fact, the *Guinness Book of World Records* has dubbed jai alai the fastest game in the world.

Jai alai was developed in the Basque Country in the 1700s, one of several games derived from the basic game of pelota. The Basques are credited with spreading jai alai around the world. (For more information on pelota, see the section on the San Francisco

Peninsula.) The sport has been played professionally in several countries: Brazil, Mexico, the Philippines, China, Cuba, Argentina, Peru, Uruguay, Indonesia, North Africa, Italy, and Belgium.

Because of the complexity and special requirements of the game, jai alai was not played seriously in the United States until it became a professional sport supported by betting. The game was first demonstrated in this country by jai alai players, or *pelotariak* from the Basque Country, at the World's Fair in St. Louis, Missouri, at the turn of the twentieth century. (The fronton for the fair was built by Ricardo Galbis, a civil engineer born in the Basque Country who made his home in Cuba. Galbis, who died in 1914, built numerous public works in Cuba, including a fronton that apparently still stands in Havana.) Jai alai was also played at the Old Hippodrome Theater in New York City in the 1930s. There was a fronton in Chicago too. But those venues did not allow gambling, and the sport eventually faltered. "As entertainment, it didn't work," said Jesus Belaustegui, a former *pelotari* and players' manager.

It wasn't until betting was permitted in Florida, in the 1930s, that jai alai took off as a professional sport in the United States. It began in Miami, where a gigantic jai alai court was built in the mid-1920s. Once Florida state officials approved pari-mutuel betting a few years later, jai alai became big business. (In pari-mutuel betting, fans bet against each other, not against the house, as in casinos. About 20 percent of every dollar goes to fronton expenses and taxes, the rest is returned to bettors in winnings.)

Eventually, during the 1950s and 1960s, the profits to be made from betting on the sport led to the construction of nine more jai alai courts in Florida. In the early 1970s pari-mutuel betting—for jai alai specifically—was permitted in Connecticut, so three professional frontons were built. In the late 1970s Rhode Island received approval for betting also, so a court was built in Newport. The 1960s and 1970s were the heyday for jai alai in this country. "In Connecticut, there were days when between the afternoon and the evening, they [the frontons] would bring in $1 million," remembers Belaustegui.

Also in the 1970s the big MGM Grand Hotel opened frontons in Reno and Las Vegas, Nevada. Pete Echeverria, head of the state Gaming Commission in Nevada at the time, was instrumental in starting up jai alai in that state. But the Nevada frontons, with their slower betting pace, apparently could not compete against the casinos. Jai alai in Reno lasted just two years, from 1978 to 1980. The Las Vegas jai alai fronton did better, lasting from 1973 to 1983.

Jai Alai Players. Jai alai players in the United States are professionals who have competed on courts around the world. A majority are Basques who trained in jai alai schools in Hegoalde—the most popular and oldest school being in the town of Markina.

A majority of the rosters of the U.S. frontons have always been comprised of Basque *pelotariak,* mostly from Bizkaia, although the sport also attracts participants from Iparralde. They usually worked six days a week, often starting at noon and not ending their day until well after midnight. Initially, most frontons were only open seasonally, but later many of them became year-round, typically closing only one month a year. Many *pelotariak* took advantage of their vacations to go back to the Basque Country.

Over time the players became increasingly frustrated as they watched the frontons rake in money while they were paid relatively low salaries. The U.S. players held a major strike in 1968, and many of them were fired. They attempted to start a union in 1975, but management at the different frontons made small concessions to head off the initiative. The fronton in Las Vegas was the first to extend health benefits to the families of the *pelotariak,* a practice that other frontons later followed, according to Jesus Belaustegui, who served as the players' manager in Las Vegas.

A union, the International Jai Alai Players Association, was finally founded in 1986. In 1988, the Basque *pelotariak* came together for another strike. There were over five hundred *pelotariak* in this country at the time. The union became part of the powerful United Auto Workers union, which gave some financial support to the players during the long strike. The *pelotariak* refused to play for three years, from 1988 to 1991, aggressively picketing thirteen of the fourteen frontons operating on the East Coast in their efforts to force the fronton owners to recognize their union. Bob Heussler, former spokesman for the Milford (Connecticut) Jai Alai, said it was the longest strike by professional players in any sport. Even the *pelotariak* never expected it to last that long. "We thought it was going to be short," said Francisco Hormaechea, a Tampa *pelotari* who has since returned to the Basque

Country. "Nobody was prepared for the effects of the strike," said Juan Elejabarrieta of Miami, adding that the stress and economic difficulties had disastrous consequences on the players, including several divorces. The *pelotariak* held out, and, eventually, fronton management conceded, recognized the unions, and hired back many of the former players. But the damage had been done. Many of the regular bettors who had frequented the frontons and were then thwarted by the picket lines for many months never returned.

The strike remains a defining event in the lives of the *pelotariak* and for U.S. jai alai, one that unfortunately did not have the hoped-for effects. "We've been playing here for sixty years, and we've never received a pension," said Eusebio Echevarria of Tampa. Many *pelotariak* returned to the Basque Country and never came back. Consequently, the East Coast Basque communities were significantly reduced in the years following the strike.

Decreasing Interest in the Game. Today the business of jai alai is on the decline in the United States. The difficulties engendered by the strike had negative repercussions for several frontons. After the strike, revenues at the frontons were significantly lower because of the decline in gambling. The facilities did not have extra money to carry out a publicity campaign to generate new fans to replace those who never came back, said jai alai expert Larry "Cachin" Blitz. Competition from the increase of gambling casinos and state lotteries also struck a blow. Only five out of ten Florida courts are left, while the three in Connecticut closed, and the only fronton in Rhode Island canceled live jai alai and turned to the simulcast version. The existing frontons are doubling their efforts to attract betting spectators by offering other amenities, such as televised sports and racing events, all in the interest of encouraging people to spend their money on jai alai. "No one would be foolish enough to say that jai alai would exist without pari-mutuel betting," said Bob Heussler. "In the same sense that Americans will never embrace soccer, they will never embrace jai alai as a legitimate sport."

Sadly, the sport may die just as it was starting to catch on among Americans. "It's not an easy sport to break into," said Heussler. Lack of exposure is one reason. About the only chance youngsters here have to see the game is when they visit the frontons with their parents. Florida allows children into its facilities if accompanied by parents, but Connecticut and Rhode Island banned children under eighteen from the frontons. Jai alai has rarely received television exposure despite years of efforts from the sport's promoters. Over the years, many sports writers have lamented the disappearance of jai alai.

On a positive note, jai alai was demonstrated in exhibition games at the 1992 Summer Olympic Games in Barcelona for the first time, because it was deemed a competitive sport at the 1924 Games in Paris.

Training. Lack of training facilities is another problem affecting the sport. The only professional fronton offering training these days is Orlando, said Blitz. The Miami and Milford training centers churned out some three hundred professional players over the years, most of who are playing at U.S. frontons. (Many of them became professional when they were called on to fill the rosters during the strike.) Most of the professional players came out of the North Miami Amateur Jai Alai facility, which was headed for years by instructor Miguel Aparicio. Florida Gaming Jai Alai (formerly known as World Jai Alai), the owner of the facility, encouraged young talent by offering free instruction every weeknight to boys between the ages of ten and sixteen. Many also participated in the U.S. Amateur Jai Alai games, and a couple went on to become world champions as well.

The training facilities in Milford, Connecticut, closed down. Official jai alai is no longer played at the amateur facility in North Miami, Florida, where many American players got their start. They use a bigger ball now and only members are allowed to play, according to the webmaster of Extreme Jai Alai, Larry "Cachin" Blitz.

The Professional Game Today. Unlike handball or jai alai in the Basque Country, in which players or teams compete against each other for an entire game of up to thirty points, in the United States, the format is completely different. Two single players or two teams will play for a point. A team wins the point when the other side misses the ball or hits it out of bounds. The losing player or team leaves the court and is quickly followed by another. Bets are placed on the teams or players who can reach seven points first. Up to fifty players will play during the course of an evening. Typically, the novice players start the early games. "You will see the best players in the later games in the program," explained Bob Heussler, an East Coast jai alai expert. The sport, in which players are known by one name, is peppered with hard-to-pronounce Basque names.

Minimum bets typically range from $1 to $3. And there's no requirement that says you have to place a bet. If you'd like to go to a fronton just to enjoy the game itself, by all means do so. If you'd like to show your support for the sport in a way other than by placing a bet, bring your friends, eat in the restaurants, or have a drink at the bar.

JAI ALAI FRONTONS

Florida has always been the primary home of the sport of jai alai in the States. It was the first place in this country where jai alai was played professionally, and at its peak, this state had ten jai alai courts.

The **Miami Jai Alai** is the largest and the oldest of the U.S. courts. The first fronton, built in Hialeah in 1924, did not last very long before it was destroyed in a hurricane. Soon thereafter a new court was built in Miami and inaugurated in 1926. Even after pari-mutuel betting became legal in Florida during the 1930s, the Miami facility continued to be the only jai alai court in the state until the 1950s. Miami Jai Alai, which seats ten thousand people, still churns with excitement and continues to be home to the best *pelotariak* on the East Coast and the South.

Not far behind are the frontons at Dania and Tampa, built during the 1950s. When the Dania fronton went up, the area was a mosquito-filled jungle. Visible from miles away with its multicolored neon lights, the fronton soon became a popular facility and was eventually engulfed by the growing metropolis of Miami.

The success of jai alai gambling led to the construction of seven more frontons in this state. Winter is the high season in Florida, when many Americans and Canadians come south to get away from cold winter weather and enjoy Florida's temperate tropical climate. For years, jai alai was played only during the winter season, between Christmas and Easter. Later, it went year-round at many frontons.

THE FUTURE OF THE SPORT

In Florida the players' strike came at a particularly bad time. "Within two weeks of the strike, the [state] lottery started," said former U.S. jai alai champ William "Billy" Schofill, past coach of the U.S. amateur jai alai team. The advent of the state lottery signaled the beginning of the downturn in the sport. "In the next few years, if something drastic doesn't happen, it's going to die," he said. Already in the past few years the frontons in West Palm Beach, Daytona Beach, Melbourne, Quincy, and Tampa have closed. Tampa was the most recent closure in 1998. The frontons in the relatively small cities of Ocala, Fort Pierce, and Orlando offer jai alai a few months out of the year. They coordinate their seasons so the *pelotariak* can rotate among them. The two hurricanes that hit Florida in 2004 devastated the Fort Pierce fronton, and, in spite of management's best efforts to make repairs, the 2005 season had to be canceled. Although the population of Dania is relatively small, it is part of the popular tourist-oriented seaside strip that extends north from Miami, so it gets its share of tourists. Miami and Dania continue year-round.

"The future of the sport is in Mexico," predicted Jesus Belaustegui in the 1990s. Mexico City has two frontons, and Acapulco has one. However, even in Mexico some foreboding signs have indicated a downturn in jai alai. A fronton in the popular seaside resort of Cancún barely lasted a year. And a fronton in Tijuana that existed for years finally closed in 2001 after it lost its betting license, said *pelotari* Larry "Cachin" Blitz, who played there. (For more on the Tijuana fronton, see the section on Southern California).

However, some glimmer of hope is in the offing. Florida legislators have been working for years to introduce slot machines to increase state revenue. The fronton owners maneuvered to have the machines located at their facilities in order to increase attendance, rather than to have separate casinos competing for their business. It was a two-step process, first seeking and then receiving statewide voter approval for slot machines, with the provision that they would be limited to racing and jai alai facilities. The jai alai players' union hired a lobbyist to tailor the bill to favor the players, and the law as written calls for them to receive a certain percentage of the slot machine revenue. On March 8, 2005, Broward County voters approved the measure to put slot machines in the Dania Jai Alai. In Dade County, voters rejected the measure, which will keep the machines out of Miami's fronton. "The slot machines alone will bring back the sport," predicted Blitz hopefully. Despite the optimism, *pelotari* Ernesto Arriaga noted, "There's still the fear that one day they might say they want the slot machines and not the frontons," reflecting on what happened in Newport, Rhode Island.

Two new frontons are being built, one of which opened in early 2006 in Florida, indicating that jai alai must be good business. A businessman built the new Hamilton Downs fronton near Jasper, Florida, next to the Georgia border. In addition to jai alai, the facility has simulcast racing, a card room, and a restaurant. According to Blitz, plans are being made in northern Texas to build a huge 12,000-seat facility and fronton. The business's Web site predicts the location will open within three years and offer jai alai, a restaurant and, eventually, an amateur program to train new players. The Web site (*www.texasjai-alai.com*) displays the colorful flags of all the places jai alai has been played, and the Basque *ikurrina* is displayed at the top. The company currently can be reached at P.O. Box 29, Mansfield, TX 76063; (817) 477-1543; or via its Web site, *www.texasjai-alai.com.*

These latest developments are encouraging to Blitz, who is a one-man campaign with his Web site Extreme Jai Alai, *www.xjaialai.com,* where you can find the latest news and game scores. The Web site also has links to practically every jai alai–related organization, article, and video in the United States and abroad. Visitors to the site can also view dozens of videos, old and new. Blitz, who builds Web sites when he's not playing jai alai, doesn't make any money off Extreme Jai Alai. His goal is "to help promote the sport," he said, noting that he gets about fifteen to twenty e-mails a day with a variety of questions.

Todd Sorensen, a jai alai columnist and promoter, noted in a 2001 article in the magazine *Gambling Times,* "I don't think jai alai can or will die. The sport is one of the world's oldest, in existence for hundreds of years. It's been an integral part of Florida since 1926 when the first permanent facility opened in Hialeah and continues to be an important part of the state's culture to this day."

Dania Jai Alai, 301 East Dania Beach Boulevard, Dania FL 33004 (954) 927-2841; *www.dania-jaialai.com*

Fort Pierce Jai Alai, 1750 South Kings Highway, Fort Pierce, FL 34945 (772) 464-7500; *www.jaialai.net*

Hamilton Downs Jai Alai, U.S. 129 at Interstate 75 (Exit 451) Jasper, FL (800) 941-4841; *www.hamiltondownsjaialai.com*

Miami Jai Alai, 3500 Northwest Thirty-seventh Avenue, Miami, FL 33142 (305) 633-6400; *www.fla-gaming.com/miami/*

Ocala Jai Alai, 4601 Northwest Highway 318, Reddick, FL 32686 (352) 591-2345; *www.ocalajaialai.com/*

Orlando Jai Alai and Race Book, 6405 South Highway 17-92 at SR 436, Fern Park, FL 32730 (407) 339-6221; *www.orlandojaialai.com*

AMATEUR JAI ALAI

The **Amateur Jai Alai** in North Miami was where many professional American players received their start. The amateur facility trained players every evening, while during the day the establishment was open to anyone who wanted to play. They had one professional-length court and two smaller ones. Today only one small court is left, and players use a bigger ball. On weekdays the fronton is open to members only, but anyone is welcome on weekends. Francisco Elorre offers training at the Orlando fronton for amateurs who want to play professionally.

North Miami Amateur Jai Alai, 1935 NE 150 Street, North Miami, FL (305) 940-8540; *www.americanjaialai.com*

BASQUE CLUBS

Basques have lived in Florida for the past seventy years, since the first fronton opened in 1924. The jai alai players on the East Coast and the South, like the sheepherders of the West, have come for a short stay, with every intention of making money and going home again. When they retired, still in their thirties or forties, many of them did move back to the Basque Country, but a few got married along the way, or started businesses with the money they made, and decided to stay here. There have been four social clubs in existence in this state, but only one has survived and it is much smaller than the ones in the West. And, unlike in the Western communities, where the Basques are in the second and third generation, in Florida the majority of the Basque club members are immigrants.

All four clubs have been renditions of gastronomic societies in Hegoalde, better known as *txokoak,* in which members gather together primarily to cook and eat a meal together. The majority of the groups are made up of men. In deference to the modern-day recognition of women's rights, the clubs have included women in their membership, but it is mostly men who get together. Because of the size of the metropolitan Miami area, it was natural that several Basques have chosen to retire or settle in the area. Miami also had a number of Basques, including former jai alai players, who fled Cuba after dictator Fidel Castro took over in 1959.

Despite the fact that Florida's largest Basque community is in Miami, the first Basque social club in Florida was established in Tampa. "We are the pioneers in Florida," said Eusebio Echevarria, a spokesman for the club when it still existed in the 1990s. The late José Luis Angulo Ibarretxe, a jai alai player who ended his career in Tampa, realized the need for a club and spearheaded the movement. He and a group of current and former jai alai players met at Blanco's Restaurant in 1983 to discuss starting a club.

They rented a location that had been partially destroyed in a fire. The group of about thirty men restored the place themselves and opened it as Euzkal Txoko in 1984. Located above some offices, the *txoko* resembled a large restaurant, with a kitchen, dining room, bar, pool tables, and even showers. *Pelotariak* made up nearly the entire membership.

The 1988 strike cut the local Basque community in half, and "it jeopardized the *txoko* too," said Echevarria. Before the strike started, there were more than sixty members. Afterward, there were as few as thirty. The club sponsored a popular paella contest, which began in 1992. Many paella enthusiasts, including local public officials, showed up for the food fest, which was publicized in the local newspaper. Unfortunately, when the Tampa fronton closed in 1998, the *txoko* disappeared as well.

Miami Clubs. After the Tampa club started, three other clubs were organized in Florida. One organization in Orlando was a short-lived effort that expired with the jai alai players' strike. In Miami, however, two other groups that predated the strike continued and finally joined as one in 1996. **Toki Ona** began with good intentions, when its members decided to separate from another group that chose to ban women from its membership. As the latter group, **Txoko Alai** functioned like a traditional gastronomic society in the Basque Country, where women and children are not allowed.

Toki Ona, which once had about twenty members, lost many because of tensions that resulted when the players strike broke out. Most of the club's members were *pelotariak,* and at least a dozen of them chose to cross the picket line. Friendships were shattered forever, and all the strike-breakers left the club. Because of their small numbers, the remaining Toki Ona members opted in 1996 to join the Txoko Alai group. "What we want is an Euskal Etxea," said club member Juan Elejabarrieta, who has a dream of joining resources with the other club to buy some property to create "*un pedacito del pueblo vasco en Miami*" (a little piece of the Basque Country in Miami), he said in Spanish. The combined club later opened its doors to women, although most of the people who gather here are men.

The members who make up Txoko Alai often get together on weekends to cook and eat a big meal together, and often to watch sporting events on their big-screen television. The club, which started in 1984, rents a nice location in a small mall with a kitchen, dining room, and bar. The members have their own keys and stop by regularly. Different groups will get together on different nights.

Txoko Alai, 4315 North West Seventh Street, Miami, FL 33126 (305) 443-1182 (weekends only)

RESTAURANTS

Most Basques in Miami will direct you to **Casa Juancho,** a Spanish restaurant on Calle Ocho in Little Havana. Casa Vasca, a former Basque place also in Little Havana, disappeared, and today Juancho's is *the* place to go. "It's the most reliable place to eat Bacalao a la Vizcaína," said caterer Bonifacio Guenechea. The fancy restaurant also serves a number of tapas. **Brasserie Les Halles,** a French bistro in upscale Coral Gables, sponsors a Basque week in October in which an array of Basque dishes is served. Gateau Basque is on the menu year-round.

Brasserie Les Halles, 2415 Ponce de Leon Boulevard, Coral Gables, FL 33134 (305) 461-1099
Casa Juancho, 2436 S.W. Eighth Street, Miami, FL 33135; *www.casajuancho.com*

BASQUE COOKING BUSINESSES

Cooking is definitely a favorite hobby of all the Basque club members. Their primary social activity is getting together to cook up a meal. In Miami, two Txoko Alai club members jumped into business ventures reflecting their culinary experience with success.

Juan Elejabarrieta and several other Basque men started their own sausage-making company in Miami, **Elore Enterprises,** in 1988. Their main product, Chorizo Quijote, is sold in major supermarkets throughout Florida. In addition, they have introduced their chorizos in New York and are also having success with sales in Mexico, Puerto Rico, and Panama.

Meanwhile, the demand for Bonifacio Guenechea's catering business, **Paella Party Creations,** which he started in 1988, is growing by leaps and bounds. His son Daniel has joined the business, which now includes sales of paella equipment, in addition to the catering of all kinds of Spanish dishes. Several bacalao dishes are available on their varied menu.

Elore Enterprises, 7224 Northwest Twenty-fifth Street, Miami, FL 33122 (305) 477-1650; *www.chorizoquijote.com*

Paella and Party Creations, 16155 Southwest 117th Avenue #8, Miami, FL 33177 (305) 252-6669; *www.paellaparty.com*

REFERENCES

Douglass, William A., and Jon Bilbao. *Amerikanuak: Basques in the New World.* Reno, Nev.: University of Nevada Press, 1975, pp. 361–62.

Louisiana

New Orleans

LOUISIANA BASQUE HISTORY

When Canadian-Basque Michel Goitia Nicholas arrived in the cosmopolitan city of New Orleans, he contacted the Center for Basque

Studies at the University of Nevada, Reno, to inquire about the Basque history in Louisiana. He was told essentially that there was none. After everything he has learned, he concludes the reply he received was because in earlier days, Basques were obscured by their French or Spanish citizenship, and that is how they were recorded in the history books. "Basques were not given the credit," he said. As part of his research, Goitia Nicholas has pored over thousands of names listed in port records, phone books, and city and street names. As he works, he refers to the five genealogy books of Basque names that he purchased in the Basque Country. He eventually hopes to write a book on the subject. His research reveals that many Basques were part of the early settlement of Louisiana, which included a great deal of French and Spanish immigration dating back to the 1700s. (The Louisiana territory, whose greatest value lay in the port of New Orleans, was owned by both France and Spain before the U.S. bought it in 1803.) For example, famous New Orleans pirate Jean Lafitte mentioned in his journal a visit to relatives in the Basque Country, according to Goitia Nicholas. More recently, the founders of the popular Zatarain spice company were from Donostia/San Sebastián. Goitia Nicholas claims the word *pirogue,* a hollowed-out canoe used frequently on Louisiana's many waterways, comes from the Basque word *piragua.* In addition, many historical names attributed to the Choctaws, natives of Mississippi, are apparently Basque.

The Cajuns, who provide a great deal of Louisiana's rich cultural heritage, have Basque connections, too, according to Goitia Nicholas. The Cajuns were descendents of French farmers and fishermen who were ousted from their settlements in Acadia, in eastern Canada, the first permanent French colony in North America. Many of them came to Louisiana because of its existing French community. More recent research has revealed that Basques were cod fishing and settling in the Acadia area as early as the 1600s, and Goitia Nicholas believes many of the Acadians were just as likely to be Basque as French.

Even the Isleños in St. Bernard Parish near New Orleans, a historical settlement of Canary Islanders that dates back to the mid- to late 1700s, believe they have some Basque heritage because of the many ethnic groups that passed through their islands off the coast of Africa on their route to the New World.

BASQUE CLUB

A Basque club of sorts cropped up in recent years in New Orleans, mainly the result of the efforts of Michel Goitia Nicolas. This tour guide and train attendant became curious about the possibility of Basques in this important port city when he saw the street name Soraburu near his house. He went on to research the Basques in Louisiana for the next five years. He compiled a huge list of possible Basques who lived in the New Orleans region and invited them all to a get-together. The local paper picked up the story and publicized the event. "I was hoping for 20 people," said Goitia Nicolas, but about 260 showed up at St. Francis Xavier Church in June 2003. A group developed, but Goitia Nicolas admits it is all moving slowly. "We're at a disadvantage in that Basques have been here one hundred, two hundred, and three hundred years, but they're just discovering their heritage," he said. One club officer who is well aware of her Basque heritage is Bertha Bidart Smith, owner of **Le Petite Chalet Basque** (*www.neworleansfrenchbandb.com*), a bed-and-breakfast inn in Metairie just outside of New Orleans. She was born in the Basque Country and was brought to California by her father, who worked as a sheepherder.

Since that large first meeting, the officers created an informal group, the **Louisiana Basque Society,** that meets about four times a year to plan activities. Their biggest event so far was a festival in April 2004, which revolved around a visit and performance by Chino's Gauden Bat dancers. West Coast Basque experts like John Ysursa and Lisa Corcostegui spoke to the crowd that gathered at the Isleños Museum in St. Bernard, just outside New Orleans.

In spite of their fascination in their heritage, Basque residents of this huge city are too busy to participate much in the group. And there is also the fact that most are far removed from their Basque heritage. Smith recalls a young man in his twenties who came to that first meeting and expressed joy at finally learning where his unusual last name came from. Most rely on Goitia Nicholas to inform them of their past Basque connections. The group has essentially no money, only a few loyal officers, and no Web site to advertise its efforts. They do not charge for membership. "We want to keep it loose and friendly," said Smith. The group often meets at her bed-and-breakfast.

After Hurricane Katrina, and the subsequent flooding in 2005, many members were displaced. Bidart Smith said she was lucky that most of the flooding was east of her bed-and-breakfast inn. She was hosting guests, many of them flood relief workers, soon after the disaster, and continued to be a point person for the Basque community. Because of damage that affected train service in the New Orleans area, Goita Nicholas was transferred to Seattle, and he was planning to return as soon as possible, she said. As for the Isleño Museum, where the group held its first festival, it is gone. "Erased is the word they are using for St. Bernard Parish," said Bidart Smith.

Louisiana Basque Society, c/o Le Petite Chalet Basque, 709 Colony Place, Metairie, LA 70003. Information: (504) 734-1183 (Bertha Bidart Smith)

APPENDIX 1: BOARDINGHOUSES STILL IN EXISTENCE

Among the remaining Basque-owned hotels that still rented rooms and served Basque food in their restaurants or dining rooms in 2004 are the following:

Basque Hotel, 1102 F Street, Fresno, CA 93706 (209) 233-2286

Centro Vasco, 13432 Central Avenue, Chino, CA 91710 (909) 628-3558

Louis' Basque Corner Restaurant, 301 E. Fourth Street, Reno, NV 89512 (702) 323-7203

Noriega Hotel, 525 Sumner Street, Bakersfield, CA 93305 (805) 322-8419

Overland Hotel, 691 South Main Street, Gardnerville, NV 89410 (702) 782-2138

Santa Fe Hotel, 235 Lake Street, Reno, NV 89501 (702) 323-7203

Shepard's Inn (formerly Santa Fe Hotel), 9345 Santa Fe Avenue, Fresno, CA 93721 (209) 266-2170

Star Hotel, 246 Silver Street, Elko, NV 89801 (702) 753-8696

Winnemucca Hotel, 95 Bridge Street, Winnemucca, NV 89445 (702) 623-2908

APPENDIX 2: SUMMER FESTIVAL CALENDAR

See the sections under the relevant city or town for more details on each event.

May

First Saturday: Fresno Basque Club Picnic
Third Sunday: Los Banos Club Picnic
Sunday Before Memorial Day: Kern County Basque Club Picnic, Bakersfield, Calif.

June

First Sunday: San Francisco Basque Club Picnic
Second Weekend: Winnemucca Festival, Winnemucca, Nev.
Second Sunday: Basque Club of Utah Picnic, Salt Lake City
Last Sunday: Sheepmen's Picnic, Bakersfield, Calif.

July

First Weekend: National Basque Festival, Elko, Nev.
First Sunday: Southern California Basque Club Picnic, Chino, Calif.
Third Sunday: Gooding Basque Association Picnic, Gooding, Idaho
Third Weekend: Reno Basque Club Festival
Last Weekend: San Ignacio Festival, Boise

August

First Saturday: Euskal Lagunak, Mountain Home, Idaho
Second Saturday: Mendiko Eskualdun Cluba Picnic, Gardnerville, Nev.
August 15: Big Horn Basque Club Festival, Buffalo, Wyo.

September

First Sunday: Chino Basque Club Picnic, Chino, Calif.
Second Sunday: Marin-Sonoma Basque Club Picnic, Penngrove, Calif.
Third Saturday: Basque Cultural Center Fall Barbecue, South San Francisco
Fourth Saturday: Rock Springs, Wyo., Festival

October

First Weekend: Las Vegas Lagun Onak Festival

GLOSSARY

aizkolariak Wood choppers

Aldudarrak People from Aldudes

arin-arin The second half of the fandango

artzainak Sheepherders

aurresku The men's dance where they kick their legs as high as they can

bakailo/bacaloa Dried, salted codfish

baserri(a) Farmhouse

Batua The unified Basque dialect

Batzarlekua The Basque government's historic headquarters in Gernika

bertsolari, bertsolariak (pl.) A Basque poet-musician; the Basque version of troubadours. They make up rhyming verses to music as they go along

bota (Spanish) Leather wine bag

briska A Spanish card game played by Boise Basque women

California'ko Eskual Herria (*The Basque Country of California*) The successor paper to *Escualdun Gazeta*

churros (Spanish) Fried pastry

croketas Fried creamed chicken snacks

Escualdun Gazeta (*Basque Gazette*) The world's first exclusively Basque-language newspaper

espartinak Espadrilles

ETA See Euzkadi 'ta Askatasuna

Euskara The Basque language

Euskal Herria The Basque Country

Euskal Kantari Eguna (the day of the Basque singer) A celebration of Basque music and singing

Euskalduna or **Eskualduna** Speaker of the Basque language; it's the word for someone who is Basque

Euzkadi 'ta Askatasuna (Basque Homeland and Freedom) Better known as ETA, it is the violent separatist group borne in Spain in 1968

Euskadi The geopolitical area of three of the four Basque provinces in Spain governed by the parliament

fandango A dance (also referred to as the *jota*)

gabon kantak Christmas carols

gateau Basque (French) A cream-filled cake

Gure Aita (Our Father) A hymn

harri mutillak (stone boys) Stones arranged usually on a high point that could be seen from miles around, as a marker for other herders

Hegoalde The Spanish side of the Basque country; includes the provinces of Araba, Gipuzkoa, Bizkaia, and Nafarroa

Hegoaldetarrak People from Hegoalde

Hizketa (Conversation) The newsletter for NABO

hotelak Boardinghouses

ikastolak Schools taught in Basque

ikurrina Basque flag; its colors are red, green, and white

Ipar-Ameriketako Euskal Dantzarien Biltzarra A U.S. Basque dance federation, similar to a large federation in the Basque Country

Iparralde The French side of the Basque Country; includes the regions of Lapurdi, Nafarroa Beherea, and Zuberoa

Iparraldetarrak People from Iparralde

irrintzi Basque yodel-like cry

jaialdi Festival

Jainkoaren Bildotsa (*Lamb of God*) A hymn

jambon (French) Ham, Basque-style

kafesnea Hot coffee and milk

kanperua Camp tender

kantxa The court where handball is played; also known as a fronton

klika Bugle corps

koskolak Lamb testicles

lauburu Basque cross

lukainka Sausage

morcilla (Spanish) Blood sausage

mus A Basque card game

North American Basque Organizations (NABO) An organization of Basque organizations

ostatuak Boardinghouses or rooming houses

pala A variation of pelota played with a wooden racket on a typical handball court

pandareta Tambourine

pelota Handball, a court game related to jai alai

pelotariak Handball players

porrusalda The second half of the fandango, or *jota*

soka tira Tug-of-war competition

solomo Pork loin

tapas Spanish appetizers

trikitixa The combination of a diatonic accordion and a tambourine in a duet called *trikitixalariak*

trinket A form of pelota played against four walls

ttun-ttun A small drum

turrón (Spanish) Bars of nougat and almonds

txapel Basque beret

txinga The weights used in weight-carrying competitions

txipiroi Squid

txipirrones en su tinta (Spanish) Squid in its own ink

txistera The basketlike extension worn on the hand for playing jai alai

txistu A flute-like instrument; it is held straight up and down

txistulari A *txistu* player

txokos Gastronomic societies in Hegoalde in which members gather together primarily to cook and eat a meal together

Vizcaíno A Basque from the province of Bizkaia. In the times of the early explorations of the New World this term was used to refer to all Basques

zahakuak Wine bags

Zazpiak Bat (Seven in One) A phrase referring to the seven Basque regions that many U.S. groups use for their name

INDEX

Page numbers in italics refer to photograph inserts